A **M**ANUAL OF NATURE CONSER

With best wishes

Mike

April 1998

A Manual of
Nature Conservation Law

Michael Fry BA, LLM
Solicitor

CLARENDON PRESS · OXFORD
1995

Oxford University Press, Walton Street, Oxford ox2 6DP

Oxford New York
Athens Auckland Bangkok Bombay
Calcutta Cape Town Dar es Salaam Delhi
Florence Hong Kong Istanbul Karachi
Kuala Lumpur Madras Madrid Melbourne
Mexico City Nairobi Paris Singapore
Taipei Tokyo Toronto
and associated companies in
Berlin Ibadan

Oxford is a trade mark of Oxford University Press

Published in the United States
by Oxford University Press Inc., New York

British Library Cataloguing in Publication Data
Data available

Library of Congress Cataloging in Publication Data
Fry, Michael (Michael J.)
A manual of nature conservation law / Michael Fry.
   p.   cm.
Includes index.
1. Nature conservation—Law and legislation—Great Britain.
I. Title.
KD1035.A3   1995   346.4104'67—dc20   [344.106467]   95–18019
ISBN 0–19–825958–1
ISBN 0–19–826048–2 (pbk.)

1 3 5 7 9 10 8 6 4 2

Set by Hope Services (Abingdon) Ltd.
Printed in Great Britain
on acid-free paper by
Biddles Ltd., Guildford and King's Lynn

Foreword

Over the last twenty years concern for the environment has become increasingly important. In the United Kingdom this anxiety has culminated in the passing of the Wildlife and Countryside Act in 1981, and the Environmental Protection Act in 1990. In these and other Acts, measures for species protection, the designation of important sites for nature conservation, and the establishment of some appropriate agencies, were introduced. In particular, the system of Sites of Special Scientific Interest and attendant negotiating procedures were put in place. Subsequent amendments have been made and more are expected in the course of the next few years. In addition to domestic legislation in the United Kingdom, measures instituted by the European Commission are having to be incorporated into British law, and here the Wildlife and Countryside Act, for example, is having to accommodate such measures as the European Species and Habitats Directive and the Birds Directive. In 1992 a global conference was held in Rio de Janeiro. Two important conventions, one on promoting sustainability and the other on biodiversity were passed and are being ratified progressively by various countries. These two conventions are also beginning to have a substantial impact on our national legislation and this is likely to become more pronounced in future.

This multiplicity of legislation is causing increasing confusion among environmentalists and has direct implications for many activities designed to protect flora and fauna and ecosystems. This manual will be invaluable in guiding all those interested in the practice of nature conservation and in the environment. It is greatly to be welcomed and is likely to prove an interesting *vade mecum* in the future.

William Wilkinson

Sir William Wilkinson
Chairman (1983–1991) of the former Nature Conservancy Council

Contents

Part III: Policy Guidance

Appendices

Use of the manual

The legislation in this manual is up to date to 1 May 1995. At the time of preparing the *Manual* the Environment Bill has been introduced into the House of Lords and enactment is expected later in 1995. The principal changes to the legislation in this manual proposed by the Bill are set out at Appendix I, p. 505.

The *Manual* covers the law of England and Wales and of Scotland. Primary and secondary legislation is set out in Parts I and II respectively, in chronological order. Lists of orders made under certain provisions are included at the end of Part II. The index enables statutory provisions relating to a particular matter to be located. In this manual, the legislation has been annotated to provide, in a convenient form, information on and references to the following points:

1. Statutory definitions and construction of words and phrases;
2. Amendments made to the legislation;
3. Commencement provisions;
4. Secondary legislation made pursuant to powers in the statutes;
5. Cases;
6. Cross-references to related and other relevant provisions; and
7. Additional notes at selected points to provide background information; for example, details of the predecessors to the Conservancy Councils are set out at section 15 of the National Parks and Access to the Countryside Act 1949, p. 15.

In the annotations, where appropriate, the authority for a statement is placed after a colon. Thus, the definition of land at section 29 of the Wildlife and Countryside Act 1981, p. 171 is set out as:

"Land" defined by s. 114(1), National Parks and Access to the Countryside Act 1949, p. 38 above: s. 52(4) below applies the definition in s. 114 of the 1949 Act.

To avoid undue repetition the annotations are arranged on the basis of sections, articles or regulations. In the above example, "land" appears several times in section 29 of the 1981 Act; the annotation is set out at the first point in the section where this word appears. Selected cases are noted which relate to the interpretation of statutory provisions. These do not comprise an exhaustive list either of the cases or of legislation which has been the subject of legal proceedings.

One detail should be noted in respect of the presentation of the legislation. In certain of the Queen's Printer copies of statutes and the printed statutory instruments italic print is not used for the scientific names of species. In keeping with scientific practice, the scientific names of species in the statutes and statutory instruments appear in italic in this manual.

Abbreviations

All ER	All England Law Reports
AONB	Area of Outstanding Natural Beauty
AOSP	Area of Special Protection for Birds
art.	Article
c.	Chapter
COD	Crown Office Digest
Crim LR	Criminal Law Review
DoE	Department of the Environment
EA	Environmental Assessment
EGLR	Estates Gazette Law Reports
ESA	Environmentally Sensitive Area
GCR	Geological Conservation Review
GDO	General Development Order
JEL	Journal of Environmental Law
JNCC	Joint Nature Conservation Committee
LNR	Local Nature Reserve
MAFF	Ministry of Agriculture, Fisheries and Food
MPG	Minerals Planning Guidance Note
NCC	Nature Conservancy Council
NCR	Nature Conservation Review
NHA	Natural Heritage Area
NNR	National Nature Reserve
OJ	Official Journal of the European Communities
p./pp.	page / pages
para.	paragraph
PPG	Planning Policy Guidance Note
pt.	Part
Ramsar Convention	The Convention on Wetlands of International Importance especially as Waterfowl Habitat, also known as the Ramsar Convention. The Convention was signed at Ramsar in Iran in 1971.
reg.	Regulation
s./ss.	section/sections
SAC	Special Area of Conservation
SCCR	Scottish Criminal Case Reports
sch.	Schedule
S.I.	Statutory Instrument
SLT	Scots Law Times
SNH	Scottish Natural Heritage

SPA	Special Protection Area
SSSI	Site of Special Scientific Interest
WLR	Weekly Law Reports

Introduction

The aim of this manual is to provide a collection of the sources of nature conservation law in one reference volume.

Some 45 years ago, following the report of the Wild Life Conservation Special Committee of 1947[1], the National Parks and Access to the Countryside Act 1949 was enacted. This can be considered as the first of the principal statutes forming part of the present-day law concerning nature conservation. More recently, at the end of October 1994, the Conservation (Natural Habitats etc.) Regulations 1994, which form the central plank of the UK Government's programme to implement the EC Habitats and Species Directive of 1992, came into force.

Over this period legislation concerning nature conservation has been amended and supplemented to a considerable degree. As regards the greater part of the legislation, it is time-consuming to piece the amended provisions together to produce the updated legislation. In addition, many significant provisions are to be found in statutes not wholly concerned with nature conservation, for example, the environmental duties set out in the water consolidation legislation of 1991. In editing this manual, the objective has been to present material relating to nature conservation in an updated and convenient format.

In common with other areas of law there is no fixed boundary defining nature conservation law. The Environmental Protection Act 1990 contains a definition of nature conservation at s. 131: "the conservation of flora, fauna or geological or physiographical features". A wide range of activity may be affected by legal provisions concerning this area and this is reflected in the breadth of the statutory provisions.

Inevitably, it is not possible to include all relevant material and readers are advised that it may be necessary to refer to legislation and other material which is not contained in this manual. In selecting material emphasis has been placed on presenting sources of general application rather than provisions relating to particular areas. Thus, in relation to land notified under s. 28 of the Wildlife and Countryside Act 1981, commonly referred to as sites of special scientific interest, in addition to the measures in the 1981 Act, the *Manual* sets out other provisions including the appointment of the advisory committee in Scotland under the Natural Heritage (Scotland) Act 1991. The *Manual* does not, however, extend to provisions which relate to more specific matters such as the installation of electric lines, applications to set aside agricultural land, and the issue of waste management licences. There are many provisions which are of considerable relevance to the practice of nature conservation, including planning measures and countryside legislation such as access to open country, country parks and, in Scotland, regional parks. The approach in this manual has been to concentrate on legislation that can be considered as directly concerned with nature conservation rather than these wider aspects. These distinctions, however, cannot be considered as capable of clear definition or imposed rigidly. Forestry, for example, may not be categorised strictly as a nature conservation area. However, in view of the importance of forestry practice on nature conservation, legislation relating to forestry is set out in the *Manual*.

It is hoped that a balance has been achieved between the somewhat competing objectives of providing a comprehensive guide whilst keeping to a manageable format. Both in this respect and in connection with the *Manual* generally the comments of readers will be greatly welcomed.

Michael Fry
May 1995

---

[1] *Conservation of Nature in England and Wales*, Cmd. 7122, HMSO, London. This report is highly respected as an analysis of nature conservation.

Part I

Primary Legislation

National Parks and Access to the Countryside Act 1949

12, 13 & 14 Geo. 6 Ch. 97

Arrangement of sections

Part I: The Countryside Commission and the Countryside Council for Wales

Part II: National Parks

Part III: Nature Conservation

Part IV: Public Rights of Way

Not reproduced

Part V: Access to Open Country

Not reproduced

Part VI: General, Financial and Supplementary

National Parks and Access to the Countryside Act 1949

An Act to make provision for National Parks and the establishment of a National Parks Commission; to confer on the Nature Conservancy and local authorities powers for the establishment and maintenance of nature reserves; to make further provision for the recording, creation, maintenance and improvement of public paths and for securing access to open country, and to amend the law relating to rights of way; to confer further powers for preserving and enhancing natural beauty; and for matters connected with the purposes aforesaid.

[16th December 1949[1]]

Part I: The National Parks Commission[2]

The Countryside Commission and the Countryside Council for Wales

1. (1) There shall be a Countryside Commission which shall exercise functions in relation to England for the purposes specified in subsection (2) below; and the Countryside Council for Wales (established by section 128 of the Environmental Protection Act 1990[3]) shall exercise corresponding functions in relation to Wales for the corresponding purposes specified in section 130(2) of the Environmental Protection Act 1990.[4]

(2) The purposes for which the functions of the Commission are exercisable are—

(*a*) the preservation and enhancement of natural beauty[5] in England, both in the areas designated under this Act as National Parks[6] or as areas of outstanding natural beauty[7] and elsewhere;

(*b*) encouraging the provision or improvement, for persons resorting to National Parks, of facilities for the enjoyment thereof and for the enjoyment of the opportunities for open-air recreation[8] and the study of nature afforded thereby.[9]

....

2. *Superseded by the Wildlife and Countryside Act 1981 (c. 69), s. 47, p. 186 below, and repealed by s. 73(1), sch. 17, pt. II, of that Act. This amendment came into force on 1 April 1982: S.I. 1982/327.*

....

---

[1] The Act came into force on the date of the Royal Assent, 16 December 1949.

[2] This part now relates to the Countryside Commission, which succeeded the National Parks Commission, and the Countryside Council for Wales.

[3] P. 229 below.

[4] P. 230 below.

[5] For the construction of references to the preservation of the natural beauty of an area see s. 114(2), p. 38 below, and the Countryside Act 1968 (c. 41), s. 21(7), p. 123 below.

[6] "National Park" has the meaning assigned to it by s. 5(3), p. 8 below: s. 114(1), p. 38 below.

[7] "Area of outstanding natural beauty" has the meaning assigned to it by s. 87(1), p. 22 below: s. 114(1), p. 37 below.

[8] The definition of open-air recreation in s. 114(1) below only applies to Part V of this Act and not to this part:

Countryside Act 1968 (c. 41), s. 21(6), p. 123 below.

[9] This section is substituted by the Environmental Protection Act 1990 (c. 43), s. 130, sch. 8, para. 1(2). This amendment came into force on 1 April 1991: S.I. 1991/685. For additional functions of the Commission and Council see the Countryside Act 1968 (c. 41), p. 112 below. On enactment in 1949 s. 1 provided for the establishment of the National Parks Commission. This body was charged with a duty similar to that set out in the present section save that by s. 1(*a*) their functions were to be exercised "for the preservation and enhancement of natural beauty in England and Wales, and particularly in the areas designated under this Act as National Parks or as areas of outstanding natural beauty". The Countryside Act 1968, s. 1, p. 114 below, provided that the National Parks Commission be known as the Countryside Commission and that their functions be enlarged.

Power of minister to give directions to Commission

3. (1) The Minister[1] may give to the Commission[2] or to the Council[3] such directions of a general character as appear to him expedient in relation to the exercise of their functions, and the Commission or Council[4] shall comply with directions given under this section.

(2) As soon as may be after giving a direction under this section the Minister shall, unless in his opinion it is against the interests of national security so to do, cause a notice setting out the direction to be published in such manner as appears to him to be requisite for informing persons and bodies of persons concerned.

4. *Superseded by the Wildlife and Countryside Act 1981 (c. 69), s. 47, p. 186 below, and repealed by s. 73(1), sch. 17, pt. II, of that Act. This amendment came into force on 1 April 1982: S.I. 1982/327.*

Part II: National Parks

Application of Part II of this Act in Wales

4A.(1) The provisions of this Part of this Act shall, subject to the next following subsection, apply to land[5] in Wales as they apply to land in England.

(2) Where a provision of this Part of this Act confers a function on the Countryside Commission as respects England (or areas of any description in England), the Countryside Council for Wales shall have the corresponding function as respects Wales (or areas of a similar description in Wales).[6]

National Parks

5. (1) The provisions of this Part of this Act shall have effect for the purpose of preserving and enhancing the natural beauty[7] of the areas specified in the next following subsection, and for the purpose of promoting their enjoyment by the public.

(2) The said areas are those extensive tracts of country in England[8] as to which it appears to the Commission[9] that by reason of—

(*a*) their natural beauty, and

(*b*) the opportunities they afford for open-air recreation[10], having regard both to their character and to their position in relation to centres of population,

it is especially desirable that the necessary measures shall be taken for the purposes mentioned in the last foregoing subsection.

(3) The said areas, as for the time being designated by order made by the Commission, and submitted to and confirmed by the Minister[11], shall be known as, and are hereinafter referred to as, National Parks[12].

---

[1] "The Minister" defined by s. 114(1), p. 38 below.

[2] "The Commission" means the Countryside Commission established by s. 1, p. 7 above: s. 114(1), p. 37 below.

[3] "The Council" means the Countryside Council for Wales: s. 114(1), p. 37 below. Words "or to the Council" inserted by the Environmental Protection Act 1990 (c. 43), s. 130, sch. 8, para. 1(3). This amendment came into force on 1 April 1991: S.I. 1991/685.

[4] Words "or Council" inserted by the Environmental Protection Act 1990 (c. 43), s. 130, sch. 8, para. 1(3).

[5] "Land" defined by s. 114(1), p. 38 below.

[6] This section inserted by the Environmental Protection Act 1990 (c. 43), s. 130, sch. 8, para. 1(4). This amendment came into force on 1 April 1991: S.I. 1991/685.

[7] For the construction of references to the preservation of the natural beauty of an area see s. 114(2), p. 38 below,

and the Countryside Act 1968 (c. 41), s. 21(7), p. 123 below.

[8] Former words "and Wales" repealed by the Environmental Protection Act 1990 (c. 43), s. 130, sch. 8, para. 1(5). This amendment came into force on 1 April 1991: S.I. 1991/685.

[9] "The Commission" means the Countryside Commission established by s. 1, p. 7 above: s. 114(1), p. 37 below. The Countryside Council for Wales has a corresponding function as respects areas in Wales: s. 4A above.

[10] The definition of open-air recreation in s. 114(1) below only applies to Part V of this Act and not to this part: Countryside Act 1968 (c. 41), s. 21(6), p. 123 below.

[11] "The Minister" defined by s. 114(1), p. 38 below.

[12] For powers to amend an order made under this section see the Wildlife and Countryside Act 1981 (c. 69), s. 45, p. 186 below.

General duties of Commission in relation to National Parks

6. (1) It shall be the duty of the Commission[1] as soon as may be after the commencement of this Act, and thereafter from time to time, to consider what areas there are in England[2] falling within subsection (2) of the last foregoing section, to determine in what order they should be designated under subsection (3) of that section, and to proceed with their designation at such times as the Commission may determine.

(2) The power of the Minister[3] to give directions under section three of this Act[4] shall extend to the giving of directions as to the order and time of designation of the said areas, notwithstanding that the directions may be of a specific character.

(3) As respects areas designated as National Parks[5], it shall be the duty of the Commission—

(*a*) to consider, generally and in relation to particular National Parks, in what way action needs to be taken under this Act and the Act of 1947[6] for the purposes specified in subsection (1) of the last foregoing section, and to make such recommendations with respect thereto to the Minister and to local authorities as may appear to the Commission to be necessary or expedient, and

(*b*) to keep under review the progress made from time to time in accomplishing the said purposes and to make to the Minister or, where the Commission deem it appropriate, to any other Minister or any local authority or other persons, such representations as appear to the Commission to be necessary or expedient as to any matter affecting the accomplishment of those purposes.

(4) Without prejudice to the generality of the last foregoing subsection, it shall be the duty of the Commission, subject to and in accordance with the following provisions of this Act in that behalf,—

(*a*) as respects any area designated as a National Park, to give advice to the appropriate planning authorities[7] as to the arrangements to be made for administering the area as a National Park;

(*b*) *Repealed by the Countryside Act 1968 (c. 41), s. 50(2), sch. 4. This amendment came into force on 3 August 1968: s. 50(3).*

(*c*) to assist such authorities in formulating proposals as to the exercise by such authorities of their powers under this Act for securing the provision of accommodation, access for open-air recreation[8] and other facilities for persons visiting National Parks and otherwise as to the exercise of their powers under this Act as respects National Parks, and to consult with such authorities with respect to the recommendations to be made by the Commission as to the payment of grants by the Minister under this Act;

---

[1] "The Commission" means the Countryside Commission established by s. 1, p. 7 above: s. 114(1), p. 37 below. The Countryside Council for Wales has a corresponding function as respects Wales: s. 4A, p. 8 above.

[2] Former words "and Wales" repealed by the Environmental Protection Act 1990 (c. 43), s. 130(1), sch. 8, para. 1(5). This amendment came into force on 1 April 1991: S.I. 1991/685.

[3] "The Minister" defined by s. 114(1), p. 38 below.

[4] P. 8 above.

[5] "National Park" has the meaning assigned to it by s. 5(3) above: s. 114(1), p. 38 below.

[6] "The Act of 1947" is defined by s. 114(1) as the Town and Country Planning Act 1947. This Act has been repealed.

References to the provisions of this Act are to be construed as references to the corresponding provisions of the consolidating Acts, namely the Town and Country Planning Act 1990 (c. 8), the Planning (Listed Buildings and Conservation Areas) Act 1990 (c. 9) and the Planning (Hazardous Substances) Act 1990 (c. 10): Planning (Consequential Provisions) Act 1990 (c. 11), s. 2, which came into force on 24 August 1990: s. 7(2).

[7] "Appropriate planning authority" defined by subsection (6), p. 10 below.

[8] The definition of open-air recreation in s. 114(1) below only applied to Part V of this Act and not to this part: Countryside Act 1968 (c. 41), s. 21(6), p. 123 below.

(d) Repealed by the Countryside Act 1968 (c. 41), s. 50(2), sch. 5. This amendment came into force on 3 August 1968: s. 50(3).

(e) to give advice where any Minister consults the Commission as to proposals for development of land[1] in a National Park, or the appropriate planning authority consult them (whether in compliance with a requirement imposed under this Act or the Act of 1947 or otherwise) in connection with the preparation or amendment of a development plan or in connection with an application for permission to develop any such land[2];

(f) to make recommendations to the Minister and, where the Commission deem it appropriate, to other Ministers as to any proposals for the development of land in a National Park, being proposals for development in a way which appears to the Commission to be inconsistent with the maintenance of the area as a Park;

(g) to notify to the Minister, or where the Commission deem it appropriate to other Ministers, the general nature of the action which will in the opinion of the Commission need to be taken as respects land in a National Park for any of the purposes specified in subsection (1) of the last foregoing section[3], in cases where it appears to the Commission that the Minister in question should be informed thereof before considering future proposals for the development of the land for other purposes; and

(h) if in any case the Commission are not satisfied that effect will be given to their recommendations or advice as to any matter mentioned in the foregoing paragraphs of this subsection, to refer the matter to the Minister and to advise the Minister as to the exercise of any powers of direction or enforcement (including powers of making orders) conferred on him by this Act or the Act of 1947.

(5) Nothing in this section shall be construed as modifying the effect of any provision of this Act whereby any specific power or duty is conferred or imposed on the Commission or whereby an obligation is imposed on any other person to consult with the Commission.

(6) In this section the expression "appropriate planning authority" means a local planning authority[4] whose area consists of or includes the whole or any part of a National Park, and includes a local authority, not being a local planning authority, by whom any powers of a local planning authority as respects a National Park are exercisable, whether under the following provisions of this Act in that behalf or otherwise; and references in this section to a Minister include references to any Board in charge of a Government department[5].

Designation and variation of National Parks

7. (1) Before making an order designating a National Park[6] the Commission[7] shall consult with every joint planning board[8], county council, county borough council and county district council[9] whose area includes any land[10] in the area to be designated a Park.

---

[1] "Land" defined by s. 114(1), p. 38 below.
[2] This paragraph applies in relation to areas of outstanding natural beauty as it applies in relation to National Parks: s. 88(1), p. 23 below.
[3] S. 5(1), p. 8 above.
[4] For statutory provisions in respect of local planning authorities see the Town and Country Planning Act 1990 (c. 8), Part I and the Local Government Act 1972 (c. 70), s. 184, sch. 17, pt. I. The Town and Country Planning Act 1990 applies by virtue of s. 114(1) below and the Planning (Consequential Provisions) Act 1990 (c. 11), s. 2.
[5] Land in a National Park may not be included in a simplified planning zone: Town and Country Planning Act 1990 (c. 80), s. 87(1).
[6] "National Park" has the meaning assigned to it by s.

5(3), p. 8 above: s. 114(1), p. 38 below.
[7] "The Commission" means the Countryside Commission established by s. 1, p. 7 above: s. 114(1), p. 37 below. The Countryside Council for Wales has a corresponding function as respects Wales: s. 4A, p. 8 above.
[8] For statutory provisions in respect of joint planning boards see the Town and Country Planning Act 1990 (c. 8), ss. 2, 4 and the Local Government Act 1972 (c. 70), s. 184, sch. 17, pt. I. The Town and Country Planning Act 1990 applies by virtue of s. 114(1) below and the Planning (Consequential Provisions) Act 1990 (c. 11), s. 2.
[9] For the construction of "county council" and "county district council" see the Local Government Act 1972 (c. 70), s. 179.
[10] "Land" defined by s. 114(1), p. 38 below.

(2) Any such order shall describe the area to be designated a Park by reference to a map and such other descriptive matter as may appear to the Commission to be requisite.

(3) The provisions in that behalf of the First Schedule to this Act shall have effect as to the making, confirmation, coming into operation and validity of any order designating a National Park.

(4) The Minister[1] may by order made after consultation with the Commission vary an order designating a National Park.

(5) Before making an order under the last foregoing subsection the Minister shall consult with every such board and council as aforesaid whose area, or any part of whose area, is comprised in the National Park, whether as existing or as proposed to be varied; and the provisions in that behalf of the First Schedule to this Act shall apply to any order under the last foregoing subsection.

(6) It shall be the duty of the Commission to secure that copies of any order such as is mentioned in this section shall be available, at the office of the Commission, at the offices of each joint planning board and local authority specified in subsection (1) or subsection (5) of this section, as the case may be, and at such other place or places in or near the Park in question as the Commission may determine, for inspection by the public at all reasonable times[2].

---

8. *Superseded by the Local Government Act 1972 (c. 70), s. 184(6), sch. 17, pt. I, and repealed by s. 272(1), sch. 30 of that Act. This amendment came into force on 1 April 1974: s. 273.*

Development plans relating to National Parks

9. (1) In preparing a development plan, or proposals for any alterations of or additions to a development plan, for any area being or including the whole or any part of a National Park[3], the local planning authority[4] shall consult with the Commission[5] and take into consideration any observations made by the Commission.

(2) Provision may be made by regulations under the Act of 1947[6] for enabling proceedings preliminary to the confirmation of orders designating a National Park and to the making of orders varying such orders to be taken concurrently with proceedings required under that Act to be taken in connection with the submission, making or amendment of development plans[7].

---

10. *Repealed by the Local Government Act 1972 (c. 70), s. 272(1), sch. 30. This amendment came into force on 1 April 1974: s. 273.*

---

[1] "The Minister" defined by s. 114(1), p. 38 below.

[2] For the exercise of functions of a local planning authority where an order is made under this section see the Town and Country Planning Act 1990 (c. 8), s. 4(3).

[3] "National Park" has the meaning assigned to it by s. 5(3), p. 8 above: s. 114(1), p. 38 below.

[4] For statutory provisions in respect of local planning authorities see the Town and Country Planning Act 1990 (c. 8), Part I and the Local Government Act 1972 (c. 70), s. 184, sch. 17, pt. I. The Town and Country Planning Act 1990 applies by virtue of s. 114(1) below and the Planning (Consequential Provisions) Act 1990 (c. 11), s. 2.

[5] "The Commission" means the Countryside Commission established by s. 1, p. 7 above: s. 114(1), p. 37 below. The Countryside Council for Wales has a corresponding function as respects areas in Wales: s. 4A, p. 8 above.

[6] "The Act of 1947" is defined by s. 114(1) as the Town and Country Planning Act 1947. This Act has been repealed. References to the provisions of this Act are to be construed as references to the corresponding provisions of the consolidating Acts, namely the Town and Country Planning Act 1990 (c. 8), the Planning (Listed Buildings and Conservation Areas) Act 1990 (c. 9), the Planning (Hazardous Substances) Act 1990 (c. 10): Planning (Consequential Provisions) Act 1990 (c. 11), s. 2, which came into force on 24 August 1990: s. 7(2).

[7] This section applies in relation to areas of outstanding natural beauty as it applies in relation to National Parks: s. 88(1), p. 23 below.

General powers of local planning authorities in relation to National Parks

11. (1) A local planning authority[1] whose area consists of or includes the whole or any part of a National Park[2] shall have power, subject to the provisions of this section, to take all such action as appears to them expedient for the accomplishment of any[3] of the purposes specified in sub-section (1) of section five of this Act[4] in relation to their area or so much thereof as is comprised in the Park.

(2) Nothing in the following provisions of this Act shall be construed as limiting the generality of the last foregoing subsection; but in so far as those provisions confer specific powers falling within that subsection those powers shall be exercised in accordance with the said provisions and subject to any limitations expressed or implied therein.

(3) *Repealed by the Countryside Act 1968 (c. 41), s. 21(1), s. 50(2), sch. 5. This amendment came into force on 3 August 1968: s. 50(3).*

(4) Without prejudice to the powers hereinafter conferred, subsection (1) of this section shall have effect only for the purpose of removing any limitation imposed by law on the capacity of a local planning authority by virtue of its constitution, and shall not authorise any act or omission on the part of such an authority which apart from that subsection would be actionable at the suit of any person on any ground other than such a limitation.[5]

....

Provision of accommodation, meals, refreshments, camping sites and parking places

12. (1) A local planning authority[6] whose area consists of or includes the whole or any part of a National Park[7] may make arrangements for securing the provision in their area (whether by the authority or by other persons)—

(*a*) of accommodation, meals and refreshments (including intoxicating liquor);

(*b*) of camping sites; and

(*c*) of parking places and means of access thereto and egress therefrom,

and may for the purposes of such arrangements erect such buildings and carry out such work as may appear to them to be necessary or expedient:

Provided that a local planning authority shall not under this section provide accommodation, meals or refreshments except in so far as it appears to them that the facilities therefor are inadequate or unsatisfactory, either generally or as respects any description of accommodation, meals or refreshments, as the case may be.[8]

(2) The functions of a local planning authority under the last foregoing subsection shall be exercisable either on land[9] in the Park or on land in the neighbourhood thereof; and where the local planning authority is a joint planning board[10], land in the neighbourhood of the Park which is in

---

[1] For statutory provisions in respect of local planning authorities see the Town and Country Planning Act 1990 (c. 8), Part I and the Local Government Act 1972 (c. 70), s. 184, sch. 17, pt. I. The Town and Country Planning Act 1990 applies by virtue of s. 114(1) below and the Planning (Consequential Provisions) Act 1990 (c. 11), s. 2.

[2] "National Park" has the meaning assigned to it by s. 5(3), p. 8 above: s. 114(1), p. 38 below.

[3] Words "of any" inserted by the Wildlife and Countryside Act 1981 (c. 69), s. 72(5). This amendment came into force on 30 November 1981: s. 74(2).

[4] P. 8 above.

[5] This section, so far as it confers power for preserving and enhancing natural beauty, applies in relation to areas of outstanding natural beauty as it applies in relation to National Parks: s. 88(1), p. 23 below. For the construction of references to the preservation of the natural beauty of an

area see s. 114(2), p. 38 below, and the Countryside Act 1968 (c. 41), s. 21(7), p. 123 below.

[6] For statutory provisions in respect of local planning authorities see the Town and Country Planning Act 1990 (c. 8), Part I and the Local Government Act 1972 (c. 70), s. 184, sch. 17, pt. I. The Town and Country Planning Act 1990 applies by virtue of s. 114(1) and the Planning (Consequential Provisions) Act 1990 (c. 11), s. 2.

[7] "National Park" has the meaning assigned to it by s. 5(3), p. 8 above: s. 114(1), p. 38 below.

[8] This subsection is extended by the Countryside Act 1968 (c. 41), s. 12(1) and (2), p. 118 below.

[9] "Land" defined by s. 114(1), p. 38 below.

[10] For statutory provisions in respect of joint planning boards see the Town and Country Planning Act 1990 (c. 8), ss. 2,4 and the Local Government Act 1972 (c. 70), s. 184, sch. 17, pt. I. The Town and Country Planning Act 1990

the area of any of the constituent authorities shall be treated for the purposes of the last foregoing subsection as in the area of the joint planning board, whether or not it is in that area.

(3) The foregoing provisions of this section shall not authorise an authority, on land in which any other person has an interest[1], without his consent to do anything which apart from this section would be actionable at his suit by virtue of that interest.

(4) A local planning authority may acquire land compulsorily for the purpose of any of their functions under this section.

Improvement of waterways for purposes of open-air recreation

13. (1) A local planning authority[2] whose area consists of or includes the whole or any part of a National Park[3] may, as respects any waterway[4] in the Park and within the area of the authority, carry out such work and do such other things as may appear to them necessary or expedient for facilitating the use of the waterway by the public for sailing, boating, bathing or fishing or other forms of recreation[5]:

Provided that a local planning authority shall not under this section provide facilities of any description except in cases where it appears to them that the facilities of that description are inadequate or unsatisfactory.[6]

(2) A local planning authority may, as respects any waterway in their area, enter into an agreement, on such terms as to payment or otherwise as may be specified in the agreement, with any other authority on whom powers of carrying out work are conferred in relation to the waterway by or under any enactment, for the exercise by the said other authority of any power of doing work conferred on the local planning authority by the last foregoing subsection.[7]

(3) Where an agreement is made under the last foregoing subsection for the exercise of any power by any such authority, other than a local planning authority, as is therein mentioned, no limitation imposed by law on the capacity of that authority by virtue of the constitution thereof shall operate so as to prevent the authority from exercising that power.[7]

(4) Where it appears to the Minister[8], as respects a waterway in the area of a local planning authority, that any power of doing work conferred on the authority by subsection (1) of this section should be exercised by any such other authority as is mentioned in subsection (2) of this section, and the local planning authority have not entered into an agreement with the said other authority under the said subsection (2), the Minister may direct that the said power shall be exercisable by the said other authority:

Provided that no direction shall be given under this subsection except after consultation with the local planning authority and the said other authority.[9]

(5) Before exercising any power conferred by or under this section an authority shall consult with such other authorities, being authorities which under any enactment have functions relating to the waterway in question, as the Minister may either generally or in any particular case direct.

(6) Where any authority consulted under the last foregoing subsection objects to a proposed exercise of powers under this section, and the objection is not withdrawn, the proposal shall not be proceeded with unless on an application in that behalf specifying the proposal and the

applies by virtue of s. 114(1) and the Planning (Consequential Provisions) Act 1990 (c. 11), s. 2.

[1] "Interest" defined by s. 114(1), p. 38 below.
[2] For statutory provisions in respect of local planning authorities see the Town and Country Planning Act 1990 (c. 8), Part I and the Local Government Act 1972 (c. 70), s. 184, sch. 17, pt. I. The Town and Country Planning Act 1990 applies by virtue of s. 114(1) and the Planning (Consequential Provisions) Act 1990 (c. 11), s. 2.
[3] "National Park" has the meaning assigned to it by s. 5(3), p. 8 above: s. 114(1), p. 38 below.
[4] "Waterway" defined by s. 114(1), p. 38 below.

[5] Words "or fishing or other forms of recreation" substituted by the Countryside Act 1968 (c. 41), s. 12(6), p. 120 below. This amendment came into force on 3 August 1968: s. 50(3).
[6] This subsection is extended by the Countryside Act 1968 (c. 41), s. 12(6), (8), p. 120 below.
[7] This subsection is extended by the Countryside Act 1968 (c. 41), s. 12(7), (8), p. 120 below.
[8] "The Minister" defined by s. 114(1), p. 38 below.
[9] This subsection is extended by the Countryside Act 1968 (c. 41), s. 12(7), (8), p. 120 below.

objection the Minister so directs, and subject to any conditions or modifications specified in the direction; and before giving a direction under this subsection the Minister shall afford to each of the authorities an opportunity of being heard by a person appointed by him for the purpose, and shall consider that person's report.

(7) The foregoing provisions of this section shall not authorise an authority to do anything on land[1], or as respects water over land, in which any other person has an interest[2], if apart from this section the doing thereof would be actionable at his suit by virtue of that interest and he does not consent to the doing thereof:

Provided that this subsection shall not apply in the case of land to which, or to water over which, the public have access by virtue of an access order under Part V of this Act, but the exercise of any power under the foregoing provisions of this section as respects such land shall be subject to the provisions in that behalf of the said Part V.

(8) A local planning authority may acquire land compulsorily for the purpose of enabling any power conferred by or under this section to be exercised.

Acquisition by Minister of land in National Parks

14. (1) Where, as respects any land[3] in a National Park[4], the Minister[5] is satisfied that it is expedient so to do, he may with the consent of the Treasury acquire the land by agreement, whether by way of purchase, lease or exchange.

(2) Unless in any particular case the Minister otherwise determines, any land acquired by the Minister under this section shall be transferred to such other persons on such trusts or subject to such conditions as may appear to him expedient for securing that the land will be managed in a suitable manner for accomplishing the purposes specified in subsection (1) of section five of this Act[6].

(3) Subject to the provisions of the last foregoing subsection, the transfer of land under that subsection may be on such terms as to payment or otherwise as may, with the consent of the Treasury, be provided for by the arrangements for the transfer; and where the arrangements so provide the Minister may defray or contribute to the cost of managing the land while it is managed in accordance with the trusts or conditions referred to in the last foregoing subsection.

(4) The Minister may defray the cost of managing any land acquired by him under this section and not transferred to other persons.

Part III[7]: Nature Conservation

Meaning of "nature reserve"

15. In this Part of this Act the expression "nature reserve" means land[8] managed for the purpose—

(a) of providing, under suitable conditions and control, special opportunities for the study of, and research into, matters relating to the fauna and flora of Great Britain and the physical conditions in which they live, and for the study of geological and physiographical features of special interest in the area, or

(b) of preserving flora, fauna or geological or physiographical features of special interest in the area,

or for both those purposes.[9]

---

[1] "Land" defined by s. 114(1), p. 38 below.
[2] "Interest" defined by s. 114(1), p. 38 below.
[3] "Land" defined by s. 114(1), p. 38 below.
[4] "National park" has the meaning assigned to it by s. 5(3), p. 8 above: s. 114(1), p. 38 below.
[5] "The Minister" defined by s. 114(1), p. 38 below.

[6] P. 8 above.
[7] This Act has effect as if s. 15 of the Countryside Act 1968 (c. 41), p. 121 below, were included in Part III: s. 15(7).
[8] "Land" defined by s. 114(1), p. 38 below.
[9] The establishment, maintenance and management of nature reserves is a function of the Nature Conservancy

Meaning of "Nature Conservancy Council"

15A. In this Part of this Act references to "the Nature Conservancy Council" are references—

(a) in relation to land[1] in England, to the Nature Conservancy Council for England[2];

(b) in relation to land in Scotland, to Scottish Natural Heritage[3]; and

(c) in relation to land in Wales, to the Countryside Council for Wales[4,5].

....

Agreements with Nature Conservancy for establishment of nature reserves

16. (1) The Nature Conservancy Council[6] may enter into an agreement with every owner[7], lessee and occupier of any land[8], being land as to which it appears to the Nature Conservancy Council expedient in the national interest that it should be managed as a nature reserve[9], for securing that it shall be so managed.

(2) Any such agreement may impose such restrictions as may be expedient for the purposes of the agreement on the exercise of rights over the land by the persons who can be bound by the agreement.

(3) Any such agreement—

(a) may provide for the management of the land in such manner, the carrying out thereon of such work and the doing thereon of such other things as may be expedient for the purposes of the agreement;

(b) may provide for any of the matters mentioned in the last foregoing paragraph being carried out, or for the cost thereof being defrayed, either by the said owner or other persons, or by the Nature Conservancy Council, or partly in one way and partly in another;

(c) may contain such other provisions as to the making of payments by the Nature Conservancy Council, and in particular for the payment by them of compensation for the effect of the

Council for England, the Countryside Council for Wales and Scottish Natural Heritage: Environmental Protection Act 1990 (c. 43), s. 132(1)(b), p. 231 below, Natural Heritage (Scotland) Act 1991 (c. 28), s. 4(7), p. 247 below.

For the statutory provision where part of a nature reserve was in England and part in Wales, or part was in England and part in Scotland, before 1 April 1991, the day appointed for the Councils to discharge their nature conservation functions, see the Environmental Protection Act 1990 (c. 43), s. 139, sch. 11, pt. II, para. 12, p. 242 below.

[1] "Land" defined by s. 114(1), p. 38 below.

[2] The Nature Conservancy Council for England, also known as English Nature, is established by the Environmental Protection Act 1990 (c. 43), s. 128, p. 229 below. For the functions of the Council see ss. 131–134, p. 230 below.

[3] Words "Scottish Natural Heritage" substituted by the Natural Heritage (Scotland) Act 1991 (c. 28), s. 4(6), sch. 2, para. 1(2). This amendment came into force on 1 April 1992: S.I. 1991/2633. Scottish Natural Heritage is established by the Natural Heritage (Scotland) Act 1991 (c. 28), s. 1, p. 245 below. For the functions of Scottish Natural Heritage see ss. 2–7, p. 245 below.

[4] The Countryside Council for Wales is established by the Environmental Protection Act 1990 (c. 43), s. 128, p. 229 below. For the functions of the Council see ss. 130–134, p. 230 below.

[5] This section inserted by the Environmental Protection Act 1990 (c. 43), s. 132(1), sch. 9, para. 1(2). The section came into force on 1 April 1991: S.I. 1991/685.

[6] For the meaning of "Nature Conservancy Council" see s. 15A above. The references in this Act to the Nature Conservancy Council are in substitution of earlier references. On enactment in 1949 the Act made reference to the Nature Conservancy. The Nature Conservancy was established by Royal Charter on 23 March 1949 "to provide scien-

tific advice on the conservation and control of the natural flora and fauna of Great Britain; to establish, maintain and manage nature reserves in Great Britain, including maintenance of physical features of scientific interest; and to organise and develop the research and scientific services related thereto".

In 1965 the Government established the Natural Environment Research Council. The Nature Conservancy surrendered its Royal Charter and became a committee of this Council. The Science and Technology Act 1965 (c. 4) substituted references to the Natural Environment Research Council in place of the references to the Nature Conservancy. The Nature Conservancy Council Act 1973 (c. 54) established the Nature Conservancy Council as an independent body and substituted the present references to the Nature Conservancy Council.

A reorganisation took place following the enactment of the Environmental Protection Act 1990 and the Natural Heritage (Scotland) Act 1991. The institutions referred to in this section were established and the Nature Conservancy Council was dissolved. For the establishment and functions of the present institutions see the Environmental Protection Act 1990 (c. 43), Part VII, p. 229 below, and the Natural Heritage (Scotland) Act 1991 (c. 28), Part I, p. 245 below.

The Secretary of State for the Environment, in a Parliamentary answer on 27 January 1994, announced a study into a proposal to bring together the Countryside Commission and the Nature Conservancy Council for England (English Nature). On 7 October 1994 the Secretary of State set out that a programme of closer working between the two organisations would be developed and that there would accordingly be no merger (DoE news release no. 572 of 7 October 1994).

[7] "Owner" defined by s. 114(1), p. 38 below.

[8] "Land" defined by s. 114(1), p. 38 below.

[9] "Nature reserve" defined by s. 15, p. 14 above.

restrictions mentioned in the last foregoing subsection, as may be specified in the agreement.

(4) Section two of the Forestry Act, 1947[1] (which empowers tenants for life and other limited owners to enter into forestry dedication covenants) shall apply to any such agreement; and where section seventy-nine of the Law of Property Act, 1925[2] (which provides that unless a contrary intention is expressed the burden of a covenant runs with the land) applies, subsections (2) and (3) of section one of the said Act of 1947[3] (which provide for enforcement against persons other than the covenantor) shall apply to any such restrictions as are mentioned in subsection (2) of this section, but with the substitution for references to the Forestry Commissioners of references to the Nature Conservancy.

(5) The following provisions shall have effect in the application of this section to Scotland:—

(a) a limited owner of land shall have power to enter into agreements under this section relating to the land;

(b) the Trusts (Scotland) Act, 1921[4], shall have effect as if among the powers conferred on trustees by section four thereof (which relates to the general powers of trustees) there were included a power to enter into agreements under this section relating to the trust estate or any part thereof;

(c) subsection (2) of section three of the Forestry Act, 1947[5], shall apply to an agreement under this section to which an owner or limited owner of land or a trustee acting under the last foregoing paragraph is a party as it applies to a forestry dedication agreement, with the substitution for the reference to the Forestry Commissioners of a reference to Scottish Natural Heritage[6];

(d) the expression "owner" incudes any person empowered under this subsection to enter into agreements relating to land;

(e) subsection (4) shall not apply.

....

Compulsory acquisition of land by Conservancy for establishment of nature reserves

17. (1) Subject to the provisions of the next following subsection, where the Nature Conservancy Council[7] are satisfied as respects any land[8] that it is expedient in the national interest that it should be managed as a nature reserve[9], they may acquire the land compulsorily.

(2) The Nature Conservancy Council shall not acquire any interest[10] in land under the last foregoing subsection unless they are satisfied that they are unable, as respects that interest, to conclude on terms appearing to them reasonable an agreement under the last foregoing section containing such provisions as in their opinion are required for securing that the land will be satisfactorily managed as a nature reserve.

....

Compulsory acquisition of land by Conservancy for maintenance of nature reserves

18. (1) Where, as respects any interest[11] in land[12], the Nature Conservancy Council[13] have entered into an agreement under the last but one foregoing section and any breach of the agreement

---

[1] The Forestry Act 1947 (c. 21) is repealed by the Forestry Act 1967 (c. 10) save for the application of ss. 1–4 for the purposes of this Act: Forestry Act 1967, s. 50, sch. 7. Sch. 6 of the 1967 Act, p. 105 below, sets out transitional provisions. S. 5 of the Forestry Act 1967, p. 69 below, makes provision for forestry dedication covenants.

[2] 1925 c. 20.

[3] The Forestry Act 1967 (c. 10), s. 5(2) makes similar provision.

[4] 1921 c. 58.

[5] The Forestry Act 1967 (c. 10), s. 5(3) makes similar provision.

[6] Words "Scottish Natural Heritage" substituted by the Natural Heritage (Scotland) Act 1991 (c. 28), s. 4(6), sch. 2, para. 1(3). This amendment came into force on 1 April 1992: S.I. 1991/2633.

[7] For the meaning of "Nature Conservancy Council" see s. 15A, p. 15 above.

[8] "Land" defined by s. 114(1), p. 38 below.

[9] "Nature reserve" defined by s. 15, p. 14 above.

[10] "Interest" defined by s. 114(1), p. 38 below.

[11] "Interest" defined by s. 114(1), p. 38 below.

[12] "Land" defined by s. 114(1), p. 38 below.

[13] For the meaning of "Nature Conservancy Council" see s. 15A, p. 15 above.

occurs which prevents or impairs the satisfactory management as a nature reserve[1] of the land to which the agreement relates, then without prejudice to any other remedy the Nature Conservancy Council may acquire that interest compulsorily.

(2) Such a breach shall not be treated as having occurred by virtue of any act or omission capable of remedy unless there has been default in remedying it within a reasonable time after notice given by the Nature Conservancy Council requiring the remedying thereof.

(3) Any dispute arising under this section whether there has been such a breach of an agreement as aforesaid shall be determined by an arbitrator appointed by the Lord Chancellor or, in the case of a dispute relating to land in Scotland, by an arbiter appointed by the Lord President of the Court of Session.

(4) Without prejudice to the operation of the Arbitration Acts, 1889 to 1934[2], as respects land in England or Wales, at any stage of the proceedings in any arbitration under the last foregoing subsection relating to land in Scotland the arbiter may, and shall if so directed by the Court of Session, state a case for the opinion of that Court on any question of law arising in the arbitration.

Declarations what areas are nature reserves

19. (1) A declaration by the Nature Conservancy Council[3] that any land[4] is the subject of an agreement entered into with them under the foregoing provisions of this Part of this Act, or has been acquired and is held by the Nature Conservancy Council, shall be sufficient evidence unless the contrary is proved, that the land is subject to such an agreement or has been so acquired and is so held, as the case may be.

(2) A declaration by the Nature Conservancy Council that any land which is subject to such an agreement as aforesaid, or is held by the Nature Conservancy Council, is being managed as a nature reserve[5] shall be conclusive of the matters declared.

(3) It shall be the duty of the Nature Conservancy Council, where any such declaration has been made and the agreement to which it relates ceases to be in force, or the land to which it relates ceases to be held by the Nature Conservancy Council or to be managed as a nature reserve, as the case may be, to make a declaration of that fact; and any such declaration shall be conclusive of the matters declared.

(4) The Nature Conservancy Council shall publish notice of any declaration under this section in such manner as appears to them best suited for informing persons concerned[6].

(5) A document purporting to be certified on behalf of the Nature Conservancy Council to be a true copy of any declaration under this section shall be receivable in evidence and shall be deemed, unless the contrary is shown, to be such a copy[7].

Byelaws for protection of nature reserves

20. (1) The Nature Conservancy Council[8] may, as respects land[9] which is being managed as a nature reserve[10] under an agreement entered into with them or land held by them which is being managed as a nature reserve, make byelaws for the protection of the reserve:

Provided that byelaws under this section shall not have effect as respects any land in a reserve unless a declaration under the last foregoing section is in force declaring that the land is being

---

[1] "Nature reserve" defined by s. 15, p. 14 above.
[2] The reference to the Arbitration Acts, 1889 to 1934, is construed as a reference to the Arbitration Act 1959 (c. 27): s. 44(3).
[3] For the meaning of "Nature Conservancy Council" see s. 15A, p. 15 above.
[4] "Land" defined by s. 114(1), p. 38 below.
[5] "Nature reserve" defined by s. 15, p. 14 above.
[6] This subsection applies to a declaration under s. 35 of

the Wildlife and Countryside Act 1981 (c. 69), s. 35(2), p. 177 below.
[7] This subsection is extended to nature reserves of national importance by the Wildlife and Countryside Act 1981 (c. 69), s. 35(2), p. 177 below.
[8] For the meaning of "Nature Conservancy Council" see s. 15A, p. 15 above.
[9] "Land" defined by s. 114(1), p. 38 below.
[10] 'Nature reserve' defined by s. 15, p. 14 above.

managed as a nature reserve and notice of the declaration has been published in pursuance of that section.

(2) Without prejudice to the generality of the last foregoing subsection, byelaws under this section—

(a) may provide for prohibiting or restricting the entry into, or movement within, nature reserves of persons, vehicles[1], boats and animals;

(b) may prohibit or restrict the killing, taking, molesting or disturbance of living creatures of any description in a nature reserve, the taking, destruction or disturbance of eggs of any such creature, the taking of, or interference with, vegetation of any description in a nature reserve, or the doing of anything therein which will interfere with the soil or damage any object in the reserve;

(c) may prohibit or restrict the shooting of birds or of birds of any description within such area surrounding or adjoining a nature reserve (whether the area be of land or of sea) as appears to the Nature Conservancy Council requisite for the protection of the reserve;

(d) may contain provisions prohibiting the depositing of rubbish and the leaving of litter in a nature reserve;

(e) may prohibit or restrict, or provide for prohibiting or restricting, the lighting of fires in a nature reserve, or the doing of anything likely to cause a fire in a nature reserve;

(f) may provide for the issue, on such terms and subject to such conditions as may be specified in the byelaws, of permits authorising entry into a nature reserve or the doing of anything therein which would otherwise be unlawful, whether under the byelaws or otherwise;

(g) may be made so as to relate either to the whole or to any part of the reserve or, in the case of byelaws made under paragraph (c) of this subsection, of any such surrounding or adjoining area as is mentioned in that paragraph, and may make different provisions for different parts thereof:

Provided that byelaws under this section shall not interfere with the exercise by any person or a right vested in him as owner[2], lessee or occupier of land in a nature reserve, or in the case of such land in Scotland as limited owner thereof, or with the exercise of any public right of way or of any functions of statutory undertakers[3], [*England and Wales*: or an internal drainage board[3] *Scotland*: of a river board or other drainage authority] or a district board for a fishery district within the meaning of the Salmon Fisheries (Scotland) Act, 1962[4], or of the Commissioners appointed under the Tweed Fisheries Act, 1857[5] or with the running of a telecommunications code system or the exercise of any right conferred by or in accordance with the telecommunications code on the operator of any such system[6,7].

(3) Where the exercise of any right vested in a person, whether by reason of his being entitled to any interest[8] in land or by virtue of a licence or agreement, is prevented or hindered by the coming into operation of byelaws under this section, he shall be entitled to receive from the Nature Conservancy compensation in respect thereof[9].

[1] "Vehicle" defined by s. 114(1), p. 38 below.
[2] "Owner" defined by s. 114(1), p. 38 below.
[3] The following are deemed to be statutory undertakers for the purposes of this Act:

The Civil Aviation Authority (CAA): Civil Aviation Act 1982 (c. 16), s. 19, sch. 2, para. 4.

A public gas supplier: Gas Act 1986 (c. 44), s. 67(1) and (3), sch. 7, para. 2(1)(vii), sch. 8, para. 33.

The National Rivers Authority, every water undertaker and every sewerage undertaker: Water Act 1989 (c. 15), s. 190(1), sch. 25, para. 1(1) and (2).

The holder of a licence under the Electricity Act 1989, s. 6(1): Electricity Act 1989 (c. 29), s. 112(1), sch. 16, para. 1(1)(vii).

[3] *England and Wales*: Words "undertakers, or an internal drainage board" substituted by the Water Act 1989 (c. 15), s.

190, sch. 25, para. 13(1). This amendment came into force on 1 September 1989: S.I. 1989/1146.
[4] 1862 c. 97.
[5] 1857 c. cxlviii.
[6] Words "or with the running of a telecommunications code system . . . any such system" inserted by the Telecommunications Act 1984 (c. 12), s. 109(1), sch. 4, para. 28(1). This amendment came into force on 5 August 1984: S.I. 1984/876.
[7] This subsection applies to byelaws made under s. 35 of the Wildlife and Countryside Act 1981 (c. 69): s. 35(4), p. 177 below.
[8] "Interest" defined by s. 114(1), p. 38 below.
[9] This subsection also applies to byelaws made under s. 35 of the Wildlife and Countryside Act 1981 (c. 690: s. 35(4), p. 177 below. For supplementary provisions concerning byelaws see s. 106, p. 33 below.

21. Establishment of nature reserves by local authorities

(1) The council of a county[1] or county borough or in Scotland[2,3] a planning authority[4] shall have power to provide, or secure the provision of, nature reserves[5] on any land[6] in their area (not being land held by, or managed in accordance with an agreement entered into with, the Nature Conservancy Council[7]) as to which it appears to the Council expedient that it should be managed as a nature reserve.

(2) and (3) Repealed by the Local Government Act 1972 (c. 70), s. 272(1), sch. 30. This amendment came into force on 1 April 1974: s. 273.

(4) The foregoing provisions of this Part of this Act shall apply to the provision of nature reserves by local authorities[8] under this section with the substitution for references to the Nature Conservancy Council of references to the local authority and as if the references in subsection (1) of sections sixteen and seventeen respectively of this Act[9] to the national interest included references to the interests of the locality.

(5) A local authority may, as respects any land which is being managed as a nature reserve by the authority, enter into an agreement with any drainage authority[10] for the exercise by the drainage authority, on such terms as to payment or otherwise as may be specified in the agreement, of any power of doing work exercisable by the local authority under the foregoing provisions of this section.

(6) A local authority shall exercise their functions under this Part of this Act in consultation with the Nature Conservancy Council.[11]

(7) Repealed by the Local Government (Scotland) Act 1973 (c. 65), s. 237(1), sch. 29. This amendment came into force on 16 May 1975: S.I. 1973/2181.

Power of drainage authorities to do work in nature reserves

22. Where the Nature Conservancy Council[12], a local authority[13] or any other person enter into an agreement with a drainage authority[14] for the doing by that authority of any work on land[15]

---

[1] a) For the construction of "the council of a county" see the Local Government Act 1972 (c. 70), s. 179.

b) The powers conferred on a county council by this section are also exercisable as respects any district by the district council and references to a local authority are construed accordingly: Local Government Act 1972 (c. 70), s. 184, sch. 17, pt. III, para. 34.

c) Under the Local Government Reorganisation (Property etc.) Order 1986, S.I. 1986/148, any land held by a metropolitan county for the purpose of this section shall vest in the local council: art. 3, sch. 1, para. 7(a). "Local council" means the council of the London borough or metropolitan district within which such land is situated or, if the land is situated in the City, the Common Council: art. 2(1). This order came into operation on 1 April 1986: art. 1(2).

d) This section has effect as if the Broads Authority were a county council: s. 111A(1), p. 37 below.

[2] Words "or in Scotland" inserted by the Local Government (Scotland) Act 1973 (c. 65), s. 214, sch. 27, para. 100. This amendment came into force on 16 May 1975: S.I. 1973/2181.

[3] Former words "general or district" repealed by the Local Government etc. (Scotland) Act 1994 (c. 39), s. 180(2), sch. 14. It is anticipated that this amendment will come into force on 1 April 1996.

[4] Words "a planning authority" substituted by the Local Government and Planning (Scotland) Act 1982 (c. 43), s. 10. This amendment came into force on 1 April 1983: 1982/1397.

[5] "Nature reserve" defined by s. 15, p. 14 above.

[6] "Land" defined by s. 114(1), p. 38 below.

[7] For the meaning of "Nature Conservancy Council" see s. 15A, p. 15 above.

[8] For the construction of "local authority" see the Local Government Act 1972 (c. 70), s. 184, sch. 17, pt. III, para. 34.

[9] P. 15–16 above.

[10] "Drainage authority" defined by s. 114(1), p. 37 below.

[11] **Cases: section 21:** Burnet v Barclay 1955 SLT 282; Evans v Godber [1974] 1 WLR 1317; [1974] 3 All ER 341.

[12] For the meaning of "Nature Conservancy Council" see s. 15A, p. 15 above.

[13] For the construction of "local authority" see the Local Government Act 1972 (c. 70), s. 184, sch. 17, pt. III, para. 34. This section has effect as if the Broads Authority were a county council: s. 111A(1), p. 37 below.

[14] "Drainage authority" defined by s. 114(1), p. 37 below.

[15] "Land" defined by s. 114(1), p. 38 below.

managed as a nature reserve[1] by, or under an agreement with, the Nature Conservancy Council or a local authority, no limitation imposed by law on the capacity of the drainage authority by virtue of the constitution thereof shall operate so as to prevent the drainage authority carrying out the agreement.

23. *This section, which provided that the Nature Conservancy Council had a duty to inform local planning authorities of areas of special scientific interest, is superseded by the Wildlife and Countryside Act 1981 (c. 69), s. 28, p. 168 below, and repealed by s. 73(1), sch. 17, pt. I save that any notification given under this section has effect as if given under s. 28(1)(a) of the Wildlife and Countryside Act 1981: s. 28(13), p. 170 below. This amendment came into force on 30 November 1981: s. 74(2).*

For statutory provisions concerning areas, or sites, of special scientific interest, also known as SSSIs, see the Wildlife and Countryside Act 1981, ss. 28 to 33, pp. 168–176 below and the additional references noted at s. 28.

24. *Repealed by the Science and Technology Act 1965 (c. 4), s. 6(3), sch. 4. This amendment came into force on 1 June 1965: S.I. 1965/1127.*

25. *Repealed by the Nature Conservancy Council Act 1973, s. 5, sch. 4. This amendment came into force on 1 November 1973: s. 1(7), S.I. 1973/1721.*

Application of Part III to Scotland

26. In the application of this Part of this Act to Scotland the expressions "owner" and "limited owner" have the same meanings as in section three of the Forestry Act, 1947[2].

Part IV: Public Rights of Way

This part is not reproduced. It is largely repealed and replaced by Part III of the Wildlife and Countryside Act 1981, the Highways Act 1980, the Rights of Way Act 1990 and other legislation. The sections of this part which are not repealed relate to long-distance routes (ss. 51–56) and the penalty for displaying on footpaths notices deterring public use (s. 57).

Part V: Access to Open Country

This part is not reproduced. It contains provisions enabling the public to have access to open country for recreation under access agreements and access orders. This part extends to England and Wales.

---

[1] "Nature reserve" defined by s. 15, p. 14 above.
[2] The Forestry Act 1947 (c. 21) is repealed by the Forestry Act 1967 (c. 10) save for the application of ss. 1–4 for the purposes of this Act: Forestry Act 1967 (c. 10), s. 50, sch. 7. Sch. 6 of the 1967 Act, p. 105 below, sets out transitional provisions. S. 3 of the Forestry Act 1947 makes provision for forestry dedication agreements. S. 3(3) provides:

"In this section the expression 'owner' in relation to any land means the proprietor thereof for his own absolute use, and the expression 'limited owner' means any person empowered by the next succeeding section to enter into forestry dedication agreements relating thereto."

The next succeeding section, s. 4, contains similar provisions to the Forestry Act 1967, sch. 2, para. 4, p. 100 below. The Forestry Act 1967, s. 5(4), p. 70 below, provides that sch. 2 to the Act empowers limited owners, trustees and others to enter into forestry dedication agreements.

Provisions concerning access to open country in Scotland are contained in Part III of the Countryside (Scotland) Act 1967 (c. 86).

Part VI: General, Financial and Supplementary

84. *Repealed by the Countryside Act 1968 (c. 41), s. 50(2), sch. 5. This amendment came into force on 3 August 1968: s. 50(3).*

General powers and duties of Commission

85. *General duty of Commission to advise on questions relating to natural beauty*

Without prejudice to their respective duties[1] relating to National Parks,[2] it shall be the duty of the Commission[3] and the Council[4]—

   (a) *Repealed by the Countryside Act 1968 (c. 41), s. 50(2), sch. 5. This amendment came into force on 3 August 1968: s. 50(3).*

   (b) in circumstances where it appears to the Minister[5] and to the Commission, or, as the case may be, to the Minister and to the Council,[6] desirable that their assistance should be generally available, to inquire into and report on such questions referred to them by any other body of persons or person;

   (c) to bring to the attention of the Minister or of local planning authorities[7] the effect on the natural beauty of such areas or places as aforesaid of developments, or developments of any class, which appear to the Commission (as respects England) or to the Council (as respects Wales)[8] to be likely to be prejudicial thereto.

Information services to be provided by Commission

86. (1) It shall be the duty of the Commission[9] to take such steps as appear to them expedient for securing that persons interested—

   (a) will be informed of the situation and extent of, and means of access to, National Parks[10], other areas, being areas of outstanding natural beauty[11], and long-distance routes for which

---

[1] Words "their respective duties" substituted by the Environmental Protection Act 1990 (c. 43), s. 130(1), sch. 8, para. 1(10)(a). This amendment came into force on 1 April 1991: S.I. 1991/685.

[2] "National Park has the meaning assigned to it by s. 5(3), p. 8 above: s. 114(1), p. 38 below.

[3] "The Commission" means the Countryside Commission established by s. 1, p. 7 above: s. 114(1), p. 37 below.

[4] Words "and the Council" inserted by the Environmental Protection Act 1990 (c. 43), s. 130(1), sch. 8, para. 1(10)(b). "The Council" means the Countryside Council for Wales: s. 114(1), p. 37 below. The Countryside Council for Wales is established by the Environmental Protection Act 1990 (c. 43), s. 128, p. 229 below. For the functions of the Council see ss. 130–134, p. 230 below.

[5] "The Minister" defined by s. 114(1), p. 38 below.

[6] Words ", or, as the case may be, to the Minister and to the Council," inserted by the Environmental Protection Act

1990 (c. 43), s. 130(1), sch. 8, para. 1(10)(c).

[7] For statutory provisions in respect of local planning authorities see the Town and Country Planning Act 1990 (c. 8), Part I and the Local Government Act 1972 (c. 70), s. 184, sch. 17, pt. I. The Town and Country Planning Act 1990 applies by virtue of s. 114(1) below and the Planning (Consequential Provisions) Act 1990 (c. 11), s. 2.

[8] Words "(as respects England) or to the Council (as respects Wales)" inserted by the Environmental Protection Act 1990 (c. 43), s. 130(1), sch. 8, para. 1(10)(d).

[9] "The Commission" means the Countryside Commission established by s. 1, p. 7 above: s. 114(1), p. 37 below. For the application of this section to the Countryside Council for Wales see s. 86A, p. 22 below.

[10] "National Park" has the meaning assigned to it by s. 5(3), p. 8 above: s. 114(1), p. 38 below.

[11] "Area of outstanding natural beauty" has the meaning assigned to it by s. 87(1) below: s. 114(1), p. 37 below.

proposals under section fifty-one of this Act have been approved, and the accommodation and facilities available for persons wishing to visit National Parks and such other areas or persons wishing to use such routes;

(b) will be able to learn about the history, natural features, flora and fauna of National Parks and the objects of architectural, archaeological[1] or historical interest therein and the opportunities for recreation available therein,

and that suitable methods of publicity are used for the prevention of damage in National Parks and such other areas as aforesaid and otherwise for encouraging a proper standard of behaviour on the part of persons visiting National Parks and such other areas; and the said methods shall include the preparation and publication of a code of conduct for the guidance of persons visiting the countryside.

(2) Without prejudice to the provisions of the last foregoing subsection, the Commission may for the purposes thereof procure the production and sale to the public of books, guides and maps, the exhibition of posters and other advertisements, the giving of lectures and the provision and exhibition of cinematograph films.

(3) For the avoidance of doubt it is hereby declared that the steps mentioned in subsection (1) of this section include the making of contributions towards expenses incurred by other bodies of persons.

86A. *Information services to be provided by Council*

The provisions of section eighty-six of this Act shall apply to the Council[2] in relation to National Parks[3] and other land[4] in Wales as they apply to the Commission in relation to National Parks and other land in England.[5]

Areas of outstanding natural beauty

Designation of areas of outstanding natural beauty

87. (1) The Commission,[6] or as the case may be, the Council[7], may, by order made as respects any area in England or Wales, not being in a National Park[8], which appears to them to be of such outstanding natural beauty that it is desirable that the provisions of this Act relating to such areas should apply thereto, designate the area for the purposes of this Act as an area of outstanding natural beauty; and references in this Act to such an area shall be construed as references to an area designated under this section[9].

(1A) The following provisions shall apply to the Council in relation to land[10] in Wales as they apply to the Commission in relation to land in England.[11]

(2) Where the Commission propose to make an order under this section they shall consult with every local authority[12] whose area includes any part of the area to which the proposed order is to relate, and shall then, before making the order, publish, in the London Gazette and in one or more local newspapers circulating in the area of every such authority as aforesaid, notice that they propose to make the order, indicating the effect of the order and stating the time within

---

[1] Word "archaeological" inserted by the Countryside Act 1968 (c. 41), s. 21(4). This amendment came into force on 3 August 1968: s. 50(3).

[2] "The Council" means the Countryside Council for Wales: s. 114(1), p. 37 below.

[3] "National Park" has the meaning assigned to it by s. 5(3), p. 8 above: s. 114(1), p. 38 below.

[4] "Land" defined by s. 114(1), p. 38 below.

[5] This section inserted by the Environmental Protection Act 1990 (c. 43), s. 130(1), sch. 8, para. 1(11). This section came into force on 1 April 1991: S.I. 1991/685.

[6] "The Commission" means the Countryside Commission established by s. 1, p. 7 above: s. 114(1), p. 37 below.

[7] Words ", or as the case may be, the Council," inserted

by the Environmental Protection Act 1990 (c. 43), s. 130(1), sch. 8, para. 1(12)(a). This amendment came into force on 1 April 1991: S.I. 1991/685. "The Council" means the Countryside Council for Wales: s. 114(1), p. 37 below.

[8] "National Park" has the meaning assigned to it by s. 5(3), p. 8 above: s. 114(1), p. 38 below.

[9] Land in an area designated under this section as an area of outstanding natural beauty may not be included in a simplified planning zone: Town and Country Planning Act 1990 (c. 8), s. 87(1).

[10] "Land" defined by s. 114(1), p. 38 below.

[11] This subsection inserted by the Environmental Protection Act 1990 (c. 43), s. 130(1), sch. 8, para. 1(12)(b).

[12] "Local authority" defined by subsection (6) below.

which and manner in which representations with respect thereto may be made to the Commission, and shall consider any representations duly made.

(3) An order under the last foregoing subsection shall not come into operation unless and until submitted to and confirmed by the Minister[1], and in submitting any such order to the Minister the Commission shall forward to him any observations made by a local authority consulted in pursuance of the last foregoing subsection and any representations duly made thereunder, other than observations or representations to which effect is given by the order as submitted to the Minister.

(4) The Minister may confirm an order submitted to him under this section either as submitted or with such modifications as he thinks expedient.

(5) Before refusing to confirm an order under this section, or determining to confirm it with modifications, the Minister shall consult with the Commission and with every local authority whose area includes any land to which the order as submitted, or as proposed to be modified, relates.

(6) In this section the expression "local authority" means a joint planning board[2], county council, county borough council or county district council[3].

(7) Without prejudice to the power of the Commission to vary an order under this section, the Minister may by order vary any such order of the Commission; and subsection (2) of this section shall apply to any order of the Minister under this subsection, with the substitution for references to the Commission of references to the Minister.

(8) It shall be the duty of the Commission to secure that copies of any order such as is mentioned in this section shall be available, at the office of the Commission, at the offices of each local authority whose area includes any part of the area to which the order relates, and at such other place or places in or near that area as the Commission may determine, for inspection by the public at all reasonable times.

....

Application to areas of outstanding natural beauty of provisions relating to National Parks

88. (1) Paragraphs[4] (*e*) of subsection (4) of section six[5], section nine[6], subsection (1) of section sixty-two, subsection (5) of section sixty-four and subsections (5) and (6) of section sixty-five of this Act shall apply in relation to areas of outstanding natural beauty[7] as they apply in relation to National Parks[8].

(2) Section eleven of this Act[9], so far as it confers powers for preserving and enhancing natural beauty[10], shall apply as aforesaid.

(2A) The provision of section 4A[11]of this Act shall apply to the provisions mentioned in the preceding subsection for the purposes of their application to areas of outstanding natural beauty as the provisions of that section apply for the purposes of Part II of this Act.[12]

---

[1] "The Minister" defined by s. 114(1), p. 38 below.

[2] For statutory provisions in respect of joint planning boards see the Town and Country Planning Act 1990 (c. 8), ss. 2, 4 and the Local Government Act 1972 (c. 70), s. 184, sch. 17, pt. I. The Town and Country Planning Act 1990 applies by virtue of s. 114(1) below and the Planning (Consequential Provisions) Act 1990 (c. 11), s. 2.

[3] For the construction of "county council" and "county district council" see the Local Government Act 1972 (c. 70), s. 179.

[4] Former words "(*d*) and" repealed by the Countryside Act 1968 (c. 41), s. 50(2), sch. 5. This amendment came into force on 3 August 1968: s. 50(3).

[5] P. 9 above.

[6] P. 11 above.

[7] "Area of outstanding natural beauty" has the meaning assigned to it by s. 87(1) above: s. 114(1), p. 37 below.

[8] "National Park" has the meaning assigned to it by s. 5(3), p. 8 above: s. 114(1), p. 38 below.

[9] P. 12 above.

[10] For the construction of references to the preservation of the natural beauty of an area see s. 114(2), p. 38 below, and the Countryside Act 1968 (c. 41), s. 21(7), p. 123 below.

[11] P. 8 above.

[12] This subsection inserted by the Environmental Protection Act 1990 (c. 43), s. 130(1), sch. 8, para. 1(13). This amendment came into force on 1 April 1991: S.I. 1991/685.

General Powers of Local Planning Authorities

Planting of trees and treatment of derelict land

89. (1) A local planning authority[1] may plant trees[2] on land in their area for the purpose of preserving or enhancing the natural beauty thereof[3].

(2) Where it appears to a local authority that any land in their area—

(a) is derelict, neglected or unsightly; or

(b) is not derelict, neglected or unsightly but is likely to become so by reason of actual or apprehended collapse of the surface as the result of the carrying out of relevant operations which have ceased to be carried out,

they may carry out, for the purpose of reclaiming or improving that land or of enabling it to be brought into use, such works on that land or any other land as appear to them expedient.

In this subsection "relevant operations" means underground mining operations other than operations for the purpose of the working and getting of coal, or of coal and other minerals worked with coal, or for the purpose of getting any product from coal in the course of working and getting coal.[4]

(2A) *Repealed by the Local Government Act 1972 (c. 70), ss. 184, 272(1), sch. 17, para. 38, sch. 30. This amendment came into force on 1 April 1974: s. 273.*

(3) The powers conferred by this section may be exercised by an authority either on land belonging to them or with the consent of all persons interested therein on other land; and in relation to such other land the said powers shall include power to make arrangements whereby the planting or work is carried out, on such terms as may be provided under the arrangements, by a person other than the authority.

(4) Nothing in the said provisions shall authorise the doing of anything in contravention of any prohibition or restriction having effect under any enactment or rule of law[5].

(5) A local authority[6] may acquire land compulsorily for the purpose of any of their functions under this section.

(6) Where a local authority[6] exercise their powers under the foregoing provisions of this section on land not belonging to the authority, the management of the land, so far as relates to anything done by the authority, may be undertaken either by the authority or by a person interested in the land, as may be agreed between the authority and the persons so interested, and on such terms as may be so agreed.

(7) In this section "local authority" means a local planning authority, the council of a county[7] not being a local planning authority, or the council of a county district.[8,9,10]

[1] For statutory provisions in respect of local planning authorities see the Town and Country Planning Act 1990 (c. 8), Part I and the Local Government Act 1972 (c. 70), s. 184. The Town and Country Planning Act 1990 applies by virtue of s. 114(1) below and the Planning (Consequential Provisions) Act 1990 (c. 11), s. 2. This section has effect as if the Broads Authority were a local planning authority: s. 111A(2), p. 37 below.

[2] For the construction of references to the planting of trees see s. 114(3), p. 38 below.

[3] For the construction of references to the preservation of the natural beauty of an area see s. 114(2), p. 38 below, and the Countryside Act 1968 (c. 41), s. 21(7), p. 123 below.

[4] This subsection substituted by the Derelict Land Act 1982 (c. 42), s. 3(1). This amendment came into force on 30 August 1982: s. 5(3). For further statutory provision see the Mineral Workings Act 1985 (c. 12), ss. 7, 8.

[5] This subsection amended by the Local Authorities (Land) Act 1963 (c. 29), s. 6(2) and the Countryside Act 1968 (c. 41), ss. 21(5), 50(2), sch. 5.

[6] Words "local authority" substituted by the Local Authorities (Land) Act 1963 (c. 29), s. 6(1). This amendment came into force on 31 July 1963, the date of the Royal Assent.

[7] Former words "or county borough" repealed by the Local Government Act 1972 (c. 70), s. 272(1), sch. 30. This amendment came into force on 1 April 1974: s. 273.

[8] For the construction of "the council of a county" and "the council of a county district" see the Local Government Act 1972 (c. 70), s. 179.

[9] Under the Local Government Reorganisation (Property etc.) Order 1986, S.I. 1986/148, any land acquired by an abolished council for the purposes of any of their functions under this section and not appropriated for the purposes of any other function shall vest in the local council: art. 3, sch.

Local authority byelaws

90. (1) A local planning authority[1] may, as respects land[2] in their area belonging to them and comprised either in a National Park[3] or area of outstanding natural beauty[4], or as respects land or a waterway[5] to which the public are given access by an agreement or order, or in consequence of acquisition, under Part V of this Act, make byelaws for the preservation of order, for the prevention of damage to the land or waterway or anything thereon or therein, and for securing that persons resorting thereto will so behave themselves as to avoid undue interference with the enjoyment of the land or waterway by other persons.

(2) *Repealed by the Local Government Act 1972 (c. 70), ss. 184, 272(1), sch. 17, para. 39, sch. 30. This amendment came into force on 1 April 1974: s. 273.*

(3) Without prejudice to the generality of subsection (1) of this section, byelaws under that subsection—

(a) may prohibit or restrict the use of the land or waterway, either generally or in any manner specified in the bye-laws, by traffic of any description so specified;

(b) may contain provisions prohibiting the depositing of rubbish and the leaving of litter;

(c) may regulate or prohibit the lighting of fires;

(d) may be made so as to relate either to the whole or to any part of the land or waterway, and may make different provisions for different parts thereof:[6]

(4) Before making byelaws under the foregoing provisions of this section as respects a National Park or area of outstanding natural beauty, the local planning authority[7] shall consult with the Commission[8] (as regards land in England) or the Council[9] (as regards land in Wales)[10].

(5) A local planning authority may, as respects parking places provided in pursuance of arrangements made by them under Part II of this Act[11], make byelaws as to the conditions of use, and charges to be made for the use, of such parking places, and for prohibiting or restricting persons from plying for hire with vehicles at such parking places.

Nothing in this subsection shall be construed as limiting the general power of a local planning authority to make charges for any services or facilities provided by them under this Act.

(6) A county council or county district council[12] shall have power to enforce byelaws made under this section by another authority as respects land in the area of the council[13].

1, para. 2. "Local council" means the council of the London borough or metropolitan district within which such land is situated or, if the land is situated in the City, the common Council: art. 2(1). This order came into operation on 1 April 1986: art. 1(2).

[10] This subsection inserted by the Local Authorities (Land) Act 1963 (c. 29), s. 6(4).

[1] For statutory provisions in respect of local planning authorities see the Town and Country Planning Act 1990 (c. 8), Part I and the Local Government Act 1972 (c. 70), s. 184. The Town and Country Planning Act 1990 applies by virtue of s. 114(1) below and the Planning (Consequential Provisions) Act 1990 (c. 11), s. 2.

[2] "Land" defined by s. 114(1), p. 38 below.

[3] "National Park" has the meaning assigned to it by s. 5(3), p. 8 above: s. 114(1), p. 38 below.

[4] "Area of outstanding natural beauty" has the meaning assigned to it by s. 87(1), p. 22 above: s. 114(1), p. 37 below.

[5] "Waterway" defined by s. 114(1), p. 38 below.

[6] This subsection is restricted by the Countryside Act 1968 (c. 41), s. 41(12), p. 128 below. The former proviso to

this subsection is repealed by the Countryside Act 1968, s. 50(2), sch. 5. This amendment came into force on 3 August 1968: s. 50(3).

[7] Words "local planning authority" substituted by the Local Government Act 1972 (c. 70), s. 272(1), sch. 17, para. 39. This amendment came into force on 1 April 1974: s. 273.

[8] "The Commission" means the Countryside Commission established by s. 1, p. 7 above: s. 114(1), p. 37 below.

[9] "The Council" means the Countryside Council for Wales: s. 114(1), p. 37 below.

[10] Words "(as regards land in England) or the Council (as regards land in Wales)" inserted by the Environmental Protection Act 1990 (c. 43), s. 130(1), sch. 8, para. 1(14). This amendment came into force on 1 April 1991: S.I. 1991/685.

[11] P. 8 above.

[12] For the construction of "county council" and "county district council" see the Local Government Act 1972 (c. 70), s. 179.

[13] This section does not apply to the Inner London boroughs or the City: London Government Act 1963 (c. 33), s. 60(5). This section is extended by the Countryside Act 1968 (c. 41), s. 41(10), p. 128 below.

Default powers of Secretary of State as to certain byelaws

91. (1) If a local planning authority[1], when required by the Secretary of State to make, as respects land[2] or a waterway[3] to which the public are given access by an agreement or order, or in consequence of acquisition, under Part V of this Act, byelaws with respect to any of the matters with respect to which they are empowered by the last foregoing section to make byelaws, do not within three months after being so required comply with the requirement to the satisfaction of the Secretary of State, he may himself make byelaws in relation to the matters, and as respects the land or waterway, in question:

Provided that before making byelaws under this section as respects a National Park[4] or area of outstanding natural beauty[5] the Secretary of State shall consult with the Commission[6] (as regards land or waterways in England) or the Council[7] (as regards land or waterways in Wales)[8].

(2) Any byelaws made by the Secretary of State under this section shall have effect as if they had been made by the local planning authority and confirmed by the Secretary of State, and the provisions of this Act and of any enactment thereby applied shall have effect in relation to the byelaws accordingly[9].

Wardens

92. (1) A local authority may appoint such number of persons as may appear to the authority to be necessary or expedient to act as wardens as respects any land[10] or waterway[11] in relation to which byelaws made by the authority are in force under the last but one foregoing section, or in relation to which the authority have power to make such byelaws[12].

(2) *Repealed by the Countryside Act 1968 (c. 41), s. 50(2), sch. 5. S. 42(4) of the Countryside Act 1968, p. 129 below, has effect in substitution for this subsection. This amendment came into force on 3 August 1968: s. 50(3).*

(3) For the purpose of exercising any function conferred on him by or under this section a warden appointed thereunder may enter upon any land, or go on any waterway, comprised in an access agreement or order in force under Part V of this Act:

Provided that this subsection shall not confer any power of entry on land which is excepted land for the purposes of the said Part V.

(4) Subject to the provisions of the last foregoing subsection, the foregoing provisions of this section shall not authorise a warden appointed by an authority thereunder, on land or a waterway in which any person other than that authority has an interest[13], without the consent of that person to do anything which apart from this section would be actionable at his suit by virtue of that interest[14].

[1] For statutory provisions in respect of local planning authorities see the Town and Country Planning Act 1990 (c. 8), Part I and the Local Government Act 1972 (c. 70), s. 184. The Town and Country Planning Act 1990 appliers by virtue of s. 114(1) below and the Planning (Consequential Provisions) Act 1990 (c. 11), s. 2.

[2] "Land" defined by s. 114(1), p. 38 below.

[3] "Waterway" defined by s. 114(1), p. 38 below.

[4] "National Park" has the meaning assigned to it by s. 5(3), p. 8 above: s. 114(1), p. 38 below.

[5] "Area of outstanding natural beauty" has the meaning assigned to it by s. 87(1), p. 22 above: s. 114(1), p. 37 below.

[6] "The Commission" means the Countryside Commission established by s. 1, p. 7 above: s. 114(1), p. 37 below.

[7] "The Council" means the Countryside Council for Wales: s. 114(1), p. 37 below. The Countryside Council for Wales is established by the Environmental Protection Act 1990 (c. 43), s. 128, p. 229 below. For the functions of the Council see ss. 130–134, p. 230 below.

[8] Words "(as regards land or waterways in England) or the Council (as regards land or waterways in Wales)" inserted by the Environmental Protection Act 1990 (c. 43), s. 130(1), sch. 8, para. 1(15). This amendment came into force on 1 April 1991: S.I. 1991/685.

[9] This section is extended by the Countryside Act 1968 (c. 41), s. 41(10), p. 128 below.

[10] "Land" defined by s. 114(1), p. 38 below.

[11] "Waterway" defined by s. 114(1), p. 38 below.

[12] This subsection is extended by the Wildlife and Countryside Act 1981 (c. 69), s. 49(2), p. 132 below.

[13] "Interest" defined by s. 114(1), p. 38 below.

[14] This section is extended by the Countryside Act 1968 (c. 41), s. 13, p. 120 below, s. 41, p. 128 and s. 42.

93–94. *Repealed by the Countryside Act 1968 (c. 41), ss. 32(11), 50(2), sch. 5. This amendment came into force on 3 August 1968: s. 50(3).*

Financial Provisions

95. *Superseded by the Wildlife and Countryside Act 1981 (c. 69), s. 47, p. 186 below, and repealed by s. 73(1), sch. 17, pt. II, of that Act. This amendment came into force on 1 April 1982: S.I. 1982/327.*

96. *Repealed by the Science and Technology Act 1965 (c. 4), s. 6(3), sch. 4. This amendment came into force on 1 June 1965: S.I. 1965/1127.*

97. *Superseded by the Derelict Land Act 1982 (c. 42), s. 1, and repealed by ss. 1(12), 5(2), sch. to that Act. This amendment came into force on 30 August 1982: s. 5(3).*

98. *Repealed by the Local Government Act 1974 (c. 7), s. 42(2), sch. 8. This amendment came into force on 1 June 1977: S.I. 1977/943.*

Contributions by local authorities

99. (1) A local authority[1] may defray or contribute towards, or undertake to defray or contribute towards, expenditure incurred or to be incurred for the purposes of this Act[2] by any other local authority.

England and Wales

(2) In this section the expression "local authority" means a local planning authority,[3] the council of a county[4] not being a local planning authority, or the council of a county district.[5]

Scotland

(2) In this section the expression "local authority" means a council constituted under section 2 of the Local Government etc. (Scotland) Act 1994.[6]

(3) Where, under subsection (4) of section thirteen of this Act[7], the Minister[8] directs that any power of a local planning authority under that section shall be exercisable by another authority, subsection (1) of this section shall apply as if that other authority were a local authority; and if

---

[1] "Local authority" defined by subsection (2) below.

[2] The reference to this Act includes reference to the Countryside Act 1968 (c. 41): s. 46(1), p. 130 below.

[3] For statutory provisions in respect of local planning authorities see the Town and Country Planning Act 1990 (c. 70), s. 184. The Town and Country Planning Act 1990 applies by virtue of s. 114(1) below and the Planning (Consequential Provisions) Act 1990 (c. 11), s. 2.

[4] Former words "or a county borough" repealed by the Local Government Act 1972 (c. 70), s. 272(1), sch. 30. This amendment came into force on 1 April 1974: s. 273.

[5] For the construction of "the council of a county" and "the council of a county district" see the Local Government Act 1972 (c. 70), s. 179. The powers conferred on a county

council by subsection (6) are also exercisable as respects any district by the district council and references to a local authority are construed accordingly: Local Government Act 1972 (c. 70), s. 184(7), sch. 17, pt. II, para. 34.

[6] Words "means a" substituted by the Local Government (Scotland) Act 1973 (c. 65), s. 214(2), sch. 27, pt. II, para. 102 which came into force on 16 May 1975: s. 214. Words "council constituted under section 2 of the Local Government etc. (Scotland) Act 1994" substituted by the Local Government etc. (Scotland) Act 1994 (c. 39), s. 180(1), sch. 13, para. 33. It is anticipated that this amendment will come into force on 1 April 1996.

[7] P. 13 above.

[8] "The Minister" defined by s. 114(1), p. 38 below.

the direction so provides the local planning authority shall be under a duty to exercise their powers under subsection (1) of this section to such extent as may be specified in the direction.

(4) *Repealed by the Highways Act 1959 (c. 25), s. 312(2), sch. 25, and the London Government Act 1963 (c. 33), s. 16(2), sch. 6, para. 70.*

(5) Any expenditure incurred under this section by a local planning authority in respect of the erection of buildings or the carrying out of work by any such other authority as is mentioned in subsection (3) of this section shall be treated for the purposes of section ninety-seven of this Act[1] as if it were expenditure incurred in the exercise of the powers of the local planning authority mentioned in paragraph (a) of subsection (1) of the said section ninety-seven.

(6) The council of a county[2] may defray or contribute towards any expenditure [*England and Wales*: incurred by the National Rivers Authority or an internal drainage board being[3] *Scotland*: incurred by a river board or other drainage authority being] expenditure incurred for the benefit of a nature reserve managed by or under an agreement with the council or in consequence of anything done in the management of such a reserve.

....

Payments out of moneys provided by Parliament

100. There shall be defrayed out of moneys provided by Parliament—

(a) the expenses under this Act of the Minister of Town and Country Planning[4],[5] and the Minister of Agriculture , Fisheries and Food[6];

(b) any increase attributable to provisions of this Act in the sums payable out of such moneys under Part I or Part II of the Local Government Act, 1948.

Supplementary Provisions

101. (1) The following provisions of this section shall have effect for applying certain provisions of this Act to Crown land, that is to say land[7] an interest[8] in which belongs to His Majesty in right of the Crown or the Duchy of Lancaster, or to the Duchy of Cornwall, and land an interest in which belongs to a Government department or is held in trust for His Majesty for the purposes of a Government department.

(2) A National Park[9] may include Crown land, and with the consent of the appropriate authority[10] the powers conferred by Part II of this Act[11] may be exercised as respects any interest in Crown land.

(3) Where a National Park includes any Crown land, the appropriate authority and the local planning authority[12] in whose area the land is situated may enter into an agreement for securing that, so far as any interest held by or on behalf of the Crown is concerned and so far as may be provided by the agreement, the land will be managed in a manner consistent with the

---

[1] P. 27 above.
[2] Former words "or county borough" repealed by the Local Government Act 1972 (c. 70), s. 272(1), sch. 30.
[3] Words "incurred by the National Rivers Authority or an internal drainage board being" substituted by the Water Act 1989 (c. 15), s. 190(1), sch. 25, para. 13(2). This amendment came into force on 1 September 1989.
[4] These functions transferred to the Secretary of State: S.I. 1970/1681 and earlier orders (see p. 38 below, note 1).
[5] Former words "the Treasury" repealed by the Science and Technology Act 1965, s. 6(3), sch. 4. This amendment came into force on 1 June 1965: S.I. 1965/1127.
[6] The reference to the Minister of Agriculture, Fisheries and Food: substituted by S.I. 1955/554 which came into

operation on 7 April 1955.
[7] "Land" defined by s. 114(1), p. 38 below.
[8] "Interest" defined by s. 114(1), p. 38 below.
[9] "National Park" has the meaning assigned to it by s. 5(3), p. 8 above: s. 114(1), p. 38 below.
[10] "The appropriate authority" defined by subsection (11) below.
[11] P. 8 above.
[12] For statutory provisions in respect of local planning authorities see the Town and Country Planning Act 1990 (c. 8), Part I and the Local Government Act 1972 (c. 70), s. 184. The Town and Country Planning Act 1990 applies by virtue of s. 114(1) below and the Planning (Consequential Provisions) Act 1990 (c. 11), s. 2.

accomplishment of either or both of the purposes specified in subsection (1) of section five of this Act[1].

(4) The appropriate authority may enter into an agreement under Part III of this Act[2] as respects an interest in Crown land held by or on behalf of the Crown, and an agreement thereunder as respects any other interest in Crown land shall not have effect unless approved by the appropriate authority.

(5) An interest in Crown land, other than one held by or on behalf of the Crown, may be acquired under the said Part III, but only with the consent of the appropriate authority.

(6) Parts IV and V of this Act shall apply to Crown land, but subject to the following modifications, that is to say,—

(a) no[3] access order shall be made as respects such land except with the consent of the appropriate authority;

(b) no such land shall be acquired under the said Part IV or V except with such consent; and

(c) if any land comprised in an access agreement or order, not being excepted land as defined for the purposes of the said Part V. becomes Crown land while it is so comprised, the access agreement or order shall cease to apply to the land unless the appropriate authority consent to the continued application thereto of the agreement or order.

(7) Section eighty-nine of this Act[4] shall apply to Crown land if the appropriate authority consents to its application thereto, but subject to the following modifications, that is to say—

(a) an interest in Crown land may be acquired for the purposes of the said section eighty-nine only with the consent of the appropriate authority;

(b) if any land affected by arrangements under subsection (3) of that section or an agreement under subsection (6) thereof becomes Crown land, the arrangements or agreement shall cease to apply to the land unless the appropriate authority consent to the continued application thereto of the arrangements or agreement.

(8) Byelaws made under this Act shall apply to Crown land if the appropriate authority consents to their application thereto.

(9) *Repealed by the Countryside Act 1968 (c. 41), s. 50(2), sch. 5. This amendment came into force on 3 August 1968: s. 50(3).*

(10) Notwithstanding anything in subsection (3) or subsection (6) of this section—

(a) an agreement authorised by the said subsection (3) and made[5] by any Government department, or an access agreement so made, shall be of no effect unless it is approved by the Treasury; and

(b) in considering whether to make or approve an agreement authorised by the said subsection (3), or an access agreement, relating to land belonging to a Government department or held in trust for His Majesty for the purposes of a Government department, the department and the Treasury shall have regard to the purposes for which the land is held by or for the department.

(11) In this section the expression "the appropriate authority", in relation to any land, means—

(a) in the case of land belonging to His Majesty in right of the Crown, the Commissioners of Crown Lands or other Government department having the management of the land in question;

---

[1] P. 8 above.

[2] P. 14 above.

[3] Former words "public path order, diversion order, extinguishment order or" repealed by the Highways Act 1959 (c. 25), s. 312(2), sch. 25 and the London Government Act 1963 (c. 33), s. 16(2), sch. 6, para. 70.

[4] P. 24 above.

[5] Former words "by the Commissioners of Crown Lands or" repealed by the Countryside Act 1968 (c. 41), ss. 47(9), 50(2), sch. 5. This amendment came into force on 3 August 1968: s. 50(3).

(b) in the case of land belonging to His Majesty in right of the Duchy of Lancaster, the Chancellor of the Duchy;

(c) in the case of land belonging to the Duchy of Cornwall, such person as the Duke of Cornwall or the possessor for the time being of the Duchy of Cornwall appoints;

(d) in the case of land belonging to a Government department or held in trust for His Majesty for the purposes of a Government department, that department;

and if any question arises under this section as to what authority is the appropriate authority in relation to any land, that question shall be referred to the Treasury, whose decision shall be final[1].

102. *Repealed by the Local Government Act 1972 (c. 70), s. 272(1), sch. 30. This amendment came into force on 1 April 1974: s. 273.*

General provisions as to acquisition of land

103. (1) Any power conferred by this Act[2] on the Nature Conservancy Council[3] (as defined in section 15A[4] of this Act)[5] or a local authority to acquire land[6] compulsorily shall be exercisable in any particular case on their being authorised so to do by the Secretary of State[7].

England and Wales

(1A) The Acquisition of Land Act 1981 shall apply to the acquisition of land under this Act, and in relation to the acquisition under this Act of any interest[8] in land the Compulsory Purchase Act 1965 shall apply with any necessary modifications.[9,10]

England and Wales

(2) *Repealed by the Acquisition of Land Act 1981 (c. 67), s. 34, sch. 6, pt. I.*

Scotland

(2) In relation to the compulsory acquisition of land under this Act by Scottish Natural Heritage[11] or a local authority, the Acquisition of Land (Authorisation Procedure) Act, 1946[12], shall apply as if this Act had been in force immediately before the commencement of that Act and as if in paragraph (a) of subsection (1) of section one thereof, in Part I of the First Schedule thereto and in the second Schedule thereto references to a local authority included references to Scottish Natural Heritage:

Provided that section two of the said Act (which confers temporary powers for the speedy acquisition of land in urgent cases) shall not apply to any such compulsory acquisition as is mentioned in this subsection.

---

[1] **Case: section 101** *Burnet v Barclay* (1955) SLT 282.

[2] The reference to this Act includes reference to the Countryside Act 1968 (c. 41): s. 46(1), p. 130 below.

[3] "Nature Conservancy Council" includes reference to the Countryside Commission and, for certain purposes, the Countryside Council for Wales: Countryside Act 1968 (c. 41), s. 46(2), p. 130 below.

[4] P. 15 above.

[5] Words "(as defined in Section 15A of this Act)" inserted by the Environmental Protection Act 1990 (c. 43), s. 132(1)(1a), sch. 9, para. 1(4). This amendment came into force on 1 April 1991: S.I. 1991/685.

[6] "Land" defined by subsection (6) below and s. 114(1), p. 38 below.

[7] This subsection inserted by the Nature Conservancy Council Act 1973 (c. 54), s. 1(1)(b), sch. 1, para. 2(1). This amendment came into force on 1 November 1973: S.I. 1973/1721.

[8] "Interest" defined by s. 114(1), p. 38 below.

[9] 1965 c. 56.

[10] This subsection inserted by the Acquisition of Land Act 1981 (c. 67), s. 34(1), sch. 4, para. 8. This amendment came into force on 30 June 1981: s. 35(3).

[11] Words "Scottish Natural Heritage" in this subsection substituted by the Natural Heritage (Scotland) Act 1991 (c. 28), s. 4(6), sch. 2, para. 1(4). This amendment came into force on 1 April 1992: S.I. 1991/2633.

[12] For construction see subsection (7) below.

(3) *Repealed by the Land Compensation Act 1961 (c. 33), s. 40(3), sch. 5 as respects England and Wales and the Land Compensation (Scotland) Act 1963 (c. 51), s. 47(3), sch. 4 as respects Scotland.*

(4) *Repealed by the Acquisition of Land Act 1981 (c. 67), s. 34, sch. 6, pt. I as respects England and Wales. This subsection did not apply to Scotland: subsection (7) below.*

(5) The following provision shall have effect, in relation to the acquisition of land under this Act, in substitution for section one hundred and fifty-seven of the Local Government Act, 1933[1] (which provides for the acquisition of land by local authorities by agreement for the purposes of their functions), that is to say, a local authority may with the consent of the Minister by agreement acquire, whether by way of purchase, lease or exchange[2], any land, whether within or without the area of the local authority, which they require for the purpose of any of their functions under this Act or any other land which they may be authorised under this Act to acquire compulsorily.

England and Wales

(6) In this section, and in any enactment in this Act which confers a power to acquire land compulsorily, the expression "land" includes any interest in land.[3]

Scotland

(6) In this section, and in any enactment in this Act which confers a power to acquire land compulsorily, the expression "land" includes any interest in land; and the provisions of the Lands Clauses Acts incorporated with this Act by virtue of paragraph 1 of the Second Schedule to the Acquisition of Land (Authorisation Procedure) Act, 1946, as applied by subsections (2) and (4) of this section, shall apply with the necessary modifications i relation to the compulsory acquisition of any interest in land, being an interest not falling within the definition of "lands" contained in the Lands Clauses Acts.

(7) In the application of this section to Scotland there shall be substituted, for references to the Acquisition of Land (Authorisation Procedure) Act, 1946, and to section one hundred and fifty-seven of the Local Government Act, 1933, respectively, references to the Acquisition of Land (Authorisation Procedure) (Scotland) Act, 1947, and to section 70 of the Local Government (Scotland) Act 1973[4] and in subsection (5) there shall be substituted for the words "whether by way of purchase, lease or exchange" the words "whether by way of purchase, feu, lease or excambion"; and subsection (4) shall not apply.

General provisions as to appropriation and disposal of land

104. (1) The following provisions of this section shall have effect with respect to the disposal or appropriation by any local authority of land[5] which has been acquired by them under this Act[6]

---

[1] *England and Wales*: S. 157 of the Local Government Act 1933 is construed as a reference to s. 120 of the Local Government Act 1972 (c. 70), s. 272(2); *Scotland*: For construction see subsection (7) below.

[2] For construction see subsection (7) below.

[3] The remainder of this subsection was repealed, as respects England and Wales, by the Acquisition of Land Act 1981 (c. 67), s. 34, sch. 6, pt. I.

[4] Words "70 of the Local Government (Scotland) Act 1973" substituted by the Local Government (Scotland) Act 1973 (c. 65), s. 214(2), sch. 27, pt. II, para. 103. This amendment came into force on 16 May 1975: s. 214(2).

[5] "Land" defined by s. 114(1), p. 38 below.

[6] The reference to this Act includes reference to the Countryside Act 1968 (c. 41) subject to sch. 2 to that Act: s. 46(1), p. 130 below.

or appropriated by them for purposes for which land can be acquired under this Act, and is for the time being held by the authority for the purposes for which it was acquired or appropriated.

(2) Subject to the provisions of subsection (5) and (6) of this section,—

(a) where any such land was acquired or appropriated by the authority for a purpose involving the disposal thereof by the authority or for a purpose which in the opinion of the authority can best be achieved by the disposal thereof, or which can be achieved consistently with the disposal thereof, they may dispose of the land to such person, in such manner and subject to such conditions as may appear to the authority to be expedient in order to secure that the land will be best dealt with having regard to the purpose for which it was acquired;

(b) where any such land is not longer required for the purpose for which it is held, the authority may dispose thereof to such person, in such manner and subject to such conditions as may appear to the authority to be expedient, having regard to the nature and situation of the land, in order to secure the best use of the land.

(3) Subject to the provisions of subsection (5) of this section, the authority may appropriate any such land, where the land is no longer required for the purpose for which it is held, for any other purpose for which the authority are or may be authorised in any capacity to acquire land under this Act or by or under any other enactment.

(4) In relation to an appropriation under the last foregoing subsection, subsections (2) and (3) of section one hundred and sixty-three of the Local Government Act, 1933[1],[2] (which relate to the operation of section sixty-eight of the Lands Clauses Consolidation Act, 1845, and to adjustments in accounts) shall have effect as they have effect in relation to appropriations under those sections respectively.

(5) The consent of the Minister[3] shall be requisite to any disposal or appropriation of land by a local authority under this section, and may be given as respects either a particular disposal or appropriation or disposals or appropriations of any class, and either subject to or free from any conditions or limitations.

(6) The consent of the Minister to a sale by a local authority under this section of the freehold in any land, or to a least by them thereunder of any land for a term of more than ninety-nine years, shall not be given unless he is satisfied that there are exceptional circumstances which render the disposal of the land in that manner expedient as mentioned in subsection (2) of this section.

(7) *and* (8) *Repealed by the Local Government Act 1974 (c. 7), ss. 35, 42(2), sch. 6, para. 6(3), sch. 8 as respects England and Wales. This amendment came into force on 1 April 1974: S.I. 1974/335. These subsections did not apply to Scotland: subsection (12) below.*

(9) In this section references to disposal of land shall be construed as references to disposal thereof in any manner (otherwise than by appropriation) whether by way of sale, exchange or lease, by the creation of any easement, right or privilege, or in any other manner, except disposal by way of gift, mortgage or charge.

(10) In relation to any such land as is mentioned in subsection (1) of this section, this section shall have effect to the exclusion of the provisions of subsection (1) of section one hundred and sixty-three and sections one hundred and sixty-four and one hundred and sixty-five of the

---

[1] S. 163(2) and (3) of the Local Government Act 1933 is construed as a reference to s. 122(4) of the Local Government Act 1972 (c. 70): s. 272(2).

[2] Former words "and subsections (2) and (3) of section one hundred and six of the London Government Act 1939"

repealed by the London Government Act 1963 (c. 33), s. 93(1), sch. 18, pt. II. This amendment came into force on 31 July 1963, the date of the Royal Assent.

[3] "The Minister" defined by s. 114(1), p. 38 below.

Local Government Act, 1933[1,2], or of sections 73 and 74 of the Local Government (Scotland) Act 1973[3].

England and Wales

(11) Section one hundred and sixty-six of the Local Government Act, 1933[4,5] (which relate to the application of capital money received from the disposal of land), and section one hundred and sixty-eight of the Local Government (Scotland) Act, 1947 (so far as it relates to the application of such money), shall have effect as respects capital money received in respect of transactions under the provisions of this section relating to the disposal of land as they have effect as respects capital money received in respect of such transactions as are mentioned in those sections respectively.

Scotland

(11) *Repealed by the Local Government (Scotland) Act 1973 (c. 65), s. 237(1), sch. 29. This amendment came into force on 16 May 1975: S.I. 1973/2181.*

(12) In the application of this section to Scotland, the following provision shall be substituted for subsection (4) of this section, that is to say—

"(4) On any appropriation being made under the last foregoing subsection proper adjustments in respect thereof shall be made in the accounts of the authority",

and the following provision shall be substituted for subsection (9) of this section, that is to say—

"(9) In this section references to disposal of land shall be construed as references to disposal thereof in any manner (otherwise than by appropriation), whether by way of sale, feu, excambion or lease, by the creation of any servitude, right or privilege, or in any other manner except disposal by way of gift or in security";

and subsections (6), (7) and (8) shall be omitted[6].

---

105. *Repealed by the Local Government Act 1974 (c. 7), ss. 35, 42(2), sch. 6, para. 6(4), sch. 8. This amendment came into force on 1 April 1974; S.I. 1874/335.*

Supplementary provisions as to byelaws

106. (1) Sections two hundred and fifty to two hundred and fifty-two of the Local Government Act, 1933[7] (which relate to the procedure for making byelaws, authorise byelaws to impose fines not exceeding five pounds, and provide for the proof of byelaws in legal proceedings) shall apply to all byelaws under this Act as if any authority having power to make them were a local authority within the meaning of the said Act of 1933[8], so, however, that in relation to byelaws made by the

[1] Ss. 163(1), 164, 165 of the Local Government Act 1933 are construed as references to s. 122(1)–(3), (5), (6), s. 123 of the Local Government Act 1972 (c. 70): s. 272(2).

[2] Former words "or of [ss. 106(1), 107 and 108] of the London Government Act 1939" repealed by the London Government Act 1963 (c. 33), s. 93(1), sch. 18, pt. II. This amendment came into force on 31 July 1963, the date of the Royal Assent.

[3] Words "or of sections 73 and 74 of the Local Government (Scotland) Act 1973" substituted by the Local Government (Scotland) Act 1973 (c. 65), s. 214, sch. 27, pt. II, para. 104. This amendment came into force on 16 May 1975: S.I. 1973/2181.

[4] S. 166 of the Local Government Act 1933 is construed as

a reference to s. 153 of the Local Government Act 1972 (c. 70), s. 153: s. 272(2).

[5] Former words "and [s. 109] of the London Government Act 1939" repealed by the London Government Act 1963 (c. 33), s. 93(1), sch. 18, pt. II. This amendment came into force on 31 July 1963, the date of the Royal Assent.

[6] This section is excluded in certain circumstances relating to the appropriation of common land: Countryside Act 1968 (c. 41): s. 9(4), sch. 2, para. 4(2).

[7] Ss. 250–252 of the Local Government Act 1933 is construed as a reference to ss. 236–238 of the Local Government Act 1972 (c. 70): s. 272(2).

[8] To be construed as the Local Government Act 1972 (c. 70): s. 272(2).

Nature Conservancy Council[1] (as defined in section 15A[2] of this Act)[3] the said sections shall apply subject to such adaptations as may be prescribed by regulations made by the Secretary of State[4].

(2) In relation to byelaws made under this Act the confirming authority for the purposes of the said section two hundred and fifty[5] shall be the Secretary of State.

(3) Any authority having power under this Act to make byelaws shall have power to enforce byelaws made by them.

(4) The following provisions shall have effect in the application of this section to Scotland:—

(a) for references to the Local Government Act, 1933, and to sections two hundred and fifty to two hundred and fifty-two thereof there shall be substituted references to the Local Government (Scotland) Act, 1973 and to sections 201 to 204 thereof[6]

(b) nothing in the last foregoing subsection shall be construed as authorising any such authority as is mentioned therein to institute proceedings in Scotland for an offence[7].

....

Supplementary provisions as to compensation under ss. 20, 46 and 70

107. (1) The following provisions shall have effect as to compensation under section twenty of this Act[8], under that section as applied by section twenty-one thereof[9,10], and under section seventy thereof.

(2) Any dispute arising on a claim for any such compensation shall be determined by the Lands Tribunal.

(3) For the purposes of any reference to the Lands Tribunal under the last foregoing subsection, section five of the Acquisition of Land (Assessment of Compensation) Act, 1919[11] (which relates to costs) shall have effect with the substitution, for references to the acquiring authority, of references to the authority from whom the compensation in question is claimed.

(4) Rules 2 to 4 of the Rules set out in section two of the said Act of 1919[12] (which provides rules for valuation on a compulsory acquisition) shall apply to the calculation of any such compensation, in so far as it is calculated by reference to the depreciation of the value of an interest in land.

(5) In the case of an interest[13] in land[14] subject to a mortgage—

(a) any such compensation in respect of the depreciation of that interest shall be calculated as if the interest were not subject to the mortgage;

(b) a claim or application for the payment of any such compensation, or an application for the recording of a claim in respect of the interest under subsection (1) of section seventy-two of this Act, may be made by any person who when the byelaws or order giving rise to the

[1] Words "Nature Conservancy Council" substituted by the Nature Conservancy Council Act 1973 (c. 54), s. 1(1)(b), sch. 1, para. 2(1). This amendment came into force on 1 November 1973: S.. 1973/1721.

[2] P. 15 above.

[3] Words "(as defined in section 15A of this Act)" inserted by the Environmental Protection Act 1990 (c. 43), s. 132(1)(a), sch. 9, para. 1(5). This amendment came into force on 1 April 1991: S.I. 1991/685.

[4] The Nature Conservancy Council (Byelaws) Regulations 1975, S.I. 1975/1970 and the Nature Conservancy Council (Byelaws) (Scotland) Regulations 1984, S.I. 1984/918 (S. 89) are made under this section.

[5] To be construed as s. 236 of the Local Government Act 1972 (c. 70): s. 272(2).

[6] Words "1973 and to section 201 to 204" substituted by the Local Government (Scotland) Act 1973 (c. 65), s. 214, sch. 27, pt. II, para. 105. This amendment came into force on 16 May 1975: s. 214(2).

[7] This section is extended by the Countryside Act 1968 (c. 41), ss. 8(5), 12(5), p. 119 below, 13(8), p. 121 below, 41(7), p.

128 below and the Wildlife and Countryside Act 1981 (c. 69), s. 35(4), p. 177 below.

[8] P. 17 above.

[9] P. 19 above.

[10] Former words "under section 46 thereof" repealed by the Highways Act 1959 (c. 25), s. 312(2), sch. 25 and the London Government Act 1963 (c. 33), s. 16(2), sch. 6, para. 70.

[11] The Acquisition of Land (Assessment of Compensation) Act 1919 is repealed by the Land Compensation Act 1961 (c. 33), s. 40(3), sch. 5. S. 5 of the 1919 Act is replaced, as respects England and Wales, by the Land Compensation Act 1961 (c. 33), s. 4 and, as respects Scotland, by the Land Compensation (Scotland) Act 1963 (c. 51), ss. 5, 11.

[12] S. 2 of the 1919 Act is replaced by the Land Compensation Act 1961 (c. 33), s. 5 as respects England and Wales and the Land Compensation (Scotland) Act 1963 (c. 51), s. 12 as respects Scotland.

[13] "Interest" defined by s. 114(1), p. 38 below.

[14] "Land" defined by s. 114(1), p. 38 below.

compensation were or was made was the mortgagee of the interest, or by any person claiming under such a person, but without prejudice to the making of a claim or application by any other person;

(c) a mortgagee shall not be entitled to any such compensation in respect of his interest as such; and

(d) any compensation payable in respect of the interest subject to the mortgage shall be paid to the mortgagee or, where there is more than one mortgagee, to the first mortgagee, and shall in either case be applied by him as if it were proceeds of sale.

(6) This section shall apply to Scotland—

(a) with the substitution for any reference to the Lands Tribunal of a reference to the Lands Tribunal for Scotland; and

(b) with the substitution respectively for any reference to a mortgage, to a mortgagee, and to the first mortgagee, of a reference to a heritable security, to the creditor in a heritable security, and to the creditor whose heritable security has priority over any other heritable securities secured on the land:

Provided that until sections one to three of the Lands Tribunal Act, 1949, come into force as respects Scotland the expression "the Lands Tribunal for Scotland" in subsection (2) of this section shall be construed as meaning an official arbiter appointed under the Acquisition of Land (Assessment of Compensation) Act, 1919, and the following provisions of the said Act of 1919, that is to say, section three thereof (which relates to procedure), section five thereof (which relates to costs) as modified by sections five and ten of the said Act of 1949, but with the substitution for references to the acquiring authority of references to the authority from whom the compensation in question is claimed, and section six thereof (which relates to the statement of special cases) as modified by section ten of the said Act of 1949, shall apply for the purposes of the arbitration.

Powers of entry

108. (1) For the purpose of surveying land[1] in connection with—

(a) the acquisition thereof or of any interest[2] therein, whether by agreement or compulsorily,

(b) *Repealed by the Highways Act 1959 (c. 25), s. 312(2), sch. 25 and the London Government Act 1963 (c. 33), s. 16(2), sch. 6, para. 70.*

(c) the making of an access order with respect thereto,

in the exercise of any power conferred by this Act[3], any person duly authorised in writing by the Minister[4] or other authority having power so to acquire the land or to make the order, as the case may be, may enter upon the land[5].

(2) For the purpose of surveying land, or of estimating its value, in connection with any claim for compensation payable under this Act by a Minister or other authority in respect of that or any other land, any person being an officer of the Valuation Office or a person duly authorised in writing by the authority from whom the compensation is claimed may enter upon the land.

(3) A person authorised under this section to enter upon any land shall, if so required, produce evidence of his authority before entering; and a person shall not under this section demand admission as of right to any land which is occupied unless at least fourteen days'[6] notice in writing of the intended entry has been given to the occupier.

[1] "Land" defined by s. 114(1), p. 38 below.
[2] "Interest" defined by s. 114(1), p. 38 below.
[3] The reference to this Act includes reference to the Countryside Act 1968 (c. 41): s. 46(1), p. 130.
[4] "The Minister" defined by s. 114(1), p. 38 below.
[5] This section is restricted, in relation to Scottish Natural Heritage, by the Natural Heritage (Scotland) Act 1991 (c. 28), s. 7(11), p. 250 below.
[6] Words "fourteen days' " substituted by the Countryside Act 1968 (c. 41), s. 46(3). This amendment came into force on 3 August 1968: s. 50(3).

(4) Any person who wilfully obstructs a person in the exercise of his powers under this section shall be liable on summary conviction to a fine not exceeding level 1 on the standard scale[1].

Application of provisions of Act of 1947 as to inquiries and service of notices

109. (1) Section one hundred and four of the Act of 1947[2] (which provides for the holding by the Minister[3] of local inquiries for the purposes of that Act) shall apply for the purposes of this Act[4].

(2) Section one hundred and five of the Act of 1947[5] and section one hundred and one of the Town and Country Planning (Scotland) Act, 1947[6] (which provide for the service of notices and other documents) shall apply to notices and other documents required or authorised to be served or given under this Act:

Provided that this subsection shall not apply to the service of any notice required or authorised to be served under the First Schedule to the Acquisition of Land (Authorisation Procedure) Act, 1946[7], or the Acquisition of Land (Authorisation Procedure) (Scotland) Act, 1947, as applied by this Act.

(3) Subsection (1) of this section shall not apply to Scotland.

Regulations and orders

110. (1) Any power conferred by this Act to make regulations shall be exercisable by statutory instrument.

(2) Any order under Part IV, V or VI of this Act may be varied or revoked by a subsequent order made in the like manner and subject to the like provisions:

Provided that, without prejudice to the making of a new access order under Part V of this Act, an access order under the said Part V shall not be varied so as to comprise land not comprised in the original order.

(3) Any regulations made under this Act shall be subject to annulment by a resolution of either House of Parliament.

Application to Isles of Scilly

111. (1) The Minister may, after consultation with the Council of the Isles of Scilly, by order provide for the application of this Act to the Isles of Scilly as if those Isles were a separate county; and any such order may provide for the application of this Act to those Isles subject to such modifications, or to the exception of such Parts or provisions thereof, as may be specified in the order[8].

(2) The power to make orders conferred by this section shall be exercisable by statutory instrument.

[1] Words "level 1 on the standard scale" substituted by the Criminal Justice Act 1982 (c. 48), ss. 38 and 46 as respects England and Wales and the Criminal Procedure (Scotland) Act 1975 (c. 21) ss. 289F, 289G, as respects Scotland. The current fine at level 1 is £200: Criminal Justice Act 1991 (c. 53), s. 17 which came into force on 1 October 1992: S.I. 1992/333, S.I. 1992/2118.

[2] "The Act of 1947" is defined by s. 114(1) as the Town and Country Planning Act 1947. This Act has been repealed. Under the Planning (Consequential Provisions) Act 1990 (c. 11), s. 2, this reference is construed as a reference to s. 320 of the Town and Country Planning Act 1990 (c. 8).

[3] Under s. 320 of the Town and Country Planning Act 1990 (c. 8) this function is conferred on the Secretary of State.

[4] The reference to this Act includes reference to the Countryside Act 1968 (c. 41): s. 46(1), p. 130 below.

[5] To be construed as a reference to s. 329 of the Town and Country Planning Act 1990 (c. 8): see note 2 above.

[6] The Town and Country Planning (Scotland) Act 1947 has been repealed. Under the Town and Country Planning (Scotland) Act 1972 (c. 52), s. 277, sch. 22, para. 1, this reference is construed as a reference to the s. 269 of the Town and Country Planning (Scotland) Act 1972.

[7] The Acquisition of Land (Authorisation Procedure) Act 1946 is repealed by the Acquisition of Land Act 1981 (c. 67), s. 34, sch. 6, pt. I which is applied by s. 103(1A), p. 30 above.

[8] The National Parks and Access to the Countryside (Isles of Scilly) Order 1973, S.I. 1973/1395, applies this Act to the Isles of Scilly as if those Isles were a separate county subject to modifications. This Order came into force on 5 September 1973. References to this Act in this section include references to the Countryside Act 1968 (c. 41): s. 46(1), p. 130 below, and s. 184 of, and sch. 17 to, the Local Government Act 1972 (c. 70): s. 184, sch. 17, para. 40.

Application to the Broads Authority

111A. (1) Sections 21 and 22 of this Act[1] shall have effect as if the Broads Authority were a country council.

(2) Sections 54 and 89 of this Act shall have effect as if the Broads Authority were a local planning authority.

(3) Part V of this Act (apart from section 69) shall have effect as if the Broads Authority were a local planning authority but as if—

(*a*) sections 61 to 63, 74 and 78 were omitted; and

(*b*) for the purposes of sections 64, 65 and 77, the Broads were a National Park.

(4) Section 69 of this Act shall have effect as if the Broads Authority were a county planning authority.

(5) In this section "the Broads" has the same meaning as in the Norfolk and Suffolk Broads Act 1988.[2,3]

Epping Forest and Burnham Beeches

112. (1) The provisions of this Act mentioned in the next following subsection shall not apply to any of the lands under the regulation and management of the Corporation of London as Conservators of Epping Forest, or acquired by, and vested in, that Corporation under the Corporation of London (Open Spaces) Act, 1878, in the area known as Burnham Beeches.

(2) The said provisions are Part II of this Act, Part V thereof, and sections eighty-seven to ninety-four thereof.[4]

National Trust land

113. No power conferred by Part V or Part VI of this Act to acquire land compulsorily shall be exercisable in respect of land belonging to the National Trust which is held by the Trust inalienably[5].

Interpretation

114. (1) In this Act the following expressions have the meanings hereby assigned to them respectively, that is to say—

"Act of 1947" means the Town and Country Planning Act, 1947[6];

"area of outstanding natural beauty" has the meaning assigned to it by subsection (1) of section eighty-seven of this Act[7];

"the Commission" means the Commission established by section one of this Act;[8]

"the Council" means the Countryside Council for Wales;[8]

"drainage authority" means the National Rivers Authority or an internal drainage board;[9]

---

[1] Pp. 19–20 above.

[2] P. 220 below.

[3] This section inserted by the Norfolk and Suffolk Broads Act 1988 (c. 4), s. 2(5), sch. 3, pt. I, para. 2. This amendment came into force on 1 April 1989: S.I. 1988/955.

[4] This section is extended by the Countryside Act 1968 (c. 41), s. 46(4), p. 131 below.

[5] This section is extended by the Countryside Act 1968 (c. 41), s. 46(5), p. 131 below.

[6] The Town and Country Planning Act 1947 is repealed by the Planning (Consequential Provisions) Act 1990 (c. 11), s. 3, sch. 1, pt. I. References to the 1947 Act are to be construed as references to the corresponding provisions of the consolidating Acts, namely the Town and Country Planning Act 1990 (c. 8), the Planning (Listed Buildings and Conservation Areas) Act 1990 (c. 9), the Planning (Hazardous Substances) Act 1990 (c. 10): Planning (Consequential Provisions) Act 1990 (c. 11), s. 2.

[7] P. 22 above.

[8] These definitions inserted by the Environmental Protection Act 1990 (c. 43), s. 130(1), sch. 8, para. 1(16). This amendment came into force on 1 April 1991: S.I. 1991/685.

[9] This definition substituted by the Water Consolidation (Consequential Provisions) Act 1991 (c. 60), s. 2(1), sch. 1, para. 7. This amendment applies to England and Wales only and came into force on 1 December 1991: s. 4(2).

"interest", in relation to land, includes any estate in land and any right over land, whether the right is exercisable by virtue of the ownership of an interest in land or by virtue of a licence or agreement, and in particular includes sporting rights;

"land" includes land covered by water and as respects Scotland includes salmon fishings;

"the Minister" as respects England and Wales means the Minister of Town and Country Planning[1], and as respects Scotland means the Secretary of State;

"National Park" has the meaning assigned to it by subsection (3) of section five of this Act[2];

"open-air recreation" does not include organized games[3];

"owner", in relation to any land, means, except in Part III of this Act[4], a person, other than a mortgagee not in possession, who, whether in his own right or as trustee or agent for any other person, is entitled to receive the rack rent of the land or, where the land is not let at a rack rent, would be so entitled if it were so let, and, in Part III of this Act, as respects England and Wales means any person being either entitled to the fee simple or being a mortgagee in possession of the land and as respects Scotland has the meaning assigned to it by section twenty-six of this Act[5];[6]

"vehicle" does not include a vessel, except any vessel adapted for use on land while it is being so used;

"waterway" means any lake, river, canal or other waters, being (in any case) waters suitable, or which can reasonably be rendered suitable, for sailing, boating, bathing or fishing;

and, except where the context otherwise requires, other expressions have the same meanings respectively as in the Act of 1947[7] or, in their application to Scotland, as in the Town and Country Planning (Scotland) Act, 1947[8].

(2) References in this Act to the preservation of the natural beauty of an area shall be construed as including references to the preservation of its flora, fauna and geological and physiographical features[9].

(3) References in this Act to the planting of trees shall be construed as including references to the planting of bushes, the planting or sowing of flowers and the sowing of grass and the laying of turf.

(4) References in this Act to any enactment shall be construed as references to that enactment as amended by or under any subsequent enactment including this Act.

....

Short title and extent

115. (1) This Act may be cited as the National Parks and Access to the Countryside Act, 1949.

(2) This Act, except Part III thereof[10] and so much of this Part thereof as relates to the said Part III, shall not extend to Scotland; and this Act shall not extend to Northern Ireland.

[1] The functions of the Minister of Town and Country Planning have been transferred to the Secretary of State. Several transfers of these functions have taken place since 1949: see S.I. 1951/142, 1951/1900, 1965/143, 1965/319, 1967/156, 1967/486, 1970/1681.

[2] P. 8 above.

[3] This definition only applies for the purposes of Part V of this Act: Countryside Act 1968 (c. 41), s. 21(6).

[4] P. 14 above.

[5] P. 20 above.

[6] Former definition of "river board" repealed by the Water Resources Act 1963 (c. 38), s. 136(2), sch. 14, pt. I. This amendment came into force on 1 April 1965: S.I. 1964/1268.

[7] See note 6, p. 37 above.

[8] The Town and Country Planning (Scotland) Act 1947 has been repealed. Under the Town and Country Planning (Scotland) Act 1972 (c. 52), s. 277, sch. 22, para. 1, references to the 1947 Act are to be construed as references to the corresponding provisions of the Town and Country Planning (Scotland) Act 1972.

[9] Words "its flora, fauna and geological and physiographical features" substituted by the Countryside Act 1968 (c. 41), s. 21(7). This amendment came into force on 3 August 1968: s. 50(3). References in this Act to the preservation of the natural beauty of an area are construed in the same way as references in the Countryside Act 1968 to the conservation of the natural beauty of an area: Countryside Act 1968 (c. 41), s. 21(7), p. 123 below.

[10] P. 14 above.

SCHEDULES

FIRST SCHEDULE

PROVISIONS AS TO MAKING, CONFIRMATION, COMING INTO OPERATION AND VALIDITY OF CERTAIN INSTRUMENTS

This Schedule is not reproduced. Part I concerns orders designating National Parks and access orders. Part II is repealed. Part III contains provisions as to the validity of orders, and of certain maps and statements prepared under Part IV of this Act. Further provisions are contained in the National Parks and Access to the Countryside Regulations 1950, S.I. 1950/1066.

SECOND SCHEDULE

GENERAL RESTRICTIONS TO BE OBSERVED BY PERSONS HAVING ACCESS TO OPEN COUNTRY OR WATERWAYS BY VIRTUE OF PART V OF ACT

This Schedule is not reproduced.

Deer (Scotland) Act 1959

7 & 8 Eliz. 2 Ch. 40

Part IV: Enforcement and Procedure

Part V: Supplementary

Deer (Scotland) Act 1959

An Act to further the conservation and control of red deer in Scotland; to prevent the illegal taking and killing of all species of deer in Scotland; and for purposes connected with the matters aforesaid.

[14th May, 1959[1]]

Part I: Conservation and Control of Red Deer

Constitution and general functions of Red Deer Commission

1. (1) There shall be constituted a commission to be called "the Red Deer Commission" (hereinafter in this Act referred to as "the Commission") which shall have the general functions[2] of furthering the conservation and control of red deer[3] or sika deer[4] or such other deer as may be specified from time to time by direction of the Secretary of State[5] and of keeping under review all matters relating to red deer or sika deer or such other deer as may be specified from time to time by direction of the Secretary of State[5], and such other functions as are conferred on them by or under this Act.

(2) The Commission shall carry out their functions in accordance with such directions of a general character as may be given by the Secretary of State.

(3) The Commission shall consist of a chairman and twelve other members appointed by the Secretary of State, and the provisions of the next following subsection shall apply to the appointment of these members other than the chairman.

(4) The members of the Commission so appointed shall be appointed as follows—

(*a*) one from nominees of[6] Scottish Natural Heritage[7]

(*aa*) one from nominees of the Natural Environment Research Council;[8]

(*b*) three from nominees of such organisations as appear to the Secretary of State to represent the interests of owners[9] of land used for agriculture[10] or forestry;

(*c*) two from nominees of such organisations as appear to the Secretary of State to represent the sporting interest in deer;

(*d*) three from nominees of such organisations as appear to the Secretary of State to represent the interests of farmers and crofters[11] (and of the persons so appointed at least one shall, in the opinion of the Secretary of State, represent the interest of farmers, and at least one shall represent the interests of crofters); and

(*e*) two from nominees of such organisations as appear to the Secretary of State to represent the interests of hill sheep farmers.

(5) For the purpose of this section the expression "crofter" has the like meaning as in the Crofters (Scotland) Act, 1955[12].

[1] This Act came into force on 14 June 1959, except for s. 21 which came into force on 21 October 1962: ss. 37(3), 21(6).

[2] "Functions" includes powers and duties: s. 20, p. 50 below.

[3] "Red deer" defined by s. 20, p. 50 below.

[4] "Sika deer" defined by s. 20, p. 50 below.

[5] Words "or sika deer or such other deer as may be specified from time to time by direction of the Secretary of State" inserted by the Deer (Amendment) (Scotland) Act 1982 (c. 19), s. 1(1). This amendment came into force on 28 July 1982: s. 16(3).

[6] Words 'one from nominees of" substituted by the Nature Conservancy Council Act 1973 (c. 54), s. 1(1)(*b*), sch. 1, para. 4. This amendment came into force on 1 November 1973: S.I. 1973/1721.

[7] Words "Scottish Natural Heritage" substituted by the Natural Heritage (Scotland) Act 1991 (c. 28), s. 4(6), sch. 2, para. 2. This amendment came into force on 1 April 1992: S.I. 1991/2633.

[8] Paragraph (*aa*) substituted by the Nature Conservancy Council Act 1973 (c. 54), s. 1(1)(*b*), sch. 1, para. 4.

[9] "Owner" defined by s. 20, p. 50 below.

[10] "Agriculture" defined by s. 20, p. 50 below.

[11] See subsection (5) and note 12 below.

[12] "Crofter" is now defined by s. 3 of the Crofters (Scotland) Act 1993 (c. 44): s. 63, sch. 6. This Act consolidates enactments relating to crofting and repeals the Crofters (Scotland) Act 1955.

(6) The provisions contained in the First Schedule[1] to this Act shall have effect in relation to the Commission.

Appointment of panels

2. (1) The Commission[2] may, with the approval of the Secretary of State, set up in any locality a panel consisting of five persons, being a chairman and four other members, two of whom shall, in the opinion of the Commission, be representative of the interests mentioned in heads (b) and (c), and two of the interests in heads (d) and (e), of subsection (4) of the last foregoing section, and of any such panel as aforesaid three shall be a quorum, and the Commission may appoint a member of the Commission or a member of the Commission's staff to act as observer to the panel for the purpose of sitting with the panel at any meeting and of taking part in their discussions and of informing the Commission of information arising during and decisions taken at such meetings; such an observer shall not be a member of the panel.[3]

(2) The Commission may refer to any such panel any matter relating to the functions[4] of the Commission, and it shall be the duty of the panel to advise the Commission on the matter.

(3) The Commission may delegate to a panel appointed under subsection (1) of this section the functions of the Commission under section six of this Act[5] so far as relating to the locality of that panel, and the panel in the exercise of the functions so delegated to them shall comply with any directions given by the Commission.

(4) In the exercise of any functions delegated to them as aforesaid, a panel shall have the like powers as the Commission in relation to that exercise.

Duty of Commission to advise Secretary of State

3. (1) It shall be the duty of the Commission[6] to advise the Secretary of State on any such matter relating to the purposes of this Act as he may refer to them, and to bring to his attention any matter relating to red deer[7] or sika deer[8] or such other deer as may be specified from time to time by direction of the Secretary of State[9] of which in the opinion of the Commission he ought to be apprised.

(2) The Commission shall make an annual report to the Secretary of State on the exercise of their functions under this Act, and the Secretary of State shall lay a copy of the report before each House of Parliament, together with such comments as he may think fit to make.

Particular powers of the Commission

4. The Commission[10] shall have power—

    (a) to advise[11] any owner of land, on the application of such owner[12], on questions relating to the carrying of stocks of red deer[13] or sika deer[14] or such other deer as may be specified from time to time by direction of the Secretary of State[15] on that land;

---

[1] P. 61 below.
[2] "The Commission" means the Red Deer Commission: s. 1(1).
[3] Words ", and the Commission may appoint . . . member of the panel" inserted by the Deer (Amendment) (Scotland) Act 1982 (c. 19), s. 2(1). This amendment came into force on 28 July 1982: s. 16(3).
[4] "Functions" defined by s. 20, p. 50 below.
[5] P. 44 below.
[6] "The Commission" means the Red Deer Commission: s. 1(1).
[7] "Red deer" defined by s. 20, p. 50 below.
[8] "Sika deer" defined by s. 20, p. 50 below.
[9] Words "or sika deer or such other deer as may be specified from time to time by direction of the Secretary of State" inserted by the Deer (Amendment) (Scotland) Act 1982 (c.

19), s. 1(1). This amendment came into force on 28 July 1982: s. 16(3).
[10] "The Commission" means the Red Deer Commission: s. 1(1).
[11] Former words "in the interests of conservation" repealed by the Deer (Amendment) (Scotland) Act 1982 (c. 19), ss. 1(3), 15(2), sch. 3. This amendment came into force on 28 July 1982: s. 16(3).
[12] "Owner" defined by s. 20, p. 50 below.
[13] "Red deer" defined by s. 20, p. 50 below.
[14] "Sika deer" defined by s. 20, p. 50 below.
[15] Words "or sika deer or such other deer as may be specified from time to time by direction of the Secretary of State" inserted by the Deer (Amendment) (Scotland) Act 1982 (c. 19), s. 1(1). This amendment came into force on 28 July 1982: s. 16(3).

(b) to collaborate with any person who is conducting any inquiry or investigation into questions of practical or scientific importance relating to red deer or sika deer or such other deer as may be specified from time to time by direction of the Secretary of State.

(c) to support and to engage in research on questions of practical or scientific importance relating to red deer or sika deer or such other deer as may be specified from time to time by direction of the Secretary of State.[1]

Returns of numbers of deer killed

5. (1) The Commission[2] for the purpose of any of their functions[3] may by notice in writing served[4] on the owner[5] or occupier[6] of any land require him to make a return in such form as the Commission may require showing the number of red deer[7] or sika deer[8,9] of each sex which to his knowledge have been killed on the land during such period (not exceeding five years) immediately preceding the service of the notice as may be specified therein.

(2) If any person on whom a notice under the foregoing subsection has been served—

(a) fails without reasonable cause to make the required return within thirty-six days after the service of the notice, or

(b) in making the return knowingly or recklessly furnishes any information which is false in a material particular,

he shall be liable on summary conviction to a fine not exceeding level 3 on the standard scale[10] or to imprisonment for a term not exceeding three months, or to both such fine and imprisonment.

Power of Commission to deal with marauding deer

6. (1) Subject to the following provisions of this section, where the Commission[11] are satisfied—

(a) that red deer[12] or sika deer[13] are, on any agricultural land[14], woodland or garden ground—

(i) causing serious damage to forestry or to agricultural production, including any crops or foodstuffs; or

(ii) causing injury to farm animals (including serious overgrazing of pastures and competing with them for supplementary feeding); and

(b) that the killing of the deer is necessary to prevent further such damage or injury,

they shall authorise in writing, subject to such conditions as may be specified in the authorisation, any person who in their opinion is competent to do so to follow and kill on any land mentioned in the authorisation such red deer or sika deer as appear to that person to be causing the damage or injury.[15]

(2) Where the Commission are satisfied that the deer which appear to be causing damage as aforesaid come from particular land, and that any person having the right to kill deer thereon will forthwith undertake the killing of the deer first-mentioned, the Commission shall make a request to that effect in writing to that person.

---

[1] Paragraph (c) inserted by the Deer (Amendment) (Scotland) Act 1982 (c. 19), s. 2(2). This amendment came into force on 28 July 1982: s. 16(3).
[2] "The Commission" means the Red Deer Commission: s. 1(1).
[3] "Functions" includes powers and duties: s. 20, p. 50 below.
[4] For the service of notices see s. 16, p. 49 below.
[5] "Owner" defined by s. 20, p. 50 below.
[6] "Occupier" defined by s. 20, p. 50 below.
[7] "Red deer" defined by s. 20, p. 50 below.
[8] "Sika deer" defined by s. 20, p. 50 below.
[9] Words "or sika deer" inserted by the Deer (Amendment) (Scotland) Act 1982 (c. 19), s. 1(2). This amendment came into force on 28 July 1982: s. 16(3).

[10] Words "level 3 on the standard scale" substituted by virtue of the Deer (Amendment) (Scotland) Act 1982 (c. 19), s. 14(1), sch. 1; Criminal Procedure (Scotland) Act 1975 (c. 21), s. 289G. The present fine at level 3 is £1,000: Criminal Justice Act 1991 (c. 53), s. 17 which came into force on 1 October 1992: S.I. 1992/333, S.I. 1992/2118.
[11] "The Commission" means the Red Deer Commission: S. 1(1).
[12] "Red deer" defined by s. 20, p. 50 below.
[13] "Sika deer" defined by s. 20, p. 50 below.
[14] "Agricultural land" defined by s. 20, p. 50 below.
[15] Subsection (1) substituted by the Deer (Amendment) (Scotland) Act 1982 (c. 19), s. 3(a). This amendment came into force on 28 July 1982: s. 16(3).

(3) Where any such request as aforesaid has been made to a person, the Commission shall not issue an authorisation under this section unless it appears to them that he has become unable or unwilling to comply with the terms of the request.

(4) An authorisation under this section shall remain in force from the date thereof for such period, not exceeding 28[1] days, as may be specified in the authorisation.

(5) Where the Commission intend to issue any such authorisation as aforesaid, it shall be their duty to give as soon as practicable to any person who in their opinion is likely to be on any land mentioned therein such warning of their intention as they consider necessary to prevent danger to that person.

(6) It shall be the duty of the Commission to give to the owner[2] of any land which is to be mentioned in an authorisation under this section such notice of their intention to issue that authorisation as may be practicable.

(7) Without prejudice to the general provisions of section sixteen of this Act[3] relating to the service of notices, any notice to be served under this section on an owner of land shall, where an agent or servant is responsible for the management or the farming of the land, be duly served if served on the said agent or servant.

(8) The Commission may make in respect of the services of any person authorised by them to follow and kill deer as aforesaid, not being one of their servants, such payments as may be agreed.

Further power of Commission to deal with marauding deer

6A. (1) Where the Commission[4] are satisfied that deer of species other than red deer[5] or sika[6] deer are causing serious damage to agricultural land[7] or to woodland and that the killing of the deer is necessary for the prevention of further such damage, they shall be entitled by their servants with the consent of the occupier[8] of the agricultural land or woodland to kill such deer as such servants may encounter in the course of their duties.

(2) The Commission shall give to the owner[9] of the agricultural land or woodland concerned such notice[10] of their intention to kill deer under this section as may be practicable.

(3) Sections 21[11] and 23(1)[12] of this Act shall not apply to the power conferred by subsection (1) above.[13]

Control schemes

7. (1) Where the Commission[14] are satisfied that red deer[15] or sika deer[16,17] have caused damage to agriculture[18] or forestry in any locality, and that for the prevention of further damage the red deer or sika deer[19] in the area in which the locality is situated should be reduced in number or exterminated, they shall determine, having due regard to the nature and character of the land in that area, what measures shall be taken for that reduction or extermination as the case may be.

(2) Thereafter it shall be the duty of the Commission to consult with such owners[20] or occupiers[21] of land, being land where red deer or sika deer[22] are established, as the Commission

---

[1] Word "28" substituted by the Deer (Amendment) (Scotland) Act 1982 (c. 19), s. 3(*b*). This amendment came into force on 28 July 1982: s. 16(3).

[2] "Owner" defined by s. 20, p. 50 below.

[3] P. 49 below.

[4] "The Commission" means the Red Deer Commission: s. 1(1).

[5] "Red deer" defined by s. 20, p. 50 below.

[6] "Sika deer" defined by s. 20, p. 50 below.

[7] "Agricultural land" defined by s. 20, p. 50 below.

[8] "Occupier" defined by s. 20, p. 50 below.

[9] "Owner" defined by s. 20, p. 50 below.

[10] For provisions concerning notices see s. 16, p. 49 below.

[11] P. 50 below.

[12] P. 50 below.

[13] This section inserted by the Deer (Amendment) (Scotland) Act 1982 (c. 19), s. 4. This amendment came into force on 28 July 1982: s. 16(3).

[14] "The Commission" means the Red Deer Commission: s. 1(1).

[15] "Red deer" defined by s. 20, p. 50 below.

[16] "Sika deer" defined by s. 20, p. 50 below.

[17] Words "or sika deer" inserted by the Deer (Amendment) (Scotland) Act 1982 (c. 19), s. 1(2). This amendment came into force on 28 July 1982: s. 16(3).

[18] "Agriculture" defined by s. 20, p. 50 below.

[19] Words "or sika deer" inserted by the Deer (Amendment) (Scotland) Act 1982 (c. 19), s. 1(2).

[20] "Owner" defined by s. 20, p. 50 below.

[21] "Occupier" defined by s. 20, p. 50 below.

[22] Words "or sika deer" inserted by the Deer (Amendment) (Scotland) Act 1982 (c. 19), s. 1(2).

consider to be substantially interested, to secure agreement on the carrying out of the measures which they have determined as aforesaid.

(3) Where after such consultations the Commission are satisfied that it is not possible to secure agreement as aforesaid or that the measures agreed on are not being carried out, they shall make a scheme (hereinafter in this Act referred to as a "control scheme") for the carrying out of such measures, and any such scheme before it comes into operation shall require confirmation by the Secretary of State.

(4) In this Act the area to which a control scheme relates as aforesaid is, in relation to that scheme, referred to as the "control area".

(5) A control scheme shall be made and confirmed in accordance with the provisions of Parts I and III of the Second Schedule to this Act[1], may be varied or revoked in accordance with the provisions of Parts II and III of the said Schedule, and Part IV of that Schedule shall apply with respect to the validity of such a scheme or any variation or revocation thereof.

Contents of control schemes

8. (1) A control scheme[2] shall—

(a) describe the control area[3] by reference to a map and specify the approximate extent of that area;

(b) specify whether the red deer[4] or sika deer[5,6] in that area or any part thereof are to be reduced in number or exterminated;

(c) specify, where the red deer or sika deer[6] are to be reduced in number, the number, and if necessary in the opinion of the Commission, the sex and class, of the animals to be killed in the control area or any part thereof, and the limit on the number of red deer or sika deer[6] of each sex to be allowed to be established in the control area or any part thereof;

(d) specify the measures which are to be taken by the owners[7] or occupiers[8] for the time being of land in the control area or any of them for the purposes of the foregoing provisions of this subsection;

(e) prescribe time limits within which the owners or occupiers are to take any such measures as aforesaid;

(f) include any incidental, consequential or supplemental provisions that may be necessary.

(2) A control scheme may specify different measures to be taken by different owners or occupiers of land in the control area, and may provide for the extension of any time limit prescribed therein.

(3) Nothing in the foregoing provisions of this section shall empower the Commission to impose on any owner or occupier of land a requirement to construct a fence on his land or on any part thereof against the movement of red deer or sika deer[9], and for the purposes of this section "fence" shall include any artificial obstruction.

Liability of owners or occupiers under control schemes

9. (1) Where any control scheme[10] has been confirmed, it shall be the duty of every owner[11] or occupier[12] of land to take such measures as the scheme may require of him in accordance with the provisions thereof.

---

[1] P. 63 below.
[2] "Control scheme" defined by s. 7(3) above.
[3] "Control area" defined by s. 7(4) above.
[4] "Red deer" defined by s. 20, p. 50 below.
[5] "Sika deer" defined by s. 20, p. 50 below.
[6] Words "or sika deer" inserted by the Deer (Amendment) (Scotland) Act 1982 (c. 19), s. 1(2). This amendment came into force on 28 July 1982: s. 16(3).

[7] "Owner" defined by s. 20, p. 50 below.
[8] "Occupier" defined by s. 20, p. 50 below.
[9] Words "or sika deer" inserted by the Deer (Amendment) (Scotland) Act 1982 (c. 19), s. 1(2).
[10] "Control scheme" defined by s. 7(3) above.
[11] "Owner" defined by s. 20, p. 50 below.
[12] "Occupier" defined by s. 20, p. 50 below.

(2) Any person who refuses or wilfully fails to comply with any requirement laid upon him by a scheme shall be guilty of an offence, and shall be liable on summary conviction to a fine not exceeding level 4 on the standard scale[1] or to imprisonment for a term not exceeding three months or to both such fine and imprisonment.

Enforcement of control schemes

10. If the Commission[2] are of the opinion that any owner[3] or occupier[4] of land upon whom a requirement is laid by a control scheme[5] has failed to carry out that requirement, it shall be the duty of the Commission to carry out the requirement if they are satisfied that it is still necessary so to do.

Recovery of expenses incurred under section 10

11. (1) Where any expenses incurred by the Commission[6] in the exercise of their functions[7] under the last foregoing section exceed the amount of the proceeds of the sale of the carcases of any red deer[8] or sika deer[9,10] killed in pursuance of that exercise, the excess shall be recoverable from the owner[11] or occupier[12] concerned by the Commission.

(2) The Commission shall furnish to any owner or occupier concerned a statement showing the expenses incurred in the exercise of their functions as aforesaid, the amount received in respect of the sale of carcases and the amount recoverable from any owner or occupier under this section; and any owner or occupier who is aggrieved by such a statement may, within one month after such a statement has been furnished to him, appeal to the Scottish Land Court who may, if it appears to them equitable so to do, vary the amount recoverable from him.

(3) Nothing in the foregoing provisions of this section shall preclude the Commission, with the approval of the Secretary of State, from waiving the right to recover expenses incurred as aforesaid in any particular case.

(4) The provisions of the Small Landholders (Scotland) Acts, 1886 to 1931, with regard to the Scottish Land Court shall, with any necessary modifications, apply for the determination of any appeal under subsection (2) of this section in like manner as those provisions apply for the determination by the Court of matters referred to them under those Acts.

Power of Commission to provide services and equipment

12. (1) The Commission[13] may be agreement with any owner[14] or occupier[15] of land assist in or undertake, whether in pursuance of a control scheme[16] or otherwise, the taking or killing of red deer[17] or sika deer[18,19] and the disposal of[20] deer or their carcases; and the agreement may make provision for the providing of equipment by the Commission.

---

[1] Words "level 4 on the standard scale" substituted by virtue of the Deer (Amendment) (Scotland) Act 1982 (c. 19), s. 14(1), sch. 1; Criminal Procedure (Scotland) Act 1975 (c. 21), s. 289G. The present fine at level 4 is £2,500: Criminal Justice Act 1991 (c. 53), s. 17 which came into force on 1 October 1992: S.I. 1992/333, S.I. 1992/2118.
[2] "The Commission" means the Red Deer Commission: s. 1(1).
[3] "Owner" defined by s. 20, p. 50 below.
[4] "Occupier" defined by s. 20, p. 50 below.
[5] "Control scheme" defined by s. 7(3), p. 46 above.
[6] "The Commission" means the Red Deer Commission: s. 1(1).
[7] "Functions" includes powers and duties: s. 20, p. 50 below.
[8] "Red deer" defined by s. 20, p. 50 below.
[9] "Sika deer" defined by s. 20, p. 50 below.

[10] Words "or sika deer" inserted by the Deer (Amendment) (Scotland) Act 1982 (c. 19), s. 1(2). This amendment came into force on 28 July 1982: s. 16(3).
[11] "Owner" defined by s. 20, p. 50 below.
[12] "Occupier" defined by s. 20, p. 50 below.
[13] "The Commission" means the Red Deer Commission: s. 1(1).
[14] "Owner" defined by s. 20, p. 50 below.
[15] "Occupier" defined by s. 20, p. 50 below.
[16] "Control scheme" defined by s. 7(3), p. 46 above.
[17] "Red deer" defined by s. 20, p. 50 below.
[18] "Sika deer" defined by s. 20, p. 50 below.
[19] Words "or sika deer" inserted by the Deer (Amendment) (Scotland) Act 1982 (c. 19), s. 1(2). This amendment came into force on 28 July 1982: s. 16(3).
[20] Former word "such" repealed by the Deer (Amendment) (Scotland) Act 1982 (c. 19), s. 15(2), sch. 3.

(2) Any agreement in pursuance of the last foregoing subsection shall, unless the Commission with the approval of the Secretary of State otherwise decide, provide for the payment of any expenses incurred by the Commission under the agreement.

Power of Commission to dispose of carcases

13. Without prejudice to the operation of the provisions of section eleven of this Act[1] relating to the disposal of the proceeds of the sale of carcases, and of section twelve of this Act, the Commission[2] shall have power to dispose by sale or otherwise of the carcases of all deer killed under their authority.

Persons acting under this Part of this Act not required to obtain game licences

14. Any person authorised or required by the Commission[3] to kill any red deer[4] or sika deer[5,6] under the provisions of this Part of this Act shall not be required to obtain for that purpose a licence to kill game.

Entry on land

15. (1) Any person duly authorised in writing by the Commission[7] shall have power at all reasonable times to enter upon any land—

(a) in pursuance of any of the functions[8] of the Commission under sections six[9], seven[10] or ten[11] of this Act;

(b) for the purpose of determining whether any of their functions under the said sections should be exercised;

(c) for the purpose of determining how far and in what manner any requirement placed on any person by virtue of this Part of this Act has been complied with;

(d) for the purpose of taking a census of red deer[12] or sika deer[13,14] in any area in pursuance of the general functions of the Commission under section 1(1)[15] of this Act.[16]

(2) Any person authorised as aforesaid by the Commission who proposes to exercise any power of entry conferred by this section shall, if so required, produce the written document authorising him so to do.

(3) Admission to any land under this section shall not be demanded as of right, unless notice[17] has been given to the owner[18] and the occupier[19] of the land that it is proposed to enter during a period, specified in the notice, not exceeding one month and beginning at least fourteen days after the giving of the notice, and entry is made on the land during the period specified in the notice:

Provided that this subsection shall not apply to any person acting in pursuance of any of the functions of the Commission under section six of this Act[20].

---

[1] P. 47 above.
[2] "The Commission" means the Red Deer Commission: s. 1(1).
[3] "The Commission" means the Red Deer Commission: s. 1(1).
[4] "Red deer" defined by s. 20, p. 50 below.
[5] "Sika deer" defined by s. 20, p. 50 below.
[6] Words "or sika deer" inserted by the Deer (Amendment) (Scotland) Act 1982 (c. 10), s. 1(2). This amendment came into force on 28 July 1982: s. 16(3).
[7] "The Commission" means the Red Deer Commission: s. 1(1).
[8] "Functions" includes powers and duties: s. 20, p. 50 below.
[9] P. 44 above.
[10] P. 45 above.

[11] P. 47 above.
[12] "Red deer" defined by s. 20, p. 50 below.
[13] "Sika deer" defined by s. 20, p. 50 below.
[14] Words "or sika deer" inserted by the Deer (Amendment) (Scotland) Act 1982 (c. 19), s. 1(2). This amendment came into force on 28 July 1982: s. 16(3).
[15] P. 42 above.
[16] Paragraph (d) inserted by the Deer (Amendment) (Scotland) Act 1967 (c. 37), s. 1. This Act came into force on 28 June 1967, the date of the Royal Assent.
[17] For provisions concerning notices see s. 16, p. 49 below.
[18] "Owner" defined by s. 20, p. 50 below.
[19] "Occupier" defined by s. 20, p. 50 below.
[20] P. 44 above.

Service of notices

16. (1) Subject to the provisions of this section, any notice for the purposes of this Act shall be in writing, and any notice or other document required or authorised by or under this Act to be given to or served on any person shall be duly given or served if it is delivered to him or left at his proper address or sent to him by post.

(2) Any such notice or other document required or authorised to be served on any person for the purposes of this Act shall be duly served, if that person is an incorporated company or body, if it is served on the clerk or secretary of that company or body.

(3) For the purposes of this section and section twenty-six of the Interpretation Act, 1889[1], the proper address of any person on whom any such notice or document is to be served shall, in the case of the clerk or secretary of any incorporated company or body, be that of the registered or principal office of such company or body, and in any other case be the last known address of the person in question.

(4) Where any notice or other document is to be given to or served on a person as being the person having any interest in land and it is not practicable after reasonable inquiry to ascertain his name or address, the notice or document may be given or served by addressing it to him by the description of the person having that interest in the land (naming it) and delivering the notice or document to some responsible person on the land or by affixing it, or a copy of it, to some conspicuous object on the land.

(5) Nothing in this section shall require the Commission[2] to give written notice of their intention to issue an authorisation in pursuance of section six of this Act[3].

Offences in relation to execution of this Part of this Act

17. A person who wilfully obstructs any person acting in the execution of this Part of this Act or of any authorisation issued thereunder shall be guilty of an offence and shall be liable on summary conviction to a fine not exceeding level 3 on the standard scale[4] or to imprisonment for a term not exceeding three months, or to both such fine and imprisonment.

Financial provisions

18. (1) The expenses of the Commission[5] shall be defrayed by the Secretary of State, and any sums received by them shall be paid to the Secretary of State.

(2) All expenses incurred by the Secretary of State under the provisions of this Act shall be defrayed out of moneys provided by Parliament, and any sums received by him under the provisions of the last foregoing subsection shall be paid into the Exchequer.

Saving of right to compensation for damage by red deer

19. Nothing in the foregoing provisions of this Act or anything done thereunder shall preclude any occupier[6] of any land from recovering any compensation for damage caused by red deer[7] or sika deer[8,9] which he would have been entitled to recover if this Act had not been passed.

---

[1] S. 7 of the Interpretation Act 1978 (c. 30) replaces s. 26 of the Interpretation Act 1889: Interpretation Act 1978, ss. 17, 22.

[2] "The Commission" means the Red Deer Commission: s. 1(1).

[3] P. 44 above.

[4] Words "level 3 on the standard scale" substituted by virtue of the Deer (Amendment) (Scotland) Act 1982 (c. 19), s. 14(1), sch. 1; Criminal Procedure (Scotland) Act 1975 (c. 21), s. 289G. The present fine at level 3 is £1,000: Criminal

Justice Act 1991 (c. 53), s. 17 which came into force on 1 October 1992: S.I. 1992/333, S.I. 1992/2118.

[5] "The Commission" means the Red Deer Commission: s. 1(1).

[6] "Occupier" defined by s. 20, p. 50 below.

[7] "Red deer" defined by s. 20, p. 50 below.

[8] "Sika deer" defined by s. 20, p. 50 below.

[9] Words "or Sika deer" inserted by the Deer (Amendment) (Scotland) Act 1982 (c. 19), s. 1(2). This amendment came into force on 28 July 1982: s. 16(3).

Interpretation of Part I

20. In this Part of this Act, unless the context otherwise requires—

"agriculture" and "agricultural land" have the like meanings as in the Agriculture (Scotland) Act, 1948;

"functions" includes powers and duties;

"occupier" in relation to any land includes any tenant or sub-tenant, whether in actual occupation of the land or not;

"owner" in relation to any land includes any person who under the Lands Clauses Acts[1] would be enabled to sell and convey the land to the promoters of an undertaking:

"red deer" means deer of the species *Cervus elaphus.*

"sika deer" means deer of the species *Cervus nippon;*

and any reference to "red deer" or "sika deer" includes any deer which is a hybrid of those species.[2]

Part II: Close Seasons

Close seasons for red deer and power to make close seasons for other species

21. (1) Subject to section thirty-three of this Act[3], no person shall take or wilfully kill or injure[4] any stag, being a red deer[5], during the period commencing on the twenty-first day of October and ending on the thirtieth day of June or any hind, being a red deer, during the period commencing on the sixteenth day of February and ending on the twentieth day of October.

(2) The Secretary of State may by order fix a period in each year during which no person shall take or wilfully kill or injure—

(*a*) any species of deer named in the order other than red deer; or

(*b*) any hybrid of any species of deer named in the order,

and he may fix a different period for males and females of the species or, as the case may be, of the hybrid so named.[6,7]

(3) Before making any such order as aforesaid the Secretary of State shall consult with any organisations that appear to him to represent persons likely to be affected by the order.

(4) For the purposes of this section "red deer" means deer of the species *Cervus elaphus.*

(5) If any person contravenes the provisions of subsection (1) of this section or of any order made under subsection (2) of this section, he shall be guilty of an offence and shall be liable on summary conviction to a fine not exceeding level 4 on the standard scale for each deer in respect of which he offence was committed[8] or to imprisonment for a term not exceeding three months,

---

[1] By the Interpretation Act 1978, s. 5, sch. 1, "Lands Clauses Acts means "in relation to Scotland, the Lands Clauses Consolidation (Scotland) Act 1845 and the Lands Clauses Consolidation Acts Amendment Act 1860, and any Acts for the time being in force amending those Acts".

[2] The definition of sika deer and the provision concerning hybrids are inserted by the Deer (Amendment) (Scotland) Act 1982 (c. 19), s. 1(4). This amendment came into force on 28 July 1982: s. 16(3).

[3] P. 59 below.

[4] Words 'or injure' inserted by the Deer (Amendment) (Scotland) Act 1982 (c.19), s.6(*a*). This amendment came into force on 28 July 1982: s.16(3).

[5] 'Red deer' defined by subsection (4) below.

[6] The Deer (Close Seasons) (Scotland) Order 1984, S.I. 1984/76 (S.5), made under this section, is at p. 322 below.

[7] This subsection substituted by the Deer (Amendment) (scotland) Act 1982 (c.19), s.6(*b*). This amendment came into force on 28 July 1982: s. 16(3).

[8] Words 'level 4 on the standard scale' substituted by virtue of the Deer (Amendment) (Scotland) Act 1982 (c.19), s.14(1), sch.1; Criminal Procedure (Scotland) Act 1975 (c.21), s.289G. The present fine at level 4 is £2,500: Criminal Justice Act 1991 (c.53), s.17 which came into force on 1 October 1992: S.I. 1992/333, S.I. 1992/2118. Words "for each deer . . . committed" substituted by the Deer (Amendment) (Scotland) Act 1982 (c. 19), s. 14 (1), sch. 1.

or to both such fine and imprisonment and to the forfeiture of any deer in respect of which the offence was committed[1].

(5A) This section does not apply to the killing of deer by any person who keeps those deer by way of business on land enclosed by a deer-proof barrier for the production of meat or foodstuffs, or skins or other by-products, or as breeding stock (or to such killing of deer by the servant or agent of any such person authorised by him for that purpose); provided that the deer are conspicuously marked to demonstrate that they are so kept.[2]

(6) This section shall come into operation on the twenty-first day of October, nineteen hundred and sixty-two.

Part III: Prevention of Illegal Taking and Killing of Deer

Prohibition of poaching

22. (1) Subject to section thirty-three of this Act[3], if any person without legal right or without permission from a person having such right takes or wilfully kills or injures[4] deer[5] on any land[6], he shall be guilty of an offence and shall be liable on summary conviction to a fine not exceeding level 4 on the standard scale for each deer in respect of which the offence was committed[7], or to imprisonment for a term not exceeding three months, or to both, and to the forfeiture of any deer illegally taken or[8] killed by him or in his possession at the time of the offence:

Provided that the provisions of this subsection shall not apply to any person taking any deer lawfully killed by him.

(2) Subject to section 33 of this Act[9], if any person without legal right to take or kill deer on any land or without permission from a person having such right removes any deer carcase from that land, he shall be guilty of an offence and liable on summary conviction to a fine not exceeding level 4 on the standard scale[10] for each carcase in respect of which the offence was committed or to imprisonment for a term not exceeding three months or to both and to the forfeiture of any carcase illegally removed by him or in his possession at the time of the offence.[11]

Unlawful taking or killing of deer

23. (1) Subject to section thirty-three of this Act[12], any person who takes or wilfully kills or injures[13] deer[14] between the expiration of the first hour after sunset and the commencement of the last hour before sunrise shall be guilty of an offence.

(2) Subject to section thirty-three of this Act, it shall be an offence to take or wilfully kill or injure[15] deer otherwise than by shooting, and shooting for the purposes of this section means

[1] Words 'and to the forfeiture of any deer in respect of which the offence was committed' added by the Deer (Amendment) (Scotland) Act 1982 (c.19), s.14(1), sch.1. This amendment came into force on 28 July 1982: s.16(3).

[2] This subsection inserted by the Deer (Amendment) (Scotland) Act 1982 (c.19), s.17. This amendment came into force on 28 July 1982: s.16(3).

[3] P. 59 below.

[4] Words 'or injuries' inserted by the Deer (Amendment) (Scotland) Act 1982 (c.19), s.6(*d*). This amendment came into force on 28 July 1982: s.16(3).

[5] 'Deer' defined by s.32, p. 58 below.

[6] 'Land' defined by s.32, p. 58 below.

[7] Words "level 4 on the standard scale" substituted by virtue of the Deer (Amendment) (Scotland) Act 1982 (c. 19), s. 14(1), sch. 1; Criminal Procedure (Scotland) Act 1975 (c. 21), s. 289G. The present fine at level 4 is £2,500: Criminal Justice Act 1991 (c. 53), s. 17 which came into force on 1 October 1992: S.I. 1992/333, S.I. 1992/2118. Words "or to imprisonment . . . or to both" substituted by the Deer (Amendment) (Scotland) Act 1982 (c. 19), s. 14(1), sch. 1.

[8] Words "taken or" inserted by the Deer (Amendment) (Scotland) Act 1982 (c. 19), s. 14(1), sch. 1. This amendment came into force on 28 July 1982: s. 16(3).

[9] P. 000 below.

[10] Words "level 4 on the standard scale" substituted by virtue of the Criminal Procedure (Scotland) Act 1975 (c. 21), s. 289G. The present fine at level 4 is £2,500: Criminal Justice Act 1991 (c. 53) , s. 17 which came into force on 1 October 1992: S.I. 1992/333, S.I. 1992/2118.

[11] This subsection inserted by the Deer (Amendment) (Scotland) Act 1982 (c. 19), s. 6(*c*). This amendment came into force on 28 July 1982: s. 16(3).

[12] P. 000 below.

[13] Words "or injures" inserted by the Deer (Amendment) (Scotland) Act 1982 (c. 19), s. 6(*d*). This amendment came into force on 28 July 1982: s. 16(3).

[14] "Deer" defined by s. 32, p. 000 below.

[15] Words "or injure" inserted by the Deer (Amendment) (Scotland) Act 1982 (c. 19), s. 6(*a*). This amendment came into force on 28 July 1982: s. 16(3).

discharging a firearm[1], as defined in the Firearms Act, 1937[2], other than a prohibited weapon.

(2A) Subject to subsection (2B) below and section 33(1) of this Act, if any person—

(a) discharges any firearm, or discharges or projects any missile, from any aircraft at any deer; or

(b) notwithstanding the provisions of section 23(5) of this Act uses any aircraft for the purpose of transporting any live deer other than in the interior of the aircraft,

he shall be guilty of an offence.

(2B) Nothing in subsection (2A)(b) above shall make unlawful anything done by, or under the supervision of, a veterinary surgeon or practitioner.

(2C) In subsection (2B) above "veterinary practitioner" means a person who is for the time being registered in the supplementary register, and "veterinary surgeon" means a person who is for the time being registered in the register of veterinary surgeons.[3]

(3) Any person guilty of an offence against subsection (1), (2) or (2A)[4] of this section shall be liable on summary conviction to a fine not exceeding level 4 on the standard scale for each deer in respect of which the offence was committed[5] or to imprisonment for a term not exceeding three months, or to both such fine and imprisonment and to the forfeiture of any deer illegally taken or killed by him or in his possession at the time of the offence[6].

(3A) Any person who uses a vehicle[7] to drive deer on unenclosed land[8] with the intention of taking, killing or injuring them shall be guilty of an offence and liable on summary conviction to a fine not exceeding level 4 on the standard scale[5] or to imprisonment for a term not exceeding 3 months or to both.[9]

(4) *Repealed by the Deer (Amendment) (Scotland) Act 1982 (c. 19), ss. 14(2), 15(2), sch. 3. This amendment came into force on 28 July 1982: s. 16(3).*

(5) Nothing in the provisions of this section shall be construed as prohibition a person having a legal right to take deer on any land[8], or a person with permission in writing from any such person as aforesaid, from taking a deer alive on that land in any manner which does not cause it unnecessary suffering.

....

Firearms and ammunition

23A. (1) The Secretary of State shall have power to make such order as he thinks fit regarding the classes of firearms[10], ammunition[11], sights and other equipment which may lawfully be used in connection with killing or taking deer[12], and the circumstances in which any class of firearms, ammunition, sights or other equipment may be so used[13].

---

[1] "Firearm" defined by s. 32, p. 58 below.
[2] The Firearms Act 1968 (c. 27) consolidates and repeals the Firearms Act 1937.
[3] Subsections (2A) to (2C) inserted by the Deer (Amendment) (Scotland) Act 1982 (c. 19), s. 8(1). This amendment came into force on 28 July 1982: s. 16(3).
[4] Words "subsection (1), (2) or (2A)" inserted by the Deer (Amendment) (Scotland) Act 1982 (c. 19), s. 8(2). This amendment came into force on 28 July 1982: s. 16(3).
[5] Words "level 4 on the standard scale" substituted by virtue of the Deer (Amendment) (Scotland) Act 1982 (c. 19), s. 14(1), sch. 1; Criminal Procedure (Scotland) Act 1975 (c. 21), s. 289G. The present fine at level 4 is £2,500: Criminal Justice Act 1991 (c. 53), s. 17 which came into force on 1 October 1992: S.I. 1992/333, S.I. 1992/2118. Words "for each deer . . . committed" substituted by the Deer (Amendment)

(Scotland) Act 1982 (c. 19), s. 14(1), sch. 1.
[6] Words "and to the forfeiture of any deer illegally taken or killed by him or in his possession at the time of the offence" added by the Deer (Amendment) (Scotland) Act 1982 (c. 19), s. 14(1), sch. 1. This amendment came into force on 28 July 1982: s. 16(3).
[7] "Vehicle" defined by s. 32, p. 58 below.
[8] "Land" defined by s. 32, p. 58 below.
[9] This subsection inserted by the Deer (Amendment) (Scotland) Act 1982 (c. 19), s. 9. This amendment came into force on 28 July 1982: s. 16(3).
[10] "Firearm" defined by s. 32, p. 58 below.
[11] "Ammunition" defined by s. 32, p. 58 below.
[12] "Deer" defined by s. 32, p. 58 below.
[13] The Deer (Firearms etc) (Scotland) Order 1985, S.I. 1985/1168 (S. 94), made under this section, is at p. 323 below.

(2) Before making an order under subsection (1) above the Secretary of State shall consult any organisations which in his opinion represent persons likely to be interested in or affected by the order.

(3) Any person who fails to comply with an order under subsection (1) above shall be guilty of an offence and liable on summary conviction to a fine not exceeding level 4 on the standard scale[1] in relation to each deer taken or killed or to imprisonment for a term not exceeding three months, or to both.

(4) No order shall be made under this section unless a draft of the order has been laid before Parliament and approved by a resolution of each House of Parliament.

(5) If any person uses any firearm or any ammunition for the purpose of wilfully injuring any deer, he shall be guilty of an offence and liable on summary conviction to a fine not exceeding level 4 on the standard scale[1] for each deer in respect of which the offence was committed or to imprisonment for a term not exceeding three months, or to both.[2]

Unlawful taking or killing of deer by two or more persons acting together

24. If two or more persons acting together do any act which would constitute an offence against any of the three[3] last foregoing sections of this Act, every such person shall be liable—

   (a) on summary conviction to a fine not exceeding in respect of each deer[4] taken or killed the statutory maximum,[5] which in this section means the prescribed sum within the meaning of section 289B(6) of the Criminal Procedure (Scotland) Act 1975[6] or to imprisonment for a term not exceeding six months or to both such fine and imprisonment;

   (b) on conviction on indictment to a fine[7] or to imprisonment for a term not exceeding two years or to both such fine and imprisonment; and

   (c) on any conviction to the forfeiture of any deer illegally taken or killed by him or in his possession at the time of the offence.[8]

Unlawful possession of deer and firearms

25. (1) If any person is found in possession of any deer[9] in circumstances which afford reasonable ground for suspecting that he has obtained possession of the deer as a result of his committing an offence against any of the provisions of Part II[10] or of any order made thereunder or of sections twenty-two to twenty-four of this Act[11], that person may be charged with unlawful possession as aforesaid of such deer.

(2) If any person is found in possession of any firearm[12] or ammunition[13] in circumstances which afford reasonable ground for suspecting that he has used the firearm or ammunition for the purpose of committing an offence against any of the provisions of sections twenty-two to twenty-four of this Act, that person may be charged with unlawful possession as aforesaid of such firearm or ammunition.

[1] Words "level 4 on the standard scale" substituted by virtue of the Criminal Procedure (Scotland) Act 1975 (c. 21), s. 289G. The present fine at level 4 is £2,500: Criminal Justice Act 1991 (c. 53), s. 17 which came into force on 1 October 1992: S.I. 1992/333, S.I. 1992/2118.

[2] This section inserted by the Deer (Amendment) (Scotland) Act 1982 (c. 19), s. 10(1). This amendment came into force on 28 July 1982: s. 16(3).

[3] Words "any of the three" substituted by the Deer (Amendment) (Scotland) Act 1982 (c. 19), s. 10(2). This amendment came into force on 28 July 1982: s. 16(3).

[4] "Deer" defined by s. 32, p. 58 below.

[5] The current statutory maximum is £5,000: Criminal Justice Act 1991 (c. 53), s. 17 which came into force on 1 October 1992: S.I. 1992/333, S.I. 1992/2118.

[6] Words "in respect of each deer taken or killed the statutory maximum, which in this section means the prescribed sum within the meaning of section 289B(6) of the Criminal Procedure (Scotland) Act 1975" inserted by the Deer (Amendment) (Scotland) Act 1982 (c. 19), s. 14(1), sch. 1. This amendment came into force on 28 July 1982: s. 16(3).

[7] Former words "not exceeding five hundred pounds' repealed by the Deer (Amendment) (Scotland) Act 1982 (c. 19), ss. 14(1), 15(2), schs. 1,3.

[8] Words "and on any conviction to the forfeiture of any deer illegally taken or killed by him or in his possession at the time of the offence" added by the Deer (Amendment) (Scotland) Act 1982 (c. 19), s. 14(1), sch. 1. This amendment came into force on 28 July 1982: s. 16(3).

[9] "Deer" defined by s. 32, p. 58 below.

[10] P. 50 above.

[11] Pp. 51–53 above.

[12] "Firearm" defined by s. 32, p. 58 below.

[13] "Ammunition" defined by s. 32, p. 58 below.

(3) Where the court is satisfied that a person charged under either or both of the two last foregoing subsections obtained possession of the deer as a result of his committing an offence against any of the provisions of Part II or of any order made thereunder or of sections twenty-two to twenty-four of this Act, or, as the case may be, that he has used any firearm or ammunition for the purpose of committing an offence against any of the provisions of the said sections twenty-two to twenty-four, that person may be convicted of unlawful possession as aforesaid and dealt with in like manner as if he had been convicted of the said offence.

(4) It shall be lawful to convict a person charged under this section on the evidence of one witness.

Part IIIA[1]: Licensing of Dealing in Venison

Licences to deal in venison

25A. (1) A council[2] may grant to any person whom they consider fit a licence to deal in venison[3] (to be known as a "venison dealer's licence").

(2) The Secretary of State shall have power by order to regulate applications for venison dealers' licences and the manner in which they are to be dealt with (including power to authorise[4] councils to charge fees in respect of such applications); and also to regulate the procedure by which venison dealers' licences may be surrendered, and the procedure for handing in of licences where a court has ordered their forfeiture or the holders have ceased to deal in venison; and in that regard he may apply any provision of Schedule 1 to the Civic Government (Scotland) Act 1982, as he thinks fit.[5]

(3) A venison dealer's licence shall be valid for 3 years (unless the dealer has been disqualified from holding a licence by reason of his conviction of an offence under this Act), and may be renewed provided that he is not at the time of application subject to such disqualification.

(4) Every[6] council which grants a venison dealer's licence shall cause to be sent to the Commission as soon as may be a copy of the licence.

(5) Every[6] council by whom venison dealers' licences are granted shall, as soon as may be after the first day of January in each year, make a return to the Commission[7] of the names and addresses of the persons who on that day held venison dealers' licences issued by the council.

Records

25B. (1) Every licenced venison dealer shall keep a book wherein shall be entered records in the prescribed form of all purchases and receipts of venison[8] by him and shall enter in such book forthwith the prescribed[9] particulars of such purchases and receipts.

(2) Any person authorised in writing in that behalf by the Secretary of State or by the Commission[10] and showing his written authority when so requested, or any constable, may inspect any book kept in pursuance of this section and it shall be the duty of the dealer to produce for inspection by such authorised person or constable such book and also all venison in

---

[1] Part IIIA is inserted by the Deer (Amendment) (Scotland) Act 1982 (c. 19), s. 11. By a commencement order made on 27 June 1984, s. 11 came into force on 1 January 1985.
[2] Word "A" substituted by the Local Government etc. (Scotland) Act 1994 (c. 39), s. 180, sch. 13, para. 53(2)(a). It is anticipated that this amendment will comeinto force on 1 April 1996.
[3] "Venison" defined by s. 25F, p. 56 below.
[4] Former words "islands and district" repealed by the Local Government etc. (Scotland) Act 1994 (c. 39), s. 180, sch. 13, para. 53(2)(b), sch. 14. It is anticipated that this amendment will come into force on 1 April 1996.
[5] The Licensing of Venison Dealers (Application Procedures etc.) (Scotland) Order 1984, S.I. 1984/922 (S.

93), is made under this section.
[6] Former words "islands or district" repealed by the Local Government etc. (Scotland) Act 1994 (c. 39), s. 180, sch. 13, para. 53(2)(c), sch. 14. It is anticipated that this amendment will come into force on 1 April 1996.
[7] "The Commission" means the Red Deer Commission: s. 1(1).
[8] "Venison" defined by s. 25F, p. 56 below.
[9] "Prescribed" defined by subsection (4) below. The Licensing of Venison Dealers (Prescribed Forms etc.) (Scotland) Order 1984, S.I. 1984/899 (S. 88), is made under this section.
[10] "The Commission" means the Red Deer Commission: s. 1(1).

the dealer's possession or under his control, or on premises or in vehicles under his control, together with all invoices, consignment notes, receipts and other documents (including copies thereof where the originals are not available) which may be required to verify any entry in such book, and to allow such authorised person or constable to take copies of such book or document or extracts therefrom.

(3) Every book kept in pursuance of subsection (1) above shall be kept until the end of the period of three years beginning with the day on which the last entry was made in the book and any such documents as are mentioned in subsection (2) above shall be kept for a period of three years beginning with the date of the entry to which they refer.

(4) For the purposes of this section "prescribed" means prescribed by order.

Reciprocal provisions

25C. A licenced venison dealer who has purchased or received venison[1] from another licensed venison dealer or from a licensed game dealer within the meaning of section 10(5) of the Deer Act 1991[2] shall be deemed to have complied with the requirements of the preceding section of this Act if he has recorded in his record book—

(*a*) that the venison was so purchased or received;

(*b*) the name and address of the other licensed venison dealer or of the licensed game dealer concerned;

(*c*) the date when the venison was so purchased or received;

(*d*) the number of carcases and sex of the venison; and

(*e*) the species of deer, provided that it is possible to identify it.

Offences

25D. (1) It shall be an offence for any person to sell[3], offer or expose for sale or have in his possession, transport or cause to be transported for the purpose of sale at any premises any venison[4] unless he is a licensed venison dealer[5] or he does so for the purpose of selling to a licensed venison dealer, or he has purchased the venison from a licensed venison dealer.

(2) A person who is guilty of an offence under subsection (1) above shall be liable on summary conviction to a fine not exceeding level 3 on the standard scale[6].

(3) If any person sells, offers or exposes for sale, or has in his possession for the purpose of sale at any premises, or transports for the purpose of sale, or purchases or offers to purchase or receives, the carcase or any part of the carcase of a deer[7] which he knows or has reason to believe has been killed unlawfully, he shall be guilty of an offence.

(4) A person who is guilty of an offence under subsection (3) above shall be liable on summary conviction to a fine not exceeding level 4 on the standard scale[8] or to imprisonment for a term not exceeding 3 months or to both.

(5) Any licensed venison dealer who fails to comply with any provision of section 25B of this Act[9], or who knowingly or recklessly makes in any book or document which he is required to keep under that section an entry which is false or misleading in any material particular, shall be

---

[1] "Venison" defined by s. 25F, p. 56 below.
[2] Words "section 10(5) of the Deer Act 1991" substituted by the Deer Act 1991 (c. 54), s. 17(5). This amendment came into force on 25 October 1991: Deer Act 1991, s. 18(3).
[3] "Sale" defined by s. 25F, p. 56 below.
[4] "Venison" defined by s. 25F, p. 56 below.
[5] "Licensed venison dealer" defined by subsection (8) below.
[6] Words "level 3 on the standard scale" substituted by virtue of the Criminal Procedure (Scotland) Act 1975 (c. 21),

s. 289G. The present fine at level 3 is £1,000: Criminal Justice Act 1991 (c. 53), s. 17 which came into force on 1 October 1992: S.I. 1992/333, S.I. 1992/2118.
[7] "Deer" defined by s. 25F, p. 56 below.
[8] Words "level 4 on the standard scale" substituted by virtue of the Criminal Procedure (Scotland) Act 1975 (c. 21), s. 289G. The present fine at level 4 is £2,500: Criminal Justice Act 1991 (c. 53), s. 17 which came into force on 1 October 1992: S.I. 1992/333, S.I. 1992/2118.
[9] P. 54 above.

guilty of an offence and liable on summary conviction to a fine not exceeding level 2 on the standard scale.[1]

(6) Any person who obstructs a person entitled under section 25B(2) of this Act to inspect any book or document or other thing in the making of such inspection shall be guilty of an offence and liable on summary conviction to a fine not exceeding level 3 on the standard scale.[2]

(7) The court by which any person is convicted of an offence under Part III[3] or IIIA[4] of this Act may disqualify him from holding or obtaining a venison dealer's licence[5] for such period as the court thinks fit.

(8) In subsection (1) above "licensed venison dealer" means the holder of a venison dealer's licence granted by the[6] council within whose area the sale, offer or exposure for sale takes place, or where the premises concerned are situated.

Transitional Provision

25E. Notwithstanding the coming into force of section 11 of the Deer (Amendment) (Scotland) Act 1982, sections 25B and 25C and subsection (1), (2), (5), (6) and (8) of section 25D of this Act shall not apply to a registered venison dealer within the meaning of the Sale of Venison (Scotland) Act 1968 until whichever is the earlier of—

(*a*) the date on which a venison dealer's licence[7] is granted to that dealer;

(*b*) the expiry of 12 months after the commencement of the said section 11,

and the said Act of 1968 shall continue to have effect in relation to such a registered venison dealer during the said period notwithstanding its repeal by the said Act of 1982[8].

Interpretation of Part IIIA

25F. In this Part of this Act—

"council" means a council constituted under section 2 of the Local Government etc. (Scotland) Act 1994;[9]

"deer" means deer of any species;

"sale" includes barter, exchange, and any other transaction by which venison is disposed of for value;

"venison" means the carcase or any edible part of the carcase of a deer.

Part IV: Enforcement and Procedure

Attempts to commit offences

26. Without prejudice to the operation of section sixty-one of the Criminal Procedure (Scotland) Act, 1887[10], and section two of the Summary Jurisdiction (Scotland) Act, 1954, any person who attempts to commit, or does any act preparatory to the commission of, an offence against Part

---

[1] Words "level 2 on the standard scale" substituted by virtue of the Criminal Procedure (Scotland) Act 1975 (c. 21), s. 289G. The present fine at level 2 is £500: Criminal Justice Act 1991 (c. 53), s. 17 which came into force on 1 October 1992: S.I. 1992/333, S.I. 1992/2118.

[2] Words "level 3 on the standard scale" substituted by virtue of the Criminal Procedure (Scotland) Act 1975 (c. 21), s. 289G. The present fine at level 3 is £1,000: Criminal Justice Act 1991 (c. 53), s. 17 which came into force on 1 October 1992: S.I. 1992/333, S.I. 1992/2118.

[3] P. 51 above.

[4] P. 54 above.

[5] "Venison dealer's licence" defined by s. 25A(1), p. 54 above.

[6] Former words "islands or district" repealed by the Local Government etc. (Scotland) Act 1994 (c. 39), s. 180, sch. 13,

para. 53(3), sch. 14. It is anticipated that this amendment will come into force on 1 April 1996.

[7] "Venison dealer's licence" defined by s. 25A(1), p. 54 above.

[8] The Sale of Venison (Scotland) Act 1968 (c. 38) is repealed by the Deer (Amendment) (Scotland) Act 1982 (c. 19), s. 15(2), sch. 3. By a commencement order made on 27 June 1984, this provision came into force on 1 January 1985.

[9] The definition of "council" inserted by the Local Government etc. (Scotland) Act 1994 (c. 39), s. 180, sch. 13, para. 53(4). It is anticipated that this amendment will come into force on 1 April 1996.

[10] The reference to s. 61 of the 1887 Act is construed as a reference to s. 63 of the Criminal Procedure (Scotland) Act 1975 (c. 21): s. 460.

II[1] or any order made thereunder or against Part III[2] of this Act shall be guilty of an offence against this Act and shall be punishable in like manner as for the said offence; except that in the case of preparatory acts, the penalty shall be a fine not exceeding level 4 on the standard scale[3] or imprisonment for a term not exceeding three months or both[4].

....

Powers of search and seizure

27. (1) A constable may seize any deer[5], firearm[6] or ammunition[7], vehicle[8] or boat liable to be forfeited on conviction of an offence under[9] this Act.

(2) A sheriff or any justice of the peace, if satisfied by information on oath that there is reasonable ground to suspect any offence against Part III[10] or section 25(D)(1) or (3)[11,12] of this Act to have been committed and that evidence of the commission of the offence is to be found on any premises or in any vehicle or boat, may grant a warrant authorising any constable at any time or times within one week from the date of such warrant to enter, if necessary by force, the said premises and every part thereof or the said vehicle or boat for the purpose of detecting the offence.

(3) A constable authorised by any such warrant as aforesaid to search any premises or any such vehicle or boat may search every person who is found in, or whom he has reasonable ground to believe to have recently left or to be about to enter, those premises or that vehicle or boat as the case may be, and may seize any article found on the premises, or in the vehicle or boat, or on any such person, which he has reasonable ground for believing to be evidence of the commission of any such offence as aforesaid.

(4) Where a constable has reasonable grounds for suspecting that an offence against Part III or section 25(D)(1) or (3) of this Act has been committed and that evidence of the commission of the offence is to be found in any vehicle or boat, and that by reason of urgency or other good cause it is impracticable to apply for a warrant to search such vehicle or boat, the said constable may stop and search that vehicle or boat and may exercise the like power of search or seizure in relation to the vehicle or boat as might be conferred under subsection (2) of this section by the warrant of the sheriff or of a justice of the peace.

(5) No female shall in pursuance of any search authorised by this section be searched except by a female.

....

Apprehension of offenders

28. If any person shall be found committing any offence against the provisions of Part III[13] or of this Part of this Act, any constable may arrest that person.

....

Cancellation of firearms certificates

28A. (1) In any case where a person is convicted of an offence provided for by any of sections 22 to 25 of this Act[14] the court shall have power (in addition to any other power) to cancel any firearm[15] or shotgun certificate held by him.

---

[1] P. 50 above.
[2] P. 51 above.
[3] Words "level 4 on the standard scale" substituted by virtue of the Deer (Amendment) (Scotland) Act 1982 (c. 19), s. 14(1), sch. 1; Criminal Procedure (Scotland) Act 1975 (c. 21), s. 289G. The present fine at level 4 is £2,500: Criminal Justice Act 1991 (c. 53), s. 17 which came into force on 1 October 1992: S.I. 1992/333, S.I. 1992/2118.
[4] Words "; except that . . . three months or both.' added by the Deer (Amendment) (Scotland) Act 1982 (c. 19), s. 14(1), sch. 1. This amendment came into force on 28 July 1982: s. 16(3).
[5] "Deer" defined by s. 32, p. 58 below.
[6] "Firearm" defined by s. 32, p. 58 below.

[7] "Ammunition" defined by s. 32, p. 58 below.
[8] "Vehicle" defined by s. 32, p. 58 below.
[9] Words "on conviction of an offence under" substituted by the Deer (Amendment) (Scotland) Act 1982 (c. 19), s. 15(1), sch. 2, para. 2. This amendment came into force on 28 July 1982: s. 16(3).
[10] P. 51 above.
[11] P. 55 above.
[12] Words "Part III or section 25D(1) or (3)" substituted by the Deer (Amendment) (Scotland) Act 1982 (c. 19), s. 14(3). This amendment came into force on 28 July 1982: s. 16(3).
[13] P. 51 above.
[14] Pp. 51–53 above.
[15] "Firearm" defined by s. 32, p. 58below.

(2) Where the court cancels a firearm or shotgun certificate under subsection (1) above—

(*a*) the court shall cause notice in writing of that fact to be sent to the chief constable by whom the certificate was granted; and

(*b*) the chief constable shall by notice in writing require the holder of the certificate to surrender it; and

(*c*) if the holder fails to surrender the certificate within twenty-one days from the date of that requirement, he shall be guilty of an offence and liable on summary conviction to a fine not exceeding level 2 on the standard scale.[1,2]

29. *Repealed by the Deer (Amendment) (Scotland) Act 1982 (c. 19), s. 15(2), sch. 3. This amendment came into force on 28 July 1982: s. 16(3).*

Disposal of deer seized under the Act

30. Where any deer[3] seized under this Part of this Act is liable to forfeiture the person by whom it is seized may sell it and the net proceeds of the sale shall be liable to forfeiture in the same manner as the deer sold:

Provided that no person shall be subject to any liability on account of his neglect or failure to exercise the powers conferred on him by this section.

Offences by bodies corporate

31. (1) When an offence against this Act or any order made thereunder which has been committed by a body corporate is proved to have been committed with the consent or connivance of, or to be attributable to any neglect on the part of, any director, manager, secretary, or other similar officer of the body corporate, or any person purporting to act in such capacity, he, as well as the body corporate, shall be deemed to be guilty of that offence and shall be liable to be proceeded against and punished accordingly.

(2) In this section the expression "director" in relation to any body corporate established by or under any enactment for the purpose of carrying on under national ownership any industry or part of an industry or undertaking, being a body corporate whose affairs are managed by the members thereof, means a member of that body corporate.

Part V: Supplementary

Interpretation of Parts III and IV

32. For the purposes of Parts III[4] and IV[5] of this Act unless the context otherwise requires—

"ammunition" has the same meaning as in section thirty-two of the Firearms Act, 1937[6];

"deer" means deer of any species and includes the carcase of any deer or any part thereof;

"firearm" has the same meaning as in section thirty-two of the Firearms Act, 1937[6];

"land" includes land covered by water, but does not include a dwelling-house or any yard, garden, outhouses and pertinents belonging thereto or usually enjoyed therewith;

---

[1] Words "level 2 on the standard scale" substituted by virtue of the Criminal Procedure (Scotland) Act 1975 (c. 21), s. 289G. The present fine at level 2 is £500: Criminal Justice Act 1991 (c. 53), s. 17 which came into force on 1 October 1992: S.I. 1992/333, S.I. 1992/2118.

[2] This section inserted by the Deer (Amendment) (Scotland) Act 1982 (c. 19), s. 15(1), sch. 2, para. 1. This amendment came into force on 28 July 1982: s. 16(3).

[3] "Deer" defined by s. 32, p. 58 below.

[4] P. 51 above.

[5] P. 56 above.

[6] S. 57(1), (2) of the Firearms Act 1968 replaces s. 32 of the Firearms Act 1937. The Firearms Act 1968 consolidates and repeals the Firearms Act 1937.

"vehicle" includes any conveyance other than a vehicle used for the purposes of a passenger transport service within the meaning of the Transport Act, 1947.

....

Exemptions for certain acts

33. (1) A person shall not be guilty of any offence against this Act or any order made thereunder in respect of any act done for the purpose of preventing suffering by an injured or diseased deer, or by any deer calf, fawn or kid[1] deprived of its mother[2].

(2) Where a person performs an act under the authority of or at the request of the Commission[3] in pursuance of section 6 of this Act[4] or in pursuance of a control scheme[5] he shall not by reason of that act be liable to be proceeded against for an offence against this Act, except that—

(a) where the person is an officer or servant of the Commission performing an act as aforesaid in pursuance of the said section 6, and the act constitutes an offence against section 23(2) of this Act[6], or

(b) where the person is any such officer or servant performing an act as aforesaid in pursuance of a control scheme, and the act constitutes an offence against either subsection (1) or (2) of the said section 23, or

(c) in the case of any other person performing an act for either of the purposes mentioned in the two last foregoing paragraphs, if the act constitutes an offence against either of the said subsections,

he shall be so liable[7].

(3) Notwithstanding section 21 of this Act[8] (close season shooting) or any order made thereunder, or anything in any agreement between an occupier of agricultural land or of enclosed woodlands and the owner thereof, it shall be lawful for—

(a) the owner in person, provided that he is duly authorised in writing by the occupier for that purpose;

(b) the owner's servants in his ordinary service, provided that they are duly authorised in writing by the occupier for that purpose;

(c) the occupier in person;

(d) the servants of the occupier in his ordinary service on the land or other persons normally resident on the land provided that they are duly authorised in writing by the occupier for that purpose; or

(e) any other person approved in writing by the Commission as a fit and competent person for the purpose who has been duly authorised in writing by the occupier for that purpose

to take or kill, and to sell or otherwise dispose of the carcases of, any deer found on any arable land, garden grounds or land laid down in permanent grass (other than moorland and unenclosed land) and forming part of that land or on enclosed woodland, as the case may be, provided that the occupier has reasonable grounds for believing that serious damage will be caused to crops, pasture, trees or human or animal foodstuffs on that land if the deer are not killed.

(3A) Any authority given under subsection (3) above shall expire—

(a) at the end of such period as the occupier may specify in it;

---

[1] Words "fawn or kid" inserted by the Deer (Amendment) (Scotland) Act 1982 (c. 19), s. 12. This amendment came into force on 28 July 1982: s. 16(3).

[2] Words "purpose of preventing suffering by an injured or diseased deer, or by any deer calf deprived of its mother" inserted by the Deer (Amendment) (Scotland) Act 1967 (c. 37), s. 2(1). This Act came into force on 28 June 1967, the date of the Royal Assent.

[3] "The Commission" means the Red Deer Commission:

s. 1(1).

[4] P. 44 above.

[5] "Control scheme" defined by s. 7(3), p. 46 above.

[6] P. 51 above.

[7] This subsection inserted by the Deer (Amendment) (Scotland) Act 1967 (c. 37), s. 2(1). This Act came into force on 28 June 1967, the date of the Royal Assent.

[8] P. 50 above.

(b) when person to whom paragraph (b) or (d) of that subsection applies ceases to be normally resident or in the owner's or, as the case may be, occupier's ordinary service;

(c) where paragraph (e) of that subsection applies, at the end of the period specified in the Commission's approval; or

(d) if the occupier revokes the authority.

(3B) Notwithstanding section 21 of this Act (close season shooting) or any order made thereunder it shall be lawful for any person authorised in writing for the purpose by the Secretary of State to take or kill deer during the close season for any scientific purpose.

(4) Notwithstanding section 23(1)[1] of this Act (night shooting) or anything contained in any agreement between an occupier of agricultural land or of enclosed woodlands and the owner thereof, it shall be lawful for the occupier in person to carry out night shooting of red deer or sika deer on such land or woodlands, provided that the occupier has reasonable grounds for believing that serious damage will be caused to crops, pasture, trees or human or animal foodstuffs on that land if the deer are not killed.

(4A) Notwithstanding anything contained in section 23(1) of this Act the Commission may authorise in writing (subject to such conditions as they may specify) any person nominated by the occupier of agricultural land or enclosed woodlands to shoot deer of any species on that land or woodlands during the period specified in the said section 23(1), provided that the Commission are satisfied—

(a) that the shooting is necessary to prevent serious damage to crops, pasture, trees or human or animal foodstuffs; and

(b) that no other method of control which might reasonably be adopted in the circumstances would be adequate; and

(c) that the person concerned is a fit and competent person to receive such authorisation.

(4B) Such authorisation as is mentioned in subsection (4A) above shall be valid for such period as the Commission may specify therein.

(4C) The owner of the agricultural land or enclosed woodlands may at any time request the occupier to inform him of the numbers of red deer[2] or sika deer[3] shot by virtue of subsection (3), (4) or (4A) above within the period of 12 months immediately preceding the request and the occupier shall comply with any such request as soon as may be.

(4D) The Commission shall prepare and publish (with power to prepare and publish a revised version from time to time) a code of practice for night shooting to which they shall have regard when exercising their powers under subsection (4A) above and it shall be a condition of any authorisation under the said subsection that the person concerned complies with the relevant provisions of the code.

(4E) In this section—

"red deer" means deer of the species Cervus elaphus and "sika deer" means deer of the species Cervus nippon;

and any reference to "red deer" or "sika deer" includes any deer which is a hybrid of those species.[4]

(5) The provisions of the last two foregoing subsections shall be construed as one with the Agriculture (Scotland) Act, 1948[5].

---

[1] P. 51 above.
[2] "Red deer" defined by subsection (4E) below.
[3] "Sika deer" defined by subsection (4E) below.
[4] Subsections (3)–(4E) inserted by the Deer (Amendment) (Scotland) Act 1982 (c. 19), s. 13(1). This amendment came into force on 28 July 1982: s. 16(3).
[5] S. 43(1) of the Agriculture (Scotland) Act 1948 (c. 45) is repealed by the Deer (Amendment) (Scotland) Act 1982 (c. 19), ss. 13(2), 15(2), sch. 3. Ss. 39 to 42 of the Agriculture (Scotland) Act 1948, so far as relating to sika deer within the meaning of the Deer (Amendment) (Scotland) Act 1982 or to any hybrid mentioned in s. 1(4) of that Act, is repealed by the Deer (Amendment) (Scotland) Act 1982, s. 15(2), sch. 3.

Application of Act to the Crown

34. This Act shall apply to land an interest in which belongs to Her Majesty in right of the Crown and land an interest in which belongs to a government department or is held in trust for Her Majesty for the purposes of a government department; but in its application to any land an interest in which belongs or is held as aforesaid this Act shall have effect subject to such modifications as may be prescribed by regulations made by the Secretary of State under this Act.

Orders, regulations, etc.

35. (1) Subject to section 23A(4) of this Act,[1] any order or regulations made under this Act shall be embodied in a statutory instrument which shall be subject to annulment in pursuance of a resolution by either House of Parliament.

(2) Any order made under this Act may be varied or revoked by a subsequent order made in the like manner.

36. *Repealed by the Statute Law Repeals Act 1974 (c. 22), s. 1, sch., pt. XI. This amendment came into force on 27 June 1974, the date of the Royal Assent.*

Short title, extent and commencement

37. (1) This Act may be cited as the Deer (Scotland) Act, 1959.

(2) This Act[2] shall extent to Scotland only.

(3) This Act, except where otherwise expressly provided, shall come into force at the expiry of one month beginning with the date of its passing[3].

SCHEDULES

FIRST SCHEDULE

(Section 1.)

PROVISIONS AS TO THE RED DEER COMMISSION

Constitution of the Commission

1. The Commission shall be a body corporate and shall have a common seal.

2. Every member of the Commission shall hold and vacate office in accordance with the terms of the instrument under which he is appointed, but notwithstanding anything in such an instrument any member of the Commission may resign his office by a notice given under his hand to the Secretary of State, and a member of the Commission who ceases to hold office shall be eligible for re-appointment to the Commission.

---

[1] Words "Subject to section 23A(4) of this Act," inserted by the Deer (Amendment) (Scotland) Act 1982 (c. 19), s. 15(1), sch. 2, para. 3. This amendment came into force on 28 July 1982: s. 16(3).
[2] Former words "except in so far as it relates to the amendment of the House of Commons Disqualification Act, 1957" repealed by the House of Commons Disqualification Act 1975 (c. 24), s. 10(2), sch. 3. This amendment came into force on 8 May 1975, the date of the Royal Assent.
[3] This Act, except for s. 21, came into force on 14 June 1959.

2A. If the Secretary of State is satisfied that the chairman of the Commission—

    (*a*) has had his estate sequestrated or has made a trust deed for behoof of his creditors or a composition contract with his creditors;

    (*b*) is incapacitated by reason of physical or mental illness;

    (*c*) has been absent from meetings of the Commission for a period of more than 3 consecutive months without the permission of the Commission or of the Secretary of State; or

    (*d*) is otherwise unable or unfit to discharge the functions of a member of the Commission, or is unsuitable to continue as the chairman.

the Secretary of State shall have power to remove him from his said office.

2B. Where a person ceases to be chairman of the Commission otherwise than on the expiry of his term of office and it appears to the Secretary of State that there are special circumstances which make it right for that person to receive compensation, the Secretary of State may make to that person a payment of such amount as the Secretary of State may, with the approval of the Treasury, determine.

2C. The Secretary of State may make such provision, if any, as he may, with the approval of the Treasury, determine for the payment of pensions to or in respect of chairmen of the Commission.[1]

3. *Repealed by the House of Commons Disqualification Act 1975 (c. 24), s. 10(2), sch. 3. This amendment came into force on 8 May 1975, the date of the Royal Assent.*

4. The Secretary of State shall pay—

    (*a*) to the Chairman of the Commission such remuneration and such allowances, and

    (*b*) to the other members of the Commission such allowances as he may with the approval of the Treasury determine.

5. The Commission may pay to the members of any panel appointed in pursuance of section two of this Act[2] the like allowances as are payable by the Secretary of State to members of the Commission under the last foregoing paragraph.

Meetings and Proceedings of the Commission

6. The quorum of the Commission shall be five or such larger number as the Commission may from time to time determine.

7. The proceedings of the Commission shall not be invalidated by any vacancy in the membership of the Commission or by any defect in the appointment of any member thereof.

8. If at any meeting of the Commission the votes are equally divided on any question, the person acting as chairman of the meeting shall have a second or casting vote.

9. Subject to the foregoing provisions of this Schedule, the Commission shall have power to regulate their own procedure and that of any panel appointed by them.

Office, Officers and Servants

10. The Commission shall have an office at which communications and notices will be received.

11. The Secretary of State may provide the services of such officers and servants as the Commission may require.

---

[1] Paragraphs 2A–2C inserted by the Deer (Amendment) (Scotland) Act 1982 (c. 19), s. 5. This amendment came into force on 28 July 1982: s. 16(3).
[2] P. 43 above.

Instruments executed or issued by the Commission

12. and 13. *Repealed by the Requirements of Writing (Scotland Act 1995 (c. 7), s. 14(2), sch. 5. This amendment came into force on 1 August 1995: s. 15(2).*

SECOND SCHEDULE

(Section 7.)

Provisions as to control schemes

PART I

Procedure for making control schemes

1. Where the Commission decide to make a control scheme[1] they shall—

    (*a*) serve on every owner[2] and every occupier[3] of land on whom the scheme proposes to impose any require-ment a copy of the said scheme, together with a notice[4] stating that any such owner or occupier may, within twenty-eight days of the service of the notice, object to the Secretary of State in such manner as may be spec-ified in the notice to the scheme or to any provision contained therein; and

    (*b*) in two successive weeks publish in the Edinburgh Gazette and in one or more newspapers circulating in the district in which the control area[5] is situated a notice stating that a control scheme has been prepared, describing the said area, naming a place within the district where a copy of the said scheme and of the map referred to therein may be inspected at all reasonable hours, and stating that any person may, within twenty-eight days of the first publication of such notice, object to the Secretary of State in such a manner as may be specified in the notice to the said scheme or to any provision contained therein.

2. If no objection is duly made under the last foregoing paragraph or if all objections so made are withdrawn, the Secretary of State may confirm the control scheme either in the form submitted to him or, subject to paragraph 4 of this Schedule, with modifications.

3. If any objection duly made as aforesaid is not withdrawn, the Secretary of State shall, before deciding whether to confirm the control scheme, cause a public inquiry to be held, and after considering the objection and the report of the person who held the inquiry may confirm the scheme either in the form submitted to him or, sub-ject to paragraph 4 of this Schedule, with modifications.

4. The control scheme shall not be confirmed with any modification unless either—

    (*a*) every person served with a copy of the scheme by virtue of paragraph 1 of this Schedule has been served with notice of the proposal to make the modification and any other person on whom the modification, if made, would impose a requirement, has been served with a notice of the proposal to make the modification along with a copy of the said scheme, and either has consented thereto or has not, before the expiry of fourteen days from the service of the notice, notified the Secretary of State in writing that he objects thereto; or

    (*b*) the modification arises from representations made at an inquiry held under paragraph 3 of this Schedule or from the findings or recommendations of the person holding that inquiry, and every person in respect of

[1] "Control scheme" defined by s. 7(3), p. 46 above.
[2] "Owner" defined by s. 20, p. 50 above.
[3] "Occupier" defined by s. 20, p. 50 above.

[4] For the service of notices see s. 16, p. 49 above.
[5] "Control area" defined by s. 7(4), p. 46 above.

whom the modification, if made, would vary or impose a requirement has been served with a copy of the scheme as aforesaid and been afforded an opportunity to appear and be heard at the inquiry.

Part II

Procedure for varying or revoking control schemes

5. On the application of the Commission[1], the Secretary of State may make a scheme varying a control scheme[2] or may revoke a control scheme.

6. Before making any such variation or revocation the Secretary of State shall—

   (a) serve on every owner[3] and every occupier[4] of land on whom the control scheme has imposed any requirement or would, if varied as proposed, impose any requirement, a draft of the scheme varying the control
   scheme or, as the case may be, an intimation of the proposed revocation together with a notice stating that
   any such owner or occupier may, within twenty-eight days of the service of the draft scheme or the intimation, as the case may be, object to the Secretary of State in such a manner as may be specified in the notice
   to the variation or revocation of the control scheme; and

   (b) in two successive weeks publish in the Edinburgh Gazette and in one or more newspapers circulating in the
   district in which the control area[5] is situated a notice stating that the control scheme is to be varied or
   revoked and that any person may, within twenty-eight days of the first publication of such notice, object in
   such manner as may be specified in the notice to the making of the variation or revocation, and in the case
   of any such variation naming a place within the district where a copy of the scheme as proposed to be varied and any map referred to therein may be inspected at all reasonable hours.

7. If no objection is duly made under the foregoing paragraph or if all objections so made are withdrawn, the Secretary of State may vary or revoke the control scheme, as the case may be.

8. If any objection duly made as aforesaid is not withdrawn, the Secretary of State shall, before deciding whether to make the variation or revocation as the case may be, cause a public inquiry to be held, and after considering the objection and the report of the person who held the inquiry may make the variation, either in the form of the draft or with modifications, or the revocation, as the case may be.

9. A variation of a control scheme shall not be made with any modification unless either—

   (a) every person served with a copy of the draft scheme by virtue of paragraph 6 of this Schedule has been served
   with notice of the proposal to make the modification and any other person on whom the modification, if
   made, would impose a requirement has been served with a notice of the proposal to make the modification
   along with a copy of the said draft scheme, and either has consented thereto or has not, before the expiry of
   fourteen days from the service of the notice, notified the Secretary of State in writing that he objects thereto;
   or

   (b) the modification arises from representations made at an inquiry held under the last foregoing paragraph or
   from the findings or recommendations of the person holding that inquiry, and every person in respect of
   whom the modification, if made, would vary or impose a requirement has been served with a copy of the
   draft scheme as aforesaid and been afforded an opportunity to appear and be heard at the inquiry.

Part III

General Procedural Provisions

10. Notwithstanding anything in paragraphs 3 or 8 of this Schedule, the Secretary of State may require any person who has made an objection to state in writing the grounds thereof, and may disregard the objection for the purposes of this Schedule if he is satisfied that the objection is frivolous.

---

[1] "The Commission" means the Red Deer Commission:
s. 1(1).
[2] "Control scheme" defined by s. 7(3), p. 46 above.

[3] "Owner" defined by s. 20, p. 50 above.
[4] "Occupier" defined by s. 20, p. 50 above.
[5] "Control area" defined by s. 7(4), p. 46 above.

11. The provisions of subsections (2) to (8) of section 210 of the Local Government (Scotland) Act 1973[1] (which relate to the holding of local inquiries) shall apply in relation to a public local inquiry held under paragraph 3 or 8 of this Schedule as they apply in relation to local inquiries held under the said section 210.[1]

PART IV

Provisions as to the validity of control schemes and of variations or revocations of such schemes

12. On confirming a control scheme[2] or on varying or revoking such a scheme the Secretary of State shall forthwith—

(a) serve on every person on whom a notice was required to be served under sub-paragraph (a) of paragraph 1 or under sub-paragraph (a) of paragraph 4 of this Schedule or, as the case may be, sub-paragraph (a) of paragraph 6 or under sub-paragraph (a) of paragraph 9 of this Schedule a notice stating that the scheme has been confirmed or, as the case may be, that a variation or revocation of such a scheme has been made;

(b) publish in the Edinburgh Gazette and in one or more newspapers circulating in the district in which the control area[3] is situated a notice stating that the scheme has been confirmed or varied or revoked, as the case may be, and naming a place within the district where a copy of the scheme or, as the case may be, the scheme as varied, and of any maps referred to therein, may be inspected at all reasonable hours.

13. If any person aggrieved by a control scheme or by any variation or revocation thereof desires to question its validity on the ground that it is not within the powers of this Act or that any requirement of this Act has not been complied with, he may, within six weeks from the date of the first publication of the notice referred to in sub-paragraph (b) of the last foregoing paragraph, make an application for the purpose to the Court of Session, and if any such application is duly made the Court, if satisfied that the scheme or any variation or revocation thereof is not within the powers of this Act or that the interests of the applicant have been substantially prejudiced by a failure to comply with any requirement of this Act, may quash the scheme or any variation or revocation thereof, either generally or in so far as it affects the applicant; but except as aforesaid the scheme or any variation or revocation thereof shall not at any time be questioned in any proceedings whatsoever.

THIRD SCHEDULE

Repealed by the Statute Law Repeals Act 1974 (c. 223), s. 1, sch. pt. XI. This amendment came into force on 27 June 1974, the date of the Royal Assent.

---

[1] Words "subsections (2) to (8) of section 210 of the Local Government (Scotland) Act 1973" and "210" substituted by the Local Government (Scotland) Act 1973 (c. 65): s. 214(2), sch. 27, pt. II, para. 143. This amendment came into force on 16 May 1975: s. 214(2).

[2] "Control scheme" defined by s. 7(3), p. 46 above.

[3] "Control area" defined by s. 7(4), p. 46 above.

Forestry Act 1967

Ch. 10

Supplementary

Part III: Administration and Finance

Advisory bodies

Acquisition and disposal of land

Finance, accounts and annual report

Part IV: General

Forestry Act 1967

An Act to consolidate the Forestry Acts 1919 to 1963 with corrections and improvements made under the Consolidation of Enactments (Procedure) Act 1949.

[22nd March 1967[1]]

Part I: Forestry and Afforestation in Great Britain

The Forestry Commission

1. (1) The Forestry Commissioners constituted under the Forestry Acts 1919 to 1945 shall continue in existence and are in this Act referred to as "the Commissioners".

(2) The Commissioners shall be charged with the general duty of promoting the interests of forestry, the development of afforestation and the production and supply of timber and other forest products in Great Britain and in that behalf shall have the powers and duties conferred or imposed on them by this Act[2].

(3) The Commissioners' general duty includes that of promoting the establishment and maintenance in Great Britain of adequate reserves of growing trees.

(3A) In discharging their functions under the Forestry Acts 1967 to 1979 the Commissioners shall, so far as may be consistent with the proper discharge of those functions, endeavour to achieve a reasonable balance between—

(a) the development of afforestation, the management of forests and the production and supply of timber, and

(b) the conservation and enhancement of natural beauty and the conservation of flora, fauna and geological or physiographical features of special interest.[3]

(4) The Commissioners shall, in exercising their functions under this Act, and also in exercising their powers under the Plant Health Act 1967[4] (which enables them to make orders for the control of timber pests and diseases), comply with such directions as may be given to them by the Ministers[5].

(5) Directions given by the Ministers for purposes of the foregoing subsection shall be given by them jointly, except in so far as they make arrangements that this subsection shall not apply.

....

Constitution, administration, etc., of Commission

2. (1) The Commissioners[6] shall consist of a chairman and not more than ten[7] other members appointed by Her Majesty by warrant under the sign manual to be Forestry Commissioners.

(2) Of the person for the time being appointed to be Forestry Commissioners—

(a) at least three shall be persons who have special knowledge and experience of forestry;

(b) at least one shall be a person who has scientific attainments and a technical knowledge of forestry; and

---

[1] This Act came into force on the date of the Royal Assent, 22 March 1967.

[2] Further powers are conferred on the Forestry Commissioners by the Countryside (Scotland) Act 1967 (c. 86), s. 58, p. 110 below, s. 65, relating to the appointment of wardens, and the Countryside Act 1968 (c. 41), s. 23, p. 123 below.

[3] This subsection inserted by the Wildlife and Countryside (Amendment) Act 1985 (c. 31), s. 4. This amendment came into force on 26 August 1985: s. 5(3).

[4] 1967 c. 8.

[5] "Minister" defined by s. 49(1), p. 97 below.

[6] "The Commissioners" means the Forestry Commissioners: s. 49(1), p. 97 below.

[7] Word "ten" substituted by the Forestry Act 1981 (c. 39), s. 5. This Act came into force on 27 July 1981, the date of the Royal Assent.

(c) at least one shall be a person who has special knowledge and experience of the timber trade.

(3) The Commissioners shall by order appoint committees for England, Scotland and Wales respectively, whose membership shall consist partly of persons who are Forestry Commissioners or officers of the Commissioners and partly of persons, not exceeding three in number, who are not Forestry Commissioners or officers of the Commissioners; and the Commissioners may delegate, subject to such restrictions or conditions as they think fit, any of their functions to a committee so appointed.

(4) Part I of Schedule 1 to this Act[1] shall have effect with respect to the Commissioners, their staff, proceedings and other related matters and to the committees appointed under subsection (3) of this section; and Part II of that Schedule[2] shall have effect with respect to the superannuation of Forestry Commissioners and officers employed by the Commissioners.

Management of forestry land

3. (1) The Commissioners[3] may manage, plant and otherwise use, for the purpose of the exercise of their functions under this Act[4], any land placed at their disposal by the Minister[5] under this Act, and—

(a) the power of the Commissioners under this subsection to manage and use any land shall, without prejudice to the generality of that power, include power to erect buildings or execute works on the land;

(b) any timber produced on land so placed at the Commissioners' disposal shall belong to the Commissioners[6].

(2) The Commissioners may undertake the management or supervision, upon such terms and subject to such conditions as may be agreed upon, or give assistance or advice in relation to the planting or management, of any woods or forests belonging to any person, including woods and forests under the management of the Crown Estate Commissioners or under the control of a government department, or belonging to a local authority.

(3) The Commissioners may—

(a) purchase or otherwise acquire standing timber, and sell or otherwise dispose of any timber belonging to them or, subject to such terms as may be mutually agreed, to a private owner, and generally promote the supply, sale, utilization and conversion of timber;

(b) establish and carry on, or aid in the establishment and carrying on, of woodland industries.

(4) In this section the expression "timber" includes all forest products.

4. *Repealed by the Forestry Act 1979 (c. 21), s. 3(2), sch. 2. This amendment came into force on 30 May 1979: s. 3(3).*

Forestry dedication covenants and agreements

5. (1) The provisions of this section shall have effect with a view to allowing land to be devoted to forestry by means of agreements entered into with the Commissioners[7], being agreements to the effect that the land shall not, except with the previous consent in writing of the Commissioners or, in the case of dispute, under direction of the Minister[8], be used otherwise than for the growing of

[1] P. 98 below.
[2] Part II, Superannuation of Forestry Commissioners and Commission staff, is not reproduced.
[3] "The Commissioners" means the Forestry Commissioners: s. 49(1), p. 97 below.
[4] The reference to the Commissioners' functions under this Act includes reference to their functions under the Countryside Act 1968 (c. 41), s. 24(1), p. 124 below.
[5] "Minister" defined by s. 49(1), p. 97 below.

[6] Further powers as respects land placed at the Commissioners' disposal are conferred, as respects Scotland, by the Countryside (Scotland) Act 1967 (c. 86), s. 58, p. 110 below, and, as respects England and Wales, by the Countryside Act 1968 (c. 41), s. 23, p. 123 below.
[7] "The Commissioners" means the Forestry Commissioners: s. 49(1), p. 97 below.
[8] "Minister" defined by s. 49(1), p. 97 below.

timber or other forest products in accordance with the rules or practice of good forestry or for purposes connected therewith; and in this Act—

(a) "forestry dedication covenant" means a covenant to the said effect entered into with the Commissioners in respect of land in England or Wales without an intention being expressed contrary to the application of section 79 of the Law of Property Act 1925[1] (under which covenants relating to land are, unless the contrary is expressed, deemed to be made on behalf of the covenantor, his successors in title and persons deriving title under him or them); and

(b) "forestry dedication agreement" means an agreement to the said effect entered into with the Commissioners in respect of land in Scotland by a person who is the proprietor thereof for his own absolute use or is empowered by this section to enter into the agreement.

(2) Where land in England or Wales is subject to a forestry dedication covenant,—

(a) the Commissioners shall, as respects the enforcement of the covenant against persons other than the covenantor, have the like rights as if they had at all material times been the absolute owners in possession of ascertained land adjacent to the land subject to the covenant and capable of being benefited by the covenant, and the covenant had been expressed to be for the benefit of that adjacent land; and

(b) section 84 of the Law of Property Act 1925 (which enables the Lands Tribunal to discharge or modify restrictive covenants) shall not apply to the covenant.

(3) A forestry dedication agreement affecting land in Scotland may be recorded in the General Register of Sasines and, on being so recorded, shall be enforceable at the instance of the Commissioners against any person having an interest in the land and against any person deriving title from him:

Provided that such an agreement shall not be so enforceable against any third party who shall have in bona fide onerously acquired right (whether completed by infeftment or not) to his interest in the land prior to the agreement being recorded as aforesaid, or against any person deriving title from such third party.

(4) Schedule 2 to this Act[2] shall have effect to empower limited owners, trustees and others to enter into forestry dedication covenants or agreements and to provide for matters arising on their doing so.

Requirements for haulage facilities

6. (1) The provisions of this section shall have effect where the Commissioners[3] are of opinion that insufficient facilities exist for the haulage of timber from any wood or forest to a road, railway or waterway.

(2) Subject to the following subsections, the Commissioners may, where they are of the said opinion, make an order that the owner and occupier of any land shall afford the necessary facilities, subject to payment by the person in whose favour the order is made of reasonable rent or wayleave and of compensation for any damage caused by the haulage, and the owner or occupier shall thereupon comply with the order.

(3) The Commissioners shall not make an order under this section until the person proposed to be required to give the said facilities has had an opportunity of being heard.

(4) A person aggrieved by an order made under this section may appeal therefrom to the Minister[4] in such manner and upon such conditions, if any, as may be prescribed[5] by the Minister, who may thereupon revoke or vary the order.

(5) The amount of rent or wayleave and compensation for damage which is payable in consequence of an order made under this section shall, in default of agreement, be assessed as follows that is to say—

[1] 1925 c. 20.
[2] P. 99 below.
[3] "The Commissioners" means the Forestry Commissioners: s. 49(1), p. 97 below.
[4] "Minister" defined by s. 49(1), p. 97 below.
[5] "Prescribed" defined by s. 35, p. 89 below.

(a) in a case relating to England and Wales, by a single arbitrator appointed by the President of the Royal Institution of Chartered Surveyors; and

(b) in a case relating to Scotland, by an arbiter appointed by the Chairman of the Scottish Committee of the said Institution.

Prevention of damage by rabbits, hares and vermin

7. (1) The provisions of this section shall have effect where the Commissioners[1] are satisfied that trees or tree plants are being, or are likely to be, damaged by rabbits, hares or vermin[2] owing to the failure or an occupier of land to destroy sufficiently the rabbits, hares or vermin on land in his occupation, or otherwise to take steps for the prevention of damage by them.

(2) The Commissioners may, where they are so satisfied authorise in writing any competent person to enter on the land and kill and take the rabbits, hares or vermin thereon; but before doing so they shall first give to the occupier and owner of the land such opportunity as the Commissioners think reasonable of destroying the rabbits, hares or vermin, or of taking steps for the prevention of the damage.

(3) The Commissioners may recover from the occupier of the land the net cost incurred by them in connection with action taken by them under the foregoing subsection.

A sum recoverable under this subsection shall, in England or Wales, be recoverable summarily as a civil debt.

(4) Anyone who obstructs a person authorised by the Commissioners in the due exercise of his powers or duties under subsection (2) above shall be liable on summary conviction to a fine not exceeding level 2 on the standard scale[3]; but the person authorised shall, if so required, produce his authority.

(5) For purposes of this section—

(a) the person entitled to kill rabbits, hares or vermin on any common land shall be deemed to be the occupier of the land; and

(b) the expression "vermin" includes squirrels.

Miscellaneous powers of Commissioners

8. The Commissioners[4] may—

(a) undertake the collection, preparation, publication and distribution of statistics relating to forestry, and promote and develop instruction and training in forestry by establishing or aiding schools or other educational institutions or in such other manner as they think fit;

(b) make, or aid in making, such inquiries, experiments and research, and collect, or aid in collecting, such information as they may think important for the purpose of promoting forestry and the teaching of forestry, and publish or otherwise take steps to make known the results of the inquiries, experiments or research and disseminate the information;

(c) make, or aid in making, such inquiries as they think necessary for the purpose of securing an adequate supply of timber and other forest products in Great Britain.

---

[1] "The Commissioners" means the Forestry Commissioners: s. 49(1), p. 97 below.

[2] "Vermin" includes squirrels: paragraph (5)(b) below.

[3] Words "level 2 on the standard scale" substituted by the Criminal Law Act 1977 (c. 45), s. 31, the Criminal Justice Act 1982 (c. 48), s. 46 as respects England and Wales and the Criminal Procedure (Scotland) Act 1975 (c. 21), ss. 289C, 289G as respects Scotland. The current fine at level 2 is £500: Criminal Justice Act 1991 (c. 53), s. 17 which came into force on 1 October 1992: S.I. 1992/333, S.I. 1992/2118.

[4] "The Commissioners" means the Forestry Commissioners: s. 49(1), p. 97 below.

8A. *General duty of Ministers*

In performing their functions under this Act the Ministers[1] shall have regard to the national interest in maintaining and expanding the forestry resources of Great Britain.[2]

Part II: Commissioners' Power to Control Felling of Trees

Restriction of felling

Requirement of licence for felling

9. (1) A felling licence[3] granted by the Commissioners[4] shall be required for the felling[5] of growing trees, except in a case where by or under the following provisions of this Part of this Act this subsection is expressed not to apply.

(**2**) Subsection (1) above does not apply—

(*a*) to the felling of trees with a diameter not exceeding 8 centimetres[6] or, in the case of coppice or underwood, with a diameter not exceeding 15 centimetres; or

(*b*) to the felling of fruit trees or trees standing or growing on land comprised in an orchard, garden, churchyard or public open space; or

(*c*) to the topping or lopping of trees or the trimming or laying of hedges.

(**3**) Subsection (1) above does not apply to the felling by any person of trees on land in his occupation or occupied by a tenant of his—

(*a*) where the trees have a diameter not exceeding 10 centimetres and the felling is carried out in order to improve the growth of other trees; or

(*b*) where the following conditions are satisfied, that is to say—

(i) the aggregate cubic content of the trees which are felled by that person without a licence (exclusive of trees to whose felling subsection (1) above does not apply) does not exceed 5 cubic metres[7] in any quarter; and

(ii) the aggregate cubic content of the trees so felled which are sold by that person whether before or after the felling (exclusive as aforesaid) does not exceed 2 cubic metres[7] in any quarter, or such larger quantity as the Commissioners may in a particular case allow.

(**4**) Subsection (1) above does not apply to any felling which—

(*a*) is for the prevention of danger or the prevention or abatement of a nuisance;

(*b*) is in compliance with any obligation imposed by or under an Act of Parliament, including this Act;

(*c*) is carried out by, or at the request of, an electricity operator, because the tree is or will be in such close proximity to an electric line or electrical plant which is kept installed or is being or is to be installed by the operator as to have the effect mentioned in paragraph 9(1)(*a*) or (*b*) of Schedule 4 to the Electricity Act 1989[8];

(*d*) is immediately required for the purpose of carrying out development authorised by planning permission granted or deemed to be granted under the Town and Country Planning Act 1990[9]

---

[1] "Minister" defined by s. 49(1), p. 97 below.

[2] This section inserted by the Forestry Act 1981 (c. 39), s. 4. This Act came into force on 27 July 1981, the date of the Royal Assent.

[3] "Felling licence" defined by s. 35, p. 89 below.

[4] "The Commissioners" means the Forestry Commissioners: s. 49(1), p. 97 below.

[5] "Felling" defined by s. 35, p. 89 below.

[6] The metric units of measurement in this section were substituted by the Forestry Act 1979 (c. 21), s. 2(1), sch. 1. This amendment came into force on 30 May 1979: s. 3(3).

[7] Words "5 cubic metres" and "2 cubic metres" in para-graph (*b*) substituted by the Forestry (Modification of Felling Restrictions) Regulations 1985: S.I. 1985/1958. These regulations came into operation on 13 December 1985.

[8] Words "an electricity operator . . . Electricity Act 1989" substituted by the Electricity Act 1989 (c. 29), s. 112(1), sch. 16, para. 13(2). This amendment came into force on 31 March 1990: S.I. 1990/117.

[9] Words "the Town and Country Planning Act 1990" substituted by the Planning (Consequential Provisions) Act 1990 (c. 11), s. 4, sch. 2, para. 14(1). This amendment came into force on 24 August 1990: s. 7(2).

or the enactments replaced by that Act, or under the Town and Country Planning (Scotland) Act 1972[1].

(5) Regulations made by the Commissioners under this Part of this Act[2] may modify subsections (2) to (4) above as follows, that is to say—

(a) they may provide for additional exceptions from the application of subsection (1) above and may in particular substitute—

   (i) in subsection (2)(a), for the reference to 8 centimetres a reference to a larger diameter;

   (ii) in subsection (3)(a), for the reference to 10 centimetres a reference to a larger diameter;

   (iii) in subsection (3)(b), for the reference to 30 cubic metres or the reference to 5.5 cubic metres in either case a reference to a larger quantity;

(b) they may substitute in subsection (2)(a) for the reference to 15 centimetres a reference to a smaller diameter; and

(c) they may restrict or suspend the exception in subsection (3)(b) and may in particular substitute, for the reference in sub-paragraph (i) to 30 cubic metres, or for the reference in sub-paragraph (ii) to 5.5 cubic metres,[3] in either case a reference to a smaller quantity;

and the said subsections shall have effect with any modification made by regulations under this subsection.

(6) In this section—

"electricity operator" means a licence holder within the meaning of Part I of the Electricity Act 1989 by whom the powers conferred by paragraph 9 (tree lopping) of Schedule 4 to that Act are exercisable;[4]

"electric line" and "electrical plant" have the same meanings as in Part I of the Electricity Act 1989;[4]

"public open space" means land laid out as a public garden or used (otherwise than in pursuance of section 193 of the Law of Property Act 1925[5] or of Part V of the National Parks and Access to the Countryside Act 1949[6] or of Part II[6] or section 48[7] of the Countryside (Scotland) Act 1967[8]) for the purpose of public recreation, or land being a disused burial ground[9];

"quarter" means the period of three months beginning with the 1st January, 1st April, 1st July or 1st October in any year;

and references to the diameter of trees shall be construed as references to the diameter, measured over the bark, at a point 1.3 metres above the ground level.[10,11]

[1] Words "the Town and Country Planning (Scotland) Act 1972" substituted by the Town and Country Planning (Scotland) Act 1972 (c. 52), s. 276(1), sch. 21, pt. II. This amendment came into force on 27 August 1972: s. 280.

[2] See note 7, p. 72 above. The Forestry (Exceptions from Restriction of Felling) Regulations 1979, S.I. 1979/792, p. 310 below, provide for additional exceptions from s. 9(1).

[3] With the exception of subsection 3(b) the metric units of measurement in this section were substituted by the Forestry Act 1979 (c. 21), s. 2(1), sch. 1. This amendment came into force on 30 May 1979: s. 3(3).

[4] These definitions substituted by the Electricity Act 1989 (c. 29), s. 112(1), para. 13(3). This amendment came into force on 31 March 1990: S.I. 1990/117.

[5] 1925 c. 20.

[6] Part V of the 1949 Act contains provisions concerning access to open country in England and Wales; Part II of the Countryside (Scotland) Act 1967 contains provisions concerning access to open country in Scotland.

[7] S. 48 of the Countryside (Scotland) Act 1967 makes provision for country parks.

[8] Words "or of Part II or section 48 of the Countryside (Scotland) Act 1967" inserted by the Countryside (Scotland) Act 1967 (c. 86), s. 58(5). This amendment came into force on 27 October 1967, the date of the Royal Assent.

[9] The definition of "public open space" is restricted by the Countryside Act 1968 (c. 41), s. 24(4), p. 124 below.

[10] Former words "and references to the cubic content of trees shall be construed as references to that content as ascertained in the prescribed manner" repealed by the Forestry Act 1979 (c. 21), s. 3(2), sch. 2. This amendment came into force on 30 Mary 1979: s. 3(3).

[11] Cases: section 9 Cullen v Jardine [1985] Crim L.R. 668; Forestry Commission v Grace and Another [1992] 1 EGLR 28.

....

Application for felling licence and decision of Commissioners thereon

10. (1) An application for a felling licence[1] may be made to the Commissioners[2] in the prescribed[3] manner by a person having such an estate or interest in the land on which the trees are growing as enables him with or without the consent of any other person, to fell[4] the trees.

(2) Subject to the provisions of this Act (and, in particular, to their duty to take advice under section 37(3)[5]), the Commissioners may on any such application grant the licence, or grant it subject to conditions, or refuse it, but shall grant it unconditionally except in a case where it appears to them to be expedient to do otherwise—

(*a*) in the interests of good forestry or agriculture or of the amenities of the district; or

(*b*) for the purpose of complying with their duty of promoting the establishment and maintenance in Great Britain of adequate reserves of growing trees.

(3) A felling licence shall continue in force for such period (not being less than one year from the date on which it is granted) as may be specified therein.

(4) If in the case of any trees the Commissioners refuse an application for a felling licence, the consequences shall be as follows:—

(*a*) except in a case to which section 14(4) below[6] applies, any person who is for the time being the owner of the trees[7] shall be entitled to compensation under and in accordance with the next following section; and

(*b*) if the land on which the trees are growing is, or in the opinion of the Commissioners will be, managed in a manner approved by them, the Commissioners may (subject to section 14(5) below[8]), if they think fit and subject to the approval of the Treasury, make to persons interested in the land advances by way of loan of such amounts, upon such terms and subject to such conditions, as they may determine.

(5) At any time after a felling licence has been refused by them in the case of any trees, the Commissioners may, if they think fit, give notice to the owner of the trees that they are prepared to grant a felling licence for the trees either unconditionally or subject to conditions described in the notice; and if the Commissioners give such a notice and an application is duly made to them for a felling licence, they shall grant a licence in accordance with the notice, subject to sections 13(2)[9] and 15[10] below.

(6) When the Commissioners refuse to grant a felling licence, they shall give notice in writing[11] to the applicant of the grounds for the refusal.

(7) Where application is made for a felling licence for trees on land which is subject to a forestry dedication covenant or agreement[12], and the licence is refused, no breach of the covenant or agreement shall be deemed to have occurred by reason of anything done or omitted in consequence of the refusal.

....

Terms of compensation on refusal of licence

11. (1) The compensation to which a person may become entitled under section 10(4)(*a*) above is for any depreciation in the value of the trees which is attributable to deterioration in the quality of the timber comprised therein in consequence of the refusal of a felling licence[13] for them.

---

[1] "Felling licence" defined by s. 35, p. 89 below.
[2] "The Commissioners" means the Forestry Commissioners: s. 49(1), p. 97 below.
[3] "Prescribed" defined by s. 35, p. 89 below. The Forestry (Felling of Trees) Regulations 1979, S.I. 1979/791, made under this section, are at p. 305 below.
[4] "Felling" defined by s. 35, p. 89 below.
[5] P. 90 below.
[6] P. 76 below.
[7] "Owner" in relation to trees defined by s. 34(1), (4), p. 88 below.
[8] P. 76 below.
[9] P. 76 below.
[10] P. 77 below.
[11] For the service of documents see s. 30, p. 86 below.
[12] "Forestry dedication covenant" and "forestry dedication agreement" have the meanings assigned to them by s. 5(1), p. 69 above: s. 49(1).
[13] "Felling licence" defined by s. 35, p. 89 below.

(2) Compensation under this section shall be recoverable from the Commissioners[1] on a claim made in the prescribed[2] manner.

(3) Claims for compensation in the case of any trees may be made from time to time in respect of deterioration taking place after the refusal of a felling licence for those trees, but—

(a) no such claim shall be made in respect of deterioration taking place more than ten years before the date of the claim; and

(b) if the trees have been felled, no such claim shall be made after the expiration of one year from the date of the felling[3].

(4) In calculating compensation,—

(a) no account shall be taken of deterioration in the quality of the timber which is attributable to neglect of the trees after the refusal of a felling licence for them; and

(b) the value of the trees at any time shall be ascertained on the basis of prices current at the date of the claim.

(5) If after refusing a felling licence the Commissioners under section 10(5) above subsequently give notice to the owner of the trees[4] that they are prepared to grant a licence, then in calculating compensation payable in consequence of the previous refusal no account shall be taken of deterioration occurring after the giving of the notice.

(6) Any question of disputed compensation shall be determined in accordance with section 31 of this Act[5].

Conditional licences

12. (1) The conditions which may under section 10(2) above[6] be attached to a felling licence[7] are such as the Commissioners[8], after consultation with the applicant for the licence, determine to be expedient for securing—

(a) the restocking or stocking with trees of the land on which the felling[9] is to take place, or of such other land as may be agreed between the Commissioners and the applicant; and

(b) the maintenance of those trees in accordance with the rules and practice of good forestry for a period not exceeding ten years.

(2) No conditions shall be imposed on the grant of a felling licence where it is for trees on land subject to a forestry dedication covenant or agreement[10] and the felling is in accordance with a plan of operations or other working plan approved by the Commissioners and in force under the covenant or agreement[11].

Deferred decision on application

13. (1) Where a person applies for a felling licence[12] and the Commissioners[13] do not within three months after receiving the application, or within such further time as may be agreed with the applicant, give notice to him of their decision on the application (including any reference of the application under section 15 of this Act[14]) the provisions of this Part of this Act shall apply in relation to the application as if it had been refused.

---

[1] "The Commissioners" means the Forestry Commissioners: s. 49(1), p. 97 below.

[2] "Prescribed" defined by s. 35, p. 89 below. The Forestry (Felling of Trees) Regulations 1979, S.I. 1979/791, made under this section, are at p. 305 below.

[3] "Felling" defined by s. 35, p. 89 below.

[4] "Owner" in relation to trees defined by s. 34(1) and (4), p. 88 below.

[5] P. 87 below.

[6] P. 74 above.

[7] "Felling licence" defined by s. 35, p. 89 below.

[8] "The Commissioners" means the Forestry Commissioners: s. 49(1), p. 97 below.

[9] "Felling" defined by s. 35, p. 89 below.

[10] "Forestry dedication covenant" and "forestry dedication agreement" have the meanings assigned to them by s. 5(1), p. 69 above: s. 49(1).

[11] Words "and the felling is in accordance with a plan of operations or other working plan approved by the Commissioners and in force under the covenant or agreement" inserted by the Trees Act 1970 (c. 43), s. 2. This amendment came into force on 29 May 1970, the date of the Royal Assent.

[12] "Felling licence" defined by s. 35, p. 89 below.

[13] "The Commissioners" means the Forestry Commissioners: s. 49(1), p. 97 below.

[14] P. 77 below.

(2) If on an application for a felling licence—

(a) the Commissioners determine to grant the licence subject to conditions; and

(b) it appears to them that the applicant is not entitled to an interest in land which would enable him to comply with those conditions;

they may give notice in writing[1] to that effect to the applicant and postpone consideration of the application until the person entitled to such an interest is joined as a party thereto.

Where a notice under this subsection is given, subsection (1) above shall apply as if, instead of referring to a period of three months after the Commissioners receive the application, it referred to a period of three months after the date on which the person entitled to such interest in the land as is mentioned in the notice is joined as a party to the application.

Tree-felling in accordance with approved working plan etc.

14. (1) The following provisions shall apply where application is made to the Commissioners[2] for a felling licence[3] and relates to the felling[4] of trees in accordance with a plan of operations or other working plan approved by the Commissioners under a forestry dedication covenant or agreement[5], or otherwise approved by them in writing for the purposes of this section.

(2) The Commissioners shall not refuse the licence unless the Minister[6] certifies that, by reason of an act of God or other emergency which has taken place or arisen since the approval of the plan, the granting of a felling licence in respect of those trees, or in respect of trees of any class which comprises those trees, would be detrimental to the national interest.

(3) If the Commissioners refuse the licence, the applicant may by notice given to the Commissioners in the prescribed[7] manner and within the prescribed time require them to buy the trees or such of them as may be specified in the notice.

(4) If a notice is served under the foregoing subsection,—

(a) no compensation shall be payable under section 11[8] in respect of any trees to which the notice relates; and

(b) the Commissioners shall be deemed to have contracted with the applicant to buy the trees on the date of the service of the notice at such prices as may in default of agreement be determined in accordance with section 31 of this Act[9], and shall fell and remove the trees at such time or times as they may determine.

(5) Where such a notice is served, and the land on which the trees are growing is subject to a forestry dedication covenant or agreement, the power of the Commissioners under section 10(4)(b) above[10] to make an advance by way of loan shall not be exercisable in respect of the trees, but this subsection shall not prejudice their power to make an advance in respect of any other trees on the land.

---

[1] For the service of documents see s. 30, p. 86 below.
[2] "The Commissioners" means the Forestry Commissioners: s. 49(1), p. 97 below.
[3] "Felling licence" defined by s. 35, p. 89 below.
[4] "Felling" defined by s. 35, p. 89 below.
[5] "Forestry dedication covenant" and "forestry dedication agreement" have the meanings assigned to them by s. 5(1), p. 69 above: s. 49(1) below.

[6] "Minister" defined by s. 49(1), p. 97 below.
[7] "Prescribed" defined by s. 35, p. 89 below. The Forestry (Felling of Trees) Regulations 1979, S.I. 1979/791, made under this section, are at p. 305 below.
[8] P. 71 above.
[9] P. 87 below.
[10] P. 74 above.

Trees subject to preservation order under Planning Acts

15. (1) If an application is made to the Commissioners[1] for a felling licence[2] in respect of trees to which a tree preservation order[3] relates, and consent under the order is required for the felling[4] of those trees, then—

(*a*) the Commissioners, if they propose to grant the licence, shall give notice in writing to the authority by whom the order was made; and

(*b*) the Commissioners may in any case refer the application to the said authority.

(2) Where the Commissioners give the notice required by subsection (1)(*a*) above and the authority within the prescribed[5] period after receipt of the notice object to the Commissioners' proposal to grant a felling licence and do not withdraw their objection, then—

(*a*) the Commissioners shall not deal with the application, but shall refer it to the Minister[6], and the application shall then be dealt with under the Town and Country Planning Acts; and

(*b*) if in pursuance of the application the Minister consents to the felling, section 9(1) of this Act[7] shall not apply so as to require a felling licence for the felling of any trees in accordance with the consent.

(3) Where the Commissioners refer an application under subjection (1)(*b*) above,—

(*a*) the application shall be dealt with under the Town and Country Planning Acts; and

(*b*) so long as the tree preservation order applying to the trees remains in force, section 9(1) shall not apply so as to require a felling licence for the felling of any trees to which the application relates.

(4) Where in the case of any trees—

(*a*) the Commissioners under this section refer an application for a felling licence to the Minister or an authority who have made a tree preservation order relating to the trees; and

(*b*) a felling licence in respect of the trees has been previously refused by the Commissioners,

no account shall be taken, in calculating any compensation payable under section 11 of this Act[8] in consequence of the previous refusal, of deterioration occurring after the date of the reference.

This subsection shall be without prejudice to section 11(5) of this Act, in a case to which that subsection applies.

(5) Except as provided by the foregoing provisions of this section, no application shall be entertained under a tree preservation order for consent thereunder in respect of the felling of trees in the case of which section 9(1) of this Act applies so as to require a felling licence.

(6) Where, in the case of trees to which a tree preservation order relates, a felling licence is granted by the Commissioners after the date on which the order comes into force, the licence shall, notwithstanding anything in that order, be sufficient authority for the felling of any trees to which the order relates.

(7) Schedule 3 to this Act[9] shall have effect for explaining the procedure applicable where this section requires an application to be dealt with under the Town and Country Planning Acts.

---

[1] "The Commissioners" means the Forestry Commissioners: s. 49(1), p. 97 below.

[2] "Felling licence" defined by s. 35, p. 89 below.

[3] "Tree preservation order" is defined by s. 35, p. 89 below as an order made or having effect as if made under s. 198 of the Town and Country Planning Act 1990 (c. 8) or s. 58 of the Town and Country Planning (Scotland) Act 1972 (c. 52). For the provisions relating to tree preservation orders in respect of England and Wales, see the Town and Country Planning Act 1990, ss. 198–210 and, in respect of Scotland, the Town and Country Planning (Scotland) Act 1972, ss. 58–60.

[4] "Felling" defined by s. 35, p. 89 below.

[5] "Prescribed" defined by s. 35, p. 89 below. The Forestry (Felling of Trees) Regulations 1979, S.I. 1979/791, made under this section, are at p. 305 below.

[6] "Minister" in this section means the Secretary of State: *England*, subsection (8) below and S.I. 1970/1681; *Wales and Scotland*, s. 49(1), p. 97 below.

[7] P. 72 above.

[8] P. 74 above.

[9] P. 100 below.

(8) In this section "the Minister", in relation to England, means the Minister of Housing and Local Government[1] and not the Minister of Agriculture, Fisheries and Food.

....

Review of refusal or conditions of licence

16. (1) The following provisions shall have effect for enabling the decision of the Commissioners[2] on an application for a felling licence[3] to be reviewed where they refuse to grant a felling licence or grant it subject to conditions.

(2) A person aggrieved by the refusal or conditions may by a notice served within the pre-scribed[4] time and in the prescribed manner request the Minister[5] to refer the matter to a committee appointed in accordance with section 27 below[6] and—

(a) the Minister shall, unless he is of opinion that the grounds for the request are frivolous, refer the matter accordingly;

(b) the committee, after compliance with section 27(3), shall thereupon make a report on the reference to the Minister.

(3) The Minister shall, after considering the committee's report, confirm the decision of the Commissioners on the application, or reverse or modify that decision and direct the Commissioners to give effect to the reversal or modification.

(4) No request may be made under this section in respect of a refusal to grant a felling licence unless a previous application for a licence in respect of the trees has been refused and the application to which the request relates is made after the following date, that is to say—

(a) where a reference under this section has been made in respect of a previous application, the third anniversary of the last such application in respect of which such a reference has been made; and

(b) in any other case, the third anniversary of the first previous application.

....

Penalty for felling without licence

17. (1) Anyone who fells[7] a tree without the authority of a felling licence, the case being one in which section 9(1) of this Act[8] applies so as to require such a licence, shall be guilty of an offence and liable on summary conviction to a fine not exceeding level 4 on the standard scale[9] or twice the sum which appears to the court to be the value of the tree, whichever is the higher.

(2) Proceedings for an offence under this section may be instituted within six months from the first discovery of the offence by the person taking the proceedings, provided that no proceedings shall be instituted more than two years after the date of the offence.[10]

....

Power of Commissioners to require restocking after unauthorised felling

17A. (1) Where a person is convicted of an offence under section 17 of this Act and he is a person having, as regards the land on which the felling[11] which gave rise to the conviction took place,

---

[1] The functions of the Minister under this section transferred to the Secretary of State: S.I. 1970/1681.

[2] "The Commissioners" means the Forestry Commissioners: s. 49(1), p. 97 below.

[3] "Felling licence" defined by s. 35, p. 89 below.

[4] "Prescribed" defined by s. 35, p. 89 below. The Forestry (Felling of Trees) Regulations 1979, S.I. 1979/791, made under this section, are at p. 305 below.

[5] "Minister" defined by s. 49(1), p. 97 below.

[6] P. 85 below.

[7] "Felling" defined by s. 35, p. 89 below.

[8] P. 72 above.

[9] Words "level 4 on the standard scale" substituted by the Civic Amenities Act 1967 (c. 69), s. 15(2), the Criminal Justice Act 1982 (c. 48), ss. 38, 46 as respects England and Wales and the Criminal Procedure (Scotland) Act 1975 (c. 21), ss. 289F, 289G as respects Scotland. The current fine at level 4 is £2,500: Criminal Justice Act 1991 (c. 53), s. 17 which came into force on 1 October 1992: S.I. 1992/333, S.I. 1992/2118.

[10] **Cases: section 17** *Cullen v Jardine* [1985] Crim L.R. 668; *Forestry Commission v Frost and Another* [1990] COD 1; *Forestry Commission v Grace and Another* [1992] 1 EGLR 28; *Campbell v Webster* [1992] SCCR 167.

[11] "Felling" defined by s. 35, p. 89 below.

such estate or interest as is mentioned in section 10(1) of this Act[1], the Commissioners[2] may serve on him a notice[3] (in this Act referred to as a "restocking notice") requiring him—

(a) to restock or stock with trees the land or such other land as may be agreed between the Commissioners and him; and

(b) to maintain those trees in accordance with the rules and practice of good forestry for a period, not exceeding ten years, specified in the notice.

(2) A restocking notice shall be served within three months after the date of the conviction or of the dismissal or withdrawal of any appeal against the conviction.

(3) Subject to the provisions of this Act, in considering whether to issue a restocking notice the Commissioners shall—

(a) have regard to the interests of good forestry and agriculture and of the amenities of the district;

(b) have regard to their duty of promoting the establishment and maintenance in Great Britain of adequate reserves of growing trees; and

(c) take into account any advice tendered by the regional advisory committee for the conservancy[4] comprising the land to which the restocking notice would relate.

(4) This section shall not apply in relation to trees to which a tree preservation order[5] relates or in relation to trees the felling of which took place before the date of coming into force of the Forestry Act 1986[6].

Appeal against restocking notice

17B. (1) A person on whom a restocking notice[7] has been served who objects to the notice or to any condition contained therein may be notice served within the prescribed[8] time and in the prescribed manner request the Minister[9] to refer the matter to a committee appointed in accordance with section 27 of this Act[10]; and—

(a) the Minister shall, unless he is of the opinion that the grounds of the request are frivolous, refer the matter accordingly; and

(b) the committee, after compliance with sub-section (3) of that section, shall thereupon make a report to the Minister.

(2) The Minister may, after considering the committee's report, direct the Commissioners[11] to withdraw the notice or to notify the objector that it shall have effect subject to such modification as the Minister shall direct.

Enforcement of restocking notice

17C. The provisions of sections 24[12] (notice to require compliance with conditions or directions), 25 (appeal against notice under section 24) and 26(1), (3) and (4) (expenses) of this Act shall apply in relation to a restocking notice[13] as they apply in relation to a felling licence[14]; and for the purposes of such application—

(a) references in those sections to a felling licence shall be construed as references to a restocking notice; and

[1] P. 74 above.
[2] "The Commissioners" means the Forestry Commissioners: s. 49(1), p. 97 below.
[3] For the service of documents see s. 30, p. 86 below.
[4] "Conservancy" defined by s. 35, p. 89 below.
[5] "Tree preservation order" defined by s. 35, p. 89 below.
[6] The Forestry Act 1986 came into force on 8 September 1986: s. 2(1).
[7] "Restocking notice" construed in accordance with s. 17A(1) above: s. 35, p. 89 below.
[8] "Prescribed" defined by s. 35, p. 89 below. The

Forestry (Felling of Trees) Regulations 1979, S.I. 1979/791, made under this section, are at p. 305 below.
[9] "Minister" defined by s. 49(1), p. 97 below.
[10] P. 85 below.
[11] "The Commissioners" means the Forestry Commissioners: s. 49(1), p. 97 below.
[12] P. 83 below.
[13] "Restocking notice" construed in accordance with s. 17A(1), p. 78 above: s. 35, p. 89 below.
[14] "Felling licence" defined by s. 35, p. 89 below.

(*b*) the reference in the said subsection (3) to the applicant for the licence shall be construed as a reference to the person on whom the restocking notice has been served.[1]

Power of Commissioners to direct felling

Felling directions

18. (1) Subject to the provisions of this Act (and, in particular, to the duty of the Commissioners[2] to take advice under section 37(3)[3]), if it appears to the Commissioners that it is expedient in the interests of good forestry, or for purposes connected with their duty of promoting the establishment and maintenance in Great Britain of adequate reserves of growing trees, that any growing trees should be felled—

(*a*) in order to prevent deterioration or further deterioration in the quality of the timber comprised therein; or

(*b*) in order to improve the growth of other trees,

they may give directions (in this Act referred to as "felling directions") to the owner of the trees[4] requiring him to fell them within such period, being not less than two years after the directions have become operative, as may be specified in the directions.

(2) In considering whether to give felling directions, the Commissioners shall have regard to the interests of agriculture and the amenity or convenience of any farm or dwelling-house or park usually occupied with a dwelling-house, or of any land held inalienably by the National Trust[5] or the National Trust for Scotland[6].

(3) Felling directions given by the Commissioners shall contain a statement of the grounds upon which they are given.

(4) A person who is given felling directions by the Commissioners may comply with the directions notwithstanding any lease, covenant or contract relating to the trees or land affected by the directions.

(5) In the case of trees to which a tree preservation order[7] relates, felling directions given by the Commissioners after the date on which the order comes into force shall, notwithstanding anything in the order, be sufficient authority for the felling.

Restrictions on Commissioners' power under s. 18

19. (1) Felling directions[8] shall not be given in the case of—

(*a*) fruit trees or trees standing or growing on land comprised in an orchard, garden, churchyard or public open space (as defined in section 9(6) above[9]);

(*b*) trees on land which is subject to a forestry dedication covenant or agreement[10]; or

(*c*) trees which are being managed to the satisfaction of the Commissioners[11] in accordance with a plan of operations or other working plan approved by them as mentioned in section 14(1) above[12], but otherwise than under a forestry dedication covenant or agreement.

(2) If an application for a felling licence[13] is made to the Commissioners in the case of trees to which a tree preservation order[14] relates and the Commissioners refer the application under

---

[1] Ss. 17A–17C inserted by the Forestry Act 1986 (c. 30), s. 1(*a*). This amendment came into force on 8 September 1986: s. 2(1).

[2] "The Commissioners" means the Forestry Commissioners: s. 49(1), p. 97 below.

[3] P. 90 below.

[4] "Owner" in relation to trees defined by s. 34(1) and (4), p. 88 below.

[5] "National Trust" and "held inalienably" defined by s. 49(1), p. 97 below.

[6] "National Trust for Scotland" and "held inalienably" defined by s. 49(1), p. 97 below.

[7] "Tree preservation order" defined by s. 35, p. 89 below.

[8] "Felling directions" defined by s. 35, p. 89 below.

[9] P. 73 above.

[10] "Forestry dedication covenant" and "forestry dedication agreement" have the meanings assigned to them by s. 5, p. 69 above: s. 49(1).

[11] "The Commissioners" means the Forestry Commissioners: s. 49(1), p. 97 below.

[12] P. 76 above.

[13] "Felling licence" defined by s. 35, p. 89 below.

[14] "Tree preservation order" defined by s. 35, p. 89 below.

section 15 above[1] to the authority who made the order, then so long as the order remains in force no felling directions shall be given in respect of the trees.

(3) If the Commissioners propose to give felling directions in respect of trees to which a tree preservation order relates, they shall give notice in writing of the proposal to the authority by whom the order was made; and if within the prescribed[2] period after the receipt of the notice the authority object to the proposal and do not withdraw the objection, the Commissioners shall not give the directions except with the consent of the Minister[3], who shall consult with the said authority before deciding whether to grant or refuse his consent.

(4) In subsection (3) above "the Minister", in relation to England, means the Minister of Housing and Local Government and not the Minister of Agriculture, Fisheries and Food[4].

Review of felling directions

20. (1) If a person to whom felling directions[5] are given in respect of any trees is aggrieved by the directions on the ground that the felling is not expedient as mentioned in section 18(1)[6], he may by notice served within the prescribed[7] time and in the prescribed manner request the Minister[8] to refer the matter to a committee appointed in accordance with section 27 below[9] and the Minister shall, unless he is of opinion that the grounds for the request are frivolous, refer the matter accordingly.

(2) The committee to whom a matter is referred under this section, after complying with section 27(3), shall thereupon make a report on the reference to the person by whom the notice was served and to the Commissioners[10], and the Commissioners shall confirm, withdraw or modify the directions in accordance with the report.

Courses open to person adversely affected by felling directions

21. (1) The provisions of this section shall have effect where a person to whom felling directions[11] are given claims that compliance with the directions would involve him in a net loss after taking into account any benefit arising therefrom in respect of other trees of which he is the owner[12].

(2) The person may by notice given to the Minister[13] in the prescribed[14] manner and within the prescribed period—

(a) if he has the right to sell the trees for immediate felling, require the Commissioners[15] to buy the trees to which the directions relate; or

(b) in any case, require the Minister to acquire his interest in the land affected by the directions.

A notice under this section requiring the Minister to acquire an interest in land shall be deemed to include an offer by the person entitled to that interest to convey to the Minister such easement or servitude or other right for the benefit of the land over adjoining land in which that person has an interest as may be agreed between that person and the Minister or as may, in default of agreement, be determined in accordance with section 31 of this Act[16].

[1] P. 77 above.
[2] "Prescribed" defined by s. 35, p. 89 below. The Forestry (Felling of Trees) Regulations 1979, S.I. 1979/791, made under this section, are at p. 305 below.
[3] "Minister" in this section means the Secretary of State: as respects England, subsection (4) below and S.I. 1970/1681; as respects Wales and Scotland, s. 49, p. 97 below.
[4] This function transferred to the Secretary of State: S.I. 1970/1681.
[5] "Felling directions" defined by s. 35, p. 89 below.
[6] P. 80 above.
[7] "Prescribed" defined by s. 35, p. 89 below. The Forestry (Felling of Trees) Regulations 1979, S.I. 1979/791, made under this section, are at p. 305 below.
[8] "Minister" defined by s. 49(1), p. 97 below.
[9] P. 85 below.
[10] "The Commissioners" means the Forestry Commissioners: s. 49(1), p. 97 below.
[11] "Felling directions" defined by s. 35, p. 89 below.
[12] "Owner" in relation to trees defined by s. 34(1) and (4), p. 88 below.
[13] "Minister" defined by s. 49(1), p. 97 below.
[14] "Prescribed" defined by s. 35, p. 89 below. The Forestry (Felling of Trees) Regulations 1979, S.I. 1979/791, made under this section, are at p. 305 below.
[15] "The Commissioners" means the Forestry Commissioners: s. 49(1), p. 97 below.
[16] P. 87 below.

(3) The Minister may within the prescribed period after receiving the notice either—

(*a*) accept the notice; or

(*b*) refer it to a committee appointed in accordance with section 27 below[1]; or

(*c*) revoke the directions to which it relates.

(4) The committee to whom a matter is referred under this section, after complying with section 27(3), shall thereupon make a report to the Minister and to the person by whom the notice under this section was given and shall state—

(*a*) whether in the opinion of the committee compliance with the felling directions would involve that person in such a loss as aforesaid; and

(*b*) if so, what modifications (if any) of the directions would be sufficient to avoid that loss.

(5) Where the committee report that compliance with the directions would not involve the person in such loss as aforesaid, the notice shall be of no effect; but in any other case the Minister may, within the prescribed period after receiving the report, either—

(*a*) accept the notice; or

(*b*) revoke the directions; or

(*c*) modify the directions in accordance with the report,

according as he thinks fit.

(6) If within the prescribed period after receiving a notice or the report of a committee under this section the Minister has not taken any such action as is authorised by subsection (3) or subsection (5) above, as the case may be, the directions to which the notice relates shall cease to have effect at the expiration of that period.

(7) In determining for the purposes of this section whether compliance with felling directions would involve a person in a net loss, regard shall be had to any compensation received by that person under a tree preservation order[2] in respect of a refusal of consent for the felling of the tree.

Consequences of acceptance by Minister of notice under s. 21

22. (1) The following shall be the consequences where a notice given by a person under section 21 is accepted by the Minister[3].

(2) The felling directions[4] in respect of which the notice was given shall cease to have effect.

(3) If the notice requires the Commissioners[5] to buy the trees to which the directions relate, the Commissioners shall be deemed to have contracted with that person to buy the trees on the date of acceptance of the notice at such price and on such terms (including terms as to the time within which the Commissioners may fell and remove the trees) as may in default of agreement be determined in accordance with section 31 of this Act[6].

(4) If the notice requires the Minister to acquire the person's interest in the land affected by the directions,—

(*a*) the Minister shall be deemed to be authorised to acquire that interest compulsorily under section 39 of this Act[7] and to have served a notice to treat in respect thereof on the date of the acceptance of the notice;

(*b*) the interest shall for that purpose include any such easement or servitude or other right as, by virtue of section 21(2)[8], the person is deemed to have offered in his notice to convey.

---

[1] P. 85 below.
[2] "Tree preservation order" defined by s. 35, p. 89 below.
[3] "Minister" defined by s. 49(1), p. 97 below.
[4] "Felling directions" defined by s. 35, p. 89 below.
[5] "The   Commissioners"   means   the   Forestry

Commissioners: s. 49(1), p. 97 below.
[6] P. 87 below.
[7] P. 91 below.
[8] P. 81 above.

(5) The power conferred by section 31(1) of the Land Compensation Act 1961[1] or section 39(1) of the Land Compensation (Scotland) Act 1963[2] to withdraw a notice to treat shall not be exercisable in the case of a notice to treat which is deemed to have been served by virtue of this section.

Proceedings in respect of felling directions

23. (1) A request under section 20 of this Act[3], and a notice under section 21 of this Act[4], may be made and given in respect of the same directions; and regulations made by the Commissioners[5] under this Part of this Act may make provision for securing—

(a) that in any such case proceedings under those sections respectively on the request and on the notice are taken concurrently;

(b) that proceedings on any such request or notice in respect of any feeling directions[6] may be postponed until the expiration of the period within which a notice or a request, as the case may be, might be given or made in respect of those directions.

(2) Felling directions shall be inoperative until the expiration of the period during which such a request or notice as aforesaid may be made or given in respect of the directions and, where a request is made or a notice is given, until the conclusions of any proceedings under section 20 or 21 pursuant to the notice or request.

Enforcement of licence conditions and felling directions

Notice to require compliance with conditions or directions

24. (1) The provisions of this section shall apply if—

(a) any works required to be carried out in accordance with conditions of a felling licence[7] are not so carried out; or

(b) any felling directions[8] given by the Commissioners[9] are not complied with.

(2) The Commissioners may give to the person responsible a notice requiring such steps as may be specified therein to be taken within such time (not being less than the prescribed[10] period after the notice has become operative) as may be so specified for remedying the default; and for purposes of this subsection, "the person responsible" is—

(a) in the case of non-compliance with conditions of a felling licence, the owner of the land[11]; and

(b) in the case of non-compliance with felling directions, the owner of the trees[12].

(3) If after the expiration of the time specified in the notice any steps required by the notice have not been taken, the Commissioners may, subject to the following section, enter on the land and take those steps.

(4) Without prejudice to the powers of the Commissioners under the foregoing subsection, a person who without reasonable excuse fails to take any steps required by a notice given to him under this section shall be guilty of an offence and be liable on summary conviction to a fine not exceeding level 5 on the standard scale[13]; and proceedings in respect of such an offence may be

[1] 1961 c. 33.
[2] 1963 c. 51.
[3] P. 81 above.
[4] P. 81 above.
[5] "The Commissioners" means the Forestry Commissioners: s. 49(1), p. 97 below. The Forestry (Felling of Trees) Regulations 1979, S.I. 1979/791, made under this section, are at p. 305 below.
[6] "Felling directions" defined by s. 35, p. 89 below.
[7] "Felling licence" defined by s. 35, p. 89 below.
[8] "Felling directions" defined by s. 35, p. 89 below.
[9] "The Commissioners" means the Forestry Commissioners: s. 49(1), p. 97 below.
[10] "Prescribed" defined by s. 35, p. 89 below. The

Forestry (Felling of Trees) Regulations 1979, S.I. 1979/791, made under this section, are at p. 305 below.
[11] "Owner" in relation to land defined by s. 34(1)–(3), p. 88 below.
[12] "Owner" in relation to trees defined by s. 34(1), (4), p. 88 below.
[13] Words "level 5 on the standard scale" substituted by the Criminal Justice Act 1982 (c. 48), ss. 39(2), 46, sch. 3 as respects England and Wales and the Criminal Procedure (Scotland) Act 1975 (c. 21), s. 289H, sch. 7D, para. 24 as respects Scotland. The current fine at level 5 is £5,000: Criminal Justice Act 1991 (c. 53), s. 17 which came into force on 1 October 1992: S.I. 1992/333, S.I. 1992/2118.

instituted within six months of the first discovery of the offence by the person taking the proceedings, provided that no proceedings shall be instituted more than two years after the date of the offence.

(5) A person who is required by a notice under this section to carry out works or take any steps may carry out those works or take the steps notwithstanding any lease, covenant or contract relating to the trees or land affected by the notice.

Appeal against notice under s. 24

25. (1) If a person to whom a notice under section 24 is given claims—

(a) that the works in question have been carried out in accordance with the conditions of the felling licence[1] or, in the case of felling directions[2], that they have been complied with; or

(b) that the steps required by the notice to be taken are not required by the conditions or directions,

he may by a notice served on the Minister[3] in the prescribed[4] manner and within the prescribed period after the receipt of the notice under section 24, request the Minister to refer the matter to a committee appointed in accordance with section 27 below[5].

(2) A notice under section 24 shall be inoperative until the expiration of the prescribed period for the purposes of subsection (1) above and, where a request to the Minister under that subsection is made, until the conclusion of any proceedings under this section in pursuance of the request.

(3) Where such a request is made by a person receiving a notice under section 24, the Minister shall, unless he is of opinion that the grounds for the request are frivolous, refer the matter accordingly to a committee so appointed.

(4) The committee to whom a matter is referred under this section, after complying with section 27(3), shall make a report on the reference to the Minister and the Minister shall, after considering the report, confirm or cancel the notice to which the reference relates.

Expenses etc. in connection with notices under s. 24

26. (1) If the Commissioners[6], in the exercise of their powers under section 24[7], enter on land and take any steps required by a notice under that section, they may recover from the person to whom the notice was given any expenses reasonably incurred in connection therewith.

(2) The Commissioners may remove and either retain or dispose of trees felled by them in the exercise of their said powers, and shall, on a claim made in the prescribed[8] manner by the owner of any trees[9] so removed, pay to him a sum equal to the value of those trees after deducting any expenses reasonably incurred by them in connection with the removal or disposal.

(3) Subject to any express agreement to the contrary, any expenses incurred by a person for the purpose of complying with a notice under section 24, and any sums paid by a person in respect of expenses of the Commissioners under that section, shall be deemed to be incurred or paid by that person—

(a) where the notice relates to works required to be carried out in pursuance of conditions of a felling licence[10], for the use and at the request of the applicant for the licence;

[1] "Felling licence" defined by s. 35, p. 89 below.
[2] "Felling directions" defined by s. 35, p. 89 below.
[3] "Minister" defined by s. 49(1), p. 97 below.
[4] "Prescribed" defined by s. 35, p. 89 below. The Forestry (Felling of Trees) Regulations 1979, S.I. 1979/791, made under this section are at p. 305 below.
[5] P. 85 below.
[6] "The Commissioners" means the Forestry Commissioners: s. 49(1), p. 97 below.
[7] P. 83 above.
[8] "Prescribed" defined by s. 35, p. 89 below. The Forestry (Felling of Trees) Regulations 1979, S.I. 1979/791, made under this section, are at p. 305 below.
[9] "Owner" in relation to trees defined by s. 34(1), (4), p. 88 below.
[10] "Felling licence" defined by s. 35, p. 89 below.

(*b*) where the notice requires compliance with felling directions[1], for the use and at the request of the person to whom the directions were given.

(4) Any sums recoverable by or from the Commissioners under this section may be recovered as a simple contract debt.

Supplementary

Committees of reference for purposes of ss. 16, 20, 21 and 25

27. (1) References in section 16, 17B[2], 20, 21 and 25 of this Act to a committee appointed in accordance with this section are to a committee consisting of—

(*a*) a chairman appointed by the Minister[3]; and

(*b*) two other members selected by the Minister from a panel of persons appointed by him, after such consultation as is provided for below, for the conservancy[4] in which the trees are growing:

Provided that no Forestry Commissioner or person employed by the Commissioners[5] shall be a member of any such committee.

(2) The consultation required by subsection (1)(*b*) above is to be with—

(*a*) the regional advisory committee for the said conservancy; and

(*b*) organisations appearing to the Minister to represent the interests of owners of woodlands and timber merchants respectively; and

(*c*) organisations concerned with the study and promotion of forestry.

(3) On any reference being made to them under this Part of this Act a committee appointed in accordance with this section shall—

(*a*) afford to the person concerned with the subject-matter of the reference an opportunity of appearing before them and of making representations to them on the matter in question;

(*b*) if they think fit, or are so required by the said person, inspect the trees or land to which the reference relates; and

(*c*) take into consideration any information furnished to them by the Commissioners as to the performance within the conservancy in which the trees are growing of their duty of promoting the establishment and maintenance in Great Britain of adequate reserves of growing trees.

For purposes of this subsection "the person concerned with the subject-matter of the reference" is the person at whose request the reference was made, except that in the case of a reference by the Minister of a notice under section 21[6] it is the person by whom the notice was given.

(4) The Minister may pay to the members of a committee appointed by him under this section such remuneration as he may, with the consent of the Treasury, determine.

....

Identification of trees

28. A person authorised by the Commissioners[7] may take such steps, whether by marking or otherwise, as the Commissioners consider necessary for identifying trees which are the subject of a felling licence[8] or felling directions[9], or in respect of which a felling licence has been refused.

---

[1] "Felling directions" defined by s. 35, p. 84 below.

[2] Words "17B" inserted by the Forestry Act 1986 (c. 30), s. 1(*b*). This amendment came into force on 8 September 1986: s. 2(1).

[3] "Minister" defined by s. 49(1), p. 97 below

[4] "Conservancy" defined by s. 35, p. 89 below.

[5] "The Commissioners" means the Forestry Commissioners: s. 49(1), p. 97 below.

[6] P. 81 above.

[7] "The Commissioners" means the Forestry Commissioners: s. 49(1), p. 97 below.

[8] "Felling licence" defined by s. 35, p. 89 below.

[9] "Felling directions" defined by s. 35, p. 89 below.

Provisions relating to mortgages, heritable securities and settled land

29. (1) Where the interest of the owner of trees[1] in England or Wales is for the time being subject to a mortgage[2]—

(*a*) a claim for any compensation or sum payable under section 11[3] or section 26 of this Act[4] in respect of the trees may be made either by the mortgagor or by the mortgagee;

(*b*) in either case the compensation or sum shall be paid to the mortgagee or, if more than one, to the first mortgagee, and shall be applied by him as if it were proceeds of the sale of the trees.

(2) Where the interest of the owner of trees in Scotland is for the time being subject to a heritable security[5],—

(*a*) a claim for any compensation or sum payable under section 11[6] or section 26 of this Act[7] in respect of the trees may be made either by the debtor in the heritable security or by the creditor in the heritable security;

(*b*) in either case the compensation or sum shall be paid to the creditor in the heritable security or, if more than one, to the creditor whose heritable security has priority over any other heritable security secured on the land, and shall be applied by him as if it were proceeds of the sale of the trees.

(3) Subject to the foregoing provisions of this section, where the owner of trees comprised in a settlement within the meaning of the Settled Land Act 1925[8] is a tenant for life who is impeachable for waste in respect of the trees, any compensation or sum payable under section 11 or section 26 of this Act in respect of the trees shall be paid to the trustees of the settlement, and shall be applied by them in accordance with section 66(2) of the Settled Land Act 1925 as if it were proceeds of sale of timber cut and sold with the consent of the trustees under that section.

Service of documents

30. (1) Any document required or authorised to be served under this Part of this Act may be served on a person either by delivering it to him, or by leaving it at his proper address, or by sending it through the post in a registered letter addressed to him at that address or in a letter sent by the recorded delivery service and so addressed.

(2) Any such document required or authorised to be served upon an incorporated company or body shall be duly served if it is served upon the secretary or clerk of the company or body.

(3) For the purposes of this section and of section 26 of the Interpretation Act 1889[9], the proper address of any person upon whom any such document as aforesaid is to be served shall, in the case of the secretary or clerk of an incorporated company or body, be that of the registered or principal office of the company or body, and in any other case be the last known address of the person to be served:

Provided that, where the person to be served has furnished an address for service, his proper address for the said purposes shall be the address furnished.

(4) If it is not practicable to ascertain the name or address of an owner[10], lessee or occupier of land on whom any such document as aforesaid is to be served, the document may be served by addressing it to him by the description of "owner", "lessee" or "occupier" of the land (describing it) to which it relates, and by delivering it to some responsible person on the land or, if there is

---

[1] "Owner" in relation to trees defined by s. 34(1) and (4), p. 88 below.

[2] "Mortgage" defined by s. 35, p. 89 below.

[3] P. 74 above.

[4] P. 84 above.

[5] "Heritable security" defined by s. 35, p. 89 below.

[6] P. 74 above.

[7] P. 84 above.

[8] 1925 c. 18.

[9] S. 7 of the Interpretation Act 1978 (c. 30) replaces s. 26 of the Interpretation Act 1889: Interpretation Act 1978, ss. 17, 22.

[10] "Owner" in relation to land defined by s. 34(1)–(3), p. 88 below.

no such person on the land to whom it may be delivered, by affixing it or a copy of it to some conspicuous part of the land.

(5) The Commissioners[1] may, for the purpose of enabling them to serve or give any document or direction under this Part of this Act, require the occupier of any land and any person who, either directly or indirectly, receives rent in respect of any land, to state in writing the nature of his interest therein and the name and address of any other person known to him as having an interest therein, whether as a freeholder or owner, mortgagee or creditor in a heritable security, lessee or otherwise; and anyone who, having been required in pursuance of this subsection to give any information, fails to give it, or knowingly makes any mis-statement in respect thereof, shall be liable on summary conviction to a fine not exceeding level 1 on the standard scale[2].

Determination of matters arising under ss. 11, 14, 21 and 22

31. (1) Where a provision of this Part of this Act requires a thing to be determined in accordance with this section, that provision shall—

(*a*) in its application to England and Wales, be taken as requiring it to be determined by the Lands Tribunal; and

(*b*) in its application to Scotland, be taken as requiring it to be determined by the Lands Tribunal for Scotland, subject however to the following subsection.

(2) Until sections 1 to 3 of the Lands Tribunal Act 1949[3] come into force as regards Scotland, the said provision shall be taken as requiring the thing in question to be determined by reference to an official arbiter appointed under Part I of the Land Compensation (Scotland) Act 1963[4]; and sections 3 and 5 of that Act shall apply, subject to any necessary modifications, in relation to the determination of any question under this Act by an arbiter so appointed.

Regulations

32. (1) The Commissioners[5] may, subject to their duty of consultation under section 37(2) below[6], by statutory instrument make regulations for prescribing anything which by this Part of this Act is authorised to be prescribed.

(2) A power conferred by this Part of this Act to prescribe the manner in which a claim or notice may be made or given thereunder shall include power to require that any particulars specified in the claim or notice shall be verified by statutory declaration.

(3) A statutory instrument containing regulations made under this Part of this Act—

(*a*) if the regulations are made under section 9(5)(*b*)[7] or (*c*), shall be of no effect unless approved by a resolution of each House of Parliament; and

(*b*) in a case not falling within the foregoing paragraph, shall be subject to annulment in pursuance of a resolution of either House of Parliament.

Application of Part II to Crown land

33. (1) In this section "Crown land" means land an interest in which belongs to Her Majesty in right of the Crown or of the Duchy of Lancaster, or to the Duchy of Cornwall, and land an interest in which belongs to a government department or is held in trust for Her Majesty for the purposes of a government department.

---

[1] "The Commissioners" means the Forestry Commissioners: s. 49(1), p. 97 below.

[2] Words "level 1 on the standard scale" substituted by the Criminal Justice Act 1967 (c. 80), s. 92(1), sch. 3, pt. 1, the Criminal Justice Act 1982 (c. 48), ss. 38, 46 as respects England and Wales and the Criminal Procedure (Scotland) Act 1975 (c. 21), ss. 289F, 289G as respects Scotland. The current fine at level 1 is £200: Criminal Justice Act 1991 (c. 53), s. 17 which came into force on 1 October 1992: S.I. 1992/333, S.I. 1992/2118.

[3] 1949 c. 42.

[4] 1963 c. 51.

[5] "The Commissioners" means the Forestry Commissioners: s. 49(1), p. 97 below.

[6] P. 90 below.

[7] P. 73 above.

(2) Subject to the following provisions of this section, the provisions of this Part of this Act shall apply in relation to Crown land and trees growing thereon to the extent only of any estate or interest therein which is for the time being held otherwise than on behalf of the Crown.

(3) Except with the consent of the appropriate authority as defined in this section,—

(a) no conditions relating to the restocking or stocking of Crown land shall be imposed on the grant of a felling licence[1];

(b) no felling directions[2] shall be given in respect of trees growing on Crown land.

(4) The Minister[3] shall not be authorised to acquire the interest of any person in Crown land by virtue of a notice under section 21[4] unless an offer has previously been made by that person to dispose of that interest to the appropriate authority on terms that the price payable therefor shall be equal to (and shall be determined in default of agreement in like manner as) the compensation which would be payable in respect of that interest if it were acquired in pursuance of such a notice, and that offer has been refused by that authority.

(5) In this section "the appropriate authority" in relation to any land means—

(a) in the case of land belonging to Her Majesty in right of the Crown, the Crown Estate Commissioners or other government department having the management of the land in question;

(b) in the case of land belonging to Her Majesty in right of the Duchy of Lancaster, the Chancellor of the Duchy;

(c) in the case of land belonging to the Duchy of Cornwall, such person as the Duke of Cornwall, or the possessor for the time being of the Duchy of Cornwall, appoints; and

(d) in the case of land belonging to a government department or held in trust for Her Majesty for the purposes of a government department, that department;

and if any question arises as to what authority is the appropriate authority in relation to any land, that question shall be referred to the Treasury, whose decision shall be final.

....

Meaning of "owner" in Part II

34. (1) In this Part of this Act the expression "owner" has the meaning ascribed to it by this section.

(2) In relation to land in England or Wales, "owner" means the person in whom for the time being is vested the legal estate in fee simple, except that where in relation to all or any of the provisions of this Part of this Act,—

(a) all persons appearing to the Minister[5] to be concerned agree, with the approval of the Minister, that some person shall be treated as the owner of land other than the person who would be so treated apart from the agreement; or

(b) on an application in that behalf to the Agricultural Land Tribunal established under Part V of the Agriculture Act 1947[6] the Tribunal determine, having regard to the respective interests of the persons interested in the land, that some person shall be treated as the owner of the land other than the person who would be so treated apart from the determination,

that person shall be so treated, but without prejudice to a subsequent agreement or determination, or to his ceasing to be so treated, if the Minister withdraws his approval under paragraph (a) of this subsection.

(3) In relation to land in Scotland, "owner" means the person who for the time being is the proprietor of the *dominium utile* or, in the case of land other than feudal land, is the owner thereof, except that where, in relation to all or any of the provisions of this Part of this Act,—

---

[1] "Felling licence" defined by s. 35, p. 89 below.
[2] "Felling directions" defined by s. 35, p. 89 below.
[3] "Minister" defined by s. 49(1), p. 97 below.
[4] P. 81 above.
[5] "Minister" defined by s. 49(1), p. 97 below.
[6] 1947 c. 48.

(a) all persons appearing to the Minister[1] to be concerned agree, with the approval of the Minister, that some person shall be treated as the owner of land other than the person who would be so treated apart from the agreement; or

(b) on an application in that behalf to the Scottish Land Court the Court determines, having regard to the respective interests of the persons interested in the land, that some person shall be treated as the owner of the land other than the person who would be so treated apart from the determination,

that person shall be so treated, but without prejudice to a subsequent agreement or determination, or to his ceasing to be so treated, if the Minister withdraws his approval under paragraph (a) of this subsection.

(4) In relation to trees, "owner" means the owner of the land on which the trees are growing and, in the case of trees which have been felled, means the person who was the owner immediately before the felling[2].

Interpretation of other expressions in Part II

35. In this Part of this Act—

"conservancy" means any area in Great Britain which may for the time being be designated by the Commissioners as a conservancy for the purpose of the performance of their functions;

"felling" includes wilfully destroying by any means;

"felling directions" means directions given by the Commissioners under section 18 of this Act[3] for the felling of trees;

"felling licence" means a licence under this Part of this Act authorising the felling of trees;

"mortgage" and "heritable security" include any charge for securing money or money's worth, and references to a mortgagee, or to a creditor or a debtor in a heritable security, shall be construed accordingly;

"prescribed" means prescribed by regulations made by the Commissioners under this Part of this Act;

"restocking notice" shall be construed in accordance with section 17A(1)[4] of this Act;[5] and

"tree preservation order" means an order made or having effect as if made under section 198 of the Town and Country Planning Act 1990[6] or section 58 of the Town and Country Planning (Scotland) Act 1972[7].

Application of Part II to London

36. This Part of this Act shall not apply to trees standing or growing on land within the area of Greater London other than the outer London Boroughs within the meaning of the London Government Act 1963[8].

---

[1] "Minister" defined by s. 49(1), p. 97 below.
[2] "Felling" defined by s. 35, below.
[3] P. 80 above.
[4] P. 78 above.
[5] This definition inserted by the Forestry Act 1986 (c. 30), s. 1(c). This amendment came into force on 8 September 1986: 2(1).
[6] Words "section 198 of the Town and Country Planning

Act 1990" substituted by the Planning (Compensation) Act 1990 (c. 11), s. 4, sch. 2, para. 14(2). This amendment came into force on 24 August 1990: s. 7(2).
[7] Words "section 58 of the Town and Country Planning (Scotland) Act 1972" substituted by the Town and Country Planning (Scotland) Act 1972 (c. 52), s. 276(1), sch. 21, pt. II. This amendment came into force on 27 August 1972: s. 280.
[8] 1963 c. 33.

Part III: Administration and Finance

Advisory bodies

Committees to advise Commissioners

37. (1) For the purpose of advising the Commissioners[1] as to the performance of their functions under section 1(3)[2] and Part II of this Act[3], and such other functions as the Commissioners may from time to time determine, the Commissioners shall continue to maintain—

(a) the central advisory committee for Great Britain known as the Home Grown Timber Advisory Committee; and

(b) a regional advisory committee for each conservancy[4] (within the meaning of Part II of this Act) in Great Britain.

(2) In relation to the performance of their duty of promoting the establishment and maintenance in Great Britain of adequate reserves of growing trees, the Commissioners shall from time to time, and as a general rule not less than quarterly, consult with the Home Grown Timber Advisory Committee; and the power of the Commissioners under section 32 of this Act[5] to make regulations shall not be exercisable except after consultation with the said Committee.

(3) The Commissioners shall—

(a) in considering whether to refuse a felling licence[6] under Part II of this Act, or to grant it unconditionally or subject to any conditions; and

(b) in considering whether to give felling directions[7] under the said Part II,

take into account any advice tendered by the regional advisory committee for the conservancy in which are growing the trees to which the felling licence applied for, or the directions proposed to be given, relate.

Composition etc. of advisory committees

38. (1) The chairman and other members of the Home Grown Timber Advisory Committee and of each regional advisory committee shall be appointed by the Commissioners[8], and shall hold and vacate office in accordance with the terms of the instrument by which they are appointed.

(2) The Home Grown Timber Advisory Committee shall consist of not more than twenty-five members, and of those members (other than the chairman)—

(a) not less than six nor more than eight shall be persons appointed by the Commissioners after consultation with organisations appearing to them to represent the interests of owners of woodlands; and

(b) not less than six nor more than eight shall be persons appointed by the Commissioners after consultation with organisations appearing to them to represent the interests of timber merchants.

(3) Each regional advisory committee shall consist of not less than seven nor more than twelve[1] members, and of those members (other than the chairman) not less than four shall be persons appointed by the Commissioners after consultation with organisations appearing to them to represent the interests of owners of woodlands and timber merchants respectively and organisations concerned with the study and promotion of forestry.

(4) The Commissioners may pay to the members of the Home Grown Timber Advisory Committee or of a regional advisory committee such allowances as they may with the consent of the Treasury determine.

---

[1] "The Commissioners" means the Forestry Commissioners: s. 49(1), p. 97 below.
[2] P. 68 above.
[3] P. 72 above.
[4] "Conservancy" defined by s. 35, p. 89 above.
[5] P. 87 above.
[6] "Felling licence" defined by s. 35, p. 89 below.
[7] "Felling directions" defined by s. 35, p. 89 below.
[8] "The Commissioners" means the Forestry Commissioners: s. 49(1), p. 97 below.

Acquisition and disposal of land

Power of Minister to acquire and dispose of land

39. (1) Subject to the provisions of this Act, the Minister[2] may acquire (by purchase, lease or exchange) land which in his opinion is suitable for afforestation or for purposes connected with forestry, together with any other land which must necessarily be acquired therewith, and may place any land acquired by him under this section at the disposal of the Commissioners[3].

(2) Subject to subsection (2A) below, the Minister may dispose for any purpose of land acquired by him under this section.

(2A) Subsection (2) above shall not apply in relation to land acquired under this section which is in the Forest of Dean; but the Minister may sell any such land if in his opinion it is not needed, or ought not to be used, for the purpose of afforestation or any purpose connected with forestry, and may exchange any such land for other land more suitable for either of the said purposes and may pay or receive money for equality of exchange.[4]

(3) The Minister shall have power, in the case of land acquired by him under this section,—

(a) to manage and use the land for such purposes as he thinks fit (this power to include that of erecting buildings and other works on the land) where it is not for the time being placed at the disposal of the Commissioners under subsection (1) above; and

(b) to let the land, or grant any interest or right in or over it.

(4) *Repealed by the Forestry Act 1981, s. 6(2), sch. This amendment came into force on 27 July 1981 the date of the Royal Assent.*

(5) *Repealed by the Requirements of Writing (Scotland) Act 1995 (*c. 7), s. 14(2), sch. 5. This amendment came into force on 1 August 1995: s. 15(2).*

(6) Schedule 4 to this Act[5] shall have effect as respects the procedure applicable where the Minister acquires land under this section, except in a case of compulsory purchase in accordance with the following section[6].

Compulsory purchase of land

40. (1) Subject to the provisions of this section, the power of the Minister[7] to acquire land by purchase under section 39 above includes a power of compulsory purchase.

(2) The following descriptions of land shall not be subject to compulsory purchase under this Act:—

(a) land which is the site of an ancient monument or other object of archæological interest;

---

[1] Word "twelve" substituted by the Forestry Act 1991 (c. 43), s. 1. This amendment came into force on 25 September 1991: s. 2(2).

[2] "Minister" defined by s. 49(1), p. 97 below.

[3] "The Commissioners" means the Forestry Commissioners: s. 49(1), p. 97 below.

[4] Subsections (2), (2A) substituted by the Forestry Act 1981 (c. 39), s. 1. This amendment came into force on 27 July 1981, the date of the Royal Assent.

[5] P. 101 below.

[6] The powers of the Minister under this section are extended, as respects Scotland, by the Countryside (Scotland) Act 1967 (c. 86), s. 59, p. 110 below and, as respects England and Wales, by the Countryside Act 1968 (c. 41), s. 23(3), p. 124 below. This Act has effect as if s. 24(2) of the Countryside Act 1968 (c. 41), p. 124 below, formed part of this section: s. 24(5).

[8] "Minister" defined by s. 49(1), p. 97 below.

(b) land which forms part of a park, garden or pleasure ground or which forms part of the home farm attached to, and usually occupied with, a mansion house or is otherwise required for the amenity or convenience of a dwelling-house;

(c) land which is the property of a local authority, that is to say,—

(i) in England or Wales, the council of a county,[1] county district[2] or rural parish, the Greater London Council[3], the Common Council of the City of London or the council of a London borough; and

(ii) in Scotland, a council constituted under section 2 of the Local Government etc. (Scotland) Act 1994[4];

(d) land which has been acquired for the purpose of their undertaking by statutory undertakers[5], that is to say persons authorised by an enactment, or by an order or scheme made under an enactment, to construct, work or carry on a railway, canal, inland navigation, dock, harbour, tramway,[6] water[7] or other public undertaking.

(3) Land shall not be subject to compulsory purchase under this Act if a forestry dedication covenant or agreement[8] is in force with respect to it and it is being used and managed in accordance with the provisions and conditions of a plan of operations approved by the Commissioners[9]; and—

(a) any question arising under this subsection whether there has been a breach of any of the provisions and conditions of a plan of operations shall be referred for determination as follows, that is to say—

(i) in a case relating to England and Wales, by an arbitrator appointed by the President of the Royal Institution of Chartered Surveyors; and

(ii) in a case relating to Scotland, by an arbiter appointed by the Chairman of the Scottish Committee of the said Institution; and

(b) such a breach shall not be treated as having occurred by virtue of any act or omission capable of remedy unless there has been default in remedying it within a reasonable time after notice given by the Commissioners requiring it to be remedied.

(4) The power of compulsory purchase under this Act shall not be exercisable in relation to land held inalienably by the National Trust[10] or by the National Trust for Scotland.[11,12]

(5) The Minister's power of compulsory purchase under this Act shall be exercisable by means of a compulsory purchase order, and—

(a) the order shall be made in accordance with Part I of Schedule 5 to this Act[13];

---

[1] Former words "county borough" repealed by the Local Authorities etc. (Miscellaneous Provisions) (No. 2) Order 1974, S.I. 1974/595, art. 3(22), sch. 1, pt. 1 which came into force on 1 April 1974.

[2] For the construction of "the council of a county" and "the council of a county district" see the Local Government Act 1972 (c. 70), s. 179(2).

[3] Words "the Greater London Council" inserted by the London Government Order 1970, S.I. 1970/211. The GLC was abolished on 1 April 1986 by the Local Government Act 1985 (c. 51), s. 1.

[4] Words "council constituted under s. 2 of the Local Government etc. (Scotland) Act 1994" inserted by the Local Government etc. (Scotland) Act 1994 (c. 39), s. 180(1), sch. 13, para. 69. It is anticipated that this amendment will come into force on 1 April 1996.

[5] The following are deemed to be statutory undertakers for the purposes of s. 40:

A public gas supplier: Gas Act 1986 (c. 44), s. 67(1), sch. 7, para. 2(1)(xviii).
The National Rivers Authority, every water undertaker and every sewerage undertaker: Water Act 1989 (c. 15), s. 190(3), sch. 27, pt. I.

The holder of a licence under s. 6(1) of the Electricity Act 1989 (c. 29): s. 112(1), sch. 16, para. 1(1)(xvii).

[6] Former words: "gas" repealed by the Gas Act 1986 (c. 44), s. 67(4), sch. 9, pt. I which came into force on 23 August 1986: S.I. 1986/1316; "electricity" repealed by the Electricity Act 1989 (c. 29), s. 112(4), sch. 18 which came into force on 31 March 1990: S.I. 1990/117.

[7] *England and Wales*: "water" repealed by the Water Act 1989 (c. 15), s. 190(3), sch. 27, pt. I. This amendment came into force on 1 September 1989: s. 194(3), S.I. 1989/1530.

[8] "Forestry dedication covenant" and "forestry dedication agreement" have the meanings assigned to them by s. 5, p. 69 above: s. 49(1).

[9] "The Commissioners" means the Forestry Commissioners: s. 49(1), p. 97 below.

[10] "National Trust" and land "held inalienably" defined by s. 49(1), p. 97 below.

[11] "National Trust for Scotland" and land "held inalienably" defined by s. 49(1), p. 97 below.

[12] This subsection substituted by the Forestry Act 1981 (c. 39), c. 2. This amendment came into force on 27 July 1981, the date of the Royal Assent.

[13] P. 102 below.

(b) Part II of that Schedule[1] shall apply with respect to the validity and date of operation of the order; and

(c) Part III of that Schedule[2] shall apply with respect to the procedure for acquiring land by compulsory purchase.

(6) If the said power of compulsory purchase is exercised in relation to land in respect of which an advance by way of grant has been made by the Commissioners—

(a) under section 4 of this Act[3]; or

(b) under section 3(3) of the Forestry Act 1919[4] at any time after the 26th March 1945,

not being in either case an advance made more than thirty years before the date of the service of the notice to treat in the exercise of that power, the amount of the compensation for the compulsory purchase shall be reduced by the amount of the advance with compound interest thereon (calculated from the date of the advance to the date on which the compensation is paid) at the rate of £3 per cent. per annum with yearly rests:

Provided that, in the case of compensation for the compulsory purchase of one of several interests in such land, the amount of the reduction in the case of each interest purchased shall be equal to a part of the advance and interest proportionate to the value of that interest as compared with the value of the land.

Finance, accounts and annual report

Forestry Fund

41. (1) The Forestry Fund constituted under section 8 of the Forestry Act 1919[5] shall continue to be maintained as heretofore.

(2) There shall be paid into the Forestry Fund out of moneys provided by Parliament such annual amounts as Parliament may determine.

(3) The following shall be paid out of the Forestry Fund:—

(a) the salaries of the Forestry Commissioners, and the salaries or remuneration of the officers and servants of the Commissioners[6];

(b) all expenses incurred by the Commissioners in the exercise of their powers and the performance of their duties under—

   (i) this Act; and

   (ii) the Plant Health Act 1967[7], and

   (iii) the Countryside (Scotland) Act 1967[8]

including the payment of allowances to the members of any committee maintained by them under this Act;

(c) any administrative expenses of the Minister under Part II of this Act (including sums required for the payment of remuneration to the members of any committee appointed by him in pursuance of section 27[9]).

(4) All sums received by the Commissioners in respect of the sale of timber, or otherwise received by them in respect of transactions carried out by them in the exercise of their powers and duties under this Act or received by them in the exercise of their powers under the Countryside (Scotland) Act 1967[10], shall be paid into the Forestry Fund.

---

[1] P. 103 below.
[2] P. 104 below.
[3] P. S. 4 has been repealed.
[4] 1919 c. 58.
[5] 1919 c. 58.
[6] "The Commissioners" means the Forestry Commissioners: s. 49(1), p. 97 below.
[7] 1967 c. 8.
[8] Words "and (iii) the Countryside (Scotland) Act 1967"

inserted by the Countryside (Scotland) Act 1967 (c. 86), s. 58(6)(a). This amendment came into force on 26 October 1967, the date of the Royal Assent.
[9] P. 85 above.
[10] Words "or received by them in the exercise of their powers under the Countryside (Scotland) Act 1967" inserted by the Countryside (Scotland) Act 1967 (c. 86), s. 58(6)(b).

(4A) There shall be paid out of the Forestry Fund into the Consolidated Fund such sums as the Ministers may from time to time with the approval of the Treasury direct.[1]

(5) The Commissioners may accept any gift made to them for all or any purposes of this Act and, subject to the terms thereof, may apply it for those purposes in accordance with regulations made by them.

(6) Payments out of and into the Forestry Fund, and all other matters relating to the Fund and money standing to the credit of the Fund, shall be made and regulated in such manner as the Treasury may, by minute to be laid before Parliament, direct.

(7) *Repealed by the Forestry Act 1981 (c. 39), ss. 3, 6(2), sch. This amendment came into force on 27 July 1981, the date of the Royal Assent.*

Finance of land acquisition, management, etc.

42. (1) Any capital payments made by the Minister[2] in acquiring land under section 39 above[3], and any expenses of the Minister in the acquisition of land thereunder, shall be defrayed out of the Forestry Fund.

(2) Where land acquired by the Minister under section 39 is for the time being placed at the disposal of the Commissioners[4]—

(a) any rent or other outgoings payable in respect of the land by the Minister shall be defrayed out of the Forestry Fund; and

(b) any sums received by the Minister from the letting of the land or the grant of any interest or right in or over it shall be paid into that Fund.

(3) Where land acquired by the Minister under section 39 is not for the time being placed at the disposal of the Commissioners, the expenses of the Minister in managing and using the land, including any rent or other outgoings payable by him in respect of the land, shall be defrayed out of moneys provided by Parliament, and—

(a) any sums received by him from the letting or use of the land, or the grant of any interest or right in or over it, shall be paid into the Exchequer; and

(b) the Minister shall pay into the Forestry Fund out of moneys provided by Parliament such periodical sums (if any) in respect of the land as may be determined by the Treasury.

(4) Any capital sums received by the Minister from the sale, lease or exchange of land acquired by him under section 39 shall be paid into the Forestry Fund.

Satisfaction of certain contingent liability to Crown Estate

43. (1) If the Minister[5] sells land which was transferred to him, or to any predecessor of his, or to the Commissioners[6], under section 1(1)(a) of the Forestry (Transfer of Woods) Act 1923[7] to an amount exceeding 2 hectares[8] at any one time, then if the sum determined under section 3 of the said Act of 1923 as the amount contingently payable by way of compensation for the transfer of rights and interests of the Crown has not been fully paid or satisfied,—

(a) the net proceeds of sale, or the portion necessary to satisfy the said sum, shall be paid by the Minister to the Crown Estate Commissioners and shall form part of the Crown Estate; and

---

[1] Subsection (4A) inserted by the Forestry Act 1981 (c. 39), s. 3. This amendment came into force on 27 July 1981, the date of the Royal Assent.

[2] "Minister" defined by s. 49(1), p. 97 below.

[3] P. 91 above.

[4] "The Commissioners" means the Forestry Commissioners: s. 49(1), p. 97 below.

[5] "Minister" defined by s. 49(1), p. 97 below.

[6] "The Commissioners" means the Forestry Commissioners: s. 49(1), p. 97 below.

[7] 1923 c. 21.

[8] Words "2 hectares" substituted by the Forestry Act 1979 (c. 21), s. 2(1), sch. 1. This amendment came into force on 30 May 1979: s. 3(3).

(*b*) the payment shall be treated as satisfying a part of that sum equal to the gross proceeds of sale or the corresponding portion of them.

(2) In the event of the hereditary revenues which are by section 1 of the Civil List Act 1952[1] directed to be carried to and made part of the Consolidated Fund ceasing at any time, whether during the present or any subsequent reign, to be carried to and made part of that Fund, there shall be paid out of the Fund to the Crown Estate Commissioners all such amounts as immediately before the commencement of this Act remained outstanding as compensation due to the Crown under section 3 of the said Act of 1923, reduced by the amount of any payments made since that commencement to the Crown Estate Commissioners pursuant to subsection (1) above or to the corresponding provision in section 8(1) of the Crown Estate Act 1961[2].

Annual accounts of Commissioners

44. (1) The Commissioners[3] shall prepare accounts in respect of each financial year (beginning with the 1st April), showing the sums paid into and the sums issued out of the Forestry Fund in that year.

(2) The Commissioners' accounts shall be in such form and manner as the Ministers with the approval of the Treasury may direct, and the Commissioners shall transmit the accounts to the Ministers at such time as the Ministers, with the said approval, may direct.

(3) The Ministers shall, on or before the 30th November in each year, transmit to the Comptroller and Auditor General the accounts prepared by the Commissioners under subsection (1) above for the financial year last ended, and the Comptroller and Auditor General shall examine and certify them and lay copies thereof, together with his report thereon, before both Houses of Parliament.

Annual report by Commissioners

45. The Commissioners[4] shall, on such day and in such form as the Ministers may direct, make to the Ministers an annual report as to their proceedings under this Act, and the Ministers shall lay the report before Parliament.

Part IV: General

Commissioners' power to make byelaws

46. (1) Subject to the provisions of this and the next following sections, the Commissioners[5] may make byelaws with respect to any land which is under their management or control and to which the public have, or may be permitted to have, access.[6]

(2) The Commissioners' byelaws may be such as appear to them to be necessary—

(*a*) for the preservation of any trees or timber on the land, or of any property of the Commissioners; and

(*b*) for prohibiting or regulating any act or thing tending to injury or disfigurement of the land or its amenities; and

(*c*) without prejudice to the generality of the foregoing, for regulating the reasonable use of the land by the public for the purposes of exercise and recreation.

(3) Byelaws under this section—

[1] 1952 c. 37.
[2] 1961 c. 55.
[3] "The Commissioners" means the Forestry Commissioners: s. 49(1), p. 97 below.
[4] "The Commissioners" means the Forestry Commissioners: s. 49(1), p. 97 below.
[5] "The Commissioners" means the Forestry Commissioners: s. 49(1), p. 97 below.
[6] The Forestry Commission Byelaws 1982, S.I. 1982/648, made under this section.

(*a*) shall not take away or injuriously affect any estate, interest, right of common or other right of a profitable or beneficial nature in, over or affecting any land, except with the consent of the person entitled thereto;

(*b*) shall not apply to a common which is subject to a scheme or regulation made in pursuance of the Metropolitan Commons Acts 1866 to 1898, or the Inclosure Acts 1845 to 1882, or the Commons Act 1899[1].

(4) Byelaws under this section shall be made by statutory instrument and a draft of a statutory instrument containing any such byelaws shall be laid before Parliament.

(5) If anyone fails to comply with, or acts in contravention of, any byelaw made under this section he shall be guilty of an offence and be liable on summary conviction as follows:—

(*a*) in the case of an offence against byelaws made by the Commissioners with respect to the New Forest, he shall be liable to a fine not exceeding level 2 on the standard scale[2]; and

(*b*) in a case not falling within the foregoing paragraph, he shall be liable to a fine not exceeding level 2 on the standard scale[2]; and

(*c*) in [*England and Wales*: the case of a continuing offence falling within either of the foregoing paragraphs[3] *Scotland*: either case] he shall be liable to a further fine not exceeding 50p.[4] for each day upon which the offence continues.[5]

(6) *Repealed by the Criminal Justice Act 1972 (c. 71), s. 64(2), sch. 6, pt. II. This amendment came into force on 1 April 1973: S.I. 1973/272.*

....

Provisions supplementary to s. 46 for New Forest and Forest of Dean

47. (1) Byelaws made by the Commissioners[6] under section 46 with respect to the New Forest or the Forest of Dean shall be without prejudice to any byelaws made under any other Act by the verderers of either Forest, but before making any such byelaws the Commissioners shall consult with the verderers of the Forest concerned.

(2) Section 1(3) of the New Forest Act 1964[7] (which applies byelaws made by the Commissioners to certain land added under that Act to the Forest) shall have effect with the substitution for the reference to section 2 of the Forestry Act 1927 of a reference to section 46 of this Act.

(3) The verderers of either of the said Forests may in their courts inquire into any offence consisting in a failure to comply with, or a contravention of, byelaws made by the Commissioners under section 46, being an offence alleged to have been committed within the Forest, and may punish any such offence so committed.

(4) As respects their jurisdiction under this section, the verderers' courts shall be deemed to be magistrates' courts, and the provisions of the Magistrates' Courts Acts 1952 and 1957[8], including provisions as to the recovery of fines and as to appeals, and the provisions of any rules made under those Acts, shall apply accordingly.

(5) The powers conferred by this section on the verderers of the New Forest and the Forest of Dean shall be in addition to, and not in derogation of, any other powers exercisable by them, and

---

[1] 1899 c. 340.

[2] Words "level 2 on the standard scale" substituted by the Criminal Justice Act 1967 (c. 80), s. 92(1), sch. 3, pt. I, the Criminal Justice Act 1982 (c. 48), ss. 39(2), 46, sch. 3 as respects England and Wales and the Criminal Procedure (Scotland) Act 1975 (c. 21), s. 289H, sch. 7D, para. 25 as respects Scotland. The current fine at level 2 is £500: Criminal Justice Act 1991 (c. 53), s. 17 which came into force on 1 October 1992: S.I. 1992/333, S.I. 1992/2118.

[3] Words "the case ... paragraphs" substituted by the Criminal Justice Act 1967 (c. 80), s. 103(1), sch. 6, para. 28. This amendment came into force on 1 January 1968: S.I. 1967/1234.

[4] Words "50p." substituted by virtue of the Decimal Currency Act 1969 (c. 47), s. 10(1).

[5] The powers to make byelaws under this section are extended, in respect of Scotland, by the Countryside (Scotland) Act 1967 (c. 86), s. 58(3), p. 110 below and, in respect of England and Wales, by the Countryside Act 1968 (c. 41), s. 23(4) p. 124 below.

[6] "The Commissioners" means the Forestry Commissioners: s. 49(1), p. 97 below.

[7] 1964 c. 83.

[8] The reference to the 1952 and 1957 Acts is construed as a reference to the Magistrates' Courts Act 1980 (c. 43): s. 154(2), sch. 8, para. 5.

shall be without prejudice to the power of any other court in relation to offences under section 46.

Powers of entry and enforcement

48. (1) An officer of the Commissioners[1] or any other person authorised by them in that behalf may (on production, if so required, of his authority) enter on and survey any land for the purpose of ascertaining whether it is suitable for afforestation or for the purpose of inspecting any timber thereon, or for any other purpose in connection with the exercise of the powers and performance of the duties of the Commissioners under this Act or the Plant Health Act 1967[2].

(2) The Commissioners may authorise an officer or servant appointed or employed by them to exercise and perform on their behalf such powers and duties as they may consider necessary for the enforcement of byelaws under section 46 of this Act[3], and in particular to remove or exclude, after due warning, from any land to which the byelaws relate a person who commits, or whom he reasonably suspects of committing, an offence against the said section or against the Vagrancy Act 1824[4].

(3) Anyone who obstructs an officer or servant appointed or employed by the Commissioners in the due exercise or performance of his powers or duties under the foregoing subsection shall be guilty of an offence and be liable on summary conviction to a fine not exceeding level 3 on the standard scale.[5]

Interpretation

49. (1) In this Act—

"the Commissioners" means the body known as "The Forestry Commissioners";

"forestry dedication covenant" and "forestry dedication agreement" have the meanings assigned to them by section 5[6];

"the Minister", except as provided by sections 15(8)[7] and 19(4)[8] and Schedule 3[9], means the Minister of Agriculture, Fisheries and Food as respects England, and a Secretary of State as respects Wales and as respects Scotland;

"National Trust" means the National Trust for Places of Historic Interest or Natural Beauty incorporated by the National Trust Act 1907[10], and "held inalienably", in relation to land belonging to the National Trust, means that the land is inalienable under section 21 of the said Act of 1907 or section 8 of the National Trust Act 1939[11];

"National Trust for Scotland" means the National Trust for Scotland for Places of Historic Interest or Natural Beauty incorporated by the Order confirmed by the National Trust for Scotland Order Confirmation Act 1935[12], and "held inalienably", in relation to land belonging to that Trust, means that the land is inalienable under section 22 of that Order.

(2) For purposes of this Act, Monmouthshire shall be deemed to be part of Wales and not of England.

(3) In this Act as it applies to Scotland any reference to the purchase of land shall be construed as including a reference to the taking of land in feu.

---

[1] "The Commissioners" means the Forestry Commissioners: s. 49(1), p. 97 below.
[2] 1967 c. 8.
[3] P. 95 above.
[4] 1824 c. 83.
[5] Words "level 3 on the standard scale" substituted by the Criminal Justice Act 1967 (c. 80), s. 92(1), sch. 3, pt. I, the Criminal Justice Act 1982 (c. 48), ss. 39(2), 46, sch. 3 as respects England and Wales and the Criminal Procedure (Scotland) Act 1975 (c. 21), s. 289H, sch. 7D, para. 26 as respects Scotland. The current fine at level 3 is £1,000: Criminal Justice Act 1991 (c. 53), s. 17 which came into force on 1 October 1992: S.I. 1992/333, S.I. 1992/2118.
[6] P. 69 above.
[7] P. 78 above.
[8] P. 81 above.
[9] P. 100 below.
[10] 1907 c. cxxxvi.
[11] 1939 c. lxxxvi.
[12] 1935 c. ii.

Transitional provisions, repeals and savings

50. (1) The transitional provisions contained in Schedule 6 to this Act[1] shall have effect.

(2) The enactments specified in the second column of Part I of Schedule 7 to this Act are hereby repealed to the extent specified in the third column of that Part of the Schedule, subject to the savings in Part II of that Schedule.

(3) Nothing in this section or in Schedule 6 or 7 to this Act shall be taken as affecting the general application of section 38 of the Interpretation Act 1889[2] with regard to the effect of repeals.

Short title and extent

51. (1) This Act may be cited as the Forestry Act 1967.

(2) This Act shall not extent to Northern Ireland.

SCHEDULES

SCHEDULE 1

(Section 2.)

THE FORESTRY COMMISSION AND ITS STAFF

PART I

ADMINISTRATION

The Commissioners

1. The Commissioners may for all purposes be described by the name of "The Forestry Commissioners".

2. (1) Each Forestry Commissioner shall hold and vacate office in accordance with the terms of his warrant of appointment, and one who vacates office shall be eligible for reappointment.

(2) There shall be paid to such Forestry Commissioners as may be determined by the Ministers, with the approval of the Treasury, such salaries or other emoluments as may be so determined.

3. The Commissioners may act by three of their number and notwithstanding a vacancy in their number, and may regulate their own procedure.

4. (1) The Commissioners shall have an official seal, which shall be officially and judicially noticed.

(2) The seal shall be authenticated by a Forestry Commissioner, or by the secretary to the Commissioners, or by some person authorised by the Commissioners to act on behalf of the secretary.

5. (1) Every document purporting to be an order or other instrument issued by the Commissioners and to be sealed with the seal of the Commissioners authenticated in manner provided by paragraph 4(2) above, or to be signed by the secretary to the Commissioners or any person authorised by the Commissioners to act on behalf of the secretary, shall be received in evidence and be deemed to be such order or instrument without further proof, unless the contrary is shown.

---

[1] P. 105 below.
[2] Ss. 16, 17 of the Interpretation Act 1978 (c. 30) replace s. 38 of the Interpretation Act 1889: Interpretation Act 1978, ss. 17, 22.

(2) The Documentary Evidence Act 1868[1], as amended by the Documentary Evidence Act 1882[2], shall apply to the Commissioners as though the Commissioners were included in the first column of the Schedule to the said Act of 1868, and the chairman or any other Commissioner, or the secretary, or any person authorised to act on behalf of the secretary, were mentioned in the second column of that Schedule, and as if the regulations referred to in those Acts included any document issued by the Commissioners.

Staff

6. (1) The Commissioners may, subject to such limit as to number as the Treasury may determine, appoint and employ such officers and servants for the purposes of this Act as the Commissioners think necessary, and may remove any officer or servant so appointed or employed.

(2) There shall be paid to officers and servants appointed or employed by the Commissioners such salaries or remuneration as the Ministers may, with the approval of the Treasury, determine.

Committees appointed under section 2(3)

7. (1) An order of the Commissioners under section 2(3) of this Act[3] appointing a committee shall make provision as to the constitution (including the terms of office of members), quorum and procedure of the committee.

(2) There shall be paid out of the Forestry Fund to the members of any committee appointed under section 2(3) who are not Forestry Commissioners or officers of the Commissioners such travelling and other allowances as the Ministers may, with the approval of the Treasury, determine.

Supplementary

8. The functions of the Ministers under this Part of this Schedule shall be exercised by them jointly, except in so far as they make arrangements that this paragraph shall not apply.

PART II

SUPERANNUATION OF FORESTRY COMMISSIONERS AND COMMISSION STAFF

Not Reproduced.

....

SCHEDULE 2[4]

(Section 5.)

CONVEYANCING AND OTHER PROVISIONS CONNECTED WITH FORESTRY DEDICATION

England and Wales

1. (1) In the case of settled land in England or Wales, the tenant for life may enter into a forestry dedication covenant[5] relating to the land or any part thereof either for consideration or gratuitously.

(2) The Settled Land Act 1925[6] shall apply as if the power conferred by sub-paragraph (1) above had been conferred by that Act; and for the purposes of section 72 of that Act (which relates to the mode of giving effect to a disposition by a tenant for life and to the operation thereof), and of any other relevant statutory provision applying to England or Wales, entering into a forestry dedication covenant shall be treated as a disposition.

(3) The foregoing provisions of this paragraph shall be construed as one with the Settled Land Act 1925[7].

---

[1] 1868 c. 37.
[2] 1882 c. 9.
[3] P. 69 above.
[4] This schedule applies to any agreement made in pursuance of the Countryside Act 1968 (c. 41), s. 15: s. 15(5), p. 122 below, and to management agreements: Wildlife and Countryside Act 1981 (c. 69), s. 39, p. 181 below.

[5] "Forestry dedication covenant" has the meaning assigned to it by s. 5, p. 69 above: s. 49(1).
[6] 1925 c. 18.
[7] Under the Endowments and Glebe Measure 1976 (No. 4), paragraph (3) ceases to apply to incumbents: s. 47(3), sch. 7.

(4) Section 28 of the Law of Property Act 1925[1] (which confers the powers of a tenant for life on trustees for sale) shall apply as if the power of a tenant for life under sub-paragraph (1) above had been conferred by the Settled Land Act 1925.

2. A university or college to which the Universities and Colleges Estates Act 1925[2] applies may enter into a forestry dedication covenant relating to any land belonging to it in England or Wales either for consideration or gratuitously, and that Act shall apply as if the power conferred by this paragraph had been conferred by that Act.

3. In the case of glebe land or other land belonging to an ecclesiastical benefice, the incumbent of the benefice and, in the case of land which is part of the endowment of any other ecclesiastical corporation, the corporation may with the consent of the Church Commissioners enter into a forestry dedication covenant relating to the land either for consideration or gratuitously, and the Ecclesiastical Leasing Acts shall apply as if the power conferred by this paragraph had been conferred by those Acts, except that the consent of the patron of an ecclesiastical benefice shall not be requisite.

Scotland

4. (1) In the case of land in Scotland, any person being—

(a) the liferenter, or

(b) the heir of entail,

in possession of the land shall have power to enter into forestry dedication agreements[3] relating to the land or any part thereof.

(2) The Trusts (Scotland) Act 1921[4] shall have effect as if among the powers conferred on trustees by section 4 thereof (which relates to the general powers of trustees) there were included a power to enter into forestry dedication agreements relating to the trust estate or any part thereof.

SCHEDULE 3

(Section 15.)

PROCEEDINGS UNDER TOWN AND COUNTRY PLANNING ACTS IN RELATION TO TREE PRESERVATION ORDERS[5]

1. Provisions of section 15 of this Act[6] requiring an application for a felling licence[7] to be dealt with under the Town and Country Planning Acts shall be construed in accordance with this Schedule.

2. Where under section 15(2)(a) an application, on being referred to the Minister[8], falls to be dealt with under the said Acts, the following shall apply:—

(a) if the tree preservation order applies section 77 of the Town and Country Planning Act 1990[9], or the corresponding provision of the Town and Country Planning Act 1947 replaced thereby, or (for Scotland) section 32 of the Town and Country Planning (Scotland) Act 1972[10], the provisions of the order and any provisions of the said Acts relating to the order shall apply as if the application—

(i) had been one made under the order for the felling of the trees; and

(ii) had been referred to the Minister in pursuance of the said section as so applied;

---

[1] 1925 c. 20.
[2] 1925 c. 24.
[3] "Forestry dedication agreement" has the meaning assigned to it by s. 5, p. 69 above: s. 49(1).
[4] 1921 c. 58.
[5] "Tree preservation order" defined by s. 35, p. 89 above.
[6] P. 77 above.
[7] "Felling licence" defined by s. 35, p. 89 above.
[8] "Minister" in this section means the Secretary of State: as respects England, para. 4 below and S.I. 1970/1681; as

respects Wales and Scotland, s. 49(1), p. 97 above.
[9] Words "section 77 of the Town and Country Planning Act 1990" substituted by the Planning (Consequential Provisions) Act 1990 (c. 11), s. 4, sch. 2, para. 14(3)(a)(i). This amendment came into force on 24 August 1990: s. 7(2).
[10] Words "section 32 of the Town and Country Planning (Scotland) Act 1972" substituted by the Town and Country Planning (Scotland) Act 1972 (c. 52), s. 276(1), sch. 21, pt. II. This Act came into force on 27 August 1972: s. 280.

(b) if the order contains no such provisions as aforesaid it shall have effect for the purposes of this paragraph as if the said section 77[1] or (for Scotland) the said section 32[2] were incorporated therein subject to such modifications as the Minister may direct.

3. Where under section 15(3)(a) of this Act[3] on application, on being referred to an authority who have made a tree preservation order, falls to be dealt with under the Town and Country Planning Acts, the provisions of the order and any provisions of the Town and Country Planning Act 1990[4] or (for Scotland) the Town and Country Planning (Scotland) Act 1972[5] relating to the order shall apply as if the application were an application made to the said authority for consent for the felling of the trees to which the application for a felling licence relates.

4. In this Schedule "the Minister", in relation to England, means the Minister of Housing and Local Government[6] and not the Minister of Agriculture, Fisheries and Food.

SCHEDULE 4

(Section 39.)

PROCEDURE FOR ACQUISITION OF LAND UNDER S. 39 BY AGREEMENT

England and Wales

1. (1) For the purpose of any acquisition by the Minister[7] land in England or Wales, where the acquisition is by agreement, Part I of the Compulsory Purchase Act 1965[8] shall apply in accordance with the following provisions of this paragraph.

(2) In the said Part I as so applied—

(a) "the acquiring authority" means the Minister;

(b) "the special Act" means section 39 of this Act[9]; and

(c) for references to land subject to compulsory purchase there shall be substituted references to land which may be acquired by agreement under the said section 39.

(3) In relation to the acquisition of land by agreement under section 39, Part I of the said Act of 1965 shall be modified as follows:—

(a) sections 4 to 8, 10, 27 and 31 shall not apply;

(b) section 30(3) shall not apply, but notices required to be served by the Minister under any provision of the said Act of 1965 as applied by this paragraph may, notwithstanding anything in section 30(1) of that Act, be served and addressed in the manner specified in section 30 of this Act[10].

Scotland

2. (1) For the purpose of any acquisition by the Minister[11] of land in Scotland, where the acquisition is by agreement, the Lands Clauses Acts[12], except the following enactments in the Lands Clauses Consolidation (Scotland) Act 1845[13], that is to say—

sections 120 to 125,
section 127, and
sections 142 and 143,

---

[1] Words "the said section 77" substituted by the Planning (Consequential Provisions) Act 1990 (c. 11), s. 4, sch. 2, para. 14(3)(a)(ii).

[2] Words "the said section 32" substituted by the Town and Country Planning (Scotland) Act 1972 (c. 52), s. 276(1), sch. 21, pt. II.

[3] P. 77 above.

[4] Words "the Town and Country Planning Act 1990" substituted by the Planning (Consequential Provisions) Act 1990 (c. 11), s. 4, sch. 2, para. 14(3)(b).

[5] Words "the Town and Country Planning (Scotland) Act 1972" substituted by the Town and Country Planning

(Scotland) Act 1972 (c. 52), s. 276(1), sch. 21, pt. II.

[6] These functions transferred to the Secretary of State: S.I. 1970/1681.

[7] "Minister" defined by s. 49(1), p. 97 above.

[8] 1965 c. 56.

[9] P. 91 above.

[10] P. 86 above.

[11] "Minister" defined by s. 49(1), p. 97 above.

[12] "Lands Clauses Acts" defined by the Interpretation Act 1978 (c. 30), s. 5, sch. 1.

[13] 1845 c. 19.

are hereby incorporated with section 39 of this Act[1], subject to the following sub-paragraphs.

(2) In construing the Lands Clauses Acts as incorporated by this paragraph, section 39 of this Act shall be deemed to be the special Act, and references to the promoters of the undertaking shall be construed as references to the Minister.

(3) Notices required to be served by the Minister under any provision of the Lands Clauses Acts as incorporated by this paragraph may, notwithstanding anything in section 18 of the Lands Clauses Consolidation (Scotland) Act 1845, be served and addressed in the manner specified in section 30 of this Act[2].

SCHEDULE 5

(Section 40.)

COMPULSORY PURCHASE

PART I

PROCEDURE FOR MAKING COMPULSORY PURCHASE ORDERS

1. A compulsory purchase order shall describe by reference to a map the land to which it applies.

2. (1) Before making a compulsory purchase order, the Minister[3] shall—

(a) publish in one or more newspapers circulating in the locality in which the land to which the order relates is situated a notice stating that a compulsory purchase order is proposed to be made; and

(b) serve a copy of the notice in such manner as he thinks fit on every owner, lessee and occupier (except tenants for a month or less period than a month) of any land to which the order relates.

(2) Section 30 of this Act[4] applies to the service of a notice under sub-paragraph (1)(b) above as it applies to the service of documents under Part II of this Act.

(3) A notice under sub-paragraph (1) above shall—

(a) describe the land,

(b) name the place where a copy of a draft of the compulsory purchase order and of the map referred to therein may be seen at all reasonable hours, and

(c) specify the time (not less than twenty-eight days from the date of the publication of the notice) within which, and the manner in which, objections to the order may be made.

3. (1) If no objection is duly made by any of the persons on whom notices are required to be served, or by any other person appearing to the Minister to be affected, or if all objections so made are withdrawn, the Minister may, if he thinks fit (but subject to sub-paragraph (3) below), make the order, either with or without modifications.

(2) In any other case the Minister shall, before making the order, cause a local inquiry to be held and shall consider any objections not withdrawn and the report of the person who held the inquiry, and may then, if he thinks fit (but subject to sub-paragraph (3) below), make the order, either with or without modifications.

(3) An order made by the Minister with modifications shall not, unless all persons interested consent, authorise him to purchase compulsorily any land which the order would not have authorised him so to purchase if it had been made without modifications.

4. Subject to paragraph 5 below, where objection to a compulsory purchase order is duly made by a person mentioned in paragraph 3(1) above and is not withdrawn before the order is made, the order shall be subject to special parliamentary procedure and the Statutory Orders (Special Procedure) Acts 1945[5] and 1965[6] shall have effect accordingly[7].

---

[1] P. 91 above.
[2] P. 86 above.
[3] "Minister" defined by s. 49(1), p. 97 above.
[4] P. 86 above.

[5] 1945 c. 18.
[6] 1965 c. 43.
[7] This paragraph does not apply to a compulsory purchase order under s. 40 of this Act for the acquisition of

5. If an objection appears to the Minister to relate exclusively to matters which can be dealt with by the tribunal by whom the compensation for the compulsory purchase would be assessed, the Minister may disregard the objection for the purposes of paragraph 3 above, and may (whether he disregards it for those purposes or not) direct that it shall be disregarded for the purposes of paragraph 4 above.

6. An inquiry in relation to a compulsory purchase order affecting land in Scotland, being an order which becomes subject to special parliamentary procedure, shall, if the Minister so directs, be held by Commissioners under the Private Legislation Procedure (Scotland) Act 1936[1]; and, where any direction has been so given,—

(a) it shall be deemed to have been give under section 2, as read with section 10, of the Statutory Orders (Special Procedure) Act 1945;

(b) the provisions of section 2(1) of that Act with regard to advertisement of notice shall be deemed to have been complied with.

Part II

Validity and Operation of Compulsory Purchase Orders

7. (1) So soon as may be after a compulsory purchase order has been made by the Minister[2], he shall—

(a) publish in one or more newspapers circulating in the locality in which the land to which the order relates is situated a notice stating that the order has been made and naming a place where a copy of the order and of the map referred to therein may be seen at all reasonable hours; and

(b) serve a like notice on every person who made an objection to the order.

(2) Section 30 of this Act[3] applies to the service of a notice under sub-paragraph (1)(b) above as it applies to the service of documents under Part II of this Act.

(3) Where the order is subject to special parliamentary procedure, the notice to be published and served by the Minister under sub-paragraph (1) above shall contain a statement that the order is to be laid before Parliament under the Statutory Orders (Special Procedure) Acts 1945[4] and 1965[5].

8. (1) Except where the order is confirmed by Act, if a person aggrieved by the order desires to question its validity on the ground that it is not within the powers of this Act or that any requirement of this Act has not been complied with, he may—

(a) in the case of an order to which the Statutory Orders (Special Procedure) Acts 1945 and 1965 apply, within a period of six weeks after the date on which the order becomes operative under those Acts; and

(b) in any other case, within a period of six weeks after the first publication of the notice of the order,

make an application for that purpose to the court.

(2) Where any such application is duly made, the court—

(a) may by interim order suspend the operation of this compulsory purchase order, either generally or in so far as it affects any property of the applicant, until the final determination of the proceedings; and

(b) if satisfied upon the hearing of the application that the order is not within the powers of this Act, or that the interests of the applicant have been substantially prejudiced by any requirement of this Act not having been complied with, may quash the order, either generally or in so far as it affects any property of the applicant.

(3) In this paragraph—

"confirmed by Act" means confirmed by Act of Parliament under section 6 of the Statutory Orders (Special Procedure) Act 1945 or (in relation to Scotland) that section and section 2(4) of the Act as read with section 10 thereof; and

"the court" means, in relation to England and Wales, the High Court and, in relation to Scotland, the Court of Session.

worked ironstone land within the ironstone district: Mineral Workings Act 1985 (c. 12), s. 6(3). "Worked ironstone land" means land which has been excavated in the course of winning and working ironstone by opencast operations, and includes land on which materials extracted in the course of such operations have been deposited; "the ironstone district" means the areas set out in Schedule 1 to the Act: s. 9. These provisions of the Mineral Workings Act 1985 came into force on 1 April 1985: s. 11(2).

[1] 1936 c. 52.
[2] "Minister" defined by s. 49(1), p. 97 above.
[3] P. 86 above.
[4] 1945 c. 18.
[5] 1965 c. 43.

9. Subject to the foregoing provisions, the order shall not be questioned by prohibition or certiorari or in any legal proceedings whatsoever either before or after the order is made.

10. The order, except where the Statutory Orders (Special Procedure) Acts 1945 and 1965 apply to it, shall become operative at the expiration of six weeks from the date on which notice of it is first published in accordance with the provisions of this Part of this Schedule.

PART III

PROCEDURE FOR ACQUISITION OF LAND BY COMPULSORY PURCHASE

England and Wales

11. (1) For the purpose of any acquisition by the Minister[1] of land in England or Wales, where the acquisition is by compulsory purchase, Part I of the Compulsory Purchase Act 1965[2] shall apply subject to and in accordance with the following provisions of this paragraph.

(2) In the said Part I as so applied—

(*a*) "the acquiring authority" means the Minister, and

(*b*) "the special Act" means section 39 of this Act[3] and the compulsory purchase order under section 40[4].

(3) In relation to compulsory purchase under this Act, Part I of the said Act of 1965 shall be modified as follows:—

(*a*) *Repealed by the Statute Law (Repeals) Act 1974 (c. 22), s. 1, sch., pt. III. This amendment came into force on 27 June 1974, the date of the Royal Assent.*

(*b*) in section 11 (power of entry after notice to treat), subsection (1) shall not apply and subsection (2) shall apply with the omission of the word "also";

Paragraphs 11(3)(c)–(e) and 11(4) repealed by the Statute Law (Repeals) Act 1974 (c. 22), s. 1, sch, pt. III.

12. As regards land in England or Wales, a compulsory purchase order under this Act may provide that section 77 of the Railways Clauses Consolidation Act 1845[5], and sections 78 to 85 of that Act as originally enacted and not as amended for certain purposes by section 15 of the Mines (Working Facilities and Support) Act 1923[6], shall be incorporated with section 39 of this Act, subject to such adaptations and modifications as may be specified in the order.

Scotland

13. (1) For the purpose of any acquisition by the Minister[7] of land in Scotland, where the acquisition is by compulsory purchase, the Lands Clauses Acts[8], except the following enactments in the Lands Clauses Consolidation (Scotland) Act 1845[9], that is to say—

sections 120 to 125,
section 127, and
sections 142 and 143,

are hereby incorporated with section 39 of this Act, subject to the modifications and adaptations specified in the following two sub-paragraphs.

---

[1] "Minister" defined by s. 49(1), p. 97 above.
[2] 1965 c. 56.
[3] P. 91 above.
[4] P. 91 above.
[5] 1845 c. 20.
[6] 1923 c. 20.
[7] "Minister" defined by s. 49(1), p. 000 below.
[8] "Lands Clauses Acts" defined by the Interpretation Act 1978 (c. 30), s. 5, sch. 1.
[9] 1845 c. 19.

(2) In construing the Lands Clauses Acts as incorporated by this paragraph, section 39 of this Act[1] and the compulsory purchase order under section 40[2] shall be deemed to be the special Act, and references to the promoters of the undertaking shall be construed as references to the Minister.

(3) Notices required to be served by the Minister under any provision of the Lands Clauses Acts as incorporated by this paragraph may, notwithstanding anything in section 18 of the Lands Clauses Consolidation (Scotland) Act 1845, be served and addressed in the manner specified in section 30 of this Act[3].

(4) For the purposes of section 116 of the Lands Clauses Consolidation (Scotland) Act 1845 (which provides that powers of compulsory purchase shall not be exercised after the expiration of the prescribed period) the prescribed period shall be three years from the coming into operation of the compulsory purchase order.

14. As regards land in Scotland, a compulsory purchase order under this Act may provide that section 70 of the Railways Clauses Consolidation (Scotland) Act 1845[4], and sections 71 to 78 of that Act as originally enacted and not as amended for certain purposes by section 15 of the Mines (Working Facilities and Support) Act 1923[5], shall be incorporated with section 39 of this Act, subject to such adaptations and modifications as may be specified in the order.

SCHEDULE 6

(Section 50.)

Transitional Provisions

1. (1) In so far as any appointment, order, regulation, byelaw, application, claim for compensation or reference made, or notice or directions given, or other thing done under an enactment repealed by this Act could have been made, given or done under a corresponding provision of this Act, it shall not be invalidated by the repeal but shall have effect as if made, given or done under that corresponding provision.

(2) Anything begun under an enactment repealed by this Act may be continued under this Act as if begun thereunder.

(3) Any reference in this Act to things done, suffered or occurring in the past shall, so far as the context requires for the purpose of continuity of operation between an enactment repealed by this Act and the corresponding enactment in this Act, be construed as including a reference to things done, suffered or occurring before the commencement of this Act.

(4) So much of any document as refers expressly or by implication to any enactment repealed by this Act shall, if and so far as the context permits, be construed as referring to this Act or the corresponding enactment therein.

(5) The generality of sub-paragraphs (1) to (4) above shall not be prejudiced by anything in the subsequent provisions of this Schedule.

2. For the purposes of sections 16(4) of this Act[6], any such anniversary of an application as is there referred to shall, in the case of an application made before the commencement of this Act and having effect as if made under this Act, be taken as falling on the date on which it would have fallen if this Act had not been passed.

3. A notice given by the Commissioners under section 11(1) of the Forestry Act 1951[7] and having effect as if given under section 24 of this Act[8] shall, in a case where the notice was by virtue of section 11(4) of that Act inoperative immediately before the commencement of this Act, remain inoperative under section 25(2) of this Act for as long as, and no longer than, it would have so remained but for the passing of this Act.

4. (1) References in this Act to land acquired by the Minister[9] thereunder shall include references to land which, immediately before the commencement of this Act, was vested in that Minister having been acquired by him or

---

[1] P. 91 above.
[2] P. 91 above.
[3] P. 86 above.
[4] 1845 c. 33.
[5] 1923 C. 20.

[6] P. 78 above.
[7] 1951 c. 61.
[8] P. 83 above.
[9] "Minister" defined by s. 49(1), p. 97 above.

any predecessor of his under section 4 of the Forestry Act 1945[1], or vested by that section in the appropriate Minister for the purposes of that Act, or transferred to the Minister by the operation of Article 9(1) of the Secretary of State for Wales and Minister of Land and Natural Resources Order 1965[2] (which Order transferred functions of the Minister of Agriculture, Fisheries and Food under the Forestry Acts 1919 to 1951 partly to the Minister of Land and Natural Resources and partly to the Secretary of State for Wales) or of Article 2 of the Ministry of Land and Natural Resources (Dissolution) Order 1967[3] (which dissolved the Ministry of Land and Natural Resources and transferred its principal functions under the said Acts to the Ministry of Agriculture, Fisheries and Food).

(2) For the purposes of this Act, any land which was immediately before the commencement of this Act for the time being placed or deemed to have been placed at the disposal of the Commissioners under the Forestry Act 1945 shall be treated as continuing after that commencement to be so placed by virtue of section 39(1) of this Act[4], without prejudice to the power of the Minister to make any other disposition with regard to that land.

5. The references to the Forestry Commissioners in section 48 of the Settled Land Act 1925[5] (which contains regulations respecting forestry leases) and in the definition of "forestry lease" in section 117 of that Act shall be construed as references to the Minister, and the reference in the said definition to the Forestry Act 1919[6] shall be construed as a reference to this Act.

6. Any power under any enactment to amend or repeal an enactment repealed by this Act includes power to amend or repeal the corresponding provision of this Act.

SCHEDULE 7

(Section 50.)

REPEALS AND SAVINGS

PART I

REPEALS

Not reproduced.

PART II

SAVINGS

1. The repeal of section 2 of the Forestry (Transfer of Woods) Act 1923[7] shall not affect any rights or liabilities of the Commissioners transferred to them under that section, in so far as any such rights and liabilities continued to subsist immediately before the commencement of this Act.

2. The repeal of section 4(5) of the Forestry Act 1945[8] shall not be taken as affecting the Minister's[9] obligation to hold land subject to any terms and conditions applicable by virtue of that subsection, so far as any obligation arising under that subsection continued to subsist immediately before the commencement of this Act; nor shall the said repeal alter the construction of any conveyance, lease or other instrument for whose construction the subsection had effect immediately before the said commencement.

[1] 1945 c. 35.
[2] S.I. 1965/319.
[3] S.I. 1967/156.
[4] P. 91 above.
[5] 1925 c. 18.

[6] 1919 c. 58.
[7] 1923 c. 21.
[8] 1945 c. 35.
[9] "Minister" defined by s. 49(1), p. 97 above.

3. The repeal of sections 1 to 4 of the Forestry Act 1947[1] shall not affect the application of any of those sections, or any part of them, for the purposes of—

the National Parks and Access to the Countryside Act 1949[2],
the Highways (Provision of Cattle Grids) Act 1950[3], or
the Highways Act 1959[4].

4. Notwithstanding the repeal of section 8(1) of the Crown Estate Act 1961[5], the powers of the Minister over land transferred as mentioned in that subsection shall not be subject to any restrictions which may have applied to the land as being part of the Royal forests, parks and chases or any of them.

[1] 1947 c. 21.
[2] P. 5 above.
[3] 1950 c. 24.

[4] 1959 c. 25.
[5] 1961 c. 55.

Countryside (Scotland) Act 1967

Ch. 86

An Act to make provision for the better enjoyment of the Scottish countryside, for the establishment of a Countryside Commission for Scotland and for the improvement of recreational and other facilities; to extend the powers of local planning authorities as respects land in their districts; to make financial provision with respect to the matters aforesaid; and for connected purposes.

[27th October 1967[1]]

Part I of the Countryside (Scotland) Act 1967, which contained provisions relating to the former Countryside Council for Scotland, has been repealed by the Natural Heritage (Scotland) Act 1991. The Countryside Council for Scotland, together with the Nature Conservancy Council for Scotland which was established under Part VII of the Environmental Protection Act 1990, have been dissolved. The nature conservation and countryside functions formerly carried out by these bodies are now exercised by Scottish Natural Heritage (SNH). For the establishment and functions of SNH see Part I of the Natural Heritage (Scotland) Act 1991, p. 245 below.

This Act now comprises the following parts:

Part II: Access to open country

This part is not reproduced.

Part III: Public paths and long-distance routes

This part is not reproduced

Part IV: Further powers of certain authorities

The following sections are reproduced from this part:

49A.   *Management agreements.*
58.   *Powers of the Forestry Commissioners.*
59.   *Extension of powers of Secretary of State under section 39 of the Forestry Act 1967.*

This part, which comprises sections 48–65, also makes provision for country parks, regional parks, camping sites and other recreational matters, byelaws and the improvement of waterways for recreation.

---

[1]   This Act came into force on 27 October 1967, the date of the Royal Assent.

Part V: General, financial and supplementary provisions

The following section is reproduced from this part:

66. *Conservation of natural beauty.*

....

Part IV: Further Powers of Certain Authorities

Management agreements

49A. (1) Scottish Natural Heritage may enter into an agreement with any person having an interest[1] in land[2] to do, or to secure the doing of, whatever in the opinion of the parties to the agreement may be necessary to secure the conservation and enhancement or to foster the understanding and enjoyment of the natural heritage of Scotland[3].

(2) A planning authority[4] may enter into an agreement with any person having an interest in land to do or to secure the doing of whatever in the opinion of the parties to the agreement may be necessary to preserve or enhance the natural beauty of the countryside or to promote the enjoyment of the countryside by the public.

(3) An agreement under subsection (1) or (2) above shall be known as a "management agreement".[5]

(4) A planning authority or Scottish Natural Heritage[6] may make such payments in respect of such agreements as are specified in the agreement.

(5) Any person, being the liferenter or the heir of entail, in possession of any land shall have power to enter into management agreements relating to the land or any part thereof.

(6) The Trusts (Scotland) Act 1921[7] shall have effect as if among the powers conferred on trustees by section 4 thereof (which relates to the general power of trustees) there were included a power to enter into management agreements relating to the trust estate or any part thereof.

(7) Subsections (8) to (10) of section 13 of this Act shall apply to management agreements as they apply to access agreements.

(8) Where any person having such an interest in any land as enables him to bind the land enters into any such agreement as aforesaid, the agreement may be registered either—

(a) in a case where the land affected by the agreement is registered in that Register, in the Land Register of Scotland, or

(b) in any other case, in the appropriate Division of the General Register of Sasines.

(9) Any agreement registered in terms of subsection (8) above shall be enforceable at the instance of the planning authority or of Scottish Natural Heritage, as the case may be, against persons deriving title to the land from the person who entered into the agreement; provided that any such agreement shall not be enforceable against a third party who shall have in good faith and for value acquired right (whether completed by infeftment or not) to the land prior to

---

[1] "Interest", in relation to land, includes any right over land, whether the right is exercisable by virtue of the ownership of an interest in land or by virtue of a licence or agreement, and in particular includes sporting and fishing rights: s. 78(1).

[2] "Land" includes land covered by water and, in relation to the acquisition or disposal of land by virtue of this Act, any right or interest in or over land: s. 78(1).

[3] For the definition of "the natural heritage of Scotland" in the Natural Heritage (Scotland) Act 1991 see s. 1(3) of that Act at p. 245 below.

[4] "Planning authority" means a general, regional or dis-

trict planning authority within the meaning of Part IX of the Local Government (Scotland) Act 1973: s. 78(1) as amended by the Local Government (Scotland) Act 1973 (c. 65), s. 172(2).

[5] Subsections (1)–(3) substituted by the Natural Heritage (Scotland) Act 1991 (c. 28), s. 27(1), sch. 10, para. 4(3). This amendment came into force on 1 April 1992: 1991/2633.

[6] Words "Scottish Natural Heritage" in this section substituted by the Natural Heritage (Scotland) Act 1991 (c. 28), s. 14(3). This amendment came into force on 1 April 1992: S.I. 1991/2633.

[7] 1921 c. 58.

the agreement being registered as aforesaid, or against any person deriving title from such third party.

(10) Notwithstanding the terms of any management agreement, it shall be open at any time to the parties to the agreement, or to persons deriving title from the parties, as the case may be, to agree to terminate it; and where any management agreement has been registered in terms of subsection (8) above, the subsequent agreement to terminate it shall be registered in the like manner.[1]

Powers of the Forestry Commissioners

58. (1) The Forestry Commissioners constituted under the Forestry Acts 1919 to 1945 (in this and the next succeeding section referred to as "the Commissioners") shall have the powers conferred on them by this section.

(2) The Commissioners may, on any land[2] placed at their disposal by the Secretary of State, provide, or arrange for or assist in the provision of tourist, recreational or sporting facilities and any equipment, facilities or works ancillary thereto, including without prejudice to that generality—

(a) accommodation for visitors;

(b) camping sites and caravan sites;

(c) places for meals and refreshments[3];

(d) picnic places, viewpoint stances, parking places, routes for nature study and footpaths;

(e) information and display centres;

(f) shops in connection with any of the aforesaid facilities;

(g) public conveniences;

and the Commissioners shall have power to make such charges as they think fit in connection with any of those facilities.

In this subsection "provide" includes manage, maintain and improve[4].

(3) The Commissioners' powers to make byelaws under section 46 of the Forestry Act 1967[5] shall include a power to make byelaws for regulating the reasonable use by the public of the facilities described in subsection (2) above, and in relation to any such matter as is described in section 54(2) above.

(4) The Commission shall have power to act as agent for the Commissioners in the exercise of their powers under subsection (2) above.

(5) *and* (6) *These subsections amend sections 9(6) and 41 of the Forestry Act 1967. These amendments are noted at the Act at pages 73 and 93 above.*

Extension of powers of Secretary of State under section 39 of the Forestry Act 1967

59. The power of the Secretary of State under section 39 of the Forestry Act 1967[6] to acquire land[7] shall include power to acquire land in proximity to land placed by him at the disposal of the Commissioners[8] where it appears to him that the land which it is proposed to acquire is

---

[1] Subsections (4)–(10) inserted by the Countryside (Scotland) Act 1981 (c. 44), s. 9. This amendment came into force on 5 November 1981: S.I. 1981/1614.

[2] "Land" includes land covered by water and, in relation to the acquisition or disposal of land by virtue of this Act, any right or interest in or over land: s. 78(1).

[3] "Refreshments" includes alcoholic liquor within the meaning of the Licensing (Scotland) Act 1976: s. 78(1) amended by the Licensing (Scotland) Act 1976 (c. 66), s. 136(1), sch. 7, para. 6.

[4] For the powers of the Secretary of State to exercise the powers conferred on the Forestry Commissioners by this subsection see s. 60 of this Act.

[5] P. 95 above.

[6] P. 91 above.

[7] "Land" includes land covered by water and, in relation to the acquisition or disposal of land by virtue of this Act, any right or interest in or over land: s. 78(1).

[8] "The Commissioners" means the Forestry Commissioners: s. 58(1), above.

reasonably required by the Commissioners for the provision of such facilities are are mentioned in subsection (2) of the last foregoing section.[1]

Part V: General, Financial and Supplementary

Conservation of natural beauty

66. In the exercise of their functions[2] relating to land[3] under any enactment[4] every Minister, government department and public body[5] shall have regard to the desirability of conserving the natural heritage of Scotland within the meaning of the Natural Heritage (Scotland) Act 1991.[6]

---

[1] Former words "and he shall have power to dispose of the land whether by way of sale, feu, lease or excambion where in his opinion it is no longer so required or where in his opinion such disposal is desirable for the purpose of securing the provision of any of those facilities by any other other body or person" repealed by the Forestry Act 1981 (c. 39), s. 6(2), sch. This amendment came into force on 27 July 1981, the date of the Royal Assent.

[2] "Function" includes power and duty: s. 78(1).

[3] "Land" includes land covered by water and, in relation to the acquisition or disposal of land by virtue of this Act, any right or interest in or over land: s. 78(1).

[4] Under s. 78(1) "enactment" has the same meaning as in the Town and Country Planning (Scotland) Act 1947 which is now construed as the Town and Country Planning (Scotland) Act 1972. Under s. 275(1) of the 1972 Act enactment "includes an enactment in any local or private Act of Parliament, and an order, rule, regulation, byelaw or scheme made under an Act of Parliament, including an order or scheme confirmed by Parliament".

[5] "Public body" includes any local authority, planning authority or statutory undertaker, and any trustees, commissioners, board or other persons who as a public body and not for their own profit act under any enactment for the improvement of any place or the production or supply of any commodity or service: s. 78(1) amended by the Local Government (Scotland) Act 1973 (c. 65), s. 172(2). The following are deemed to be statutory undertakers for the purposes of this section:

A public gas supplier Gas Act (c. 44), s. 67(1), sch. 7, para. 2(1)(xx).

The holder of a licence under the Electricity Act 1989 who is entitled to exercise any power conferred by sch. 3 or 4 of that Act: Electricity Act 1989 (c. 29), s. 112(1), sch. 16, para. 2(1).

Under s. 78(1) "statutory undertakers" has the meaning assigned to it by s. 113 of the Town and Country Planning (Scotland) Act 1947 which is construed as a reference to s. 275(1) of the Town and Country Planning (Scotland) Act 1972.

[6] Words "the natural heritage of Scotland within the meaning of the Natural Heritage (Scotland) Act 1991" inserted by the Natural Heritage (Scotland) Act 1991 (c. 28), s. 27(1), sch. 10, para. 4(7). This amendment came into force on 1 April 1992: S.I. 1991/2633. "The natural heritage of Scotland" is defined by s. 1(3) of the 1991 Act at p. 245 below.

Countryside Act 1968

Ch. 41

Arrangement of sections

Traffic regulation orders

Financial

Supplemental

Countryside Act 1968

An Act to enlarge the functions of the Commission established under the National Parks and Access to the Countryside Act 1949, to confer new powers on local authorities and other bodies for the conservation and enhancement of natural beauty and for the benefit of those resorting to the countryside and to make other provision for the matters dealt with in the Act of 1949 and generally as respects the countryside, and to amend the law about trees and woodlands, and footpaths and bridleways, and other public paths.

[3rd July 1968[1]]

The Countryside Commission

General functions of the Commission

1. (1) The National Parks Commission shall in future be known as the "Countryside Commission" and shall exercise functions in relation to England.

(1A) The functions of the Countryside Commission[2] (in this Act referred to as "the Commission") in England and the corresponding functions of the Countryside Council for Wales[3] (in this Act referred to as "the Council") in Wales shall be enlarged in accordance with this Act.[4]

(2) The functions conferred by this Act on the said Commission (in this Act referred to as "the Commission") are to be exercised for the conservation and enhancement of the natural beauty and amenity of the countryside[5], and encouraging the provision and improvement, for persons resorting to the countryside, of facilities for the enjoyment of the countryside and of open-air recreation and the study of nature[6] in the countryside; and the purposes for which the functions of the Council in Wales are to be exercised are the corresponding purposes specified in section 130(2) of the Environmental Protection Act 1990.[7]

(3) The Commission and the Council shall each[8] have power—

(a) to make such charges for any of their services as they think fit,

(b) to accept any gift or contribution made to them for the purposes of any of their functions, and, subject to the terms of the gift or contribution and to the provisions of the National Parks and Access to the Countryside Act 1949[9] (in this Act referred to as "the Act of 1949") and this Act, to apply it for those purposes, and

(c) to do all such things as are incidental to, or conducive to the attainment of the purposes of, any of their functions.

---

[1] This Act came into force on 3 August 1968: s. 50(3), p. 133 below.

[2] For further statutory provision relating to the Countryside Commission see the National Parks and Access to the Countryside Act 1949, s. 1, p. 7 above and the Wildlife and Countryside Act 1981, s. 47, sch. 13, pp. 186–211 below.

[3] The Countryside Council for Wales is established by the Environmental Protection Act 1990 (c. 43), s. 128, p. 229 below.

[4] Subsections (1) and (1A) substituted by the Environmental Protection Act 1990 (c. 43), s. 130(1), sch. 8, para. 2(2)(a). This amendment came into force on 1 April 1991: S.I. 1991/685.

[5] For the construction of references to the conservation of the natural beauty of an area see s. 49(4), p. 133 below.

[6] Words "and the study of nature" inserted by the Environmental Protection Act 1990 (c. 43), s. 130(1), sch. 8, para. 2(2)(b)(i).

[7] P. 230 below. Words "; and the purposes . . . Environmental Protection Act 1990" inserted by the Environmental Protection Act 1990 (c. 43), s. 130(1), sch. 8, para. 2(2)(b)(ii).

[8] Words "and the Council shall each" substituted by the Environmental Protection Act 1990 (c. 43), s. 130(1), sch. 8, para. 2(2)(c).

[9] P. 5 above.

(4) *Repealed by the Wildlife and Countryside Act 1981 (c. 69), s. 73(1), sch. 17, pt. II. This amendment came into force on 28 September 1982: S.I. 1982/1217.*

(5) In section 1[1] of the Act of 1949 for the words "National Parks Commission" there shall be substituted the words "Countryside Commission".[2,3]

(6) *Repealed by the House of Commons Disqualifications Act 1975 (c. 24), s. 10(2), sch. 3. This amendment came into force on 8 May 1975, the date of the Royal Assent.*

New functions of the Commission

2. (1) The Commission[4] and the Council[5] each[6] shall have the general duties imposed by this section, but nothing in this section shall be construed as modifying the effect of any provision of this Act or of the Act of 1949[7] whereby any general or specific power or duty is conferred or imposed on the Commission or Council[8], or whereby an obligation is imposed on any other person to consult with the Commission or Council.[8]

(2) The Commission and the Council[9] shall keep under review all matters relating to—

(a) the provision and improvement of facilities for the enjoyment of the countryside,

(b) the conservation and enhancement of the natural beauty and amenity of the countryside[10], and

(c) the need to secure public access to the countryside for the purposes of open-air recreation,

and shall consult with such local planning authorities[11] and other bodies as appear to the Commission or Council[12] to have an interest in those matters.

(3) The Commission and the Council[13] shall encourage, assist, concert or promote the implementation of any proposals with respect to those matters made by any person or body, being proposals which the Commission or Council[12] consider to be suitable.

(4) The Commission and the Council[14] shall advise any Minister[15] having functions under this Act, or any other Minister or any public body[16], on such matters relating to the countryside as he

---

[1] Former words "and 2(1)" repealed by the Wildlife and Countryside Act 1981 (c. 69), s. 73(1), sch. 17, pt. II.

[2] The amendment made to s. 1 of the National Parks and Access to the Countryside Act 1949, p. 7 above, by the Environmental Protection Act 1990 (c. 43) includes this substitution.

[3] Former words "and in section 4(1) of the Act of 1949 (Commission's annual report) the reference to the Commission's functions under the Act of 1949 shall include a reference to their functions under this Act" repealed by the Wildlife and Countryside Act 1981 (c. 69), s. 73(1), sch. 17, pt. II.

[4] "The Commission" means the Countryside Commission: s. 49(2), p. 132 below.

[5] "The Council" means the Countryside Council for Wales: s. 49(2), p. 132 below.

[6] Words "and the Council shall each" substituted by the Environmental Protection Act 1990 (c. 43), s. 130(1), sch. 8, para. 2(3)(a). This amendment came into force on 1 April 1991: S.I. 1991/685.

[7] The National Parks and Access to the Countryside Act 1949 (c. 97), p. 5 above.

[8] Words "or Council" inserted by the Environmental Protection Act 1990 (c. 43), s. 130(1), sch. 8, para. 2(3)(b).

[9] Words "and the Council" inserted by the Environmental Protection Act 1990 (c. 43), s. 130(1), sch. 8, para. 2(3)(b).

[10] For the construction of references to the conservation of the natural beauty of an area see s. 49(4), p. 133 below.

[11] For statutory provisions in respect of local planning authorities see the Town and Country Planning Act 1990 (c. 8), Part I and the Local Government Act 1972 (c. 70), s. 184, sch. 17, pt. I. The Town and Country Planning Act 1990 applies by virtue of s. 49(1), p. 132 below, National Parks and Access to the Countryside Act 1949 (c. 97), s. 114(1) and the Planning (Consequential Provisions) Act 1990 (c. 11), s. 2.

[12] Words "or Council" inserted by the Environmental Protection Act 1990 (c. 43), s. 130(1), sch. 8, para. 2(3)(b).

[13] Words "and the Council" inserted by the Environmental Protection Act 1990 (c. 43), s. 130(1), sch. 8, para. 2(3)(b).

[14] Words "and the Council" inserted by the Environmental Protection Act 1990 (c. 43), s. 130(1), sch. 8, para. 2(3)(c).

[15] "The Minister" defined by s. 49(2), p. 132 below.

[16] "Public body" defined by s. 49(2), p. 132 below. The definition includes statutory undertakers. The National Rivers Authority, every water undertaker and every sewerage undertaker are deemed to be statutory undertakers for the purposes of this section in so far as references in this section to a public body are to be construed as references to a statutory undertaker: Water Act 1989 (c. 15), s. 190(1), sch. 25, para. 1(1), (2).

or they may refer to the Commission or Council[1], or as the Commission or Council[1] may think fit.

(5) Where it appears to the Commission or to the Council[2] that the provision and improvement of facilities for enjoyment of the countryside or the conservation and enhancement of the natural beauty and amenity of the countryside presents special problems or requires special professional or technical skill, the Commission or, as the case may be, the Council[3]—

(a) shall notify their opinion to the appropriate local planning authority or other public body, and

(b) on the application of any such authority or other body in any case where it appears to the Commission or Council[4] expedient having regard to the provisions of section 1(2) of this Act, and to the provisions of section 5(1) of the Act of 1949[5] (general provisions as respects National Parks), shall place the services of officers or servants of the Commission or Council[4], or the services of consultants engaged by the Commission or Council[4], at the disposal of the authority or other body for such period as may be agreed between them, and on such terms as to payment or otherwise, as may be so agreed with the approval of the Minister.

(6) The Commission and the Council[6] shall make to local planning authorities and other public bodies, as respects the exercise of the powers of making byelaws conferred by this Act and the Act of 1949, recommendations as to the matters in respect of which byelaws should be made.

(7) The Commission and the Council[7] shall carry out, or commission the carrying out of, such inquiries, investigations or researches, either on their own account or jointly with other persons, as the Commission or Council[8] may deem necessary or expedient for the purposes of any of their functions.

(8) The Commission and the Council[7] shall provide, or assist in the provision of, publicity and information services relating to the countryside, to places of beauty or interest therein, or the functions of the Commission or Council[8], and shall take such steps as appear to them expedient for securing that suitable methods of publicity are used for the prevention of damage in the countryside and for informing persons resorting to the countryside of their rights and obligations.[9]

(9) The Commission and the Council[7] shall make to the Minister such recommendations as the Commission or Council[8] think proper in respect of applications by local authorities for Exchequer grants under[10] the Act of 1949.

....

3. (1) *Superseded by s. 47 of the Wildlife and Countryside Act 1981 (c. 69), p. 186 below, and repealed by s. 73(1), sch. 17, pt. II of that Act. This amendment came into force on 1 April 1982: S.I. 1982/327.*

....

Experimental projects or schemes

[1] Words "or Council" inserted by the Environmental Protection Act 1990 (c. 43), s. 130(1), sch. 8, para. 2(3)(c).

[2] Words "or to the Council" inserted by the Environmental Protection Act 1990 (c. 43), s. 130(1), sch. 8, para. 2(3)(d).

[3] Words "or, as the case may be, the Council" inserted by the Environmental Protection Act 1990 (c. 43), s. 130(1), sch. 8, para. 2(3)(d).

[4] Words "or Council" inserted by the Environmental Protection Act 1990 (c. 43), s. 130(1), sch. 8, para. 2(3)(e).

[5] P. 8 above.

[6] Words "and the Council" inserted by the Environmental Protection Act 1990 (c. 43), s. 130(1), sch. 8, para. 2(3)(f).

[7] Words "and the Council" inserted by the Environmental Protection Act 1990 (c. 43), s. 130(1), sch. 8, para. 2(3)(g).

[8] Words "or Council" inserted by the Environmental Protection Act 1990 (c. 43), s. 130(1), sch. 8, para. 2(3)(g).

[9] Words "informing persons . . . obligations" inserted by the Wildlife and Countryside Act 1981 (c. 69), s. 72(7). This amendment came into force on 30 November 1981: the Wildlife and Countryside Act 1981, s. 74(2).

[10] Former words "this Act or" repealed by the Local Government Act 1974 (c. 9), s. 42(2), sch. 8. This amendment came into force on 1 April 1974: S.I. 1974/335.

4. (1) The Commission[1] and the Council,[2,3] after consultation with such local authorities and other bodies as appear to the Commission or Council[4] to have an interest, may from time to time make and carry out or promote the carrying out of any experimental scheme designed to facilitate the enjoyment of the countryside, or to conserve or enhance its natural beauty[5] or amenity, which—

(a) in relation to the countryside generally or to any particular area involves the development or application of new methods, concepts or techniques, or the application or further development of existing methods, concepts or techniques; and

(b) is designed to illustrate the appropriateness of the scheme in question for the countryside generally or for any particular area.[6]

(3) For the purpose of their functions under the foregoing provisions of this section the Commission or, as the case may be, the Council[7] may—

(a) with the approval of the Minister[8] acquire land[9] by agreement, or may be authorised by the Minister in a particular case to acquire land compulsorily,

(b) hold and manage land, and with the approval of the Minister and subject to the subsequent provisions of this section, dispose of or otherwise deal with land,

(c) erect buildings and carry out works or other operations on land,

(d) provide equipment, facilities and services on or in connection with land or with the use of land,

(e) hold, manage, maintain, hire, let or otherwise dispose of such works, equipment, facilities or services,

(f) exercise any powers to carry out work or to provide facilities or services conferred by this Act or the Act of 1949[10] on local authorities or local planning authorities[11],

(g) with the approval of the Minister and the Treasury, acquire by agreement and carry on or set up and carry on, directly or through an agent, or themselves carry on as agent, any business or undertaking relevant to the experimental project or scheme, and, subject to the approval of the Minister and the Treasury, may dispose of any such business or undertaking.

(4) The disposal of land under this section may be by way of sale or exchange, or by the letting of land or the granting of any interest[12] in or right over land, but the Commission or Council[13] shall not under this section dispose of land by way of gift.

(5) The powers conferred by paragraphs (c) to (f) of subsection (3) above may be exercised by the Commission or by the Council[14]—

(a) on land belonging to them, or

---

[1] "The Commission" means the Countryside Commission: s. 49(2), p. 132 below.

[2] "The Council" means the Countryside Council for Wales: s. 49(2), p. 132 below.

[3] Words "and the Council" inserted by the Environmental Protection Act 1990 (c. 43), s. 130(1), sch. 8, para. 2(4)(a). This amendment came into force on 1 April 1991: S.I. 1991/685.

[4] Words "or Council" inserted by the Environmental Protection Act 1990 (c. 43), s. 130(1), sch. 8, para. 2(4)(a).

[5] For the construction of references to the conservation of the natural beauty of an area see s. 49(4), p. 133 below.

[6] This subsection substitutes former subsections (1) and (2): Wildlife and Countryside Act 1981 (c. 69), s. 40. This amendment came into force on 30 November 1981: Wildlife and Countryside Act 1981 (c. 69), s. 74(2).

[7] Words "or, as the case may be, the Council" inserted by the Environmental Protection Act 1990 (c. 43), s. 130(1), sch. 8, para. 2(4)(b).

[8] "The Minister" defined by s. 49(2), p. 132 below.

[9] "Land" defined by s. 49(2), p. 132 below.

[10] The National Parks and Access to the Countryside Act 1949 (c. 97), p. 5 above.

[11] For statutory provisions in respect of local planning authorities see the Town and Country Planning Act 1990 (c. 8), Part I and the Local Government Act 1972 (c. 70), s. 184, sch. 17, pt. I. The Town and Country Planning Act 1990 applies by virtue of s. 49(1), p. 132 below, National Parks and Access to the Countryside Act 1949 (c. 97), s. 114(1) and the Planning (Consequential Provisions) Act 1990 (c. 11), s. 2.

[12] "Interest" defined by s. 114(1), National Parks and Access to the Countryside Act 1949, p. 38 above: s. 49(1), p. 132 below applies the definition in s. 114 of the 1949 Act.

[13] Words "or Council" inserted by the Environmental Protection Act 1990 (c. 43), s. 130(1), sch. 8, para. 2(4)(c).

[14] Words "or by the Council" inserted by the Environmental Protection Act 1990 (c. 43), s. 130(1), sch. 8, para. 2(4)(d).

(b) on such terms as may be agreed with the owners[1] and any other persons whose authority is required for the purpose, on other land,

and an agreement under paragraph (b) above may provide for the making by the Commission or Council[2] of payments in consideration of the making of the agreement and payments by way of contribution towards expenditure incurred by the persons making the agreement in consequence thereof.

(6) The provisions of this section, except for that authorising compulsory purchase of land, shall have effect only for the purpose of removing any limitation imposed by law on the capacity of the Commission or of the Council[3], and shall not authorise any act or omission on the part of the Commission or Council[4] which, apart from the said provisions of this section, would be actionable at the suit of any person on any ground other than such a limitation.

....

5. *Repealed by the Local Government Act 1974 (c. 7), ss. 42(2), sch. 8. This amendment came into force on 1 April 1974: S.I. 1974/335. S. 9 of the 1974 Act supersedes this section and makes provision for the Countryside Commission to give financial assistance by way of grant or loan in respect of the attainment of any of the purposes of this Act or the National Parks and Access to the Countryside Act 1949.*

New powers of local authorities

6–10. *These sections, which are not reproduced, contain provisions relating to country parks and commons, powers exercisable over or near common land, and camping and picnic sites.*

....

Nature conservation, National Parks and access to open country

Conservation of natural beauty

11. In the exercise of their functions relating to land[5] under any enactment every Minister, government department and public body[6] shall have regard to the desirability of conserving the natural beauty and amenity of the countryside[7].

....

Facilities in or near National Parks

12. (1) A local planning authority[8] whose area consists of or includes the whole or any part of a National Park[9] may, at the request of, and in accordance with terms laid down by, the Commission or, as the case may be, the Council[10], make arrangements for securing the provision in the area of the local planning authority (whether by the authority or by other persons) of study

---

[1] "Owners" defined by s. 114(1), National Parks and Access to the Countryside Act 1949, p. 38 above: s. 49(1) below applies the definition in s. 114 of the 1949 Act.

[2] Words "or Council" inserted by the Environmental Protection Act 1990 (c. 43), s. 130(1), sch. 8, para. 2(4)(d).

[3] Words "or of the Council" inserted by the Environmental Protection Act 1990 (c. 43), s. 130(1), sch. 8, para. 2(4)(e).

[4] Words "or Council" inserted by the Environmental Protection Act 1990 (c. 43), s. 130(1), sch. 8, para. 2(4)(e).

[5] "Land" defined by s. 49(2), p. 132 below.

[6] "Public body" defined by s. 49(2), p. 132 below. The definition includes statutory undertakers. The following are deemed to be statutory undertakers for the purposes of this section:

A public gas supplier: Gas Act (c. 44), s. 67(1), sch. 7, para. 2(1)(xxii).

The holder of a licence under the Electricity Act 1989 who is entitled to exercise any power conferred by sch. 3 or 4 of that Act: Electricity Act 1989 (c. 29), s. 112(1), sch. 16,

para. 2(1).

[7] For the construction of references to the conservation of the natural beauty of an area see s. 49(4), p. 133 below.

[8] For statutory provisions in respect of local planning authorities see the Town and Country Planning Act 1990 (c. 8), Part I and the Local Government Act 1972 (c. 70), s. 184, sch. 17, pt. I. The Town and Country Planning Act 1990 applies by virtue of s. 49(1), p. 132 below, National Parks and Access to the Countryside Act 1949 (c. 97), s. 114(1) and the Planning (Consequential Provisions) Act 1990 (c. 11), s. 2.

[9] "National Park" defined by s. 114(1), National Parks and Access to the Countryside Act 1949, by which it has the meaning assigned to it by s. 5(3), p. 8 above: s. 49(1), p. 132 below applies the definition in s. 114 of the 1949 Act.

[10] Words "or, as the case may be, the Council" inserted by the Environmental Protection Act 1990 (c. 43), s. 130(1), sch. 8, para. 2(6)(a). This amendment came into force on 1 April 1991: S.I. 1991/685.

centres and other facilities for learning about the history, natural features, flora and fauna of the National Park and the objects of architectural, archaeological or historical interest therein; and section 12 of the Act of 1949[1] (provision of facilities in National Parks) shall have effect as if the functions of local planning authorities under this subsection were functions conferred by subsection (1) of that section.

Expenses incurred by a local planning authority under this subsection shall be expenses towards which the Commission or the Council[2] may make contributions under section 86 of the Act of 1949[3] (information services) and no grant shall be payable under paragraph (a) or paragraph (e) of section 97(1) of the Act of 1949[4] in respect of expenses incurred by the local planning authority under this subsection, or expenses in or in connection with the acquisition of land[5] for the purposes of this subsection.

(2) The functions conferred by subsection (1) of the said section 12 of the Act of 1949 shall include the making of arrangements for securing the provision in their area (whether by the authority or by other persons)—

(a) of public sanitary conveniences in proper and convenient situations, and

(b) of receptacles for refuse or litter, and services for the regular emptying and cleansing of those receptacles.

(3) A local planning authority whose area consists of or includes any part of a National Park which is bounded by the sea, or by any waterway[6] which is not part of the sea, may, on land which is in or in the neighbourhood of the National Park, carry out such work and do such other things as may appear to them necessary or expedient for facilitating the use of the waters so adjoining the National Park by the public for sailing, boating, bathing and fishing and other forms of recreation:

Provided that a local planning authority shall not under this subsection provide facilities of any description except in cases where it appears to them that the facilities of that description are inadequate or unsatisfactory.

(4) The works which a local planning authority may carry out under subsection (3) above include the construction of jetties and other works wholly or partly in the sea or in other waters.

The local planning authority, before acting under this subsection, shall consult with and seek the consent of the National Rivers Authority and such[7] authorities, being authorities which under any enactment have functions relating to the part of the sea or other waters in question, as the Minister[8] may either generally or in any particular case direct, and Schedule 1 to this Act[9] shall have effect where any authority so consulted withhold their consent.

(5) A local planning authority may make byelaws regulating the use of works carried out by them under subsection (3) above in the waters bounding a National Park and of any facilities or services provided in connection with the works, but before making any such byelaws the local planning authority shall consult the Commission (if the National Park is in England) or the Council (if the National Park is in Wales)[10].

Provided that byelaws made under this subsection shall not interfere with the exercise of any functions relating to the waters or land to which the byelaws apply which are exercisable by any authority under any enactment.

Section 106 of the Act of 1949[11] (supplementary provisions as to byelaws) shall have effect as if byelaws under this subsection were byelaws under that Act.

---

[1] P. 12 above.
[2] Words "or the Council" inserted by the Environmental Protection Act 1990 (c. 43), s. 130(1), sch. 8, para. 2(6)(a).
[3] P. 21 above.
[4] P. 27 above.
[5] "Land" defined by s. 49(2), p. 132 below.
[6] "Waterway" defined by s. 114(1), National Parks and Access to the Countryside Act 1949, p. 38 above: s. 49(1), p. 132 below applies the definition in s. 114 of the 1949 Act.
[7] Words "of the National Rivers Authority and such" substituted by the Water Act 1989 (c. 15), s. 190(1), sch. 25, para. 37(2). This amendment came into force on 1 September 1989: S.I. 1989/1146.
[8] "The Minister" defined by s. 49(2), p. 132 below.
[9] P. 133 below.
[10] Words "(if the National Park . . . Wales)" inserted by the Environmental Protection Act 1990 (c. 43), s. 130(1), sch. 8, para. 2(6)(b).
[11] P. 33 above.

Expenses incurred by a local planning authority under this subsection shall be expenses towards which the Commission or the Council[2] may make contributions under section 86 of the Act of 1949[3] (information services) and no grant shall be payable under paragraph (*a*) or paragraph (*e*) of section 97(1) of the Act of 1949[4] in respect of expenses incurred by the local planning authority under this subsection, or expenses in or in connection with the acquisition of land[5] for the purposes of this subsection.

(2) The functions conferred by subsection (1) of the said section 12 of the Act of 1949 shall include the making of arrangements for securing the provision in their area (whether by the authority or by other persons)—

(*a*) of public sanitary conveniences in proper and convenient situations, and

(*b*) of receptacles for refuse or litter, and services for the regular emptying and cleansing of those receptacles.

(3) A local planning authority whose area consists of or includes any part of a National Park which is bounded by the sea, or by any waterway[6] which is not part of the sea, may, on land which is in or in the neighbourhood of the National Park, carry out such work and do such other things as may appear to them necessary or expedient for facilitating the use of the waters so adjoining the National Park by the public for sailing, boating, bathing and fishing and other forms of recreation:

Provided that a local planning authority shall not under this subsection provide facilities of any description except in cases where it appears to them that the facilities of that description are inadequate or unsatisfactory.

(4) The works which a local planning authority may carry out under subsection (3) above include the construction of jetties and other works wholly or partly in the sea or in other waters.

The local planning authority, before acting under this subsection, shall consult with and seek the consent of the National Rivers Authority and such[7] authorities, being authorities which under any enactment have functions relating to the part of the sea or other waters in question, as the Minister[8] may either generally or in any particular case direct, and Schedule 1 to this Act[9] shall have effect where any authority so consulted withhold their consent.

(5) A local planning authority may make byelaws regulating the use of works carried out by them under subsection (3) above in the waters bounding a National Park and of any facilities or services provided in connection with the works, but before making any such byelaws the local planning authority shall consult the Commission (if the National Park is in England) or the Council (if the National Park is in Wales)[10].

Provided that byelaws made under this subsection shall not interfere with the exercise of any functions relating to the waters or land to which the byelaws apply which are exercisable by any authority under any enactment.

Section 106 of the Act of 1949[11] (supplementary provisions as to byelaws) shall have effect as if byelaws under this subsection were byelaws under that Act.

(6) The Act of 1949 shall have effect as if subsections (3) and (4) above formed part of section

---

[1] P. 13 above.
[2] P. 13 above.
[3] 1949 c. 74.
[4] S. 9 of the Harbours Act 1964 is repealed by the Ports (Finance) Act 1985 (c. 30), s. 6, sch.
[5] For statutory provisions in respect of local planning authorities see the Town and Country Planning Act 1990 (c. 8), Part I and the Local Government Act 1972 (c. 70), s. 184, sch. 17, pt. I. The Town and Country Planning Act 1990 applies by virtue of s. 49(1), p. 132 below, National Parks and Access to the Countryside Act 1949 (c. 97), s. 114(1) and the Planning (Consequential Provisions) Act 1990 (c. 11), s. 2.

[6] "National Park" defined by s. 114(1), National Parks and Access to the Countryside Act 1949, by which it has the meaning assigned to it by s. 5(3), p. 8 above: s. 49(1), p. 132 below applies the definition in s. 114 of the 1949 Act.
[7] "Lake" defined by subsection (13) below.
[8] "Boat" defined by s. 49(2), p. 132 below.
[9] For the construction of references to the conservation of the natural beauty of an area see s. 49(4), p. 133 below.
[10] Pp.7–8 above.
[11] Words "(if the National Park . . . in Wales)" inserted by the Environmental Protection Act 1990 (c. 43), s. 130(1), sch. 8, para. 2(7). This amendment came into force on 1 April 1991: S.I. 1991/685.

(5) Byelaws under this section shall not be made so as to extinguish any public right of way over any waters, but, except as otherwise expressly provided, any byelaws under this section shall apply to persons exercising any such public right of way as they apply to other persons.

(6) Byelaws under this section—

(a) shall be of no effect if and in so far as inconsistent with any rules under the Merchant Shipping Act 1894[1] which are in force as respects the water to which the byelaws apply.

(b) shall not interfere with any functions relating to the water or land[2] to which the byelaws apply which are exercisable by any authority under any enactment.

(7) This section shall not apply to any lake owned or managed by any statutory undertakers[3].

(8) Section 106 of the Act of 1949[4] (supplementary provisions as to byelaws) shall have effect as if byelaws under this section were byelaws under that Act.

(9) Subsections (1) and (2), and subject to the next following subsection subsection (4), of section 92 of the Act of 1949[5] (appointment of wardens of land for which byelaws may be made under section 90 of that Act[6]) shall have effect as if the power of making byelaws conferred by this section was contained in the said section 90.

(10) For the purpose of securing compliance with any byelaws made under this section, a warden appointed under the said section 92 as applied by this section may enter upon any land, or go on any water, whether or not within the area where the byelaws are in force.

(11) Where two or more local planning authorities' areas consist of or include part of a National Park, the powers conferred by this section may be exercised by them, or any of them, jointly, or may by agreement between them be exercised by one local planning authority in the part of the National Park in the area of another.

(12) Byelaws made by a local planning authority under this section may be enforced by any local authority in the area of that other local authority.

(13) In this section "lake" includes any expanse of water other than a river or canal.

....

14. *Superseded by s. 42 of the Wildlife and Countryside Act 1981 (c. 69), p. 183 below, and repealed by s. 73(1), sch. 17, pt. I of that Act. This amendment came into force on 30 November 1981: s. 74(2).*

....

Areas of special scientific interest

15. (1) This section has effect as respects land[7,8] which is or forms part of an area which in the opinion of the Nature Conservancy Council[9] (in this section referred to as "the Council") is of special interest by reason of its flora, fauna, or geological or physiographical features.

(2) Where, for the purpose of conserving those flora, fauna or geological or physiographical features, it appears to the Council expedient[10] to do so, the Council may enter into an agreement with the owners[11], lessees and occupiers of any such land (or of any adjacent

---

[1] 1894 c. 60.

[2] "Land" defined by s. 49(2), p. 132 below.

[3] Words "managed by any statutory undertakers" substituted by the Water Act 1989 (c. 15), s. 190(1), sch. 25, para. 37(3). This amendment came into force on 1 September 1989: S.I. 1989/1146. The National Rivers Authority, every water undertaker and every sewerage undertaker are deemed to be statutory undertakers for the purposes of this section: Water Act 1989, s. 190(1), sch. 25, para. 1(1) and (2).

[4] P. 33 above.

[5] P. 26 above,

[6] P. 25 above.

[7] "Land" defined by s. 49(2), p. 132 below.

[8] Former words "which is not for the time being managed as a nature reserve but" repealed by the Wildlife and Countryside Act 1981 (c. 69), ss. 72(8), 73(1), sch. 17, pt. I.

This amendment came into force on 30 November 1981: s. 74(2).

[9] "Nature Conservancy Council" and "the Council" defined by subsection (6A) below. Words "Nature Conservancy Council" substituted by the Nature Conservancy Council Act 1973 (c. 54), s. 1(1)(b), 1(7), sch. 1, para. 9. This amendment came into force on 1 November 1973: S.I. 1973/1721.

[10] Former words "in the national interest" repealed by the Environmental Protection Act 1990 (c. 43), ss. 132(1)(a), 162(2), sch. 9, para. 4(2)(a), sch. 16, pt. VI. This amendment came into force on 1 April 1991: S.I. 1991/685.

[11] "Owners" defined by s. 114(1), National Parks and Access to the Countryside Act 1949, p. 38 above: s. 49(1), p. 132 below applies the definition in s. 114 of the 1949 Act.

land)[1] which imposes restrictions on the exercise of rights over land by the persons who can be bound by the agreement.

(3) Any such agreement—

(a) may provide for the carrying out on the land of such work and the doing thereon of such other things as may be expedient for the purposes of the agreement,

(b) may provide for any of the matters mentioned in paragraph (a) above being carried out, or for the cost thereof being defrayed, either by the owners or other persons, or by the Council, or partly in one way and partly in another, and

(c) may contain such other provisions as to the making of payments by the Council as may be specified in the agreement.

(4) Where section 79 of the Law of Property Act 1925[2] (burden of covenant running with the land) applies to any such restrictions as are mentioned in subsection (2) of this section, the Council shall have the like rights as respects the enforcement of the restrictions as if the Council had at all material times been the absolute owner in possession of ascertained land adjacent to the land in respect of which the restriction is sought to be enforced, and capable of being benefited by the restriction, and the restriction had been expressed to be for the benefit of that adjacent land.

Section 84 of the Law of Property Act 1925 (discharge or modification of restrictive covenants) shall not apply to such a restriction.

(5) Schedule 2 to the Forestry Act 1967[3] (powers of tenants for life and other limited owners to enter into forestry dedication covenants or agreements) shall apply to any agreement made in pursuance of this section as it applies to such a covenant or agreement.

(6) This section shall apply to Scotland but there shall be substituted for subsection (4) the following subsection—

(4) An agreement under this section may be recorded in the Register of Sasines, and if so recorded shall be enforceable at the instance of the Council against any person having an interest[4] in the land and against any person deriving title from him:

Provided that such an agreement shall not be enforceable against any third party who shall have in good faith and for value acquired right (whether completed by infeftment or not) to his interest in the land prior to the agreement being recorded as aforesaid, or against any person deriving title from such third party.

(6A) In this section references to "the Nature Conservancy Council" or "the Council" are references to the Nature Conservancy Council for England,[5] Scottish Natural Heritage[6] or the Council,[7] according as the land in question is in England, Scotland or Wales.[8]

(7) The Act of 1949 shall have effect as if this section were included in Part III of that Act[9,10].

....

16–20. *Sections 16, 18 and 20, which are not reproduced, relate to access agreements and orders made under the provisions of Part V of the National Parks and Access to the Countryside Act*

[1] Words "(or of any adjacent land)" inserted by the Environmental Protection Act 1990 (c. 43), s. 132(1)(a), sch. 9, para. 4(2)(a).

[2] 1925 c. 20.

[3] P. 99 above.

[4] "Interest" defined by s. 114(1), National Parks and Access to the Countryside Act 1949, p. 38 above: s. 49(1), p. 132 below applies the definition in s. 114 of the 1949 Act.

[5] The Nature Conservancy Council for England, also known as English Nature, is established by the Environmental Protection Act 1990 (c. 43), s. 128, p. 229 below.

[6] Scottish Natural Heritage is established by the Natural Heritage (Scotland) Act 1991 (c. 28), s. 1, p. 245 below.

Words "Scottish Natural Heritage" substituted by the Natural Heritage (Scotland) Act 1991 (c. 28), s. 4(6), sch. 2, para. 3. This amendment came into force on 1 April 1992: S.I. 1991/2633.

[7] "The Council" means the Countryside Council for Wales: s. 49(2), p. 132 below. The Council is established by the Environmental Protection Act 1990 (c. 43), s. 128, p. 229 below.

[8] This subsection inserted by the Environmental Protection Act 1990 (c. 43), s. 132(1)(a), sch. 9, para. 4(2)(b).

[9] P. 14 above.

[10] **Case: section 15** *Nature Conservancy Council v Deller* [1992] 2 EGLR 11.

1949. Part V of the 1949 Act is not included in this manual. Sections 17 and 19 have been repealed.

Amendments of Act of 1949

21. **(1)–(5)** *These subsections amend the National Parks and Access to the Countryside Act 1949. The amendments made by subsections (1), (4) and (5) are noted at the appropriate points in the 1949 Act. Subsections (2) and (3) make amendments to sections of the Act which are not included in this manual.*

(6) The definition of the expression "open-air recreation" in section 114(1) of the Act of 1949[1] (which excludes organised games from that expression) shall apply only for the purposes of Part V of that Act.

(7) In subsection (2) of the said section 114[2] (definition of preservation of natural beauty) for the words "the characteristic natural features, flora and fauna thereof" there shall be substituted the words "its flora, fauna and geological and physiographical features", and (with a view to facilitating the consolidation of the appropriate parts of this Act and the Act of 1949) references in the Act of 1949 to the preservation of the natural beauty of an area shall be construed in the same way as references in this Act to the conservation of the natural beauty of an area.

22. *Repealed by the Water Act 1989 (c. 15), s. 190(3), sch. 27, pt. I. This amendment came into force on 1 September 1989: S.I. 1989/1530.*

Trees and woodlands

Provision of facilities by Forestry Commissioners

23. **(1)** The Forestry Commissioners constituted under the Forestry Acts 1919 to 1945 (in this section referred to as "the Commissioners") shall have the powers conferred on them by this section.

(2) The Commissioners[3] may, on any land[4] placed at their disposal by the Minister of Agriculture, Fisheries and Food or the Secretary of State for Wales, provide, or arrange for or assist in the provision of, tourist, recreational or sporting facilities and any equipment, facilities or works ancillary thereto, including without prejudice to that generality—

(*a*) accommodation for visitors,

(*b*) camping sites and caravan sites,

(*c*) places for meals and refreshments,

(*d*) picnic places, places for enjoying views, parking places, routes for nature study and footpaths[5],

(*e*) information and display centres,

(*f*) shops in connection with any of the aforesaid facilities,

(*g*) public conveniences,

and the Commissioners shall have power to make such charges as they think fit in connection with any of those facilities.

In this subsection "provide" includes manage, maintain and improve.

---

[1] P. 38 above.
[2] P. 38 above.
[3] For the exercise of the Commissioners' powers in respect of the New Forest see the New Forest Act 1970

(c. 21), s. 1.
[4] "Land" defined by s. 49(2), p. 132 below.
[5] "Footpath" defined by s. 49(2), p. 132 below.

(3) The power of the Minister of Agriculture, Fisheries and Food and the Secretary of State for Wales under section 39 of the Forestry Act 1967[1] to acquire land shall include power to acquire land in proximity to land placed by him at the disposal of the Commissioners where it appears to him that the land which it is proposed to acquire is reasonably required by the Commissioners for the provision of such facilities as are mentioned in subsection (2) above.[2]

(4) The Commissioners' powers to make byelaws under section 46 of the Forestry Act 1967[3] shall include power to make byelaws for regulating the reasonable use by the public of the facilities described in subsection (2) above, and in relation to any such matter as is described in section 41(3) of this Act[4].

(5) The Countryside Commission and the Countryside Council for Wales shall each[5] have power to act as agent for the Commissioners in the exercise of their powers under subsection (2) above.

(6) All expenses incurred by the Commissioners in the exercise of their powers under this section shall be paid out of the Forestry Fund, and all sums received by the Commissioners in the exercise of their powers under this section shall be paid into the Forestry Fund.

Amendments of Forestry Act 1967

24. (1) Without prejudice to the provisions of section 11 of this Act[6], the said Commissioners[7] may, on any land placed at their disposal by the Minister (as defined in the Forestry Act 1967[8]), plant, care for and manage trees in the interests of amenity, and in section 3(1) of the Forestry Act 1967[9] (management of forestry land) the reference to the Commissioners' functions under that Act shall include a reference to their functions under this subsection.

(2) The said Minister may acquire, whether by purchase, feu, lease, exchange or excambion, land which in his opinion ought to be used for planting trees in the interests of amenity, or partly for that purpose and partly for afforestation, together with any other land which must necessarily be acquired therewith, and may place any land acquired by him under this subsection at the disposal of the Commissioners.

(3) *Repealed by the Forestry Act 1981 (c. 39), s. 6(2), sch. This amendment came into force on 27 July 1981, the date of the Royal Assent.*

(4) The definition of "public open space" in section 9(6) of the Forestry Act 1967[10] shall not include a country park provided under section 7 of this Act, or a park or pleasure ground in the Lee Valley Regional Park which in the opinion of the Minister serves the purpose set out in section 6(1) of this Act when the considerations in paragraphs (*a*) and (*b*) of that subsection are taken into account.

(5) This section shall be construed as one with the Forestry Act 1967, and that Act shall have effect as if subsections (2)[11] above formed part of section 39 of that Act[12].

25–26. Repealed by the Town and Country Planning Act 1971 (c. 78), s. 292(2), sch. 25 which came

---

[1] P. 91 above.
[2] Former words "Either of the said Ministers shall have power to dispose of land acquired by him, whether by way of sale, lease or exchange, where in his opinion it is no longer so required, or where in his opinion the disposal is desirable for the purpose of securing the provision of any of those facilities by any other body or person." repealed by the Forestry Act 1981 (c. 39), s. 6(2), sch. This amendment came into force on 27 July 1981, the date of the Royal Assent.
[3] P. 95 above.
[4] P. 127 below.
[5] Words "and the Countryside Council for Wales shall

each" substituted by the Environmental Protection Act 1990 (c. 43), s. 130(1), sch. 8, para. 2(8). This amendment came into force on 1 April 1991: S.I. 1991/685.
[6] P. 118 above.
[7] The Forestry Commissioners.
[8] P. 97 above.
[9] P. 69 above.
[10] P. 73 above.
[11] Former words "and (3)" repealed by the Forestry Act 1981 (c. 39), s. 6(2), sch. This amendment came into force on 27 July 1981, the date of the Royal Assent.
[12] P. 91 above.

into force on 1 April 1972: s. 294, in respect of England and Wales, and the Town and Country Planning (Scotland) Act 1972 (c. 52), s. 277(2), sch. 23 which came into force on 27 August 1972: s. 280, in respect of Scotland.

Public rights of way

Sections 27, 30, 31, concerning public rights of way, are not reproduced. Sections 28 and 29 have been repealed.

Traffic regulation orders

32. *Repealed by the Road Traffic Regulation Act 1984 (c. 27), s. 146, sch. 14. This amendment came into force on 26 September 1984: s. 145(1).*

Financial

33–35. *Repealed by the Local Government Act 1974 (c. 9), s. 42(2), sch. 8. This amendment came into force on 1 April 1979: S.I. 1978/1583.*

36. *Repealed by the Derelict Land Act 1982 (c. 42), s. 5(2), sch. This amendment came into force on 30 August 1982: s. 5(3).*

Supplemental

Protection for interests in countryside

37. In the exercise of their functions under this Act, the Act of 1949 and the Wildlife and Countryside Act 1981[1] it shall be the duty of every Minister, and of the Commission[2], the Council,[3] the Nature Conservancy Council for England[4,5] and local authorities to have due regard to the needs of agriculture and forestry and to the economic and social interests of rural areas.

Avoidance of pollution

38. In the exercise of their functions under this Act and the Act of 1949[6] it shall be the duty of the Commission[7], the Council[8,9], the Forestry Commission and local authorities to have due regard to the protection against pollution of any water, whether on the surface or underground, which

[1] Words "the Act of 1949 and the Wildlife and Countryside Act 1981" substituted by the Wildlife and Countryside Act 1981 (c. 69), s. 72(9). This amendment came into force on 30 November 1981: s. 74(2).

[2] "The Commission" means the Countryside Commission: s. 49(2), p. 132 below.

[3] "The Council" means the Countryside Council for Wales: s. 49(2), p. 132 below.

[4] Words ", the Council, the Nature Conservancy Council for England" substituted by the Environmental Protection Act 1990 (c. 43), s. 132(1)(a), sch. 9, para. 4(3). This amendment came into force on 1 April 1991: S.I. 1991/685.

[5] Former words "and the Nature Conservancy Council for Scotland" repealed by the Natural Heritage (Scotland) Act 1991 (c. 28), s. 27(2), sch. 11. This amendment came into force on 1 April 1992: S.I. 1991/2633.

[6] The National Parks and Access to the Countryside Act 1949 (c. 97), p. 5 above.

[7] "The Commission" means the Countryside Commission: s. 49(2), p. 132 below.

[8] "The Council" means the Countryside Council for Wales: s. 49(2), p. 132 below.

[9] Words ", the Council" inserted by the Environmental Protection Act 1990 (c. 43), s. 130(1), sch. 8, para. 2(9). This amendment came into force on 1 April 1991: S.I. 1991/685.

belongs to the National Rivers Authority or a water undertaker or which that Authority or a water undertaker is[1] for the time being authorised to take.

39. *Repealed by the Local Government Act 1972 (c. 70), s. 272(1), sch. 30. This amendment came into force on 1 April 1974: s. 273.*

National parks joint planning board: expenses of members or officers

40. (1) This section has effect as respects any National Park joint planning board, that is to say a joint planning board constituted under section 2 of the Town and Country Planning Act 1990[2] for an area which consists of or includes any part of a National Park[3].

(2) Any such board may defray—

(a) any travelling or other expenses reasonably incurred by or on behalf of members or officers of the board, or of any committee of the board, in attending a conference or meeting convened by one or more local planning authorities[4] whose areas includes the whole or part of a National Park, or by any association of such authorities, being a conference or meeting for the purpose of discussing any matter connected with the discharge of functions exercisable by local planning authorities in respect of National Parks;

(b) any travelling or other expenses reasonably incurred by or on behalf of members or officers of the board, or of any committee of the board, in making official or courtesy visits, whether inside or outside the United Kingdom, on behalf of the board;

(c) any expenses incurred in the reception and entertainment by way of official courtesy of distinguished persons residing in or visiting the board's area, and of persons representative of or connected with other local planning authorities or bodies concerned with matters relating to the countryside, whether inside or outside the United Kingdom, and in the supply of information to any such persons.

(3) In the case of a visit within the United Kingdom, the amount defrayed in respect of the expenses of a member of the board shall not exceed the payments which he would have been entitled to receive by way of travelling allowance or subsistence allowance under section 113 of the Local Government Act 1948[5] if the making of the visit had been an approved duty of that member within the meaning of that section.

Power to make byelaws and related provisions about wardens

41. (1) A local authority may as respects—

(a) a country park provided by the local authority under section 7 of this Act (on land[6] belonging to the local authority or other land), or

(b) any land as respects which the local authority have exercised powers conferred by section 9 of this Act, or

(c) a picnic site provided by the local authority under section 10 of this Act,

---

[1] Words "the National Rivers Authority . . . water undertaker is" substituted by the Water Act 1989 (c. 15), s. 190(1), sch. 25, para. 37(5). This amendment came into force on 1 September 1989: S.I. 1989/1146.

[2] Words "section 2 of the Town and Country Planning Act 1990" substituted by the Planning (Consequential Provisions) Act 1990, s. 4, sch. 2, para. 20. This amendment came into force on 24 August 1990: s. 7(2). This section has effect as if the Broads Authority were a National Park joint planning board and the Broads were a National Park: s. 47A(4), p. 132 below.

[3] "National Park" defined by s. 114(1), National Parks and Access to the Countryside Act 1949, by which it has the meaning assigned to it by s. 5(3), p. 8 above: s. 49(1), p. 132

below applies the definition in s. 114 of the 1949 Act.

[4] For statutory provisions in respect of local planning authorities see the Town and Country Planning Act 1990 (c. 8), Part I and the Local Government Act 1972 (c. 70), s. 184, sch. 17, pt. I. The Town and Country Planning Act 1990 applies by virtue of s. 49(1), p. 132 below, National Parks and Access to the Countryside Act 1949 (c. 97), s. 114(1) and the Planning (Consequential Provisions) Act 1990 (c. 11), s. 2.

[5] S. 113 of the Local Government Act 1948 is construed as a reference to s. 174 of the Local Government Act 1972 (c. 70): s. 272.

[6] "Land" defined by s. 49(2), p. 132 below.

(d) a trunk road picnic area as respects which functions of the Minister stand delegated to the local authority under section 113(1) of the Highways Act 1980, or are functions of the local authority by virtue of an agreement under section 113(3) of that Act,[1]

make byelaws for the preservation of order, for the prevention of damage to the land or anything thereon or therein, and for securing that persons resorting thereto will so behave themselves as to avoid undue interference with the enjoyment of the land by other persons.

(1A) The power of a local authority under subsection (1)(d) above is exercisable only in so far as any conditions attached to the relevant delegation or, as the case may be, included in the relevant agreement do not otherwise provide.[1]

(2) The Commission[2] and the Council[3] may each[4] as respects any land held by them for the purposes of section 4 of this Act[5], or as respects land to which the public have rights of access pursuant to an agreement under section 4(5)(b) of this Act, make byelaws for the preservation of order and the other purposes mentioned in subsection (1) above.

(3) Without prejudice to the generality of the foregoing provisions of this section, byelaws under those provisions—

(a) may prohibit or restrict the use of the land or of any waterway[6] comprised therein, either generally or in any manner specified in the byelaws, by traffic of any description so specified,

(b) may contain provisions prohibiting the depositing of rubbish and the leaving of litter,

(c) may regulate or prohibit the lighting of fires,

(d) may regulate sailing, boating, bathing and fishing and other forms of recreation on waterways,

(e) may prohibit the use of any waterway comprised in a country park by boats[7] which are not for the time being registered with the local authority in such manner as the byelaws may provide.

(f) may be made so as to relate either to the whole or to any part of the land or of any waterway comprised therein, and may make different provisions for different parts thereof,

and the byelaws may authorise the making of reasonable charges in respect of the registration of boats in pursuance of the byelaws.

(4) Byelaws made under this section shall not interfere with the exercise of any public right of way or of any functions relating to the land or waterway to which the byelaws apply which are exercisable by any authority under any enactment or with the running of a telecommunications code system or the exercise of any right conferred by or in accordance with the telecommunications code on the operator of any such system[8].

(5) Before a local authority make byelaws under the foregoing provisions of this section as respects a National Park[9] or area of outstanding natural beauty[10], the local authority shall consult the Commission (as respects a park or area in England) or the Council (as respects a park or area in Wales)[11].

---

[1] Paragraph (d) and subsection (1A) inserted by the Highways Act 1980 (c. 66), s. 342. This amendment came into force on 1 January 1981: s. 345.

[2] "The Commission" means the Countryside Commission s. 49(2), p. 132 below.

[3] "The Council" means the Countryside Council for Wale: s. 49(2), p. 132 below.

[4] Words "and the Council may each" substituted by the Environmental Protection Act 1990 (c. 43), s. 130(1), sch. 8, para. 2(10)(a). This amendment came into force on 1 April 1991: S.I. 1991/685.

[5] P. 117 above.

[6] "Waterway" defined by s. 114(1), National Parks and Access to the Countryside Act 1949, p. 38 above: s. 49(1), p. 132 below applies the definition in s. 114 of the 1949 Act.

[7] "Boat" defined by s. 49(2), p. 132 below.

[8] Words "or with the running ... any such system" inserted by the Telecommunications Act 1984 (c. 12), s. 109, sch. 4, para. 48. This amendment came into force on 5 August 1984: S.I. 1984/876.

[9] "National Park" defined by s. 114(1), National Parks and Access to the Countryside Act 1949, by which it has the meaning assigned to it by s. 5(3), p. 8 above: s. 49(1), p. 132 below applies the definition in s. 114 of the 1949 Act.

[10] "Area of outstanding natural beauty" defined by s. 114(1), National Parks and Access to the Countryside Act 1949, by which it has the meaning assigned to it by s. 87(1), p. 22 above: s. 49(1), p. 132 below applies the definition in s. 114 of the 1949 Act.

[11] Words "(as respects a park ... in Wales)" inserted by the Environmental Protection Act 1990 (c. 43), s. 130(1), sch. 8, para. 2(1)(b).

(6) A county council or county district council[1] shall have power to enforce byelaws made under this section by another authority as respects land in the area of the council.

(7) Section 106 of the Act of 1949[2] (supplementary provisions as to byelaws) shall have effect as if byelaws under this section were byelaws under that Act.

(8) Subsections (1) and (2), and subject to the next following subsection subsection (4), of section 92 of the Act of 1949[3] (appointment of wardens for land for which byelaws may be made under section 90 of that Act[4]) shall have effect as if the power of making byelaws conferred by this section was contained in the said section 90, and as if the Commission and the Council were local authorities.[5]

(9) For the purposes of exercising any function conferred on him by the said section 92 as applied by subsection (8) above a warden appointed under that section may enter upon any land, or go on any waterway, as respects which byelaws under this section are in force, although the land or waterway does not belong to the local authority, the Commission or the Council.[6]

(10) Sections 90, 91 and 92 of the Act of 1949 shall have effect as if any path[7] which is a means of access to land to which the public are given access by an agreement or order, or in consequence of acquisition, under Part V of the Act of 1949 was included in that land.

(11) In subsection (10) above "path" means a public path, or a road used as a public path (as those expressions are defined in section 27(6) of the Act of 1949) or any other path, not being a highway at the side of a public road, which the public have the right to use, or are permitted to use, as a means of access to land to which the public are given access under Part V of the Act of 1949.

(12) Byelaws made under section 90(3) of the Act of 1949 shall not interfere with the exercise of any public right of way or with any authority having under any enactment functions relating to the land or waterway to which the byelaws apply or with the running of a telecommunications code system or the exercise of any right conferred by or in accordance with the telecommunications code on the operator of any such system[8].

....

Wardens

42. (1) A local planning authority[9] whose area consists of or includes the whole or any part of a National Park[10] may appoint such number of persons as may appear to the authority to be necessary or expedient to act as wardens as respects any land[11] within the National Park to which section 193 of the Law of Property Act 1925[12] (common land) for the time being applies, whether or not within the area of the local planning authority.

(2) Before a local planning authority first exercise their powers under subsection (1) above as respects any land, they shall, if practicable, consult the person entitled to the soil of the land.

(3) The foregoing subsections shall be construed as one with section 92 of the Act of 1949[13] and shall be subject to subsection (4) of that section (saving for interests of landowners).

---

[1] For the construction of "county council' and "county district council" see the Local Government Act 1972 (c. 70), s. 179.

[2] P. 33 above.

[3] P. 26 above.

[4] P. 25 above.

[5] Words "and the Council were local authorities" substituted by the Environmental Protection Act 1990 (c. 43), s. 130(1), sch. 8, para. 2(1)(c).

[6] Words ", the Commission or the Council" substituted by the Environmental Protection Act 1990 (c. 43), s. 130(1), sch. 8, para. 2(10)(d).

[7] "Path" defined by subsection (11) below.

[8] Words "or with the running ... any such system" inserted by the Telecommunications Act 1984 (c. 12), s. 109, sch. 4, para. 48. This amendment came into force on 5 August 1984: S.I. 1984/876.

[9] For statutory provisions in respect of local planning authorities see the Town and Country Planning Act 1990 (c. 8), Part I and the Local Government Act 1972 (c. 70), s. 184, sch. 17, pt. I. The Town and Country Planning Act 1990 applies by virtue of s. 49(1), p. 132 below, National Parks and Access to the Countryside Act 1949 (c. 97), s. 114(1) and the Planning (Consequential Provisions) Act 1990 (c. 11), s. 2.

[10] "National Park" defined by s. 114(1), National Parks and Access to the Countryside Act 1949, by which it has the meaning assigned to it by s. 5(3), p. 8 above: s. 49(1), p. 132 below applies the definition in s. 114 of the 1949 Act.

[11] "Land" defined by s. 49(2), p. 132 below.

[12] 1925 c. 20.

[13] P. 26 above.

(4) The purposes for which wardens may be appointed by an authority under the said section 92 (as amended by this Act) as respects any land or waters are—

(a) to secure compliance with any byelaws, with the provisions of section 87 of the Environmental Protection Act 1990[1] and with any requirements imposed by or under section 193 of the Law of Property Act 1925,

(b) to advise and assist the public, and

(c) to perform such other duties (if any) in relation to the land or waters as the authority may determine.

This subsection shall have effect in substitution for subsection (2) of the said section 92.

General provisions as to local authority powers conferred by Act

43. (1) A local authority[2] shall make available any facilities and services provided by them under this Act for those who do not normally reside in the area of the local authority as freely as for those who do.

(2) A local authority shall have power to make reasonable charges for any facilities or services provided by them under this Act and may arrange for any facilities or services which they have power to provide under this Act to be provided by some other person, and, where they make arrangements for any such facilities or services to be provided by some other person, may authorise that person to make reasonable charges.

(3) The services and facilities for which charges may be made under subsection (2) above include the use of any camping site, picnic site or parking place, of any waterway[3] comprised in a country park, and of any part of a country park set aside for any particular form of recreation.

(4) Any power of a local authority under this Act to provide buildings or other premises for any purpose shall include power to equip them with such furniture and apparatus as may be reasonably necessary to enable them to be used for that purpose.

(5) Any power of a local authority under this Act to provide buildings or other premises, or any services or facilities, or anything else, shall include power to enter into agreements with any other authority or person for the use, on such terms as may be agreed, of anything, or any facilities or services, provided by, or under the control of, that other authority or person and, if it appears convenient, for the services of any staff employed in connection therewith.

Power to amend local Acts concerning local authorities

44. (1) The Minister[4] may, subject to the provisions of this section, by order repeal or amend any provision in any local Act passed before this Act and relating to any local authority[5] where it appears to him that that provision is inconsistent with, or has become unnecessary in consequence of, any provision of this Act.

(2) Before making an order under this section the Minister shall consult with each local authority affected by the proposed order.

(3) An order made under this section—

(a) shall not repeal or amend any enactment so far as it relates to the water undertaking of a local authority,

(b) may contain such transitional, supplemental or incidental provisions as appear to the Minister to be expedient, and

---

[1] Words "section 87 of the Environmental Protection Act 1990" inserted by the Environmental Protection Act 1990 (c. 43), s. 162(1), sch. 15, para. 11. This amendment came into force on 1 April 1991: S.I. 1991/1042.

[2] This section has effect as if the Broads Authority were a local authority: s. 47A(5), p. 132 below.

[3] "Waterway" defined by s. 114(1), National Parks and Access to the Countryside Act 1949, p. 38 above: s. 49(1), p. 132 below applies the definition in s. 114 of the 1949 Act.

[4] "The Minister" defined by s. 49(2), p. 132 below.

[5] This section has effect as if the Broads Authority were a local authority: s. 47A(5), p. 132 below.

(c) shall be made by statutory instrument subject to annulment in pursuance of a resolution of either House of Parliament.

Agreements with landowners

45. (1) This section has effect as respects any power conferred by this Act on the Commission[1], the Council[2] or any local authority[3] to enter into agreements with landowners and other persons having interests[4] in land[5].

(2) Schedule 2 to the Forestry Act 1967[6] (powers of tenants for life and other limited owners to enter into forestry dedication covenants) shall apply to any such agreement as it applies to such a covenant.

(3) Where a landowner, or other person having an interest in the land, by the agreement grants or agrees to grant any right as respects the land, the grant or agreement shall be binding upon any person deriving title or otherwise claiming under the grantor to the same extent as it is binding upon the grantor notwithstanding that it would not have been binding upon that person apart from the provisions of this subsection.

(4) Any such agreement may be made either irrevocably or subject to such provisions for revocation or variation as may be specified in the agreement.

(5) For the purposes of any enactment or rule of law as to the circumstances in which the dedication of a highway or the grant of an easement may be presumed, or may be established by prescription, the use by the public or by any person of a way across land at any time while it is the subject of any such agreement shall be disregarded.

Application of general provisions of Act of 1949

46. (1) In the following provisions of the Act of 1949[7] references to that Act shall include references to this Act—

section 99(1)[8] (power of local authority to contribute to expenses of another local authority),

section 103[9] (acquisition of land),

section 104[10] (appropriation and disposal of land by local authorities) but subject to Schedule 2 to this Act,

section 108[11] (entry to survey land in connection with its acquisition),

section 109[12] (local inquiries and service of documents),

section 111[13] (Isles of Scilly).

(2) In subsections (1)[14] of the said section 103 of the Act of 1949 references to the Nature Conservancy Council[15] shall include references to the Commission and any reference to the Nature Conservancy Council, so far as referring to the Countryside Council for Wales for purposes connected with their nature conservation functions (within the meaning of section 131 of the Environmental Protection Act 1990[16]) shall include a reference to that Council for purposes

---

[1] "The Commission" means the Countryside Commission: s. 49(2), p. 132 below.

[2] "The Council" means the Countryside Council for Wales: s. 49(2), p. 132 below. Words ", the Council" inserted by the Environmental Protection Act 1990 (c. 43), s. 130(1), sch. 8, para. 2(11). This amendment came into force on 1 April 1991: S.I. 1991/685.

[3] This section has effect as if the Broads Authority were a local authority: s. 47A(5), p. 132 below.

[4] "Interest" defined by s. 114(1), National Parks and Access to the Countryside Act 1949, p. 38 above: s. 49(1), p. 132 below applies the definition in s. 114 of the 1949 Act.

[5] "Land" defined by s. 49(2), p. 132 below.

[6] P. 99 above.

[7] The National Parks and Access to the Countryside Act 1949 (c. 97), p. 5 above.

[8] P. 27 above.

[9] P. 30 above.

[10] P. 31 above.

[11] P. 35 above.

[12] P. 36 above.

[13] P. 36 above.

[14] Former words "and (2)" repealed by the Environmental Protection Act 1990 (c. 43), s. 162(2), sch. 16, pt. VI. This amendment came into force on 1 April 1991: S.I. 1991/685.

[15] Words "Nature Conservancy Council" substituted by the Nature Conservancy Council Act 1973 (c. 54), s. 1(1)(b), sch. 1, para. 9. This amendment came into force on 1 November 1973: S.I. 1973/1721.

[16] P. 230 below.

connected with their countryside functions (whether conferred by this Act, the Act of 1949 or otherwise)[1].

(3) In section 108(3) of the Act of 1949 (seven days' notice to be given of intended entry) for the words "seven days' " there shall be substituted the words "fourteen days' ", and this amendment shall have effect both for the purposes of the Act of 1949 and of this Act.

(4) Section 112 of the Act of 1949[2] (Epping Forest and Burnham Beeches) shall have effect as if the provisions of this Act about experimental projects or schemes, country parks, common land and camping and picnic sites were mentioned in the said section 112(2).

(5) Section 113 of the Act of 1949[3] (National Trust Land) shall have effect as if the provisions of this Act about experimental projects or schemes, country parks, common land and camping and picnic sites were contained in Part VI of the Act of 1949[4].

Crown land

47. (1) The following provisions of this section shall have effect for applying certain provisions of this Act to Crown land, that is to say land[5] an interest[6] in which belongs to Her Majesty in right of the Crown or the Duchy of Lancaster, or to the Duchy of Cornwall, and land an interest in which belongs to a Government department or is held in trust for Her Majesty for the purposes of a Government department.

(2) Any power under this Act to acquire land compulsorily may be exercised to acquire an interest in Crown land, other than one held by or on behalf of the Crown, but only with the consent of the appropriate authority[7].

(3) Subject to subsection (4) below, the appropriate authority may enter into an agreement under section 4(5)(*b*)[8] or section 7(3)(*b*) of this Act as respects an interest in Crown land held by or on behalf of the Crown, and any such agreement as respects any other interest in Crown land shall not have effect unless approved by the appropriate authority.

(4) Notwithstanding anything in subsection (3) above—

(*a*) an agreement authorised by the said subsection (3) and made by any Government department shall be of no effect unless it is approved by the Treasury, and

(*b*) in considering whether to make or approve an agreement so authorised and relating to land belonging to a Government department or held in trust for Her Majesty for the purposes of a Government department, the department and the Treasury shall have regard to the purposes for which the land is held by or for the department.

(5) *Repealed by the Highways Act 1980 (c. 66), s. 343(3), sch. 25. This amendment came into force on 1 January 1981: s. 345(2).*

(6) If any land subject to an agreement to which section 45 of this Act applies[9] becomes Crown land, subsection (3) of that section shall cease to apply to that agreement unless the appropriate authority consent to its continued application to the agreement.

(7) Byelaws made under this Act shall apply to Crown land if the appropriate authority consent to their application thereto.

(8) Section 101(11) of the Act of 1949[10] shall apply for the construction of references in this section to "the appropriate authority".

(9) Agreements made by the Crown Estate Commissioners shall not require the approval of the Treasury under section 101(10)(*a*) of the Act of 1949 and accordingly in that paragraph, as

[1] Words "and any reference . . . or otherwise)" inserted by the Environmental Protection Act 1990 (c. 43), s. 130(1), sch. 8, para. 2(12). This amendment came into force on 1 April 1991: S.I. 1991/685.

[2] P. 37 above.

[3] P. 37 above.

[4] P. 21 above.

[5] "Land" defined by s. 49(2), p. 132 below.

[6] "Interest" defined by s. 114(1), National Parks and Access to the Countryside Act 1949, p. 38 above: s. 49(1), p. 132 below applies the definition in s. 114 of the 1949 Act.

[7] For "appropriate authority" see subsection (8) below.

[8] P. 117 above.

[9] P. 130 above.

[10] P. 29 above.

originally enacted, the words "by the Commissioners of Crown Lands or" shall cease to have effect.

Application to the Broads Authority

47A. (1) Sections 6 to 9 of this Act shall have effect as if the Broads Authority were a local authority.

(2) Sections 10, 18 and 20 of this Act shall have effect as if the Broads Authority were a local planning authority.

(3) Section 16 of this Act shall have effect as if the Broads Authority were a local planning authority and the Broads were a National Park.

(4) Section 40 of this Act[1] shall have effect as if the Broads Authority were a National Park joint planning board and the Broads were a National Park.

(5) Sections 43 to 45[2] shall have effect as if the Broads Authority were a local authority.

(6) In this section "the Broads" has the same meaning as in the Norfolk and Suffolk Broads Act 1988.[3]

Expenses and payments into Exchequer

48. (1) There shall be defrayed out of money provided by Parliament—

(*a*) any sums required for the payment of grants under this Act, or any other expenses of a Minister under this Act, and

(*b*) any increase attributable to the provisions of this Act in the sums payable out of such money under any other Act.

(2) There shall be paid into the Exchequer any sums required to be so paid in consequence of any of the provisions of this Act.

Interpretation

49. (1) Section 114 of the Act of 1949[4] shall apply for the construction of this Act.

(2) In this Act, unless the context otherwise requires—

"the Act of 1949" means the National Parks and Access to the Countryside Act 1949[5];

"boat" includes any hover vehicle or craft being a vehicle or craft designed to be supported on a cushion of air and which is used on or over water;

"bridleway" and "footpath" have the meanings given by section 329(1) of the Highways Act 1980[6];

"the Commission" means the Countryside Commission;[7]

"the Council" means the Countryside Council for Wales;[7]

"land" includes any interest in or right over land;

"the Minister", as respects Wales and Monmouthshire, means the Secretary of State, and otherwise means the Minister of Housing and Local Government[8];

"public body" includes any local authority or statutory undertaker, and any trustees, commissioners, board or other persons, who, as a public body and not for their own profit, act under

---

[1] P. 126 above.
[2] Pp. 129–130 above.
[3] This section inserted by the Norfolk and Suffolk Broads Act 1988 (c. 4), s. 2(5), sch. 3, pt. I, para. 6. This amendment came into force on 1 April 1989: S.I. 1988/955.
[4] P. 37 above.
[5] P. 5 above.
[6] Words "section 329(1) of the Highways Act 1980" substituted by the Highways Act 1980 (c. 66), s. 343(2), sch. 24, para. 17(*b*). This amendment came into force on 1 January

1981: s. 345(2).
[7] The definitions of the Commission and the Council inserted by the Environmental Protection Act 1990 (c. 43), s. 130(1), sch. 8, para. 2(13). This amendment came into force on 1 April 1991: S.I. 1991/685.
[8] The functions of the Minister of Housing and Local Government were transferred to the Secretary of State by the Secretary of State for the Environment Order 1970: S.I. 1970/1681.

any enactment for the improvement of any place or the production or supply of any commodity or service;[1]

(3) In this Act "parish" means a rural parish.[2]

(4) References in this Act to the conservation of the natural beauty of an area shall be construed as including references to the conservation of its flora, fauna and geological and physiographical features.

Short title, repeals, commencement and extent

50. (1) This Act may be cited as the Countryside Act 1968.

(2) The enactments mentioned in Schedule 5 to this Act shall be repealed to the extent specified in the third column of that Schedule.

(3) This Act shall come into force at the expiration of a period of one month beginning with the date on which it is passed[3].

(4) *Repealed by the House of Commons Disqualification Act 1975 (c. 24), s. 10(2), sch. 3. This amendment came into force on 8 May 1975, the date of the Royal Assent.*

(5) This Act, except subsections (1), (3)[4] of this section, sections 15, 24, 25, 26, 32, 37, 46(3) and so much of sections 46(1), 48, and 49 as relates to the first-mentioned sections, shall not extent to Scotland, and[5] this Act shall not extend to Northern Ireland.

SCHEDULES

SCHEDULE 1

(Sections 7, 12 and 16.)

PROPOSALS SUBMITTED TO STATUTORY UNDERTAKERS AND OTHER AUTHORITIES

1. This Schedule has effect where any authority are consulted in accordance with section 9, section 12(4)[6] or section 16(7) of this Act.

2. (1) If the authority withhold their consent to the proposals about which they are consulted, the proposals shall not be proceeded with unless, on an application in that behalf specifying the proposals and the grounds for withholding consent, the Minister[7] so directs, and subject to any conditions or modifications specified in the direction.

(2) Before giving a direction under this paragraph the Minister shall afford to the objecting authority, and the authority by whom the proposals are made, an opportunity of being heard by a person appointed by him for the purpose, and shall consider that person's report.

---

[1] Former definitions of "river authority" and "statutory water undertakers" repealed by the Water Act 1973 (c. 37), s. 40(3), sch. 9. This amendment came into force on 1 April 1973: s. 40(3).

[2] Former words "and references to a parish and a parish council shall be construed as including references to a borough which has been included in a rural district and the council of such a borough respectively" repealed by the Local Government Act 1972 (c. 70), s. 272(1), sch. 30. This

amendment came into force on 1 April 1974: s. 273.

[3] This Act came into force on 3 August 1968.

[4] Former words "and (4)" repealed by the House of Commons Disqualification Act 1975 (c. 24), s. 10(2), sch. 3.

[5] Former words "subject to subsection (4) above" repealed by the House of Commons Disqualification Act 1975 (c. 24), s. 10(2), sch. 3.

[6] P. 119 above.

[7] "The Minister" defined by s. 49(2), p. 132 above.

(3) This Schedule shall apply with the necessary modifications where the Minister in accordance with section 16(8) of this Act consults any authority as respects an access order to be made by him.

....

Schedule 2 concerns the procedure for taking common land under section 9 of this Act.

Schedule 3 relates to the part of this Act concerning public rights of way which is not reproduced. The schedule is largely repealed.

Schedule 4 is repealed by the Local Government Act 1972 (c. 70), s. 272(1), sch. 30. This amendment came into force on 1 April 1974: s. 273.

Schedule 5 sets out the enactments repealed under section 50(2) of this Act.

....

Conservation of Seals Act 1970

Ch. 30

Conservation of Seals Act 1970

An Act to provide for the protection and conservation of seals in England and Wales and Scotland and in the adjacent territorial waters.

[29th May 1970[1]]

Prohibited methods of killing seals

1. (1) Subject to section 9(2)[2] and section 10[3] of this Act, if any person—

   (a) uses for the purpose of killing or taking any seal any poisonous substance; or

   (b) uses for the purpose of killing, injuring or taking any seal any firearm[4] other than a rifle using ammunition[5] having a muzzle energy of not less than 600 footpounds and a bullet weighing not less than 45 grains,

   he shall be guilty of an offence.

   (2) The Secretary of State may by order amend paragraph (b) of subsection (1) of this section by adding any firearm or ammunition to, or by altering the description of, or by substituting any other firearm or ammunition for, the firearm or ammunition mentioned in that subsection.

Close seasons for seals

2. (1) There shall be an annual close season for grey seals, that is to say seals of the species known as *Halichoerus grypus*, extending from 1st September to 31st December both inclusive and an annual close season for common seals, that is to say seals of the species known as *Phoca vitulina*, extending from 1st June to 31st August both inclusive.

   (2) Subject to sections 9[6] and 10[7] of this Act, if any person wilfully kills, injures or takes a seal during the close season prescribed by subsection (1) of this section for seals of the species so killed, injured or taken he shall be guilty of an offence.

Orders prohibiting killing seals

3. (1) Where, after consultation with the Council[8], it appears to the Secretary of State necessary for the proper conservation of seals he may by order prohibit with respect to any area specified in the order the killing, injuring or taking of the seals of both or either of the species mentioned in section 2 of this Act[9].

   (2) Subject to sections 9[10] and 10[11] of this Act, if any person wilfully kills, injures or takes a seal in contravention of an order made under subsection (1) of this section he shall be guilty of an offence.

Apprehension of offenders and powers of search and seizure

4. (1) A constable may stop any person he suspects with reasonable cause of committing an offence under this Act and may—

---

[1] This Act came into force on 29 August 1970: s. 17(4).
[2] P. 138 below.
[3] P. 138 below.
[4] "Firearm" defined by s. 15, p. 140 below.
[5] "Ammunition" defined by s. 15, p. 140 below.
[6] P. 137 below.
[7] P. 138 below.
[8] "The Council" defined by s. 15, p. 140 below.
[9] The Conservation of Seals (Common Seals) (Shetland Islands Area) Order 1991, S.I. 1991/2638, p. 331 below, and the Conservation of Seals (England) Order 1993, S.I. 1993/2876, p. 332 below, are made under this section.
[10] P. 137 below.
[11] P. 138 below.

(a) without warrant arrest that person if he fails to give his name and address to the constable's satisfaction[1];

(b) without warrant search any vehicle or boat which that person may be using at that time; and

(c) seize any seal, seal skin, firearm[2], ammunition[3] or poisonous substance which is liable to be forfeited under section 6 of this Act.

(2) A constable may sell or otherwise dispose of any seal seized under this section and the net proceeds of any sale shall be liable to forfeiture in the same manner as the seal sold:

Provided that no constable shall be subject to any liability on account of his neglect or failure in the exercise of the powers conferred on him by this subsection.

Penalties

5. (1) Any person guilty of an offence under section 11(7)[4] of this Act shall be liable on summary conviction to a fine not exceeding level 3 on the standard scale.[5]

(2) Any person guilty of any other offence under this Act shall be liable on summary conviction to a fine not exceeding level 4 on the standard scale.[6]

Forfeitures

6. The court by which a person is convicted of an offence under this Act may order the forfeiture of any seal or seal skin in respect of which that offence was committed or of any seal, seal skin, firearm[7], ammunition[8] or poisonous substance in his possession at the time of the offence.

Jurisdiction of courts

7. Where any offence under this Act is committed at some place on the sea coast or at sea outside the area of any commission of the peace, the place of the commission of the offence shall, for the purposes of the jurisdiction of any court, be deemed to be any place where the offender is found or to which he is first brought after the commission of the offence.

Attempt to commit offence

8. (1) Any person who attempts to commit an offence under this Act shall be guilty of an offence.

(2) Any person who, for the purpose of committing an offence under this Act, has in his possession any poisonous substance or any firearm[9] or ammunition[10] the use of which is prohibited by section 1(1)(b)[11] of this Act shall be guilty of an offence.

General exceptions

9. (1) A person shall not be guilty of an offence under section 2[12] or 3[13] of this Act by reason only of—

[1] *England & Wales*: Para. (a) repealed by the Police and Criminal Evidence Act 1984 (c. 60), s. 119(2), sch. 7, pt. I. This amendment came into force on 1 January 1986: S.I. 1985/1934.

[2] "Firearm" defined by s. 15, p. 140 below.

[3] "Ammunition" defined by s. 15, p. 140 below.

[4] P. 140 below.

[5] Words "level 3 on the standard scale" substituted by the Criminal Justice Act 1982 (c. 48), ss. 38, 46 as respects England and Wales and the Criminal Procedure (Scotland) Act 1975 (c. 21), ss. 289F, 289G as respects Scotland. The current fine at level 3 is £1,000: Criminal Justice Act 1991 (c. 53), s. 17 which came into force on 1 October 1992: S.I. 1992/333, S.I. 1992/2118.

[6] Words "level 4 on the standard scale" substituted by the

Criminal Law Act 1977 (c. 45), s. 31(1), sch. 6; the Criminal Justice Act 1982 (c. 48), s. 46 as respects England and Wales and the Criminal Procedure (Scotland) Act 1975 (c. 21), ss. 289C, 289G, sch. 7C as respects Scotland. The current fine at level 4 is £2,500: Criminal Justice Act 1991 (c. 53), s. 17 which came into force on 1 October 1992: S.I. 1992/333, S.I. 1992/2118.

[7] "Firearm" defined by s. 15, p. 140 below.

[8] "Ammunition" defined by s. 15, p. 140 below.

[9] "Firearm" defined by s. 15, p. 140 below.

[10] "Ammunition" defined by s. 15, p. 140 below.

[11] P. 136 above.

[12] P. 136 above.

[13] P. 136 above.

(*a*) the taking or attempted taking of any seal which had been disabled otherwise than by his act and was taken or to be taken solely for the purpose of tending it and releasing it when no longer disabled;

(*b*) the unavoidable killing or injuring of any seal as an incidental result of a lawful action;

(*c*) the killing or attempted killing of any seal to prevent it from causing damage to a fishing net or fishing tackle in his possession or in the possession of a person at whose request he killed or attempted to kill the seal, or to any fish for the time being in such fishing net, provided that at the time the seal was in the vicinity of such net or tackle.

(2) A person shall not be guilty of an offence under section 1,[1] 2 or 3 of this Act by reason only of the killing of any seal which had been so seriously disabled otherwise than by his act that there was no reasonable chance of its recovering.

....

Power to grant licences

10. (1) A licence may be granted to any person by the Secretary of State authorising that person, notwithstanding anything in the foregoing provisions of this Act, but subject to compliance with any conditions specified in the licence,—

(*a*) for scientific or educational purposes to kill or take within an area specified in the licence by any means so specified other than by the use of strychnine any number of seals so specified;

(*b*) for the purposes of any zoological gardens or collection specified in the licence to take within an area specified in the licence by any means so specified any number of seals so specified;

(*c*) for—

    (i) the prevention of damage to fisheries;

    (ii) the reduction of a population surplus of seals for management purposes;[2]

    (iii) the use of a population surplus of seals as a resource; or

    (iv) the protection of flora or fauna in an area to which subsection (4) of this section applies,[3]

to kill or take within any area specified in the licence by any means so specified other than by the use of strychnine any number of seals so specified.

(2) A licence granted under this section may be revoked at any time by the Secretary of State and, without prejudice to any other liability of a penalty which he may have incurred under this or any other Act, any person who contravenes or fails to comply with any condition imposed on the grant of a licence under this section shall be guilty of an offence.

(3) The Secretary of State—

(*a*) shall consult the Council[4] before granting a licence under this Act; and

(*b*) except in relation to the prevention of damage to fisheries shall not without the consent of the Nature Conservancy Council[5] grant a licence to kill or take seals in an area to which sub-section (4) of this section applies.[6]

(4) This subsection applies to any area which—

(*a*) is a nature reserve within the meaning of section 15 of the National Parks and Access to the Countryside Act 1949[7];

---

[1] P. 136 above.

[2] Former word "or" repealed by the Wildlife and Countryside Act 1981 (c. 69), ss. 12, 73(1), sch. 7, para. 7(1), sch. 17, pt. II. This amendment came into force on 16 February 1982: S.I. 1982/44.

[3] Sub-paragraph (iv) inserted by the Wildlife and Countryside Act 1981 (c. 69), s. 12, sch. 7, para. 7(1). This amendment came into force on 16 February 1982: S.I. 1982/44.

[4] "The Council" defined by s. 15, p. 140 below.

[5] "Nature Conservancy Council" defined by subsection (5) below. Words "the Nature Conservancy Council" substituted by the Nature Conservancy Council Act 1973 (c. 54), s. 1(1)(*b*), sch. 1, para. 10. This amendment came into force on 1 November 1973: S.I. 1973/1721.

[6] Words "an area to which subsection (4) of this section applies" substituted by the Wildlife and Countryside Act 1981 (c. 69), s.12, sch. 7, para. 7(2).

[7] P. 14 above.

(b) has been notified under section 28(1) of the Wildlife and Countryside Act 1981[1] (areas of special scientific interest);

(c) is an area to which section 29(3) of that Act[2] (special protection for certain areas of special scientific interest) applies; or

(d) has been designated as a marine nature reserve under section 36 of that Act.[3,4]

(5) In this section a reference to "the Nature Conservancy Council" is a reference to the Nature Conservancy Council for England[5], Scottish Natural Heritage[6] or the Countryside Council for Wales[7], according as the area in question is in or is in waters adjacent to England, Scotland or Wales.[8]

Entry upon land

11. (1) The Secretary of State[9] may, after consultation with the Council[10], authorise in writing any person to enter upon any land[11] for the purpose of—

(a) obtaining information relating to seals for the purpose of any of the functions of the Secretary of State under this Act;

(b) killing or taking seals for the purpose of preventing damage to fisheries by seals.

(2) Any such authorisation shall specify—

(a) the land to be entered upon;

(b) the period, not exceeding 8 weeks, during which the power of entry upon the land may be exercised;

(c) the purpose of the entry;

(d) the number, species and age of seals that may be killed or taken where the purpose of the entry is to prevent damage to fisheries by seals.

(3) Any such authorisation may impose other conditions on the exercise by the person authorised of the power of entry or the manner of giving effect to the authorisation.

(4) The Secretary of State shall give not less than 48 hours' notice[12], or in the case of an authorisation to enter upon land for the purpose of killing or taking seals not less than 28 days' notice, to the occupier of any land of his intention to issue an authorisation and of the purpose of the authorisation; and in the case of an authorisation to enter upon land for the purpose of killing or taking seals the Secretary of State shall have regard to any representations that might be made by the occupier and shall not issue the authorisation if before the expiration of the notice the occupier satisfies the Secretary of State that he has killed or taken the number of seals which the Secretary of State proposes to specify in the authorisation.

(5) Any seals killed or taken by a person authorised under this section to enter upon land shall belong to the Secretary of State and may be disposed of as the Secretary of State thinks fit.

(6) Any person authorised under this section to enter upon any land shall, if required by the occupier of that land, produce his authority and may take with him upon that land such other persons as may be necessary.

---

[1] P. 168 below.
[2] P. 171 below.
[3] P. 178 below.
[4] Subsection (4) inserted by the Wildlife and Countryside Act 1981 (c. 69), s. 12, sch. 7, para. 7(3).
[5] The Nature Conservancy Council for England, also known as English Nature, is established by the Environmental Protection Act 1990 (c. 43), s. 128, p. 229 below.
[6] Scottish Natural Heritage is established by the Natural Heritage (Scotland) Act 1991 (c. 28), s. 1, p. 245 below. Words "Scottish Natural Heritage" substituted by the Natural Heritage (Scotland) Act 1991 (c. 28), s. 4(6), sch. 2, para. 4. This amendment came into force on 1 April 1992:

S.I. 1991/2633.
[7] The Countryside Council for Wales is established by the Environmental Protection Act 1990 (c. 43), s. 128, p. 229 below.
[8] Subsection (5) inserted by the Environmental Protection Act 1990 (c. 43), s. 132(1)(a), sch. 9, para. 5. This amendment came into force on 1 April 1991: S.I. 1991/685.
[9] *England & Wales:* "The Secretary of State" includes a reference to the Minister of Agriculture, Fisheries and Food: subsection (8) below.
[10] "The Council" defined by s. 15, p. 140 below.
[11] "Land" includes land covered by water: subsection (8) below.
[12] For provisions as to notice see s. 12, p. 140 below.

(7) If any person wilfully obstructs any person authorised by the Secretary of State exercising a power of entry under this section, he shall be guilty of an offence.

(8) Any reference in this section to the Secretary of State shall, in relation to England and Wales, be deemed to include a reference to the Minister of Agriculture, Fisheries and Food and any reference to land shall include land covered by water.

Giving of notice

12. (1) Any notice required by this Act to be given to any person shall be duly given if it is delivered to him, or left at his proper address, or sent to him by post.

(2) Any such notice required to be given to an incorporated company or body shall be duly given if given to the secretary or clerk of the company or body.

(3) For the purposes of this section and of section 26 of the Interpretation Act 1889[1] the proper address of any person to whom any such notice is to be given shall, in the case of the secretary or clerk of any incorporated company or body, be that of the registered or principal office of the company or body, and in any other case be the last-known address of the person in question.

(4) Where any such notice is to be given to a person as being the person having an interest in land, and it is not practicable after reasonable enquiry to ascertain his name or address, the notice may be given by addressing it to him by the description of the person having that interest in the land (naming it), and delivering the notice to some responsible person on the land or by affixing it, or a copy of it, to some conspicuous object on the land.

Duty of the Council

13. The Council[2] shall provide the Secretary of State with scientific advice on matters related to the management of seal populations.

Orders

14. (1) The power of the Secretary of State to make orders under this Act shall be exercisable by statutory instrument; and any statutory instrument made by virtue of this Act shall be subject to annulment in pursuance of a resolution of either House of Parliament.

(2) Any order made under this Act may be varied or revoked by a subsequent order made in the like manner.

Interpretation

15. In this Act unless the context otherwise requires—

"ammunition" has the same meaning as in the Firearms Act 1968[3];

"the Council" means the Natural Environment Research Council;

"firearm" has the same meaning as in the Firearms Act 1968.

Repeal

16. (1) The Grey Seals Protection Act 1932[4] and the reference to section 2(1) of that Act in Schedule 3 to the Criminal Justice Act 1967[5] are hereby repealed.

---

[1] S. 7 of the Interpretation Act 1978 (c. 30) replaces s. 26 of the Interpretation Act 1889: Interpretation Act 1978, ss. 17, 22.
[2] "The Council" defined by s. 15, below.
[3] 1968 c. 27.
[4] 1932 c. 23.
[5] 1967 c. 80.

(2) Notwithstanding the repeal of the Grey Seals Protection Act 1932 all prosecutions and proceedings in respect of offences under that Act committed before the coming into force of this Act may be continued, commenced, taken or prosecuted as if this Act had not been passed.

Short title, area of application, extent and commencement

17. (1) This Act may be cited as the Conservation of Seals Act 1970.

(2) Nothing done outside the seaward limits of the territorial waters adjacent to Great Britain shall constitute an offence under this Act.

(3) This Act shall not extend to Northern Ireland.

(4) This Act shall come into force at the expiry of 3 months beginning with the date of its passing[1].

---

[1] The Act accordingly came into force on 29 August 1970.

Forestry Act 1979

Ch. 21

An Act to re-state the power of the Forestry Commissioners to make grants and loans; and to provide for the metrication of enactments relating to forestry and forest lands.

[29th March 1979[1]]

Finance for forestry

1. (1) The Forestry Commissioners may, with the Treasury approval, make grants and loans to owners and lessees of land for and in connection with the use and management of the land for forestry purposes.

(2) Any such grant or loan shall be made out of the Forestry Fund and be on such terms and conditions as the Commissioners think fit.

(3) In the application of this section to land in Scotland which constitutes or is part of a common grazing for which a grazings committee or a grazings constable has been appointed under section 24 of the Crofters (Scotland) Act 1955[2], the references to owners and lessees shall be construed as references to the grazings committee or, as the case may be, the grazings constable[3].

2. *This section, and schedule 1, amend the Forestry Act 1967. The amendments are noted at the appropriate points in the 1967 Act.*

Citation, etc.

3. (1) This Act may be cited as the Forestry Act 1979; and the Forestry Act 1967[4] and this Act may be cited together as the Forestry Acts 1967 and 1979.

(2) The Forestry Act 1967 is repealed to the extent specified in Schedule 2 to this Act[5].

(3) This Act comes into force at the expiration of two months from the date on which it is passed.

(4) This Act does not extend to Northern Ireland.

---

[1] This Act came into force on 30 May 1979: s. 3(3) below.
[2] S. 24 of the Crofters (Scotland) Act 1955 is replaced by s. 47 of the Crofters (Scotland) Act 1993 (c. 44): s. 63, Sch. 6. The 1993 Act consolidates enactments relating to crofting and repeals the Crofters (Scotland) Act 1955.
[3] Subsection (3) inserted by the Crofter Forestry (Scotland) Act 1991 (c. 18), s. 3(1). This amendment came into force on 1 April 1992: S.I. 1992/504.
[4] P. 66 above.
[5] S. 4 and part of s. 9(6) of the Forestry Act 1967 are repealed by s. 3(2) and sch. 2.

Wildlife and Countryside Act 1981

Ch. 69

Part II: Nature Conservation, Countryside and National Parks

Nature conservation

Countryside

National Parks

Miscellaneous and supplemental

Part III: Public Rights of Way

Part IV: Miscellaneous and General

Schedules:

Wildlife and Countryside Act 1981

An Act to repeal and re-enact with amendments the Protection of Birds Acts 1954 to 1967 and the Conservation of Wild Creatures and Wild Plants Act 1975; to prohibit certain methods of killing or taking wild animals; to amend the law relating to protection of certain mammals; to restrict the introduction of certain animals and plants; to amend the Endangered Species (Import and Export) Act 1976; to amend the law relating to nature conservation, the countryside and National Parks and to make provision with respect to the Countryside Commission; to amend the law relating to public rights of way; and for connected purposes.

[30th October 1981[1]]

Part I: Wildlife[2]

Protection of birds

Protection of wild birds, their nests and eggs

1. (1) Subject to the provisions of this Part, if any person intentionally—

 (*a*) kills, injures or takes any wild bird[3];

 (*b*) takes, damages or destroys the nest of any wild bird while that nest is in use or being built; or

 (*c*) takes or destroys[4] an egg of any wild bird,

 he shall be guilty of an offence.

 (2) Subject to the provisions of this Part, if any person has in his possession or control—

 (*a*) any live or dead wild bird or any part of, or anything derived from, such a bird; or

 (*b*) an egg of a wild bird or any part of such an egg,

 he shall be guilty of an offence.

 (3) A person shall not be guilty of an offence under subsection (2) if he shows that—

 (*a*) the bird or egg had not been killed or taken, or had been killed or taken otherwise than in contravention of the relevant provisions; or

 (*b*) the bird, egg or other thing in his possession or control had been sold[5] (whether to him or any other person) otherwise than in contravention of those provisions;

 and in this subsection "the relevant provisions" means the provisions of this Part and of orders made under it and, in the case of a bird or other thing falling within subsection (1)(*a*), the provisions of the Protection of Birds Acts 1954 to 1967 and of orders made under those Acts.

 (4) Any person convicted of an offence under subsection (1) or (2) in respect of—

 (*a*) a bird included in Schedule 1[6] or any part of, or anything derived from, such a bird;

 (*b*) the nest of such a bird; or

 (*c*) an egg of such a bird or any part of such an egg,

 shall be liable to a special penalty[7].

---

[1] This Act came into force on various dates noted at the parts and sections below.

[2] This part, except ss. 12 and 19A, came into force on 28 September 1982: S.I. 1982/1217.

[3] "Wild bird" defined by s. 27(1), p. 167 below, and sub-section (6) below.

[4] "Destroy" defined by s. 27(1), p. 166 below.

[5] "Sale" defined by s. 27(1), p. 166 below.

[6] P. 192 below; see subsection (7) below.

[7] For penalties see s. 21, p. 162 below.

(5) Subject to the provisions of this Part, if any person intentionally—

(a) disturbs any wild bird included in Schedule 1 while it is building a nest or is in, on or near a nest containing eggs or young; or

(b) disturbs dependent young of such a bird,

he shall be guilty of an offence and liable to a special penalty.

(6) In this section "wild bird" does not include any bird which is shown to have been bred in captivity[1].

(7) Any reference in this Part to any bird included in Schedule 1 is a reference to any bird included in Part I and, during the close season[2] for the bird in question, any bird included in Part II of that Schedule[3].

....

Exceptions to s. 1

2. (1) Subject to the provisions of this section, a person shall not be guilty of an offence under section 1 by reason of the killing or taking of a bird included in Part I of Schedule 2[4] outside the close season[5] for that bird, or the injuring of such a bird outside that season in the course of an attempt to kill it.

(2) Subject to the provisions of this section, an authorised person[6] shall not be guilty of an offence under section 1 by reason of—

(a) the killing or taking of a bird included in Part II of Schedule 2[7], or the injuring of such a bird in the course of an attempt to kill it;

(b) the taking, damaging or destruction of a nest of such a bird; or

(c) the taking or destruction[8] of an egg of such a bird.

(3) Subsections (1) and (2) shall not apply in Scotland on Sundays or on Christmas Day; and subsection (1) shall not apply on Sundays in any area of England and Wales which the Secretary of State may by order prescribe for the purposes of that subsection.[9]

(4) In this section and section 1 "close season" means—

(a) in this case of capercaillie and (except in Scotland) woodcock, the period in any year commencing with 1st February and ending with 30th September;

(b) in the case of snipe, the period in any year commencing with 1st February and ending with 11th August;

(c) in the case of wild duck and wild geese in or over any area below high-water mark of ordinary spring tides, the period in any year commencing with 21st February and ending with 31st August;

(d) in any other case, subject to the provisions of this Part, the period in any year commencing with 1st February and ending with 31st August.

(5) The Secretary of State may by order made with respect to the whole or any specified part of Great Britain vary the close season for any wild bird[10] specified in the order.

(6) If it appears to the Secretary of State expedient that any wild birds included in Part II of Schedule 1 or Part I of Schedule 2 should be protected during any period outside the close season for those birds, he may by order made with respect to the whole or any specified part of Great Britain declare any period (which shall not in the case of any order exceed fourteen days) as a period of special protection for those birds; and this section and section 1 shall have effect as if

---

[1] For "bred in captivity" see s. 27(2), p. 167 below.
[2] "Close season" defined by s. 2(4) below.
[3] **Cases: section 1** *Kirkland v Robinson* [1987] Crim LR 643; *Robinson v Everett and W & FC Bonham & Son Ltd* [1988] Crim LR 699.
[4] P. 194 below.
[5] "Close season" defined by subsection (4) below.

[6] "Authorised person" defined by s. 27(1), p. 165 below.
[7] P. 195 below.
[8] "Destruction" defined by s. 27(1), p. 166 below.
[9] Orders made under the corresponding provision of the Protection of Birds Act 1954, which is replaced by this subsection, are listed at p. 396 below.
[10] "Wild bird" defined by s. 27(1), p. 167 below.

any period of special protection declared under this subsection for any birds formed part of the close season for those birds.

(7) Before making an order under subsection (6) the Secretary of State shall consult a person appearing to him to be a representative of persons interested in the shooting of birds of the kind proposed to be protected by the order.

Areas of special protection

3. (1) The Secretary of State may by order[1] make provision with respect to any area specified in the order providing for all or any of the following matters, that is to say—

   (*a*) that any person who, within that area or any part of it specified in the order, at any time or during any period so specified, intentionally—

   (i) kills, injures or takes any wild bird[2] or any wild bird so specified;

   (ii) takes, damages or destroys the nest of such a bird while that nest is in use or being built;

   (iii) takes or destroys[3] an egg of such a bird;

   (iv) disturbs such a bird while it is building a nest or is in, on or near a nest containing eggs or young; or

   (v) disturbs dependent young of such a bird,

   shall be guilty of an offence under this section;

   (*b*) that any person who, except as may be provided in the order, enters into that area or any part of it specified in the order at any time or during any period so specified shall be guilty of an offence under this section;

   (*c*) that where any offence under this Part, or any such offence under this Part as may be specified in the order, is committed within that area, the offender shall be liable to a special penalty[4].

(2) An authorised person[5] shall not by virtue of any such order be guilty of an offence by reason of—

   (*a*) the killing or taking of a bird included in Part II of Schedule 2[6], or the injuring of such a bird in the course of an attempt to kill it;

   (*b*) the taking, damaging or destruction of the nest of such a bird;

   (*c*) the taking or destruction of an egg of such a bird; or

   (*d*) the disturbance of such a bird or dependent young of such a bird.

(3) The making of any order under this section with respect to any area shall not affect the exercise by any person of any right vested in him, whether as owner, lessee or occupier[7] of any land in that area or by virtue of a licence or agreement.

(4) Before making any order under this section the Secretary of State shall give particulars of the intended order either by notice in writing to every owner and every occupier of any land included in the area with respect to which the order is to be made or, where the giving of such a notice is in his opinion impracticable, by advertisement in a newspaper circulating in the locality[8] in which that area is situated.

(5) The Secretary of State shall not make an order under this section unless—

   (*a*) all the owners and occupiers aforesaid have consented thereto;

---

[1] Areas of special protection for birds established by order under this section are listed at p. 397 below.
[2] "Wild bird" defined by s. 27(1), p. 167 below.
[3] "Destroy" defined by s. 27(1), p. 166 below.
[4] For penalties see s. 21, p. 162 below.
[5] "Authorised person" defined by s. 27(1), p. 165 below.

[6] P. 195 below.
[7] "Occupier" defined by s. 27(1), p. 166 below.
[8] Word "locality" substituted by the Local Government (Wales) Act 1994 (c. 19), s. 66(6), sch. 16, para. 65(1). It is planned that this amendment will come into force on 1 April 1996.

(b) no objections thereto have been made by any of those owners or occupiers before the expiration of a period of three months from the date of the giving of the notice or the publication of the advertisement; or

(c) any such objections so made have been withdrawn.

Exceptions to ss. 1 and 3

4. (1) Nothing in section 1[1] or in any order made under section 3 shall make unlawful—

(a) anything done in pursuance of a requirement by the Minister of Agriculture, Fisheries and Food or the Secretary of State under section 98 of the Agriculture Act 1947[2], or by the Secretary of State under section 39 of the Agriculture (Scotland) Act 1948[3];

(b) anything done under, or in pursuance of an order made under, section 21 or 22 of the Animal Health Act 1981[4]; or

(c) except in the case of a wild bird[5] included in Schedule 1[6] or the nest or egg of such a bird, anything done under, or in pursuance of an order made under, any other provision of the said Act of 1981.

(2) Notwithstanding anything in the provisions of section 1 or any order made under section 3, a person shall not be guilty of an offence by reason of—

(a) the taking of any wild bird if he shows that the bird had been disabled otherwise than by his unlawful act and was taken solely for the purpose of tending it and releasing it when no longer disabled;

(b) the killing of any wild bird if he shows that the bird had been so seriously disabled otherwise than by his unlawful act that there was no reasonable chance of its recovering; or

(c) any act made unlawful by those provisions if he shows that the act was the incidental result of a lawful operation and could not reasonably have been avoided.

(3) Notwithstanding anything in the provisions of section 1 or any order made under section 3, an authorised person[7] shall not be guilty of an offence by reason of the killing or injuring of any wild bird, other than a bird included in Schedule 1, if he shows that his action was necessary for the purpose of—

(a) preserving public health or public or air safety;

(b) preventing the spread of disease; or

(c) preventing serious damage to livestock[8], foodstuffs for livestock, crops, vegetables, fruit, growing timber, or fisheries[9].

Prohibition of certain methods of killing or taking wild birds

5. (1) Subject to the provisions of this Part, if any person—

(a) sets in position any of the following articles, being an article which is of such a nature and is so placed as to be calculated to cause bodily injury to any wild bird[10] coming into contact therewith, that is to say, any spring, trap, gin, snare, hook and line, any electrical device for killing, stunning or frightening or any poisonous, poisoned or stupefying substance;

(b) uses for the purpose of killing or taking any wild bird any such article as aforesaid, whether or not of such a nature and so placed as aforesaid, or any net, baited board, bird-lime or substance of a like nature to bird-lime;

---

[1] P. 146 above.
[2] 1947 c. 48.
[3] 1948 c. 45.
[4] 1981 c. 22.
[5] "Wild bird" defined by s. 27(1), p. 167 below.
[6] P. 192 below.

[7] "Authorised person" defined by s. 27(1), p. 165 below.
[8] "Livestock" defined by s. 27(1), p. 166 below.
[9] **Case: section 4** *Robinson v Everett and W & FC Bonham & Son Ltd* [1988] Crim LR 699.
[10] "Wild bird" defined by s. 27(1), p. 167 below. In this section "wild bird" includes any game bird.

    (*c*) uses for the purpose of killing or taking any wild bird—

        (i) any bow or crossbow;

      (ii) any explosive other than ammunition for a firearm[1];

    (iii) any automatic or semi-automatic weapon[2];

    (iv) any shot-gun of which the barrel has an internal diameter at the muzzle of more than one and three-quarter inches;

     (v) any device for illuminating a target or any sighting device for night shooting;

    (vi) any form of artificial lighting or any mirror or other dazzling device;

   (vii) any gas or smoke not falling within paragraphs (*a*) and (*b*); or

  (viii) any chemical wetting agent;

    (*d*) uses as a decoy, for the purpose of killing or taking any wild bird, any sound recording or any live bird of other animal whatever which is tethered, or which is secured by means of braces or other similar appliances, or which is blind, maimed or injured;

    (*e*) uses any mechanically propelled vehicle[3] in immediate pursuit of a wild bird for the purpose of killing or taking that bird; or

    (*f*) knowingly causes or permits to be done an act which is mentioned in the foregoing provisions of this subsection and which is not lawful under subsection (5)[4].

he shall be guilty of an offence and be liable to a special penalty[5].

(2) Subject to subsection (3), the Secretary of State may by order, either generally or in relation to any kind of wild bird specified in the order, amend subsection (1) by adding any method of killing or taking wild birds or by omitting any such method which is mentioned in that subsection.

(3) The power conferred by subsection (2) shall not be exerciseable, except for the purpose of complying with an international obligation, in relation to any method of killing or taking wild birds which involves the use of a firearm.

(4) In any proceedings under subsection (1)(*a*) it shall be a defence to show that the article was set in position for the purpose of killing or taking, in the interests of public health, agriculture, forestry, fisheries or nature conservation, any wild animals[6] which could be lawfully killed or taken by those means and that he took all reasonable precautions to prevent injury thereby to wild birds.

(4A) In any proceedings under subsection (1)(*f*) relating to an act which is mentioned in subsection (1)(*a*) it shall be a defence to show that the article was set in position for the purpose of killing or taking, in the interests of public health, agriculture, forestry, fisheries or nature conservation, any wild animals which could be lawfully killed or taken by those means and that he took or caused to be taken all reasonable precautions to prevent injury thereby to wild birds[7].

(5) Nothing in subsection (1) shall make unlawful—

    (*a*) the use of a cage-trap or net by an authorised person[8] for the purpose of taking a bird included in Part II of Schedule 2[9];

    (*b*) the use of nets for the purpose of taking wild duck in a duck decoy which is shown to have been in use immediately before the passing of the Protection of Birds Act 1954[10]; or

    (*c*) the use of a cage-trap or net for the purpose of taking any game bird[11] if it is shown that the taking of the bird is solely for the purpose of breeding;

---

[1] "Firearm" defined by s. 27(1), p. 166 below.

[2] "Automatic weapon" and "semi-automatic weapon" defined by s. 27(1), p. 166 below.

[3] "Vehicle" defined b s. 27(1), p. 166 below.

[4] Paragraph (*f*) inserted by the Wildlife and Countryside (Amendment) Act 1991 (c. 39), s. 1(3). This amendment came into force on 25 September 1991: s. 3(3), (4).

[5] For penalties see s. 21, p. 162 below.

[6] "Wild animal" defined by s. 27(1), p. 167 below.

[7] Subsection (4A) inserted by the Wildlife and Countryside (Amendment) Act 1991 (c. 39), s. 1(4).

[8] "Authorised person" defined by s. 27(1), p. 165 below.

[9] P. 195 below.

[10] 1954 c. 30.

[11] "Game bird" defined by s. 27(1), p. 166 below.

but nothing in this subsection shall make lawful the use of any net for taking birds in flight or the use for taking birds on the ground of any net which is projected or propelled otherwise than by hand[1].

Sale etc. of live or dead wild birds, eggs etc.

6. (1) Subject to the provisions of this Part, if any person—

   (*a*) sells[2], offers or exposes for sale, or has in his possession or transports for the purpose of sale, any live wild bird[3] other than a bird included in Part I of Schedule 3[4], or an egg of a wild bird or any part of such an egg; or

   (*b*) publishes or causes to be published any advertisement[5] likely to be understood as conveying that he buys or sells, or intends to buy or sell, any of those things,

   he shall be guilty of an offence.

   (2) Subject to the provisions of this Part, if any person who is not for the time being registered in accordance with regulations made by the Secretary of State[6]—

   (*a*) sells, offers or exposes for sale, or has in his possession or transports for the purpose of sale, any dead wild bird other than a bird included in Part II or III of Schedule 3[7], or any part of, or anything derived from, such a wild bird; or

   (*b*) publishes or causes to be published any advertisement likely to be understood as conveying that he buys or sells, or intends to buy or sell, any of those things,

   he shall be guilty of an offence.

   (3) Subject to the provisions of this Part, if any person shows or causes or permits to be shown for the purposes of any competition or in any premises in which a competition is being held—

   (*a*) any live wild bird other than a bird included in Part I of Schedule 3; or

   (*b*) any live bird one of whose parents was such a wild bird,

   he shall be guilty of an offence.

   (4) Any person convicted of an offence under this section in respect of—

   (*a*) a bird included in Schedule 1[8] or any part of, or anything derived from, such a bird; or

   (*b*) an egg of such bird or any part of such an egg,

   shall be liable to a special penalty[9].

   (5) Any reference in this section to any bird included in Part I of Schedule 3 is a reference to any bird included in that Part which was bred in captivity[10] and has been ringed or marked in accordance with regulations made by the Secretary of State; and regulations so made may make different provision for different birds or different provisions of this section[11].

   (6) Any reference in this section to any bird included in Part II or III of Schedule 3 is a reference to any bird included in Part II and, during the period commencing with 1st September in any year and ending with 28th February of the following year, any bird included in Part III of that Schedule.

   (7) The power of the Secretary of State to make regulations under subsection (2) shall include power—

   (*a*) to impose requirements as to the carrying out by a person registered in accordance with the regulations of any act which, apart from the registration, would constitute an offence under this section; and

---

[1] **Case: section 5** *Robinson v Hughes* [1987] Crim LR 644.
[2] "Sale" defined by s. 27(1), p. 166 below.
[3] "Wild bird" defined by s. 27(1), p. 167 below.
[4] P. 195 below; see subsection (5) below.
[5] "Advertisement" defined by s. 27(1), p. 165 below.
[6] The Wildlife and Countryside (Registration to Sell etc. Certain Dead Wild Birds) Regulations 1982, S.I. 1982/1219 as amended by S.I. 1991/479, made under this section, are

at p. 313 below.
[7] P. 195 below; see subsection (6) below.
[8] P. 192 below.
[9] For penalties see s. 21, p. 162 below.
[10] For "bred in captivity" see s. 27(2), p. 167 below.
[11] The Wildlife and Countryside (Ringing of Certain Birds) Regulations 1982, S.I. 1982/1220, made under this section, are at p. 316 below.

(*b*) to provide that any contravention of the regulations shall constitute such an offence.

(8) Regulations under subsection (2) shall secure that no person shall become or remain registered—

(*a*) within five years of his having been convicted of an offence under this Part for which a special penalty is provided; or

(*b*) within three years of his having been convicted of any other offence under this Part so far as it relates to the protection of birds or other animals or any offence involving their ill-treatment,

no account being taken for this purpose of a conviction which has become spent by virtue of the Rehabilitation of Offenders Act 1974[1].

(9) Any person authorised in writing by the Secretary of State may, at any reasonable time and (if required to do so) upon producing evidence that he is authorised, enter and inspect any premises where a registered person keeps any wild birds for the purpose of ascertaining whether an offence under this section is being, or has been, committed on those premises.

(10) Any person who intentionally obstructs a person acting in the exercise of the power conferred by subsection (9) shall be guilty of an offence.

Registration etc. of certain captive birds

7. (1) If any person keeps or has in his possession or under his control any bird included in Schedule 4[2] which has not been registered and ringed or marked in accordance with regulations made by the Secretary of State[3], he shall be guilty of an offence and be liable to a special penalty[4].

(2) The power of the Secretary of State to make regulations under subsection (1) shall include power—

(*a*) to impose requirements which must be satisfied in relation to a bird included in Schedule 4 before it can be registered in accordance with the regulations; and

(*b*) to make different provision for different birds or different descriptions of birds.

(3) If any person keeps or has in his possession or under his control any bird included in Schedule 4—

(*a*) within five years of his having been convicted of an offence under this Part for which a special penalty is provided; or

(*b*) within three years of his having been convicted of any other offence under this Part so far as it relates to the protection of birds or other animals or any offence involving their ill-treatment,

he shall be guilty of an offence.

(4) If any person knowingly disposes of or offers to dispose of any bird included in Schedule 4 to any person—

(*a*) within five years of that person's having been convicted of such an offence as is mentioned in paragraph (*a*) of subsection (3); or

(*b*) within three years of that person's having been convicted of such an offence as is mentioned in paragraph (*b*) of that subsection,

he shall be guilty of an offence.

(5) No account shall be taken for the purpose of subsections (3) and (4) of any conviction which has become spent for the purpose of the Rehabilitation of Offenders Act 1974[5].

---

[1] 1974 c. 53.
[2] P. 196 below.
[3] The Wildlife and Countryside (Registration and Ringing of Certain Captive Birds) Regulations 1982, S.I. 1982/1221,

as amended by S.I. 1991/478, S.I. 1994/1152, made under this section, are at p. 318 below.
[4] For penalties see s. 21, p. 162 below.
[5] 1974 c. 53.

(6) Any person authorised in writing by the Secretary of State may, at any reasonable time and (if required to do so) upon producing evidence that he is authorised, enter and inspect any premises where any birds included in Schedule 4 are kept for the purpose of ascertaining whether an offence under this section is being, or has been, committed on those premises.

(7) Any person who intentionally obstructs a person acting in the exercise of the power conferred by subsection (6) shall be guilty of an offence.

Protection of captive birds

8. (1) If any person keeps or confines any bird whatever in any cage or other receptacle which is not sufficient in height, length or breadth to permit the bird to stretch its wings freely, he shall be guilty of an offence and be liable to a special penalty[1].

(2) Subsection (1) does not apply to poultry[2], or to the keeping or confining of any bird—

(a) while that bird is in the course of conveyance, by whatever means;

(b) while that bird is being shown for the purposes of any public exhibition or competition if the time during which the bird is kept or confined for those purposes does not in the aggregate exceed 72 hours; or

(c) while that bird is undergoing examination or treatment by a veterinary surgeon or veterinary practitioner.

(3) Every person who—

(a) promotes, arranges, conducts, assists in, receives money for, or takes part in, any event whatever at or in the course of which captive birds are liberated by hand or by any other means whatever for the purpose of being shot immediately after their liberation; or

(b) being the owner or occupier[3] of any land, permits that land to be used for the purposes of such an event,

shall be guilty of an offence and be liable to a special penalty.

Protection of other animals

Protection of certain wild animals

9. (1) Subject to the provisions of this Part, if any person intentionally kills, injures or takes any wild animal[4] included in Schedule 5[5], he shall be guilty of an offence.

(2) Subject to the provisions of this Part, if any person has in his possession or control any live or dead wild animal included in Schedule 5 or any part of, or anything derived from, such an animal, he shall be guilty of an offence.

(3) A person shall not be guilty of an offence under subsection (2) if he shows that—

(a) the animal had not been killed or taken, or had been killed or taken otherwise than in contravention of the relevant provisions; or

(b) the animal or other thing in his possession or control had been sold[6] (whether to him or any other person) otherwise than in contravention of those provisions;

and in this subsection "the relevant provisions" means the provisions of this Part and of the Conservation of Wild Creatures and Wild Plants Act 1975[7].

(4) Subject to the provisions of this Part, if any person intentionally—

(a) damages or destroys, or obstructs access to, any structure or place which any wild animal included in Schedule 5 uses for shelter or protection; or

---

[1] For penalties see s. 21, p. 162 below.
[2] "Poultry" defined by s. 27(1), p. 166 below.
[3] "Occupier" defined by s. 27(1), p. 166 below.
[4] "Wild animal" defined by s. 27(1), (3), p. 167 below.

[5] P. 197 below.
[6] "Sale" defined by s. 27(1), p. 166 below.
[7] 1975 c. 48.

(b) disturbs any such animal while it is occupying a structure or place which it uses for that purpose,

he shall be guilty of an offence.

(5) Subject to the provisions of this Part, if any person—

(a) sells[1], offers or exposes for sale, or has in his possession or transports for the purpose of sale, any live or dead wild animal included in Schedule 5, or any part of, or anything derived from, such an animal; or

(b) publishes or causes to be published any advertisement[2] likely to be understood as conveying that he buys or sells, or intends to buy or sell, any of those things,

he shall be guilty of an offence.

(6) In any proceedings for an offence under subsection (1), (2) or (5)(a), the animal in question shall be presumed to have been a wild animal unless the contrary is shown.

....

Exceptions to s. 9

10. (1) Nothing in section 9 shall make unlawful—

(a) anything done in pursuance of a requirement by the Minister of Agriculture, Fisheries and Food or the Secretary of State under section 98 of the Agriculture Act 1947[3], or by the Secretary of State under section 39 of the Agriculture (Scotland) Act 1948[4]; or

(b) anything done under, or in pursuance of an order made under, the Animal Health Act 1981[5].

(2) Nothing in subsection (4) of section 9 shall make unlawful anything done within a dwelling-house.

(3) Notwithstanding anything in section 9, a person shall not be guilty of an offence by reason of—

(a) the taking of any such animal if he shows that the animal had been disabled otherwise than by his unlawful act and was taken solely for the purpose of tending it and releasing it when no longer disabled;

(b) the killing of any such animal if he shows that the animal had been so seriously disabled otherwise than by his unlawful act that there was no reasonable chance of its recovering; or

(c) any act made unlawful by that section if he shows that the act was the incidental result of a lawful operation and could not reasonably have been avoided.

(4) Notwithstanding anything in section 9, an authorised person[6] shall not be guilty of an offence by reason of the killing or injuring of a wild animal[7] included in Schedule 5[8] if he shows that his action was necessary for the purpose of preventing serious damage to livestock[9], foodstuffs for livestock, crops, vegetables, fruit, growing timber or any other form of property or to fisheries.

(5) A person shall not be entitled to rely on the defence provided by subsection (2) or (3)(c) as respects anything done in relation to a bat otherwise than in the living area of a dwelling house unless he had notified the Nature Conservancy Council[10] for the area in which the house is situated or, as the case may be, the act is to take place[11] of the proposed action or operation and allowed them a reasonable time to advise him as to whether it should be carried out and, if so, the method to be used.

---

[1] "Sale" defined by s. 27(1), p. 166 below.
[2] "Advertisement" defined by s. 27(1), p. 165 below.
[3] 1947 c. 48.
[4] 1948 c. 45.
[5] 1981 c. 22.
[6] "Authorised person" defined by s. 27(1), p. 165 below.
[7] "Wild animal" defined by s. 27(1) and (3), p. 167 below.
[8] P. 197 below.

[9] "Livestock" defined by s. 27(1), p. 166 below.
[10] For "the Nature Conservancy Council" see s. 27(3A), p. 167 below.
[11] Words "for the area in which the house is situated or, as the case may be, the act is to take place" inserted by the Environmental Protection Act 1990 (c. 43), s. 132(1)(a), sch. 9, para. 11(2). This amendment came into force on 1 April 1991: S.I. 1991/685.

(6) An authorised person shall not be entitled to rely on the defence provided by subsection (4) as respects any action taken at any time if it had become apparent, before that time, that that action would prove necessary for the purpose mentioned in that subsection and either—

(a) a licence under section 16[1] authorising that action had not been applied for as soon as reasonably practicable after that fact had become apparent; or

(b) an application for such a licence had been determined.

Prohibition of certain methods of killing or taking wild animals

11. (1) Subject to the provisions of this Part, if any person—

(a) sets in position any self-locking snare which is of such a nature and so placed as to be calculated to cause bodily injury to any wild animal[2] coming into contact therewith;

(b) uses for the purpose of killing or taking any wild animal any self-locking snare, whether or not of such a nature or so placed as aforesaid, any bow or crossbow or any explosive other than ammunition for a firearm[3];

(c) uses as a decoy, for the purpose of killing or taking any wild animal, any live mammal or bird whatever; or

(d) knowingly causes or permits to be done an act which is mentioned in the foregoing provisions of this section,[4]

he shall be guilty of an offence.

(2) Subject to the provisions of this Part, if any person—

(a) sets in position any of the following articles, being an article which is of such a nature and so placed as to be calculated to cause bodily injury to any wild animal included in Schedule 6[5] which comes into contact therewith, that is to say, any trap or snare, any electrical device for killing or stunning or any poisonous, poisoned or stupefying substance;

(b) uses for the purpose of killing or taking any such wild animal any such article as aforesaid, whether or not of such a nature and so placed as aforesaid, or any net;

(c) uses for the purpose of killing or taking any such wild animal—

   (i) any automatic or semi-automatic weapon[6];

   (ii) any device for illuminating a target or sighting device for night shooting;

   (iii) any form of artificial light or any mirror or other dazzling device; or

   (iv) any gas or smoke not falling within paragraphs (a) and (b);

(d) uses as a decoy, for the purpose of killing or taking any such wild animal, any sound recording;

(e) uses any mechanically propelled vehicle[7] in immediate pursuit of any such wild animal for the purpose of driving, killing or taking that animal; or

(f) knowingly causes or permits to be done an act which is mentioned in the foregoing provisions of this subsection,[8]

he shall be guilty of an offence.

(3) Subject to the provisions of this Part, if any person—

(a) sets in position or knowingly causes or permits to be set in position[9] any snare which is of

---

[1] P. 158 below.

[2] "Wild animal" defined by s. 27(1) and (3), p. 167 below.

[3] "Firearm" defined by s. 27(1), p. 166 below.

[4] Paragraph (d) inserted by the Wildlife and Countryside (Amendment) Act 1991 (c. 39), s. 2(2)(b). This amendment came into force on 25 September 1991: s. 3(3), (4).

[5] P. 200 below.

[6] "Automatic weapon" and "semi-automatic weapon"

defined by s. 27(1), p. 166 below.

[7] "Vehicle" defined by s. 27(1), p. 166 below.

[8] Paragraph (f) inserted by the Wildlife and Countryside (Amendment) Act 1991 (c. 39), s. 2(3)(b).

[9] Words "or knowingly causes or permits to be set in position" inserted by the Wildlife and Countryside (Amendment) Act 1991 (c. 39), s. 2(4).

such a nature and so placed as to be calculated to cause bodily injury to any wild animal coming into contact therewith; and

(b) while the snare remains in position fails, without reasonable excuse, to inspect it, or cause it to be inspected, at least once every day,

he shall be guilty of an offence.

(4) The Secretary of State may, for the purpose of complying with an international obligation, by order, either generally or in relation to any kind of wild animal specified in the order, amend subsection (1) or (2) by adding any method of killing or taking wild animals or by omitting any such method as is mentioned in that subsection.

(5) In any proceedings for an offence under subsection (1)(b) or (c) or (2)(b), (c), (d) or (e), and in any proceedings for an offence under subsection (1)(d) or 2(f) relating to an act which is mentioned in any of those paragraphs[1] the animal in question shall be presumed to have been a wild animal unless the contrary is shown.

(6) In any proceedings for an offence under subsection (2)(a) it shall be a defence to show that the article was set in position by the accused for the purpose of killing or taking, in the interests of public health, agriculture, forestry, fisheries or nature conservation, any wild animals which could be lawfully killed or taken by those means and that he took all reasonable precautions to prevent injury thereby to any wild animals included in Schedule 6.

(7) In any proceedings for an offence under subsection (2)(f) relating to an act which is mentioned in subsection (2)(a) it shall be a defence to show that the article was set in position for the purpose of killing or taking, in the interests of public health, agriculture, forestry, fisheries or nature conservation, any wild animals which could be lawfully killed or taken by those means and that he took or caused to be taken all reasonable precautions to prevent injury thereby to any wild animals included in Schedule 6.[2]

Protection of certain mammals

12. Schedule 7, which amends the law relating to the protection of certain mammals, shall have effect[4].

Protection of plants

Protection of wild plants

13. (1) Subject to the provisions of this Part, if any person—

(a) intentionally picks[5], uproots[6] or destroys any wild plant[7] included in Schedule 8[8]; or

(b) not being an authorised person[9], intentionally uproots any wild plant not included in that Schedule,

he shall be guilty of an offence.

(2) Subject to the provisions of this Part, if any person—

(a) sells[10], offers or exposes for sale, or has in his possession or transports for the purpose of sale, any live or dead wild plant included in Schedule 8, or any part of, or anything derived from, such a plant; or

(b) publishes or causes to be published any advertisement[11] likely to be understood as conveying that he buys or sells, or intends to buy or sell, any of those things,

---

[1] Words "and in any proceedings for an offence under subsection (1)(d) or (2)(f) relating to an act which is mentioned in any of those paragraphs" inserted by the Wildlife and Countryside (Amendment) Act 1991 (c. 39), s. 2(5).

[2] Subsection (7) inserted by the Wildlife and Countryside (Amendment) Act 1991 (c. 39), s. 2(6).

[4] This section came into force on 16 February 1982: S.I. 1982/44. Schedule 7 is not reproduced. The amendments made by Schedule 7 to the Conservation of Seals Act 1970 (c.

30) are noted at the appropriate points within the Act.

[5] "Pick" defined by s. 27(1), p. 166 below.

[6] "Uproot" defined by s. 27(1), p. 166 below.

[7] "Wild plant" defined by s. 27(1), p. 167 below.

[8] P. 201 below.

[9] "Authorised person" defined by s. 27(1), p. 165 below.

[10] "Sale" defined by s. 27(1), p. 166 below.

[11] "Advertisement" defined by s. 27(1), p. 165 below.

he shall be guilty of an offence.

(3) Notwithstanding anything in subsection (1), a person shall not be guilty of an offence by reason of any act made unlawful by that subsection if he shows that the act was an incidental result of a lawful operation and could not reasonably have been avoided.

(4) In any proceedings for an offence under subsection (2)(*a*), the plant in question shall be presumed to have been a wild plant unless the contrary is shown.

Miscellaneous

Introduction of new species etc.

14. (1) Subject to the provisions of this Part, if any person releases or allows to escape into the wild any animal[1] which—

(*a*) is of a kin which is not ordinarily resident in and is not a regular visitor to Great Britain in a wild state; or

(*b*) is included in Part I of Schedule 9[2],

he shall be guilty of an offence.

(2) Subject to the provisions of this Part, if any person plants or otherwise causes to grow in the wild any plant which is included in Part II of Schedule 9[3], he shall be guilty of an offence.

(3) Subject to subsection (4), it shall be a defence to a charge of committing an offence under subsection (1) or (2) to prove that the accused took all reasonable steps and exercised all due diligence to avoid committing the offence.

(4) Where the defence provided by subsection (3) involves an allegation that the commission of the offence was due to the act or default of another person, the person charged shall not, without leave of the court, be entitled to rely on the defence unless, within a period ending seven clear days before the hearing, he has served on the prosecutor a notice giving such information identifying or assisting in the identification of the other person as was then in his possession.

(5) Any person authorised in writing by the Secretary of State may, at any reasonable time and (if required to do so) upon producing evidence that he is authorised, enter any land for the purpose of ascertaining whether an offence under subsection (1) or (2) is being, or has been, committed on that land; but nothing in this subsection shall authorise any person to enter a dwelling.

(6) Any person who intentionally obstructs a person acting in the exercise of the power conferred by subsection (5) shall be guilty of an offence.

....

Endangered species (import and export)

15. (1) The Endangered Species (Import and Export) Act 1976 shall have effect subject to the amendments provided for in Schedule 10; and in that Schedule "the 1976 Act" means that Act.[4]

(2) The functions of the Nature Conservancy Councils[5] shall include power to advise or assist—

(*a*) any constable;

(*b*) any officer commissioned or other person appointed or authorised by the Commissioners of Customs and Excise to exercise any function conferred on the Commissioners by the said Act of 1976; or

(*c*) any person duly authorised by the Secretary of State under section 7(3) of that Act,

in, or in connection with, the enforcement of that Act or any order made under it.

---

[1] For "animal" see s. 27(3), p. 167 below.
[2] P. 204 below.
[3] P. 205 below.
[4] Schedule 10 to this Act and the Endangered Species (Import and Export) Act 1976 are not reproduced in this Manual.

[5] For "Nature Conservancy Councils" see s. 27(3A), p. 167 below. Word "Councils" substituted by the Environmental Protection Act 1990 (c. 43), s. 132(1)(*a*), sch. 9, para. 11(3). This amendment came into force on 1 April 1991: 1991/685.

Supplemental

Power to grant licences

16. (1) Sections 1[1], 5[2], 6(3)[3], 7[4] and 8[5] and orders under section 3[6] do not apply to anything done—

(*a*) for scientific or educational purposes;

(*b*) for the purpose of ringing or marking, or examining any ring or mark on, wild birds[7];

(*c*) for the purpose of conserving wild birds;

(*d*) for the purpose of protecting any collection of wild birds;

(*e*) for the purposes of falconry or aviculture[8];

(*f*) for the purposes of any public exhibition or competition;

(*g*) for the purposes of taxidermy;

(*h*) for the purpose of photography;

(*i*) for the purposes of preserving public health or public or air safety;

(*j*) for the purpose of preventing the spread of disease; or

(*k*) for the purposes of preventing serious damage to livestock[9], foodstuffs for livestock, crops, vegetables, fruit, growing timber or fisheries,

if it is done under and in accordance with the terms of a licence granted by the appropriate authority[10].

(2) Section 1[11] and orders under section 3[12] do not apply to anything done for the purpose of providing food for human consumption in relation to—

(*a*) a gannet on the island of Sula Sgeir; or

(*b*) a gull's egg or, at any time before 15th April in any year, a lapwing's egg,

if it is done under and in accordance with the terms of a licence granted by the appropriate authority.

(3) Sections 9(1)[13], (2) and (4), 11(1)[14] and (2) and 13(1)[15] do not apply to anything done—

(*a*) for scientific or educational purposes;

(*b*) for the purpose of ringing or marking, or examining any ring or mark on, wild animals[16];

(*c*) for the purpose of conserving wild animals or wild plants[17] or introducing them to particular areas;

(*d*) for the purpose of protecting any zoological or botanical collection;

(*e*) for the purpose of photography;

(*f*) for the purpose of preserving public health or public safety;

(*g*) for the purpose of preventing the spread of disease; or

(*h*) for the purpose of preventing serious damage to livestock, foodstuffs for livestock, crops, vegetables, fruit, growing timber or any other form of property or to fisheries,

if it is done under and in accordance with the terms of a licence granted by the appropriate authority.

(4) The following provisions, namely—

---

[1] P. 146 above.
[2] P. 150 above.
[3] P. 151 above.
[4] P. 152 above.
[5] P. 153 above.
[6] P. 148 above.
[7] "Wild bird" defined by s. 27(1), p. 167 below. In this section "wild bird" includes any game bird.
[8] "Aviculture" defined by s. 27(1), p. 166 below.
[9] "Livestock" defined by s. 27(1), p. 166 below.

[10] "The appropriate authority" defined by subsection (9) below.
[11] P. 146 above.
[12] P. 148 above.
[13] P. 153 above.
[14] P. 155 above.
[15] P. 156 above.
[16] "Wild animal" defined by s. 27(1) and (3), p. 167 below.
[17] "Wild plant" defined by s. 27(1), p. 167 below.

(*a*) section 6(1)[1] and (2);

(*b*) sections 9(5)[2] and 13(2)[3]; and

(*c*) section 14[4],

do not apply to anything done under and in accordance with the terms of a licence granted by the appropriate authority.

(5) Subject to subsection (6), a licence under the foregoing provisions of this section—

(*a*) may be, to any degree, general or specific;

(*b*) may be granted either to persons of a class or to a particular person;

(*c*) may be subject to compliance with any specified conditions;

(*d*) may be modified or revoked at any time by the appropriate authority; and

(*e*) subject to paragraph (*d*), shall be valid for the period stated in the licence;

and the appropriate authority may charge therefore such reasonable sum (if any) as they may determine.

(6) A licence under subsection (1), (2) or (3) which authorises any person to kill wild birds or wild animals—

(*a*) shall specify the area within which, and the methods by which the wild birds or wild animals may be killed; and

(*b*) subject to subsection (5)(*d*), shall be valid for the period, not exceeding two years, stated in the licence.

(7) It shall be a defence in proceedings for an offence under section 8(*b*) of the Protection of Animals Act 1911[5] or section 7(*b*) of the Protection of Animals (Scotland) Act 1912[6] (which restrict the placing on land of poison and poisonous substances) to show that—

(*a*) the act alleged to constitute the offence was done under and in accordance with the terms of a licence issued under subsection (1) or (3); and

(*b*) any conditions specified in the licence were complied with.

(8) For the purposes of a licence granted under the foregoing provisions of this section, the definition of a class of persons may be framed by reference to any circumstances whatever including, in particular, their being authorised by any other person.

(9) In this section "the appropriate authority" means—

(*a*) in the case of a licence under paragraph (*a*), (*b*) or (*c*) of subsection (1), either the Secretary of State after consultation with whichever one of the advisory bodies[7] he considers is best able to advise him as to whether the licence should be granted, or the relevant Nature Conservancy Council[8];

(*b*) in the case of a licence under any of paragraphs (*d*) to (*g*) of subsection (1), subsection (2) or paragraph (*a*) or (*b*) of subsection (4), the Secretary of State after such consultation as aforesaid;

(*c*) in the case of a licence under paragraph (*h*) of subsection (1) or any of paragraphs (*a*) to (*e*) of subsection (3), the relevant Nature Conservancy Council;

(*d*) in the case of a licence under paragraph (*i*), (*j*) or (*k*) of subsection (1) or paragraph (*f*), (*g*) or (*h*) of subsection (3) or a licence under paragraph (*c*) of subsection (4) which authorises anything to be done in relation to fish or shellfish, the agriculture Minister[9]; and

---

[1] P. 151 above.
[2] P. 154 above.
[3] P. 156 above.
[4] P. 157 above.
[5] 1911 c. 27.
[6] 1912 c. 14.
[7] "Advisory body" defined by s. 23, p. 163 below: s. 27(1).

[8] For "relevant Nature Conservancy Council" see subsection (11) below and s. 27(3A), p. 167 below. Word "relevant" in this subsection inserted by the Environmental Protection Act 1990 (c. 43), s. 132(1)(*a*), sch. 9, para. 11(4)(*a*). This amendment came into force on 1 April 1991: S.I. 1991/685.
[9] "Agriculture Minister" defined by s. 27(1), p. 165 below.

(e) in the case of any other licence under paragraph (c) of subsection (4), the Secretary of State.

(10) The agriculture Minister—

(a) shall from time to time consult with each of the Nature Conservancy Councils[1] as to the exercise in the area of that Council[2] of his functions under this section; and

(b) shall not grant a licence of any description unless he has been advised by the relevant nature Conservancy Council[3] as to the circumstances in which, in their opinion, licences of that description should be granted.

(11) For the purposes of this section a reference to a relevant Nature Conservancy Council is a reference to the Nature Conservancy Council for the area in which it is proposed to carry on the activity requiring a licence.[4]

....

False statements made for obtaining registration or licence etc.

17. A person who, for the purposes of obtaining, whether for himself or another, a registration in accordance with regulations made under section 6(2)[5] or 7(1)[6] or the grant of a licence under section 16—

(a) makes a statement or representation, or furnishes a document or information, which he knows to be false in a material particular; or

(b) recklessly makes a statement or representation, or furnishes a document or information, which is false in a material particular,

shall be guilty of an offence.

....

Attempts to commit offences etc.

18. (1) Any person who attempts to commit an offence under the foregoing provisions of this Part shall be guilty of an offence and shall be punishable in like manner as for the said offence.

(2) Any person who for the purposes of committing an offence under the foregoing provisions of this Part, has in his possession anything capable of being used for committing the offence shall be guilty of an offence and shall be punishable in like manner as for the said offence.

....

Enforcement

19. (1) If a constable suspects with reasonable cause that any person is committing or has committed an offence under this Part, the constable may without warrant—

(a) stop and search that person if the constable suspects with reasonable cause that evidence of the commission of the offence is to be found on that person;

(b) search or examine any thing which that person may then be using or have in his possession if the constable suspects with reasonable cause that evidence of the commission of the offence is to be found on that thing;

(c) arrest that person if he fails to give his name and address to the constable's satisfaction[7];

(d) seize and detain for the purposes of proceedings under this Part any thing which may be evidence of the commission of the offence or may be liable to be forfeited under section 21[8].

---

[1] For "Nature Conservancy Councils" see s. 27(3A), p. 167 below. Words "each of the Nature Conservancy Councils" substituted by the Environmental Protection Act 1990 (c. 43), s. 132(1)(a), sch. 9, para. 11(4)(b).
[2] Words "in the area of that Council" inserted by the Environmental Protection Act 1990 (c. 43), s. 132(1)(a), sch. 9, para. 11(4)(b).
[3] Words "relevant Nature Conservancy" inserted by the Environmental Protection Act 1990 (c. 43), s. 132(1)(a), sch. 9, para. 11(4)(c).

[4] Subsection (11) inserted by the Environmental Protection Act 1990 (c. 43), s. 132(1)(a), sch. 9, para. 11(4)(d).
[5] P. 151 above.
[6] P. 152 above.
[7] *England and Wales*: Paragraph (c) repealed by the Police and Criminal Evidence Act 1984 (c. 60), s. 119(2), sch. 7, pt. I. This amendment came into force on 1 January 1986: S.I. 1985/1934.
[8] P. 162 below.

(2) If a constable suspects with reasonable cause that any person is committing an offence under this Part, he may, for the purpose of exercising the powers conferred by subsection (1) [*England and Wales*: or arresting a person, in accordance with section 25 of the Police and Criminal Evidence Act 1984, for such an offence[1]], enter any land other than a dwelling-house.

(3) If a justice of the peace is satisfied by information on oath that there are reasonable grounds for suspecting that—

(a) an offence under section 1[2], 3[3], 5[4], 7[5] or 8[6] in respect of which this Part or any order made under it provides for a special penalty; or

(b) an offence under section 6[7], 9[8], 11(1)[9] or (2), 13[10] or 14[11],

has been committed and that evidence of the offence may be found on any premises, he may grant a warrant to any constable (with or without other persons) to enter upon and search those premises for the purpose of obtaining that evidence.

In the application of this subsection to Scotland, the reference to a justice of the peace includes a reference to the sheriff[12].

Evidence in Scotland as to taking or destruction of eggs

19A. In any proceedings in Scotland for an offence under section 1(1)(c)[13] of, or by virtue of section 3(1)(a)(iii)[14] of, this Act, the accused may be convicted on the evidence of one witness.[15]

Summary prosecutions

20. (1) This section applies to—

(a) any offence under section 1(1)[16] or 3(1)[17] involving the killing or taking of any wild bird[18] or the taking of an egg of such a bird;

(b) any offence under section 9(1)[19] involving the killing or taking of any wild animal[20]; and

(c) any offence under section 13(1)[21] involving the picking[22] uprooting[23] or destruction of any wild plant[24].

(2) Summary proceedings for an offence to which this section applies may be brought within a period of six months from the date on which evidence sufficient in the opinion of the prosecutor to warrant the proceedings came to his knowledge; but no such proceedings shall be brought by virtue of this section more than two years after the commission of the offence.

(3) For the purpose of this section a certificate signed by or on behalf of the prosecutor and stating the date on which such evidence as aforesaid came to his knowledge shall be conclusive evidence of that fact; and a certificate stating that matter and purporting to be so signed shall be deemed to be so signed unless the contrary is proved.

---

[1] Words "or arresting . . . offence" inserted by the Police and Criminal Evidence Act 1984 (c. 60), s. 119(1), sch. 6, pt. I, para. 25. This amendment came into force on 1 January 1986: S.I. 1985/1934.

[2] P. 146 above.

[3] P. 148 above.

[4] P. 149 above.

[5] P. 152 above.

[6] P. 153 above.

[7] P. 151 above.

[8] P. 153 above.

[9] P. 155 above.

[10] P. 156 above.

[11] P. 157 above.

[12] **Case: section 19** *Whitelaw v Haining* [1992] S.L.T. 956.

[13] P. 146 above.

[14] P. 148 above.

[15] This section inserted by the Prisoners and Criminal Proceedings (Scotland) Act 1993 (c. 9), s. 36. This amendment came into force on 18 September 1993: S.I. 1993/2050.

[16] P. 146 above.

[17] P. 148 above.

[18] "Wild bird" defined by s. 27(1), p. 167 below.

[19] P. 153 above.

[20] "Wild animal" defined by s. 27(1) and (3), p. 167 below.

[21] P. 156 above.

[22] "Pick" defined by s. 27(1), p. 166 below.

[23] "Uproot" defined by s. 27(1), p. 166 below.

[24] "Wild plant" defined by s. 27(1), p. 167 below.

Penalties, forfeitures etc.

21. (1) Subject to subsection (5), a person guilty of an offence under section 1, 3, 5, 6, 7 or 8[1] shall be liable on summary conviction—

(a) in a case where this Part or any order made under it provides that he shall be liable to a special penalty, to a fine not exceeding level 5 on the standard scale[2];

(b) in any other case, to a fine not exceeding level 3 on the standard scale[3].

(2) Subject to subsection (5), a person guilty of an offence under section 9[4] or 11(1) or (2)[5] shall be liable on summary conviction to a fine not exceeding level 5 on the standard scale.[2]

(3) Subject to subsection (5), a person guilty of an offence under section 11(3)[6], 13[7] or 17[8] shall be liable on summary conviction to a fine not exceeding level 4 on the standard scale.[9]

(4) A person guilty of an offence under section 14[10] shall be liable—

(a) on summary conviction, to a fine not exceeding the statutory maximum;

(b) on conviction on indictment, to a fine.

(5) Where an offence to which subsection (1), (2) or (3) applies was committed in respect of more than one bird, nest, egg, other animal[11], plant or other thing, the maximum fine which may be imposed under that subsection shall be determined as if the person convicted had been convicted of a separate offence in respect of each bird, nest, egg, animal, plant or thing.

(6) The court by which any person is convicted of an offence under this Part—

(a) shall order the forfeiture of any bird, nest, egg, other animal, plant or other thing in respect of which the offence was committed; and

(b) may order the forfeiture of any vehicle[12], animal, weapon or other thing which was used to commit the offence and, in the case of an offence under section 14, any animal or plant which is of the same kind as that in respect of which the offence was committed and was found in his possession.

(7) Any offence under this Part shall, for the purpose of conferring jurisdiction, be deemed to have been committed in any place where the offender is found or to which he is first brought after the commission of the offence.

Power to vary Schedules

22. (1) The Secretary of State may by order, either generally or with respect to particular provisions of this Part, particular areas of Great Britain or particular times of the year, add any bird to, or remove any bird from, any of or any Part of Schedules 1 to 4[13].

(2) An order under subsection (1) adding any bird to Part II of Schedule 1 or Part I of Schedule 2 may prescribe a close season in the case of that bird for the purposes of sections 1 and 2; and any close season so prescribed shall commence on a date not later than 21st February and end on a date not earlier than 31st August.

---

[1] Ss. 1–8 are at pp. 146–153 above.

[2] Words "level 5 on the standard scale" substituted by the Criminal Justice Act 1982 (c. 48), ss. 37, 46 as respects England and Wales and the Criminal Procedure (Scotland) Act 1975 (c. 21), s. 289G as respects Scotland. The current fine at level 5 is £5,000: Criminal Justice Act 1991 (c. 53), s. 17 which came into force on 1 October 1992: S.I. 1992/333, S.I. 1992/2118.

[3] Words "level 3 on the standard scale" substituted by the Criminal Justice Act (c. 48), ss. 37, 46 as respects England and Wales and the Criminal Procedure (Scotland) Act 1975 (c. 21), s. 289G as respects Scotland. The current fine at level 3 is £1,000: Criminal Justice Act 1991 (c. 53), s. 17 which came into force on 1 October 1992: S.I. 1992/333, S.I. 1992/2118.

[4] P. 153 above.

[5] P. 155 above.

[6] P. 155 above.

[7] P. 156 above.

[8] P. 160 above.

[9] Words "level 4 on the standard scale" substituted by the Criminal Justice Act 1982 (c. 48), ss. 37, 46 as respects England and Wales and the Criminal Procedure (Scotland) Act 1975 (c. 21), s. 289G as respects Scotland. The current fine at level 4 is £2,500: Criminal Justice Act 1991 (c. 53), s. 17 which came into force on 1 October 1992: S.I. 1992/333, S.I. 1992/2118.

[10] P. 157 above.

[11] For "animal" see s. 27(3), p. 167 below.

[12] "Vehicle" defined by s. 27(1), p. 166 below.

[13] The Schedules commence at p. 192 below.

(3) The Secretary of State may, on a representation made jointly to him by the Nature Conservancy Councils,[1] by order, either generally or with respect to particular provisions of this Part, particular areas of Great Britain or particular times of the year—

(a) add to Schedule 5 or Schedule 8 any animal or plant which, in his opinion, is in danger of extinction in Great Britain or is likely to become so endangered unless conservation measures are taken; and

(b) remove from Schedule 5 or Schedule 8 any animal or plant which, in his opinion, is no longer so endangered or likely to become so endangered,

and the functions of the Nature Conservancy Councils under this subsection shall be special functions of the Councils for the purposes of section 133 of the Environmental Protection Act 1990[2].

(4) The Secretary of State may, for the purpose of complying with an international obligation, by order, either generally or with respect to particular provisions of this Part or particular times of the year—

(a) add any animals to, or remove any animals from, Schedule 5 or Schedule 6; and

(b) add any plants to, or remove any plants from, Schedule 8.

(5) The Secretary of State may by order, either generally or with respect to particular areas of Great Britain—

(a) add any animals to, or remove any animals from, Part I of Schedule 9; and

(b) add any plants to, or remove any plants from, Part II of that Schedule.

Advisory bodies and their functions

23. (1) The Secretary of State may—

(a) establish any body or bodies, consisting in each case of such members as he may from time to time appoint;

(b) assign to any body or bodies the duty referred to in subsection (4).

(2) Without prejudice to his power under subsection (1), the Secretary of State shall, as soon as practicable after the commencement date[3],—

(a) establish at least one body under paragraph (a) of subsection (1); or

(b) assign to at least one body, under paragraph (b) of that subsection, the duty referred to in subsection (4).

(3) A reference in this Part to an advisory body is a reference to a body which is established under subsection (1) or to which the duty there referred to is assigned under that subsection.

(4) It shall be the duty of an advisory body to advise the Secretary of State on any question which he may refer to it or on which it considers it should offer its advice—

(a) in connection with the administration of this Part; or

(b) otherwise in connection with the protection of birds or other animals[4] or plants.

(5) In so far as it does not have power to do so apart from this subsection, an advisory body may publish reports relating to the performance by it of its duty under subsection (4).

(6) Before appointing a person to be a member of an advisory body established under subsection (1)(a), the Secretary of State shall consult such persons or bodies as he thinks fit.

[1] For "the Nature Conservancy Councils" see s. 27(3A), p. 167 below. Words "jointly to him by the Nature Conservancy Councils" substituted by the Environmental Protection Act 1990 (c. 43), s. 132(1)(a), sch. 9, para. 11(5). This amendment came into force on 1 April 1991: S.I. 1991/685.

[2] P. 232 below. Words "and the functions ... Environ-mental Protection Act 1990" inserted by the Environmental Protection Act 1990 (c. 43), s. 132(1)(a), sch. 9, para. 11(5).

[3] "The commencement date" defined by s. 71, p. 191 below. The commencement date of this section is 28 September 1982: S.I. 1982/1217.

[4] For "animal" see s. 27(3), p. 167 below.

(7) The Secretary of State may, out of moneys provided by Parliament and to such an extent as may be approved by the Treasury, defray or contribute towards the expenses of an advisory body established under subsection (1)(a).

....

Functions of Nature Conservancy Council

24. (1) The Nature Conservancy Councils, acting jointly,[1] may at any time and shall five years after 30th October 1991[2] and every five years thereafter, review Schedules 5 and 8[3] and advise the Secretary of State whether, in their opinion,—

(a) any animal should be added to, or removed from, Schedule 5;

(b) any plant should be added to, or removed from, Schedule 8.

and the functions of the Nature Conservancy Councils under this subsection shall be special functions of the Councils for the purposes of section 133 of the Environmental Protection Act 1990.[4]

(2) Advice may be given under subsection (1) either generally or with respect to particular provisions of this Part, particular areas of Great Britain or particular times of the year; and any advice so given shall be accompanied by a statement of the reasons which led to that advice being given.[5]

(3) The Secretary of State shall lay before each House of Parliament a copy of any advice so given and the statements accompanying it.[6]

(4) The functions of the Nature Conservancy Councils[7] shall include power to advise or assist—

(a) any constable;

(b) any proper officer of a local authority[8]; or

(c) any person duly authorised by the Secretary of State under section 6(9)[9], 7(6)[10] or 14(5)[11],

in, or in connection with, the enforcement of the provisions of this Part or any order or regulations made under it.

....

Functions of local authorities

25. (1) Every local authority[12] shall take such steps as they consider expedient for bringing to the attention of the public and of schoolchildren in particular the effect of—

(a) the provisions of this Part; and

(b) any order made under this Part affecting the whole or any part of their area.

(2) A local authority in England and Wales may institute proceedings for any offence under this Part or any order made under it which is committed within their area.

---

[1] For "Nature Conservancy Councils" see s. 27(3A), p. 167 below. Words "Councils, acting jointly" substituted by the Environmental Protection Act 1990 (c. 43), s. 132(1)(a), sch. 9, para. 11(6)(a). This amendment came into force on 1 April 1991: S.I. 1991/685.

[2] Words "30th October 1991" substituted by the Environmental Protection Act 1990 (c. 43), s. 132(1)(a), sch. 9, para. 11(6)(a).

[3] Pp. 197–201 below.

[4] P. 232 below. Words "and the functions . . . Environmental Protection Act 1990" inserted by the Environmental Protection Act 1990 (c. 43), s. 132(1)(a), sch. 9, para. 11(6)(a).

[5] Words "to that advice being given." substituted by the Environmental Protection Act 1990 (c. 43), s. 132(1)(a), sch. 9, para. 11(6)(b).

[6] Subsection (3) substituted by the Environmental Protection Act 1990 (c. 43), s. 132(1)(a), sch. 9, para. 11(6)(c).

[7] Words "Nature Conservancy Councils" substituted by the Environmental Protection Act 1990 (c. 43), s. 132(1)(a), sch. 9, para. 11(6)(d).

[8] "Local authority" defined by s. 27(1), p. 166 below.

[9] P. 152 above.

[10] P. 153 above.

[11] P. 157 above.

[12] "Local authority" defined by s. 27(1), p. 166 below.

Regulations, orders, notices etc.

26. (1) Any power to make regulations or orders under this Part shall be exercisable by statutory instrument.

(2) A statutory instrument containing regulations under this Part, or an order under a provision of this Part other than sections 2(6)[1], 3[2], 5[3] and 11[4], shall be subject to annulment in pursuance of a resolution of either House of Parliament.

(3) No order under section 5[5] or 11[6] shall be made unless a draft of the order has been laid before and approved by a resolution of each House of Parliament.

(4) Before making any order under this Part, the Secretary of State—

(a) except in the case of an order under section 2(6)[7], shall give to any local authority[8] affected and, except in the case of an order under section 3[9], any other person affected, by such means as he may think appropriate, an opportunity to submit objections or representations with respect to the subject matter of the order;

(b) except in the case of an order under section 22(3)[10], shall consult with whichever one of the advisory bodies[11] he considers is best able to advise him as to whether the order should be made; and

(c) may, if he thinks fit, cause a public inquiry to be held.

(5) Notice of the making of an order under this Part shall be published by the Secretary of State—

(a) if the order relates in whole or in part to England and Wales, in the London Gazette; and

(b) if the order relates in whole or in part to Scotland, in the Edinburgh Gazette.

(6) The Secretary of State shall give consideration to any proposals for the making by him of an order under this Part with respect to any area which may be submitted to him by a local authority whose area includes that area.

Interpretation of Part I

27. (1) In this Part, unless the context otherwise requires—

"advertisement" includes a catalogue, a circular and a price list;

"advisory body" has the meaning given by section 23[12];

"agriculture Minister" means the Minister of Agriculture, Fisheries and Food or the Secretary of State;

"authorised person" means—

(a) the owner or occupier[13], or any person authorised by the owner or occupier, of the land on which the action authorised is taken;

(b) any person authorised in writing by the local authority[14] for the area within which the action authorised is taken;

(c) as respects anything done in relation to wild birds[15], any person authorised in writing by any of the following bodies, that is to say, any of the Nature Conservancy Councils[16], a water

---

[1] P. 147 above.
[2] P. 148 above.
[3] P. 150 above.
[4] P. 155 above.
[5] P. 149 above.
[6] P. 155 above.
[7] P. 147 above.
[8] "Local authority" defined by s. 27(1), p. 166 below.
[9] P. 148 above.
[10] P. 163 above.
[11] "Advisory body" defined by s. 23, p. 163 above: s.

27(1).
[12] P. 163 above.
[13] "Occupier" defined below.
[14] "Local authority" defined below.
[15] "Wild bird" defined below.
[16] For "Nature Conservancy Councils" see subsection (3A) below. Words "any of the Nature Conservancy Councils" substituted by the Environmental Protection Act 1990 (c. 43), s. 132(1)(a), sch. 9, para. 11(7)(a). This amendment came into force on 1 April 1991: S.I. 1991/685.

authority or any other statutory water undertakers,[1] a district board for a fishery district within the meaning of the Salmon Fisheries (Scotland) Act 1862[2] or a local fisheries committee constituted under the Sea Fisheries Regulation Act 1966[3];

(d) any person authorised in writing by the National Rivers Authority, a water undertaker or a sewerage undertaker;[4]

so, however, that the authorisation of any person for the purposes of this definition shall not confer any right of entry upon any land;

"automatic weapon" and "semi-automatic weapon" do not include any weapon the magazine of which is incapable of holding more than two rounds;

"aviculture" means the breeding and rearing of birds in captivity;

"destroy", in relation to an egg, includes doing anything to the egg which is calculated to prevent it from hatching, and "destruction" shall be construed accordingly;

"domestic duck" means any domestic form of duck;

"domestic goose" means any domestic form of goose;

"firearm" has the same meaning as in the Firearms Act 1968[5];

"game bird" means any pheasant, partridge, grouse (or moor game), black (or heath) game or ptarmigan;

"livestock" includes any animal which is kept—

(a) for the provision of food, wool, skins or fur;

(b) for the purpose of its use in the carrying on of any agricultural activity; or

(c) for the provision or improvement of shooting or fishing;

"local authority" means—

(a) in relation to England[6], a county, district or London borough council[7];

(aa) in relation to Wales, a county council or county borough council;[8]

(b) in relation to Scotland, a Council constituted under section 2 of the Local Government etc. (Scotland) Act 1994;[9]

"occupier", in relation to any land other than the foreshore, includes any person having any right of hunting, shooting, fishing or taking game or fish;

"pick", in relation to a plant, means gather or pluck any part of the plant without uprooting it;

"poultry" means domestic fowls, geese[10], ducks[11], guinea-fowls, pigeons and quails, and turkeys;

"sale" includes hire, barter and exchange and cognate expressions shall be construed accordingly;

"uproot", in relation to a plant, means dig up or otherwise remove the plant from the land on which it is growing;

"vehicle" includes aircraft, hovercraft and boat;

---

[1] *England & Wales*: Former words "a water authority or any other statutory water undertakers," repealed by the Water Act 1989 (c. 15), s. 190(3), sch. 27, pt. I. This amendment came into force on 1 September 1989: s. 194(3), S.I. 1989/1530.
Scotland: "Water authority" defined below.
[2] 1862 c. 97.
[3] 1966 c. 38.
[4] *England & Wales*: Paragraph (d) inserted by the Water Act 1989 (c. 15), s. 190(1), sch. 25, para. 66(1). This amendment came into force on 1 September 1989: S.I. 1989/1146.
[5] 1968 c. 27.
[6] Former words "and Wales" repealed by the Local Government (Wales) Act 1994 (c. 19), s. 66(6), (8), sch. 16, para. 65(2), sch. 18. It is planned that this amendment will

come into force on 1 April 1996.
[7] "London borough council" defined by s. 71, p. 191 below. Former words "and the Greater London Council" repealed by the Local Government Act 1985 (c. 51), s. 102(2), sch. 17. This amendment came into force on 1 April 1986: ss. 1(2), 102(3), 105.
[8] Paragraph (aa) inserted by the Local Government (Wales) Act 1994 (c. 19), s. 66(6), sch. 16, para. 65(2).
[9] Words "Council ... 1994" inserted by the Local Government etc. (Scotland) Act 1994 (c. 39), s. 180(1), sch. 13, para. 125(2). It is anticipated that this amendment will come into force on 1 April 1996.
[10] "Domestic goose" defined above.
[11] "Domestic duck" defined above.

"water authority", in relation to Scotland, has the same meaning as in the Water (Scotland) Act 1980[1];

"wild animal" means any animal (other than a bird) which is or (before it was killed or taken) was living wild;

"wild bird" means any bird of a kind which is ordinarily resident in or is a visitor to Great Britain in a wild state but does not include poultry[2] or, except in sections 5[3] and 16[4], any game bird[5];

"wild plant" means any plant which is or (before it was picked, uprooted or destroyed) was growing wild and is of a kind which ordinarily grows in Great Britain in a wild state.

(2) A bird shall not be treated as bred in captivity for the purposes of this Part unless its parents were lawfully in captivity when the egg was laid.

(3) Any reference in this Part to an animal of any kind includes, unless the context otherwise requires, a reference to an egg, larva, pupa, or other immature stage of an animal of that kind.

(3A) Any reference in this Part to the Nature Conservancy Councils is a reference to the Nature Conservancy Council for England[6], Scottish Natural Heritage[7] and the Countryside Council for Wales.[8],[9]

(4) This Part shall apply to the Isles of Scilly as if the Isles were a county and as if the Council of the Isles were a county council.

(5) This Part extends to the territorial waters adjacent to Great Britain, and for the purposes of this Part any part of Great Britain which is bounded by territorial waters shall be taken to include the territorial waters adjacent to that part.

Part II: Nature Conservation, Countryside and National Parks

Construction of references to Nature Conservancy Council

27A. In this Part reference to "the Nature Conservancy Council" are, unless the contrary intention appears, references—

(a) in relation to land in, or land covered by waters adjacent to, England, to the Nature Conservancy Council for England;[10]

(b) in relation to land in, or land covered by waters adjacent to, Scotland, to Scottish Natural Heritage;[11] and

(c) in relation to land in, or land covered by waters adjacent to, Wales, to the Countryside Council for Wales;[12]

and references to "the Council" shall be construed accordingly.[13]

---

[1] 1980 c. 45.

[2] "Poultry" defined above.

[3] P. 149 above.

[4] P. 158 above.

[5] "Game bird" defined above.

[6] The Nature Conservancy Council for England, also known as English Nature, is established by the Environmental Protection Act 1990 (c. 43), s. 128, p. 229 below.

[7] Scottish Natural Heritage is established by the Natural Heritage (Scotland) Act 1991 (c. 28), s. 1, p. 245 below. Words "Scottish Natural Heritage" substituted by the Natural Heritage (Scotland) Act 1991 (c. 28), s. 4(6), sch. 2, para. 8(2). This amendment came into force on 1 April 1992: S.I. 1991/2633.

[8] The Countryside Council for Wales is established by the Environmental Protection Act 1990 (c. 43), s. 128, p. 229 below.

[9] Subsection (3A) inserted by the Environmental

Protection Act 1990 (c. 43), s. 132(1)(a), sch. 9, para. 11(7)(b).

[10] The Nature Conservancy Council for England, also known as English Nature, is established by the Environmental Protection Act 1990 (c. 43), s. 128, p. 229 below.

[11] Scottish Natural Heritage is established by the Natural Heritage (Scotland) Act 1991 (c. 28), s. 1, p. 245 below. Words "Scottish Natural Heritage" substituted by the Natural Heritage (Scotland) Act 1991 (c. 28), s. 4(6), sch. 2, para. 8(3). This amendment came into force on 1 April 1992: S.I. 1991/2633.

[12] The Countryside Council for Wales is established by the Environmental Protection Act 1990 (c. 43), s. 128, p. 229 below.

[13] This section inserted by the Environmental Protection Act 1990 (c. 43), s. 132(1)(a), sch. 9, para. 11(8). This section came into force on 1 April 1991: S.I. 1991/685.

Nature conservation

Areas of special scientific interest

28. (1) Where the Nature Conservancy Council[1] are of the opinion that any area of land[2] is of special interest by reason of any of its flora, fauna, or geological or physiographical features, it shall be the duty of the Council[3] to notify[4] that fact—

(a) to the local planning authority[5] in whose area the land is situated;

(b) to every owner[6] and occupier of any of that land; and

(c) to the Secretary of State[7].

(2) A notification under subsection (1) shall specify the time (not being less than three months from the date of the giving of the notification) within which, and the manner in which, representations or objections with respect thereto may be made; and the Council shall consider any representation or objection duly made.[8]

(3) *Repealed by the Wildlife and Countryside (Service of Notices) Act 1985 (c. 59), s. 1(2). This amendment came into force on 25 July 1985, the date of the Royal Assent.*

(4) A notification under subsection (1)(b) shall specify—

(a) the flora, fauna, or geological or physiographical features by reason of which the land is of special interest; and

(b) any operations appearing to the Council to be likely to damage that flora or fauna or those features.

(4A) Where a notification under subsection (1) has been given, the Council may within the period of nine months beginning with the date on which the notification was served on the Secretary of State either—

(a) give notice to the persons mentioned in subsection (1) withdrawing the notification; or

(b) give notice to those persons confirming the notification (with or without modifications[9]);

and the notification shall cease to have effect—

(i) on the giving of notice of its withdrawal under paragraph (a) of this subsection to any of the persons mentioned in subsection (1), or

(ii) if not withdrawn or confirmed by notice under paragraph (a) or (b) of this subsection within the said period of nine months, at the end of that period.

(4B) The Council's power under subsection (4A)(b) to confirm a notification under subsection (1) with modifications shall not be exercised so as to add to the operations specified in the notification or extend the area to which it applies.

(4C) As from the time when there is served on the owner or occupier of any land which has been notified under subsection (1)(b) a notice under subsection (4A) confirming the notification with modifications, the notification shall have effect in its modified form in relation to so much (if any) of that land as remains subject to it.[10]

---

[1] For "the Nature Conservancy Council" see s. 27A above: s. 52(1), p. 189 below.
[2] "Land" defined by s. 114(1), National Parks and Access to the Countryside Act 1949, p. 38 above: s. 52(4) below applies the definition in s. 114 of the 1949 Act.
[3] For "The Council" see s. 27A, p. 167 above.
[4] S. 70A, p. 191 below, provides for the service of notices.
[5] "Local planning authority" defined by s. 52(2), p. 189 below, and subsection (13A) below.
[6] "Owner" defined by s. 114(1), National Parks and Access to the Countryside Act 1949, p. 38 above: s. 52(4), p.

189 below applies the definition in s. 114 of the 1949 Act.
[7] Where a notification is in force the land may not be included in a simplified planning zone: Town and Country Planning Act 1990 (c. 8), s. 87 (England and Wales); Town and Country Planning (Scotland) Act 1972 (c. 52), s. 21E.
[8] This subsection inserted by the Wildlife and Countryside (Amendment) Act 1985 (c. 31), s. 2(2). This amendment came into force on 26 August 1985: s. 5(3).
[9] "Modifications" defined by s. 71, p. 191 below.
[10] Subsections (4A)–(4C) inserted by the Wildlife and Countryside (Amendment) Act 1985 (c. 31), s. 2(4).

(5) The owner or occupier of any land which has been notified under subsection (1)(*b*) shall not while the notification remains in force[1] carry out, or cause or permit to be carried out, on that land any operation specified in the notification unless—

(*a*) one of them has, after service on him of the notification[2], given the Council written notice of a proposal to carry out the operation specifying its nature and the land on which it is proposed to carry it out; and

(*b*) one of the conditions specified in subsection (6) is fulfilled.

(6) The said conditions are—

(*a*) that the operation is carried out with the Council's written consent;

(*b*) that the operation is carried out in accordance with the terms of an agreement under section 16 of the 1949 Act[3] or section 15 of the 1968 Act[4]; and

(*c*) that four[5] months have expired from the giving of the notice under subsection (5).

(6A) If before the expiry of the four months referred to in subsection (6)(*c*) the relevant person[6] agrees with the Council in writing that, subject to subsection (6B), the condition specified in paragraph (*c*) of subsection (6) shall not apply in relation to the operation mentioned in subsection (5)(*a*), then, subject to subsection (6B), subsection (5) shall as from the date of the agreement have effect in relation to the operation in question (as regards both the owner and the occupier of the land) as if paragraph (*c*) of subsection (6) were omitted.

(6B) If after an agreement has been made with the Council under subsection (6A) the relevant person (whether a party to the agreement or not) gives the Council written notice that he wishes to terminate the agreement, then as from the giving of the notice subsection (5) shall have effect in relation to the operation in question (as regards both the owner and the occupier of the land) as if paragraph (*c*) of subsection (6) specified the condition that one month or, if the notice under this subsection specifies a longer period, that longer period has expired from the giving of the notice under this subsection.

(6C) In subsections (6A) and (6B) "the relevant person"—

(*a*) in a case where the notice under subsection (5) was given by the owner of the land in question, means the owner of that land;

(*b*) in a case where that notice was given by the occupier of that land, means the occupier of that land.[7]

(7) A person who, without reasonable excuse, contravenes subsection (5) shall be liable on summary conviction to a fine not exceeding level 4 on the standard scale.[8]

(8) It is a reasonable excuse in any event for a person to carry out an operation if—

(*a*) the operation was authorised by a planning permission granted on an application under Part III of the Town and Country Planning Act 1990[9] or Part III of the Town and Country Planning (Scotland) Act 1972[10],[11]; or

[1] Words "while the notification remains in force" inserted by the Wildlife and Countryside (Amendment) Act 1985 (c. 31), s. 2(5)(*a*).

[2] Words "after service on him of the notification" substituted by the Wildlife and Countryside (Amendment) Act 1985 (c. 31), s. 2(5)(*b*).

[3] P. 15 above.

[4] P. 121 above.

[5] Words "four months" substituted by the Wildlife and Countryside (Amendment) Act 1985 (c. 31), s. 2(6).

[6] "Relevant person" defined by subsection (6C) below.

[7] Subsection (6A)–(6C) inserted by the Wildlife and Countryside (Amendment) Act 1985 (c. 31), s. 2(7).

[8] Words "level 4 on the standard scale" substituted by the Criminal Justice Act 1982 (c. 48), ss. 37, 46 as respects England and Wales and the Criminal Procedure (Scotland) Act 1975 (c. 21), s. 289G as respects Scotland. The current fine at level 4 is £2,500: Criminal Justice Act 1991 (c. 53), s. 17 which came into force on 1 October 1992: S.I. 1992/333, S.I. 1992/2118.

[9] 1990 c. 8. Words "Part III of the Town and Country Planning Act 1990" substituted by the Planning (Consequential Provisions) Act 1990 (c. 11), s. 4, sch. 2, para. 54(1). This amendment came into force on 24 August 1990: s. 7(2).

[10] 1972 c. 52.

[11] For consultation requirements before granting planning permission see *England and Wales*: Town and Country Planning (General Development Procedure Order) 1995: S.I. 1995/419, art. 10(1)(u); *Scotland*: Town and Country Planning (General Development Procedure) (Scotland) Order 1992: S.I. 1992/224, art. 15 (amended by S.I. 1994/3294).

(*b*) the operation was an emergency operation particulars of which (including details of the emergency) were notified to the Council as soon as practicable after the commencement of the operation.

(9) The Council shall have power to enforce the provisions of this section; but nothing in this subsection shall be construed as authorising the Council to institute proceedings in Scotland for an offence.

(10) Proceedings in England and Wales for an offence under subsection (7) shall not, without the consent of the Director of Public Prosecutions, be taken by a person other than the Council.

(11) A notification under subsection (1)(*b*) of land in England and Wales shall be a local land charge.

(12) The Council shall compile and maintain a register of notifications in respect of each local planning authority in Scotland.

(12A) There shall be included in any such register as is mentioned in subsection (12)—

(*a*) copies of all notifications given under subsection (1) which relate wholly or partly to land situated within the district of the authority;

(*b*) copies of all plans referred to in any such notification; and

(*c*) copies of all notices served under subsection (4A) which relate to any such notification.

(12B) Each local planning authority in Scotland shall keep a copy of the register relating to their district available at their principal office for free public inspection, and may similarly keep, at such of their other offices as they think fit, a copy of such part of the register as appears to them to relate to the area in which the office is situated.[1]

(13) Section 23 of the 1949 Act (which is superseded by this section) shall cease to have effect; but any notification given under that section shall have effect as if given under subsection (1)(*a*).

(13A) For the purposes of this section "local planning authority", in relation to land within the Broads[2], includes the Broads Authority.[3,4]

(14) *Repealed by the Wildlife and Countryside (Amendment) Act 1985 (c. 31), s. 2(9). This amendment came into force on 26 August 1985: S. 5(3).*

---

[1] Subsections (12), (12A) and (12B) substituted by the Wildlife and Countryside (Amendment) Act 1985 (c. 31), s. 2(8).

[2] "The Broads" defined by s. 71, p. 191 below.

[3] The "Broads Authority" is established by the Norfolk and Suffolk Broads Act 1988 (c. 4), s. 1, p. 221 below.

[4] Subsection 13A inserted by the Norfolk and Suffolk Broads Act 1988 (c. 4), s. 2(5), sch. 3, para. 31(1). This amendment come into force on 1 April 1989: S.I. 1988/955.

Supplementary notes

1. Section 2(10), (11) of the Wildlife and Countryside (Amendment) Act 1985 (c. 31) provides for the application of the amendments made by that Act in respect of notifications given before the commencement of the Act and for related transitional applications.

2. For the statutory provision where part of an area of special scientific interest was in England and part in Wales, or part was in England and part in Scotland, before 1 April 1991, the day appointed for the Councils established under s. 128 of the Environmental Protection Act 1990 (c. 43) to discharge their nature conservation functions, see the Environmental Protection Act 1990 (c. 43), s. 139, sch. 11, pt. II, para. 12, p. 000 below.

3. This section came into force on 30 November 1981: s. 74(1), p. 192 below.

References to further statutory provision

1. Countryside Act 1968 (c. 41), s. 15, areas of special scientific interest, p. 121 above.

2. Conservation of Seals Act 1970 (c. 30), s. 10, power to grant licences, p. 138 above.

3. Water Industry Act 1991 (c. 56), s. 4, environmental duties with respect to sites of special interest, p. 277 below; s. 156, restrictions on disposals of land, p. 279 below.

4. Water Resources Act 1991 (c. 57), s. 17, environmental duties with respect to sites of special interest, p. 285 below.

5. Land Drainage Act 1991 (c. 59), s. 61C, duties with respect to sites of special scientific interest, p. 290 below.

6. Natural Heritage (Scotland) Act 1991 (c. 28), s. 12, advisory committee on SSSIs, p. 252 below.

Cases: section 28

R v Poole Borough Council ex P Beebee: [1991] JEL 293

Southern Water Authority v Nature Conservancy Council: [1992] 1 WLR 775, [1992] 3 All ER 481, [1993] JEL 109.

Special protection for certain areas of special scientific interest

29. (1) Where it appears to the Secretary of State expedient to do so—

(a) in the case of any land[1] to which this paragraph applies, for the purpose of securing the survival in Great Britain of any kind of animal or plant or of complying with an international obligation; or

(b) in the case of any land to which this paragraph applies, for the purpose of conserving any of its flora, fauna, or geological or physiographical features,

he may, after consultation with the Nature Conservancy Council[2], by order apply subsection (3) to that land; and the provisions of Schedule 11[3] shall have effect as to the making, confirmation and coming into operation of orders under this section.

An order made under this section may be amended or revoked by a subsequent order so made.

(2) Paragraphs (a) and (b) of subsection (1) apply to any land which in the opinion of the Secretary of State is—

(a) of special interest; and

(b) in the case of paragraph (b) of that subsection, of national importance,

by reason of any of its flora, fauna, or geological or physiographical features.

(3) Subject to subsection (4), no person shall carry out on any land to which this subsection applies any operation which—

(a) appears to the Secretary of State to be likely to destroy or damage the flora, fauna, or geological or physiographical features by reason of which the land is land to which paragraph (a) or, as the case may be, paragraph (b) of subsection (1) applies; and

(b) is specified in the order applying this subsection to the land.

(4) Subsection (3) shall not apply in relation to any operation carried out, or caused or permitted to be carried out, by the owner[4] or occupier of the land if—

(a) one of them has, after the making of the order[5], given the Council[6] written[7] notice of a proposal to carry out the operation, specifying its nature and the land on which it is proposed to carry it out; and

(b) one of the conditions specified in subsection (5) is fulfilled.

(5) The said conditions are—

(a) that the operation is carried out with the Council's written consent;

(b) that the operation is carried out in accordance with the terms of an agreement under section 16 of the 1949 Act[8] or section 15 of the 1968 Act[9]; and

(c) subject to subsections (6) and (7), that three months have expired from the giving of the notice under subsection (4).

(6) If before the expiration of the period mentioned in paragraph (c) of subsection (5) the Council offer to enter into an agreement for the acquisition of the interest[10] of the person who gave the notice under subsection (4) or an agreement under section 16 of the 1949 Act or section 15 of the 1968 Act providing for the making by them of payments to that person, that paragraph shall have effect as if for the said period there were substituted—

---

[1] "Land" defined by s. 114(1), National Parks and Access to the Countryside Act 1949, p. 38 above: s. 52(4), p. 189 below applies the definition in s. 114 of the 1949 Act.

[2] For "the Nature Conservancy Council" see s. 27A, p. 167 above. S. 52(1), p. 189 below.

[3] P. 206 below.

[4] "Owner" defined by s. 114(1), National Parks and Access to the Countryside Act 1949, p. 38 above: s. 52(4) below applies the definition in s. 114 of the 1949 Act.

[5] Words "making of the order" substituted by the Environmental Protection Act 1990 (c. 43), s. 132(1)(a), sch.

9, para. 11(9). This amendment came into force on 1 April 1991: S.I. 1991/685.

[6] For "the Council" see s. 27A, p. 167 above: S. 52(1), p. 189 below.

[7] Word "written" inserted by the Environmental Protection Act 1990 (c. 43), s. 132(1)(a), sch. 9, para. 11(10).

[8] P. 15 above.

[9] P. 121 above.

[10] "Interest" defined by s. 114(1), National Parks and Access to the Countryside Act 1949, p. 38 above: s. 52(4), p. 189 below applies the definition in s. 114 of the 1949 Act.

(a) where the agreement is entered into before the expiration of twelve months from the giving of the notice, the period expiring on the day on which it is entered into;

(b) in any other case, twelve months from the giving of the notice or three months from rejection or withdrawal of the offer to enter into the agreement, whichever period last expires.

(7) If before the expiration of the period mentioned in paragraph (c) of subsection (5), or that paragraph as it has effect by virtue of subsection (6), an order is made for the compulsory acquisition by the Council of the interest of the person who gave the notice under subsection (4), that paragraph shall have effect as if for the said period there were substituted the period expiring—

(a) in the case of an order which is confirmed, on the day on which the Council enter on the land;

(b) in any other case, on the day on which the order is withdrawn or the Secretary of State decides not to confirm it.

(8) A person who, without reasonable excuse, contravenes subsection (3) shall be liable—

(a) on summary conviction, to a fine not exceeding the statutory maximum;

(b) on conviction on indictment to a fine.

(9) It is a reasonable excuse in any event for a person to carry out an operation if—

(a) the operation was authorised by a planning permission granted on an application under Part III of the Town and Country Planning Act 1990[1] or Part III of the Town and Country Planning (Scotland) Act 1972[2,3]; or

(b) the operation was an emergency operation particulars of which (including details of the emergency) were notified to the Council as soon as practicable after the commencement of the operation.

(10) An order made under this section in relation to land in Scotland shall be registered either—

(a) in a case where the land affected by the order is registered in that Register, in the Land Register of Scotland; or

(b) in any other case, in the appropriate Division of the General Register of Sasines.

(11) A report submitted by the Council to the Secretary of State under paragraph 20 of Schedule 6 to the Environmental Protection Act 1990[4] or under section 10(2) of the Natural Heritage (Scotland) Act 1991[5] for any year shall set out particulars of any areas of land as respects which orders under this section have come into operation during that year[6,7].

Compensation where order is made under s. 29

30. (1) Subsection (2) applies where an order is made under section 29 and subsection (3) applies where—

(a) notice of a proposal to carry out an operation is duly given to the Nature Conservancy Council[8] under subsection (4) of that section; and

---

[1] 1990 c. 8. Words "Part III of the Town and Country Planning Act 1990" substituted by the Planning (Consequential Provisions) Act 1990 (c. 11), s. 4, sch. 2, para. 54(1). This amendment came into force on 24 August 1990: s. 7(2).

[2] 1972 c. 52.

[3] For consultation requirements before granting planning permission see *England and Wales*: Town and Country Planning (General Development Procedure Order) 1995: S.I. 1995/419, art. 10(1)(u); *Scotland*: Town and Country Planning (General Development Procedure) (Scotland) Order 1992: S.I. 1992/224, art. 15 (amended by S.I. 1994/3294).

[4] P. 237 below. Words "paragraph 20 of Schedule 6 to the Environmental Protection Act 1990" substituted by the Environmental Protection Act 1990 (c. 43), s. 132(1)(a), sch.

9, para. 11(11).

[5] Words "or under section 10(2) of the Natural Heritage (Scotland) Act 1991" inserted by the Natural Heritage (Scotland) Act 1991 (c. 28), s. 4(6), sch. 2, para. 8(4). This amendment came into force on 1 April 1992: S.I. 1991/2633.

[6] This section came into force on 6 September 1982: S.I. 1982/1136.

[7] **Cases: section 29** *Sweet v Secretary of State for the Environment and the Nature Conservancy Council* [1989] JEL 245; *North Uist Fisheries Ltd v Secretary of State for Scotland* [1992] JEL 241; *R v Secretary of State for the Environmental, ex parte Upton Brickworks Ltd* [1992] COD 301.

[8] For "the Nature Conservancy Council" see s. 27A, p. 167 above: s. 52(1), p. 189 below.

(*b*) paragraph (*c*) of subsection (5) of that section has effect as modified by subsection (6) or (7) of that section.

(2) The Council[1] shall pay compensation to any person having at the time of the making of the order an interest[2] in land[3] comprised in an agricultural unit[4] comprising land to which the order relates who, on a claim made to the Council within the time and in the manner prescribed by regulations under this section[5], shows that the value of his interest is less than what it would have been if the order had not been made; and the amount of the compensation shall be equal to the different between the two values.

(3) The Council shall pay compensation to any person having at the time of the giving of the notice an interest in land to which the notice relates who, on a claim made to the Council within the time and in the manner prescribed by regulations under this section[5], shows that—

(*a*) he has reasonably incurred expenditure which has been rendered abortive, or expenditure in carrying out work which has been rendered abortive, by reason of paragraph (*c*) of subsection (5) of section 29 having effect as modified by subsection (6) or (7) of that section; or

(*b*) he has incurred loss or damage which is directly attributable to that paragraph having effect as so modified;

but nothing in this subsection shall entitle any such person to compensation in respect of any reduction in the value of his interest in the land.

(4) For the purposes of subsection (2)—

(*a*) an interest in land shall be valued as at the time when the order is made;

(*b*) where a person, by reason of his having more than one interest in land, makes more than one claim under that subsection in respect of the same order, his various interests shall be valued together;

(*c*) section 10 of the Land Compensation Act 1973[6] (mortgages, trusts for sale and settlements) or section 10 of the Land Compensation (Scotland) Act 1973[2] (restricted interests in land) shall apply in relation to compensation under that subsection as it applies in relation to compensation under Part I of that Act.

(5) For the purposes of assessing any compensation payable under subsection (2), the rules set out in section 5 of the Land Compensation Act 1961[8] or section 12 of the Land Compensation (Scotland) Act 1963[9] shall, so far as applicable and subject to any necessary modifications[10], have effect as they have effect for the purpose of assessing compensation for the compulsory acquisition of an interest in land.

(6) No claim shall be made under subsection (2) in respect of any order under section 29 unless the Secretary of State has given notice under paragraph 6(1) or (2) of Schedule 11[11] of his decision in respect of the order; and, without prejudice to subsection (4)(*a*), that decision will be taken into account in assessing the compensation payable in respect of the order.

(7) Compensation under this section shall carry interest, at the rate for the time being prescribed under section 32 of the Land Compensation Act 1961 or section 40 of the Land Compensation (Scotland) Act 1963, from the date of the claim until payment.

(8) Except in so far as may be provided by regulations under this section, any question of disputed compensation under this section shall be referred to and determined by the Lands Tribunal or the Lands Tribunal for Scotland.

---

[1] For "The Council" see s. 27A, p. 167 above: s. 52(1), p. 189 below.

[2] "Interest" defined by s. 114(1), National Parks and Access to the Countryside Act 1949, p. 38 above: s. 52(4), p. 189 below applies the definition in s. 114 of the 1949 Act.

[3] "Land" defined by s. 114(1), National Parks and Access to the Countryside Act 1949, p. 38 above: s. 52(4), p. 189 below applies the definition in s. 114 of the 1949 Act.

[4] "Agricultural unit" defined by subsection (11) below.

[5] The Wildlife and Countryside (Claims for Compensation under section 30) Regulations 1982, S.I. 1982/1346, made under this section, are at p. 321 below.

[6] 1973 c. 26.

[7] 1973 c. 56.

[8] 1961 c. 33.

[9] 1963 c. 51.

[10] "Modifications" defined by s. 71, p. 191 below.

[11] P. 207 below.

(9) In relation to the determination of any such question, the provisions of sections 2 and 4 of the Land Compensation Act 1961 or sections 9 and 11 of the Land Compensation (Scotland) Act 1963 (procedure and costs) shall apply, subject to any necessary modifications and to the provisions of any regulations under this section.

(10) Regulations under this section shall be made by the Secretary of State and shall be made by statutory instrument subject to annulment in pursuance of a resolution of either House of Parliament.

(11) In this section "agricultural unit" means land which is occupied as a unit for agricultural purposes, including any dwelling-house or other building occupied by the same person for the purpose of farming the land[1].

Restoration where order under s. 29 is contravened

31. (1) Where the operation in respect of which a person is convicted of an offence under section 29[2] has destroyed or damaged any of the flora, fauna, or geological or physiographical features by reason of which the land[3] on which it was carried out is of special interest, the court by which he is convicted, in addition to dealing with him in any other way, may make an order requiring him to carry out, within such period as may be specified in the order, such operations for the purpose of restoring the land to its former condition as may be so specified.

(2) An order under this section made on conviction on indictment shall be treated for the purposes of sections 30 and 42(1) and (2) of the Criminal Appeal Act 1968[4] (effect of appeals on orders for the restitution of property) as an order for the restitution of property; and where by reason by the quashing by the Court of Appeal of a person's conviction any such order does not take effect, and on appeal to the House of Lords the conviction is restored by that House, the House may make any order under this section which could be made on his conviction by the court which convicted him.

(3) In the case of an order under this section made by a magistrates' court the period specified in the order shall not begin to run—

(a) in any case until the expiration of the period for the time being prescribed by law for the giving of notice of appeal against a decision of a magistrates' court;

(b) where notice of appeal is given within the period so prescribed, until determination of the appeal.

(4) At any time before an order under this section has been complied with or fully complied with, the court by which it was made may, on the application of the person against whom it was made, discharge or vary the order if it appears to the court that a change in circumstances has made compliance or full compliance with the order impracticable or unnecessary.

(5) If, within the period specified in an order under this section, the person against whom it was made fails, without reasonable excuse, to comply with it, he shall be liable on summary conviction—

(a) to a fine not exceeding level 5 on the standard scale[5]; and

(b) in the case of a continuing offence, to a further fine not exceeding £100 for each day during which the offence continues after conviction.

(6) If, within the period specified in an order under this section, any operations specified in the order have not been carried out, the Nature Conservancy Council[6] may enter the land and carry

---

[1] This section came into force on 6 September 1982: S.I. 1982/1136.

[2] P. 171 above.

[3] "Land" defined by s. 114(1), National Parks and Access to the Countryside Act 1949, p. 38 above: s. 52(4), p. 189 below applies the definition in s. 114 of the 1949 Act.

[4] 1968 c. 19.

[5] Words "level 5 on the standard scale" substituted by the Criminal Justice Act 1982 (c. 48), ss. 37, 46 as respects England and Wales and the Criminal Procedure (Scotland) Act 1975 (c. 21), s. 289G as respects Scotland. The current fine at level 5 is £5,000: Criminal Justice Act 1991 (c. 53), s. 17 which came into force on 1 October 1992: S.I. 1992/333, S.I. 1992/2118.

[6] For "Nature Conservancy Council" see s. 27A, p. 167 above: s. 52(1), p. 189 below.

out those operations and recover from the person against whom the order was made any expenses reasonably incurred by them in doing so.

(7) In the application of this section to Scotland—

(a) subsections (2) and (3) shall not apply; and

(b) for the purposes of any appeal or review, an order under this section is a sentence.[1]

Duties of agriculture Ministers with respect to areas of special scientific interest

32. (1) Where an application for a farm capital grant[2] is made as respects expenditure incurred or to be incurred for the purpose of activities on land[3] notified under section 28(1)[4] or land to which section 29(3)[5] applies, the appropriate Minister[6]—

(a) shall, so far as may be consistent with the purposes of the grant provisions,[7] so exercise his functions thereunder as to further the conservation of the flora, fauna, or geological or physiographical features by reason of which the land is of special interest; and

(b) where the Nature Conservancy Council[8] have objected to the making of the grant on the ground that the activities in question have destroyed or damaged or will destroy or damage that flora or fauna or those features, shall not make the grant except after considering the objection and, in the case of land in England, after consulting with the Secretary of State.

(2) Where, in consequence of an objection by the Council[9], an application for a grant as respects expenditure to be incurred is refused on the ground that the activities in question will have such an effect as is mentioned in subsection (1)(b), the Council shall, within three months of their receiving notice of the appropriate Minister's decision, offer to enter into, in the terms of a draft submitted to the applicant, an agreement under section 16 of the 1949 Act[10] or section 15 of the 1968 Act[11]—

(a) imposing restrictions as respects those activities; and

(b) providing for the making of them of payments to the applicant.

(3) In this section—

"the appropriate Minister" means the Minister responsible for determining the application;

"farm capital grant" means—

(a) a grant under a scheme made under section 29 of the Agriculture Act 1970[12]; or

(b) a grant under regulations made under section 2(2) of the European Communities Act 1972[13] to a person carrying on an agricultural business within the meaning of those regulations in respect of expenditure incurred or to be incurred for the purposes of or in connection with that business, being expenditure of a capital nature or incurred in connection with expenditure of a capital nature;

"grant provisions" means—

(i) in the case of such a grant as is mentioned in paragraph (a) above, the scheme under which the grant is made and section 29 of the Agriculture Act 1970; and

---

[1] This section came into force on 6 September 1982: S.I. 1982/1136.

[2] "Farm capital grant" defined by subsection (3) below. Words "a farm capital grant" substituted by the Agriculture Act 1986 (c. 49), s. 20(2)(a). This amendment came into force on 25 September 1986: s. 24(2).

[3] "Land" defined by s. 114(1), National Parks and Access to the Countryside Act 1949, p. 38 above: s. 52(4), p. 189 below applies the definition in s. 114 of the 1949 Act.

[4] P. 168 above.

[5] P. 171 above.

[6] "Appropriate Minister" defined by subsection (3) below.

[7] "Grant provisions" defined by subsection (3) below. Words "the grant provisions" substituted by the Agriculture Act 1986 (c. 49), s. 20(2)(b).

[8] For "the Nature Conservancy Council" see s. 27A, p. 167 above: s. 52(1), p. 189 below.

[9] For "the Council" see s. 27A, p. 167 above: s. 52(1), p. 189 below.

[10] P. 15 above.

[11] P. 121 above.

[12] 1970 c. 40.

[13] 1972 c. 68.

(ii) in the case of such a grant as is mentioned in paragraph (*b*) above, the regulations under which the grant is made and the Community instrument in pursuance of which the regulations were made.[1,2]

Ministerial guidance as respects areas of special scientific interest

33. (1) The Ministers[3] shall from time to time, after consultation with the Nature Conservancy Councils[4] and such persons appearing to them to represent other interests concerned as they consider appropriate—

(*a*) prepare codes containing such recommendations, advice and information as they consider proper for the guidance of—

(i) persons exercising functions under sections 28 to 32; and

(ii) persons affected or likely to be affected by the exercise of any of those functions; and

(*b*) revise any such code by revoking, varying, amending or adding to the provisions of the code in such manner as the Ministers think fit.

(2) A code prepared in pursuance of subsection (1) and any alterations proposed to be made on a revision of such a code shall be laid before both Houses of Parliament forthwith after being prepared; and the code or revised code, as the case may be, shall not be issued until the code or the proposed alterations have been approved by both Houses.

(3) Subject to subsection (2), the Ministers shall cause every code prepared or revised in pursuance of subsection (1) to be printed, and may cause copies of it to be put on sale to the public at such price as the Ministers may determine[5].

Limestone pavement orders

34. (1) Where the Nature Conservancy Council[6] or the Commission[7] are of the opinion that any land[8] in the countryside which comprises a limestone pavement[9] is of special interest by reason of its flora, fauna or geological or physiographical features, it shall be the study of the Council[10] or the Commission to notify that fact to the local planning authority[11] in whose area the land is situated.

(2) Where it appears to the Secretary of State or the relevant authority[12] that the character or appearance of any land notified under subsection (1) would be likely to be adversely affected by the removal of the limestone or by its disturbance in any way whatever, the Secretary of State or that authority may make an order (in this section referred to as a "limestone pavement order") designating the land and prohibiting the removal or disturbance of limestone on or in it; and the provisions of Schedule 11[13] shall have effect as to the making, confirmation and coming into operation of limestone pavement orders.

(3) The relevant authority may, after consultation with the Council and the Commission, amend or revoke a limestone pavement order made by the authority; and the Secretary of State may, after such consultation as aforesaid, amend or revoke any such order made by him or that authority but, in the case of an order made by that authority, only after consultation with that authority.

---

[1] Subsection (3) substituted by the Agriculture Act 1986 (c. 49), s. 20(3).

[2] This section came into force on 28 February 1983: S.I. 1983/87.

[3] "The Ministers" defined by s. 52(1), p. 189 below.

[4] "Nature Conservancy Councils" defined by s. 52(1), p. 189 below. Word "Councils" substituted by the Environmental Protection Act 1990 (c. 43), s. 132(1)(*a*), sch. 9, para. 11(12). This amendment came into force on 1 April 1991: S.I. 1991/685.

[5] This section came into force on 30 November 1981: S. 74(2) below.

[6] For "the Nature Conservancy Council" see s. 27A, p. 167 above: s. 52(1), p. 189 below.

[7] The Countryside Commission: subsection (6) below.

[8] "Land" defined by s. 114(1), National Parks and Access to the Countryside Act 1949, p. 38 above: s. 52(4), p. 189 below applies the definition in s. 114 of the 1949 Act.

[9] "Limestone pavement" defined by subsection (6) below.

[10] For "the Council" see s. 27A, p. 167 above: s. 52(1), p. 189 below.

[11] "Local planning authority" defined by s. 52(2), p. 189 below.

[12] "Relevant authority" defined by subsection (6) below.

[13] P. 206 below.

(**4**) If any person without reasonable excuse removes or disturbs limestone on or in any land designated by a limestone pavement order he shall be liable—

(*a*) on summary conviction, to a fine not exceeding the statutory maximum;

(*b*) on conviction on indictment, to a fine.

(**5**) It is a reasonable excuse in any event for a person to remove or disturb limestone or cause or permit its removal or disturbance, if the removal or disturbance was authorised by a planning permission granted on an application under Part III of the Town and Country Planning Act 1990[1] or Part III of the Town and Country Planning (Scotland) Act 1972[2].

(**6**) In this section—

"the Commission" means the Countryside Commission in relation to England[3,4];

"limestone pavement" means an area of limestone which lies wholly or partly exposed on the surface of the ground and has been fissured by natural erosion;

"the relevant authority" means—

(*a*) in relation to a non-metropolitan county in England,[5] the county planning authority and, in relation to any other area in England, the local planning authority;

(*aa*) in relation to any area in Wales, the local planning authority;[7]

(*b*) in relation to Scotland, the authority exercising district planning functions.[8,9]

....

National nature reserves

35. (**1**) Where the Nature Conservancy Council[10] are satisfied that any land[11] which—

(*a*) is being managed as a nature reserve[12] under an agreement entered into with the Council[13];

(*b*) is held by the Council and is being managed by them as a nature reserve; or

(*c*) is held by an approved body[14] and is being managed by that body as a nature reserve,

is of national importance, they may declare that land to be a national nature reserve.

(**2**) A declaration by the Council that any land is a national nature reserve shall be conclusive of the matters declared; and subsections (4) and (5) of section 19 of the 1949 Act[15] shall apply in relation to any such declaration as they apply in relation to a declaration under that section.

(**3**) On the application of the approved body concerned, the Council may, as respect any land which is declared to be a national nature reserve under subsection (1)(*c*), make byelaws for the protection of the reserve.

(**4**) Subsections (2) and (3) of section 20[15] and section 106[16] of the 1949 Act shall apply in relation to byelaws under this section as they apply in relation to byelaws under the said section 20.

---

[1] 1990 c. 8. Words "Part III of the Town and Country Planning Act 1990" substituted by the Planning (Consequential Provisions) Act 1990 (c. 11), s. 4, sch. 2, para. 54(1). This amendment came into force on 24 August 1990: s. 7(2).

[2] 1972 c. 52.

[3] Former words "and Wales" repealed by the Environmental Protection Act 1990 (c. 43), ss. 130(1), 162(2), sch. 8, para. 6(2), sch. 16, pt. VI. This amendment came into force on 1 April 1991: S.I. 1991/685.

[4] Former words "and the Countryside Commission for Scotland in relation to Scotland" repealed by the Natural Heritage (Scotland) Act 1991 (c. 28), s. 27(2), sch. 11. This amendment came into force on 1 April 1992: S.I. 1991/2633.

[5] Words "in England" inserted by the Local Government (Wales) Act 1994 (c. 19), s. 66(6), sch. 16, para. 65(3). It is planned that this amendment will come into force on 1 April 1996.

[7] Paragraph (*aa*) inserted by the Local Government

(Wales) Act 1994 (c. 19), s. 66(6), sch. 16, para. 65(3).

[8] The definition of "relevant authority" amended by the Local Government Act 1985 (c. 51), s. 7(1), sch. 3, para. 7(2). This amendment came into force on 1 April 1986: ss. 1(2), 2.

[9] This section came into force on 30 November 1981: s. 74(2), p. 192 below.

[10] For "Nature Conservancy Council" see s. 27A, p. 000 above: s. 52(1), p. 167 below.

[11] "Land" defined by s. 114(1), National Parks and Access to the Countryside Act 1949, p. 38 above: s. 52(4), p. 189 below applies the definition in s. 114 of the 1949 Act.

[12] "Nature reserve" defined by subsection (5) below.

[13] For "the Council" see s. 27A, p. 167 above: s. 52(1), p. 189 below.

[14] "Approved body" defined by subsection (5) below.

[15] P. 17 above.

[16] P. 17 above.

[17] P. 33 above.

(5) In this section—

"approved body" means a body approved by the Council for the purposes of this section;

"nature reserve" has the same meaning as in Part III of the 1949 Act[1,2].

....

Marine nature reserves

36. (1) Where, in the case of any land[3] covered (continuously or intermittently) by tidal waters or parts of the sea which are landward of the baselines from which the breadth of the territorial sea adjacent to Great Britain is measured or are seaward of those baselines up to distance of three nautical miles[4], it appears to the Secretary of State expedient, on an application made by the Nature Conservancy Council[5], that the land and waters covering it should be managed by the Council[6] for the purpose of—

(*a*) conserving marine flora or fauna or geological or physiographical features of special interest in the area; or

(*b*) providing, under suitable conditions and control, special opportunities for the study of, and research into, matters relating to marine flora and fauna and the physical conditions in which they live, or for the study of geological and physiographical features of special interest in the area,

he may by order designate the area comprising that land and those waters as a marine nature reserve; and the Council shall manage any area so designated for either or both of those purposes[7].

(2) An application for an order under this section shall be accompanied by—

(*a*) a copy of the byelaws which, if an order is made, the Council propose making under section 37 for the protection of the area specified in the application; and

(*b*) a copy of any byelaws made or proposed to be made for the protection of that area by a relevant authority[8];

and an order made on the application shall authorise the making under that section of such of the byelaws proposed to be made by the Council as may be set out in the order with or without modifications[9].

(3) Byelaws the making of which is so authorised—

(*a*) shall not require the Secretary of State's consent under subsection (1) of section 37; and

(*b*) notwithstanding anything in the provisions applied by subsection (4) of that section, shall take effect on their being made.

(4) The provisions of Schedule 12[10] shall have effect as to the making, validity and date of coming into operation of orders under this section; and an order made under this section may be amended or revoked by a subsequent order so made.

(5) The powers exercisable by the Council for the purpose of managing an area designated as a marine nature reserve under this section shall include power to install markers indicating the existence and extent of the reserve.

---

[1] See s. 15, National Parks and Access to the Countryside Act 1949, p. 14 above.

[2] This section came into force on 30 November 1981: s. 74(2), p. 192 below.

[3] "Land" defined by s. 114(1), National Parks and Access to the Countryside Act 1949, p. 38 above: s. 52(4), p. 189 below applies the definition in s. 114 of the 1949 Act.

[4] Words "which are landward . . . three nautical miles" substituted by the Territorial Sea Act 1987 (c. 49), s. 3(1), sch. 1, para. 6(*a*). This amendment came into force on 15 May 1987: S.I. 1987/1270.

[5] For "the Nature Conservancy Council" see s. 27A, p. 167 above: s. 52(1), p. 189 below.

[6] For "the Council" see s. 27A, p. 167 above: s. 52(1), p. 189 below.

[7] An Order in Council may amend subsection (1) so that other parts of the territorial sea adjacent to Great Britain may be included in an order under the subsection: Territorial Sea Act 1987 (c. 49), s. 3(2)(*b*).

[8] "Relevant authority" defined by subsection (7) below.

[9] "Modifications" defined by s. 71, p. 191 below.

[10] P. 208 below.

(6) Nothing in this section or in byelaws made under section 37 shall interfere with the exercise of any functions of a relevant authority, any functions conferred by or under an enactment (whenever passed) or any right of any person (whenever vested).

(7) In this section—

"enactment" includes an enactment contained in a local Act;

"local authority" means—

(a) in relation to England and Wales, a county council, a county borough council[1], a district council,[2] or a London borough council;

(b) in relation to Scotland, a council constituted under section 2 of the Local Government etc. (Scotland) Act 1994[3];

"nautical miles" means international nautical miles of 1,852 metres;[4]

"relevant authority" means a local authority, [England and Wales: the National Rivers Authority, a water undertaker, a sewerage undertaker,[5] Scotland: a water authority or any other statutory water undertakers,] an internal drainage board, a navigation authority, a harbour authority,[6] a lighthouse authority, a conservancy authority, a river purification board, a district board for a fishery district within the meaning of the Salmon Fisheries (Scotland) Act 1862[7], or a local fisheries committee constituted under the Sea Fisheries Regulation Act 1966[8].

Byelaws for protection of marine nature reserves

37. (1) The Nature Conservancy Council[10] may, with the consent of the Secretary of State make byelaws for the protection of any area designated as a marine nature reserve under section 36.

(2) Without prejudice to the generality of subsection (1), byelaws made under this section as respects a marine nature reserve—

(a) may provide for prohibiting or restricting, either absolutely or subject to any exceptions—

  (i) the entry into, or movement within, the reserve of persons and vessels[11];

  (ii) the killing, taking, destruction, molestation or disturbance of animals or plants of any description[12] in the reserve, or the doing of anything therein which will interfere with the sea bed or damage or disturb any object in the reserve; or

  (iii) the depositing of rubbish in the reserve;

(b) may provide for the issue, on such terms and subject to such conditions as may be specified in the byelaws, of permits authorising entry into the reserve or the doing of anything which would otherwise be unlawful under the byelaws; and

(c) may be so made as to apply either generally or with respect to particular parts of the reserve or particular times of the year.

(3) Nothing in byelaws made under this section shall—

---

[1] Words "a county borough council" inserted by the Local Government (Wales) Act 1994 (c. 19), s. 66(6), sch. 16, para. 65(4). It is planned that this amendment will come into force on 1 April 1996.

[2] Former words "the Greater London Council" repealed by the Local Government Act 1985 (c. 51), s. 102(2), sch. 17. This amendment came into force on 1 April 1986: ss. 1(2), 102(3), 105(1).

[3] Words "council ... 1994" substituted by the Local Government etc. (Scotland) Act 1994 (c. 39), s. 180(1), sch. 13, para. 125(3). It is anticipated that this amendment will come into force on 1 April 1996.

[4] Definition of "nautical miles" inserted by the Territorial Sea Act 1987 (c. 49), s. 3(1), sch. 1, para. 6(b).

[5] England and Wales: Words "the National Rivers Authority, a water undertaker, a sewerage undertaker," sub-stituted by the Water Act 1989 (c. 15), s. 190(1), sch. 25, para. 66(2). This amendment came into force on 1 September 1989: S.I. 1989/1146.

[6] Former words "a pilotage authority" repealed by the Pilotage Act 1987 (c. 21), s. 32(5), sch. 3. This amendment came into force on 1 October 1988: S.I. 1988/1137.

[7] 1862 c. 97.

[8] 1966 c. 38.

[9] This section came into force on 30 November 1987: s. 74(2), p. 192 below.

[10] For "the Nature Conservancy Council" see s. 27A, p. 167 above: s., 52(1), p. 189 below.

[11] "Vessels" defined by subsection (10) below.

[12] For "animals or plants of any description" see subsection (11) below.

(a) prohibit or restrict the exercise of any right of passage by a vessel other than a pleasure boat[1]; or

(b) prohibit, except with respect to particular parts of the reserve at particular times of the year, the exercise of any such right by a pleasure boat.

(4) Nothing in byelaws so made shall make unlawful—

(a) anything done for the purpose of securing the safety of any vessel, or of preventing damage to any vessel or cargo, or of saving life;

(b) the discharge of any substance from a vessel; or

(c) anything done more than 30 metres below the sea bed.

(5) Sections 236 to 238 of the Local Government Act 1972[2] or sections 202 to 204 of the Local Government (Scotland) Act 1973[3] (which relate to the procedure for making byelaws, authorise byelaws to impose fines not exceeding the amount there specified and provide for the proof of byelaws in legal proceedings) shall apply to byelaws under this section as if the Council were a local authority within the meaning of the said Act of 1972 or the said Act of 1973, so however that in relation to such byelaws the said sections shall apply subject to such modifications[4] (including modifications increasing the maximum fines which the byelaws may impose) as may be prescribed by regulations made by the Secretary of State[5].

Regulations under this subsection shall be made by statutory instrument which shall be subject to annulment in pursuance of a resolution of either House of Parliament.

(6) In relation to byelaws under this section the confirming authority for the purposes of the said section 236 or the said section 202 shall be the Secretary of State.

(7) The Secretary of State may, after consultation with the Council, direct them—

(a) to revoke any byelaws previously made under this section; or

(b) to make any such amendments of any byelaws so made as may be specified in the direction.

(8) The Council shall have power to enforce byelaws made under this section; but nothing in this subsection shall be construed as authorising the Council to institute proceedings in Scotland for an offence.

(9) Proceedings in England and Wales for an offence under byelaws made under this section shall not, without the consent of the Director of Public Prosecutions, be taken by a person other than the Council.

(10) In this section "vessel" includes a hovercraft and any aircraft capable of landing on water and "pleasure boat" shall be construed accordingly.

(11) References in this section to animals or plants of any description include references to eggs, seeds, spores, larvae or other immature stages of animals or plants of that description[6].

....

38. *Repealed by the Environmental Protection Act 1990 (c. 43), s. 162(2), sch. 16, pt. VI. This amendment came into force on 1 April 1991: S.I. 1991/685.*

....

[1] "Pleasure boat" defined by subsection (10) below.
[2] 1972 c. 70.
[3] 1973 c. 65.
[4] "Modifications" defined by s. 71, p. 191 below.
[5] The Wildlife and Countryside (Byelaws for Marine Nature Reserves) Regulations 1986, S.I. 1986/143, are made under this section and modify ss. 236–238 of the Local Government Act 1972.
[6] This section came into force on 30 November 1981: s. 74(2), p. 192 below.

Countryside

Management agreements with owners and occupiers of land

39. (**1**) A relevant authority[1] may, for the purpose of conserving or enhancing the natural beauty or amenity of any land[2] which is both in the countryside and within their area or promoting its enjoyment by the public, make an agreement (in this section referred to as a "management agreement") with any person having an interest[3] in the land with respect to the management of the land during a specified term or without limitation of the duration of the agreement.

(**2**) Without prejudice to the generality of subsection (1), a management agreement—

(*a*) may impose on the person having an interest in the land restrictions as respects the method of cultivating the land, its use for agricultural purposes or the exercise of rights over the land and may impose obligations on that person to carry out works or agricultural or forestry operations or do other things on the land;

(*b*) may confer on the relevant authority power to carry out works for the purpose of performing their functions under the 1949 Act[4] and the 1968 Act[5]; and

(*c*) may contain such incidental and consequential provisions (including provisions for the making of payments by either party to the other) as appear to the relevant authority to be necessary or expedient for the purposes of the agreement.

(**3**) The provisions of a management agreement with any person interested in the land shall, unless the agreement otherwise provides, be binding on persons deriving title under or from that person and be enforceable by the relevant authority against those persons accordingly.

(**4**) Schedule 2 to the Forestry Act 1967[8] (power for tenant for life and others to enter into forestry dedication covenants) shall apply to management agreements as it applies to forestry dedication covenants.

(**5**) In this section "the relevant authority" means—

(*a*) as respects land[7] in a National Park[8], and outside a metropolitan county[9] the county planning authority;

(*aa*) as respects land within the Broads,[10] the Broads Authority[11];

(*b*) *Repealed by the Local Government Act 1985 (c. 51), s. 102(2), sch. 17. This amendment came into force on 1 April 1986: ss. 1(2), 102(3), 105(1).*

(*c*) as respects any other land, the local planning authority[12].

(**6**) The powers conferred by this section on a relevant authority shall be in addition to and not in derogation of any powers conferred on such an authority by or under any enactment[13].

---

[1] "Relevant authority" defined by subsection (5) below.

[2] For the construction of references to the conservation of the natural beauty of an any land see s. 52(3), p. 189 below. "Land" defined by s. 114(1), National Parks and Access to the Countryside Act 1949, p. 38 above: s. 52(4), p. 189 below applies the definition in s. 114 of the 1949 Act.

[3] "Interest" defined by s. 114(1), National Parks and Access to the Countryside Act 1949, p. 38 above: s. 52(4), p. 189 below applies the definition in s. 114 of the 1949 Act.

[4] P. 5 above.

[5] P. 112 above.

[6] P. 99 above.

[7] It is proposed in the Environment Bill that a prospective amendment made here by the Local Government (Wales) Act 1994, along with s. 39(5)(a), be repealed.

[8] "National Park" defined by s. 114(1), National Parks and Access to the Countryside Act 1949, by which it has the meaning assigned to it by s. 5(3), p. 8 above: s. 52(4), p. 189 below applies the definition s. 114 of the 1949 Act.

[9] Words "and outside a metropolitan county" inserted by the Local Government Act 1985 (c. 51), s. 7(1), sch. 3, para. 7(3). This amendment came into force on 1 April 1986: ss. 1(2), 2, 105(1).

[10] "The Broads" defined by s. 71, p. 191 below.

[11] The "Broads Authority" is established by the Norfolk and Suffolk Broads Act 1988 (c. 4), s. 1, p. 221 below. Paragraph (*aa*) inserted by the Norfolk and Suffolk Broads Act 1988 (c. 4), s. 2(5), sch. 3, para. 31(2). This amendment came into force on 1 April 1989: S.I. 1988/955.

[12] "Local planning authority" defined by s. 52(2), p. 189 below.

[13] This section came into force on 30 November 1981: s. 74(2), p. 192 below.

40. *This section substitutes a replacement subsection 4(1), at p. 117 above, for the former subsections 4(1) and (2) of the Countryside Act 1968 (c. 41).*

Duties of agriculture Ministers with respect to the countryside

41. (1) *Repealed by the Agriculture Act 1986 (c. 41), s. 24(5), sch. 4. This amendment came into force on 25 September 1986: s. 24(2).*

(2) In the exercise of his general duty under section 4(2) of the Small Landholders (Scotland) Act 1911[1] of promoting the interests of agriculture and other rural industries, and without prejudice to the generality of that duty, the Secretary of State shall make provision, through such organisation as he considers appropriate, for the giving of—

(a) advice to persons carrying on agricultural businesses[2] on the conservation and enhancement on the natural beauty and amenity of the countryside[3];

(b) advice to such persons on diversification into other enterprises of benefit to the rural economy; and

(c) advice to government departments and other bodies exercising statutory functions on the promotion and furtherance of such diversification as is mentioned in paragraph (b).[4]

(3) Where an application for a farm capital grant[5] is made as respects expenditure incurred or to be incurred for the purposes of activities on land[6] which is in a National Park[7] or an area specified for the purposes of this subsection by the Ministers[8], the appropriate Minister[9]—

(a) shall, so far as may be consistent with the purposes of the grant provisions[10] so exercise his functions thereunder as to further the conservation and enhancement of the natural beauty and amenity of the countryside and to promote its enjoyment by the public; and

(b) where the relevant authority[11] have objected to the making of the grant on the ground that the activities in question have had or will have an adverse effect on the natural beauty or amenity of the countryside or its enjoyment by the public, shall not make the grant except after considering the objection and, in the case of land in England, after consulting with the Secretary of State;

and this subsection shall have effect, in its application to Scotland, as if references to the amenity of the countryside were omitted.

(4) Where, in consequence of an objection by the relevant authority, an application for a grant as respects expenditure to be incurred is refused on the ground that the activities in question will have such an effect as is mentioned in subsection (3)(b), the relevant authority shall, within three months of their receiving notice of the appropriate Minister's decision, offer to enter into, in the terms of a draft submitted to the applicant, a management agreement[12]—

---

[1] 1911 c. 49.

[2] "Agricultural business" defined by subsection (5) below.

[3] For the construction of references to the conservation of the natural beauty of any land see s. 52(3), p. 189 below.

[4] Paragraphs (a), (b) and (c) inserted by the Agriculture Act 1986 (c. 41), s. 24(4), sch. 3, para. 4.

[5] "Farm capital grant" defined by s. 32(3), p. 175 above: subsection (5) below. Words "a farm capital grant" substituted by the Agriculture Act 1986 (c. 41), s.20(4)(a).

[6] "Land" defined by s. 114(1), National Parks and Access to the Countryside Act 1949, p. 38 above: s. 52(4), p. 189 below applies the definition in s. 114 of the 1949 Act.

[7] "National Park" defined by: s. 114(1), National Parks and Access to the Countryside Act 1949, by which it has the meaning assigned to it by s. 5(3), p. 8 above: s. 52(4), p. 189 below applies the definition in s. 114 of the 1949 Act; subsection (5A) below.

[8] "The Ministers" defined by s. 52(1), p. 189 below.

[9] "The appropriate Minister" defined by s. 32(3), p. 175 above: subsection (5) below.

[10] "Grant provisions" defined by s. 32(3), p. 175 above: subsection (5) below. Words "the grant provisions" substituted by the Agriculture Act 1986 (c. 41), s. 20(4)(b).

[11] "Relevant authority" defined by subsection (5) below.

[12] "Management agreement" defined by subsection (5) below.

(a) imposing restrictions as respects those activities; and

(b) providing for the making by them of payments to the applicant.

(5) In this section—

"agricultural business" has the same meaning as in section 29 of the Agriculture Act 1970[1];

"the appropriate Minister", "farm capital grant" and "grant provisions" have the same meanings as in section 32;[2,3]

"management agreement"—

(a) in relation to England and Wales, means an agreement under section 39[4];

(b) in relation to Scotland, means an agreement under section 49A of the Countryside (Scotland) Act 1967[5];

"the relevant authority"—

(a) in relation to England and Wales, has the same meaning as in section 39;

(b) in relation to Scotland, means the authority exercising district planning functions.

(5A) For the purposes of this section the Broads[6] shall be treated as a National Park.[7]

(6) Subsection (2) extends only to Scotland[8,9].

National Parks

Notification of agricultural operations on moor and health in National Parks

42. (1) The Ministers[10] may, if satisfied that it is expedient to do so, by order apply subsection (2) to any land[11] which is comprised in a National Park[12] and which appears to them to consist of or include moor or heath.

(2) Subject to subsection (3), no person shall—

(a) by ploughing or otherwise convert into agricultural land[13] any land to which this subsection applies and which is moor or heath which has not been agricultural land at any time within the preceding 20 years; or

(b) carry out on any such land any other agricultural operation or any forestry operation which (in either case) appears to the Ministers to be likely to affect its character or appearance and is specified in the order applying this subsection to that land[14].

(3) Subsection (2) shall not apply in relation to any operation carried out, or caused or permitted to be carried out, by the owner[15] or occupier of the land if—

(a) one of them has, after the coming into force of the order, given the local[16] planning authority written notice of a proposal to carry out the operation, specifying its nature and the land on which it is proposed to carry it out; and

(b) one of the conditions specified in subsection (4) is satisfied.

---

[1] 1970 c. 40.
[2] P. 175 above.
[3] These definitions substituted by the Agriculture Act 1986 (c. 41), s. 20(5).
[4] P. 181 above.
[5] P. 109 above.
[6] "The Broads" defined by s. 71, p. 191 below.
[7] This subsection inserted by the Norfolk and Suffolk Broads Act 1988 (c. 4), s. 2(5), sch. 3, para. 31(3). This amendment came into force on 1 April 1989: S.I. 1988/955.
[8] Former words "Subsection (1) extends only to England and Wales and" repealed by the Agriculture Act 1986 (c. 41), s. 24(5), sch. 4.
[9] This section came into force on 28 February 1983: S.I. 1983/87.
[10] "The Ministers" defined by s. 52(1), p. 189 below.
[11] "Land" defined by s. 114(1), National Parks and Access to the Countryside Act 1949, p. 38 above: s. 52(4), p. 189

below applies the definition in s. 114 of the 1949 Act.
[12] "National Park" defined by s. 114(1), National Parks and Access to the Countryside Act 1949, by which it has the meaning assigned to it by s. 5(3), p. 8 above: s. 52(4), p. 189 below applies the definition in s. 114 of the 1949 Act.
[13] "Agricultural land" defined by s. 52(1), p. 189 below.
[14] The Dartmoor National Park (Restriction of Agricultural Operations) Order 1991, S.I. 1991/1616, applies this subsection to an area at Cator Common within the Dartmoor National Park.
[15] "Owner" defined by s. 114(1), National Parks and Access to the Countryside Act 1949, p. 000 above: s. 52(4), p. 38 below applies the definition in s. 114 of the 1949 Act.
[16] "Local planning authority" defined by s. 52(2), p. 189 below. Words "local planning authority" in this section substituted by the Local Government Act 1985 (c. 51), s. 7(1), sch. 3, para. 7(4). This amendment came into force on 1 April 1986: ss. 1(2), 2, 105(1).

(4) The said conditions are—

(a) that the local planning authority have given their consent to the carrying out of the operation;

(b) where that authority have neither given nor refused their consent, that three months have expired from the giving of the notice; and

(c) where that authority have refused their consent, that twelve months have expired from the giving of the notice.

(5) A person who, without reasonable excuse, contravenes subsection (2) shall be liable—

(a) on summary conviction, to a fine not exceeding the statutory maximum;

(b) on conviction on indictment, to a fine.

(6) Where the local planning authority are given notice under this section in respect of any land, the authority shall forthwith send copies of the notice to the Ministers, the Nature Conservancy Council[1] and the Countryside Commission.

(7) In considering for the purposes of this section whether land has been agricultural land within the preceding 20 years, no account shall be taken of any conversion of the land into agricultural land which was unlawful under the provisions of this section or section 14 of the 1968 Act.

(8) An order under this section shall be made by statutory instrument which shall be subject to annulment in pursuance of a resolution of either House of Parliament.

(9) The said section 14 (which is superseded by this section) shall cease to have effect; but this section shall have effect as if any order under that section in force immediately before the coming into force of this section had been made under this section[2].

....

Maps of National Parks showing certain areas of moor or heath

43. Maps of National Parks showing certain areas of moor or heath.

(1) Every local planning authority[3] whose area comprises the whole or any part of a National Park[4] shall—

(a) before the expiration of the period of two years beginning with the relevant date,[5] prepare a map of the Park or the part thereof showing any areas to which this section applies whose natural beauty[6] it is, in the opinion of the authority, particularly important to conserve; and

(b) at intervals of not more than five years[7] review the particulars contained in the map and make such revisions thereof (if any) as may be requisite.

(1A) In considering under subsection (1) whether any area to which this section applies is one whose natural beauty it is particularly important to conserve, a local planning authority shall act in accordance with the guidelines from time to time issued[8] under subsection (1B).

(1B) The Countryside Commission and the Countryside Council for Wales shall each[9] issue guidelines for the guidance of local planning authorities in considering as mentioned in

---

[1] For "Nature Conservancy Council" see s. 27A, p. 167 above: s. 52(1), p. 189 below.

[2] This section came into force on 30 November 1981: s. 74(2) p. 192 below.

[3] Words "local planning authority" in this section substituted by the Local Government Act 1985 (c. 51), s. 7(1), sch. 3, para. 7(4). This amendment came into force on 1 April 1986: ss. 1(2), 2, 105(1).

[4] "National Park" defined by s. 114(1), National Parks and Access to the Countryside Act 1949, by which it has the meaning assigned to it by s. 5(3), p. 8 above: s. 52(4), p. 189 below applies the definition in s. 114 of the 1949 Act.

[5] "The relevant date" defined by subsection (3) below. Words "the relevant date" substituted by the Wildlife and Countryside (Amendment) Act 1985 (c. 31), s. 3(2)(a). This

amendment came into force on 26 August 1985: s. 5(3).

[6] Words "to which this section applies whose natural beauty" substituted by the Wildlife and Countryside (Amendment) Act 1985 (c. 31), s. 3(2)(b).

[7] Words "at intervals of not more than five years" substituted by the Wildlife and Countryside (Amendment) Act 1985 (c. 31), s. 3(3).

[8] Former words "by the Countryside Commission" repealed by the Environmental Protection Act 1990 (c. 43), ss. 130(1), 162(2), sch. 8, para. 6(3), sch. 16, pt. VI.. This amendment came into force on 1 April 1991: S.I. 1991/685.

[9] Words "and the Countryside Council for Wales shall each" inserted by the Environmental Protection Act 1990 (c. 43), s. 130(1), sch. 8, para. 6(3)(a).

subsection (1A), and the Commission and the Council may each[1] from time to time revise any guidelines so issued.

(1C) Before issuing or revising any guidelines under subsection (1B) the Commission or, as the case may be, the Council[2] shall consult such bodies as appear to them to represent interests concerned; and before preparing or revising any map under subsection (1) a local planning authority shall consult such bodies as appear to the authority to represent interests concerned with matters affecting the Park or part of the Park in question.[3]

(2) The authority shall cause a map prepared or revised in pursuance of subsection (1) to be printed, and shall cause copies thereof to be put on sale to the public at such price as the authority may determine.

(3) This section applies to any area of mountain, moor, heath, woodland, down, cliff or foreshore (including any bank, barrier, dune, beach, flat or other land adjacent to the foreshore); and in this section "the relevant date" means the date of issue of the first guidelines under subsection (1B).[4,5]

Grants and loans for purposes of National Parks

44. (1) Without prejudice to section 11 of the 1949 Act[6] (general powers of local planning authorities in relation to National Parks), a local planning authority[7] may give financial assistance by way of grant or loan, or partly in one way and partly in the other, to any person in respect of expenditure incurred by him in doing anything which in the opinion of the authority is conducive to the attainment, in any National Park[8] the whole or part of which is comprised in that authority's area, or any of the following purposes, that is to say, the conservation and enhancement of the natural beauty[9] of that Park and the promotion of its enjoyment by the public.

(2) On making a grant or loan under this section a local planning authority may impose such conditions as they think fit, including (in the case of a grant) conditions for repayment in specified circumstances.

(3) A local planning authority shall so exercise their powers under subsection (2) as to ensure that any person receiving a grant or loan under this section in respect of premises to which the public are to be admitted, whether on payment or otherwise, shall, in the means of access both to and within the premises, and in the parking facilities and sanitary conveniences to be available (if any), make provision, insofar as it is in the circumstances both practicable and reasonable, for the needs of members of the public visiting the premises who are disabled.

(4) For the purposes of this section the Broads Authority[10] shall be treated as a county planning authority and the Broads[11] as a National Park.[12,13]

---

[1] Words "the Commission and the Council may each" inserted by the Environmental Protection Act 1990 (c. 43), s. 130(1), sch. 8, para. 6(3)(*a*).

[2] Words "or, as the case may be, the Council" inserted by the Environmental Protection Act 1990 (c. 43), s. 130(1), sch. 8, para. 6(3)(*b*).

[3] Subsections (1A)–(1C) inserted by the Wildlife and Countryside (Amendment) Act 1985 (c. 31), s. 3(4).

[4] Subsection (3) inserted by the Wildlife and Countryside (Amendment) Act 1985 (c. 31), s. 3(5).

[5] This section came into force on 30 November 1981: s. 74(2), p. 192 below.

[6] P. 12 above.

[7] Words "local planning authority" in this section substituted by the Local Government Act 1985 (c. 51), s. 7(1), sch. 3, para. 7(4). This amendment came into force on 1 April

1986: ss. 1(2), 2, 105(1).

[8] "National Park" defined by s. 114(1), National Parks and Access to the Countryside Act 1949, by which it has the meaning assigned to it by s. 5(3), p. 8 above: s. 52(4), p. 189 below applies the definition in s. 114 of the 1949 Act.

[9] For the construction of references to the conservation of the natural beauty of any land see s. 52(3), p. 189 below.

[10] The "Broads Authority" is established by the Norfolk and Suffolk Broads Act 1988 (c. 4), s. 1, p. 221 below.

[11] "The Broads" defined by s. 71, p. 191 below.

[12] Subsection (4) inserted by the Norfolk and Suffolk Broads Act 1988 (c. 4), s. 2(5), sch. 3, para. 31(4). This amendment came into force on 1 April 1989: S.I. 1988/955.

[13] This section came into force on 30 November 1981: s. 74(2), p. 192 below.

Power to vary order designating National Park

45. (1) The Countryside Commission (as well as the Secretary of State) shall have power to make an order amending an order made under section 5 of the 1949 Act[1] designating a National Park[2] in England[3], and—

(*a*) section 7(5) and (6) of that Act[4] (consultation and publicity in connection with orders under section 5 or 7) shall apply to an order under this section as they apply to an order under section 7(4) of that Act with the substitution for the reference in section 7(5) to the Secretary of State of a reference to the Countryside Commission; and

(*b*) Schedule 1 to that Act[5] (procedure in connection with the making and confirmation of orders under section 5 or 7) shall apply to an order under this section as it applies to an order designating a National Park.

(2) Subsection (1) shall apply to the Countryside Council for Wales, in relation to any National Park in Wales, as it applies to the Countryside Commission in relation to any National Park in England.[6,7]

46. *This section amends Schedule 17 to the Local Government Act 1972 (c. 70).*

Miscellaneous and supplemental

Provisions with respect to the Countryside Commission

47. (1) Schedule 13[8] shall have effect as respects the Countryside Commission.

(2) The Secretary of State may, with the approval of the Treasury, make to the Countryside Commission or to the Countryside Council for Wales[9] out of moneys provided by Parliament grants of such amount and subject to such conditions (if any) as he may, with the approval of the Treasury, think fit.

(3) Sections 2, 4 and 95 of the 1949 Act[10] and section 3 of the 1968 Act[11] (which are superseded by this section) shall cease to have effect.[12]

48. *Repealed by the Water Act 1989 (c. 15), s. 190(3), sch. 27, pt. I. This amendment came into force on 1 September 1992: s. 194(3), S.I. 1989/1530.*

Extension of power to appoint wardens

49. (1) This section applies to any land[13] in a National Park[14] or in the countryside if—

(*a*) the public are allowed access to the land; and

---

[1] P. 8 above.

[2] "National Park" defined by s. 114(1), National Parks and Access to the Countryside Act 1949, by which it has the meaning assigned to it by s. 5(3), p. 8 above: s. 52(4), p. 189 below applies the definition in s. 114 of the 1949 Act.

[3] Words "in England" inserted by the Environmental Protection Act 1990 (c. 43), s. 130(1), sch. 8, para. 6(4). This amendment came into force on 1 April 1981: S.I. 1991/685.

[4] P. 11 above.

[5] Not reproduced.

[6] Subsection (2) inserted by the Environmental Protection Act 1990 (c. 43), s. 130(1), sch. 8, para. 6(4).

[7] This section came into force on 30 November 1981: s. 74(2), p. 192 below.

[8] P. 211 below.

[9] Words "or to the Countryside Council for Wales" inserted by the Environmental Protection Act 1990 (c. 43), s. 130(1), sch. 8, para. 6(5). This amendment came into force on 1 April 1991: S.I. 1991/685.

[10] The National Parks and Access to the Countryside Act 1949 (c. 97): s. 71, p. 191 below.

[11] The Countryside Act 1968 (c. 41): s. 71, p. 191 below.

[12] This section came into force on 1 April 1982: S.I. 1982/327.

[13] "Land" defined by s. 114(1), National Parks and Access to the Countryside Act 1949, p. 38 above: s. 52(4), p. 189 below applies the definition in s. 114 of the 1949 Act.

[14] "National Park" defined by s. 114(1), National Parks and Access to the Countryside Act 1949, by which it has the meaning assigned to it by s. 5(3), p. 8 above: s. 52(4), p. 189 below applies the definition in s. 114 of the 1949 Act.

(*b*) there is no power under any of the provisions of the 1949 Act[1] and the 1968 Act[2] for a local authority, a local planning authority[3], the Countryside Council for Wales[4] or the Countryside Commission to appoint wardens as respects that land.

(**2**) Subject to subsections (3) and (4) the power conferred on a local authority by section 92(1) of the 1949 Act[5] (appointment of wardens) shall include a power, exercisable only with the agreement of the owner[6] and of the occupier of any land to which this section applies, to appoint persons to act as wardens as respects that land.

(**3**) The only purpose for which wardens may be appointed by virtue of subsection (2) is to advise and assist the public.

(**4**) Notwithstanding the provisions of section 41(8) of the 1968 Act[7] (Countryside Commission or the Countryside Council for Wales[8] to be local authority for purposes of section 92 of the 1949 Act), nothing in this section shall be construed as conferring on the Countryside Commission or the Countryside Council for Wales[8] any additional power to appoint wardens[9].

Payments under certain agreements offered by authorities

50. (**1**) This section applies where—

(*a*) the Nature Conservancy Council[10] offer to enter into an agreement under section 16 of the 1949 Act[11] or section 15 of the 1968 Act[12] providing for the making by them of payments to—

  (i) a person who has given notice under section 28(5)[13] or 29(4)[14]; or

  (ii) a person whose application for farm capital grant[15] has been refused in consequence of an objection by the Council[16]; or

(*b*) the relevant authority[17] offer to enter into a management agreement[18] providing for the making by them of payments to a person whose application for a farm capital grant has been refused in consequence of an objection by the authority.

(**2**) Subject to subsection (3), the said payments shall be of such amounts as may be determined by the offeror in accordance with guidance given by the Ministers[19].

(**3**) If the offeree so requires within one month of receiving the offer, the determination of those amounts shall be referred to an arbitrator (or, in Scotland, an arbiter) to be appointed, in default of agreement, by the Secretary of State; and where the amounts determined by the arbitrator exceed those determined by the offeror, the offeror shall—

(*a*) amend the offer so as to give effect to the arbitrator's (or, in Scotland, the arbiter's) determination; or

(*b*) except in the case of an offer made to a person whose application for a farm capital grant has been refused in consequence of an objection by the offeror, withdraw the offer.

---

[1] The National Parks and Access to the Countryside Act 1949 (c. 97): s. 71, p. 191 below.
[2] The Countryside Act 1968 (c. 41): s. 71, p. 191 below.
[3] "Local planning authority" defined by s. 52(2), p. 189 below.
[4] Words ", the Countryside Council for Wales" inserted by the Environmental Protection Act 1990 (c. 43), s. 130(1), sch. 8, para. 6(6). This amendment came into force on 1 April 1991: S.I. 1991/685.
[5] P. 26 above.
[6] "Owner" defined by s. 114(1), National Parks and Access to the Countryside Act 1949, p. 189 above: s. 52(4), p. 189 below applies the definition in s. 114 of the 1949 Act.
[7] P. 128 above.
[8] Words "or the Countryside Council for Wales" inserted by the Environmental Protection Act 1990 (c. 43), s. 130(1), sch. 8, para. 6(6).
[9] This section came into force on 30 November 1981:

s. 74(2), p. 192 below.
[10] For "the Nature Conservancy Council" see s. 27A, p. 167 above: s. 52(1), p. 189 below.
[11] P. 15 above.
[12] P. 121 above.
[13] P. 169 above.
[14] P. 171 above.
[15] "Farm capital grant" defined by s. 32(3), p. 175 above: subsection (4) below.
[16] For "the Council" see s. 27A, p. 167 above: s. 52(1), p. 189 below.
[17] "Relevant authority" defined by s. 41(5), p. 183 above: subsection (4) below.
[18] "Management agreement" defined by s. 41(5), p. 183 above: subsection (4) below.
[19] "The Ministers" defined by s. 52(1), p. 189 below. Guidance is set out in Circular 4/83 (DOE), 6/83 (Welsh Office) which is currently under review.

(4) In this section—

"farm capital grant" has the same meaning as in section 32[1];

"management agreement" and "the relevant authority" have the same meanings as in section 41[2,3].

....

Powers of entry

51. (1) Any person authorised in writing by the relevant authority[4] may, at any reasonable time and (if required to do so) upon producing evidence that he is authorised, enter any land[5] for any of the following purposes—

(a) to ascertain whether an order should be made in relation to that land under section 29[6] or if an offence under that section is being, or has been, committed on that land;

(b) to ascertain the amount of any compensation payable under section 30[7] in respect of an interest[8] in that land;

(c) to ascertain whether an order should be made in relation to that land under section 34[9] or if an offence under that section is being, or has been, committed on that land;

(d) to ascertain whether an order should be made in relation to that land under section 42[10] or if an offence under that section is being, or has been, committed on that land;

but nothing in this subsection shall authorise any person to enter a dwelling.

(2) In subsection (1) "the relevant authority" means—

(a) for the purposes of paragraphs (a) and (b) of that subsection, the Nature Conservancy Council[11];

(b) he purposes of paragraph (c) of that subsection, the Secretary of State or the relevant authority within the meaning of section 34;

(c) for the purposes of paragraph (d) of that subsection, the Ministers[12] or the local planning authority[13].

(3) A person shall not demand admission as of right to any land which is occupied unless either—

(a) 24 hours notice of the intended entry has been given to the occupier; or

(b) the purpose of the entry is to ascertain if an offence under section 29, 34 or 42 is being, or has been, committed on that land.

(4) Any person who intentionally obstructs a person acting in the exercise of any power conferred by subsection (1) shall be liable on summary conviction to a fine not exceeding level 3 on the standard scale.[14,15]

---

[1] The definition of farm capital grant substituted by the Agriculture Act 1986 (c. 49), s. 20(6). This amendment came into force on 25 September 1986: s. 24(2).

[2] This section came into force on 30 November 1981: s. 74(2), p. 192 below.

[3] **Cases: section 50** *Cameron v Nature Conservancy Council* [1991] S.L.T. (Lands Tr) 85; *Thomas and another v The Countryside Council for Wales* [1994] 1 EGLR 17.

[4] "Relevant authority" defined by subsection (2) below.

[5] "Land" defined by s. 114(1), National Parks and Access to the Countryside Act 1949, p. 38 above: s. 52(4), p. 189 below applies the definition in s. 114 of the 1949 Act.

[6] P. 171 above.

[7] P. 172 above.

[8] "Interest" defined by s. 114(1), National Parks and Access to the Countryside Act 1949,. p. 38 above: s. 52(4), p. 189 below applies the definition in s. 114 of the 1949 Act.

[9] P. 176 above.

[10] P. 183 above.

[11] For "Nature Conservancy Council" see s. 27A, p. 167 above: s. 52(1), p. 189 below.

[12] "The Ministers" defined by s.52(1) below.

[13] "Local planning authority" defined by s. 52(2), p. 189 below. Words "local planning authority" substituted by the Local Government Act 1985 (c. 51), s. 7(1), sch. 3, para. 7(4). This amendment came into force on 1 April 1986: ss. 1(2), 2, 105(1).

[14] Words "level 3 on the standard scale" substituted by the Criminal Justice Act 1982 (c. 48), ss. 37, 46 as respects England and Wales and the Criminal Procedure (Scotland) Act 1975 (c. 21), s. 289G as respects Scotland. The current fine at level 3 is £1,000: Criminal Justice Act 1991 (c. 53), s. 17 which came into force on 1 October 1992: S.I. 1992/333, S.I. 1992/2118.

[15] This section came into force on 30 November 1981: s. 74(2), p. 192 below.

Interpretation of Part II

52. (1) In this Part, unless the context otherwise requires,—

"agricultural land" does not include land which affords rough grazing for livestock but is not otherwise used as agricultural land;

"the Ministers", in the application of this Part to England, means the Secretary of State and the Minister of Agriculture, Fisheries and Food, and, in the application of this Part to Scotland or Wales, means the Secretary of State.

"the Nature Conservancy Councils" means the Nature Conservancy Council for England, Scottish Natural Heritage[1] and the Countryside Council for Wales;

and references to "the Nature Conservancy Council" shall be construed in accordance with section 27A.[2]

(2) In the application of this part to England (except as respects a metropolitan county or Greater London)[3] references to a local planning authority shall be construed—

(a) in sections 42, 43, 44[4] and 51(2)(c)[5] as references to a county planning authority; and

(b) in any other provision, as references to a county planning authority and a district planning authority;[6]

and in the application of this Part to Scotland references to a local planning authority shall be construed as references to a regional planning authority, a general planning authority and a district planning authority.

(3) References in this Part to the conservation of the natural beauty of any land shall be construed as including references to the conservation of its flora, fauna and geological and physiographical features.

(4) Section 114 of the 1949 Act[7] shall apply for the construction of this Part.

(5) Any power or duty which under this Part (except sections 41 and 42(1))[8] falls to be exercised or performed by or in relation to the Ministers[9] may, in England, be exercised or performed by or in relation to either of them[10].

Part III: Public Rights of Way

Not Reproduced.

Part IV: Miscellaneous and General

Application to Crown

67. (1) Subject to the following provisions of this section, Part II[11], except section 51, and Part III shall apply to Crown land, that is to say, land an interest in which belongs to Her Majesty in the

---

[1] Words "Scottish Natural Heritage" substituted by the Natural Heritage (Scotland) Act 1991 (c. 28), s. 4(6), sch. 2, para. 8(5). This amendment came into force on 1 April 1992: S.I. 1991/2633.

[2] The definition of the Nature Conservancy Council(s) inserted by the Environmental Protection Act 1990 (c. 43), s. 132(1)(a), sch. 9, para. 11(13). This amendment came into force on 1 April 1991: S.I. 1991/685.

[3] Former words "and to Wales" repealed by the Local Government (Wales) Act 1994 (c. 19), s. 66(8), sch. 16, para. 65(6), sch. 18. It is planned that this amendment will come into force on 1 April 1996.

[4] Ss. 42–44 are at pp. 183–185 above.

[5] P. 188 above.

[6] This part of subsection (2), relating to England, substituted by the Local Government Act 1985 (c. 51), s. 7(1), sch. 3, para. 7(5). This amendment came into force on 1 April 1986: ss. 1(2), 2, 105(1).

[7] P. 37 above.

[8] Ss. 41 and 42(1) are at pp. 182–183 above.

[9] "The Ministers" defined above.

[10] This section came into force on 30 November 1981: s. 74(2), p. 192 below.

[11] P. 167 above.

right of the Crown or the Duchy or Lancaster or to the Duchy of Cornwall, and land an interest in which belongs to a Government department or is held in trust for Her Majesty for the purposes of a Government department.

(2) No order shall be made under section 29[1], 34[2], 36[3] or 42[4] in relation to Crown land unless the appropriate authority[5] has consented to the making of that order.

(3) An agreement under section 39[6] as respects any interest in Crown land, other than an interest held by or on behalf of the Crown, shall not have effect unless approved by the appropriate authority.

(4) Section 101(11) of the 1949 Act[7] (Crown land) shall apply for the construction of references in this section to the appropriate authority[8].

Application to the Isles of Scilly

68. The Secretary of State may, after consultation with the Council of the Isles of Scilly, by order made by statutory instrument provide for the application of the provisions of Part II or III to the Isles of Scilly as if those Isles were a separate county; and any such order may provide for the application of those provisions to those Isles subject to such modifications as may be specified in the order[9],[10].

Offences by bodies corporate etc.

69. (1) Where a body corporate is guilty of an offence under this Act and that offence is proved to have been committed with the consent or connivance of, or to be attributable to any neglect on the part of, any director, manager, secretary or other similar officer of the body corporate or any person who was purporting to act in any such capacity he, as well as the body corporate, shall be guilty of that offence and shall be liable to be proceeded against and punished accordingly.

(2) Where the affairs of a body corporate are managed by its members subsection (1) shall apply in relation to the acts and defaults of a member in connection with his functions of management as if he were a director of the body corporate[11].

Financial provisions

70. (1) There shall be defrayed out of money provided by Parliament—

(a) any administrative expenses incurred by any Minister of the Crown under this Act; and

(b) any increase attributable to the provisions of this Act in the sums payable out of money so provided under any other enactment.

(2) Any sums received by a Minister of the Crown under this Act shall be paid into the Consolidated Fund[11].

[1] P. 171 above.
[2] P. 176 above.
[3] P. 178 above.
[4] P. 183 above.
[5] For "appropriate authority" see subsection (4) below.
[6] P. 181 above.
[7] P. 29 above.
[8] This section came into force on 30 November 1981: s. 74(2), p. 192 below.
[9] By the Wildlife and Countryside (isles of Scilly) Order 1983, S.I. 1983/512, the provisions of Part II (p. 167 above) and Part III apply to the Isles of Scilly as if those Isles were a separate county. These provisions apply with the modification that a reference to the Council of the Isles is substituted for any reference to a county council, county planning authority, local authority or local planning authority. This order came into operation on 5 May 1983.
[10] This section came into force on 30 November 1981: s. 74(2), p. 192 below.
[11] This section came into force on 30 November 1981: s. 74(2), p. 192 below.

Service of notices

70A. (1) Subject to subsection (2), section 329 of the Town and Country Planning Act 1990[1] and section 269 of the Town and Country Planning (Scotland) Act 1972[2] (which provide for the service of notices and other documents) shall apply to notices and other documents required or authorised to be served or given under this Act.

(2) Subsections (2) and (3) of the said section 329[3] shall not apply to a notice required to be served under paragraph 2 of Schedule[3].

(3) This section shall not affect the operating of paragraph 2(4) of Schedule 11 or paragraph 3(4) of Schedule 15.[4]

General interpretation

71. In this Act—

"the 1949 Act" means the National Parks and Access to the Countryside Act 1949[5];

"the 1968 Act" means the Countryside Act 1968[6];

"the Broads" has the same meaning as in the Norfolk and Suffolk Broads Act 1988.[7]

"the commencement date", in relation to any provision of this Act and any area, means the date of the coming into force of that provision in that area;

"London borough council" includes the Common Council of the City of London;

"modifications" includes additions, alterations and omissions, and cognate expressions shall be construed accordingly;

8,9

72. *This section makes minor amendments to various Acts. The amendments made to the National Parks and Access to the Countryside Act, 1949 (c. 97) and the Countryside Act 1968 (c. 41) are noted at the appropriate points in those Acts.*

Repeals and savings

73. (1) The enactments mentioned in Schedule 17 are hereby repealed to the extent specified in the third column of that Schedule.

(2) Nothing in the repeals made by this section shall affect the operation of sections 27 to 32 of the 1949 Act[10] in relation to any survey begun before the commencement date.

(3) Nothing in the repeals made by this section shall affect the operation of sections 33 and 34 of the 1949 Act and Parts II, III and IV of Schedule 3 to the 1968 Act[11] in relation to any review begun before the commencement date[12].

---

[1] 1990 c. 8. Words "section 329 of the Town and Country Planning Act 1990" substituted by the Planning (Consequential Provisions) Act 1990 (c. 11), s. 4, sch. 2, para. 54(2)(a). This amendment came into force on 24 August 1990: s. 7(2).

[2] 1972 c. 52.

[3] Words "Subsections (2) and (3) of the said section 329" substituted by the Planning (Consequential Provisions) Act 1990 (c. 11), s. 4, sch. 2, para. 54(2)(b).

[4] This section inserted by the Wildlife and Countryside (Service of Notices) Act 1985 (c. 59), s. 1(1). This amendment came into force on 25 July 1985, the date of the Royal Assent.

[5] P. 5 above.

[6] P. 112 above.

[7] P. 220 below. The definition of the Broads inserted by the Norfolk and Suffolk Broads Act 1988 (c. 4), s. 2(5), sch. 3, para. 31(5). This amendment came into force on 1 April 1989: S.I. 1989/955.

[8] Former definition of "statutory maximum" repealed by the Statute Law (Repeals) Act 1993 (c. 50), s. 1, sch. 1, pt. XIV. This amendment came into force on 5 November 1993, the date of the Royal Assent.

[9] This section came into force on 30 November 1981: s. 74(2), p. 192 below.

[10] The National Parks and Access to the Countryside Act 1949 (c. 97): s. 71, above.

[11] The Countryside Act 1968 (c. 41): s. 71, above.

[12] Subsections (2) and (3) of this section came into force on 30 November 1981: s. 74(2), p. 192 below.

(4) *Repealed by the Protection of Badgers Act 1992 (c. 51), s. 15(2). This amendment came into force on 16 October 1992: s. 15(3).*

Short title commencement and extent

74. (1) This Act any be cited as the Wildlife and Countryside Act 1981.

(2) The following provisions of this Act, namely—

Part II, except sections 29 to 32, 41 and 46 to 48 and Schedule 13;

sections 59 to 62 and 65 and 66; and

Part IV, except section 72(4), (6) and (14) and section 73(1) so far as relating to Part II of Schedule 17,

shall come into force on the expiration of the period of one month beginning with the passing of this Act.

(3) The remaining provisions of this Act shall come into force on such day as the Secretary of State may by order made by statutory instrument appoint and different days may be appointed under this subsection for different provisions, different purposes or different areas.

(4) An order under subsection (3) may make such transitional provision as appears to the Secretary of State to be necessary or expedient in connection with the provisions thereby brought into force.

(5) The following provisions of this Act, namely—

sections 39, 40 and 42 to 49 and Schedule 13; and Part III,

do not extend to Scotland.

(6) This Act, except section 15(1) and Schedule 10 and, so far as regards any enactment mentioned in Schedule 17 that so extends, section 73 and that Schedule, does not extend to Northern Ireland[1].

SCHEDULES

SCHEDULE 1[2]

(Sections 1, 2, 4, 6, 19 and 22)

BIRDS WHICH ARE PROTECTED BY SPECIAL PENALTIES

PART I

AT ALL TIMES

Common name	Scientific name
Avocet	*Recurvirostra avosetta*
Bee-eater	*Merops apiaster*
Bittern	*Botaurus stellaris*
Bittern, Little	*Ixobrychus minutus*
Bluethroat	*Luscinia svecica*
Brambling	*Fringilla montifringilla*
Bunting, Cirl	*Emberiza cirlus*
Bunting, Lapland	*Calcarius lapponicus*

[1] This section came into force on 30 November 1981: subsection (2).

[2] This schedule came into force on 28 September 1982: S. I. 1982/1217.

Common name	Scientific name
Bunting, Snow	*Plectrophenax nivalis*
Buzzard, Honey	*Pernis apivorus*
Chough	*Pyrrhocorax pyrrhocorax*
Corncrake	*Crex crex*
Crake, Spotted	*Porzana porzana*
Crossbills (all species)	*Loxia*
Curlew, Stone	*Burhinus oedicnemus*
Divers (all species)	*Gavia*
Dotterel	*Charadrius morinellus*
Duck, Long-tailed	*Clangula hyemalis*
Eagle, Golden	*Aquila chrysaetos*
Eagle, White-tailed	*Haliaetus albicilla*
Falcon, Gyr	*Falco rusticolus*
Fieldfare	*Turdus pilaris*
Firecrest	*Regulus ignicapillus*
Garganey	*Anas querquedula*
Godwit, Black-tailed	*Limosa limosa*
Goshawk	*Accipiter gentilis*
Grebe, Black-necked	*Podiceps nigricollis*
Grebe, Slavonian	*Podiceps auritus*
Greenshank	*Tringa nebularia*
Gull, Little	*Larus minutus*
Gull, Mediterranean	*Larus melanocephalus*
Harriers (all species)	*Circus*
Heron, Purple	*Ardea purpurea*
Hobby	*Falco subbuteo*
Hoopoe	*Upupa epops*
Kingfisher	*Alcedo atthis*
Kite, Red	*Milvus milvus*
Merlin	*Falco columbarius*
Oriole, Golden	*Oriolus oriolus*
Osprey	*Pandion haliaetus*
Owl, Barn	*Tyto alba*
Owl, Snowy	*Nyctea scandiaca*
Peregrine	*Falco peregrinus*
Petrel, Leach's	*Oceanodroma leucorhoa*
Phalarope, Red-necked	*Phalaropus lobatus*
Plover, Kentish	*Charadrius alexandrinus*
Plover, Little Ringed	*Charadrius dubius*
Quail, Common	*Coturnix coturnix*
Redstart, Black	*Phoenicurus ochruros*
Redwing	*Turdus iliacus*
Rosefinch, Scarlet	*Carpodacus erythrinus*
Ruff	*Philomachus pugnax*
Sandpiper, Green	*Tringa ochropus*
Sandpiper, Purple	*Calidris maritima*
Sandpiper, Wood	*Tringa glareola*
Scaup	*Aythya marila*
Scoter, Common	*Melanitta nigra*
Scoter, Velvet	*Melanitta fusca*
Serin	*Serinus serinus*
Shorelark	*Eremophila alpestris*
Shrike, Red-backed	*Lianius collurio*
Spoonbill	*Platalea leucorodia*
Stilt, Black-winged	*Himantopus himantopus*
Stint, Temminck's	*Calidris temminickii*
Swan, Bewick's	*Cygnus bewickii*
Swan, Whooper	*Cygnus cygnus*
Tern, Black	*Chlidonias niger*

Common name	Scientific name
Tern, Little	*Sterna albifrons*
Tern, Roseate	*Sterna dougallii*
Tit, Bearded	*Panurus biarmicus*
Tit, Crested	*Parus cristatus*
Treecreeper, Short-toed	*Certhia brachydactyla*
Warbler, Cetti's	*Cettia cetti*
Warbler, Dartford	*Sylvia undata*
Warbler, Marsh	*Acrocephalus palustris*
Warbler, Savi's	*Locustella luscinioides*
Whimbrel	*Numenius phaeopus*
Woodlark	*Lullula arborea*
Wryneck	*Jynx torquilla*

PART II

DURING THE CLOSE SEASON

Common name	Scientific name
Goldeneye	*Bucephala clangula*
Goose, Greylage (in Outer Hebrides, Caithness, Sutherland and Wester Ross only)	*Anser anser*
Pintail	*Anas acuta*

NOTE. The common name or names given in the first column of this Schedule are included by way of guidance only; in the event of any dispute or proceedings, the common name or names shall not be taken into account.

SCHEDULE 2[1]

BIRDS WHICH MAY BE KILLED OR TAKEN

PART I

OUTSIDE THE CLOSE SEASON

Common name	Scientific name
Capercaillie	*Tetraeo urogallus*
Coot	*Fulica atra*
Duck, Tufted	*Aythya fuligula*
Gadwall	*Anas strepera*
Goldeneye	*Bucephala clangula*
Goose, Canada	*Branta canadensis*
Goose, Greylag	*Anser Anser*
Goose, Pink-footed	*Anser brachyrhynchus*
Goose, White-fronted (in England and Wales only)	*Anser albifrons*
Mallard	*Anas platyrhynchos*
Moorhen	*Gallinula chloropus*
Pintail	*Anas acuta*
Plover, Golden	*Pluvialis apricaria*
Pochard	*Aythya ferina*
Shoveler	*Anas clypeata*
Snipe, Common	*Gallinago gallinago*
Teal	*Anas crecca*
Wigeon	*Anas penelope*
Woodcock	*Scolopax rusticola*

[1] This schedule came into force on 28 September 1982: S.I. 1982/1217.

PART II

BY AUTHORISED PERSONS AT ALL TIMES

Common name	*Scientific name*

There are now no birds listed in Part II of Schedule 2. Thirteen species of birds formerly listed were removed by the Wildlife and Countryside Act 1981 (Variation of Schedules 2 and 3) Order 1992: S.I. 1992/3010, art. 2. This order came into force on 1 January 1993.

NOTE. The common name or names given in the first column of this Schedule are included by way of guidance only; in the event of any dispute or proceedings, the common name or names shall not be taken into account.

SCHEDULE 3[1]

(Sections 6 and 22)

BIRDS WHICH MAY BE SOLD

PART I

ALIVE AT ALL TIMES IF RINGED AND BRED IN CAPTIVITY

Common name	*Scientific name*
Blackbird	*Turdus merula*
Brambling	*Fringilla montifringilla*
Bullfinch	*Pyrrhula pyrrhula*
Bunting, Reed	*Emberiza schoeniclus*
Chaffinch	*Fringilla coelebs*
Dunnock	*Prunella modularis*
Goldfinch	*Carduelis carduelis*
Greenfinch	*Carduelis chloris*
Jackdaw	*Corvus monedula*
Jay	*Garrulus glandarius*
Linnet	*Carduelis cannabina*
Magpie	*Pica pica*
Owl, Barn	*Tyto alba*
Redpoll	*Carduelis flammea*
Siskin	*Carduelis spinus*
Starling	*Sturnus vulgaris*
Thrush, Song	*Turdus philomelos*
Twite	*Carduelis flavirostris*
Yellowhammer	*Emberiza citrinella*

PART II

DEAD AT ALL TIMES

Common name[2]	*Scientific name*[2]
Woodpigeon	*Columba palumbus*

[1] This schedule came into force on 28 September 1982: S.I. 1982/1217.

[2] The Feral Pigeon, *Columba livia*, was removed from Part II of Schedule 3 by the Wildlife and Countryside Act 1981 (Variation of Schedules 2 and 3) Order 1992: S.I. 1992/3010, art. 3. This order came into force on 1 January 1993.

PART III

DEAD FROM 1ST SEPTEMBER TO 28TH FEBRUARY

Common name	Scientific name
Capercaillie	Tetrao urogallus
Coot	Fulica atra
Duck, Tufted	Aythya fuligula
Mallard	Anas platyrhynchos
Pintail	Anas acuta
Plover, Golden	Pluvialis apricaria
Pochard	Aythya ferina
Shoveler	Anas clypeata
Snipe, Common	Gallinago gallinago
Teal	Anas crecca
Wigeon	Anas penelope
Woodcock	Scolopax rusticola

NOTE. The common name or names given in the first column of this Schedule are included by way of guidnce only; in the event of any dispute or proceedings, the common name or names shall not be taken into account.

SCHEDULE 4[1]

(Sections 7 and 22)

BIRDS WHICH MUST BE REGISTERED AND RINGED IF KEPT IN CAPTIVITY

Common name	Scientific name
Bunting, Cirl	Emberiza cirlus
Bunting, Lapland	Calcarius lapponicus
Bunting, Snow	Plectrophenax nivalis
Buzzard, Honey	Pernis apivorus
Eagle, Adalbert's	Aquila adalberti
Eagle, Golden	Aquila chrysaetos
Eagle, Great Philippine	Pithecophaga jefferyi
Eagle, Imperial	Aquila heliaca
Eagle, New Guinea	Harpyopsis novaeguineae
Eagle, White-tailed	Haliaeetus albicilla
Chough	Pyrrhocorax pyrrhocorax
Crossbills (all species)	Loxia spp
Falcon, Barbary	Falco pelegrinoides
Falcon, Gyr	Falco rusticolus
Falcon, Peregrine	Falco peregrinus
Fieldfare	Turdus pilaris
Firecrest	Regulus ignicapillus
Fish-Eagle, Madagascar	Haliaeetus vociferoides
Forest-Falcon, Plumbeous	Micrastur plumbeus
Goshawk	Accipiter gentilis
Harrier, Hen	Circus cyaneus
Harrier, Marsh	Circus aeruginosus
Harrier, Montagu's	Circus pygargus
Hawk, Galapagos	Buteo galapagoensis
Hawk, Grey-backed	Leucopternis occidentalis
Hawk, Hawaiian	Buteo solitarius
Hawk, Ridgway's	Buteo ridgwayi

[1] This schedule came into force on 28 September 1982: S.I. 1982/1217.

Common name	Scientific name
Hawk, White-necked	*Leucopternis lacernulata*
Haw-Eagle, Wallace's	*Spizaetus nanus*
Hobby	*Falco subbuteo*
Honey-Buzzard, Black	*Henicopernis infuscatus*
Kestrel, Lesser	*Falco naumanni*
Kestrel, Mauritius	*Falco punctatus*
Kite, Red	*Milvus milvus*
Merlin	*Falco columbarius*
Oriole, Golden	*Oriolus oriolus*
Osprey	*Pandion haliaetus*
Redstart, Black	*Phoenicurus ochruros*
Redwing	*Turdus iliacus*
Sea-Eagle, Pallas'	*Haliaeetus leucoryphus*
Sea-Eagle, Steller's	*Haliaeetus pelagicus*
Serin	*Serinus serinus*
Serpent-Eagle, Andaman	*Spilornis elgini*
Serpent-Eagle, Madagascar	*Eutriorchis astur*
Serpent-Eagle, Mountain	*Spilornis kinabaluensis*
Shorelark	*Eremophila alpestris*
Shrike, Red-backed	*Lanius collurio*
Sparrowhawk, New Britain	*Acceipiter brachyurus*
Sparrowhawk, Gundlach's	*Accipiter gundlachi*
Sparrowhawk, Imitator	*Accipiter imitator*
Sparrowhawk, Small	*Accipiter nanus*
Tit, Bearded	*Panurus biarmicus*
Tit, Crested	*Parus cristatus*
Warbler, Cetti's	*Cettia cetti*
Warbler, Dartford	*Sylvia undata*
Warbler, Marsh	*Acrocephalus palustris*
Warbler, Savi's	*Locustella luscinioides*
Woodlark	*Lullula arborea*
Wryneck	*Jynx torquilla*

Any bird one of whose parents or other lineal ancestor was a bird of a kind specified in the above list.[1]

NOTE. The common name or names given in the first column of this Schedule are included by way of guidance only; in the event of any dispute or proceedings, the common name or names shall not be taken into account.

SCHEDULE 5[2]

(Sections 9, 10, 22 and 24)

ANIMALS WHICH ARE PROTECTED

Common name	Scientific name
Adder (in respect of section 9(1) so far as it relates to killing and injuring and in respect of section 9(5))[3]	*Vipera berus*
Anemone, Ivell's Sea[4]	*Edwardsia ivelli*
Anemone, Starlet Sea[4]	*Nematosella vectensis*
Apus[4]	*Triops cancriformis*

[1] Thirty-seven species of birds and the species of Falcons and Hawks not in this list were removed by the Wildlife and Countryside Act 1981 (Variation of Schedule 4) Order 1994: S.I. 1994/1151, art. 2. Words "Any bird one of whose parents . . . this Schedule", adding hybrids to the Schedule, inserted by S.I. 1994/1151, art. 3. This order came into force on 24 May 1994.

[2] This schedule came into force on 28 September 1982:

S.I. 1982/1217.

[3] The Adder, *Vipera berus*, was listed in respect of s. 9(1) so far as it relates to killing and injuring by S.I. 1991/367 which came into force on 27 March 1991; it has been listed since enactment in respect of s. 9(5).

[4] These animals were added by S.I. 1988/288 which came into force on 18 March 1988.

Common name	Scientific name
Bats, Horseshoe (all species)	*Rhinolophidae*
Bats, Typical (all species)	*Vespertilionidae*
Beetle[1]	*Graphoderus zonatus*
Beetle[1]	*Hypebaeus flavipes*
Beetle[1]	*Paracymus aeneus*
Beetle, Lesser Silver Water[1]	*Hydrochara caraboides*
Beetle, Mire Pill (in respect of section 9(4)(*a*) only)[1]	*Curimopsis nigrita*
Beetle, Rainbow Leaf	*Chrysolina cerealis*
Beetle, Violet Click[2]	*Limoniscus violaceus*
Burbot	*Lota lota*
Butterfly, Northern Brown Argus[3] (in respect of section 9(5) only)	*Aricia artaxerxes*
Butterfly, Adonis Blue[3] (in respect of section 9(5) only)	*Lysandra bellargus*
Butterfly, Chalkhill Blue[3] (in respect of section 9(5) only)	*Lysandra coridon*
Butterfly, Large Blue	*Maculinea arion*
Butterfly, Silver-studded Blue[3] (in respect of section 9(5) only)	*Plebejus argus*
Butterfly, Small Blue[3] (in respect of section 9(5) only)	*Cupido minimus*
Butterfly, Large Copper[3] (in respect of section 9(5) only)	*Lycaena dispar*
Butterfly, Purple Emperor[3] (in respect of section 9(5) only)	*Apatura iris*
Butterfly, Duke of Burgundy Fritillary[3] (in respect of section 9(5) only)	*Hamearis lucina*
Butterfly, Glanville Fritillary[3] (in respect of section 9(5) only)	*Melitaea cinxia*
Butterfly, Heath Fritillary	*Mellicta athalia* (*otherwise known as Melitaea athalia*)
Butterfly, High Brown Fritillary[4]	*Argynnis adippe*
Butterfly, Marsh Fritillary[3] (in respect of section 9(5) only)	*Eurodryas aurinia*
Butterfly, Pearl-bordered Fritillary[3] (in respect of section 9(5) only)	*Boloria euphrosyne*
Butterfly, Black Hairstreak[3] (in respect of section 9(5) only)	*Strymonidia pruni*
Butterfly, Brown Hairstreak[3] (in respect of section 9(5) only)	*Thecla betulae*
Butterfly, White Letter Hairstreak[3] (in respect of section 9(5) only)	*Stymonida w-album*
Butterfly, Large Heath[3] (in respect of section 9(5) only)	*Coenonympha tullia*
Butterfly, Mountain Ringlet[3] (in respect of section 9(5) only)	*Erebia epiphron*
Butterfly, Chequered Skipper[3] (in respect of section 9(5) only)	*Carterocephalus palaemon*
Butterfly, Lulworth Skipper[3] (in respect of section 9(5) only)	*Thymelicus acteon*
Butterfly, Silver Spotted Skipper[3] (in respect of section 9(5) only)	*Hesperia comma*
Butterfly, Swallowtail	*Papilio machaon*

[1] These animals were added by S.I. 1992/2350 which came into force on 29 October 1992.

[2] These animals were added by S.I. 1988/288 which came into force on 18 March 1988.

[3] These butterflies were added by S.I. 1989/906 which came into force on 28 June 1989.

[4] The High Brown Fritillary, *Agrynnis adippe*, was added by S.I. 1992/2350 which came into force on 29 October 1992; it had been added in respect of section 9(5) only by S.I. 1989/906.

Common name	*Scientific name*
Butterfly, Large Tortoiseshell[1] (in respect of section 9(5) only)	*Nymphalis polychloros*
Butterfly, Wood White[1] (in respect of section 9(5) only)	*Leptidea sinapis*
Cat, Wild[2]	*Felis silvestris*
Cicada, New Forest[2]	*Cicadetta montana*
Crayfish, Atlantic Stream (only in respect of section 9(1) so far as it relates to taking and in respect of section 9(5))[3]	*Austropotamobius pallipes*
Cricket, Field	*Gryllus campestris*
Cricket, Mole	*Gryllotalpa gryllotalpa*
Dolphin, all species[4]	*Cetacea*
Dormouse[2]	*Muscardinus avellanarius*
Dragonfly, Norfolk Aeshna	*Aeshna isosceles*
Frog, Common (in respect of section 9(5) only)	*Rana temporaria*
Grasshopper, Wart-biter	*Decticus verrucivorus*
Hatchet Shell, Northern[5]	*Thyasira gouldi*
Lagoon Snail[5]	*Paludinella littorina*
Lagoon Snail, De Folin's[5]	*Caecum armoricum*
Lagoon Worm, Tentacled[5]	*Alkmaria romijni*
Leech, Medicinal[2]	*Hirudo medicinalis*
Lizard, Sand	*Lacerta agilis*
Lizard, Viviparous (in respect of section 9(1) so far as it relates to killing and injuring and in respect of section 9(5))[6]	*Lacerta vivipara*
Marten, Pine[2]	*Martes martes*
Mat, Trembling Sea: see under Sea-Mat below	
Moth, Barberry Carpet	*Pareulype berberata*
Moth, Black-veined	*Siona lineata (otherwise known as Idaea lineata)*
Moth, Essex Emerald	*Thetidia smaragdaria*
Moth, New Forest Burnet	*Zygaena viciae*
Moth, Reddish Buff	*Acosmetia caliginosa*
Moth, Sussex Emerald[5]	*Thalera fimbrialis*
Moth, Viper's Bugloss[2]	*Hadena irregularis*
Mussell, Freshwater Pearl (only in respect of section 9(1) so far as it relates to killing and injuring)[7]	*Margaritifera margaritifera*
Newt, Great Crested (otherwise known as Warty newt)	*Triturus cristatus*
Newt, Palmate (in respect of section 9(5) only)	*Triturus helveticus*
Newt, Smooth (in respect of section 9(5) only)	*Triturus vulgaris*
Otter, Common	*Lutra lutra*
Porpoise, all species[4]	*Cetacea*
Sandworm, Lagoon[2]	*Armandia cirrhosa*
Sea Fan, Pink (in respect of section 9(1), 9(2) and 9(5) only)[5]	*Eunicella verrucosa*
Sea-mat, Trembling[2]	*Victorella pavida*
Sea Slug, Lagoon[5]	*Tenellia adspersa*
Shad, Allis (only in respect of section 9(1))[8]	*Alosa alosa*

[1] These butterflies were added by S.I. 1989/906 which came into force on 28 June 1989.

[2] These animals were added by S.I. 1998/288 which came into force on 18 March 1988.

[3] The Atlantic Stream Crayfish, *Austropotamobius pallipes*, was added by S.I. 1988/288 which came into force on 18 March 1988.

[4] All species of dolphin and all species of porpoise were added by S.I. 1988/288 which came into force on 18 March 1988; two species of dolphin and one species of porpoise had been listed since enactment.

[5] These animals were added by S.I. 1992/2350 which came into force on 29 October 1992.

[6] These animals were added in respect of s. 9(1) so far as it relates to killing and injuring by S.I. 1988/288 which came into force on 18 March 1988; since enactment they had been listed in respect of s. 9(5).

[7] The Freshwater Peal Mussell, *Margaritifera margaritifera*, was added by S.I. 1991/367 which came into force on 27 March 1991.

[8] The Allis Shad, *Alosa alosa*, was added by S.I. 1991/367 which came into force on 27 March 1991.

Common name	Scientific name
Shrimp, Fairy[1]	Chirocephalus diaphanus
Shrimp, Lagoon Sand[1]	Gammarus insensibilis
Slow-worm (in respect of section 9(1) so far as it relates to killing and injuring and in respect of section 9(5))[2]	Anguis fragilis
Snail, Glutinous	Myxas glutinosa
Snail, Sandbowl	Catinella arenaria
Snake, Grass (in respect of section 9(1) so far as it relates to killing and injuring and in respect of section 9(5)[2]	Natrix helvetica (otherwise known as Natrix natrix)
Snake, Smooth	Coronella austriaca
Spider, Fen Raft	Dolomedes plantarius
Spider, Ladybird	Eresus niger
Sturgeon[3]	Acipenser sturio
Squirrel, Red	Sciurus vulgaris
Toad, Common (in respect of section 9(5) only)	Bufo bufo
Toad, Natterjack	Bufo calamita
Turtles, Marine (all species)[1]	Dermochelyidae and Cheloniidae
Vendace[1]	Coregonus albula
Walrus[1]	Odobenus rosmarus
Whale (all species)[1]	Cetacea
Whitefish[1]	Coregonus lavaretus

The Carthusian Snail *Monacha cartusiana* and the Chequered Skipper Butterfly *Carterocephalus palaemon* were removed from schedule 5 by S.I. 1988/288 which came into force on 18 March 1988.

NOTE. The common name or names given in the first column of this Schedule are included by way of guidance only; in the event of any dispute or proceedings, the common name or names shall not be taken into account.

SCHEDULE 6[4]

(Sections 11 and 22)

ANIMALS WHICH MAY NOT BE KILLED OR TAKEN BY CERTAIN METHODS

Common name	Scientific name
Badger	Meles meles
Bats, Horseshoe (all species)	Rhinolophidae
Bats, Typical (all species)	Vespertilionidae
Cat, Wild	Felis silvestris
Dolphin, Bottle-nosed	Tursiops truncatus (otherwise known as Tursiops tursio)
Dolphin, Common	Delphinus delphis
Dormice (all species)	Gliridae
Hedgehog	Erinaceus europaeus
Marten, Pine	Martes martes
Otter, Common	Lutra lutra
Polecat	Mustela putorius
Porpoise, Harbour (otherwise known as Common Porpoise)	Phocaena phocaena
Shrews (all species)	Soricidae
Squirrel, Red	Sciurus vulgaris

NOTE. The common name or names given in the first column of this Schedule are included by way of guidance only; in the event of any dispute or proceedings, the common name or names shall not be taken into account.

[1] These animals were added by S.I. 1998/288 which came into force on 18 March 1988.

[2] These animals were added in respect of s. 9(1) so far as it relates to killing and injuring by S.I. 1988/288 which came into force on 18 March 1988; since enactment they had been listed in respect of s. 9(5).

[3] These animals were added by S.I. 1992/2350 which came into force on 29 October 1992.

[4] This Schedule came into force on 28 September 1982: S.I. 1982/1217.

SCHEDULE 8[1]

(Sections 13, 22 and 24)

PLANTS WHICH ARE PROTECTED

Common name	Scientific name
Adder's-tongue, Least[2]	*Ophioglossum lusitanicum*
Alison, Small	*Alyssum alyssoides*
Blackwort[3]	*Southbya nigrella*
Broomrape, Bedstraw	*Orobanche caryophyllacea*
Broomrape, Oxtongue	*Orobanche loricata*
Broomrape, Thistle	*Orobanche reticulata*
Cabbage, Lundy[2]	*Rhynchosinapis wrightii*
Calamint, Wood	*Calamintha sylvatica*
Caloplaca, Snow[3]	*Caloplaca nivalis*
Catapyrenium, Tree[3]	*Catapyrenium psoromoides*
Catchfly, Alpine	*Lychnis alpina*
Catillaria, Laurer's[3]	*Catellaria laureri*
Centaury, Slender[3]	*Centaurium tenuiflorum*
Cinquefoil, Rock	*Potentilla rupestris*
Cladonia, Upright Mountain[3]	*Cladonia stricta*
Clary, Meadow[3]	*Salvia pratensis*
Club-rush, Triangular	*Scirpus triquetrus*
Colt's foot, Purple[2]	*Homogyne alpina*
Cotoneaster, Wild	*Cotoneaster integerrimus*
Cottongrass, Slender[2]	*Eriophorum gracile*
Cow-wheat, Field	*Melampyrum arvense*
Crocus, Sand[2]	*Romulea columnae*
Crystalwort, Lizard[3]	*Riccia bifurca*
Cudweed, Broad-leaved[3]	*Filago pyramidata*
Cudweed, Jersey	*Gnaphalium luteoalbum*
Cudweed, Red-tipped[2]	*Filago lutescens*
Diapensia	*Diapensia lapponica*
Dock, Shore[3]	*Rumex rupestris*
Earwort, Marsh[3]	*Jamesoniella undulifolia*
Eryngo, Field	*Eryngium campestre*
Fern, Dickie's Bladder	*Cystopteris dickieana*
Fern, Killarney	*Trichomanes speciosum*
Flapwort, Norfolk[3]	*Lieocolea rutheana*
Fleabane, Alpine[2]	*Erigeron borealis*
Fleabane, Small[2]	*Pulicaria vulgaris*
Frostwort, Pointed[3]	*Gymnomitrion apiculatum*
Galingale, Brown	*Cyperus fuscus*
Gentian, Alpine	*Gentiana nivalis*
Gentian, Dune[3]	*Gentianella uliginosa*
Gentian, Early[3]	*Gentianella anglica*
Gentian, Fringed[2]	*Gentianella ciliata*
Gentian, Spring	*Gentiana verna*
Germander, Cut-leaved[2]	*Teucrium botrys*
Germander, Water	*Teucrium scordium*
Gladiolus, Wild	*Gladiolus illyricus*
Goosefoot, Stinking[2]	*Chenopodium vulvaria*
Grass-poly[2]	*Lythrum hyssopifolia*
Grimmia, Blunt-leaved[3]	*Grimmia unicolor*

[1] This schedule came into force on 28 September S.I. 1982/1217.

[2] These plants added by S.I. 1982/288 which came into force on 18 March 1988.

[3] These plants added by S.I. 1992/2350 which came into force on 29 October 1992.

Common name	Scientific name
Gyalecta, Elm[2]	*Gyalecta ulmi*
Hare's-ear, Sickle-leaved	*Bupleurum falcatum*
Hare's ear, Small	*Bupleurum baldense*
Hawk's-beard, Stinking[1]	*Crepis foetida*
Hawkweed, Northroe[2]	*Hieracium northroense*
Hawkweed, Shetland[2]	*Hieracium zetlandicum*
Hawkweed, Weak-leaved[2]	*Hieracium attenuatifolium*
Heath, Blue	*Phyllodoce caerulea*
Helleborine, Red	*Cephalanthera rubra*
Helleborine, Young's[1]	*Epipactis youngiana*
Horsetail, Branched[1]	*Equisetum ramosissimum*
Hound's-tongue, Green[1]	*Cynoglossum germanicum*
Knawel, Perennial	*Scleranthus perennis*
Knotgrass, Sea	*Polygonum maritimum*
Lady's-slipper	*Cypripedium calceolus*
Lecanactis, Churchyard[2]	*Lecanactis hemisphaerica*
Lecanora, Tarn[2]	*Lecanora archariana*
Lecidea, Copper[2]	*Lecidea inops*
Leek, Round-headed	*Allium sphaerocephalon*
Lettuce, Least	*Lactuca saligna*
Lichen, Arctic Kidney[2]	*Nephroma arcticum*
Lichen, Ciliate Strap[2]	*Heterodermia leucomelos*
Lichen, Coralloid Rosette[2]	*Heterodermia propagulifera*
Lichen, Ear-lobed Dog[2]	*Peltigera lepidophora*
Lichen, Forked Hair[2]	*Bryoria furcellata*
Lichen, Golden Hair[2]	*Teloschistes flavicans*
Lichen, Orange Fruited Elm[2]	*Caloplaca luteoalba*
Lichen, River Jelly[2]	*Collema dichotomum*
Lichen, Scaly Breck[2]	*Squamarina lentigera*
Lichen, Stary Breck[2]	*Buellia asterella*
Lily, Snowdon	*Lloydia serotina*
Liverwort[2]	*Petallophyllum ralfsi*
Liverwort, Lindenberg's Leafy[2]	*Adelanthus lindenbergianus*
Marsh-mallow, Rough	*Althaea hirsuta*
Marshwort, Creeping[1]	*Apium repens*
Milk-parsley, Cambridge[1]	*Selinum carvifolia*
Moss[2]	*Drepanocladius vernicosus*
Moss, Alpine Copper[2]	*Mielichoferia mielichoferi*
Moss, Baltic Bog[2]	*Sphagnum balticum*
Moss, Blue Dew[2]	*Saelania glaucescens*
Moss, Blunt-levaed Bristle[2]	*Orthotrichum obtusifolium*
Moss, Bright Green Cave[2]	*Cyclodictyon laetevirens*
Moss, Cordate Beard[2]	*Barbula cordata*
Moss, Cornish Path[2]	*Ditrichum cornubicum*
Moss, Derbyshire Feather[2]	*Thamnobryum angustifolium*
Moss, Dune Threat[2]	*Bryum mamillatum*
Moss, Glaucous Beard[2]	*Barbula glauca*
Moss, Green Shield[2]	*Buxbaumia viridis*
Moss, Hair Silk[2]	*Plagiothecium piliferum*
Moss, Knothole[2]	*Zygodon forsteri*
Moss, Large Yellow Feather[2]	*Scorpidium turgescens*
Moss, Millimetre[2]	*Micromitrium tenerum*
Moss, Multifruited River[2]	*Cryphaea lamyana*
Moss, Nowell's Limestone[2]	*Zygodon gracilis*
Moss, Rigid Apple[2]	*Bartramia stricta*
Moss, Round-leaved Feather[2]	*Rhyncostegium rotundifolium*
Moss, Schleicher's Thread[2]	*Bryum schleicheri*

[1] These plants added by S.I. 1982/288 which came into force on 18 March 1988.

[2] These plants added by S.I. 1992/2350 which came into force on 29 October 1992.

Common name	Scientific name
Moss, Triangular Pygmy[2]	*Acaulon triquetrum*
Moss, Vaucher's Feather[2]	*Hypnum vaucheri*
Mudwort, Welsh[2]	*Limosella australis*
Naiad, Holly-leaved[1]	*Najas marina*
Naiad, Slender[2]	*Najas flexilis*
Orache, Stalked[2]	*Halimione pedunculata*
Orchid, Early Spider	*Ophrys sphegodes*
Orchid, Fen	*Liparis loeselii*
Orchid, Ghost	*Epipogium aphyllum*
Orchid, Lapland Marsh[2]	*Dactylorhiza lapponica*
Orchid, Late Spider	*Ophrys fuciflora*
Orchid, Lizard	*Himantoglossum hircinum*
Orchid, Military	*Orchis militaris*
Orchid, Monkey	*Orchis simia*
Pannaria, Caledonia[2]	*Pannaria ignobilis*
Parmelia, New Forest[2]	*Parmelia minarum*
Parmentaria, Oil Stain[2]	*Parmentaria chilensis*
Pear, Plymouth	*Pyrus cordata*
Penny-cress, Perfoliate[2]	*Thlaspi perfoliatum*
Pennyroyal[1]	*Mentha pulegium*
Pertusaria, Alpine Moss[2]	*Pertusaria bryontha*
Physcia, Southern Grey[2]	*Physcia tribacioides*
Pigmyweed[1]	*Crassula aquatica*
Pine, Ground[2]	*Ajuga chamaepitys*
Pink, Cheddar	*Dianthus gratianopolitanus*
Pink, Childling	*Petroraghia nanteuilii*
Plantain, Floating Water[2]	*Luronium natans*
Pseudocyphellaria, Ragged[2]	*Pseudocyphellaria lacerata*
Psora, Rusty Alpine[2]	*Psora rubiformis*
Ragwort, Fen[1]	*Senecio paludosus*
Ramping-fumitory, Martin's[1]	*Fumaria martinii*
Rampion, Spiked[2]	*Phyteuma spicatum*
Restharrow, Small[1]	*Ononis reclinata*
Rock-cress, Alpine[1]	*Arabis alpina*
Rock-cress, Bristol[1]	*Arabis stricta*
Rustworth, Western[2]	*Marsupella profunda*
Sandwort, Norwegian	*Arenaria norvegica*
Sandwort, Teesdale	*Minuartia stricta*
Saxifrage, Drooping	*Saxifraga cernua*
Saxifrage, Marsh[2]	*Saxifrage hirulus*
Saxifrage, Tufted	*Saxifraga cespitosa*
Solenopsora, Serpentine[2]	*Solenopsora liparina*
Solomon's-seal, Whorled	*Polygonatum verticillatum*
Sow-thistle, Alpine	*Cicerbita alpina*
Spearwort, Adder's-tongue	*Ranunculus ophioglossifolius*
Speedwell, Fingered[1]	*Veronica triphyllos*
Speedwell, Spiked	*Veronica spicata*
Starfruit	*Gagea bohemica*
Star-of-Bethlehem, Early[1]	*Damasonium alisma*
Stonewort, Bearded[2]	*Chara canescens*
Stonewort, Foxtail[1]	*Lamprothamnium papulosum*
Strapwort[1]	*Corrigiola litoralis*
Turpswort[2]	*Geocalyx graveolens*
Violet, Fen	*Viola persicifolia*
Viper's-grass[1]	*Scorzonera humilis*
Water-plantain, Ribbon leaved	*Alisma gramineum*
Wood-sedge, Starved	*Carex depauperata*

[1] These plants added by S.I. 1982/288 which came into force on 18 March 1988.

[2] These plants added by S.I. 1992/2350 which came into force on 29 October 1992.

Common name	Scientific name
Woodsia, Alpine	Woodsia alpina
Woodsia, Oblong	Woodsia ilvensis
Wormwood, Field	Artemisia campestris
Woundwort, Downy	Stachys germanica
Woundwort, Limestone	Stachys alpina
Yellow-rattle, Greater	Rhinanthus serotinus

Note. The common name or names given in the first column of this Schedule are included by way of guidance only; in the event of any dispute or proceedings, the common name or names shall not be taken into account.[1]

SCHEDULE 9[2]

(Sections 14 and 22)

ANIMALS AND PLANTS TO WHICH SECTION 14 APPLIES

PART I

ANIMALS WHICH ARE ESTABLISHED IN THE WILD

Common name	Scientific name
Bass, Large-mouthed Black	Micropterus salmoides
Bass, Rock	Ambloplites rupestris
Bitterling	Rhodeus sericeus
Budgerigar	Melopsittacus undulatus
Capercaillie	Tetrao urogallus
Coypu	Myocastor coypus
Crayfish, Noble[3]	Astacus astacus
Crayfish, Signal[3]	Pacifastacus leniusculus
Crayfish, Turkish[3]	Astacus leptocdactylus
Deer, Sika[3]	Cervus nippon
Dormouse, Fat	Glis glis
Duck, Carolina Wood	Aix sponsa
Duck, Mandarin	Aix galericulata
Duck, Ruddy	Oxyura jamaicensis
Eagle, White-tailed	Haliaetus albicilla
Flatworm, New Zealand[3]	Artiposthia triangulata
Frog, Edible	Rana esculenta
Frog, European Tree (otherwise known as Common tree frog)	Hyla arborea
Frog, Marsh	Rana ridibunda
Gerbil, Mongolian	Meriones unguiculatus
Goose, Canada	Branta canadensis
Goose, Egyptian	Alopochen aegyptiacus
Heron, Night	Nycticorax nycticorax
Lizard, Common Wall	Podarcis muralis
Marmot, Prairie (otherwise known as Prairie dog)	Cynomys
Mink, American	Mustela vison
Newt, Alpine	Triturus alpestris

[1] The following plants were removed from schedule 8 by S.I. 1992/2350 which came into force on 29 October 1992:

Common Name	Scientific Name
Lavender, Sea	Limonium paradoxum
	Limonium recurvum
Spurge, Purple	Euphorbia peplis

[2] This schedule came into force on 28 September 1982: S.I. 1982/1217.

[3] These animals added by S.I. 1992/320 which came into force on 17 March 1992.

Common name	Scientific name
Newt, Italian Crested[1]	*Triturus carnifex*
Owl, Barn[2]	*Tyto alba*
Parakeet, Ring-necked	*Psittacula krameri*
Patridge, Chukar	*Alectoris chukar*
Partridge, Rock	*Alectoris graeca*
Pheasant, Golden	*Chrysolophus pictus*
Pheasant, Lady Amherst's	*Chrysolophus amherstiae*
Pheasant, Reeves'	*Syrmaticus reevesii*
Pheasant, Silver	*Lophura nycthemera*
Porcupine, Crested	*Hystrix cristata*
Porcupine, Himalayan	*Hystrix hodgsonii*
Pumpkinseed (otherwise known as Sun-fish or Pond-perch)	*Lepomis gibbosus*
Quail, Bobwhite	*Colinus virginianus*
Rat, Black	*Rattus rattus*
Snake, Aesculapian[1]	*Elaphe longissima*
Squirrel, Grey	*Sciurus carolinensis*
Terrapin, European Pond	*Emys orbicularis*
Toad, African Clawed	*Xenopus laevis*
Toad, Midwife	*Alytes obstetricans*
Toad, Yellow-bellied	*Bombina variegata*
Wallaby, Red-necked	*Macropus rufogriseus*
Wels (otherwise known as European catfish)	*Silurus glanis*
Zander	*Stizostedion lucioperca*

PART II

PLANTS

Common name	Scientific name
Hogweed, Giant	*Heracleum mantegazzianum*
Kelp, Giant	*Macrocystis pyrifera*
Kep, Giant[3]	*Macrocystis angustifolia*
Kelp, Giant[3]	*Macrocystis integrifolia*
Kelp, Giant[3]	*Macrocystis laevis*
Kelp, Japanese[3]	*Laminaria japonica*
Knotweed, Japanese	*Polygonum cuspidatum*
Seafingers, Green[3]	*Codium fragile tomentosoides*
Seaweed, California Red[3]	*Pikea californica*
Seaweed, Hooked Asparagus[3]	*Asparagopsis armata*
Seaweed, Japanese	*Sargassum muticum*
Seaweeds, Laver (except native species)[3]	*Porphyra spp except—*
	p. amethystea
	p.leucosticta
	p. linearis
	p. miniata
	p. purpurea
	p. umbilicalis
Wakame[3]	*Undaria pinnatifida*

NOTE. The common name or names given in the first column of this Schedule are included by way of guidance only; in the event of any dispute or proceedings, the common name or names shall not be taken into account.

[1] These animals added by S.I. 1992/320 which came into force on 17 March 1992.
[2] The Barn Owl, *Tyto alba*, added by S.I. 1992/2674 which came into force on 25 November 1992.
[3] These plants added by S.I. 1992/320 which came into force on 17 March 1992.

SCHEDULE 11[1]

(Sections 29 and 34)

PROCEDURE IN CONNECTION WITH CERTAIN ORDERS UNDER PART II

Coming into operation

1. (1) An original order[2] or a restrictive amending order[3] shall take effect on its being made.

(2) It shall be the duty of the Secretary of State to consider every original order or restrictive amending order made by him or a relevant authority[4], and any such order shall cease to have effect nine months after it is made unless the Secretary of State has previously given notice under paragraph 6 that he has considered it and does not propose to amend or revoke it or he has amended or revoked it or, in the case of an order made by such an authority, the authority has revoked it.

(3) An amending or revoking order[5], other than a restrictive amending order, made by a relevant authority shall be submitted by the authority to the Secretary of State for confirmation and shall not take effect until confirmed by him.

(4) Subject to paragraphs 3(1) and 4(4), an amending or revoking order, other than a restrictive amending order, made by the Secretary of State shall not take effect until confirmed by him.

(5) An amending or revoking order requiring confirmation shall, by virtue of this sub-paragraph, stand revoked if the Secretary of State gives notice under paragraph 6 that the order is not to be confirmed.

Publicity for orders

2. (1) Where an order takes effect immediately, the authority making the order (whether the relevant authority or the Secretary of State) shall give notice—

(a) setting out the order or describing its general effect and in either case stating that it has taken effect;

(b) naming a place in the area in which the land[6] to which the order relates is situated where a copy of the order may be inspected free of charge at all reasonable hours; and

(c) specifying the time (not being less than 28 days from the date of the first publication of the notice) within which, and the manner in which, representations or objections with respect to the order may be made.

(2) Where an order requires confirmation, the authority making the order shall give notice—

(a) setting out the order or describing its general effect and in either case stating that it has been made and requires confirmation; and

(b) stating in relation to it the matters specified in sub-paragraph (1)(b) and (c).

(3) Subject to sub-paragraph (4), the notice to be given under sub-paragraph (1) or (2) shall be given—

(a) by publication in the Gazette[7] and also at least one local newspaper circulating in the area in which the land to which the order relates is situated;

(b) by serving a like notice on every owner[8] and occupier of any of that land; and

(c) in the case of a notice given by the Secretary of State, by serving a like notice on the relevant authority in whose area the land to which the order relates is situated.

(4) The Secretary of State may, in any particular case, direct that it shall not be necessary to comply with sub-paragraph (3)(b); but if he so directs in the case of any land, then in addition to publication the notice shall be addressed to "The owners and any occupiers" of the land (describing it) and a copy or copies of the notice shall be affixed to some conspicuous object or objects on the land.

---

[1] In relation to section 29, this schedule came into force on 6 September 1982: S.I. 1982/1136; in relation to section 34 this schedule came into force on 30 November 1981: s. 74(2), p. 192 above.

[2] "Order" in this schedule means an order under s. 29 or s. 34. "Original order" means an order other than an amending or revoking order: para. 8, p. 208 below.

[3] "Restrictive amending order" defined by paragraph 8, p. 208 below.

[4] "Relevant authority" has the same meaning as in s. 34(6), p. 177 above; para. 8 below.

[5] "Amending or revoking order" defined by para. 8, p. 208 below.

[6] "Land" defined by s. 114(1), National Parks and Access to the Countryside Act 1949, p. 38 above: s. 52(4), p. 189 above applies the definition in s. 114 of the 1949 Act.

[7] "Gazette" defined by para. 8, p. 208 below.

[8] "Owner" defined by s. 114(1), National Parks and Access to the Countryside Act 1949, p. 38 above: s. 52(4), p. 189 above applies the definition in s. 114 of the 1949 Act.

Unopposed orders

3. (1) Where an order made by a relevant authority takes effect immediately and no representations or objections are duly made in respect of it or any so made are withdrawn,—

(a) the Secretary of State shall as soon as practicable after considering it decide either to take no action on the order or to make an order amending or revoking it (subject, however, to paragraph 5); and

(b) the amending or revoking order shall take effect immediately, but it shall not require confirmation and no representation or objection with respect to it shall be entertained.

(2) Where an order requiring confirmation is made and no representations or objections are duly made in respect of it or any so made are withdrawn, the Secretary of State may confirm the order (with or without modifications).

Opposed orders

4. (1) If any representation or objection duly made with respect to an order is not withdrawn, then, as soon as practicable in the case of an order having immediate effect and before confirming an order requiring confirmation, the Secretary of State shall either—

(a) cause a local inquiry to be held; or

(b) afford any person by whom a representation or objection has been duly made and not withdrawn an opportunity of being heard by a person appointed by the Secretary of State for the purpose.

(2) On considering any representations or objections duly made and the report of any person appointed to hold the inquiry or to hear representations or objections, the Secretary of State—

(a) shall, if the order has already taken effect, decide either to take no action on the order or to make an order (subject, however, to paragraph 5) amending or revoking the order as the Secretary of State thinks appropriate in the light of the report, representations or objections, without consulting the relevant authority where that authority made the order; or

(b) if the order requires confirmation, may confirm it (with or without modifications).

(3) The provisions of subsections (2) to (5) of section 250 of the Local Government Act 1972[1] or subsections (4) to (8) of section 210 of the Local Government (Scotland) Act 1973[2] (which relate to the giving of evidence at, and defraying the cost of, local inquiries) shall apply in relation to any inquiry held under this paragraph as they apply in relation to a local inquiry which a Minister causes to be held under subsection (1) of that section.

(4) An amending or revoking order made by virtue of this paragraph shall take effect immediately, but it shall not require confirmation and no representation or objection with respect to it shall be entertained.

Restriction on power to amend orders or confirm them with modifications

5. The Secretary of State shall not by virtue of paragraph 3(1) or 4(2) amend an order which has taken effect, or confirm any other order with modifications, so as to extend the area to which an original order applies.

Notice of final decision on orders

6. (1) The Secretary of State shall as soon as practicable after making an order by virtue of paragraph 3(1) or 4(2) give notice—

(a) setting out the order or describing its general effect and in either case stating that it has taken effect; and

(b) stating the name of the place in the area in which the land to which the order relates is situated where a copy of the order may be inspected free of charge at all reasonable hours.

(2) The Secretary of State shall give notice of any of the following decisions of his as soon as practicable after making the decision—

(a) a decision under paragraph 3(1) or 4(2) to take no action on an order which has already taken effect;

(b) a decision to confirm or not to confirm an order requiring confirmation under this Schedule.

(3) A notice under this paragraph of a decision to confirm an order shall—

(a) set out the order as confirmed or describe its general effect, and in either case state the day on which the order took effect;

---

[1] 1972 c. 70.   [2] 1973 c. 65.

(*b*) State the name of the place in the area in which the land to which the order relates is situated where a copy of the order as confirmed may be inspected free of charge at all reasonable hours.

(4) A notice under this paragraph shall be given by publishing it in accordance with paragraph 2(3) and serving a copy of it on any person on whom a notice was required to be served under paragraph 2(3) or (4).

Proceedings for questioning validity of orders

7. (1) This paragraph applies to any order which has taken effect and as to which the Secretary of State has given notice under paragraph 6 of a decision of his to take no action or to amend the order in accordance with paragraph 3 or 4; and in this paragraph "the relevant notice" means any such notice.

(2) If any person is aggrieved by an order to which this paragraph applies and desires to question its validity on the ground that it is not within the powers of section 29[1] or 34[2], as the case may be, or that any of the requirements of this Schedule have not been complied with in relation to it, he may within six weeks from the date of the relevant notice make an application to the Court under this paragraph.

(3) On any such application the Court may, if satisfied that the order is not within those powers or that the interests of the applicant have been substantially prejudiced by a failure to comply with any of those requirements—

(*a*) in England and Wales, quash the order, or any provision of the order, either generally or in so far as it affects the interests of the applicant; or

(*b*) in Scotland, make such declarator as seems to the Court to be appropriate.

(4) Except as provided by this paragraph, the validity of an order shall not be questioned in any legal proceedings whatsoever.

(5) In this paragraph "the Court" means the High Court in relation to England and Wales and the Court of Session in relation to Scotland[3].

Interpretation

8. In this Schedule—

"amending order" and "revoking order" mean an order which amends or, as the case may be, revokes a previous order;

"the Gazette" means—

(*a*) if the order relates in whole or in part to England and Wales, the London Gazette;

(*b*) if the order relates in whole or in part to Scotland, the Edinburgh Gazette;

"order" means an order under section 29[4] or 34[5];

"original order" means an order other than an amending or revoking order;

"the relevant authority" has the same meaning as in section 34:

"restrictive amending order" means an amending order which extends the area to which a previous order applies.

SCHEDULE 12[6]

PROCEDURE IN CONNECTION WITH ORDERS UNDER SECTION 36[7]

Consultation

1. Before making an order[8], the Secretary of State shall consult with such persons as he may consider appropriate.

Publicity for draft orders

2. (1) Before making an order, the Secretary of State shall prepare a draft of the order and give notice—

(*a*) stating that he proposes to make the order and the general effect of it;

[1] P. 171 above.
[2] P. 176 above.
[3] **Case: schedule** 11 *R v Secretary of State for the Environment, ex parte Upton Brickworks Ltd* [1992] COD 301.
[4] P. 171 above.
[5] P. 176 above.
[6] This schedule came into force on 30 November 1981: s. 74(2), p. 192 above.
[7] P. 178 above.
[8] "Order" in this schedule means an order under s. 36: para. 9(1) below.

(*b*) naming a place in the area[1] in which the land[2] to which the draft order relates is situated where a copy of the draft order, and of any byelaws made or proposed to be made by a relevant authority[3] for the protection of the area specified in the draft order, may be inspected free of charge, and copies thereof may be obtained at a reasonable charge, at all reasonable hours; and

(*c*) specifying the time (not being less than 28 days from the date of the first publication of the notice) within which, and the manner in which, representations or objections with respect to the draft order may be made.

(2) Subject to sub-paragraph (3), the notice to be given under sub-paragraph (1) shall be given—

(*a*) by publication in the Gazette[4] and also at least one local newspaper circulating in the area in which the land to which the draft order relates is situated;

(*b*) by serving a like notice on—

(i) every person in whom is vested an interest[5] in or right over any of that land;

(ii) every relevant authority whose area includes any of that land; and

(iii) such other bodies as may be prescribed[6] or as the Secretary of State may consider appropriate; and

(*c*) by causing a copy of the notice to be displayed in a prominent position—

(i) at council offices[7] in the locality of the land to which the draft order relates; and

(ii) at such other places as the Secretary of State may consider appropriate.

(3) The Secretary of State may, in any particular case, direct that it shall not be necessary to comply with sub-paragraph (2)(*b*)(i).

(4) Subject to sub-paragraph (3), sub-paragraph (2)(*b*) and (*c*) shall be complied with not less than 28 days before the expiration of the time specified in the notice.

Unopposed orders

3. If no representations or objections are duly made, or if any so made are withdrawn, the Secretary of State may make the order with or without modifications[8].

Opposed orders

4. (1) If any representation or objection duly made is not withdrawn the Secretary of State shall, before making the order, either—

(*a*) cause a local inquiry to be held; or

(*b*) afford any person by whom a representation or objection has been duly made and not withdrawn an opportunity of being heard by a person appointed by the Secretary of State for the purpose.

(2) On considering any representations or objections duly made and the report of the person appointed to hold the inquiry or hear representations or objections, the Secretary of State may make the order with or without modifications.

Restriction on power to make orders with modifications

5. (1) The Secretary of State shall not make an order with modifications so as—

(*a*) to affect land not affected by the draft order; or

(*b*) to authorise the making of any byelaw not authorised by the draft order.

except after complying with the requirements of sub-paragraph (2).

(2) The said requirements are that the Secretary of State shall—

(*a*) give such notice as appears to him requisite of his proposal so to modify the order, specifying the time (which shall not be less than 28 days from the date of the first publication of the notice) within which, and the manner in which, representations or objections with respect to the proposal may be made;

[1] "Area" includes district: para. 9(1), p. 210 below.
[2] "Land" defined by para. 9(2), p. 211 below.
[3] "Relevant authority" defined by s. 36(7), p. 179 above: para. 9(1), p. 211 below.
[4] "Gazette" defined by para. 9(1), p. 210 below.
[5] "Interest" defined by s. 114(1), National Parks and Access to the Countryside Act 1949, p. 38 above: s. 52(4), p. 189 above applies the definition in s. 114 of the 1949 Act.
[6] "Prescribed" defined by para. 9(1), p. 211 below.
[7] "Council offices" defined by para. 9(1), p. 210 below.
[8] "Modifications" defined by s. 71, p. 191 above.

(b) hold a local inquiry or afford any person by whom any representation or objection has been duly made and not withdrawn an opportunity of being heard by a person appointed by the Secretary of State for the purpose; and

(c) consider the report of the person appointed to hold the inquiry or to hear representations or objections.

Local inquiries

6. (1) The provisions of subsection (2) to (5) of section 250 of the Local Government Act 1972[1] or subsections (4) to (8) of section 210 of the Local Government (Scotland) Act 1973[2]which relate to the giving of evidence at, and defraying the cost of, local inquiries) shall apply in relation to any inquiry held under paragraph 4 or 5 as they apply in relation to a local inquiry which a Minister causes to be held under subsection (1) of that section.

(2) A local inquiry caused to be held under paragraph 4 or 5 before the making of an order may be held concurrently with any local inquiry caused to be held before the confirmation of byelaws made by a relevant authority for the protection of the area specified in the order.

Notice of making of orders

7. (1) As soon as practicable after an order is made, the Secretary of State shall give notice—

(a) describing the general effect of the order as made and stating the date on which it took effect; and

(b) naming a place in the area in which the land to which the order relates is situated where a copy of the order as made may be inspected free of charge, and copies thereof may be obtained at a reasonable charge, at all reasonable hours.

(2) A notice under sub-paragraph (1) shall be given—

(a) by publication in the manner required by paragraph 2(2)(a);

(b) by serving a like notice on any persons on whom notices were required to be served under paragraph 2(2)(b); and

(c) by causing like notices to be displayed in the like manner as the notices required to be displayed under paragraph 2(2)(c).

Proceedings for questioning validity of orders

8. (1) If any person is aggrieved by an order which has taken effect and desires to question its validity on the ground that it is not within the powers of section 36[3] or that any of the requirements of this Schedule have not been complied with in relation to it, he may within 42 days from the date of publication of the notice under paragraph 7 make an application to the Court under this paragraph.

(2) On any such application the Court may, if satisfied that the order is not within those powers or that the interests of the applicant have been substantially prejudiced by a failure to comply with those requirements—

(a) in England and Wales, quash the order, or any provision of the order, either generally or in so far as it affects the interests of the applicant; or

(b) in Scotland, make such declarator as seems to the Court to be appropriate.

(3) Except as provided by this paragraph, the validity of an order shall not be questioned in any legal proceedings whatever.

(4) In this paragraph "the Court" means the High Court in relation to England and Wales and the Court of Session in relation to Scotland.

9. (1) In this Schedule—

"area" includes district or Welsh county or county borough[4];

"council offices" means offices or buildings acquired or provided by a local authority;

"the Gazette" means—

(a) if the order relates in whole or in part to England and Wales, the London Gazette;

(b) if the order relates in whole or in part to Scotland, the Edinburgh Gazette;

"order" means an order under section 36;

---

[1] 1972 c. 70.
[2] 1973 c. 65.
[3] P. 000 above.
[4] Words "or Welsh county or county borough" inserted by the Local Government (Wales) Act 1994 (c. 19), s. 66(6), sch. 16, para. 65(10). It is planned that this amendment will come into force on 1 April 1996.

"prescribed" means prescribed by regulations made by the Secretary of State;

and expressions to which a meaning is assigned by section 36 have the same meanings in this Schedule as in that section.

(2) References in this Schedule to land include references to any waters covering it; and for the purposes of this Schedule any area in Great Britain which is bounded by tidal waters or parts of the sea shall be taken to include—

(a) the waters adjacent to that area up to the seaward limits of territorial waters; and

(b) the land covered by the said adjacent waters.

(3) Regulations under this Schedule shall be made by statutory instrument which shall be subject to annulment in pursuance of a resolution of either House of Parliament.

SCHEDULE 13[1]

(Section 47)

PROVISIONS WITH RESPECT TO THE COUNTRYSIDE COMMISSION

Status

1. The Commission shall be a body corporate.

2. The Commission shall not be regarded as the servant or agent of the Crown, or as enjoying any status, immunity or privilege of the Crown; and the Commission's property shall not be regarded as property of, or property held on behalf of, the Crown.

Members

3. (1) The Commission shall consist of a chairman and such number of other members as the Secretary of State may determine, of whom one may be appointed to be deputy chairman.

(2) The members of the Commission shall be appointed by the Secretary of State and shall hold and vacate office in accordance with such terms as may be prescribed by or under regulations made by the Secretary of State and, on vacating office, shall be eligible for re-appointment.[2]

(3) Regulations under sub-paragraph (2) shall be made by statutory instrument which shall be subject to annulment in pursuance of a resolution of either House of Parliament.

(4) A member may at any time by notice in writing to the Secretary of State resign his office.

4. (1) The Commission—

(a) shall pay to their members such remuneration and allowances (if any) as the Secretary of State may, with the approval of the Minister[3], determine; and

(b) as regards any member in whose case the Secretary of State may, with the approval of the Minister, so determine, shall pay such pension[4] to or in respect of him, or make such payments towards the provision of such pension as the Secretary of State may, with the Minister's approval, determine.

(2) If a person ceases to be a member of the Commission, and it appears to the Secretary of State that there are special circumstances which make it right that he should receive compensation, the Secretary of State may, with the approval of the Minister, require the Commission to pay to that person a sum of such amount as the Secretary of State may, with the Minister's approval, determine.

---

[1] This schedule came into force on 1 April 1982: S.I. 1982/327.

[2] The National Parks and Access to the Countryside (National Parks Commission) Regulations 1949, S.I. 1949/2361, make provision concerning the tenure and vacation of office of members of the Commission.

[3] "The Minister" means the Minister for Civil Service: para. 16, p. 214 below.

[4] "Pension" includes allowance or gratuity: para. 16, p. 214 below.

5. *Repealed by the Environmental Protection Act 1990 (c. 43), s. 162(2), sch. 16, pt. VI. This amendment came into force on 1 April 1991: S.I. 1991/685.*

Procedure

6. The procedure (including the quorum) of the Commission shall be such as they may determine.

7. The validity of any proceeding of the Commission shall not be affected by any vacancy among the members thereof or by any defect in the appointment of a member thereof.

Staff

8. (1) The Commission shall appoint—

(*a*) with the approval of the Secretary of State, a chief officer and

(*b*) such number of other employees as they may with the approval of the Secretary of State and the Minister determine.

(2) The Commission shall pay to their employees such remuneration and allowances as they may with the approval of the Secretary of State and the Minister determine.

(3) In the case of any person to be employed by them on and after the appointed day[1] who immediately before that day was a civil servant, the Commission shall ensure that, so long as he is engaged in duties reasonably comparable to those in which he was engaged immediately before the coming into force of this Schedule, the terms and conditions of his employment, taken as a whole, are not less favourable than those which he then enjoyed.

(4) In relation to any person who—

(*a*) is a civil servant before the appointed day; and

(*b*) is as from that day employed by the Commission,

Schedule 13 to the Employment Protection (Consolidation) Act 1978[2] (ascertainment, for the purposes of that Act and section 119 of the Employment Protection Act 1975[3], of the length of an employee's period of employment and whether that employment has been continuous) shall have effect as if his service as a civil servant had been employment under the Commission.

9. (1) The Commission shall in the case of such of their employees as they may with the approval of the Secretary of State and the Minister determine,—

(*a*) pay such pension to or in respect of them;

(*b*) make such payments towards the provision of such pensions; or

(*c*) provide and maintain such schemes (whether contributory or not) for the payment of such pensions,

as they may with the approval of the Secretary of State and the Minister determine.

(2) In this paragraph any reference to the payment of pensions to or in respect of the Commission's employees includes a reference to the payment of pensions by way of compensation to or in respect of any of the Commission's employees who suffer loss of office or employment or loss or dimunition of emoluments.

10. (1) Employment with the Commission shall be included among the kinds of employment to which a superannuation scheme under section 1 of the Superannuation Act 1972[4] can apply, and accordingly in Schedule 1 to that Act (in which those kinds of employment are listed) the words "Countryside Commission" shall be inserted after the words "Monopolies Commission".

(2) The Commission shall pay to the Minister at such times in each financial year[5] as may be determined by the Minister, subject to any directions of the Treasury, sums of such amounts as he may so determine for the purposes of this paragraph as being equivalent to the increase during the year of such liabilities of his under the Principal Civil Service Pension Scheme as are attributable to the provision of pensions to or in respect of

---

[1] The appointed day was 1 April 1982, para. 16 S.I. 1982/327: below, 1 April 1982: para. 16 below, S.I. 1982/327.
[2] 1978 c. 44.
[3] 1975 c. 71.
[4] 1972 c. 11.
[5] "Financial year" defined by para. 16, p. 214 below.

persons who are, or have been, in the service of the Commission in so far as that increase results from the service of those persons during that financial year and to the expense to be incurred in administering those pensions.

Accounts and report

11. (1) The Commission shall keep proper accounts and other records, and shall prepare for each financial year[1] a statement of account in such form as the Secretary of State with the approval of the Treasury may direct and submit those statements of account to the Secretary of State at such time as he may with the approval of the Treasury direct.

(2) The Secretary of State shall, as respects each financial year, send the Commission's statement of accounts to the Comptroller and Auditor General not later than the end of November following the year.

(3) The Comptroller and Auditor General shall examine, certify and report on the statement of accounts and lay copies of it, together with his report, before each House of Parliament.

12. The Commission shall furnish the Secretary of State with such returns, accounts and other information with respect to their property and activities or proposed activities as he may from time to time require, and shall afford to the Secretary of State facilities for the verification of information so furnished and for that purpose permit any person authorised in that behalf by the Secretary of State to inspect and make copies of the Commission's accounts, books, documents or papers and give that person such explanation of them as he may reasonably require.

13. (1) The Commission shall, as soon as possible after the end of each financial year, make to the Secretary of State a report on the discharge by them of their functions under the 1949 Act[2], the 1968 Act[3] and this Act during that year.

(2) Without prejudice to the generality of sub-paragraph (1), but subject to the provisions of sub-paragraph (3), the report of the Commission for any year shall include—

(a) a statement of the action taken by the Commission to promote the enjoyment of the countryside by members of the public who are disabled; and

(b) a record of all questions with which the Commission have been concerned during that year and which appear to the Commission to be of general public interest, indicating the purport of any representations or recommendations made by the Commission with respect thereto, and the conclusions (if any) reached thereon.

(3) The report of the Commission for any year shall set out any direction given by the Secretary of State during that year under section 3 of the 1949 Act[4] unless the Secretary of State has notified to the Commission his opinion that it is against the interests of national security so to do.

(4) The Secretary of State shall lay a copy of every report of the Commission under this paragraph before each House of Parliament.

Land

14. The Commission, for the purpose of providing themselves with office or other accommodation in connection with the exercise of any of their functions, may, with the approval of the Secretary of State, acquire land[4], erect and maintain buildings or other structures thereon, and, when the land is no longer required for such purpose, dispose of it.

15. Any land occupied by the Commission shall, for the purpose of any rate on property, be treated as if it were property occupied by or on behalf of the Crown for public purposes.

---

[1] "Financial year" defined by para. 16, p. 214 below.

[2] The National Parks and Access to the Countryside Act 1949 (c. 97: s. 71 above.

[3] The Countryside Act 1968 (c. 41): s. 71 above.

[4] P. 8 above.

[5] "Land" defined by s. 114(1), National Parks and Access to the Countryside Act 1949, p. 38 above: s. 52(4), p. 189 above applies the definition in s. 114 of the 1949 Act.

Interpretation

16. In this Schedule—

"appointed day" means the day appointed for the coming into force of this Schedule;

"the Commission" means the Countryside Commission;

"financial year" means the period commencing with the appointed day and ending with 31st March following that day, and each successive period of twelve months;

"the Minister" means the Minister for the Civil Service;

"pension" includes allowance or gratuity.

Agriculture Act 1986

Ch. 49

An Act to make further provision relating to agriculture and agricultural and other food products, horticulture and the countryside; and for connected matters.

25th July 1986[1]]

The following sections are reproduced from this Act:

Sections 1 and 18(7) extend to England and Wales only; sections 17–19, save for section 18(7), extend to England, Wales and Scotland.

Provision of agricultural services and goods

Provision of services and goods connected with agriculture and countryside

1. (1) The Minister[2] may make provision for the supply to any person of any services or goods relating to—

    (*a*) the production and marketing of agricultural[3] produce and other food[4];

    (*b*) the conservation and enhancement of the natural beauty and amenity of the countryside[5]; or

    (*c*) any other agricultural activity or other enterprise of benefit to the rural economy.

(2) The provision which may be made under this section includes, in particular, provision for—

    (*a*) the giving of information, advice, instruction and training;

    (*b*) the undertaking of research and development;

    (*c*) the examination or testing of any substance;

    (*d*) the supply of veterinary services and of goods required for veterinary purposes;

    (*e*) the performance of any service required in connection with the drainage of agricultural land.

(3) The provision which may be made under this section includes provision for any services or goods mentioned in subsection (1) above to be supplied—

    (*a*) through any person with whom the Minister enters into a contract for the making of the supply; or

    (*b*) through any organisation established by him for the purposes of this section.[6]

(4) Any services or goods provided by virtue of this section may be provided free of charge or for such reasonable charge as the Ministers[6] may determine.

---

[1] The sections reproduced below came into force on 25 September 1986: s. 24(2).

[2] "The Minister" defined by subsection (6) below.

[3] "Agriculture" defined by subsection (6) below.

[4] "Food" defined by subsection (6) below.

[5] "Conservation of the natural beauty of the countryside" defined by subsection (5) below.

[6] Subsection (3) substituted by the Deregulation and Contracting Out Act 1994 (c. 40), s. 76, sch. 16, para. 14. This amendment came into force on 3 January 1995: s. 82(2).

[7] "Ministers" defined by subsection (6) below.

(5) For the purposes of this section the conservation of the natural beauty of the countryside includes the conservation of flora and fauna and geological and physiographical features.

(6) In this section—

"agriculture" has the same meaning as in the Agriculture Act 1947[1];

"food" has the same meaning as in the Food Safety Act 1990;[2] and

"the Minister" means—

(a) in relation to services or goods provided in England, the Minister of Agriculture, Fisheries and Food; and

(b) in relation to services or goods provided in Wales, the Secretary of State.

and "the Ministers" means those Ministers acting jointly[3].

Conservation

Duty to balance interests in exercise of agricultural functions

17. (1) In discharging any functions connected with agriculture[4] in relation to any land the Minister[5] shall, so far as is consistent with the proper and efficient discharge of those functions, have regard to and endeavour to achieve a reasonable balance between the following considerations—

(a) the promotion and maintenance of a stable and efficient agricultural industry;

(b) the economic and social interests of rural areas;

(c) the conservation and enhancement of the natural beauty and amenity of the countryside (including its flora and fauna and geological and physiographical features) and of any features of archaeological interest there; and

(d) the promotion of the enjoyment of the countryside by the public.

(2) In this section—

"agriculture" has the same meaning as in the Agriculture Act 1947[6] or, in Scotland, the Agriculture (Scotland) Act 1948[7]; and

"the Minister" means—

(a) in relation to land in England, the Minister of Agriculture, Fisheries and Food; and

(b) in relation to land in Wales or Scotland, the Secretary of State[8].

Designation and management of environmentally sensitive areas

18. (1) If it appears to the Minister[9] that it is particularly desirable—

(a) to conserve and enhance the natural beauty of an area;

(b) to conserve the flora or fauna or geological or physiographical features of an area; or

(c) to protect buildings or other objects of archaeological, architectural or historic interest in an area,

and that the maintenance or adoption of particular agricultural[10] methods is likely to facilitate such conservation, enhancement or protection, he may, with the consent of the Treasury and after consulting the persons mentioned in subsection (2) below as to the inclusion of the area in the order and the features for which conservation, enhancement or protection is desirable, by order designate that area as an environmentally sensitive area[11].

---

[1] 1947 c. 48.

[2] Words "Food Safety Act 1990" substituted by the Food Safety Act 1990 (c. 16), s. 59(1), sch. 3, para. 35. This amendment came into force on 1 January 1991: S.I. 1990/2372.

[3] This section does not extend to Scotland: s. 24(6).

[4] "Agriculture" defined by subsection (2) below. Any function conferred on a Minister of the Crown by or under the Farm Land and Rural Development Act 1988, s. 1 (grants in respect of farm businesses) and s. 2 (grants in respect of farm woodlands) is to be treated as a function connected with agriculture for the purpose of this section: Farm Land and Rural Development Act 1988 (c. 16), s. 4(3).

[5] "The Minister" defined by subsection (2) below.

[6] 1947 c. 48.

[7] 1948 c. 45.

[8] This section extends to England, Wales and Scotland.

[9] "The Minister" defined by subsection (11) below.

[10] "Agricultural" defined by subsection (11) below.

[11] A list of the orders made under this section designating environmentally sensitive areas is at p. 399 below.

(2) The persons referred to in subsection (1) above are—

(a) in the case of an area in England, the Secretary of State, the Countryside Commission and the Nature Conservancy Council for England[1];

(b) in the case of an area in Wales, the Countryside Council for Wales;[2] and

(c) in the case of an area in Scotland, Scottish Natural Heritage.[3]

(3) If the Minister considers that any of the purposes mentioned in paragraphs (a) to (c) of subsection (1) above is likely to be facilitated in a designated area by doing so, he may make an agreement with any person having an interest in agricultural land in, or partly in, the area by which that person agrees in consideration of payments to be made by the Minister to manage the land in accordance with the agreement.

(4) An order under this section designating an area may specify—

(a) the requirements as to agricultural practices, methods and operations and the installation or use of equipment which must be included in agreements under subsection (3) above as respects land in the area;

(aa) the requirements as to public access which may be included in such agreements;[4]

(b) the period of minimum period for which requirements included in such agreements under paragraph (a) or paragraph (aa) above must be imposed;[5]

(c) the provisions which must be included in such agreements concerning the breach of such requirements; and

(d) the rates or maximum rates at which payments may be made by the Minister under such agreements and the matters in respect of which such payments may be made.

(5) Subject to the foregoing provisions of this section, an agreement under subsection (3) above may contain such provisions as the Minister thinks fit and, in particular, such provisions as he considers are likely to facilitate such conservation enhancement or protection as is mentioned in subsection (1) above.

(6) The Minister shall not make an agreement with any person under subsection (3) above in respect of any land unless that person has certified to the Minister—

(a) that no person other than he is the owner of the land; or

(b) that he has notified any other person who is an owner of the land of his intention to make an agreement under subsection (3) above in respect of the land;

and in this subsection references to the owner of the land are to the estate owner in respect of the fee simple in the land or, in Scotland, the owner of the dominium utile.[6]

(7) The provisions of an agreement under subsection (3) above with any person interested in any land in England or Wales shall, unless the agreement otherwise provides, be binding on persons deriving title under or from that person and be enforceable by the Minister against those persons accordingly.

(8) Where agreements have been made under subsection (3) above with persons having an interest in land in a designated area the Minister shall arrange for the effect on the area as a

---

[1] The Nature Conservancy Council for England, also known as English Nature, is established by the Environmental Protection Act 1990 (c. 43), s. 128, p. 229 below. Words "for England" inserted by the Environmental Protection Act 1990 (c. 43), s. 132(1)(a), sch. 9, para. 13(a). This amendment came into force on 1 April 1991: S.I. 1991/685.

[2] The Countryside Council for Wales is established by the Environmental Protection Act 1990 (c. 43), s. 128, p. 229 below. Words "Countryside Council for Wales" substituted by the Environmental Protection Act 1990 (c. 43), s. 132(1)(a), sch. 9, para. 13(b).

[3] Scottish Natural Heritage is established by the Natural Heritage (Scotland) Act 1991 (c. 28), s. 1, p. 245 below. Para.

(c) substituted by the Natural Heritage (Scotland) Act 1991 (c. 28), s. 27(1), sch. 10, para. 12. This amendment came into force on 1 April 1992: S.I. 1991/2633.

[4] Para. (aa) inserted by the Agriculture Act 1986 (Amendment) Regulations 1994: S.I. 1994/249, reg. 2(a). The regulations came into force on 1 March 1994: reg. 1.

[5] Words "requirements included . . . must be imposed" substituted by the Agriculture Act 1986 (Amendment) Regulations 1994: S.I. 1994/249, reg. 2(b).

[6] Words "the owner of the dominium utile" substituted by the Agricultural Holdings (Scotland) Act 1991 (c. 55), s. 88(1), sch. 11, para. 45. This amendment came into force on 25 September 1991: s. 89(2).

whole of the performance of the agreements to be kept under review and shall from time to time publish such information as he considers appropriate about those effects.

(9) Schedule 2 to the Forestry Act 1967[1] (power for tenant for life and others to enter into forestry dedication covenants, or, in Scotland, forestry dedication agreements) shall apply to agreements under subsection (3) above as it applies to forestry dedication covenants or, as the case may be, forestry dedication agreements.

(10) This section applies to land an interest in which belongs to Her Majesty in right of the Crown or to the Duchy of Lancaster, the Duchy of Cornwall or a Government department or which is held in trust for Her Majesty for the purposes of a Government department, but no agreement under subsection (3) above shall be made as respects land to which this subsection applies without the consent of the appropriate authority[2].

(11) In this section—

"agricultural" has the same meaning as in the Agriculture Act 1947[3] or, in Scotland, the Agriculture (Scotland) Act 1948[4];

"the appropriate authority" has the same meaning as in section 101(11) of the National Parks and Access to the Countryside Act 1949[5];

"the Minister" means—

(a) in relation to an area in England, the Minister of Agriculture, Fisheries and Food; and

(b) in relation to an area in Wales or Scotland, the Secretary of State.

(12) The power to make an order under this section shall be exercisable by statutory instrument and any statutory instrument containing such an order shall be subject to annulment in pursuance of a resolution of either House of Parliament[6].

(13) *This subsection relates to Northern Ireland.*

Supplementary provisions regarding agreements under s. 18(3) in Scotland

19. (1) Where a person having an interest of a kind described in section 18(3) above in land in Scotland, being an interest which enables him to bind the land, enters into an agreement under that subsection—

(a) where the land is registered in the Land Register of Scotland, the agreement may be registered in that Register;

(b) in any other case the agreement may be recorded in the appropriate Division of the General Register of Sasines.

(2) An agreement registered or recorded under subsection (1) above shall be enforceable at the instance of the Secretary of State against persons deriving title to the land (including any person acquiring right to a tenancy by assignation or succession) from the person who entered into the agreement; provided that such an agreement shall not be enforceable against a third party who shall have in good faith and for value acquired right (whether completed by infeftment or not) to the land prior to the agreement being registered or recorded as aforesaid, or against any person deriving title from such third party.

(3) Notwithstanding the terms of any agreement registered or recorded under subsection (1) above, the parties to the agreement or any persons deriving title from them may at any time agree to terminate it; and such an agreement to terminate it shall be registered or recorded in the same manner as was the original agreement.

---

[1] P. 99 above.
[2] "Appropriate authority" defined by subsection (11) below.
[3] 1947 c. 58.
[4] 1948 c. 45.
[5] P. 29 above.
[6] This section extends to England, Wales and, save for subsection (7), Scotland.

(4) A grazings committee appointed under section 24 of the 1955 Act[1] may, with the consent of a majority of the crofters ordinarily resident in the township, enter into an agreement under section 18(3) above in relation to any part of the common grazings and may agree to the revocation or variation of any such agreement, and such agreement, revocation or variation shall be binding upon all their successors.

(5) In the case of an agreement of a kind referred to in subsection (4) above, the payments by the Secretary of State shall be made to the grazings committee and shall be applied by them either—

(a) by division among the crofters who share in the common grazings in proportion to their respective rights therein; or

(b) subject to subsection (6) below, in carrying out works for the improvement of the common grazings or the fixed equipment required in connection therewith.

(6) A grazings committee to whom such a payment as is referred to in subsection (5) above has been made and who are proposing to apply the payment in carrying out works in accordance with paragraph (b) of that subsection shall give notice in writing to each crofter sharing in the common grazings of their proposals; and any such crofter may within one month of the date of such notice make representations in respect of the proposals to the Crofters Commission who may approve them with or without modifications or reject them.

(7) "Crofter" and other expressions used in any of subsections (4) to (6) above and in section 3 of the Crofters (Scotland) Act 1955 have the same meaning in this section as they have in that section as read with section 15(6) of the Crofters (Scotland) Act 1961.[2,3]

....

20. *This section amends the Wildlife and Countryside Act 1981. The amendments are noted at s. 29, p. 171 above, and s. 41, p. 182 above.*

....

[1] Words "the 1955 Act" substituted by the Agricultural Holdings (Scotland) Act 1991 (c. 55), s. 88(1), sch. 11, para. 46. This amendment came into force on 25 September 1991: s. 89(2). "The 1955 Act" is defined by s. 23A of the Agriculture Act 1986 as the Crofters (Scotland) Act 1955. S. 24 of the Crofters (Scotland) Act 1955 is replaced by s. 47 of the Crofters (Scotland) Act 1993 (c. 44): s. 63, sch. 6. The 1993 Act consolidates enactments relating to crofting and repeals the Crofters (Scotland) Act 1955.

[2] S. 3 of the Crofters (Scotland) Act 1955 is replaced by s. 3 of the Crofters (Scotland) Act 1993 (c. 44); s. 15(6) of the Crofters (Scotland) Act 1961 is replaced by s. 47(1) of the Crofters (Scotland) Act 1993: s. 63, sch. 6 of the 1993 Act.

[3] This section extends to England, Wales and Scotland.

Norfolk and Suffolk Broads Act 1988

Ch. 4

Part I of this Act is reproduced.

Arrangement of sections

Part I: The Broads Authority

Norfolk and Suffolk Broads Act 1988

An Act to establish an authority to be known as the Broads Authority; to make provision with respect to its powers; to make provision with respect to the area commonly known as the Broads and with respect to the Great Yarmouth Port and Haven and its Commissioners; to provide for the making of grants to the Authority by the Secretary of State; and for connected purposes.

[15th March 1988[1]]

Part I: The Broads Authority

The Broads Authority

1. (1) There shall be a body corporate, to be known as the Broads Authority, which shall perform the functions conferred on it by this Act.

(2) In this Act the Broads Authority is referred to as "the Authority".

(3) The Authority shall consist of—

(*a*) eighteen members appointed as follows—
四 by Norfolk County Council;
two by Suffolk County Council;
two by Broadland District Council;
two by Great Yarmouth Borough Council;
two by North Norfolk District Council;
two by Norwich City Council;
two by South Norfolk District Council;
two by Waveney District Council;

(*b*) fifteen members appointed as follows—
two by the Countryside Commission[2];
one by the Nature Conservancy Council for England[3];
two by the Great Yarmouth Port and Haven Commissioners;
one by the National Rivers Authority[4];
nine by the Secretary of State; and

(*c*) two members appointed by the Authority from those members of its Navigation Committee (established under section 9 of this Act) who are not already members of the Authority.

(4) A member appointed by a participating authority (that is to say by one of the local authorities mentioned in subsection (3)(*a*) above) shall be appointed from among the members of that authority.

(5) Not less than three of the members appointed by the Secretary of State shall be appointed by him after consultation with such bodies appearing to him to represent boating interests as he considers appropriate.

---

[1] S. 1 of the Act came into force on 15 March 1988: s. 26(1); ss. 2–7 came into force on 1 April 1989: S.I. 1988/955.

[2] The Countryside Commission is established by the Countryside Act 1968 (c. 41), s. 1, p. 114 above.

[3] The Nature Conservancy Council for England, also known as English Nature, is established by the Environmental Protection Act 1990 (c. 43), s. 128, p. 229 below.

Words "for England" inserted by the Environmental Protection Act 1990 (c. 43), s. 132(1)(*a*), sch. 9, para. 15. This amendment came into force on 1 April 1991: S.I. 1991/685.

[4] Words "National Rivers Authority" inserted by the Water (Local Statutory Provisions) (Consequential Amendments) Order 1989, S.I. 1989/1380, art. 4, which came into force on 1 September 1989.

(6) Not less than two of the members appointed by the Secretary of State shall be appointed by him after consultation with such bodies appearing to him to represent farming and landowning interests as he considers appropriate.

(7) Schedule 1 to this Act shall have effect for the purposes of supplementing this section[1].

Functions of Authority: general

2. (1) It shall be the general duty of the Authority[2] to manage the Broads[3] for the purposes of—

(a) conserving and enhancing the natural beauty of the Broads[4];

(b) promoting the enjoyment of the Broads by the public; and

(c) protecting the interests of navigation.

(2) So far as it relates to navigation, subsection (1) above is subject to the Commissioners'[5] functions in respect of navigation within the Haven[6].

(3) In this Act "the Broads" means, subject to—

(a) the variations made by Part I of Schedule 2[7] to this Act; and

(b) any variation made in accordance with the provisions of Part II of that Schedule[8];

the area coloured pink on the deposited map[9].

(4) In discharging its functions, the Authority shall have regard to—

(a) the national importance of the Broads as an area of natural beauty and one which affords opportunities for open-air recreation;

(b) the desirability of protecting the natural resources of the Broads from damage; and

(c) the needs of agriculture and forestry and the economic and social interests of those who live or work in the Broads.

(5) Part I of Schedule 3 to this Act shall have effect to amend certain provisions of the law relating to planning and connected matters, the main purpose of the amendments being to provide for the Authority to be the sole district planning authority in respect of the Broads.

(6) The Authority shall have the miscellaneous functions set out in Part II of Schedule 3[10].

(7) The Authority shall have power to do anything which is necessary or expedient for the purpose of enabling it to carry out its functions, or for incidental purposes, including power—

(a) to acquire, manage, reclaim and dispose of land or other property;

(b) to carry out any building or other operations; and

(c) to carry on any business or undertaking.

---

[1] Schedule 1, which is not included in this work, contains provisions relating to the appointment and replacement of members of the Authority, meetings of the Authority, chairman and vice-chairman and the Authority's chief officer.

[2] "The Authority" means the Broads Authority: s. 1(2), p. 221 above.

[3] "The Broads" are defined by subsection (3) below.

[4] References to conserving the natural beauty of an area include references to conserving its flora, fauna and geological and physiographical features: s. 2(2).

[5] "The Commissioners" means the Great Yarmouth Port and Haven Commissioners: s. 25(1).

[6] "The Haven" means, subject to s. 25(3) and sch. 7, para. 5, the area of the Haven of Great Yarmouth as defined in s. 5 of the Great Yarmouth Port and Haven Act 1866 (1866 c. ccxlvii): s. 25(1). S. 25(3) defines the boundary between the Haven and the navigation area, as defined in s. 8(1), and

sch. 7 contains transitional provisions.

[7] Part I of Schedule 2 varies the area coloured pink on the deposited map.

[8] Part II of Schedule 2 contains provisions for varying by order the area constituting the Broads.

[9] "The deposited map" means the set of maps dated November 1986 deposited in connection with the Norfolk and Suffolk Broads Bill in the office of the Clerk of the Parliaments and the Private Bill Office of the House of Commons: s. 25(1).

[10] The miscellaneous functions in Part II of Schedule 3 concern land drainage, water, discharge of trade and sewage effluent, staithes, common land, open spaces, provision of facilities, caravan sites, conservation of buildings, derelict land, compulsory acquisitions, refuse disposal, litter, footpaths and bridleways, tree preservation and publication of information.

The Broads Plan

3. (1) The Authority[1] shall, before the end of the period of three years beginning with the operative date[2], prepare and publish a plan (to be known as "the Broads Plan") setting out its policy with respect to the exercise of its functions.

(2) The Authority shall review the Broads Plan at least once in every five years.

(3) If, as a result of any such review, the Authority is of the opinion that it is appropriate to vary the Broads Plan, it shall do so in such manner as it thinks fit.

(4) The Authority shall publish a report on the result of any review carried out under this section and the report shall set out the variations (if any) which the Authority has made following the review.

(5) Before preparing or varying the Broads Plan the Authority shall—

(*a*) publish a draft of its proposals; and

(*b*) consult each of the appointing authorities[3], the internal drainage board for each internal drainage district which is wholly or partly within the Broads[4] and such other bodies as appear to it to represent interests likely to be concerned.

(6) The Authority shall send to the Secretary of State a copy of any plan, or variation, published under this section.

Conservation of areas of natural beauty

4. (1) The Authority[5] shall—

(*a*) before the end of the period of two years beginning with the operative date[6], prepare a map showing any areas within the Broads whose natural beauty it is, in the opinion of the Authority, particularly important to conserve[7]; and

(*b*) at least once in every five years, review the particulars shown on the map and make such variations (if any) as it considers necessary.

(2) The Authority shall cause any map prepared or varied under this section to be printed and copies of it to be on sale to the public at such reasonable prices as the Authority may determine.

(3) Before preparing or varying any such map, the Authority shall consult—

(*a*) the Nature Conservancy Council for England[8]; and

(*b*) such bodies as appear to the Authority to represent persons who have an interest in matters affecting the area, or any part of the area, in question.

(4) The Countryside Commission shall issue, and from time to time review, guidance for the Authority with respect to the exercise of its functions under this section; and in considering for the purposes of this section whether any area is one the natural beauty of which it is particularly important to conserve, the Authority shall act in accordance with that guidance.

(5) Before issuing, or reviewing, any guidance under subsection (4) above, the Countryside Commission shall consult—

(*a*) the Nature Conservancy Council for England[8]; and

(*b*) such bodies appearing to the Commission to represent interests concerned as it considers appropriate.

---

[1] "The Authority" means the Broads Authority: s. 1(2) above.

[2] The operative date is 1 April 1989: s. 25(1), S.I. 1988/955.

[3] "Appointing authority" means any of the persons mentioned in s. 1(3)(*a*) or (*b*) above: s. 25(1).

[4] "The Broads" has the meaning given by s. 2(3) above: s. 25(1).

[5] "The Authority" means the Broads Authority: s. 1(2) above.

[6] The operative date is 1 April 1989: s. 25(1), S.I. 1988/955.

[7] References to conserving the natural beauty of an area include references to conserving its flora, fauna and geological and physiographical features: s. 25(2).

[8] Words "for England" inserted by the Environmental Protection Act 1990 (c. 43), s. 132(1)(*a*), sch. 9, para. 15. This amendment came into force on 1 April 1991: S.I. 1991/685.

Notification of certain operations within the Broads

5. (1) Where they are satisfied that it is expedient to do so, the Ministers[1] may by order specify, for the purposes of this section—

(a) such areas of grazing marsh, fen marsh, reed bed or broad-leaved woodland; and

(b) such operations appearing to them likely to affect the character or appearance of one or other of the areas so specified;

as they think fit.

(2) No person shall carry out on any land which is within an area so specified any operation which is so specified unless he has, after the making of the order, given written notice to the Authority[2] specifying both the nature of the proposed operation and the area in which it is proposed to carry it out and—

(a) the Authority has consented in writing to the carrying out of the operation; or

(b) the Authority has neither given nor refused such consent and a period of three months beginning with the date on which the notice required by this subsection was duly given has expired; or

(c) the Authority has refused its consent and a period of twelve months beginning with that date has expired.

(3) Any person who contravenes subsection (2) above without reasonable excuse shall be liable—

(a) on summary conviction, to a fine not exceeding the statutory maximum[3];

(b) on conviction on indictment, to a fine.

(4) Where the Authority is given any notice under this section it shall forthwith send copies of the notice to the Ministers, the Nature Conservancy Council for England[4] and the Countryside Commission.

(5) Any person authorised in writing by the Ministers may, at any reasonable time and (if required to do so) on producing evidence that he is authorised, enter any land for the purpose of assisting the Ministers in deciding whether or not to make an order under this section affecting that land.

(6) Any person authorised in writing by the Authority may, at any reasonable time and (if required to do so) on producing evidence that he is authorised, enter any land for the purpose of ascertaining whether an offence has been committed under this section.

(7) Nothing in subsection (5) or (6) above shall authorise any person to enter a dwelling.

(8) Where any person intends to exercise his right of entry under this section in respect of land which is occupied he shall, except where his purpose is to ascertain if an offence has been committed under this section, give reasonable notice to the occupier.

(9) Any person intentionally obstructing another in the exercise of the right of entry conferred by this section shall be liable on summary conviction to a fine not exceeding level two on the standard scale[5].

Byelaws: general

6. (1) The Authority[6] may make byelaws under this section for the purpose of securing that persons resorting to land to which the byelaws apply do not—

---

[1] "The Ministers" means the Secretary of State and the Minister of Agriculture, Fisheries and Food, acting jointly: s. 25(2).

[2] "The Authority" means the Broads Authority: s. 1(2), p. 221 above.

[3] The present statutory maximum fine is £5,000: Criminal Justice Act 1991 (c. 53), s. 17(2)(c) which came into force on 1 October 1992: S.I. 1992/333.

[4] Words "for England" inserted by the Environmental Protection Act 1990 (c. 43), s. 132(1)(a), sch. 9, para. 15. This amendment came into force on 1 April 1991: S.I. 1991/685.

[5] The present fine at level 2 on the standard scale is £500: Criminal Justice Act 1991 (c. 53): s. 17 which came into force on 1 October 1992: S.I. 1992/333.

[6] "The Authority" means the Broads Authority: s. 1(2), p. 221 above.

(a) damage the land or anything in, on or under it; or

(b) interfere unduly with the enjoyment of the land by other persons.

(2) Byelaws under this section may only be made in respect of land within the Broads[1]—

(a) of which the Authority is the owner or occupier;

(b) to which the general public have a right of access; or

(c) which is commonly used by the general public.

(3) Byelaws under this section may, in particular—

(a) prohibit or restrict the use of land (other than any highway or other road or any land within the navigation area[2] or the Haven[3]), either generally or in any manner specified in the byelaws, by traffic of any description so specified;

(b) contain provisions prohibiting the depositing of rubbish and the leaving of litter;

(c) regulate or prohibit the lighting of fires; and

(d) make provision as to the conditions of use of parking places provided by the Authority and prohibit or restrict persons from plying for hire with vehicles at any such parking places.

(4) Before making, varying or revoking any byelaws under this section, the Authority shall consult the Countryside Commission.

(5) Subsections (3) to (8) and (11) of section 236, and section 238, of the Local Government Act 1972[4] (procedure for making byelaws) shall apply in relation to byelaws made by the Authority under this section as they apply in relation to byelaws made by a local authority; but the Secretary of State may confirm the byelaws with such modifications as he thinks fit.

(6) Where the Secretary of State proposes to make any such modification which appears to him to be substantial, he shall inform the Authority and require it to take such steps as he considers necessary for informing persons likely to be concerned with the modification.

(7) Where the Secretary of State has informed the Authority of his intention to make a modification which appears to him to be substantial, he shall not confirm the byelaws until such period has elapsed as he thinks reasonable for the Authority, and for others who have been informed of his proposal, to consider and comment on it.

(8) The Secretary of State may hold a local inquiry before deciding whether or not to confirm any byelaws made under this section.

(9) Section 12 of the Local Government (Miscellaneous Provisions) Act 1982[5] (enforcement of byelaws) shall apply in relation to byelaws under this section as if the Authority were a relevant local authority.

(10) Any byelaws made under this section may provide for any person contravening any of their provisions to be guilty of an offence and liable—

(a) on summary conviction to such fine (not exceeding level three on the standard scale[6]) as may be specified in the byelaws; and

(b) in the case of a continuing offence, such further fine (not exceeding one tenth of level three for each day during which the offence continues after conviction) as may be so specified.

(11) The Authority may, for the purpose of advising and assisting members of the public using the Broads and of securing compliance with any byelaws made under this Act, appoint one or more of its officers to act as wardens.

---

[1] "The Broads" has the meaning given by section 2(3), p. 222 above.

[2] "The navigation area" has the meaning given by s. 8(1): s. 25(2). S. 8(1) defines stretches of specified rivers, and their banks, as the navigation area.

[3] "The Haven" means, subject to s. 25(3) and sch. 7, para. 5, the area of the Haven of Great Yarmouth as defined in s. 5 of the Great Yarmouth Port and Haven Act 1866 (1866 c.

ccxlvii): s. 25(1). S. 25(3) defines the boundary between the Haven and the navigation area, as defined in s. 8(1), and sch. 7 contains transitional provisions.

[4] 1972 c. 70.

[5] 1982 c. 30.

[6] The present fine at level 3 on the standard scale is £1,000: Criminal Justice Act 1991 (c. 53): s. 17 which came into force on 1 October 1992: S.I. 1992/333.

Alteration of constitution of Authority

7. (1) Where the Authority[1] has, following the passing by it of a special resolution[2], made a written proposal to the Secretary of State—

(*a*) for the appointment of one or more additional members of the Authority by a specified[3] appointing authority[4] or by some other specified body or individual;

(*b*) for a variation in the number of members of the Authority who may be appointed by a specified appointing authority;

(*c*) for an appointing authority to cease to be entitled to appoint to membership of the Authority; or

(*d*) for the appointment of one or more of the members of the Authority to be made jointly by two or more appointing authorities;

the Secretary of State may, if he thinks fit, by order amend[5] this Act in such manner as he considers necessary or expedient for the purpose of giving effect to the proposal.

(2) Where the area which constitutes the Broads for the purposes of this Act is varied by an order made under Schedule 2 to this Act, the Secretary of State may, if he thinks fit, by order amend this Act (so far as it is concerned with the constitution of the Authority) in such manner as he considers necessary or expedient in consequence of the order under Schedule 2.

(3) Before making any order under this section, the Secretary of State shall consult each of the appointing authorities and such bodies appearing to him to represent boating interests as he considers appropriate.

(4) Any order under this section may, in addition to making any provision which is authorised by section 24(3) of this Act, amend any local enactment in such manner as the Secretary of State thinks necessary or expedient in consequence of giving effect to the proposal in question or (as the case may be) of the order under Schedule 2.

(5) In this section—

"amend" includes repeal;

"special resolution" means a resolution of the Authority—

(*a*) passed at a meeting specially convened for the purpose; and

(*b*) in favour of which at least three quarters of the members of the Authority voted at that meeting; and

"specified" means specified in the proposal in question.

The remainder of this Act, which is not reproduced, comprises the following parts:

Part II: Navigation

In relation to the navigation area, defined by s. 8(1) as stretches of specified rivers and their banks, the Broads Authority has the following functions relating to nature conservation:

(i) *The Authority may make byelaws under s. 10 for "the good management of the navigation area, the conservation of its natural beauty and amenities and the promotion of its use for purposes of recreation": see s. 10(3), (4).*

---

[1] "The Authority" means the Broads Authority: s. 1(2), p. 221 above.

[2] "Special resolution" defined by subsection (5) below.

[3] "Specified" defined by subsection (5) below.

[4] "Appointing authority" means any of the persons mentioned in s. 1(3)(*a*) or (*b*) above: s. 25(2).

[5] "Amend" includes repeal: subsection (5) below.

(ii) *The Authority may close to navigation any area at the edge of any waterway or restrict navigation in any such area to specified classes of vessel: see s. 10(5), sch. 5, pt. I, paras. 13, 14, 16.*

Part III: Finance

Part IV: Miscellaneous and supplemental provisions

Environmental Protection Act 1990

Ch. 43

Arrangement of sections

Environmental Protection Act 1990

An Act to . . . make provision for the abolition of the Nature Conservancy Council and for the creation of councils to replace it and discharge the functions of that Council and, as respects Wales, of the Countryside Commission . . .[1]

[1st November 1990]

Part VII of the Act is reproduced below.[2]

Part VII[3]: Nature Conservation in Great Britain and Countryside Matters in Wales

New Councils for England, Scotland and Wales

Creation and constitution of new Councils

128. (1) There shall be two[4] councils, to be called the Nature Conservancy Council for England[5,6], and the Countryside Council for Wales (in this Part referred to as "the Councils").

(2) The Councils shall have the following membership, that is to say—

(a) the Nature Conservancy Council for England shall have not less than 10 nor more than 14 members;

(b) *Repealed by the Natural Heritage (Scotland) Act 1991 (c. 28), s. 27(2), sch. 11. This amendment came into force on 1 April 1992: S.I. 1991/2633.*

(c) the Countryside Council for Wales shall have not less than 8 nor more than 12 members;

and those members shall be appointed by the Secretary of State.

(3) The Secretary of State may by order amend paragraph (a), (b) or (c) of subsection (2) above so as to substitute for the number for the time being specified as the maximum membership of a Council such other number as he thinks appropriate.

(4) The Councils shall establish a committee to be called the Joint Nature Conservation Committee (in this Part referred to as "the joint committee")[7].

(5) Schedules 6[8] and 7[9] to this Act shall have effect with respect to the constitution and proceedings of the Councils and of the joint committee and related matters[10].

---

[1] Extract from the long title.

[2] Sections 128 to 139, save for the amendments made by sections 128, 130 and 132 came into force on 5 November 1990: S.I. 1990/2226. The amendments made by sections 128, 130 and 132 came into force on 1 April 1991: S.I. 1991/685.

[3] Except as regards the joint committee and the provisions noted, this Part does not extend to Scotland: Natural Heritage (Scotland) Act 1991 (c. 28), s. 4(1). This amendment came into force on 1 April 1992: S.I. 1991/2633.

[4] Word "two" substituted by the Natural Heritage (Scotland) Act 1991 (c. 28), s. 4(6), sch. 2, para. 10(4). This amendment came into force on 1 April 1992: S.I. 1991/2633.

[5] The Nature Conservancy Council for England also operates under the name English Nature.

[6] Former words "the Nature Conservancy Council for Scotland" repealed by the Natural Heritage (Scotland) Act 1991 (c. 28), s. 27(2), sch. 11.

[7] Subsection (4) extends to Scotland; the reference to "the Councils" includes a reference to Scottish Natural Heritage: Natural Heritage (Scotland) Act 1991 (c. 28), s. 4(2), p. 246 below.

[8] P. 235 below.

[9] P. 238 below.

[10] Subsection (5) in so far as it relates to schedule 7 extends to Scotland; the reference to "the Councils" includes a reference to Scottish Natural Heritage: Natural Heritage (Scotland) Act 1991 (c. 28), s. 4(2), p. 246 below.

Grants by Secretary of State to new Councils

129. (1) The Secretary of State may with the approval of the Treasury make to the Councils[1] grants of such amounts as the Secretary of State thinks fit.

(2) A grant under this section may be made subject to such conditions (including in particular conditions as to the use of the money for purposes of the joint committee) as the Secretary of State may with the approval of the Treasury think fit.

Countryside matters

Countryside functions of Welsh Council

130. (1) The Countryside Council for Wales shall, in place of the Commission established under section 1 of the National Parks and Access to the Countryside Act 1949 (so far as concerns Wales), have such of the functions under the Acts amended by Schedule 8 to this Act (which relates to countryside matters) as are assigned to them in accordance with the amendments effected by that Schedule[2].

(2) The Countryside Council for Wales shall discharge those functions—

(a) for the conservation and enhancement of natural beauty in Wales and of the natural beauty and amenity of the countryside in Wales, both in the areas designated under the National Parks and Access to the Countryside Act 1949 as National Parks or as areas of outstanding natural beauty and elsewhere;

(b) for encouraging the provision or improvement, for persons resorting to the countryside in Wales, of facilities for the enjoyment thereof and for the enjoyment of the opportunities for open-air recreation and the study of nature afforded thereby;

and shall have regard to the social and economic interests of rural areas in Wales.

(3) The reference in subsection (2) above to the conservation of the natural beauty of the countryside includes the conservation of its flora, fauna and geological and physiographical features.

(4) The Countryside Council for Wales and the Countryside Commission shall discharge their respective functions under those Acts (as amended by Schedule 8) on and after a day to be appointed[3] by an order made by the Secretary of State.

Nature conservation in Great Britain

Nature conservation functions: preliminary

131. (1) For the purposes of nature conservation[4], and fostering the understanding thereof, the Councils[5] shall, in place of the Nature Conservancy Council established under the Nature Conservancy Council Act 1973[6], have the functions conferred on them by sections 132 to 134 below (which are in this Part referred to as "nature conservation functions").

(2) It shall be the duty of the Councils in discharging their nature conservation functions to take appropriate account of actual or possible ecological changes.

(3) The Councils shall discharge their nature conservation functions on and after a day to be appointed by an order made by the Secretary of State[7].

(4) The Secretary of State may give the Councils, or any of them, directions of a general or specific character with regard to the discharge of any of their nature conservation functions other than those conferred on them by section 132(1)(a) below.

---

[1] "The Councils" defined by s. 128(1), p. 229 above.

[2] The amendments made by Schedule 8 to the Acts set out in this manual are noted at the appropriate points within those Acts.

[3] The day appointed was 1 April 1991: S.I. 1991/685.

[4] "Nature conservation" defined by subsection (6) below.

[5] "The Councils" defined by s. 128(1), p. 229 above, and subsection (5) below.

[6] 1973 c. 54.

[7] The day appointed was 1 April 1991: S.I. 1991/685.

(5) Any reference in this section to the Councils includes a reference to the joint committee[1] and, accordingly, directions under subsection (4) above may be given to the joint committee as respects any of the functions dischargeable by them (other than under section 133(2)(*a*)).

(6) In this Part "nature conservation" means the conservation of flora, fauna or geological or physiographical features[2].

General functions of the Councils

132. (1) The Councils[3] shall each have the following functions, namely—

(*a*) such of the functions previously discharged by the Nature Conservancy Council under the Acts amended by Schedule 9 to this Act[4] as are assigned to them in accordance with the amendments effected by that Schedule;

(*b*) the establishment, maintenance and management of nature reserves (within the meaning of section 15 of the National Parks and Access to the Countryside Act 1949[5]) in their area;

(*c*) the provision of advice for the Secretary of State or any other Minister on the development and implementation of policies for or affecting nature conservation[6] in their area;

(*d*) the provision of advice and the dissemination of knowledge to any persons about nature conservation in their area or about matters arising from the discharge of their functions under this section or section 134 below;

(*e*) the commissioning or support (whether by financial means or otherwise) of research which in their opinion is relevant to any of their functions under this section or section 134 below;

and the Councils shall, in discharging their functions under this section, have regard to any advice given to them by the joint committee[7] under section 133(3) below.

(2) The Councils shall each have power—

(*a*) to accept any gift or contribution made to them for the purposes of any of the functions conferred on them by subsection (1) above or section 134 below and, subject to the terms of the gift or contribution, to apply it to those purposes.

(*b*) to initiate and carry out such research directly related to those functions as it is appropriate that they should carry out instead of commissioning or supporting other persons under paragraph (*e*) of that subsection;

and they may do all such other things as are incidental or conducive to those functions including (without prejudice to the generality of this provision) making charges and holding land or any interest in or right over land.

(3) Nothing in this section or in the Natural Heritage (Scotland) Act 1991 (in so far as it relates to the nature conservation functions of Scottish Natural Heritage)[8] shall be taken as preventing any of the Councils—

(*a*) if consulted by another of the Councils about a matter relating to the functions of that other Council, from giving that other Council any advice or information which they are able to give; or

(*b*) from giving advice or information to the joint committee about any matter relating to any of the functions conferred by section 133(2) and (3) below[9].

---

[1] "The joint committee" means the Joint Nature Conservation Committee: s. 128(4), p. 229 above.

[2] This section in so far as it relates to the joint committee extends to Scotland: the Natural Heritage (Scotland) Act 1991 (c. 28), s. 4(3).

[3] "The Councils" defined by s. 128(1), p. 229 above.

[4] The amendments made by Schedule 9 to the Acts set out in this manual are noted at the appropriate points within those Acts.

[5] P. 14 above.

[6] "Nature conservation" defined by s. 131(6) above.

[7] "The joint committee" means the Joint Nature Conservation Committee: s. 128(4), p. 229 above.

[8] Words "or in the Natural Heritage (Scotland) Act 1991 ... Scottish Natural Heritage)" inserted by the Natural Heritage (Scotland) Act 1991 (c. 28), s. 4(6), sch. 2, para. 10(5). This amendment came into force on 1 April 1992: S.I. 1991/2633.

[9] Subsection (3) extends to Scotland; the reference to "the Councils" includes a reference to Scottish Natural Heritage: Natural Heritage (Scotland) Act 1991 (c. 28), s. 4(2), p. 246 below.

Special functions of Councils

133. (1) The Councils[1] shall jointly have the following functions which may, however, be discharged only through the joint committee[2]; and in this section the functions so dischargeable are referred to as "special functions".

(2) The special functions of the Councils are—

(a) such of the functions previously discharged by the Nature Conservancy Council under the Wildlife and Countryside Act 1981 as are assigned to the Councils jointly as special functions in accordance with the amendments to that Act effected by Schedule 9 to this Act[3];

(b) the provision of advice for the Secretary of State or any other Minister on the development and implementation of policies for or affecting nature conservation for Great Britain as a whole[4] or nature conservation[5] outside Great Britain;

(c) the provision of advice and the dissemination of knowledge to any persons about nature conservation for Great Britain as a whole or nature conservation outside Great Britain;

(d) the establishment of common standards throughout Great Britain for the monitoring of nature conservation and for research into nature conservation and the analysis of the resulting information;

(e) the commissioning or support (whether by financial means or otherwise) of research which in the opinion of the joint committee is relevant to any matter mentioned in paragraphs (a) to (d) above;

and section 132(2) above shall apply to the special functions as it applies to the functions conferred by subsection (1) of that section.

(3) The joint committee may give advice or information to any of the Councils on any matter arising in connection with the functions of that Council under section 132 above or, as the case may be, the nature conservation functions of Scottish Natural Heritage[6] which, in the opinion of the committee, concerns nature conservation for Great Britain as a whole or nature conservation outside Great Britain.

(4) For the purposes of this section, references to nature conservation for Great Britain as a whole are references to—

(a) any nature conservation matter of national or international importance or which otherwise affects the interests of Great Britain as a whole; or

(b) any nature conservation matter which arises throughout Great Britain and raises issues common to England, Scotland and Wales.

and it is immaterial for the purposes of paragraph (a) above that a matter arises only in relation to England, to Scotland or to Wales.

(5) The Secretary of State may, as respects any matter arising in connection with—

(a) any special function of the Councils, or

(b) the function of the joint committee under subsection (3) above,

give directions to any of the Councils requiring that Council (instead of the joint committee) to discharge that function in relation to that matter[7].

---

[1] "The Councils" defined by s. 128(1) above. The references to "the Councils" in this section includes a reference to Scottish Natural Heritage: Natural Heritage (Scotland) Act 1991 (c. 28), s. 4(4)(a), p. 246 below.

[2] "The joint committee" means the Joint Nature Conservation Committee: s. 128(4), p. 229 above.

[3] The functions assigned to the Councils jointly as special functions in accordance with sch. 9 are those set out at the Wildlife and Countryside Act 1981, s. 22(3), p. 163 above, and s. 24(1), p. 164 above.

[4] "Nature conservation for Great Britain as a whole" defined by subsection (4) below.

[5] "Nature conservation" defined by s. 131(6), p. 231 above.

[6] Words "or, as the case may be, the nature conservation functions of Scottish Natural Heritage" inserted by the Natural Heritage (Scotland) Act 1991 (c. 28), s. 4(4)(b). This amendment came into force on 1 April 1992: S.I. 1991/2633.

[7] This section extends to Scotland and in discharging its nature conservation functions Scottish Natural Heritage shall have regard to any advice given to it by the joint committee under subsection (3): Natural Heritage (Scotland) Act 1991 (c. 28), s. 4(4), p. 246 below.

Grants and loans by the Councils

134. (1) The Councils[1] may each, with the consent of or in accordance with a general authorisation given by the Secretary of State, give financial assistance by way of grant or loan (or partly in one way and partly in the other) to any person in respect of expenditure incurred or to be incurred by him in doing anything which in their opinion is conducive to nature conservation[2] or fostering the understanding of nature conservation.

(2) No consent or general authorisation shall be given by the Secretary of State under subsection (1) above without the approval of the Treasury.

(3) On making a grant or loan a Council may impose such conditions as they think fit, including (in the case of a grant) conditions for repayment in specified circumstances.

(4) The Councils shall exercise their powers under subsection (3) above so as to ensure that any person receiving a grant or loan under this section in respect of premises to which the public are to be admitted (on payment or otherwise) shall, in the means of access both to and within the premises, and in the parking facilities and sanitary conveniences to be available (if any), make provision, so far as it is in the circumstances both practicable and reasonable, for the needs of members of the public visiting the premises who are disabled.

Transfer of property, rights and liabilities to new Councils

Schemes for the transfer of property etc. of the Nature Conservancy Council

135. (1) The Nature Conservancy Council shall make one or more schemes ("transfer schemes") for the division of all their property, rights and liabilities (other than rights and liabilities under the contracts of employment of their staff and in respect of the provision of pensions, allowances or gratuities) between the Councils[3].

(2) On the date appointed by a transfer scheme, the property, rights and liabilities of the Nature Conservancy Council which are the subject of the scheme shall , by virtue of this subsection, become property, rights and liabilities of the Councils to which they are allocated by the scheme.

(3) Part I of Schedule 10 to this Act[4] shall have effect in relation to transfer schemes under this section.

(4) The rights and liabilities of the Nature Conservancy Council in respect of the provision of pensions, allowances and gratuities for or in respect of their members and employees or their former members or employees shall, on the date appointed under section 131(3) above[5], by virtue of this subsection, become rights and liabilities of the Secretary of State.

Transfer to Welsh Council of certain property etc. of Countryside Commission

136. (1) The Countryside Commission shall make one or more schemes ("transfer schemes") for allocating to the Countryside Council for Wales so much of their property, rights and liabilities (other than rights and liabilities under the contracts of employment of their staff) as the Commission consider appropriate having regard to the countryside functions conferred on the Council by section 130 above[6].

(2) On the date appointed by a transfer scheme, the property, rights and liabilities of the Countryside Commission which are the subject of the scheme shall, by virtue of this subsection, become property, rights and liabilities of the Countryside Council for Wales.

[1] "The Councils" defined by s. 128(1), p. 229 above.
[2] "Nature conservation" defined by s. 131(6), p. 231 above.
[3] "The Councils" defined by s. 128(1), p. 229 above.
[4] Part I of Schedule 10, which is not reproduced, made provision for transfer schemes concerning the former Nature Conservancy Council.
[5] P. 230 above. The date appointed was 1 April 1991: S.I. 1991/685.
[6] P. 230 above.

(3) Part II of Schedule 10 to this Act[1] shall have effect in relation to transfer schemes under this section.

Employment by new Councils of staff of existing bodies

Offers of employment to employees of Nature Conservancy Council and certain employees of Countryside Commission

137. (1) Any person who immediately before the date appointed under section 131(3) above[2] is employed by the Nature Conservancy Council shall be entitled to receive an offer of employment from one of the Councils (to be determined in accordance with proposals made by the Nature Conservancy Council).

(2) Subsection (1) above does not apply to a person whose contract of employment with the Nature Conservancy Council terminates on the day immediately preceding the date appointed under section 131(3) above.

(3) The Countryside Council for Wales shall also make an offer of employment to any person who—

(a) is, immediately before the date appointed under section 130(4) above, employed by the Countryside Commission; and

(b) is a person the Commission has proposed should receive such an offer.

(4) Part III of Schedule 10 to this Act[3] shall have effect with respect to offers and proposals under this section.

Dissolution of Nature Conservancy Council

Winding up and dissolution of Nature Conservancy Council

138. (1) On the date appointed under section 131(3) above[4] the chairman and other members of the Nature Conservancy Council shall cease to hold office and after that date—

(a) the Council shall consist only of a chairman appointed by the Secretary of State and such one or more other persons as may be so appointed; and

(b) the Council shall have only the following functions, namely—

(i) anything which falls to be done by the Council under any transfer scheme under section 135 above;

(ii) the preparation of such accounts and reports as the Secretary of State may direct;

and such other functions as are necessary for winding up their affairs.

(2) The Secretary of State may, by order, after consultation with the Nature Conservancy Council and the Councils, dissolve the Nature Conservancy Council on a day specified in the order as soon as he is satisfied that nothing remains to be done by that Council[5].

(3) The Secretary of State may pay to persons who cease to hold office by virtue of subsection (1) above such sums by way of compensation for loss of office, or loss or diminution of pension rights, as the Secretary of State may, with the approval of the Treasury, determine.

Transitional provisions and savings

Transitional provisions and savings

139. Schedule 11 to this Act[6] (which contains transitional provisions and savings relating to this Part) shall have effect.

---

[1] Part II of Schedule 10, which is not reproduced, made provision for transfer schemes under this section concerning the Countryside Commission.

[2] P. 230 above. The date appointed was 1 April 1991: S.I. 1991/685.

[3] Part III of Schedule 10, which is not reproduced, made provision for the employment of staff under this section.

[4] P. 230 above. The date appointed was 1 April 1991: S.I. 1991/685.

[5] The Nature Conservancy Council was dissolved on 21 December 1991: S.I. 1991/2923.

[6] P. 239 below.

SCHEDULE 6

(Section 128)

THE NATURE CONSERVANCY COUNCILS FOR ENGLAND AND SCOTLAND AND THE COUNTRYSIDE COUNCIL FOR WALES: CONSTITUTION [1]

Preliminary

1. In this Part of this Schedule any reference to the council is a reference to each of the Councils established by section 128 of this Act[2].

Constitution and membership

2. The council shall be a body corporate.

3. (1) The council shall not be regarded as the servant or agent of the Crown, or as enjoying any status, immunity or privilege of the Crown; and the council's property shall not be regarded as property of, or property held on behalf of, the Crown.

    (2) Sub-paragraph (1) above has effect subject to paragraph 18 below.

4. (1) The Secretary of State shall appoint one of the members of the council to be chairman of the council and may appoint a member to be deputy chairman.

    (2) The chairman, deputy chairman and other members of the council shall hold and vacate office in accordance with the terms of their appointment.

    (3) A member of the council may, by notice in writing addressed to the Secretary of State, resign his membership, and the chairman and deputy chairman of the council may by such a notice resign their office as such without resigning their membership.

5. A member of the council who ceases to be a member or ceases to be chairman or deputy chairman of the council shall be eligible for reappointment.

6. The Secretary of State may remove a member of the council from membership if he has—

    (*a*) become bankrupt or made an arrangement with his creditors or, in Scotland, had his estate sequestrated or made a trust deed for behoof of his creditors or a composition contract; or

    (*b*) been absent from meetings of the council for a period longer than six consecutive months without the permission of the council;

    or if he is, in the opinion of the Secretary of State unable or unfit to discharge the functions of a member.

Remuneration and allowances for members of council

7. (1) The council shall—

    (*a*) pay to their members such remuneration and allowances (if any); and

    (*b*) as regards any member or former member in whose case the Secretary of State may so determine, pay such pension, allowance or gratuity to or in respect of him, or make such payments towards the provision of such pension, allowance or gratuity,

    as the Secretary of State may with the approval of the Treasury determine.

    (2) If a person ceases to be a member of the council, and it appears to the Secretary of State that there are special circumstances which make it right that he should receive compensation, the Secretary of State may require

---

[1] For the constitution of Scottish Natural Heritage see the Natural Heritage (Scotland) Act 1991 (c. 28), s. 1, p. 245   below and sch. 1, p. 256.
[2] P. 229 above.

the council to pay to that person a sum of such amount as the Secretary of State may with the approval of the Treasury determine.

Staff

8. (1) There shall be a chief officer of the council.

(2) The first appointment of a chief officer shall be made by the Secretary of State after consultation with the chairman of the council (if there is a person holding that office when the appointment is made); and the council shall, with the approval of the Secretary of State, make the subsequent appointments.

9. The council may appoint such number of other employees as they may, with the approval of the Secretary of State given with the consent of the Treasury, determine.

10. The council shall pay to the chief officer and their other employees such remuneration and allowances as the council may, with the approval of the Secretary of State given with the consent of the Treasury, determine.

11. The council shall, in the case of such of their employees or former employees as they may, with the approval of the Secretary of State given with the consent of the Treasury, determine—

(a) pay such pensions, allowances or gratuities to or in respect of those employees.

(b) make such payments towards provision of such pensions, allowances or gratuities, or

(c) provide and maintain such schemes (whether contributory or not) for the payment of such pensions, allowances or gratuities,

as they may, with the approval of the Secretary of State given with the consent of the Treasury, determine.

Proceedings

12. (1) The council may regulate their own procedure (including making provision in relation to quorum).

(2) The proceedings of the council and any committee of the council shall not be invalidated by any vacancy amongst their members or by any defect in the appointment of any such member.

Delegation of powers

13. (1) Anything authorised or required by or under any enactment to be done by the council may be done by any committee of theirs which, or by any member or employee of the council who, is authorised (generally or specially) for the purpose by the council.

(2) Nothing in sub-paragraph (1) above shall prevent the council from doing anything that a committee, member or employee has been authorised to do.

Committees

14. (1) The council may appoint persons who are not members of the council to be members of any committee established by the council (in addition to any members of the council).

(2) The council shall pay to a person so appointed such remuneration and allowances (if any) as the Secretary of State may with the approval of the Treasury determine.

(3) The council may regulate the procedure of any committee of theirs.

Documents

15. (1) This paragraph applies in England and Wales only.

(2) The application of the seal of the council shall be authenticated by the signature of any member or employee of the council who is authorised (generally or specially) for the purpose by the council.

(3) Any document purporting to be an instrument made or issued by the council and to be duly executed under the seal of the council, or to be signed or executed by a person authorised for the purpose by the council, shall be received in evidence and treated, without further proof, as being so made or issued unless the contrary is shown.

16. *Repealed by the Natural Heritage (Scotland) Act 1991 (c. 28), s. 27(2), sch. 11. This amendment came into force on 1 April 1991: S.I. 1991/2633.*

Public Records

17. In Schedule 1 to the Public Records Act 1958[1] (definition of public records), in Part II of the Table at the end of paragraph 3 (organisations whose records are public records) there shall be inserted in the appropriate places entries relating to the Countryside Council for Wales and the Nature Conservancy Council for England.

Land

18. (1) For the purposes of the application of any enactment or rule of law to land an interest in which belongs to the council, and which is managed as a nature reserve, the council shall be deemed to be a Government department; and any other land occupied by them shall be deemed, for the purpose of any rate on property, to be property occupied by or on behalf of the Crown for public purposes.

(2) In sub-paragraph (1) above "interest" and "land" have the meanings assigned to them by section 114 of the National Parks and Access to the Countryside Act 1949[2].

Reports, accounts etc.

19. The council shall—

(a) furnish the Secretary of State with such returns, accounts and other information with respect to their property and activities or proposed activities as he may from time to time require;

(b) afford to the Secretary of State facilities for the verification of information so furnished; and

(c) for the purpose of such verification, permit any person authorised in that behalf by the Secretary of State to inspect and make copies of the council's accounts, books, documents or papers and give that person such explanation of anything he is entitled to inspect as he may reasonably require.

20. (1) The council shall—

(a) as soon as possible after the 31st March following the date appointed under section 131(3) of this Act[3] make to the Secretary of State a report on the exercise and performance of their functions down to that date, and

(b) make a similar report to him as to each period of twelve months thereafter as soon as possible after its end;

and a copy of each such report shall be laid before each House of Parliament by the Secretary of State.

(2) Without prejudice to the generality of sub-paragraph (1) above, the report of the Countryside Council for Wales for any year shall include a statement of the action taken by the Council to promote the enjoyment of the countryside by members of the public who are disabled.

21. (1) The council shall keep proper accounts and other records, and shall prepare for each financial year a statement of account in such form as the Secretary of State with the approval of the Treasury may direct and submit those statements of account to the Secretary of State at such time as he may with the approval of the Treasury direct.

(2) The Secretary of State shall, on or before 30th November in any year, transmit to the Comptroller and Auditor General the statements of account of the council for the financial year last ended.

(3) The Comptroller and Auditor General shall examine and certify the statements of account transmitted to him under this paragraph, and lay copies of them together with his report thereon before each House of Parliament.

(4) In this paragraph "financial year" means the period beginning with the day appointed under section 131(3) of this Act and ending with the 31st March following that date and each period of twelve months thereafter.

---

[1] 1958 c. 51.
[2] P. 38 above.

[3] P. 230 above. The date appointed was 1 April 1991: S.I. 1991/685.

22–25. *These paragraphs, which are not reproduced, make amendments to the Superannuation Act 1965 (c. 74), the Parliamentary Commissioner Act 1967 (c. 13), the House of Commons Disqualification Act 1975 (c. 24) and the Inheritance Tax Act 1984 (c. 51).*

SCHEDULE 7

(Section 128)

THE JOINT NATURE CONSERVATION COMMITTEE

Preliminary

1. In this Schedule—

"chairman" means (except in paragraph 2(1) below) the chairman of the committee;

"the committee" means the Joint Nature Conservation Committee; and

"council" means a council established by section 128(1) of this Act[1].

Membership

2. (1) The committee shall consist of eleven voting members, namely—

(*a*) a chairman appointed by the Secretary of State;

(*b*) three members appointed by the Secretary of State;

(*c*) the chairman of each council and one other member of each council appointed by that council; and

(*d*) the chairman of the Countryside Commission;

and two non-voting members appointed by the Department of the Environment for Northern Ireland.

(2) The committee may appoint any voting member to be deputy chairman.

3. The chairman and the three members appointed by the Secretary of State shall be persons who are not members of any of the councils and shall hold and vacate office in accordance with the terms of their appointments.

4. (1) The three members appointed by the Secretary of State shall be persons appearing to the Secretary of State to have experience in or scientific knowledge of nature conservation[2]; and the Secretary of State shall, in determining who to appoint, have regard to any recommendations made to him by the chairman.

(2) Before appointing such a member the Secretary of State shall consult the chairman and such persons having scientific knowledge of nature conservation as the Secretary of State considers appropriate.

Remuneration and allowances for members

5. (1) The councils shall—

(*a*) pay to the chairman such remuneration and allowances; and

(*b*) pay such pension, allowance or gratuity to or in respect of the chairman or make such payments towards the provision of such pension, allowance or gratuity;

as the Secretary of State may with the approval of the Treasury determine.

(2) If a person ceases to be chairman and it appears to the Secretary of State that there are special circumstances which make it right that he should receive compensation, the Secretary of State may require the councils to pay to that person a sum of such amount as the Secretary of State may with the approval of the Treasury determine.

---

[1] In this schedule "council" includes Scottish Natural Heritage: Natural Heritage (Scotland) Act 1991 (c. 28), s. 4(2), p. 246 below.

[2] For the definition of "nature conservation" applied to Part VII of this Act see s. 131(6), p. 231 above.

6. The councils shall pay to the three members appointed by the Secretary of State, and to the non-voting members, such remuneration and allowances as the Secretary of State may with the approval of the Treasury determine.

Staff etc. and expenses

7. (1) The councils shall provide the committee with such staff, accommodation and other facilities, and such financial resources, as the councils, after consultation with the committee, consider appropriate for the proper discharge of the functions conferred by section 133(2) and (3) of this Act[1].

(2) The expenses of the committee shall be defrayed by the councils in such proportions as the councils may agree.

(3) In default of agreement between the councils as to any question arising under sub-paragraph (1) or (2) above the Secretary of State shall determine that question.

Proceedings

8. (1) The committee may regulate their own procedure (including making provision in relation to the quorum of voting members).

(2) The proceedings of the committee shall not be invalidated by any vacancy amongst their members or defect in the appointment of any member.

Delegation of functions

9. (1) Anything authorised or required to be done by the committee may be done by any member of the committee, by any council or by any employee of a council who is authorised (generally or specially) for the purpose by the committee.

(2) Nothing in sub-paragraph (1) above shall prevent the committee from doing anything that another person has been authorised to do.

10. (1) The committee shall—

(a) as soon as possible after 31st March following the date appointed under section 131(3) of this Act[2] make to the Secretary of State a report on their activities down to that date; and

(b) make a similar report to him as to each period of twelve months thereafter as soon as possible after its end;

and a copy of each such report shall be laid before each House of Parliament by the Secretary of State.

(2) The committee shall, at the same time as they make a report under subparagraph (1) above, send a copy of it to each of the councils.

SCHEDULE 11

(Section 139)

TRANSITIONAL PROVISIONS AND SAVINGS FOR PART VII

PART I

COUNTRYSIDE FUNCTIONS

Preliminary

1. In this Part of this Schedule—

"the appointed day" means the day appointed under section 130(4) of this Act[3];

---

[1] P. 232 above.
[2] P. 230 above. The date appointed was 1 April 1991: S.I. 1991/685.
[3] P. 230 above. The date appointed was 1 April 1991: S.I. 1991/685.

"the Commission" means the Countryside Commission;

"the Council" means the Countryside Council for Wales;

"relevant", in relation to anything done by or in relation to the Commission before the appointed day, means anything which, if it were to be done on or after the appointed day, would be done by or in relation to the Council or, as the case may be, by or in relation to both the Commission (so far as concerning England) and the Council (so far as concerning Wales).

Continuity of exercise of functions

2. (1) Any relevant thing done by or in relation to the Commission before the appointed day shall, so far as is required for continuing its effect on and after that date, have effect as if done by or in relation to the Council or, as the case may be, by or in relation to both the Council and the Commission.

(2) Any relevant thing which, immediately before the appointed day, is in the process of being done by or in relation to the Commission may be continued by or in relation to the Council or, as the case may be, by or in relation to both the Council and the Commission.

Construction of references to the Countryside Commission

3. (1) This paragraph applies to any provision of any agreement, or of any instrument or other document, subsisting immediately before the appointed day[1] which refers (in whatever terms) to the Commission[2] and does so (or is to be construed as doing so) in relation to, or to things being done in or in connection with, Wales.

(2) Any provision to which this paragraph applies shall, subject to subparagraphs (3) and (4) below, have effect on and after the appointed day with the substitution for, or the inclusion in, any reference to the Commission of a reference to the Council[3], according as the reference concerns Wales only or concerns both England and Wales.

(3) Any provision to which this paragraph applies which refers in general terms to members of or to persons employed by or agents of the Commission shall have effect on and after the appointed day with the substitution for, or the inclusion in, any such reference of a reference to members of or persons employed by or agents of the Council, according as the reference concerns Wales only or concerns both England and Wales.

(4) Any provision to which this paragraph applies which refers to a member or employee of the Commission shall have effect on and after the appointed day with the substitution for, or the inclusion in, any such reference of—

(a) a reference to such person as the Council may appoint, or

(b) in default of appointment, to the member or employee of the Council who corresponds as nearly as may be to the member or employee in question,

according as the reference concerns Wales only or concerns both England and Wales.

4. (1) This paragraph applies to any provision of a local Act passed, or subordinate legislation made, before the appointed day which refers (in whatever terms) to the Commission and relates to, or to things being done in or in connection with, Wales.

(2) The Secretary of State may by order make such consequential modifications of any provision to which this paragraph applies as appear to him to be necessary or expedient.

(3) Subject to any exercise of the power conferred by sub-paragraph (2) above, any provision to which this paragraph applies shall have effect on and after the appointed day with the substitution for, or inclusion in, any reference to the Commission of a reference to the Council, according as the reference concerns Wales only or concerns both England and Wales.

Existing areas of outstanding natural beauty and long distance routes

5. (1) This paragraph applies to—

(a) any area of land which immediately before the appointed day[4] is an area of outstanding natural beauty designated under section 87 of the 1949 Act[5] of which part is in England and part is in Wales (referred to as "the two parts" of such an area); and

[1] "Appointed day" defined by para. 1 above.
[2] "The Commission" means the Countryside Commission: para. 1 above.
[3] "The Council" means the Countryside Council for Wales: para. 1 above.
[4] "Appointed day" defined by para. 1, p. 239 above.
[5] P. 22 above.

(b) any long distance route under Part IV of that Act of which some parts are in England and other parts in Wales.

(2) On and after the appointed day the two parts of an area to which this paragraph applies shall be treated as if each were a distinct area of outstanding natural beauty; and accordingly, so far as may be necessary for the purpose of applying paragraphs 2 and 3 above, anything done by or in relation to the Commission in relation to both parts of that area shall be treated as having been done in relation to the part in Wales by or in relation to the Council.

(3) On and after the appointed day any route to which this paragraph applies shall not cease, by virtue of this Part of this Act to be a single route for the purposes of Part IV of the 1949 Act; but any function which before that day is exercisable by or in relation to the Commission shall, on and after that day be exercisable by or in relation to the Commission (so far as concerns parts of the route in England) and by or in relation to the Council (so far as concerns parts of the route in Wales).

(4) On or after the appointed day the Commission and the Council shall each exercise any function of theirs in relation to an area or route to which this paragraph applies only after consultation with the other; and the Commission and the Council may make arrangements for discharging any of their functions in relation to such an area or route jointly.

PART II

NATURE CONSERVATION FUNCTIONS

Preliminary

6. In this Part of this Schedule—

"appointed day" means the date appointed under section 131(3) of this Act[1];

"appropriate new council" shall be construed in accordance with paragraph 7 below; and

"new council" means a council established by section 128(1) of this Act.

7. (1) In this Part of this Schedule a reference to "the appropriate new council" is, in relation to or to things done in connection with property, rights or liabilities of the Nature Conservancy Council which are transferred by section 135(2) of this Act[2] to a new council, a reference to that new council.

(2) Subject to sub-paragraph (1) above, a reference in this Part of this Schedule to "the appropriate new council" is, in relation to anything else done before the appointed day by or in relation to the Nature Conservancy Council in the exercise of or in connection with any function of theirs (other than a function corresponding to a special function of the new councils)—

(a) a reference to the new council by whom the nature conservation function corresponding to that function is exercisable on and after that date; or

(b) where the thing done relates to a matter affecting the area of more than one new council, a reference to each new council by whom the nature conservation function corresponding to that function is exercisable on and after that date;

and in relation to anything done in the exercise of or in connection with any function of the Nature Conservancy Council corresponding to a special function of the new councils a reference to "the appropriate new council" is a reference to the joint committee or, where directions under section 133(5) of this Act have been given, the new council by whom the corresponding special function is dischargeable (on behalf of the new councils) on and after that day.

(3) Any question arising under this paragraph as to which new council is the appropriate new council in relation to any particular function of the Nature Conservancy Council may be determined by a direction given by the Secretary of State.

Continuity of exercise of functions

8. (1) Anything done (or deemed by any enactment to have been done) by or in relation to the Nature Conservancy Council before the appointed day[3] shall, so far as is required for continuing its effect on and after that date, have effect as if done by or in relation to the appropriate new council[4].

---

[1] P. 230 above. The date appointed was 1 April 1991: S.I. 1991/685.

[2] P. 233 above.

[3] "Appointed day" defined by para. 6 above.

[4] "Appropriate new council" construed in accordance with para. 7 above: para. 6.

(2) Anything which immediately before the appointed day is in the process of being done by or in relation to the Nature Conservancy Council may be continued by or in relation to the appropriate new council as if it had been done by or in relation to that council.

Construction of references to the Nature Conservancy Council

9. (1) This paragraph applies to any agreement, any instrument and any other document subsisting immediately before the appointed day[1] which refers (in whatever terms) to the Nature Conservancy Council, other than a scheme provided by that Council under paragraph 12 of Schedule 3 to the Nature Conservancy Council Act 1973[2].

(2) Any agreement, instrument or other document to which this paragraph applies shall have effect on and after the appointed day with the substitution—

(a) for any reference to the Nature Conservancy Council of a reference to the appropriate new council[3];

(b) for any reference in general terms to members of or to persons employed by or agents of the Nature Conservancy Council of a reference to members of or persons employed by or agents of the appropriate new council; and

(c) for any reference to a member or officer of the Nature Conservancy Council of a reference to such person as the appropriate new council may appoint or, in default of appointment, to the member or employee of that council who corresponds as nearly as may be to the member or officer in question.

10. (1) This paragraph applies to any provision of a local Act passed, or subordinate legislation made, before the appointed day which refers (in whatever terms) to the Nature Conservancy Council.

(2) The Secretary of State may by order make such consequential modifications of any provision to which this paragraph applies as appear to him to be necessary or expedient.

(3) Subject to any exercise of the power conferred by sub-paragraph (2) above, any provision to which this paragraph applies shall have effect on and after the appointed day with the substitution for each reference to the Nature Conservancy Council of a reference to such one or more of the new councils as may be appropriate, according as the provision relates to, or to things being done in or in connection with, England, Scotland or Wales.

Pensions for Nature Conservancy Council staff

11. (1) The repeal by this Act of paragraph 12 of Schedule 3 to the Nature Conservancy Council Act 1973 shall not affect the operation on and after the appointed day of any scheme provided by the Nature Conservancy Council for the payment to or in respect of its officers of pensions, allowances or gratuities.

(2) Any such scheme shall have effect on and after the appointed day with the substitution for any reference to the Nature Conservancy Council of a reference to the Secretary of State.

Existing nature reserves and areas of special scientific interest

12. (1) This paragraph applies to any land which, immediately before the appointed day is—

(a) a nature reserve (within the meaning of Part III of the 1949 Act[4]) which is managed by, or under an agreement entered into with, the Nature Conservancy Council or which is the subject to a declaration under section 35 of the 1981 Act[5]; or

(b) an area of special scientific interest which has been notified by the Nature Conservancy Council under section 28(1) of the 1981 Act[6] or is treated by section 28(13) of that Act as having been notified under section 28(1)(a) of that Act or is an area to which an order under section 29(1) of that Act[7] relates;

and of which part is in England and part is in Wales or, as the case may be, part is in England and part is in Scotland (referred to as "the two parts" of such a reserve or area).

(2) On and after the appointed day[8], the two parts of any reserve or area to which this paragraph applies shall be treated as if each were a distinct nature reserve or area of special scientific interest; and accordingly, so far

---

[1] "Appointed day" defined by para. 6, p. 241 above.
[2] 1973 c. 54.
[3] "Appropriate new council" construed in accordance with para. 7, p. 241 above: para. 6.
[4] P. 14 above.
[5] P. 177 above.
[6] P. 168 above.
[7] P. 171 above.
[8] "Appointed day" defined by para. 6, p. 241 above.

as may be necessary for the purpose of applying paragraphs 8 and 9 above, anything done by or in relation to the Nature Conservancy Council affecting both parts of that reserve or area shall be treated as having been done by or in relation to each of the two parts separately.

(3) On and after the appointed day the new council[1] exercising functions as respects either part of a reserve or area to which this paragraph applies shall exercise those functions only after consultation with the new council exercising functions as respects the other part; and those councils may make arrangements for discharging any of those functions jointly[2].

Part III
Supplementary

13. Paragraphs 3, 4, 5, 8, 9, 10 and 12 above are without prejudice to any provision made by or under this Part of this Act in relation to any particular functions, property, rights or liabilities; and, in particular, nothing in this Schedule applies in relation to contracts of employment made by the Countryside Commission or the Nature Conservancy Council.

14. The Secretary of State may, in relation to any particular functions of the Countryside Commission or the Nature Conservancy Council, by order exclude, or modify or supplement any provision of this Schedule or make such other transitional provision as he may think necessary or expedient.

15. In this Schedule "the 1949 Act" means the National Parks and Access to the Countryside Act 1949[3] and "the 1981 Act" means the Wildlife and Countryside Act 1981[4].

---

[1] References to the new council, as regards the exercise of functions in part of a nature reserve or area of scientific interest in Scotland, are construed as references to Scottish Natural Heritage: Natural Heritage (Scotland) Act 1991 (c. 28), s. 4(8), p. 247 below. This amendment came into force on 1 April 1992: S.I. 1991/2633.

[2] Paragraph 12 extends to Scotland: Natural Heritage (Scotland) Act 1991 (c. 28), s. 4(8), p. 247 below.

[3] P. 5 above.

[4] P. 143 above.

Natural Heritage (Scotland) Act 1991

Ch. 28

Arrangement of sections

Part I: Scottish Natural Heritage

Natural Heritage (Scotland) Act 1991

An Act to establish Scottish Natural Heritage; to make provision as to the management of water resources in Scotland; and for connected purposes.

[27th June 1991[1]]

Part I: Scottish Natural Heritage

Establishment of SNH

Scottish Natural Heritage

1. (1) There shall be established a body to be known as "Scottish Natural Heritage" (in this Part of this Act referred to as "SNH") whose general aims and purposes shall be—

   (*a*) to secure the conservation and enhancement of; and

   (*b*) to foster understanding and facilitate the enjoyment of,

   the natural heritage of Scotland; and SNH shall have regard to the desirability of securing that anything done, whether by SNH or any other person, in relation to the natural heritage of Scotland is undertaken in a manner which is sustainable.

   (2) Schedule 1 to this Act[2] shall have effect with respect to the constitution and proceedings of and other matters relating to Scottish Natural Heritage.

   (3) For the purposes of this Act, "the natural heritage of Scotland" includes the flora and fauna of Scotland, its geological and physiographical features, its natural beauty and amenity; and references to "natural heritage" shall be construed accordingly[3].

Functions of SNH

General functions of Scottish Natural Heritage

2. (1) SNH[4] shall have the following general functions—

   (*a*) the provision of advice to the Secretary of State or any other minister on the development and implementation of policies for or affecting the natural heritage of Scotland[5];

   (*b*) the provision of advice and the dissemination of knowledge to any persons (including the provision and promotion of publicity and information services) about the natural heritage (including its use and enjoyment) and any matters arising from the discharge of its functions;

   (*c*) the commissioning or support (whether by financial means or otherwise) of research which in its opinion is relevant to any of its functions or, in the case of research which is directly related to its functions, if it considers it appropriate to do so initiating and carrying out such research itself;

   (*d*) the power to accept any gift or contribution made to it for the purposes of any of its functions and, subject to the terms of such gift or contribution, it shall apply the gift or contribution to those purposes;

   (*e*) the power to form or promote or join with any other person in forming or promoting companies (within the meaning of the Companies Act 1985[6]);

---

[1] The Act came into force on various dates which are noted at the sections below.

[2] P. 256 below.

[3] This section came into force on 27 November 1991: S.I.

1991/2633.

[4] "SNH" means Scottish Natural Heritage: s. 1(1).

[5] "The natural heritage of Scotland" defined by s. 1(3).

[6] 1985 c. 6.

(f) the power to form partnerships with other persons; and

(g) the power to do all such other things as are incidental or conducive to the discharge of its functions including (without prejudice to the generality of this paragraph) the power to make charges for any service undertaken by it and the power to acquire, hold and dispose of land or any interest in or right over land.

(2) SNH may, and if so requested by the Secretary of State or any general, regional or district planning authority shall, advise the Secretary of State or, as the case may be, the authority in relation to any matter arising under the Town and Country Planning (Scotland) Act 1972[1] which affects the natural heritage of Scotland[2].

Duty to take account of certain matters

3. (1) Subject to subsection (2) below, it shall be the duty of SNH[3] in exercising its functions to take such account as may be appropriate in the circumstances of—

(a) actual or possible ecological and other environmental changes to the natural heritage of Scotland[4];

(b) the needs of agriculture, fisheries and forestry;

(c) the need for social and economic development in Scotland or any part of Scotland;

(d) the need to conserve sites and landscapes of archaeological or historical interest;

(e) the interests of owners and occupiers of land; and

(f) the interests of local communities.

(2) Paragraphs (b) to (f) of subsection (1) above shall not apply as regards any function exercised by SNH in pursuance of any of paragraphs (b) to (e) of section 133(2) of the Environmental Protection Act 1990[5] (special functions to be exercised through the joint committee)[6].

Nature conservation functions

4. (1) Except as regards the joint committee within the meaning of Part VII of the Environmental Protection Act 1990[7] and subject to the following provisions of this section, Part VII of that Act shall not extend to Scotland.

(2) Sections 128(4)[8], 128(5) (in so far as it relates to Schedule 7) and 132(3)[9] of that Act shall continue to extend to Scotland and any reference in those sections to "the Councils" shall include a reference to SNH[10].

(3) Section 131 of that Act[11], in so far as it relates to the joint committee mentioned in subsection (1) above, shall continue to extend to Scotland.

(4) Section 133 of that Act[12] shall continue to extend to Scotland and—

(a) the references to "the Councils" shall include a reference to SNH; and

(b) in subsection (3) after the words "section 132 above" there shall be inserted the words "or, as the case may be, the nature conservation functions of Scottish Natural Heritage",

and in discharging its nature conservation functions, SNH shall have regard to any advice given to it by the joint committee under the said subsection (3).

---

[1] 1972 c. 52.
[2] Subsection (1) came into force on 27 November 1991; subsection (2) came into force on 1 April 1992: S.I. 1991/2633.
[3] "SNH" means Scottish Natural Heritage: s. 1(1), p. 245 above.
[4] "The natural heritage of Scotland" defined by s. 1(3), p. 245 above.
[5] P. 232 above.

[6] This section came into force on 27 November 1991: S.I. 1991/2633.
[7] P. 229 above.
[8] P. 229 above.
[9] P. 231 above.
[10] "SNH" means Scottish Natural Heritage: s. 1(1), p. 245 above.
[11] P. 230 above.
[12] P. 232 above.

(5) The amendments made by Schedule 9 to that Act to enactments extending to Scotland shall continue to extend to Scotland.

(6) SNH shall have the functions previously discharged by the Nature Conservancy Council for Scotland under the enactments amended by Schedule 2 to this Act in accordance with those enactments as so amended.

(7) SNH shall be responsible for the establishment, maintenance and management of nature reserves (within the meaning of section 15 of the National Parks and Access to the Countryside Act 1949[1]) in Scotland.

(8) Paragraph 12 of Schedule 11 to the said Act of 1990[2] shall continue to extend to Scotland; and references to a new council shall, as regards the exercise of functions in part of a nature reserve or area of scientific interest in Scotland, be construed as references to SNH.

(9) In this section "nature conservation" means the conservation of flora, fauna or geological or physiographical features.

(10) Subject to anything in this section and Schedules 2 and 10 to this Act[3], for any reference in any enactment (including an enactment contained in a local or private Act and any order, regulation or other instrument having effect by virtue of an Act) to the Nature Conservancy Council for Scotland there shall be substituted a reference to Scottish Natural Heritage[4].

Development projects or schemes

5. (1) SNH[5] may prepare proposals with respect to any area for a development project or scheme which is designed to achieve the conservation or enhancement of or which fosters understanding or enjoyment of the natural heritage of Scotland[6].

(2) Proposals prepared under subsection (1) above in relation to any area shall—

(a) in relation to that area involve the application of new or developed methods, concepts or techniques; and

(b) be designed to illustrate the appropriateness of such a project or scheme to that area or other areas of a similar nature or which present similar problems to that area.

(3) SNH may undertake, promote or coordinate, either by itself or in conjunction with any other authority or person, measures to implement the proposals mentioned in subsection (1) above.

(4) Where SNH has prepared a proposal for a development project or scheme for any area which involves the compulsory acquisition of land under subsection (6)(a) below, a compulsory purchase order for that purpose shall be subject to special parliamentary procedure in any case where an objection has been duly made by the owner of the land and has not been withdrawn.

(5) In subsection (4) above "owner" shall have the same meaning as in the Acquisition of Land (Authorisation Procedure) (Scotland) Act 1947[7].

(6) For the purposes of its function under subsection (3) above, SNH may—

(a) acquire land compulsorily;

(b) exercise any powers to carry out work or provide services or facilities conferred by the Countryside (Scotland) Act 1967[8] on local authorities or planning authorities;

(c) with the approval of the Secretary of State and the Treasury, acquire by agreement and carry on or set up and carry on, directly or through an agent, or themselves carry on as agent, any business or undertaking, and, subject to such approval, may dispose of any such business or undertaking.

---

[1] P. 14 above.
[2] P. 242 above.
[3] Schedules 2 and 10 amend legislation; the amendments made to the legislation in this manual are noted where the amendments occur.
[4] This section came into force on 1 April 1992: S.I. 1991/2633.

[5] "SNH" means Scottish Natural Heritage: s. 1(1), p. 245 above.
[6] "The natural heritage of Scotland" defined by s. 1(3), p. 245 above.
[7] 1947 c. 42.
[8] P. 108 above.

(7) The power conferred by paragraph (*b*) or subsection (6) above—

(*a*) may be exercised by SNH either on or in connection with land belonging to it, or with the consent of all persons having an interest therein, on or in connection with other land; and

(*b*) shall be exercisable in relation to land not belonging to it on such terms as may be arranged by agreement with the persons having an interest in the land.

(8) Where any person having such an interest in the land as enables him to bind the land enters into any such agreement as is mentioned in subsection (7) above, the agreement—

(*a*) in a case where the land affected by the agreement is registered in the Land Register of Scotland, may be registered in that register;

(*b*) in any other case, may be recorded in the appropriate Division of the General Register of Sasines.

and if so registered or recorded shall be enforceable at the instance of SNH against persons deriving title to the land from the person who entered into the agreement:

Provided that any such agreement shall not be enforceable against a third party who has in good faith and for value acquired right (whether completed by infeftment or not) to the land prior to the agreement being registered or recorded or against any person deriving title from such a third party.

(9) The Acquisition of Land (Authorisation Procedure) (Scotland) Act 1947 shall apply in relation to the compulsory acquisition of land under this section as if this section had been in force immediately before the commencement of that Act, and in relation to such acquisition of land, SNH shall be treated as if it were a local authority within the meaning of that Act.

(10) No land may be compulsorily acquired under this section unless the acquisition is authorised by the Secretary of State.

(11) Any power to acquire land under this section shall include power to acquire a servitude or other right in or over land by the creation of a new right[1].

....

Natural Heritage Areas

6. (1) Where it appears to SNH[2], after consultation with such persons as it thinks fit, that an area is of outstanding value to the natural heritage of Scotland[3], and that special protection measures are appropriate for it, it may recommend to the Secretary of State that the area be designated as a Natural Heritage Area.

(2) Where the Secretary of State receives a recommendation under subsection (1) above he may designate the area by a direction under this subsection as a Natural Heritage Area.

(3) Where the Secretary of State proposes to make a direction under subsection (2) above he shall publish notice of the proposal in the Edinburgh Gazette and in at least one newspaper circulating in an area which includes the proposed area.

(4) Before making a direction under subsection (2) above, the Secretary of State shall consider any representations received by him about the proposal within three months of the date which is the later of the dates on which the publication under subsection (3) above of notice relating to the proposal occurs.

(5) Where the Secretary of State makes a direction under subsection (2) above he shall publish notice of the designation in the Edinburgh Gazette and in at least one newspaper circulating in an area which includes the Area.

(6) Where it appears to SNH, after consultation with such persons as it thinks fit, that it is no longer appropriate that an area which has been designed as a Natural Heritage Area or any part of

---

[1] This section came into force on 1 April 1992: S.I. 1991/2633.
[2] "SNH" means Scottish Natural Heritage: s. 1(1), p. 245

above.
[3] "The natural heritage of Scotland" defined by s. 1(3), p. 245 above.

it should continue to be so designated it may recommend to the Secretary of State that the designation be cancelled or, as the case may be, varied.

(7) Where the Secretary of State receives a recommendation under subsection (6) above he may, by a direction under this subsection, cancel or, as the case may be, vary the designation of the Natural Heritage Area; and subsections (3) to (5) above shall apply to a direction proposed to be made under this subsection as they apply to a direction proposed to be made under subsection (2) above, and for the purposes of such application the reference in subsection (3) to the proposed area shall be construed as a reference to the Area.

(8) Section 262C of the Town and Country Planning (Scotland) Act 1972[1] (National Scenic Areas) shall be amended as follows—

(a) in subsection (3) for the words "National Scenic Area" there shall be substituted the words "Natural Heritage Area under section 6 of the Natural Heritage (Scotland) Act 1991"; and

(b) in subsection (4) for the words "National Scenic Area" there shall be substituted the words "Natural Heritage Area".

(9) Notwithstanding the repeal by section 27 of and Schedule 11 to this Act of subsections (1) and (2) of the said section 262C or the amendment by this section of subsections (3) and (4) of that section, any area which, at the date of such repeal, was designated as a National Scenic Area shall continue to be so designated and, until such designation is cancelled by a direction under the said section 262C, the provisions of that section shall continue to have effect in relation to the area as if they had not been repealed or, as the case may be, amended[2].

Powers of entry

7. (1) For the purpose of surveying land in connection with—

(a) the exercise or the proposed exercise of any of the functions of SNH[3] under this Act or any other enactment in relation to land;

(b) the making of an access order by SNH under Part II of the Countryside (Scotland) Act 1967[4]; or

(c) the acquisition under this Act or any other enactment of land or of any interest in land whether by agreement or compulsorily,

any person duly authorised in writing by SNH may, at any reasonable time, enter upon the land.

(2) For the purpose of surveying land, or of estimating its value, in connection with any claim for compensation payable by SNH by virtue of—

(a) Part II of the Countryside (Scotland) Act 1967; or

(b) this Part of this Act,

in respect of that or any other land, any person being an officer of the Valuation Office of the Inland Revenue Department or a person duly authorised in writing by SNH may, at any reasonable time, enter upon the land.

(3) A person authorised under this section to enter upon any land shall, if so required by the occupier or anyone acting on his behalf, produce evidence of his authority, and shall not demand admission as of right to any land which is occupied unless at least fourteen days' notice in writing of the intended entry has been given to the occupier and, where practicable, to the owner[5].

(4) The power conferred on SNH in connection with the exercise of its functions under section 5 of this Act shall be construed as including power to search and bore for the purpose of ascertaining the nature of the soil or subsoil or the presence of minerals.

---

[1] 1972 c. 52.
[2] This section came into force on 1 April 1992: S.I. 1991/2633.
[3] "SNH" means Scottish Natural Heritage: s. 1(1), p. 245 above.
[4] 1967 c. 86.
[5] For the service of documents see s. 25, p. 254 below.

(5) No works authorised by subsection (4) above shall be carried out unless notice of the intention to do so has been included in a notice under subsection (3) above, and if the land in question is held by any statutory undertaker and such undertaker objects to the proposed works on the ground that carrying out such works would be seriously detrimental to the carrying on of their undertaking, the works shall not be carried out except with the authority of the appropriate Minister (within the meaning of section 213(1) of the Town and Country Planning (Scotland) Act 1972)[1].

(6) Subject to subsection (7) below, if the sheriff is satisfied that there is a reasonable ground for entry upon any land which a person is entitled to enter in pursuance of this section and—

(a) that admission to that land has been refused;

(b) that such refusal is apprehended; or

(c) that the land is unoccupied or the occupier is temporarily absent,

then the sheriff may grant a warrant authorising that person to enter the land, if necessary using such force as is reasonable in all the circumstances, and a warrant issued in pursuance of this section shall continue in force until the purpose for which the entry is required has been satisfied.

(7) Without prejudice to subsection (3) above, in any case to which paragraph (a) or (b) of subsection (6) above applies the sheriff shall not grant a warrant unless he is satisfied that a notice of the intended entry has been served on the occupier of the land and, where practicable, on the owner not less than fourteen days before the demand for entry was made.

(8) A person entering upon any land by virtue of this section may take with him such other persons and such equipment as may be necessary, and on leaving any land upon which he has so entered, being either unoccupied land, or land from which the occupier is temporarily absent, shall leave it as effectively secured against unauthorised entry as he found it.

(9) A person who wilfully obstructs any person acting in the exercise of his powers under this section shall be guilty of an offence and shall be liable on summary conviction to a fine not exceeding level 3 on the standard scale[2].

(10) It shall be the duty of SNH to compensate any person who has sustained damage by reason of— ·

(a) the exercise by a person authorised by SNH of any powers conferred on him by virtue of this section; or

(b) the failure of a person so authorised to perform the duty imposed on him by subsection (8) above,

except where the damage is attributable to the fault of the person who sustained it; and any dispute as to a person's entitlement to compensation in pursuance of this subsection or as to the amount of the compensation shall be determined by arbitration.

(11) SNH shall not authorise any person to exercise a power to enter land under section 108 of the National Parks and Access to the Countryside Act 1949[3]; but nothing in this subsection shall affect the validity of anything done in pursuance of an authorisation granted before the date of coming into force of this section by the Nature Conservancy Council for Scotland[4].

Grants and loans

Government grants to Scottish Natural Heritage

8. (1) The Secretary of State may, with the approval of the Treasury, make to SNH[5] grants of such amounts as he thinks fit.

---

[1] 1972 c. 52.
[2] The present fine at level 3 is £1,000: Criminal Justice Act 1991 (c. 53), s. 17 which came into force on 1 October 1991: S.I. 1992/333; S.I. 1992/2118.
[3] P. 35 above.

[4] This section came into force on 1 April 1992: S.I. 1991/2633.
[5] "SNH" means Scottish Natural Heritage: s. 1(1), p. 245 above.

(2) A grant under this section may be made subject to such conditions (including, in particular, conditions as to the use of the money for the purposes of the Joint Nature Conservation Committee established in pursuance of section 128(4) of the Environmental Protection Act 1990[1]) as the Secretary of State may, with the approval of the Treasury, determine[2].

Grants and loans

9. (1) SNH[3] may, with the consent of or in accordance with a general authorisation given by the Secretary of State, give financial assistance by way of grant or loan (or partly in one way and partly in the other) to any person, including a public body, in respect of expenditure incurred or to be incurred by him in doing anything which, in the opinion of SNH, is conducive to the attainment of its general aims and purposes as mentioned in section 1(1) of this Act[4].

(2) No consent or general authorisation shall be given by the Secretary of State under subsection (1) above without the approval of the Treasury.

(3) On making a grant or loan SNH may impose such conditions as it thinks fit, including (in the case of a grant) conditions for repayment in specified circumstances.

(4) SNH shall exercise its powers under subsection (3) above so as to ensure that any person receiving a grant or loan under this section in respect of premises to which the public are to be admitted (on payment or otherwise) shall, in the means of access both to and within the premises, and in the parking facilities and sanitary conveniences to be available (if any), make provision, so far as it is in the circumstances both practicable and reasonable, for the needs of members of the public visiting the premises who are disabled.[5]

Miscellaneous

Reports, accounts etc.

10. (1) SNH[6] shall—

(a) furnish the Secretary of State with such returns, accounts and other information with respect to its property and activities or proposed activities as he may, from time to time, require;

(b) afford to the Secretary of State facilities for the verification of information so furnished; and

(c) for the purpose of such verification, permit any person authorised in that behalf by the Secretary of State to inspect and make copies of the accounts, books, documents or papers of SNH and to give that person such explanation of anything he is entitled to inspect as he may reasonably require.

(2) SNH shall—

(a) as soon as possible after the 31st March following the date upon which section 1 of this Act comes into force make to the Secretary of State a report on the exercise and performance of its functions to that date; and

(b) make a similar report to him as to each period of twelve months thereafter as soon as possible after the end of such period,

and a copy of every such report shall be laid before each House of Parliament by the Secretary of State:

Provided that if the date upon which the said section 1 comes into force falls on a day after 30th September and before 31st March, the first report of SNH under this section shall be for the period ending with the next succeeding 31st March[7].

---

[1] P. 229 above.
[2] This section came into force on 27 November 1991: S.I. 1991/2633.
[3] "SNH" means Scottish Natural Heritage: s. 1(1), p. 245 above.
[4] P. 245 above.

[5] This section came into force on 1 April 1992: S.I. 1991/2633.
[6] "SNH" means Scottish Natural Heritage: s. 1(1), p. 245 above.
[7] S. 1 came into force on 27 November 1991. The first report of SNH covered the period ending 31 March 1993.

(3) SNH shall keep proper accounts and other records, and shall prepare for each financial year[1] a statement of account in such form as the Secretary of State with the approval of the Treasury may direct and shall submit those statements of account to the Secretary of State at such time as he may with the approval of the Treasury direct.

(4) The Secretary of State shall, on or before the 30th November in any year, transmit to the Comptroller and Auditor General the statement of account of SNH for the financial year last ended.

(5) The Comptroller and Auditor General shall examine and certify the statements of account transmitted to him under subsection (4) above, and shall lay copies of them together with his report thereon before each House of Parliament.

(6) In this section "financial year" means the period beginning with the date upon which section 1 of this Act comes into force and ending with the 31st March following that date and each period of twelve months thereafter:

Provided that if the date upon which the said section 1 comes into force falls on a day after 30th September and before 31st March, the first financial year of SNH shall end with the next succeeding 31st March[2].

Directions by Secretary of State

11. (1) Subject to subsection (3) below, the Secretary of State may give SNH[3] directions of a general or specific character with regard to the discharge of its functions; and it shall be the duty of SNH to comply with any such directions.

(2) A direction given under this section may be varied or revoked by a subsequent direction so given.

(3) The Secretary of State shall not give directions under this section in respect of functions conferred on SNH by virtue of section 4(6) of this Act[4,5].

Advisory Committee on SSSIs

12. (1) The Secretary of State shall appoint a committee (in this section referred to as "the Committee") which shall have the function of giving advice to SNH[6] on such matters concerning areas of special scientific interest as are specified in this section.

(2) The chairman and members of the Committee shall be appointed by the Secretary of State from among persons who are not members of SNH or of any committee appointed by it having scientific qualifications and experience in relation to flora or fauna or the geological or physiographical features of land.

(3) The chairman and members of the Committee shall be appointed upon such terms and for such periods as the Secretary of State may determine and they shall be paid by SNH such remuneration and allowances as the Secretary of State may, with the consent of the Treasury, determine.

(4) The Secretary of State may, from time to time, give directions to the Committee as to its procedure.

(5) Where SNH has given notification to the owner or occupier of any land under subsection (1) of section 28 of the Wildlife and Countryside Act 1981[7] (areas of special scientific interest) that the land is or forms part of an area of special interest and has received from the owner or occupier of the land, within the time specified in subsection (2) of that section, representations or

---

[1] "Financial year" defined by subsection (6) below.

[2] This section came into force on 27 November 1991: S.I. 1991/2633.

[3] "SNH" means Scottish Natural Heritage: s. 1(1), p. 245 above.

[4] P. 247 above.

[5] This section came into force on 27 November 1991: S.I. 1991/2633.

[6] "SNH" means Scottish Natural Heritage: s. 1(1), p. 245 above.

[7] P. 168 above.

objections relating to any reason specified in the notification in pursuance of subsection (4)(*a*) of that section and the owner or occupier does not agree to withdraw such representations or objections, it shall refer the matter to the Committee.

(6) Where, as regards any land in respect of which a notification has been given under subsection (1) of the said section 28 before the commencement of this section, SNH receives representations from the owner or occupier of the land that any reason specified in the notification in pursuance of the said subsection (4)(*a*) has ceased to be valid and, within six months of such representations having been made, they have not been withdrawn—

(*a*) in the case of a notification given since the commencement of section 2 of the Wildlife and Countryside (Amendment) Act 1985[1] or in the case of a notice of proposed notification given before such commencement, where objections or representations were duly made in pursuance of subsection (2) of the said section 28 at the time the notification or, as the case may be, notice was given; and

(*b*) in any other case, where not less than 10 years have elapsed since the date the notification or, as the case may be, notice was given,

it shall refer the matter to the Committee.

(7) SNH shall not confirm a notification to which subsection (5) above applies or come to a decision on representations to which subsection (6) above applies without having received and considered the advice of the Committee on the matter; and in any case where a matter has been referred to the Committee SNH shall send a copy of the Committee's advice to any owner or occupier who has made objections or representations at the time when it notifies the owner or occupier of the confirmation of a notification or, as the case may be, its decision on the matter.

(8) Where representations are made to SNH in respect of a notification relating to any land in circumstances other than those mentioned in subsection (5) or (6) above, SNH shall refer the representations to the Committee where not less than 10 years have elapsed from whichever is the later of the date of the notification or the date of any earlier representations made in respect of the notification[2].

Access to open country

13. Part II of the Countryside (Scotland) Act 1967 shall be amended in accordance with Schedule 3 to this Act to enable SNH to enter into access agreements or to make access orders under that Part of that Act[3].

Dissolution of bodies

14. (1) On a date to be appointed by the Secretary of State—

(*a*) the Nature Conservancy Council for Scotland; and

(*b*) the Countryside Commission for Scotland,

shall each be dissolved.

(2) On the date appointed for the purposes of subsection (1) above, all heritable or moveable property wherever situated held by each of the Nature Conservancy Council for Scotland and the Countryside Commission for Scotland immediately before that date shall be transferred to and vest in SNH and all rights, liabilities and obligations of both the Nature Conservancy Council for Scotland and the Countryside Commission for Scotland to which either of them were entitled or subject immediately before that date shall, on that date, be transferred to to SNH.

---

[1] The Wildlife and Countryside (Amendment) Act 1985 came into force on 26 August 1985: s. 5(3).
[2] This section came into force on 1 April 1992: S.I. 1991/2633.
[3] This section came into force on 1 April 1992: S.I. 1991/2633.

(3) In the Countryside (Scotland) Act 1967 for the words "the Commission" where they occur there shall be substituted the words "Scottish Natural Heritage".

(4) Subject to anything in this section and Schedule 10 to this Act[1], for any reference in any enactment (including an enactment contained in a local or private Act and any order, regulation or other instrument having effect by virtue of an Act) to the Countryside Commission for Scotland there shall be substituted a reference to Scottish Natural Heritage.

(5) Schedule 4 to this Act[2] shall have effect for the purpose of making transitional provisions and savings in consequence of the dissolution of the Nature Conservancy Council for Scotland and the Countryside Commission for Scotland under subsection (1) above[3].

Parts II and III are not reproduced. Part II contains provisions relating to irrigation and Part III contains provisions relating to drought.

Part IV: General

Finance

23. There shall be defrayed out of money provided by Parliament—

    (a) any expenses of the Secretary of State incurred under this Act; and

    (b) any increase attributable to this Act in the sums so payable under any other enactment[4].

24. *S. 24, relating to rights of entry and inspection under Parts II and III, is not reproduced.*

Service of documents

25. (1) Any document required or authorised by virtue of this Act to be served on any person may be served—

    (a) by delivering it to him or by leaving it at his proper address or by sending it by post to him at that address; or

    (b) if the person is a body corporate, by serving it in accordance with paragraph (a) above on the secretary or clerk of that body; or

    (c) if the person is a partnership, by serving it in accordance with paragraph (a) above on a partner or a person having the control or management of the partnership business.

    (2) For the purpose of this section and section 7 of the Interpretation Act 1978[5] (which relates to the service of documents by post) in its application to this section, the proper address of any person on whom a document is to be served shall be his last known address, except that—

    (a) in the case of service on a body corporate or its secretary or clerk, it shall be the address of the registered or principal office of the body;

    (b) in the case of service on a partnership or a partner or a person having the control or management of a partnership business, it shall be the address of the principal office of the partnership;

    and for the purposes of this subsection the principal office of a company registered outside the United Kingdom or of a partnership carrying on business outside the United Kingdom is its principal office within the United Kingdom.

---

[1] Schedule 10 amends legislation; the amendments made to the legislation in this manual are noted where the amendments occur.

[2] P. 259 below.

[3] Subsections (1), (2) and (5) came into force on 27 November 1991; subsections (3) and (4) came into force on 1 April 1992: S.I. 1991/2633.

[4] This section came into force on 1 October 1991: S.I. 1991/2187.

[5] 1978 c. 30.

(3) If a person to be served by virtue of this Act with any document by another has specified to that other an address within the United Kingdom other than his proper address (as determined in pursuance of subsection (2) above) as the one at which he or someone on his behalf will accept documents of the same description as that document, that address shall also be treated as his proper address for the purpose of this section and for the purpose of the said section 7 in its application to this section.

(4) Where under any provision of this Act any document is required to be served on the owner or on the occupier of any land then—

(a) if the name or address of the owner or, as the case may be, of the occupier of the land cannot after reasonable inquiry be ascertained; or

(b) in the case of service on the occupier, if the land appears to be or is unoccupied,

that document may be served either by leaving it in the hands of a person who is or appears to be resident or employed on the land or by leaving it conspicuously affixed to some building or object on the land.

(5) This section shall not apply to any document in relation to the service of which provision is made by rules of court[1].

Offences by persons other than natural persons

26. (1) Where an offence under this Act which has been committed by a body corporate is proved to have been committed with the consent or connivance of, or to be attributable to the negligence of, any director, manager, secretary or other similar officer of the body corporate or any person who was purporting to act in any such capacity, he as well as the body corporate shall be guilty of that offence and be liable to be proceeded against and punished accordingly.

(2) Where the affairs of a body corporate are managed by its members subsection (1) above shall apply in relation to the acts and defaults of a member in connection with his functions of management as if he were a director of the body corporate.

(3) Where an offence under this Act is committed by a partnership or by an unincorporated association (other than a partnership) and is proved to have been committed with the consent or connivance of, or to be attributable to the negligence of, a partner in the partnership or, as the case may be, a person concerned in the management or control of the association, he (as well as the partnership or association) shall be guilty of the offence and shall be liable to be proceeded against and punished accordingly[2].

27. *S. 27, relating to consequential and miscellaneous amendments and repeals, is not reproduced.*

Short title, commencement and extent

28. (1) This Act may be cited as the Natural Heritage (Scotland) Act 1991.

(2) This Act shall come into force on such date as the Secretary of State may, by order made by statutory instrument appoint and different days may be so appointed for different provisions or for different purposes.

(3) An order under subsection (2) above may make such transitional provision as appears to the Secretary of State necessary or expedient in connection with the provision brought into force by the order.

(4) Subject to subsection (5) below, this Act extends to Scotland only.

[1] This section came into force on 1 October 1991: S.I. 1991/2187.   [2] This section came into force on 1 October 1991: S.I. 1991/2187.

(5) Section 4(2)[1] and (4) of this Act and so much of sections 4(10) and 27 of and Schedules 2, 10 and 11 to this Act as relates to enactments extending to England and Wales shall extend also to England and Wales[2].

SCHEDULES

SCHEDULE 1

(Section 1)

CONSTITUTION AND PROCEEDINGS OF SCOTTISH NATURAL HERITAGE

Incorporation and status

1. SNH[3] shall be a body corporate and shall have a common seal.

2. (1) SNH shall not—
    (a) be regarded as a servant or agent of the Crown;
    (b) have any status, immunity or privilege of the Crown;
    (c) be exempt from any tax, duty, rate, levy or other charge whatsoever whether general or local,
    and its property shall not be regarded as property of, or held on behalf of, the Crown.
    (2) Sub-paragraph (1) above shall have effect subject to paragraph 19 below.

Membership

3. The members of SNH shall be not less than eight, nor more than twelve, persons appointed by the Secretary of State.

4. In making appointments under paragraph 3 above, the Secretary of State shall have regard to the desirability of ensuring that the membership of SNH contains at any time, so far as is practicable, persons of knowledge or experience relevant to the principal areas of activity of SNH.

5. The Secretary of State shall satisfy himself—
    (a) before he appoints a person to be a member that the person will have no such financial or other interest as is likely to affect prejudicially the performance of his functions as a member: and
    (b) from time to time that each person so appointed continues, and has continued, to have no such interest.

6. A person in respect of whom the Secretary of State requires to be satisfied as is mentioned in paragraph 5 above shall, whenever requested by the Secretary of State to do so, furnish the Secretary of State with such information as the Secretary of State may consider necessary for the purposes of fulfilling that requirement.

7. Subject to this paragraph and paragraphs 9 and 10 below, each member of SNH—
    (a) shall hold and vacate office in accordance with the terms of his appointment;
    (b) may, by notice in writing to the Secretary of State, resign his membership; and
    (c) after ceasing to hold office shall be eligible for reappointment as a member.

---

[1] P. 246 above.
[3] This section came into force on 27 November 1991: S.I. 1991/2633.

[3] "SNH" means Scottish Natural Heritage: s. 1(1), p. 245 above.

8. The Secretary of State may, by order made by statutory instrument subject to annulment in pursuance of a resolution of either House of Parliament, amend paragraph 3 above so as to substitute for the numbers for the time being specified as, respectively, the minimum and maximum membership of SNH such other numbers as he thinks fit.

9. The Secretary of State may remove a member from office if he is satisfied that the member—

(a) has been adjudged bankrupt, has made an arrangement with his creditors, has had his estate sequestrated or has granted a trust deed for his creditors or a composition contract;

(b) is incapacitated by physical or mental illness;

(c) has been absent from meetings of SNH for a period longer than three months without the permission of SNH; or

(d) is otherwise unable or unfit to discharge his functions as a member or is unsuitable to continue as a member.

Chairman and Deputy Chairman

10. (1) The Secretary of State shall appoint one of the members of SNH to be chairman and, after consulting the chairman, shall appoint one of the members to be deputy chairman.

(2) The chairman and deputy chairman shall hold and vacate office in terms of their appointment.

(3) A member of SNH who is chairman or deputy chairman may resign his office by notice in writing to the Secretary of State; but if the chairman or deputy chairman ceases to be a member of SNH (whether or not on giving notice under paragraph 7(b) above) he shall cease to be its chairman or, as the case may be, deputy chairman.

Remuneration and allowances

11. (1) SNH shall—

(a) pay to its members such remuneration and allowances (if any); and

(b) as regards any member or former member in whose case the Secretary of State may so determine, pay such pension, allowance or gratuity to or in respect of him, or make such payments towards the provision of such pension, allowance or gratuity,

as the Secretary of State may, with the approval of the Treasury, determine.

(2) If a person ceases to be a member of SNH, and it appears to the Secretary of State that there are special circumstances which make it right that he should receive compensation, the Secretary of State may require SNH to pay to that person a sum of such amount as the Secretary of State may, with the approval of the Treasury, determine.

Staff

12. (1) There shall be a chief officer of SNH.

(2) The Secretary of State shall, after consultation with the chairman or person designated to be chairman (if there is a person holding or designated to hold that office), make the first appointment of the chief officer of SNH on such terms and conditions as he may, with the consent of the Treasury, determine; and thereafter SNH may, with the approval of the Secretary of State, make subsequent appointments to that office on such terms and conditions as it may, with the approval of the Secretary of State given with the consent of the Treasury, determine.

13. Subject to paragraph 3 of Schedule 4 to this Act, SNH may appoint on such terms and conditions as it may, with the approval of the Secretary of State given with the consent of the Treasury, determine such other employees as it thinks fit.

14. (1) SNH shall, in the case of such of its employees or former employees as it may, with the approval of the Secretary of State given with the consent of the Treasury, determine—

(a) pay such pensions, allowances or gratuities to or in respect of those employees;

(*b*) make such payments towards provision of such pensions, allowances or gratuities; or

(*c*) provide and maintain such schemes (whether contributory or not) for the payment of such pensions allowances or gratuities,

as it may, with the approval of the Secretary of State given with the consent of the Treasury, determine.

(2) The reference in sub-paragraph (1) above to pensions, allowances or gratuities in respect of employees of SNH includes a reference to pensions, allowances or gratuities by way of compensation to or in respect of any such employee who suffers loss of office or employment.

(3) If an employee of SNH becomes a member of SNH and was by reference to his employment by SNH a participant in a pension scheme established and administered by it for the benefit of its employees—

(*a*) SNH may determine that his service as a member shall be treated for the purposes of the scheme as service as an employee of SNH whether or not any benefits are to be payable to or in respect of him by virtue of paragraph 11 above; but

(*b*) if SNH determines as aforesaid, any discretion as to the benefits payable to or in respect of him which the scheme confers on SNH shall be exercised only with the consent of the Secretary of State given with the approval of the Treasury.

Proceedings

15. (1) SNH may regulate its own procedure (including making provision in relation to the quorum for its meetings and the meetings of any committee appointed by it).

(2) The proceedings of SNH and of any committee appointed by it shall not be invalidated by any vacancy amongst its members or the members of such committee or by any defect in the appointment of such member.

Committees

16. (1) SNH may appoint persons who are not members of it to be members of any committee established by it:

Provided that no such committee shall consist entirely of persons who are not members of SNH.

(2) SNH shall pay to a person so appointed such remuneration and allowances (if any) as the Secretary of State may, with the consent of the Treasury, determine.

(3) SNH may regulate the procedure of any committee established by it and any such committee shall comply with any directions given to them by it.

Delegation of powers

17. (1) Anything authorised or required by or under any enactment to be done by SNH may be done by any of its committees which, or by any of its members or employees who, is authorised (generally or specifically) for the purpose by SNH.

(2) Nothing in sub-paragraph (1) above shall prevent SNH from doing anything that a committee, member or employee has been authorised to do.

Documents

18. *Repealed by the Requirements of Writing (Scotland) Act 1995 (c. 7), s. 14(2), sch. 5. This amendment came into force on 1 August 1995: s. 15(2).*

Land

19. (1) For the purposes of the application of any enactment or rule of law to land an interest in which belongs to SNH, and which is managed as a nature reserve, SNH shall be deemed to be a Government department; and any other land occupied by it shall be deemed, for the purpose of any rate on property, to be property occupied by or on behalf of the Crown for public purposes.

(2) In sub-paragraph (1) above "interest" and "land" have the meanings assigned to them by section 114 of the National Parks and Access to the Countryside Act 1949[1,2].

SCHEDULE 4

(Section 14)

TRANSITIONAL ARRANGEMENTS ON THE DISSOLUTION OF EXISTING BODIES

Preliminary

1. In this Schedule—

"the appointed day" means the date appointed for the purposes of section 14(1) of this Act;

"the Commission" means the Countryside Commission for Scotland;

"the Council" means the Nature Conservancy Council for Scotland;

"relevant" in relation to anything done by or in relation to the Commission or, as the case may be, the Council before the appointed day, means anything which, if it were to be done on or after the appointed day, would be done by or in relation to SNH.

Preparation of accounts and reports

2. (1) The requirement imposed on—

(a) the Council by paragraphs 20 and 21 of Schedule 6 to the Environmental Protection Act 1990[3]; and

(b) the Commission by section 71 of the Countryside (Scotland) Act 1967,

to prepare accounts and a report shall become, with effect from the appointed day, a requirement imposed on SNH[4].

(2) Where the appointed day is a date other than 31st March, the requirement—

(a) as regards the accounts and report of the Council; and

(b) as regards the accounts of the Commission,

shall relate to the preparation of accounts and a report or, as the case may be, accounts for the period beginning with 1st April immediately preceding the appointed day and ending on that day, and for the reference in the said paragraph 21 and section 71 to 30th November there may be substituted such other date as the Secretary of State may, in the order appointing the appointed day, determine.

(3) Where the appointed day is a date other than 31st December, the requirement as regards the report of the Commission shall relate to the preparation of the report for the period beginning with 1st January immediately preceding the appointed day and ending on that day.

....

Paragraphs 3 to 6, which are not reproduced, relate to the employment by SNH of persons formerly employed by the Countryside Commission for Scotland and the Nature Conservancy Council for Scotland.

....

Continuity of exercise of functions

7. (1) Any relevant[5] thing done by or in relation to the Council or, as the case may be, the Commission before the appointed day shall, so far as is required for continuing its effect on and after that date, have effect as if done by or in relation to SNH.

(2) Any relevant thing which, immediately before the appointed day, is in the process of being done by or in relation to the Council or, as the case may be, the Commission may be continued by or in relation to SNH.

---

[1] P. 38 above.
[2] This schedule came into force on 27 November 1991: S.I. 1991/2633.
[3] P. 237 above.

[4] "SNH" means Scottish Natural heritage: s. 1(1), p. 245 above.
[5] "Relevant" defined by para. 1 above.

Construction of references to the Council and the Commission

8. (1) This paragraph applies to any agreement, any instrument and any other document, subsisting immediately before the appointed day which refers (in whatever terms) to the Council or, as the case may be, the Commission.

(2) Any agreement, instrument or other document to which this paragraph applies shall have effect on and after the appointed day with the substitution—

(a) for any reference to the Council or, as the case may be, the Commission of a reference to SNH;

(b) for any reference in general terms to members of or to persons employed by or agents of the Council, or as the case may be, the Commission of a reference to members of or persons employed by or agents of SNH; and

(c) for any reference to a member or officer of the Council or, as the case may be, the Commission of a reference to such person as SNH may appoint or, in default of appointment, to the member or officer of SNH who corresponds as nearly as may be to the member or officer in question.

9. The Secretary of State may, by order, make such consequential modifications of any provision of any local or private Act passed, or subordinate legislation made, before the appointed day which refers to the Council or, as the case may be, the Commission as appear to him to be necessary or expedient.

Supplementary

10. (1) The Secretary of State may, in relation to any particular functions of the Council or the Commission, by order exclude or modify or supplement any provision of this Schedule or make such other transitional provision as he may think necessary or expedient.

(2) Nothing in this paragraph or in paragraph 8 or 9 above shall apply in relation to contracts of employment made by the Council or the Commission[1].

[1] This schedule came into force on 27 November 1991: S.I. 1991/2633.

Deer Act 1991

Ch. 54

Deer Act 1991

An Act to consolidate certain enactments relating to deer with amendments to give effect to recommendations of the Law Commission.

[25th July 1991[1]]

Offences relating to deer

Poaching of deer

1. (1) Subject to subsection (3) below, if any person enters any land without the consent of the owner or occupier or other lawful authority in search or pursuit of any deer[2] with the intention of taking, killing or injuring it, he shall be guilty of an offence.

    (2) Subject to subsection (3) below, if any person while on any land—

    (*a*) intentionally takes, kills or injures, or attempts to take, kill or injure, any deer,

    (*b*) searches for or pursues any deer with the intention of taking, killing or injuring it, or

    (*c*) removes the carcase of any deer,

    without the consent of the owner or occupier of the land or other lawful authority, he shall be guilty of an offence.

    (3) A person shall not be guilty of an offence under subsection (1) or subsection (2) above by reason of anything done in the belief that—

    (*a*) he would have the consent of the owner or occupier of the land if the owner or occupier knew of his doing it and the circumstances of it; or

    (*b*) he has other lawful authority to do it.

    (4) If any authorised person suspects with reasonable cause that any person is committing or has committed an offence under subsection (1) or subsection (2) above on any land, he may require that person—

    (*a*) to give his full name and address; and

    (*b*) to quit that land forthwith;

    and any person who fails to comply with a requirement under this subsection shall be guilty of an offence.

    (5) In subsection (4) above "authorised person", in relation to any land, means the owner or occupier of the land or any person authorised by the owner or occupier, and includes any person having the right to take or kill deer on the land.

....

Taking or killing of certain deer in close season

2. (1) Subject to sections 6 to 8 below[3] and to subsection (3) below, if any person takes or intentionally kills any deer of a species and description mentioned in Schedule 1 to this Act[4] during the prescribed close season, he shall be guilty of an offence.

    (2) The prescribed close season, in relation to a particular deer, is the close season prescribed by Schedule 1 to this Act in relation to deer of that species and description.

    (3) Where—

---

[1] This Act came into force on 25 October 1991: s. 18(3), p. 270 below.

[2] "Deer" defined by s. 16, p. 270 below.

[3] Pp. 264–266 below.

[4] P. 271 below.

(a) any person, by way of business, keeps deer[1] on land enclosed by a deer-proof barrier for the production of meat or other foodstuffs or skins or other by-products, or as breeding stock, and

(b) those deer are conspicuously marked in such a way as to identify them as deer kept by that person as mentioned in the preceding paragraph,

the killing of any of those deer by that person, or by any servant or agent of that person authorised by him for the purpose, shall not constitute an offence under this section.

(4) The Secretary of State may by order amend Schedule 1 to this Act by the addition of any species not mentioned in that Schedule and of a close season for any description of deer of that species, or by varying or deleting any such addition.

(5) Before making any order under subsection (4) above the Secretary of State shall consult any organisations that appear to him to represent persons likely to be interested in or affected by the order.

Taking or killing of deer at night

3. Subject to sections 6[2] and 8[3] below, if any person takes or intentionally kills any deer[4] between the expiry of the first hour after sunset and the beginning of the last hour before sunrise, he shall be guilty of an offence.

Use of prohibited weapons and other articles

4. (1) Subject to sections 6[5] and 8[6] below, if any person—

(a) sets in position any article which is a trap, snare, or poisoned or stupefying bait and is of such a nature and so placed as to be calculated to cause bodily injury to any deer[7] coming in contact with it, or

(b) uses for the purpose of taking or killing any deer any trap, snare or poisoned or stupefying bait, or any net,

he shall be guilty of an offence.

(2) Subject to sections 6 to 8 below, if any person uses for the purpose of taking or killing or injuring any deer—

(a) any firearm[8] or ammunition[9] mentioned in Schedule 2 to this Act[10],

(b) any arrow, spear or similar missile, or

(c) any missile, whether discharged from a firearm or otherwise, carrying or containing any poison, stupefying drug or muscle-relaxing agent,

he shall be guilty of an offence.

(3) The Secretary of State may by order amend Schedule 2 to this Act by adding any firearm or ammunition or by altering the description of, or deleting, any firearm or ammunition for the time being mentioned in that Schedule.

(4) Subject to subsection (5) below, if any person—

(a) discharges any firearm, or projects any missile, from any mechanically propelled vehicle[11] at any deer, or

(b) uses any mechanically propelled vehicle for the purpose of driving deer,

he shall be guilty of an offence.

---

[1] "Deer" defined by s. 16, p. 270 below.
[2] P. 264 below.
[3] P. 265 below.
[4] "Deer" defined by s. 16, p. 270 below.
[5] P. 264 below.
[6] P. 265 below.

[7] "Deer" defined by s. 16, p. 270 below.
[8] "Firearm" defined by s. 16, p. 270 below.
[9] "Ammunition" defined by s. 16, p. 270 below.
[10] P. 271 below.
[11] "Vehicle" defined by s. 16, p. 270 below.

(5) An act which, apart from this subsection, would constitute an offence under subsection (4) above shall not constitute such an offence if it is done—

(a) by, or with the written authority of, the occupier of any enclosed land where deer are usually kept; and

(b) in relation to any deer on that land.

Attempts to commit certain offences, etc.

5. (1) Any person who attempts to commit an offence under any of sections 2 to 4 above[1] shall be guilty of an offence.

(2) If any person, for the purpose of committing an offence under any of sections 2 to 4 above, has in his possession—

(a) any article the use of which is prohibited by section 4(1)(b), section 4(2)(b) or section 4(2)(c) above, or

(b) any firearm[2] or ammunition[3],

he shall be guilty of an offence.

General exceptions to certain provisions of this Act

6. (1) Nothing in section 2[4] or section 3[5] above shall make unlawful anything done in pursuance of a requirement by the Minister of Agriculture, Fisheries and Food under section 98 of the Agriculture Act 1947[6].

(2) A person shall not be guilty of an offence under section 2 or section 3 above by reason of any act done for the purpose of preventing the suffering of an injured or diseased deer[7].

(3) A person shall not be guilty of an offence under section 4(1)(a)[8] or section 4(1)(b) above by reason of setting in position, or using, any trap or net for the purpose of preventing the suffering of an injured or diseased deer.

(4) A person shall not be guilty of an offence under section 4(2)(a) above by reason of the use of any smooth-bore gun for the purpose of killing any deer if he shows that the deer had been so seriously injured otherwise than by his unlawful act, or was in such a condition, that to kill it was an act of mercy.

(5) A person shall not be guilty of an offence under section 4(2)(a) above by reason of the use as a slaughtering instrument, for the purpose of killing any deer, of a smooth-bore gun which—

(a) is of not less gauge than 12 bore;

(b) has a barrel less than 24 inches (609.6 millimetres) in length; and

(c) is loaded with a cartridge purporting to contain shot none of which is less than .203 inches (5.16 millimetres) in diameter (that is to say, size AAA or any larger size).

Exceptions for occupiers etc. of land where deer are

7. (1) Subject to subsection (3) below, a person to whom this section applies shall not be guilty of an offence under section 2 above[9] by reason of—

(a) the taking or killing of any deer[10] by means of shooting, or

---

[1] Pp. 262–264 above.
[2] "Firearm" defined by s. 16, p. 270 below.
[3] "Ammunition" defined by s. 16, p. 270 below.
[4] P. 262 above.
[5] P. 263 above.
[6] 1947 c. 48.
[7] "Deer" defined by s. 16, p. 270 below.
[8] P. 263 above.
[9] P. 262 above.
[10] "Deer" defined by s. 16, p. 270 below.

(*b*) the injuring of any deer by means of shooting in an attempt to take or kill it,

on any cultivated land, pasture or enclosed woodland.

(2) Subject to subsection (3) below, a person to whom this section applies shall not be guilty of an offence under section 4(2)(*a*) above[1] by reason of the use, for the purpose of taking or killing any deer on any land, of any smooth-bore gun of not less gauge than 12 bore which is loaded with—

(*a*) a cartridge containing a single non-spherical projectile weighing not less than 22.68 grammes (350 grains); or

(*b*) a cartridge purporting to contain shot each of which is .203 inches (5.16 millimetres) in diameter (that is to say, size AAA).

(3) A person to whom this section applies shall not be entitled to rely on the defence provided by subsection (1) or subsection (2) above as respects anything done in relation to any deer on any land unless he shows that—

(*a*) he had reasonable grounds for believing that deer of the same species were causing, or had caused, damage to crops, vegetables, fruit, growing timber or any other form of property on the land;

(*b*) it was likely that further damage would be so caused and any such damage was likely to be serious; and

(*c*) his action was necessary for the purpose of preventing any such damage.

(4) The persons to whom this section applies are—

(*a*) the occupier of the land on which the action is taken;

(*b*) any member of the occupier's household normally resident on the occupier's land, acting with the written authority of the occupier;

(*c*) any person in the ordinary service of the occupier on the occupier's land, acting with the written authority of the occupier; and

(*d*) any person having the right to take or kill deer on the land on which the action is taken or any person acting with the written authority of a person having that right.

(5) The Secretary of State and the agriculture Minister[2] acting jointly may by order, either generally or in relation to any area or any species and description of deer specified in the order,—

(*a*) repeal subsection (2) above or amend it by adding any firearm[3] or ammunition[4] or by altering the description of, or deleting, any firearm or ammunition for the time being mentioned in it;

(*b*) amend subsection (3) above by adding any further conditions which must be satisfied or by varying or deleting any conditions so added.

(6) Before making any order under subsection (5) above the Secretary of State and the agriculture Minister shall consult organisations that appear to them to represent persons likely to be interested in or affected by the order.

(7) In this section "agriculture Minister" means—

(*a*) in relation to England, the Minister of Agriculture, Fisheries and Food; and

(*b*) in relation to Wales, the Secretary of State.

....

Exceptions for persons licensed by the Nature Conservancy Council for England or the Countryside Council for Wales

8. (1) A licence may be granted to any person by the Nature Conservancy Council for England[5] exempting that person, and any persons acting with his written authority, from sections 2 to 4[6]

[1] P. 263 above.
[2] "Agriculture Minister" defined by subsection (7) below.
[3] "Firearm" defined by s. 16, p. 270 below.
[4] "Ammunition" defined by s. 16, p. 270 below.
[5] The Nature Conservancy Council for England, also

known as English Nature, is established by the Environmental Protection Act 1990 (c. 43), s. 128, p. 229 above.
[6] Pp. 262–264 above.

above in respect of any of the acts specified in subsection (3) below which are done in England for the purpose of removing deer[1] from one area to another or of taking deer alive for scientific or educational purposes.

(2) A licence may be granted to any person by the Countryside Council for Wales[2] exempting that person, and any persons acting with his written authority, from sections 2 to 4 above[3] in respect of any of the acts specified in subsection (3) below which are done in Wales for the purpose of removing deer from one area to another or of taking deer alive for scientific or educational purposes.

(3) The acts referred to in subsections (1) and (2) above are—

(a) using any net, trap, stupefying drug or muscle-relaxing agent of a type authorised by the licence;

(b) using any missile carrying or containing such stupefying drug or muscle-relaxing agent and discharging any such missile by any means authorised by the licence.

(4) A licence granted under subsection (1) above may be revoked at any time by the Nature Conservancy Council for England and a licence granted under subsection (2) above may be revoked at any time by the Countryside Council for Wales; and a licence granted under either of those subsections may be granted subject to conditions.

(5) Without prejudice to any other liability to a penalty which he may have incurred under this or any other Act, any person who contravenes or fails to comply with any condition imposed on the grant of a licence under subsection (1) or subsection (2) above shall be guilty of an offence.

....

Penalties for offences relating to deer

9. (1) Subject to subsection (2) below, a person guilty of an offence under any of the preceding provisions of this Act shall be liable on summary conviction to a fine not exceeding level 4 on the standard scale[4] or to imprisonment for a term not exceeding three months or to both.

(2) Where an offence under any of the preceding provisions of this Act was committed in respect of more than one deer the maximum fine which may be imposed under subsection (1) above shall be determined as if the person convicted had been convicted of a separate offence in respect of each deer.

Offences relating to venison etc.

Offences relating to sale and purchase etc. of venison

10. (1) If any person who is not a licensed game dealer[5]—

(a) at any time during the prohibited period sells or offers or exposes for sale[6], or has in his possession for sale, any venison[7] to which this paragraph applies, or

(b) at any time sells or offers or exposes for sale any venison otherwise than to a licensed game dealer,

he shall be guilty of an offence and liable on summary conviction to a fine not exceeding level 3 on the standard scale[8].

(2) Paragraph (a) of subsection (1) above applies to any venison which comes from a deer of a species and description in relation to which a close season is prescribed by Schedule 1 to this Act[9]; and the prohibited period, in relation to any such venison, is the period beginning with the expiry of the tenth day, and ending with the expiry of the last day, of that close season.

---

[1] "Deer" defined by s. 16, p. 270 below.
[2] The Countryside Council for Wales is established by the Environmental Protection Act 1990 (c. 43), s. 128, p. 229 above.
[3] Pp. 262–264 above.
[4] The present fine at level 4 on the standard scale is £2,500: Criminal Justice Act 1991 (c. 53), s. 17 which came into force on 1 October 1992: S.I. 1992/333.

[5] "Licensed game dealer" defined by subsection (5) below.
[6] "Sale" and "sell" defined by subsection (5) below.
[7] "Venison" defined by s. 16, p. 270 below.
[8] The present fine at level 3 on the standard scale is £1,000: Criminal Justice Act 1991 (c. 53), s. 17 which came into force on 1 October 1992: S.I. 1992/333.
[9] P. 271 below.

(3) If any person—

(a) sells or offers or exposes for sale, or has in his possession for sale, or

(b) purchases[1] or offers to purchase or receives,

any venison which comes from a deer to which this subsection applies, he shall be guilty of an offence and liable on summary conviction to a fine not exceeding level 4 on the standard scale[2] or to imprisonment for a term not exceeding three months or to both.

(4) Subsection (3) above applies to any deer—

(a) which has been taken or killed in circumstances which constitute an offence under any of the preceding provisions of this Act; and

(b) which the person concerned knows or has reason to believe has been so taken or killed.

(5) In this section—

"licensed game dealer" means a person licensed to deal in game under the Game Act 1831[3] and the Game Licences Act 1860[4], and includes a servant of such a person; and

"sale" includes barter and exchange, and "sell" and "purchase" shall be construed accordingly.

Licensed game dealers to keep records

11. (1) Every licensed game dealer[5] who sells or offers or exposes for sale[6], or has in his possession for sale, any venison[7] shall—

(a) in accordance with the provisions of this section keep or cause to be kept a book containing records (in this section referred to as a "record book"); and

(b) subject to subsection (3) below, enter or cause to be entered in his record book forthwith full particulars of all his purchases and receipts of venison;

and, subject to subsection (2) below, those records shall be in the form set out in Schedule 3 to this Act[8] or a form substantially to the same effect.

(2) The Secretary of State may by order vary the form in which records are required to be kept under this section.

(3) Where a licensed game dealer has purchased[9] or received venison from another licensed game dealer, or from a venison dealer licensed under Part IIIA of the Deer (Scotland) Act 1959[10], he need record in his record book only—

(a) that the venison was so purchased or received;

(b) the name and address of the other licensed game dealer or the venison dealer so licensed;

(c) the date when the venison was so purchased or received; and

(d) the total weight of the venison.

(4) Any authorised officer[11], on producing, if so required, his written authority, and any constable, may inspect—

(a) the record book of a licensed game dealer,

(b) any venison in the licensed game dealer's possession or under his control, or on premises or in vehicles[12] under his control, and

---

[1] "Purchase" defined by subsection (5) below.

[2] The present fine at level 4 on the standard scale is £2,500: Criminal Justice Act 1991 (c. 53), s. 17 which came into force on 1 October 1992: S.I. 1992/333.

[3] 1831 c. 32.

[4] 1860 c. 90.

[5] "Licensed game dealer" defined by s. 10(5) above: subsection (9) below.

[6] "Sale" and "sell" defined by s. 10(5) above: subsection

(9) below.

[7] "Venison" defined by s. 16, p. 270 below.

[8] P. 272 below.

[9] "Purchase" defined by s. 10(5) above: subsection (9) below.

[10] P. 54 above.

[11] "Authorised officer" defined by subsection (9) below.

[12] "Vehicle" defined by s. 16, p. 270 below.

(c) any invoices, consignment notes, receipts and other documents which relate to entries in the record book (including, where the originals are not available, copies),

and may take copies of, or extracts from, the record book and any such documents.

(5) A record book shall be kept until the end of the period of three years beginning with the day on which the last entry was made in the book, and any such documents as are mentioned in subsection (4)(c) above shall be kept until the end of the period of three years beginning with the date of the entry to which they relate.

(6) Any licensed game dealer who, without reasonable excuse, fails to comply with the provisions of this section shall be guilty of an offence.

(7) If any person—

(a) intentionally obstructs any authorised officer or constable making an inspection under this section, or

(b) knowingly or recklessly makes or causes to be made in a record book any entry which is false or misleading in a material particular,

he shall be guilty of an offence.

(8) A person guilty of an offence under this section shall be liable on summary conviction to a fine not exceeding level 2 on the standard scale[1].

(9) In this section—

"authorised officer" means any officer of the council of a Welsh county or county borough,[2] district or London borough, or of the Common Council of the City of London, who is authorised by them in writing to exercise the powers conferred by this section;

"licensed game dealer" has the same meaning as in section 10 above; and

"sale" has the same meaning as in that section, and "sell" and "purchase" shall be construed accordingly.

Enforcement etc.

Powers of search, arrest and seizure

12. (1) If a constable suspects with reasonable cause that any person is committing or has committed an offence under this Act, the constable may without warrant—

(a) stop and search that person if the constable suspects with reasonable cause that evidence of the commission of the offence is to be found on that person;

(b) search or examine any vehicle[3], animal, weapon or other thing which that person may then be using if the constable suspects with reasonable cause that evidence of the commission of the offence is to be found on that vehicle, animal, weapon or other thing;

(c) seize and detain for the purposes of proceedings under this Act anything which is evidence of the commission of the offence and any deer[4], venison[5], vehicle, animal, weapon or other thing which is liable to be forfeited under section 13 below.

(2) For the purposes of—

(a) exercising the powers conferred by subsection (1) above, or

(b) arresting a person, in accordance with section 25 of the Police and Criminal Evidence Act 1984[6] (general arrest conditions), for an offence under this Act,

a constable may enter any land other than a dwelling-house.

---

[1] The present fine at level 2 on the standard scale is £500: Criminal Justice Act 1991 (c. 53), s. 17 which came into force on 1 October 1992: S.I. 1992/333.
[2] Words "Welsh county or county borough," inserted by the Local Government (Wales) Act 1994 (c. 19), s. 66(6), sch. 16, para. 92. It is planned that this amendment will come into force on 1 April 1996.
[3] "Vehicle" defined by s. 16, p. 270 below.
[4] "Deer" defined by s. 16, p. 270 below.
[5] "Venison" defined by s. 16, p. 270 below.
[6] 1984 c. 60.

(3) A constable may sell any deer or venison seized under this section and the net proceeds of the sale shall be liable to be detained and forfeited in the same manner as the deer or venison sold; but he shall not be subject to any liability on account of his neglect or failure to exercise the powers conferred on him by this subsection.

Forfeitures and disqualifications

13. (1) The court by which a person is convicted of any offence under this Act may order the forfeiture of—

(a) any deer[1] or venison[2] in respect of which the offence was committed or which was found in that person's possession;

(b) any vehicle[3], animal, weapon or other thing which was used to commit the offence or which was capable of being used to take, kill or injure deer and was found in his possession.

(2) Where the offence of which the person is convicted is an offence under any of sections 1[4], 10[5] and 11[6] above or under subsection (3)(c) below, the court (without prejudice to its powers under subsection (1) above)—

(a) may disqualify that person for holding or obtaining a licence to deal in game for such period as the court thinks fit; and

(b) may cancel any firearm or shotgun certificate held by him.

(3) Where the court cancels a firearm or shotgun certificate under subsection (2)(b) above—

(a) the court shall cause notice in writing of that fact to be sent to the chief officer of police by whom the certificate was granted; and

(b) the chief officer of police shall by notice in writing require the holder of the certificate to surrender it; and

(c) if the holder fails to surrender the certificate within twenty-one days from the date of that requirement, he shall be guilty of an offence and liable on summary conviction to a fine not exceeding level 2 on the standard scale[7].

Offences by bodies corporate

14. (1) Where an offence under any of sections 1[8], 10[9] and 11[10] above which has been committed by a body corporate is proved to have been committed with the consent or connivance of, or to be attributable to any neglect on the part of, any director, manager, secretary or other similar officer of the body corporate or any person who was purporting to act in any such capacity, he as well as the body corporate shall be guilty of that offence and be liable to be proceeded against and punished accordingly.

(2) Where the affairs of a body corporate are managed by its members, subsection (1) above shall apply in relation to the acts and defaults of a member in connection with his functions of management as if he were a director of the body corporate.

Supplementary

Orders

15. (1) Any power to make orders under this Act shall be exercisable by statutory instrument.

---

[1] "Deer" defined by s. 16, p. 270 below.
[2] "Venison" defined by s. 16, p. 270 below.
[3] "Vehicle" defined by s. 16, p. 270 below.
[4] P. 262 above.
[5] P. 266 above.
[6] P. 267 above.

[7] The present fine at level 2 on the standard scale is £500: Criminal Justice Act 1991 (c. 53), s. 17 which came into force on 1 October 1992: S.I. 1992/333.
[8] P. 262 above.
[9] P. 266 above.
[10] P. 267 above.

(2) A statutory instrument containing an order made under any of sections 2(4)[1], 4(3)[2] and 11(2)[3] above shall be subject to annulment in pursuance of a resolution of either House of Parliament.

(3) No order shall be made under section 7(5)[4] above unless a draft of the order has been laid before and approved by a resolution of each House of Parliament.

Interpretation

16. In this Act, unless the context otherwise requires,—

"ammunition" and "firearm" have the same meaning as in the Firearms Act 1968[5];

"deer" means deer of any species and includes the carcase of any deer or any part thereof;

"vehicle" includes an aircraft, hovercraft or boat; and

"venison" includes imported venison and means—

(*a*) any carcase of a deer, or

(*b*) any edible part of the carcase of a deer,

which has not been cooked or canned.

Transitional provisions, consequential amendment and repeals

17. (1) Anything done under any provision of the Deer Act 1963[6] or the Deer Act 1980[7] shall have effect as if it had been done under the corresponding provision of this Act.

(2) Without prejudice to the generality of subsection (1) above, a licence granted by the Nature Conservancy Council under section 11 of the Deer Act 1963 which, by virtue of paragraph 8 of Schedule 11 to the Environmental Protection Act 1990[8], has effect as if granted by the Nature Conservancy Council for England or the Countryside Council for Wales, shall be treated as if it had been granted under subsection (1) or, as the case may be, subsection (2) of section 8 above[9].

(3) Where a licence granted under section 11 of the Deer Act 1963 contains a reference to an enactment repealed by this Act, the licence shall be construed as referring, or, as the context requires, as including a reference to, the corresponding provision of this Act.

(4) Where a period of time specified in an enactment repealed by this Act is current at the commencement of this Act, this Act shall have effect as if the corresponding provision thereof had been in force when that period began to run.

(5) In section 25C of the Deer (Scotland) Act 1959 for the words "section 2(4) of the Deer Act 1980" there shall be substituted "section 10(5) of the Deer Act 1991"[10].

(6) The enactments specified in Schedule 4 to this Act are hereby repealed to the extent specified in the third column of that Schedule.

Short title, extent and commencement

18. (1) This Act may be cited as the Deer Act 1991.

(2) With the exception of section 17(5) above, which extends to Scotland only, this Act extends to England and Wales only.

(3) This Act shall come into force at the end of the period of three months beginning with the day on which it is passed[11].

---

[1] P. 263 above.
[2] P. 263 above.
[3] P. 267 above.
[4] P. 265 above.
[5] 1968 c. 27.
[6] 1963 c. 36. This Act is repealed by sch. 4.

[7] 1980 c. 49. This Act is repealed by sch. 4.
[8] P. 241 above.
[9] P. 265 above.
[10] This amendment is noted at p. 55 above.
[11] This Act came into force on 25 October 1991.

SCHEDULES

SCHEDULE 1

(Section 2)

CLOSE SEASONS

RED DEER [*Cervus elaphus*]

Stags	1st May to 31st July inclusive
Hinds	1st March to 31st October inclusive

FALLOW DEER [*Dama dama*]

Buck	1st May to 31st July inclusive
Doe	1st March to 31st October inclusive

ROE DEER [*Capreolus capreolus*]

Buck	1st November to 31st March inclusive
Doe	1st March to 31st October inclusive

SIKA DEER [*Cervus nippon*]

Stags	1st May to 31st July inclusive
Hinds	1st March to 31st October inclusive

SCHEDULE 2

(Section 4)

PROHIBITED FIREARMS AND AMMUNITION

Firearms

1. Any smooth-bore gun.

2. Any rifle having a calibre of less than .240 inches or a muzzle energy of less than 2,305 joules (1,700 foot pounds).

3. Any air gun, air rifle or air pistol.

Ammunition

4. Any cartridge for use in a smooth-bore gun.

5. Any bullet for use in a rifle other than a soft-nosed or hollow-nosed bullet.

SCHEDULE 3

(Section 11)

FORM OF RECORD TO BE KEPT BY LICENSED GAME DEALERS

Date of purchase or receipt*	Species	Means by which the deer was killed†	Particulars of carcases purchased or received						Particulars of parts of carcases purchased or received			Particulars of seller, or in the case of a receipt the source‡ from which receipt obtained, and registration number of vehicle delivering venison
			Male		Female		Total		Number (of parts)	Description (of parts)	Weight	
			No.	Weight	No.	Weight	No.	Weight				

* Where the venison comes from deer killed by the dealer, enter date of killing.

† If killed by rifle or smooth-bore gun, enter "rifle" or "smooth-bore gun".

‡ Where the venison comes from deer killed by the dealer, enter name of premises or place in which killed.

Water Industry Act 1991

Ch. 56

An Act to consolidate enactments relating to the supply of water and the provision of sewerage services, with amendments to give effect to recommendations of the Law Commission.

[25th July 1991[1]]

The following sections are reproduced from this Act.

Part I: Preliminary

General duties

Part VI: Undertakers' powers and works

Chapter I: Undertakers' powers

Powers in relation to land

The sections reproduced from this Act extend to England and Wales only: s. 223(3). The complete parts and chapters of the Act are not reproduced. Part I of the Act comprises sections 1–26 and Part VI comprises sections 155–192, of which chapter 1 comprises sections 155–173.

Part I: Preliminary

General duties

General duties with respect to water industry

2. (1) This section shall have effect for imposing duties on the Secretary of State and on the Director[2] as to when and how they should exercise and perform the following powers and duties, that is to say—

   (a) in the case of the Secretary of State, the powers and duties conferred or imposed on him by virtue of the provisions of this Act relating to the regulation of relevant undertakers[3]; and

   (b) in the case of the Director, the powers and duties conferred or imposed on him by virtue of any of those provisions, by the provisions relating to the financial conditions of requisitions or by the provisions relating to the movement of certain pipes.

---

[1] This Act came into force on 1 December 1991: s. 223(2).
[2] "The Director" means the Director General of Water Services: ss. 1(1), 219(1).

[3] "Relevant undertaker" means a water undertaker or sewerage undertaker: s. 219(1).

(2) The Secretary of State or, as the case may be, the Director shall exercise and perform the powers and duties mentioned in subsection (1) above in the manner that he considers is best calculated—

(a) to secure that the functions[1] of a water undertaker and of a sewerage undertaker are properly carried out as respects every area of England and Wales; and

(b) without prejudice to the generality of paragraph (a) above, to secure that companies holding appointments under Chapter I of Part II of this Act as relevant undertakers are able (in particular, by securing reasonable returns on their capital) to finance the proper carrying out of the functions of such undertakers.

(3) Subject to subsection (2) above, the Secretary of State or, as the case may be, the Director shall exercise and perform the powers and duties mentioned in subsection (1) above in the manner that he considers is best calculated—

(a) to ensure that the interests of every person who is a customer or potential customer of a company which has been or may be appointed under Chapter 1 of Part II of this Act to be a relevant undertaker are protected as respects the fixing and recovery by that company of water and drainage charges and, in particular—

   (i) that the interests of customers and potential customers in rural areas are so protected; and

   (ii) that no undue preference is shown, and that there is no undue discrimination, in the fixing of those charges;

(b) to ensure that the interests of every such person are also protected as respects the other terms on which any services are provided by that company in the course of the carrying out of the functions of a relevant undertaker and as respects the quality of those services;

(bb) to ensure that the interests of every such person are also protected as respects any activities of that company which are not attributable to the exercise of functions of a relevant undertaker, or as respects any activities of any person appearing to the Secretary of State or (as the case may be) the Director to be connected with that company, and in particular by ensuring—

   (i) that transactions are carried out at arm's length; and

   (ii) that that company, in relation to the exercise of its functions as a relevant undertaker, maintains and presents accounts in a suitable form and manner;[2]

(c) to ensure that the interests of every such person are further protected as respects benefits that could be secured for them by the application in a particular manner of any of the proceeds of any disposal (including a disposal before the Secretary of State and the Director became subject to the duties imposed by virtue of this paragraph) of any of that company's protected land or of any interest or right in or over any of that land;

(d) to promote economy and efficiency on the part of any such company in the carrying out of the functions of a relevant undertaker; and

(e) to facilitate effective competition, with respect to such matters as he considers appropriate, between persons holding or seeking appointments under that Chapter.

(4) In performing his duty under subsection (3) above, so far as it requires him to do anything in the manner which he considers is best calculated to ensure that the interests of the customers and potential customers of any company are protected as respects the quality of any services provided by that company in the course of the carrying out of the functions of a relevant undertaker, the Secretary of State or, as the case may be, the Director shall take into account, in particular, the interests of those who are disabled or of pensionable age.

---

[1] "Functions", in relation to a relevant undertaker, means the functions of the undertaker under or by virtue of any enactment and shall be construed subject to s. 217 of this Act: s. 219(1).

[2] Paragraph (bb) inserted by the Competition and Service (Utilities) Act 1992 (c. 43), s. 50. This amendment came into force on 1 July 1992: Commencement No. 1 Order 1992.

(5) In this section the references to water and drainage charges are references to—

(a) any charges in respect of any services provided in the course of the carrying out of the functions of a relevant undertaker; and

(b) amounts of any other description which such an undertaker is authorised by or under any enactment to require any of its customers or potential customers to pay.

(6) For the purposes of this section—

(a) the reference in subsection (1) above to the provisions of this Act relating to the regulation of relevant undertakers is a reference to the provisions contained in Part II of this Act (except section 28 and Schedule 4), or in any of sections 38, 39, 95, 96, 153, 181, 182, 193 to 195 and 201 to 203 below;

(b) the reference in that subsection to the provisions relating to the financial conditions of requisitions is a reference to the provisions contained in sections 42, 43, 48, 99 and 100 below; and

(c) the reference in that subsection to the provisions relating to the movement of certain pipes is a reference to the provisions of section 185 below.

General environmental and recreational duties

3. (1) It shall be the duty of each of the following, that is to say—

(a) the Secretary of State;

(b) the Minister of Agriculture, Fisheries and Food;

(c) the Director[1]; and

(d) every company holding an appointment as a relevant undertaker[2],

in formulating or considering any proposals relating to any functions of a relevant undertaker[3] (including, in the case of such a company, any functions which, by virtue of that appointment, are functions of the company itself) to comply with the requirements imposed in relation to the proposals by subsections (2) and (3) below.

(2) The requirements imposed by this subsection in relation to any such proposals as are mentioned in subsection (1) above are—

(a) a requirement, so far as may be consistent—

(i) with the purposes of any enactment[4] relating to the functions of the undertaker; and

(ii) in the case of the Secretary of State and the Director, with their duties under section 2 above,

so to exercise any power conferred with respect to the proposals on the person subject to the requirement as to further the conservation and enhancement of natural beauty and the conservation of flora, fauna and geological or physiographical features of special interest;

(b) a requirement to have regard to the desirability of protecting and conserving buildings[5], sites and objects of archaeological, architectural or historic interest; and

(c) a requirement to take into account any effect which the proposals would have on the beauty or amenity of any rural or urban area or on any such flora, fauna, features, buildings, sites or objects.

(3) The requirements imposed by this subsection in relation to any such proposals as are mentioned in subsection (1) above are, subject to the requirements imposed by subsection (2) above—

---

[1] "The Director" means the Director General of Water Services: ss. 1(1), 219(1).

[2] "Relevant undertaker" means a water undertaker or sewerage undertaker: s. 219(1).

[3] "Functions", in relation to a relevant undertaker, means the functions of the undertaker under or by virtue of

any enactment and shall be construed subject to s. 217 of this Act: s. 219(1). For the construction of "functions of a relevant undertaker" see subsection (9) below.

[4] "Enactment" includes an enactment contained in this Act or in any Act passed after this Act: s. 219(1).

[5] "Building" includes structure: subsection (1) below.

(a) a requirement to have regard to the desirability of preserving for the public any freedom of access to areas of woodland, mountains, moor, heath, down, cliff or foreshore and other places of natural beauty;

(b) a requirement to have regard to the desirability of maintaining the availability to the public of any facility for visiting or inspection any building, site or object of archaeological, architectural or historic interest; and

(c) a requirement to take into account any effect which the proposals would have on any such freedom of access or on the availability of any such facility.

(4) Subsections (1) to (3) above shall apply so as to impose duties on the Director and any company holding an appointment as a relevant undertaker in relation to any proposal relating to—

(a) the functions of the NRA[1]; or

(b) the functions of an internal drainage board,

as they apply in relation to any proposals relating to the functions of such an undertaker; and for the purposes of this subsection the reference in subsection (2)(a) above to the functions of the undertaker shall have effect as a reference to the functions of the NRA or, as the case may be, of the internal drainage board in question.

(5) Subject to obtaining the consent of any navigation authority[2], harbour authority[3] or conservancy authority[4] before doing anything which causes navigation which is subject to the control of that authority to be obstructed or otherwise interfered with, it shall be the duty of every company holding an appointment as a relevant undertaker to take such steps as are—

(a) reasonably practicable; and

(b) consistent with the purposes of the enactments relating to the functions of the undertaker in question,

for securing, so long as that company has rights to the use of water or land associated with water, that those rights are exercised so as to ensure that the water or land is made available for recreational purposes and is so made available in the best manner.

(6) It shall be the duty of a company holding an appointment as a relevant undertaker, in determining what steps to take in performance of any duty imposed by virtue of subsection (5) above, to take into account the needs of persons who are chronically sick or disabled.

(7) The obligations under this section of a company holding an appointment as a relevant undertaker shall be enforceable under section 18 below[5] by the Secretary of State.

(8) Nothing in this section or the following provisions of this Act shall require recreational facilities made available by a relevant undertaker to be made available free of charge.

(9) References in this section to the functions of a relevant undertaker shall be construed, without prejudice to section 156(7) below[6], as if those functions included the management, by a company holding an appointment as such an undertaker, of any land for the time being held by that company for any purpose whatever (whether or not connected with the carrying out of the functions of a relevant undertaker).

(10) In this section "building" includes structure.

[1] "The NRA" means the National Rivers Authority: s. 219(1).

[2] "Navigation authority" means any person who has a duty or power under any enactment to work, maintain, conserve, improve or control any canal or other inland navigation, navigable river, estuary, harbour or dock: s. 219(1).

[3] "Harbour authority" means a person who is a harbour authority within the meaning of the Prevention of Oil Pollution Act 1971 (c. 60) and is not a navigation authority: s. 219(1).

[4] "Conservancy authority" means any person who has a duty or power under any enactment to conserve, maintain or improve the navigation of a tidal water, and is not a harbour authority or navigation authority: s. 219(1).

[5] S. 18 contains provisions enabling the Secretary of State to make an enforcement order. Ss. 19–22 make further provision in respect of enforcement orders.

[6] P. 280 below.

Environmental duties with respect to sites of special interest

4. **(1)** Where the Nature Conservancy Council for England[1] or the Countryside Council for Wales[2] are of the opinion that any area of land in England or, as the case may be, in Wales—

(*a*) is of special interest by reason of its flora, fauna or geological or physiographical features; and

(*b*) may at any time be affected by schemes, works, operations or activities of a relevant undertaker[3],

that Council shall notify the fact that the land is of special interest for that reason to every relevant undertaker whose works, operations or activities may affect the land.

(2) Where a National Park authority[4] or the Broads Authority[5] is of the opinion that any area of land in a National Park or in the Broads[6]—

(*a*) is land in relation to which the matters for the purposes of which section 3 above has effect are of particular importance; and

(*b*) may at any time be affected by schemes, works, operations or activities of a relevant undertaker,

the National Park authority or Broads Authority shall notify the fact that the land is such land, and the reasons why those matters are of particular importance in relation to the land, to every relevant undertaker whose works, operations or activities may affect the land.

(3) Where a relevant undertaker has received a notification under subsection (1) or (2) above with respect to any land, that undertaker shall consult the notifying body before carrying out any works, operations or activities which appear to that undertaker to be likely—

(*a*) to destroy or damage any of the flora, fauna, or geological or physiographical features by reason of which the land is of special interest; or

(*b*) significantly to prejudice anything the importance of which is one of the reasons why the matters mentioned in subsection (2) above are of particular importance in relation to that land.

(4) Subsection (3) above shall not apply in relation to anything done in an emergency where particulars of what is done and of the emergency are notified to the Nature Conservancy Council for England, the Countryside Council for Wales, the National Park authority in question or, as the case may be, the Broads Authority as soon as practicable after that thing is done.

(5) The obligations under this section of a relevant undertaker shall be enforceable under section 18 below by the Secretary of State.

(6) In this section—

"the Broads" has the same meaning as in the Norfolk and Suffolk Broads Act 1988[7]; and

"National Park authority" means a National Park Committee or a joint or special planning board for a National Park;

and section 3(9) above shall apply, as it applies in relation to that section, for construing (in accordance with section 6 below[8]) any references in this section to a relevant undertaker.

Codes of practice with respect to environmental and recreational duties

5. **(1)** The Secretary of State may by order approve any code of practice issued (whether by him or by another person) for the purpose of—

---

[1] The Nature Conservancy Council for England, also known as English Nature, is established by the Environmental Protection Act 1990 (c. 43), s. 128, p. 229 above.

[2] The Countryside Council for Wales is established by the Environmental Protection Act 1990 (c. 43), s. 128, p. 229 above.

[3] "Relevant undertaker" means a water undertaker or sewerage undertaker: s. 219(1); see subsection (6) below.

[4] "National Park authority" defined by subsection (6) below.

[5] The Broads Authority is established by the Norfolk and Suffolk Broads Act 1988, s. 1, p. 221 above.

[6] "The Broads" defined by subsection (6) below.

[7] P. 220 above.

[8] Section 6 makes provision in respect of the appointment of water and sewerage undertakers.

(a) giving practical guidance to relevant undertakers[1] with respect to any of the matters for the purposes of which sections 3 and 4 above have effect; and

(b) promoting what appear to him to be desirable practices by such undertakers with respect to those matters,

and may at any time by such an order approve a modification[2] of such a code or withdraw his approval of such a code or modification[3].

(2) A contravention of a code of practice as for the time being approved under this section shall not of itself constitute a contravention of any requirement imposed by section 3 or 4 above or give rise to any criminal or civil liability; but the Secretary of State and the Minister of Agriculture, Fisheries and Food shall each be under a duty to take into account whether there has been or is likely to be any such contravention in determining when and how he should exercise his powers in relation to any relevant undertaker by virtue of this Act, any of the other consolidation Acts[4] or the Water Act 1989[5].

(3) The power of the Secretary of State to make an order under this section shall be exercisable by statutory instrument subject to annulment in pursuance of a resolution of either House of Parliament.

(4) The Secretary of State shall not make an order under this section unless he has first consulted—

(a) the NRA[6];

(b) the Countryside Commission[7], the Nature Conservancy Council for England[8] and the Countryside Council for Wales[9];

(c) the Historic Buildings and Monuments Commission for England;

(d) the Sports Council and the Sports Council for Wales; and

(e) such relevant undertakers and other persons as he considers it appropriate to consult.

(5) In this section "the other consolidation Acts" means the Water Resources Act 1991[10], the Statutory Water Companies Act 1991[11], the Land Drainage Act 1991[12] and the Water Consolidation (Consequential Provisions) Act 1991[13].

---

[1] "Relevant undertaker" means a water undertaker or sewerage undertaker: s. 219(1).

[2] "Modifications" includes additions, alterations and omissions, and cognate expressions shall be construed accordingly: s. 219(1).

[3] The Water and Sewerage (Conservation, Access and Recreation) (Code of Practice) Order 1989, S.I. 1989/1152, made under the provisions of the Water Act 1989 from which this section is derived, approves the Code of Practice on Conservation, Access and Recreation. The explanatory note sets out that copies of the Code are available for inspection at and may be obtained from the Department of the Environment, Romney House, 43 Marsham Street, London SW1P 3PY, and at the Welsh Office, Cathays Park, Cardiff CF1 3NQ.

[4] "The other consolidation Acts" defined by subsection (5) below.

[5] 1989 c. 15.

[6] "The NRA" means the National Rivers Authority: s. 219(1).

[7] For the establishment and functions of the Countryside Commission see the National Parks and Access to the Countryside Act 1949 (c. 97), s. 1, p. 7 above and the Countryside Act 1968 (c. 41), s. 1, p. 114 above.

[8] The Nature Conservancy Council for England, also known as English Nature, is established by the Environmental Protection Act 1990 (c. 43), s. 128, p. 229 above.

[9] The Countryside Council for Wales is established by the Environmental Protection Act 1990 (c. 43), s. 128, p. 229 above.

[10] 1991 c. 57.

[11] 1991 c. 58.

[12] 1991 c. 59.

[13] 1991 c. 60.

Part VI: Undertakers' powers and works

Chapter I: Undertakers' Powers

Powers in relation to land

Restriction on disposals of land

156. (1) A company holding an appointment under Chapter I of Part II of this Act[1] shall not dispose[2] of any of its protected land[3], or of any interest or right in or over any of that land, except with the consent of, or in accordance with a general authorisation given by, the Secretary of State.

(2) A consent or authorisation for the purposes of this section—

(*a*) shall be set out in a notice[4] served by the Secretary of State on the company which is or may be authorised, by virtue of the provision contained in the notice, to dispose of land or of interests or rights in or over land or, as the case may be, on every such company; and

(*b*) in the case of an authorisation, may be combined with an authorisation for the purposes of section 157 of the Water Resources Act 1991[5].

(3) A consent or authorisation for the purposes of this section may be given on such conditions as the Secretary of State considers appropriate.

(4) Without prejudice to the generality of subsection (3) above and subject to subsection (5) below, the conditions of a consent or authorisation for the purposes of this section may include—

(*a*) a requirement that, before there is any disposal, an opportunity of acquiring the land in question, or an interest or right in or over that land, is to be made available, in such manner and on such terms as may be specified in or determined under provision contained in the notice setting out the consent or authorisation, to such person as may be so specified or determined;

(*b*) a requirement that the company making the disposal has complied with such of the conditions of its appointment under Chapter I of Part II of this Act as relate to the disposal of its protected land or of any interest or right in or over that land;

(*c*) a requirement that the company, before making a disposal in a case in which the land in question is situated in a National Park, in the Broads[6] or in an area of outstanding natural beauty or special scientific interest[7], should do one or both of the following, that is to say—

(i) consult with the Countryside Commission[8] (as respects land in England) or the Countryside Council for Wales[9] (as respects land in Wales) and, in the case of an area

---

[1] Chapter I, Part II relates to appointments as a water or sewerage undertaker (a "relevant undertaker").

[2] "Disposal", in relation to land or any interest or right in or over land, includes the creation of such an interest or right and a disposal effected by means of the surrender or other termination of any such interest or right and cognate expressions shall be construed accordingly: s. 219(1).

[3] "Protected land", in relation to a company holding an appointment under Chapter I of Part II of this Act, means any land which, or any interest or right in or over which—

(*a*) was transferred to that company in accordance with a scheme under Schedule 2 to the Water Act 1989 (c. 15) or, where that company is a statutory water company, was held by that company at any time during the financial year ending with 31st March 1990;

(*b*) is or has at any time on or after 1 September 1989 been held by that company for purposes connected with the carrying out of its functions as a water undertaker or sewerage undertaker (including any functions which for the purposes for which section 218 above has effect are taken to be such functions by virtue of subsection (6) or

(7) of that section); or

(*c*) has been transferred to that company in accordance with a scheme under Schedule 2 to this Act from another company in relation to which that land was protected land when the other company held an appointment under that Chapter: s. 219(1).

Note: It appears that the reference in (*b*) to section 218 should be to section 217.

[4] "Notice" means notice in writing: s. 219(1).

[5] 1991 c. 57.

[6] "The Broads" defined by subsection (8) below.

[7] "Area of outstanding natural beauty or special scientific interest" defined by subsection (8) below.

[8] For the establishment and functions of the Countryside Commission see the National Parks and Access to the Countryside Act 1949 (c. 97), s. 1, p. 7 above and the Countryside Act 1968 (c. 41), s. 1, p. 114 above.

[9] The Countryside Council for Wales is established by the Environmental Protection Act 1990 (c. 43), s. 128, p. 229 above.

of special scientific interest in England, with the Nature Conservancy Council for England[1]; and

> (ii) enter into such agreements under section 39 of the Wildlife and Countryside Act 1981[2](management agreements) or such covenants under subsection (6) below as the Secretary of State may determine;

(d) provision requiring determinations under or for the purposes of the consent or authorisation to be made, in such cases as are mentioned in paragraph (c) above, either by the Countryside Commission or the Countryside Council for Wales or only after consultation with that Commission or Council.

(5) A consent or authorisation shall not be given on any such condition as is mentioned in subsection (4)(a) above except where the Secretary of State is satisfied that the condition will have effect in relation only to—

(a) land which, or any interest in or right over which, was acquired by the relevant undertaker in question, or any predecessor of that undertaker, either compulsorily or at a time when the undertaker or that predecessor was authorised to acquire it compulsorily; or

(b) land situated in a National Park, in the Broads or in an area of outstanding natural beauty or special scientific interest.

(6) Where a company holding an appointment under Chapter I of Part II of this Act is proposing, in such a case as is mentioned in subsection (4)(c) above, to dispose of, or of any interest or right in or over, any of its protected land, it may enter into a covenant with the Secretary of State by virtue of which it accepts obligations with respect to—

(a) the freedom of access to the land that is to be afforded to members of the public or to persons of any description; or

(b) the use or management of the land;

and a covenant under this subsection shall bind all persons deriving title from or under that company and shall be enforceable by the Secretary of State accordingly.

(7) Section 3 above[3] shall have effect for the purposes of this section as if every proposal which—

(a) is made by a company holding an appointment as a relevant undertaker with respect to land in a National Park, in the Broads or in an area of outstanding natural beauty or special scientific interest, or with respect to any interest or right in or over any such land; and

(b) is a proposal for which the Secretary of State's consent or authorisation is required under this section,

were a proposal relating to the functions of such an undertaker.

(8) In this section—

"area of outstanding natural beauty or special scientific interest" means an area which—

(a) is for the time being designated as an area of outstanding natural beauty for the purposes of the National Parks and Access to the Countryside Act 1949[4]; or

(b) is an area in relation to which a notification given, or having effect as if given, under section 28 of the Wildlife and Countryside Act 1981[5] (areas of special scientific interest) for the time being has effect;

and the reference in subsection (4)(c) above to an area of special scientific interest shall, accordingly, be construed as a reference to an area such as is mentioned in paragraph (b) of this definition; and

"the Broads" has the same meaning as in the Norfolk and Suffolk Broads Act 1988[6].

---

[1] The Nature Conservancy Council for England, also known as English Nature, is established by the Environmental Protection Act 1990 (c. 43), s. 128, p. 229 above.
[2] P. 181 above.

[3] P. 275 above.
[4] See s. 87 of the 1949 Act at p. 22 above.
[5] P. 168 above.
[6] P. 220 above.

Water Resources Act 1991

Ch. 57

Note: *At the time of preparing this manual the Environment Bill is before Parliament. The Bill sets out, among other matters, provisions for the transfer of the functions of the National Rivers Authority to the Environment Agency. Following enactment of the Environment Act, the National Rivers Authority will be abolished, pursuant to the Act, on the transfer date. The sections set out below will be largely repealed and new provisions will be contained in Part I of the Environment Act 1995. The present plan is that the functions of the National Rivers Authority, together with other functions, will be transferred to the Environment Agency on 1 April 1996.[1] A note on the Environment Bill is at Appendix I, p. 505 below.*

An Act to consolidate enactments relating to the National Rivers Authority and the matters in relation to which it exercises functions, with amendments to give effect to recommendations of the Law Commission.

[25th July 1991[2]]

The following sections are reproduced from this Act.

Part I: Preliminary

Chapter I: The National Rivers Authority

Chapter III: General Duties

Subject to subsections (4) to (6) of section 2 and to the extension, by virtue of any other enactment, of any provision of this Act to the territorial sea, the sections reproduced from this Act extend to England and Wales only: s. 225(3). The complete chapters of Part I of the Act are not reproduced. Part I comprises sections 1–18, of which chapter I comprises sections 1–5 and chapter III comprises sections 15–18.

---

[1] Department of Environment news release 576 of 13 October 1994.

[2] This Act came into force on 1 December 1991: s. 225(1).

Part I: Preliminary

Chapter I: The National Rivers Authority

The National Rivers Authority

1. (1) There shall continue to be a body corporate, known as the National Rivers Authority, for the purpose of carrying out the functions specified in section 2 below.

(2) The Authority shall consist of not less than eight nor more than fifteen members of whom—

(a) two shall be appointed by the Minister[1], and

(b) the others shall be appointed by the Secretary of State.

(3) The Secretary of State shall designate one of the members appointed by him as the chairman of the Authority and may, if he thinks fit, designate another member of the Authority (whether or not appointed by him) as the deputy chairman of the Authority.

(4) In appointing a person to be a member of the Authority, the Secretary of State or, as the case may be, the Minister shall have regard to the desirability of appointing a person who has experience of, and has shown capacity in, some matter relevant to the functions of the Authority.

(5) The Authority shall not be regarded—

(a) as the servant or agent of the Crown, or as enjoying any status, immunity or privilege of the Crown; or

(b) by virtue of any connection with the Crown, as exempt from any tax, duty, rate, levy or other charge whatsoever, whether general or local;

and the Authority's property shall not be regarded as property of, or property held on behalf of, the Crown.

(6) The provisions of Schedule 1 to this Act shall have effect with respect to the Authority.

....

The Authority's functions

2. (1) The functions of the Authority[2] are—

(a) its functions with respect to water resources by virtue of Part II of this Act;

(b) its functions with respect to water pollution by virtue of Part III of this Act;

(c) its functions with respect to flood defence and land drainage by virtue of Part IV of this Act and the Land Drainage Act 1991[3] and the functions transferred to the Authority by virtue of section 136(8) of the Water Act 1989[4] and paragraph 1(3) of Schedule 15 to that Act (transfer of land drainage functions under local statutory provisions and subordinate legislation);

(d) its functions with respect to fisheries by virtue of Part V of this Act, the Diseases of Fish Act 1937[5], the Sea Fisheries Regulation Act 1966[6], the Salmon and Freshwater Fisheries Act 1975[7] and other enactments[8] relating to fisheries.

(e) the functions as a navigation authority[9], harbour authority[10] or conservancy authority[11]

---

[1] "The Minister" means the Minister of Agriculture, Fisheries and Food: s. 221(1).

[2] "The Authority" means the National Rivers Authority: s. 221(1).

[3] 1991 c. 59.

[4] 1989 c. 15.

[5] 1937 c. 33.

[6] 1966 c. 38.

[7] 1975 c. 51.

[8] "Enactment" includes an enactment contained in this Act or in any Act passed after this Act: s. 221(1).

[9] "Navigation authority" means any person who has a duty or power under any enactment to work, maintain, con- serve, improve or control any canal or other inland naviga- tion, navigable river, estuary, harbour or dock: s. 221(1).

[10] "Harbour authority" (except in the flood defence pro- visions of this Act, in which it has the same meaning as in the Merchant Shipping Act 1894, c. 60) means a person who is a harbour authority within the meaning of the Prevention of Oil Pollution Act 1971 (c. 60) and is not a navigation authority: s. 221(1).

[11] "Conservancy authority" means any person who has a duty or power under any enactment to conserve, maintain or improve the navigation of a tidal water and is not a navi- gation authority or harbour authority: s. 221(1).

which were transferred to the Authority by virtue of Chapter V of Part III of the Water Act 1989 or paragraph 23(3) of Schedule 13 to that Act or which are transferred to the Authority by any order or agreement under Schedule 2 to this Act; and

(*f*) the functions assigned to the Authority by any other enactment.

(2) Without prejudice to its duties under section 16 below[1], it shall be the duty of the Authority, to such extent as it considers desirable, generally to promote—

(*a*) the conservation and enhancement of the natural beauty and amenity of inland and coastal waters[2] and of land associated with such waters;

(*b*) the conservation of flora and fauna which are dependent on an aquatic environment; and

(*c*) the use of such waters and land for recreational purposes;

and it shall be the duty of the Authority, in determining what steps to take in performance of the duty imposed by virtue of paragraph (*c*) above, to take into account the needs of persons who are chronically sick or disabled.

(3) It shall be the duty of the Authority to make arrangements for the carrying out of research and related activities (whether by the Authority or others) in respect of matters to which the functions of the Authority relate.

(4) The provisions of this Act relating to the functions of the Authority under Chapter II or Part II of this Act[3], and the related water resources provisions so far as they relate to other functions of the Authority, shall not apply to so much of any inland waters as—

(*a*) are part of the River Tweed;

(*b*) are part of the River Esk or River Sark at a point where either of the banks of the river is in Scotland; or

(*c*) are part of any tributary stream of the River Esk or the River Sark at a point where either of the banks of the tributary stream is in Scotland.

(5) The functions of the Authority specified in subsection (1)(*c*) above extend to the territorial sea adjacent to England and Wales in so far as—

(*a*) the area of any regional flood defence committee includes any area of that territorial sea; or

(*b*) section 165(2) or (3)[4] below provides for the exercise of any power in the territorial sea.

(6) The area in respect of which the Authority shall carry out its functions relating to fisheries shall be the whole of England and Wales, together with—

(*a*) such part of the territorial sea adjacent to England and Wales as extends for six miles from the baselines from which the breadth of that sea is measured; and

(*b*) in the case of Part V of this Act, the Diseases of Fish Act 1937 and the Salmon and Freshwater Fisheries Act 1975, so much of the River Esk, with its banks and tributary streams up to their source, as is situated in Scotland.

but, in the case of Part V of this Act and those Acts, excluding the River Tweed.

(7) In this section—

"miles" means international nautical miles of 1,852 metres; and

"the River Tweed" means "the river" within the meaning of the Tweed Fisheries Amendment Act 1859[5], as amended by byelaws.

---

[1] P. 284 below.
[2] "Inland waters" means the whole or any part of—

(*a*) any river, stream or other watercourse (within the meaning of Chapter II of Part II of this Act), whether natural or artificial and whether tidal or not;

(*b*) any lake or pond, whether natural or artificial, or any reservoir or dock, in so far as the lake, pond, reservoir or dock does not fall within paragraph (*a*) of this definition; and

(*c*) so much of any channel, creek, bay, estuary or arm of the sea as does not fall within paragraph (*a*) or (*b*) of this definition: s. 221(1).

[3] Chapter II of Part II contains provisions relating to abstraction and impounding.
[4] Section 165 contains general powers to carry out flood defence and drainage works.
[5] 1859 c. lxx.

The remainder of chapter I, comprising sections 3–5, is not reproduced. These sections make provision for incidental functions and incidental general powers of the NRA and Ministerial directions to the NRA.

Chapter III: General Duties

General duties with respect to the water industry

15. (1) It shall be the duty of the Authority[1], in exercising any of its powers under any enactment[2], to have particular regard to the duties imposed, by virtue of the provisions of Parts II to IV of the Water Industry Act 1991[3], on any water undertaker or sewerage undertaker which appears to the Authority to be or to be likely to be affected by the exercise of the power in question.

(2) It shall be the duty of each of the Ministers[4], in exercising—

(a) any power conferred by virtue of this Act, the Land Drainage Act 1991[5], the Water Industry Act 1991[6] or the Water Act 1989[7] in relation to, or to decisions of, the Authority; or

(b) any power which, but for any direction given by one of the Ministers, would fall to be exercised by the Authority,

to take into account the duty imposed on the Authority by subsection (1) above.

General environmental and recreational duties

16. (1) It shall be the duty of each of the Ministers[8] and of the Authority[9], in formulating or considering any proposals relating to any functions of the Authority—

(a) so far as may be consistent—

(i) with the purposes of any enactment[10] relating to the functions of the Authority; and

(ii) in the case of the Secretary of State, with his duties under section 2 of the Water Industry Act 1991[11],

so to exercise any power conferred on him or it with respect to the proposals as to further the conservation and enhancement of natural beauty and the conservation of flora, fauna and geological or physiographical features of special interest;

(b) to have regard to the desirability of protecting and conserving buildings[12], sites and objects of archaeological, architectural or historic interest; and

(c) to take into account any effect which the proposals would have on the beauty or amenity of any rural or urban area or on any such flora, fauna, features, buildings, sites or objects.

(2) Subject to subsection (1) above, it shall be the duty of each of the Ministers and of the Authority, in formulating or considering any proposals relating to the functions of the Authority—

(a) to have regard to the desirability of preserving for the public any freedom of access to areas of woodland, mountains, moor, heath, down, cliff or foreshore and other places of natural beauty;

---

[1] "The Authority" means the National Rivers Authority: s. 221(1).

[2] "Enactment" includes an enactment contained in this Act or in any Act passed after this Act: s. 221(1).

[3] Part II of the Water Industry Act 1991 (c. 56) contains provisions relating to the appointment and regulation of undertakers, Part III provisions relating to water supply and Part IV provisions relating to sewerage services.

[4] "The Ministers" means the Secretary of State and the Minister of Agriculture, Fisheries and Food: s. 221(1).

[5] 1991 c. 59.

[6] 1991 c. 56.

[7] 1989 c. 15.

[8] "The Ministers" means the Secretary of State and the Minister of Agriculture, Fisheries and Food: s. 221(1).

[9] "The Authority" means the National Rivers Authority: s. 221(1).

[10] "Enactment" includes an enactment contained in this Act or in any Act passed after this Act: s. 221(1).

[11] P. 273 above.

[12] "Building" includes structure: subsection (7) below.

(b) to have regard to the desirability of maintaining the availability to the public of any facility for visiting or inspecting any building, site or object of archaeological, architectural or historic interest; and

(c) to take into account any effect which the proposals would have on any such freedom of access or on the availability of any such facility.

(3) Subsections (1) and (2) above shall apply so as to impose duties on the Authority in relation to—

(a) any proposals relating to the functions of a water undertaker or sewerage undertaker;

(b) any proposals relating to the management, by the company holding an appointment as such an undertaker, of any land for the time being held by that company for any purpose whatever (whether or not connected with the carrying out of the functions of a water undertaker or sewerage undertaker); and

(c) any proposal which by virtue of section 156(7) of the Water Industry Act 1991[1] (disposals of protected land) falls to be treated for the purposes of section 3 of that Act[2] as a proposal relating to the functions of a water undertaker or sewerage undertaker,

as they apply in relation to proposals relating to the Authority's own functions but as if, for that purpose, the reference in subsection (1)(a) above to enactments relating to the functions of the Authority were a reference to enactments relating to that to which the proposal relates.

(4) Subject to obtaining the consent of any navigation authority[3], harbour authority[4] or conservancy authority[5] before doing anything which causes navigation which is subject to the control of that authority to be obstructed or otherwise interfered with, it shall be the duty of the Authority to take such steps as are—

(a) reasonably practicable; and

(b) consistent with the purposes of the enactments relating to the functions of the Authority,

for securing, so long as the Authority has rights to the use of water or land associated with water, that those rights are exercised so as to ensure that the water or land is made available for recreational purposes and is so made available in the best manner.

(5) It shall be the duty of the Authority, in determining what steps to take in performance of any duty imposed by virtue of subsection (4) above, to take into account the needs of persons who are chronically sick or disabled.

(6) Nothing in this section or the following provisions of this Act shall require recreational facilities made available by the Authority to be made available free of charge.

(7) In this section "building" includes structure.

Environmental duties with respect to sites of special interest

17. (1) Where the Nature Conservancy Council for England[6] or the Countryside Council for Wales[7] are of the opinion that any area of land in England or, as the case may be, in Wales—

(a) is of special interest by reason of its flora, fauna or geological or physiographical features; and

---

[1] P. 280 above.

[2] P. 275 above.

[3] "Navigation authority" means any person who has a duty or power under any enactment to work, maintain, conserve, improve or control any canal or other inland navigation, navigable river, estuary, harbour or dock: s. 221(1).

[4] "Harbour authority" (except in the flood defence provisions of this Act, in which it has the same meaning as in the Merchant Shipping Act 1894, c. 60) means a person who is a harbour authority within the meaning of the Prevention of Oil Pollution Act 1971 (c. 60) and is not a navigation authority: s. 221(1).

[5] "Conservancy authority" means any person who has a duty or power under any enactment to conserve, maintain or improve the navigation of a tidal water and is not a navigation authority or harbour authority: s. 221(1).

[6] The Nature Conservancy Council for England, also known as English Nature, is established by the Environmental Protection Act 1990 (c. 43), s. 128, p. 229 above.

[7] The Countryside Council for Wales is established by the Environmental Protection Act 1990 (c. 43), s. 128, p. 229 above.

(b) may at any time be affected by schemes, works, operations or activities of the Authority[1] or by an authorisation given by the Authority,

that Council shall notify the fact that the land is of special interest for that reason to the Authority.

(2) Where a National Park authority[2] or the Broads Authority[3] is of the opinion that any area of land in a National Park or in the Broads[4]—

(a) is land in relation to which the matters for the purposes of which sections 2(2)[5] and 16 above have effect are of particular importance; and

(b) may at any time be affected by schemes, works, operations or activities of the Authority or by an authorisation given by the Authority,

the National Park authority or Broads Authority shall notify the fact that the land is such land, and the reasons why those matters are of particular importance in relation to the land, to the Authority.

(3) Where the Authority has received a notification under subsection (1) or (2) above with respect to any land, it shall consult the notifying body before carrying out or authorising any works, operations or activities which appear to the Authority to be likely—

(a) to destroy or damage any of the flora, fauna, or geological or physiographical features by reason of which the land is of special interest; or

(b) significantly to prejudice anything the importance of which is one of the reasons why the matters mentioned in subsection (2) above are of particular importance in relation to that land.

(4) Subsection (3) above shall not apply in relation to anything done in an emergency where particulars of what is done and of the emergency are notified to the Nature Conservancy Council for England, the Countryside Council for Wales, the National Park authority in question or, as the case may be, the Broads Authority as soon as practicable after that thing is done.

(5) In this section—

"the Broads" has the same meaning as in the Norfolk and Suffolk Broads Act 1988[6]; and

"National Park authority" means a National Park Committee or a joint or special planning board for a National Park.

Codes of practice with respect to environmental and recreational duties

18. (1) Each of the Ministers[7] shall have power by order to approve any code of practice issued (whether by him or by another person) for the purpose of—

(a) giving practical guidance to the Authority[8] with respect to any of the matters for the purposes of which sections 2(2)[9], 16[10] and 17 above have effect; and

(b) promoting what appear to him to be desirable practices by the Authority with respect to those matters,

and may at any time by such an order approve a modification[11] of such a code or withdraw his approval of such a code or modification[12].

---

[1] "The Authority" means the National Rivers Authority: s. 221(1).

[2] "National Park authority" defined by subsection (5) below.

[3] The Broads Authority is established by the Norfolk and Suffolk Broads Act 1988, s. 1, p. 221 above.

[4] "The Broads" defined by subsection (5) below.

[5] P. 283 above.

[6] P. 220 above.

[7] "The Ministers" means the Secretary of State and the Minister of Agriculture, Fisheries and Food: s. 221(1).

[8] "The Authority" means the National Rivers Authority: s. 221(1).

[9] P. 283 above.

[10] P. 284 above.

[11] "Modifications" includes additions, alterations and omissions, and cognate expressions shall be construed accordingly: s. 221(1).

[12] The Water and Sewerage (Conservation, Access and Recreation) (Code of Practice) Order 1989, S.I. 1989/1152, made under the provisions of the Water Act 1989 from which this section is derived, approves the Code of Practice on Conservation, Access and Recreation. The explanatory note sets out that copies of the Code are available for inspection at and may be obtained from the Department of the Environment, Romney House, 43 Marsham Street,

(2) A contravention of a code of practice as for the time being approved under this section shall not of itself constitute a contravention of any requirement imposed by section 2(2), 16 or 17 above or give rise to any criminal or civil liability; but each of the Ministers shall be under a duty to take into account whether there has been or is likely to be any such contravention in determining when and how he should exercise his powers in relation to the Authority by virtue of this Act, the Land Drainage Act 1991[1], the Water Industry Act 1991[2] or the Water Act 1989[3].

(3) The power of each of the Ministers to make an order under this section shall be exercisable by statutory instrument subject to annulment in pursuance of a resolution of either House of Parliament.

(4) Neither of the Ministers shall make an order under this section unless he has first consulted—

(a) the Authority;

(b) the Countryside Commission[4], the Nature Conservancy Council for England[5] and the Countryside Council for Wales[6];

(c) the Historic Buildings and Monuments Commission for England;

(d) the Sports Council and the Sports Council for Wales; and

(e) such water undertakers, sewerage undertakers and other persons as he considers it appropriate to consult.

London SW1P 3PY, and at the Welsh Office, Cathays Parks, Cardiff CF1 3NQ.

[1] 1991 c. 59.
[2] 1991 c. 56.
[3] 1989 c. 15.
[4] For the establishment and functions of the Countryside Commission see the National Parks and Access to the Countryside Act 1949 (c. 97), s. 1, p. 7 above and the Countryside Act 1968 (c. 41), s. 1, p. 114 above.

[5] The Nature Conservancy Council for England, also known as English Nature, is established by the Environmental Protection Act 1990 (c. 43), s. 128, p. 229 above.

[6] The Countryside Council for Wales is established by the Environmental Protection Act 1990 (c. 43), s. 128, p. 229 above.

Land Drainage Act 1991

Ch. 59

An Act to consolidate the enactments relating to internal drainage boards, and to the functions of such boards and of local authorities in relation to land drainage, with amendments to give effect to recommendations of the Law Commission.

[25th July 1991]

The following sections are reproduced from this Act.

Part IVA: Duties with Respect to the Environment and Recreation[1]

The Land Drainage Act 1991 extends to England and Wales only: s. 76(3) of the 1991 Act; Land Drainage Act 1994, s. 3(3).

Part IVA: Duties with Respect to the Environment and Recreation

Duties in relation to drainage boards

61A. (1) It shall be the duty of an internal drainage board[2], of each of the Ministers[3] and of the NRA[4], in formulating or considering any proposals relating to any functions of such a board—

    (*a*) so far as may be consistent—

        (i) with the purposes of any enactment relating to the functions of such a board; and

        (ii) in the case of the Secretary of State, with his duties under section 2 of the Water Industry Act 1991[5],

    so to exercise any power conferred with respect to the proposals on the board, that Minister or, as the case may be, the NRA as to further the conservation and enhancement of natural beauty and the conservation of flora, fauna and geological or physiographical features of special interest;

    (*b*) to have regard to the desirability of protecting and conserving buildings[6], sites and objects of archaeological, architectural or historical interest; and

    (*c*) to take into account any effect which the proposals would have on the beauty or amenity of any rural or urban area or on any such flora, fauna, features, buildings, sites or objects.

---

[1] Part IVA inserted by the Land Drainage Act 1994 (c. 25), s. 1. This amendment came into force on 21 September 1994: s. 3(2).

[2] Part I of this Act contains provisions relating to internal drainage boards.

[3] "The Ministers" means the Minister of Agriculture, Fisheries and Food and the Secretary of State, and in rela-

tion to anything which falls to be done by the Ministers, means those Ministers acting jointly: s. 72(1).

[4] "The NRA" means the National Rivers Authority: s. 72(1).

[5] P. 273 above.

[6] "Building" includes structure: subsection (7) below.

(2) Subject to subsection (1) above, it shall be the duty of an internal drainage board, of each of the Ministers and of the NRA, in formulating or considering any proposals relating to any functions of such a board—

(a) to have regard to the desirability of preserving for the public any freedom of access to areas of woodland, mountains, moor, heath, down, cliff or foreshore and other places of natural beauty;

(b) to have regard to the desirability of maintaining the availability to the public of any facility for visiting or inspecting any building, site or object of archaeological, architectural or historic interest; and

(c) to take into account any effect which the proposals would have on any such freedom of access or on the availability of any such facility.

(3) Subsections (1) and (2) above shall apply so as to impose duties on an internal drainage board in relation to—

(a) any proposals relating to the functions of the NRA or of a water undertaker or sewerage undertaker;

(b) any proposals relating to the management, by the company holding an appointment as such an undertaker, of any land for the time being held by that company for any purpose whatever (whether or not connected with the carrying out of the functions of a water undertaker or sewerage undertaker); and

(c) any proposal which by virtue of section 156(7) of the Water Industry Act 1991[1] (disposals of protected land) falls to be treated for the purposes of section 3 of that Act[2] as a proposal relating to the functions of a water undertaker or sewerage undertaker,

as they apply in relation to proposals relating to the functions of an internal drainage board but as if, for that purpose, the reference in subsection (1)(a) above to enactments relating to the functions of such a board were a reference to enactments relating to that to which the proposal relates.

(4) Subject to obtaining the consent of any navigation authority[3], harbour authority[4] or conservancy authority[5] before doing anything which causes navigation which is subject to the control of that authority to be obstructed or otherwise interfered with, it shall be the duty of an internal drainage board to take such steps as are—

(a) reasonably practicable; and

(b) consistent with the purposes of the enactments relating to the functions of that board,

for securing, so long as that board have rights to the use of water or land associated with water, that those rights are exercised as to ensure that the water or land is made available for recreational purposes and is so made available in the best manner.

(5) It shall be the duty of every internal drainage board, in determining what steps to take in performance of any duty imposed by virtue of subsection (4) above, to take into account the needs of persons who are chronically sick or disabled.

(6) Nothing in this section (or any other provision of this Act) shall require recreational facilities made available by an internal drainage board to be made available free of charge.

(7) In this section—

"building" includes structure; and

"harbour authority" means a harbour authority within the meaning of the Prevention of Oil Pollution Act 1971[6].

[1] P. 280 above.
[2] P. 275 above.
[3] "Navigation authority" means any person who has a duty or power under any enactment to work, maintain, conserve, improve or control any canal or other inland navigation, navigable river, estuary, harbour or dock: s. 72(1).
[4] "Harbour authority" defined by subsection (7) below.
[5] "Conservancy authority" means any person who has a duty or power under any enactment to conserve, maintain or improve the navigation of a tidal water and is not a navigation authority or a harbour authority within the meaning of the Prevention of Oil Pollution Act 1971 (c. 60).
[6] 1971 c. 60.

Duties in relation to local authorities

61B. (1) It shall be the duty of a local authority[1], of each of the Ministers[2] and of the NRA[3], in formulating or considering any proposals relating to any functions of a local authority under this Act—

(*a*) so far as may be consistent—

(i) with the purposes of this Act; and

(ii) in the case of the Secretary of State, with his duties under section 2 of the Water Industry Act 1991[4],

so to exercise any power conferred with respect to the proposals on the local authority, that Minister or, as the case may be, the NRA as to further the conservation and enhancement of natural beauty and the conservation of flora, fauna and geological or physiographical features of special interest;

(*b*) to have regard to the desirability of protecting and conserving buildings, sites and objects of archaeological, architectural or historic interest; and

(*c*) to take into account any effect which the proposals would have on the beauty or amenity of any rural or urban area or on any such flora, fauna, features, buildings, sites or objects.

(2) Subject to subsection (1) above, it shall be the duty of a local authority, of each of the Ministers and of the NRA, in formulating or considering any proposals relating to any functions of a local authority under this Act—

(*a*) to have regard to the desirability of preserving for the public any freedom of access to areas of woodland, mountains, moor, heath, down, cliff or foreshore and other places of natural beauty;

(*b*) to have regard to the desirability of maintaining the availability to the public of any facility for visiting or inspecting any building, site or object of archaeological, architectural or historic interest; and

(*c*) to take into account any effect which the proposals would have on any such freedom of access or on the availability of any such facility.

(3) In this section "building" includes structure.

Duties with respect to sites of special scientific interest

61C. (1) Where the Nature Conservancy Council for England[5] or the Countryside Council for Wales[6] are of the opinion that any area of land in England or, as the case may be, in Wales—

(*a*) is of special interest by reason of its flora, fauna or geological or physiographical features; and

(*b*) may at any time be affected—

(i) by works, operations or activities of an internal drainage board, or

(ii) by works, operations or activities of a local authority under this Act,

that Council shall notify the fact that the land is of special interest for that reason to every internal drainage board and local authority whose works, operations or activities may affect the land.

---

[1] "Local authority" means the council of a county, county borough, district or London borough or the Common Council of the City of London: s. 72(1).

[2] "The Ministers" means the Minister of Agriculture, Fisheries and Food and the Secretary of State, and in relation to anything which falls to be done by the Ministers, means those Ministers acting jointly: s. 72(1).

[3] "The NRA" means the National Rivers Authority: s. 72(1).

[4] P. 273 above.

[5] The Nature Conservancy Council for England, also known as English Nature, is established by the Environmental Protection Act 1990 (c. 43), s. 128, p. 229 above.

[6] The Countryside Council for Wales is established by the Environmental Protection Act 1990 (c. 43), s. 128, p. 229 above.

(2) Where a National Park authority or the Broads Authority[1] is of the opinion that any area of land in a National Park or in the Broads[2]—

(a) is land in relation to which the matters for the purposes of which section 61A or 61B above has effect are of particular importance; and

(b) may at any time be affected—

  (i) by works, operations or activities of an internal drainage board, or

  (ii) by works, operations or activities of a local authority under this Act,

the National Park authority or Broads Authority shall notify the fact that the land is such land, and the reasons why those matters are of particular importance in relation to the land, to every internal drainage board and local authority whose works, operations or activities may affect the land.

(3) Where an internal drainage board or local authority have received a notification under subsection (1) or (2) above with respect to any land, the board or authority shall consult the notifying body before carrying out any works, operations or activities, or in the case of the authority any works operations or activities under this Act, which appear to the board or authority to be likely—

(a) to destroy or damage any of the flora, fauna, or geological or physiographical features by reason of which the land is of special interest; or

(b) significantly to prejudice anything the importance of which is one of the reasons why the matters mentioned in subsection (2) above are of particular importance in relation to that land.

(4) Subsection (3) above shall not apply in relation to anything done in an emergency where particulars of what is done and of the emergency are notified to the Nature Conservancy Council for England, the Countryside Council for Wales, the National Park authority in question or, as the case may be, the Broads Authority as soon as practicable after that thing is done.

(5) In this section—

"the Broads" has the same meaning as in the Norfolk and Suffolk Broads Act 1988[3]; and

"National Park authority" means a National Park Committee or a joint or special planning board for a National Park.

....

Ministerial directions to drainage boards

61D. (1) Where the relevant Minister[4], considers that any works, operations or activities which are being, or are about to be, carried out by an internal drainage board are likely to destroy or seriously damage—

(a) any flora or fauna or any geological or physiographical feature of special interest; or

(b) any building, structure, site or object of archaeological, architectural or historic interest,

which in his opinion is of national or international importance, the relevant Minister may give such directions as he considers appropriate to the internal drainage board with respect to the exercise and performance of their functions.

---

[1] The Broads Authority is established by the Norfolk and Suffolk Broads Act 1988, s. 1, p. 221 above.

[2] "The Broads" defined by subsection (5) below.

[3] P. 220 above.

[4] "The relevant Minister"—

(a) in relation to internal drainage districts which are neither wholly nor partly in Wales or to the boards for such districts, means the Minister;

(b) in relation to internal drainage districts which are partly in Wales or to the boards for such districts, means the Ministers;

(c) in relation to internal drainage districts which are wholly in Wales or to the boards for such districts, means the Secretary of State: s. 72(1);

"The Minister" means the Minister of Agriculture, Fisheries and Food: s. 72(1);

"The Ministers" means the Minister and the Secretary of State, and in relation to anything which falls to be done by the Ministers, means those Ministers acting jointly: s. 72(1).

(2) Except in an emergency, the relevant Minister shall not give directions to an internal drainage board under this section unless he has first consulted the board.

(3) It shall be the duty of an internal drainage board to comply with any direction which they are given under this section.

....

Codes of practice

61E. (1) The Ministers[1] may by order approve any code of practice issued (whether by them or by another person) for the purpose of—

(*a*) giving practical guidance—

   (i) to internal drainage boards with respect to any of the matters for the purposes of which sections 61A and 61C above have effect; and

   (ii) to local authorities with respect to any of the matters for the purposes of which sections 61B and 61C also have effect; and

(*b*) promoting what appear to the Ministers to be desirable practices by internal drainage boards or, as the case may be, local authorities with respect to those matters,

and may at any time by order approve a modification of such a code or withdraw their approval of such a code or modification.

(2) A contravention of a code of practice as for the time being approved under this section shall not of itself—

(*a*) constitute a contravention of any requirement imposed by section 61A, 61B or 61C above; or

(*b*) give rise to any criminal or civil liability;

but each of the Ministers shall be under a duty to take into account whether there has been or is likely to be any such contravention in determining when and how he should exercise his powers in relation to an internal drainage board or local authority under this Act.

(3) The power of the Ministers to make an order under this section shall be exercisable by statutory instrument subject to annulment in pursuance of a resolution of either House of Parliament.

(4) The Ministers shall not make an order under this section unless they have first consulted—

(*a*) the NRA[2];

(*b*) the Countryside Commission[3], the Nature Conservancy Council for England[4] and the Countryside Council for Wales[5];

(*c*) the Historic Buildings and Monuments Commission for England; and

(*d*) such other persons or bodies as the Ministers consider it appropriate to consult.

---

[1] "The Ministers" means the Minister of Agriculture, Fisheries and Food and the Secretary of State, and in relation to anything which falls to be done by the Ministers, means those Ministers acting jointly: s. 72(1).

[2] "The NRA" means the National Rivers Authority: s. 72(1).

[3] For the establishment and functions of the Countryside Commission see the National Parks and Access to the Countryside Act 1949 (c. 97), s. 1, p. 7 above and the Countryside Act 1968 (c. 41), s. 1, p. 114 above.

[4] The Nature Conservancy Council for England, also known as English Nature, is established by the Environmental Protection Act 1990 (c. 43), s. 128, p. 229 above.

[5] The Countryside Council for Wales is established by the Environmental Protection Act 1990 (c. 43), s. 128, p. 229 above.

Sea Fisheries (Wildlife Conservation) Act 1992

Ch. 36

An Act to require appropriate Ministers and relevant bodies to have regard to the conservation of flora and fauna in the discharge of their functions under the Sea Fisheries Acts.

[16th March 1992[1]]

Conservation in the exercise of sea fisheries functions

1. (1) In discharging any functions conferred or imposed on him or them by or under the Sea Fisheries Acts, the Minister or Ministers or any relevant body shall, so far as is consistent with the proper and efficient discharge of those functions—

(a) have regard to the conservation of marine flora and fauna; and

(b) endeavour to achieve a reasonable balance between that consideration and any other considerations to which he is or they are required to have regard.

(2) In this section—

"enactment" does not include an enactment contained in Northern Ireland legislation;

"the Minister or Ministers" means any one of the following or any two or more of them acting jointly, namely—

(a) the Minister of Agriculture, Fisheries and Food;

(b) the Secretaries of State respectively concerned with the sea fishing industry in Scotland, Wales and Northern Ireland; and

(c) the Department of Agriculture for Northern Ireland;

"relevant body" means any local fisheries committee constituted under the Sea Fisheries Regulation Act 1966[2] or any authority exercising the powers of such a committee;

"the Sea Fisheries Acts" means any enactments for the time being in force relating to sea-fishing, including any enactment relating to fishing in the sea for shellfish, salmon or migratory trout.

Short title, commencement and extent

2. (1) This Act may be cited as the Sea Fisheries (Wildlife Conservation) Act 1992.

(2) This Act shall come into force at the end of the period of two months beginning with the day on which it is passed.

(3) This Act extends to Northern Ireland.

---

[1] This Act came into force on 16 May 1992: s. 2(2).   [2] 1966 c. 38.

Protection of Badgers Act 1992

Ch. 51

Arrangement of sections

Protection of Badgers Act 1992

An Act to consolidate the Badgers Act 1973, the Badgers Act 1991 and the Badgers (Further Protection) Act 1991.

[16th July 1992[1]]

Offences

Taking, injuring or killing badgers

1. (1) A person is guilty of an offence if, except as permitted by or under this Act, he wilfully kills, injures or takes, or attempts to kill, injure or take, a badger[2].

(2) If, in any proceedings for an offence under subsection (1) above consisting of attempting to kill, injure or take a badger, there is evidence from which it could reasonably be concluded that at the material time the accused was attempting to kill, injure or take a badger, he shall be presumed to have been attempting to kill, injure or take a badger unless the contrary is shown.

(3) A person is guilty of an offence if, except as permitted by or under this Act, he has in his possession or under his control any dead badger or any part of, or anything derived from, a dead badger.

(4) A person is not guilty of an offence under subsection (3) above if he shows that—

(a) the badger had not been killed, or had been killed otherwise than in contravention of the provisions of this Act or of the Badgers Act 1973[3]; or

(b) the badger or other thing in his possession or control had been sold[4] (whether to him or any other person) and, at the time of the purchase, the purchaser had had no reason to believe that the badger had been killed in contravention of any of those provisions.

(5) If a person is found committing an offence under this section on any land it shall be lawful for the owner or occupier of the land, or any servant of the owner or occupier, or any constable, to require that person forthwith to quit the land and also to give his name and address; and if that person on being so required wilfully remains on the land or refuses to give his full name or address he is guilty of an offence.

Cruelty

2. (1) A person is guilty of an offence if—

(a) he cruelly ill-treats a badger[5];

(b) he uses any badger tongs in the course of killing or taking, or attempting to kill or take, a badger;

(c) except as permitted by or under this Act, he digs for a badger; or

(d) he uses for the purpose of killing or taking a badger any firearm[6] other than a smooth bore weapon of not less than 20 bore or a rifle using ammunition[7] having a muzzle energy not less than 160 footpounds and a bullet weighing not less than 38 grains.

---

[1] This Act came into force on 16 October 1992: s. 15(3).
[2] "Badger" defined by s. 14, p. 301 below.
[3] 1973 c. 57.
[4] "Sale" defined by s. 14, p. 301 below.

[5] "Badger" defined by s. 14, p. 301 below.
[6] "Firearm" defined by s. 14, p. 301 below.
[7] "Ammunition" defined by s. 14, p. 301 below.

(2) If in any proceedings for an offence under subsection (1)(c) above there is evidence from which it could reasonably be concluded that at the material time the accused was digging for a badger he shall be presumed to have been digging for a badger unless the contrary is shown.

Interfering with badger setts

3. A person is guilty of an offence if, except as permitted by or under this Act, he interferes with a badger sett[1] by doing any of the following things—

    (a) damaging a badger sett or any part of it;

    (b) destroying a badger sett;

    (c) obstructing access to, or any entrance of, a badger sett;

    (d) causing a dog to enter a badger sett; or

    (e) disturbing a badger[2] when it is occupying a badger sett,

intending to do any of those things or being reckless as to whether his actions would have any of those consequences.

Selling and possession of live badgers

4. A person is guilty of an offence if, except as permitted by or under this Act, he sells[3] a live badger[4] or offers one for sale or has a live badger in his possession or under his control.

Marking and ringing

5. A person is guilty of an offence if, except as authorised by a licence under section 10 below[5], he marks, or attaches any ring, tag or other marking device to, a badger[6] other than one which is lawfully in his possession by virtue of such a licence.

Exceptions and licences

General exceptions

6. A person is not guilty of an offence under this Act by reason only of—

    (a) taking or attempting to take a badger[7] which has been disabled otherwise than by his act and is taken or to be taken solely for the purpose of tending it;

    (b) killing or attempting to kill a badger which appears to be so seriously injured or in such a condition that to kill it would be an act of mercy;

    (c) unavoidably killing or injuring a badger as an incidental result of a lawful action;

    (d) doing anything which is authorised under the Animals (Scientific Procedures) Act 1986[8].

Exceptions from s. 1

7. (1) Subject to subsection (2) below, a person is not guilty of an offence under section 1(1) above[9] by reason of—

    (a) killing or taking, or attempting to kill or take, a badger[10]; or

    (b) injuring a badger in the course of taking it or attempting to kill or take it,

if he shows that his action was necessary for the purpose of preventing serious damage to land, crops, poultry or any other form of property.

---

[1] "Badger sett" defined by s. 14, p. 301 below.
[2] "Badger" defined by s. 14, p. 301 below.
[3] "Sale" defined by s. 14, p. 301 below.
[4] "Badger" defined by s. 14, p. 301 below.
[5] P. 298 below.
[6] "Badger" defined by s. 14, p. 301 below.
[7] "Badger" defined by s. 14, p. 301 below.
[8] 1986 c. 14.
[9] P. 295 above.
[10] "Badger" defined by s. 14, p. 301 below.

(2) The defence provided by subsection (1) above does not apply in relation to any action taken at any time if it had become apparent, before that time, that the action would prove necessary for the purpose there mentioned and either—

(a) a licence under section 10 below[1] authorising that action had not been applied for as soon as reasonably practicable after that fact had become apparent; or

(b) an application for such a licence had been determined.

Exceptions from s. 3

8. (1) Subject to subsection (2) below, a person is not guilty of an offence under section 3 above[2] if he shows that his action was necessary for the purpose of preventing serious damage to land, crops, poultry or any other form of property.

(2) Subsection (2) of section 7 above applies to the defence in subsection (1) above as it applies to the defence in subsection (1) of that section.

(3) A person is not guilty of an offence under section 3(a), (c) or (e) above if he shows that his action was the incidental result of a lawful operation and could not reasonably have been avoided.

(4) A person is not guilty of an offence under section 3(a), (c) or (e) above by reason of obstructing any entrance of a badger sett[3] for the purpose of hunting foxes with hounds if he—

(a) takes no action other than obstructing such entrances;

(b) does not dig into the tops or sides of the entrances;

(c) complies with subsection (5) below as to the materials used for obstructing the entrances and with subsection (6) below as to how and when they are to be placed and removed; and

(d) is acting with the authority of the owner or occupier of the land and the authority of a recognised Hunt[4].

(5) The materials used shall be only—

(a) untainted straw or hay, or leaf-litter, bracken or loose soil; or

(b) a bundle of sticks or faggots, or paper sacks either empty or filled with untainted straw or hay or leaf-litter, bracken or loose soil.

(6) The materials shall not be packed hard into the entrances and—

(a) if they are of the kind mentioned in paragraph (a) of subsection (5) above, they shall not be placed in the entrances except on the day of the hunt or after midday on the preceding day;

(b) if they are of the kind mentioned in paragraph (b) of that subsection, they shall not be placed in the entrances except on the day of the hunt and shall be removed on the same day.

(7) A person is not guilty of an offence under section 3(a), (c) or (e) above by reason of his hounds barking at a badger sett provided they are withdrawn as soon as reasonably practicable.

(8) Each recognised Hunt shall keep a register of the persons authorised to act under subsection (4) above.

(9) In this section "recognised Hunt" means a Hunt recognised by the Masters of Fox Hounds Association, the Association of Masters of Harriers and Beagles or the Central Committee of Fell Packs.

Exceptions from s. 4

9. A person is not guilty of an offence under section 4 above[5] by reason of having a live badger[6] in his possession or under his control if—

---

[1] P. 298 below.
[2] P. 296 below.
[3] "Badger sett" defined by s. 14, p. 301 below.

[4] "Recognised Hunt" defined by subsection (9) below.
[5] P. 296 above.
[6] "Badger" defined by s. 14, p. 301 below.

(a) it is in his possession or under his control, as the case may be, in the course of his business as a carrier; or

(b) it has been disabled otherwise than by his act and taken by him solely for the purpose of tending it and it is necessary for that purpose for it to remain in his possession or under his control, as the case may be.

....

Licences

10. (1) A licence may be granted to any person by the appropriate Conservancy Council[1] authorising him, notwithstanding anything in the foregoing provisions of this Act, but subject to compliance with any conditions specified in the licence—

(a) for scientific or educational purposes or for the conservation of badgers[2]—

 (i) to kill or take, within an area specified in the licence by any means so specified, or to sell, or to have in his possession, any number of badgers so specified; or

 (ii) to interfere with any badger sett[3] within an area specified in the licence by any means so specified;

(b) for the purpose of any zoological gardens or collection specified in the licence, to take within an area specified in the licence by any means so specified, or to sell, or to have in his possession, any number of badgers so specified;

(c) for the purpose of ringing and marking, to take badgers within an area specified in the licence, to mark such badgers or to attach to them any ring, tag or other marking device as specified in the licence;

(d) for the purpose of any development as defined in section 55(1) of the Town and Country Planning Act 1990[4] or, as respects Scotland, section 19(1) of the Town and Country Planning (Scotland) Act 1972[5], to interfere with a badger sett within an area specified in the licence by any means so specified;

(e) for the purpose of the preservation, or archaeological investigation, of a monument scheduled under section 1 of the Ancient Monuments and Archaeological Areas Act 1979[6], to interfere with a badger sett within an area specified in the licence by any means so specified;

(f) for the purpose of investigating whether any offence has been committed or gathering evidence in connection with proceedings before any court, to interfere with a badger sett within an area specified in the licence by any means so specified.

(2) A licence may be granted to any person by the appropriate Minister[7] authorising him, notwithstanding anything in the foregoing provisions of this Act, but subject to compliance with any conditions specified in the licence—

(a) for the purpose of preventing the spread of disease, to kill or take badgers, or to interfere with a badger sett, within an area specified in the licence by any means so specified;

(b) for the purpose of preventing serious damage to land, crops, poultry or any other form of property, to kill or take badgers, or to interfere with a badger sett, within an area specified in the licence by any means so specified;

(c) for the purpose of any agricultural or forestry operation, to interfere with a badger sett within an area specified in the licence by any means so specified;

(d) for the purpose of any operation (whether by virtue of the Land Drainage Act 1991[8] or otherwise) to maintain or improve any existing watercourse or drainage works, or to construct new works required for the drainage of any land, including works for the purpose of defence

---

[1] "Appropriate Conservancy Council" defined by subsection (4) below.
[2] "Badger" defined by s. 14, p. 301 below.
[3] "Badger sett" defined by s. 14, p. 301 below.
[4] 1990 c. 8.
[5] 1972 c. 52.
[6] 1979 c. 46.
[7] "Appropriate Minister" defined by subsection (5) below.
[8] 1991 c. 59.

against sea water or tidal water, to interfere with a badger sett within an area specified in the licence by any means so specified.

(3) A licence may be granted to any person either by the appropriate Conservancy Council or the appropriate Minister authorising that person, notwithstanding anything in the foregoing provisions of this Act, but subject to compliance with any conditions specified in the licence, to interfere with a badger sett within an area specified in the licence by any means so specified for the purpose of controlling foxes in order to protect livestock, game or wild life.

(4) In this section "the appropriate Conservancy Council" means, in relation to a licence for an area—

(a) in England, the Nature Conservancy Council for England[1];

(b) in Wales, the Countryside Council for Wales[2]; and

(c) in Scotland, Scottish Natural Heritage[3].

(5) In this section "the appropriate Minister" means in relation to a licence for an area—

(a) in England, the Minister of Agriculture, Fisheries and Food; and

(b) in Wales or in Scotland, the Secretary of State.

(6) The appropriate Minister shall from time to time consult with the appropriate Conservancy Council as to the exercise of his functions under subsection (2)(b), (c) or (d) above and shall not grant a licence of any description unless he has been advised by the appropriate Conservancy Council as to the circumstances in which, in that Council's opinion, licences of that description should be granted.

(7) In relation to Scottish Natural Heritage subsection (6) above shall have effect with the omission of the reference to subsection (2)(c) and (d).

(8) A licence granted under this section may be revoked at any time by the authority by whom it was granted, and without prejudice to any other liability to a penalty which he may have incurred under this or any other Act, a person who contravenes or fails to comply with any condition imposed on the grant of a licence under this section is guilty of an offence.

(9) A licence under this section shall not be unreasonably withheld or revoked.

(10) It shall be a defence in proceedings for an offence under section 8(b) of the Protection of Animals Act 1911[4] or section 7(b) of the Protection of Animals (Scotland) Act 1912[5] (each of which restricts the placing on land of poison and poisonous substances) to show that—

(a) the act alleged to constitute the offence was done under the authority of a licence granted under subsection (2)(a) above; and

(b) any conditions specified in the licence were complied with.

Enforcement and penalties

Powers of constables

11. Where a constable has reasonable grounds for suspecting that a person is committing an offence under the foregoing provisions of this Act, or has committed an offence under those provisions or those of the Badgers Act 1973[6] and that evidence of the commission of the offence is to be found on that person or any vehicle or article he may have with him, the constable may—

(a) without warrant stop and search that person and any vehicle or article he may have with him;

---

[1] The Nature Conservancy Council for England, also known as English Nature, is established by the Environmental Protection Act 1990 (c. 43), s. 128, p. 229 above.

[2] The Countryside Council for Wales is established by the Environmental Protection Act 1990 (c. 43), s. 128, p. 229 above.

[3] Scottish Natural Heritage is established by the Natural Heritage (Scotland) Act 1991 (c. 28), s. 1, p. 245 above.

[4] 1911 c. 27.

[5] 1912 c. 14.

[6] 1973 c. 57.

(*b*) seize and detain for the purposes of proceedings under any of those provisions anything which may be evidence of the commission of the offence or may be liable to be forfeited under section 12(4) below;

(*c*) in Scotland arrest that person without warrant if he fails to give his full name and address to the constable's satisfaction.

Penalties and forfeiture

12. (1) A person guilty of an offence under section 1(1)[1] or (3), 2[2] or 3[3] above is liable on summary conviction to imprisonment for a term not exceeding six months or a fine not exceeding level 5 on the standard scale[4] or both; and a person guilty of an offence under section 4[5], 5[6] or 10(8)[7] above or 13(7) below is liable on summary conviction to a fine not exceeding that level.

(2) Where an offence was committed in respect of more than one badger[8] the maximum fine which may be imposed under subsection (1) above shall be determined as if the person convicted had been convicted of a separate offence in respect of each badger.

(3) A person guilty of an offence under section 1(5) above[9] is liable on summary conviction to a fine not exceeding level 3 on the standard scale[10].

(4) The court by which a person is convicted of an offence under this Act shall order the forfeiture of any badger or badger skin in respect of which the offence was committed and may, if they think fit, order the forfeiture of any weapon or article in respect of or by means of which the offence was committed.

Powers of court where dog used or present at commission of offence

13. (1) Where a dog has been used in or was present at the commission of an offence under sections 1(1)[11], 2[12] or 3[13] above, the court, on convicting the offender, may, in addition to or in substitution for any other punishment, make either or both of the following orders—

(*a*) an order for the destruction or other disposal of the dog;

(*b*) an order disqualifying the offender, for such period as it thinks fit, for having custody of a dog.

(2) Where the court makes an order under subsection (1)(*a*) above, it may—

(*a*) appoint a person to undertake the destruction or other disposal of the dog and require any person having custody of the dog to deliver it up for that purpose; and

(*b*) order the offender to pay such sum as the court may determine to be the reasonable expenses of destroying or otherwise disposing of the dog and of keeping it pending its destruction or disposal.

(3) Where an order under subsection (1)(*a*) above is made in relation to a dog owned by a person other than the offender, the owner of the dog may appeal to the Crown Court against the order.

(4) A dog shall not be destroyed pursuant to an order under subsection (1)(*a*) above—

(*a*) until the end of the period within which notice of appeal to the Crown Court against the order can be given; and

(*b*) if notice of appeal is given in that period, until the appeal is determined or withdrawn,

---

[1] P. 295 above.
[2] P. 295 above.
[3] P. 296 above.
[4] The present fine at level 5 on the standard scale is £5,000: Criminal Justice Act 1991 (c. 53), s. 17 which came into force on 1 October 1992: S.I. 1992/333, S.I. 1992/2118.
[5] P. 296 above.
[6] P. 296 above.
[7] P. 299 above.

[8] "Badger" defined by s. 14, p. 301 below.
[9] P. 295 above.
[10] The present fine at level 3 on the standard scale is £1,000: Criminal Justice Act 1991 (c. 53), s. 17 which came into force on 1 October 1992: S.I. 1992/333, S.I. 1992/2118.
[11] P. 295 above.
[12] P. 295 above.
[13] P. 296 above.

unless the owner of the dog gives notice to the court which made the order that he does not intend to appeal against it.

(5) A person who is disqualified for having custody of a dog by virtue of an order made under subsection (1)(*b*) above may, at any time after the end of the period of one year beginning with the date of the order, apply to the court that made it (or any magistrates' court acting for the same petty sessions area as that court) for a direction terminating the disqualification.

(6) On an application under subsection (5) above the court may—

(*a*) having regard to the applicant's character, his conduct since the disqualification was imposed and any other circumstances of the case, grant or refuse the application; and

(*b*) order the applicant to pay all or any part of the costs of the application;

and where an application in respect of an order is refused no further application in respect of that order shall be entertained if made before the end of the period of one year beginning with the date of the refusal.

(7) Any person who—

(*a*) has custody of a dog in contravention of an order under subsection (1)(*b*) above; or

(*b*) fails to comply with a requirement imposed on him under subsection (2)(*a*) above,

is guilty of an offence.

(8) A sum ordered to be paid by an order under subsection (2)(*b*) above shall be recoverable summarily as a civil debt.

(9) In the application of this section to Scotland—

(*a*) in subsection (3), for the words "Crown Court against the order" there shall be substituted the words "High Court of Justiciary against the order within the period of seven days beginning with the date of the order";

(*b*) for subsection (4)(*a*) there shall be substituted—

"(*a*) until the end of the period of seven days beginning with the date of the order"; and

(*c*) in subsection (5), the words "(or any magistrates' court acting for the same petty sessions area as that court)" shall be omitted.

Interpretation

14. In this Act—

"ammunition" has the same meaning as in the Firearms Act 1968[1];

"badger" means any animal of the species *Meles meles*;

"badger sett" means any structure or place which displays signs indicating current use by a badger;

"firearm" has the same meaning as in the Firearms Act 1968;

"sale" includes hire, barter and exchange and cognate expressions shall be construed accordingly.

Short title, repeals, commencement and extent

15. (1) This Act may be cited as the Protection of Badgers Act 1992.

(2) The enactments mentioned in the Schedule to this Act are repealed to the extent specified in the third column of that Schedule.

(3) This Act shall come into force at the end of the period of three months beginning with the day on which it is passed[2].

(4) This Act does not extend to Northern Ireland.

[1] 1968 c. 27.

[2] This Act came into force on 16 October 1992.

Local Government etc. (Scotland) Act 1994

Ch. 39

Part II: Water and Sewerage Re-organisation

Section 62 of this Act makes provision for the establishment of new water and sewerage authorities, the East of Scotland Water Authority, the West of Scotland Water Authority, and the North of Scotland Water Authority. These authorities are to be the water and sewerage authorities for their area from 1 April 1996. Section 65 imposes duties in respect of the conservation of natural beauty, flora and fauna and geological or physiographical features of special interest on the Secretary of State and the new authorities. Section 73 of the Act is reproduced below. At the time of preparing this manual section 73 has not been brought into force.

Environmental protection

Duty of new authorities as respects Natural Heritage Area or area of special interest

73. (1) Where an area of land ("the relevant land")—

   (a) has been designated under section 6(2) of the Natural Heritage (Scotland) Act 1991[1] ("the 1991 Act") as a Natural Heritage Area; or

   (b) is, in the opinion of Scottish Natural Heritage ("the environmental authority"), of special interest by reason of its flora, fauna or geological or physiographical features,

and the environmental authority consider that it may at any time be affected by schemes, works, operations or activities of a new water and sewerage authority ("the relevant authority"), the environmental authority shall by written notice advise the relevant authority that they so consider; but they shall forthwith notify the relevant authority of any cancellation or variation, under section 6(7) of the 1991 Act, of the designation or if they cease to be of the opinion mentioned in paragraph (b) above.

(2) Where the relevant authority intend to carry out any scheme, work, operation or activity which appears to them likely to, as the case may be—

   (a) prejudice significantly the value of the relevant land, or any part of it, as a Natural Heritage Area (the designation mentioned in subsection (1)(a) above not having been cancelled or so varied as no longer to apply to the part in question); or

   (b) destroy or damage any of the flora, fauna or features, by reference to which the environmental authority formulated their opinion under subsection (1)(b) above as respects the special interest of the relevant land (notification of their ceasing to be of that opinion not having been given),

the relevant authority shall consult with the environmental authority before commencing the scheme, work, operation or activity.

(3) Subsection (2) above shall not apply in relation to anything done by the relevant authority in an emergency if particulars of what is done and of the emergency are notified by them to the environmental authority as soon as is practicable after the thing is done.

(4) Any expression not defined in this Act but used both in this section and in the 1991 Act, shall be construed in accordance with that Act.

---

[1] P. 248 above. "Natural Heritage Area" is defined by s. 6 of the Natural Heritage (Scotland) Act 1991.

Part II

Secondary Legislation

The Forestry (Felling of Trees) Regulations 1979

S.I. 1979 No. 791

The Forestry Commissioners, in exercise of the powers conferred upon them by sections 10(1), 11(2), 14(3), 15(2), 16(2), 19(3), 20(1), 21(2), (3) and (5), 23(1), 24(2), 25(1), 26(2) and 32(1) and (2) of the Forestry Act 1967[1], and of every other power enabling them in that behalf, and after consultation with the Home Grown Timber Advisory Committee, hereby make the following Regulations:

Citation, commencement and extent

1. (1) These Regulations may be cited as the Forestry (Felling of Trees) Regulations 1979 and shall come into operation on 9th August 1979.

(2) These Regulations shall apply to Great Britain.

Revocation of previous regulations

2. The Forestry (Felling of Trees) Regulations 1951[2] are hereby revoked.

Interpretation

3. (1) In these Regulations, unless the context otherwise requires, the following expressions have the meanings hereby assigned to them respectively, that is to say—

"the Act" means the Forestry Act 1967;

"the appropriate Minister" means the Minister of Agriculture, Fisheries and Food as respects England, the Secretary of State for Scotland as respects Scotland and the Secretary of State for Wales as respects Wales;

"the Commissioners" means the Forestry Commissioners;

"the Conservator" means, in relation to the service of any document, the Commissioners' Conservator of Forests for the conservancy in which the trees to which the document relates are or were growing; and

"licence" means a licence under Part II of the Act[3] authorising the felling of trees.

(2) Any reference in these Regulations to a form denoted by a number shall be construed as a reference to the form so numbered in Schedule 1 hereto or a form substantially to the like effect.

Application for felling licence

4. Any application for a felling licence made under section 10(1) of the Act[4] shall be—

(a) in the form set out in Schedule 2 hereto, which shall be supplied by the Commissioners[5] on request, or in a form substantially to the like effect;

(b) accompanied by an Ordnance Survey map signed and dated by the applicant showing the area to which the application relates on a scale not smaller than one to ten thousand or six inches

[1] P. 66 above.
[2] S.I. 1951/1726.
[3] P. 72 above.
[4] P. 74 above.
[5] "The Commissioners" means the Forestry Commissioners: reg. 3(1) above.

to one mile, and with the National Grid reference of the north west corner of the area marked on the map.[1]

Claims for compensation

5. Any claim for compensation made under section 11(2) of the Act[2] (which relates to compensation for refusal of a licence[3]) shall be in Form 1, if the land on which the trees concerned are or were growing is situate in England or Wales, or in Form 2, if the land is situate in Scotland, and shall be sent to the Conservator[4].

Notices under section 14 of the Act

6. Any notice under section 14(3) of the Act[5] (which relates to the right of an applicant for a licence[6] authorising the felling of trees in accordance with a plan approved by the Commissioners[7] to require them to buy the trees if the licence is refused) shall be in Form 3 and shall be sent to the Conservator[8] within three months after the receipt by the applicant for the licence of the Commissioners' notice of refusal thereof.

Prescribed period under section 15 of the Act

7. For the purposes of section 15(2) of the Act[9] (which provides the procedure to be followed where the Commissioners[10] propose to grant a licence[11] in respect of any felling of trees for which consent is required under a tree preservation order and give the requisite notice in writing of the proposal to the authority by whom the order was made and the authority within the prescribed period after the receipt of the notice object to the proposal and do not withdraw the objection) the prescribed period shall be one month.

Review of refusal of licence or conditions of licence

8. (1) Any notice under section 16(2) of the Act[12] (which relates to the review of a refusal of a licence[13] or of the conditions subject to which a licence has been granted) shall be served on the appropriate Minister[14] within three months after—

(*a*) in the case of a refusal of which notice has been given under section 10(6) of the Act[15], the receipt of that notice by the applicant for the licence;

(*b*) in the case where refusal is deemed to take place by virtue of section 13(1) of the Act[16], the expiration of the period specified in that section; and

(*c*) in the case of the grant of a licence subject to conditions, the receipt of the licence by the applicant therefor.

(2) Any notice under section 16(2) of the Act shall be in Form 4, 5 or 6 according as the case falls within sub-paragraph (*a*), (*b*) or (*c*) of the preceding paragraph of this Regulation.

---

[1] Reg. 4 substituted by the Forestry (Felling of Trees) (Amendment) Regulations 1987, S.I. 1987/632, reg. 2(1). This amendment came into force on 1 May 1987: reg. 1.

[2] P. 75 above.

[3] "Licence" defined by reg. 3(1), p. 305 above.

[4] "Conservator" defined by reg. 3(1), p. 305 above.

[5] P. 76 above.

[6] "Licence" defined by reg. 3(1), p. 305 above.

[7] "The Commissioners" means the Forestry Commissioners: reg. 3(1), p. 305 above.

[8] "Conservator" defined by reg. 3(1), p. 305 above.

[9] P. 77 above.

[10] "The Commissioners" means the Forestry Commissioners: reg. 3(1), p. 305 above.

[11] "Licence" defined by reg. 3(1), p. 305 above.

[12] P. 78 above.

[13] "Licence" defined by reg. 3(1), p. 305 above.

[14] "Appropriate Minister" defined by reg. 3(1), p. 305 above.

[15] P. 74 above.

[16] P. 75 above.

Appeal against restocking notice

8A. Any notice under section 17B(1) of the Act[1] (which relates to appeal against a restocking notice) shall be served on the appropriate Minister[2] within three months after the receipt of the restocking notice by the person on whom that notice has been served by the Commissioners under section 17A of the Act (power to require restocking after unauthorised felling) and shall be in Form 6A.[3]

Prescribed period under section 19 of the Act

9. For the purposes of section 19(3) of the Act[4] (which provides the procedure to be followed where the Commissioners[5] propose to give felling directions in respect of trees to which a tree preservation order relates and give the requisite notice in writing of the proposal to the authority by whom the order was made and the authority within the prescribed period after the receipt of the notice object to the proposal and do not withdraw the objection) the prescribed period shall be one month.

Review of felling directions

10. Any notice under section 20(1) of the Act[6] (which relates to the review of felling directions given by the Commissioners[7]) shall be served on the appropriate Minister[8] within three months after the receipt of the directions to which it relates and shall be in Form 7.

Notices and prescribed periods under section 21 of the Act

11. (1) Any notice under section 21(2) of the Act[9] (which relates to the right of a person to whom felling directions are given to require his trees or his interest in land to be acquired) shall be given to the appropriate Minister[10] within three months after the receipt of the directions to which it relates and shall be in Form 8.

(2) For the purposes of section 21(3) of the Act (which provides that, where a notice is given under section 21(2) of the Act, the appropriate Minister may within the prescribed period after receiving it take certain action) the prescribed period shall be three months, in the reckoning of which no account shall be taken of the time during which, in pursuance of paragraph (2) of the next following Regulation, proceedings on the notice are postponed.

(3) For the purposes of section 21(5) of the Act (which provides that, where the committee referred to therein have made a report to the appropriate Minister, he may in certain cases and within the prescribed period after receiving it take certain action) the prescribed period shall be three months.

Proceedings in respect of felling directions

12. (1) Where a request has been duly made under section 20(1) of the Act[11] (which relates to the review of felling directions given by the Commissioners[12]) any proceedings on that request in respect of the felling directions to which it relates may be postponed—

---

[1] P. 79 above.
[2] "Appropriate Minister" defined by reg. 3(1), p. 305 above.
[3] Reg. 8A inserted by the Forestry (Felling of Trees) (Amendment) Regulations 1987, S.I. 1987/632, reg. 2(2). This amendment came into force on 1 May 1987: reg. 1.
[4] P. 80 above.
[5] "The Commissioners" means the Forestry Commissioners: reg. 3(1), p. 305.
[6] P. 81 above.
[7] "The Commissioners" means the Forestry Commissioners: reg. 3(1), p. 305 above.
[8] "Appropriate Minister" defined by reg. 3(1), p. 305 above.
[9] P. 81 above.
[10] "Appropriate Minister" defined by reg. 3(1), p. 305 above.
[11] P. 81 above.
[12] "The Commissioners" means the Forestry Commissioners: reg. 3(1), p. 305 above.

(*a*) until a notice has been duly given in respect of those directions under section 21(2) of the Act[1] (which relates to the right of a person to whom felling directions are given to require his trees or his interest in land to be acquired) or

(*b*) until the expiration of the period within which such a notice might be given,

whichever event first happens.

(2) Where a notice has been duly given under section 21(2) of the Act, any proceedings on that notice in respect of the felling directions to which it relates may be postponed—

(*a*) until a request has been duly made in respect of those directions under section 20(1) of the Act or

(*b*) until the expiration of the period within which such a notice might be given.

whichever event first happens.

(3) Where such a request and such a notice are duly made and given in respect of the same directions, the appropriate Minister[2] may arrange for any proceedings before a committee on the notice to be taken concurrently with any proceedings before a committee on the request.

Prescribed period under section 24(2) of the Act

13. For the purposes of section 24(2) of the Act[3] (which, as adapted by section 17C of the Act, provides that in the event of failure to carry out works in accordance with conditions of a licence[4] or to comply with felling directions or a restocking notice, the Commissioners[5] may give notice to the owner of the land or the owner of the trees, as the case may be, requiring such steps as may be specified in the notice to be taken within such time (not being less than the prescribed period after the notice has become operative) as may be so specified for remedying the default) the prescribed period shall be three months.[6]

Notices under section 25 of the Act

14. Any notice under section 25(1) of the Act[7] (which, as adapted by section 17C of the Act, relates to a request for the review of a requirement that the steps specified in a notice (including a restocking notice) given under section 24(2) of the Act shall be taken) shall be in Form 9 and shall be served on the appropriate Minister[8] within three months after the receipt by the owner of the land or the owner of the trees, as the case may be, of the notice under section 24(2) of the Act.[9]

Claims under section 26 of the Act

15. Any claim made under section 26(2) of the Act[10] (which provides for payment by the Commissioners[11] to the owner of the trees removed by them) shall be in Form 10 if the land on which the trees concerned were growing is situate in England or Wales, or in Form 11, if the land is situate in Scotland, and shall be sent to the Conservator[12].

---

[1] P. 81 above.

[2] "Appropriate Minister" defined by reg. 3(1), p. 305 above.

[3] P. 83 above.

[4] "Licence" defined by reg. 3(1), p. 305 above.

[5] "The Commissioners" means the Forestry Commissioners: reg. 3(1), p. 305 above.

[6] Reg. 13 substituted by the Forestry (Felling of Trees) (Amendment) Regulations 1987, S.I. 1987/632, reg. 2(3). This amendment came into force on 1 May 1987: reg. 1.

[7] P. 84 above.

[8] "Appropriate Minister" defined by reg. 3(1), p. 305 above.

[9] Reg. 14 substituted by the Forestry (Felling of Trees) (Amendment) Regulations 1987, S.I. 1987/632, reg. 2(3).

[10] P. 84 above.

[11] "The Commissioners" means the Forestry Commissioners: reg. 3(1), p. 305 above.

[12] "Conservator" defined by reg. 3(1), p. 305 above.

Verification of claims and notices

16. The Commissioners[1] or the appropriate Minister[2], as the case may be, may require any particulars specified in any claim or notice (including a notice of appeal against a restocking notice) made or given under the Act to be verified by statutory declaration.[3]

In witness whereof the Official Seal of the Forestry Commissioners is hereunto affixed on 9th July 1979.

The Schedules to this order, which are not reproduced, are:

Schedule 1

Form 1: Claim for compensation (England and Wales)

Form 2: Claim for compensation (Scotland)

Form 3: Notice requiring purchase of trees under section 14

Form 4: Request for review of refusal of a licence

Form 5: Request for review of refusal of a licence

Form 6: Request for review of conditions of a licence

Form 6A: Notice of objection in relation to a restocking notice[4]

Form 7: Request for review of felling directions

Form 8: Notice requiring purchase of trees or land under section 21(2)

Form 9: Request for review of section 24 Notice[5]

Form 10: Claim for value of trees felled by the Forestry Commissioners (England and Wales)

Form 11: Claim for value of trees felled by the Forestry Commissioners (Scotland)

Schedule 2

Form: Application for licence to fell growing trees

As set out in Regulation 4, this form is available from the Commissioners on request.

---

[1] "The Commissioners" means the Forestry Commissioners: reg. 3(1), p. 305 above.
[2] "Appropriate Minister" defined by reg. 3(1), p. 305 above.

[3] Reg. 16 substituted by the Forestry (Felling of Trees) (Amendment) Regulations 1987, S.I. 1987/632, reg. 2(4).
[4] Form inserted by S.I. 1987/632.
[5] New form substituted by S.I. 1987/632.

The Forestry (Exceptions from Restriction of Felling) Regulations 1979

S.I. 1979 No. 792

The Forestry Commissioners, in exercise of the powers conferred upon them by sections 9(5)(*a*)[1] and 32(1) of the Forestry Act 1967, and of every other power enabling them in that behalf, and after consultation with the Home Grown Timber Advisory Committee, hereby make the following Regulations:

Citation, commencement and extent

1. (1) These Regulations may be cited as the Forestry (Exceptions from Restriction of Felling) Regulations 1979 and shall come into operation on 9th August 1979.

(2) These Regulations shall apply to Great Britain.

Revocation

2. The Forestry (Exceptions from Restriction of Felling) Regulations 1951[2], the Forestry (Exception from Restriction of Felling) Regulations 1972[3], the Forestry (Exception from Restriction of Felling) Regulations 1974[4] and the Forestry (Exception from Restriction of Felling) (Amendment) Regulations 1977[5] are hereby revoked.

Interpretation

3. In these Regulations, unless the context otherwise requires, the following expressions have the meanings hereby assigned to them respectively, that is to say—

"the Act" means the Forestry Act 1967;

"the Minister" means the Minister of Agriculture, Fisheries and Food as respects England, the Secretary of State for Scotland as respects Scotland and the Secretary of State for Wales as respects Wales;

"the Commissioners" means the Forestry Commissioners;

"aerodrome" means any area of land or water designed, equipped, set a part or commonly used for affording facilities for the landing and departure of aircraft;

"licence" means a licence under Part II of the Act[6] authorising the felling of trees; and

"statutory undertakers" means persons authorised by any enactment to carry on any railway, light railway, tramway, road transport, water transport, canal, inland navigation, dock, harbour, power or lighthouse undertaking, or any undertaking for the supply of[7] hydraulic power or water, and public gas suppliers within the meaning of Part I of the Gas Act 1986.[8]

---

[1] P. 73 above.
[2] S.I. 1951/1725.
[3] S.I. 1974/1817.
[4] S.I. 1972/91.
[5] S.I. 1974/1817.
[6] P. 1972/91.
[7] Former words "electricity" omitted by the Electricity Act 1989 (Consequential Modifications of Subordinate Legislation) Order 1990, S.I. 1990/526, which came into force on 31 March 1990; "gas" omitted by the Gas Act 1986 (Consequential Modifications of Subordinate Legislation) Order 1986, S.I. 1986/1356, which came into force on 23 August 1986.

[8] Words ", and public gas suppliers ... Gas Act 1986" inserted by the Gas Act 1986 (Consequential Modifications of Subordinate Legislation) Order 1986, S.I. 1986/1356, which came into force on 23 August 1986.

Exceptions from restriction of felling

4. The following shall be exceptions from the application of section 9(1) of the Act[1] (which prohibits the felling of growing trees unless a licence[2] is in force authorising the felling) additional to the exceptions specified in section 9(2), (3) and (4) of the Act and accordingly no licence shall be required in respect of—

(1) the felling of any tree where the Secretary of State for Defence or the Secretary of State for Trade has certified that the tree obstructs the approach of aircraft to, or their departure from, any aerodrome[3] or hinders the safe and efficient use of air navigational or aircraft landing installations;

(2) the felling by statutory undertakers[4] of trees on land in their occupation which obstruct the construction of any works required for the purposes of the undertaking of those undertakers or of trees which interfere with the maintenance or operation of any works vested in those undertakers;

(3) the felling of any tree by, or at the request of, a water authority established under the Water Act 1973, or an internal drainage board for the purposes of the Land Drainage Act 1976[5], where the tree interferes or would interfere with the exercise of any functions of that authority or board;

(4) the felling of any tree of the genus *Ulmus* which is affected by the disease in elms caused by the fungus *Ceratocystis ulmi* and commonly known as Dutch elm disease to such an extent that the greater part of the crown of the tree is dead;

(5) the felling of trees on land which is subject to an agreement entered into with the Commissioners[6], being an agreement to which section 5(1) of the Act[7] refers, namely an agreement to the effect that the land shall not, except with the previous consent in writing of the Commissioners or, in the case of dispute, under direction of the Minister[8], be used otherwise than for the growing of timber or other forest products in accordance with the rules or practice of good forestry or for purposes connected therewith: provided that this exception shall not apply unless—

(a) the agreement is a forestry dedication covenant or a forestry dedication agreement registered in the General Register of Sasines, and the following conditions are fulfilled, that is to say—

   (i) any positive covenants or terms on the part of the owner of the land contained in the same document as the said forestry dedication covenant or agreement are at the time of the felling binding on the person who is then the owner of the land; and

   (ii) the felling is in accordance with a plan of operations approved by the Forestry Commissioners under such document;

or

(b) the agreement, being an agreement relating to land situate in England or Wales, is not made under seal or, being an agreement relating to land situate in Scotland, is a forestry dedication agreement not registered in the General Register of Sasines, and the following conditions are fulfilled, that is to say—

   (i) the land is at the time of the felling owned by the person or persons who entered into the agreement with the Commissioners or by the survivor or survivors of such persons; and

   (ii) the felling is in accordance with a plan of operations approved by the Commissioners under the agreement;

(6) the felling of trees in accordance with a plan of operations approved by the Commissioners as part of an agreement entered into between the Commissioners and an applicant for participation

---

[1] P. 72 above.
[2] "Licence" defined by reg. 3, p. 310 above.
[3] "Aerodrome" defined by reg. 3, p. 310 above.
[4] "Statutory undertaker" defined by reg. 3, p. 310 above.
[5] See also the Land Drainage Act 1991 (c. 59): Water Consolidation (Consequential Provisions) Act 1991 (c. 60),

s. 2, sch. 2, pt. 1, para. 1.
[6] "The Commissioners" means the Forestry Commissioners: reg. 3, p. 310 above.
[7] P. 69 above.
[8] "The Minister" defined by reg. 3, p. 310 above.

in the Forestry Grant Scheme or the Broadleaved Woodland Grant Scheme or the Woodland Grant Scheme (being schemes under which the Commissioners enter into agreements to make grants pursuant to section 1 of the Forestry Act 1979[1] for and in connection with the use and management of land for forestry purposes), where the felling is carried out or authorised by a person who has entered into that agreement or has subsequently agreed with the Commissioners to observe it.[2]

In Witness whereof the Official Seal of the Forestry Commissioners is hereunto affixed on 9th July 1979.

[1] P. 142 above.
[2] Para. 6 substituted by the Forestry (Exceptions from Restriction of Felling) (Amendment) Regulations 1988, S.I. 1988/970, reg. 2. This amendment came into force on 28 June 1988: reg. 1.

Wildlife and Countryside (Registration to Sell etc. Certain Dead Wild Birds) Regulations 1982

S.I. 1982 No. 1219

The Secretary of State for the Environment as respects England, the Secretary of State for Scotland as respects Scotland and the Secretary of State for Wales as respects Wales, in exercise of the powers conferred by section 6(2), (7) and (8) of the Wildlife and Countryside Act 1981[1], hereby make the following regulations:

Title, commencement and interpretation

1. (1) These regulations may be cited as the Wildlife and Countryside (Registration to Sell etc. Certain Dead Wild Birds) Regulations 1982, and shall come into operation on 28th September 1982.

(2) In these regulations—

"registered person" means a person registered in accordance with these regulations;

"the Act" means the Wildlife and Countryside Act 1981; and

"the Secretary of State" means the Secretary of State for the Environment.

(3) Any reference in these regulations to a dead wild bird to which these regulations apply is a reference to any dead wild bird to which section 6(2) of the Act applies.

Registration

2. (1) The Secretary of State shall maintain a register for the purposes of section 6(2)[1] of the Act.

(2) An application for registration shall be made by the person seeking registration on a form obtained from the Secretary of State.

(3) The Secretary of State may make such reasonable charge for registration as he thinks fit.

3. (1) Where any person becomes registered—

(a) within five years of his having been convicted of an offence under Part I of the Act for which a special penalty is provided; or

(b) within three years of his having been convicted of any other offence under the said Part I so far as it relates to the protection of birds or other animals or any offence involving their ill-treatment,

his registration shall be void; provided that no account shall be taken for this purpose of a conviction which has become spent by virtue of the Rehabilitation of Offenders Act 1974.

(2) Where any registered person is convicted as mentioned in paragraph (1) above, his registration shall cease to have effect.

(3) Any person who has been convicted as mentioned in paragraph (1) above (and whose conviction is not required by that paragraph to be left out of account) shall when applying for registration notify the Secretary of State of his conviction and supply details thereof.

[1] P. 151 above.

(4) Any person—

(*a*) who has applied for registration (and whose application is still under consideration); or

(*b*) who is a registered person,

and who is convicted as mentioned in paragraph (1) above, shall immediately notify the Secretary of State of his conviction and supply details thereof.

4. Any registration effected before 1st April 1991 shall cease to have effect on 1st September 1992, and any registration effected on or after 1st April 1991 shall cease to have effect at the expiration of a period of three years beginning with the day on which the registration is effected.[1]

Obligations of registered persons

5. Any registered person who has in his possession any dead wild bird[2] to which these regulations apply shall maintain a record relating to such bird in the form set out in Schedule 1[3] to these regulations.

6. Any registered person who has in his possession any dead wild bird to which these regulations apply shall ensure that there is at all times affixed to the skin or, where there is no skin, to the skeleton[4] of the bird a mark which enables that bird to be identified by reference to the record required by regulation 5.

7. Any registered person who sells any dead wild bird to which these regulations apply shall ensure that at the time of the sale there is affixed to the skin or, where there is no skin, to the skeleton[5] of the bird a mark obtained from the Secretary of State:

Provided that where, for the purpose of display—

(*a*) the bird is mounted in a sealed case, the mark shall instead of being affixed to the skin or skeleton[6] of the bird be affixed in a visible position to the case;

(*b*) the bird is mounted otherwise than as mentioned in paragraph (*a*) above, the mark shall instead of being affixed to the skin or skeleton[6] of the bird be affixed in a visible position to the mount or base upon which the bird is displayed;

and where two or more birds are mounted together, the mark relating to each bird shall be affixed as close as possible to the bird to which it relates.

8. Any registered person who sells a dead wild bird to which these regulations apply shall supply the Secretary of State with information relating to the sale in the form set out in Schedule 2 to these regulations.

9. Any registered person who effects a permanent change of address shall, within twenty-eight days of so doing, inform the Secretary of State of his new address.

---

[1] Regulation 4 substituted by the Wildlife and Countryside (Registration to Sell etc. Certain Dead Wild Birds) (Amendment) Regulations 1991, S.I. 1991/479, which came into force on 1 April 1991, reg. 2.

[2] "Dead wild bird" defined by reg. 1(3), p. 313 above.

[3] Words "Schedule 1" substituted by S.I. 1991/479, reg. 3.

[4] Words "or, where there is no skin, to the skeleton" inserted by S.I. 1991/479, reg. 4.

[5] Words "or, where there is no skin, to the skeleton" inserted by S.I. 1991/479, reg. 5(*a*).

[6] Words "or skeleton" inserted by S.I. 1991/479, reg. 5(*b*).

Offences

10. Any person who, without reasonable excuse, contravenes the provisions of regulations 3(3) or (4), 5, 6, 7, 8 or 9 shall be guilty of an offence under section 6 of the Act[1].

The Schedules to this order, which are not reproduced, are:

  Schedule 1: (Model record of) The Register of Birds Received.

  Schedule 2: Register of Birds Sold.

---

[1] P. 151 above.

Wildlife and Countryside (Ringing of Certain Birds) Regulations 1982

S.I. 1982 No. 1220

The Secretary of State for the Environment as respects England, the Secretary of State for Scotland as respects Scotland and the Secretary of State for Wales as respects Wales, in exercise of the powers conferred by section 6(5) of the Wildlife and Countryside Act 1981[1], hereby make the following regulations:

Title, commencement, interpretation and application

1. (1) These regulations may be cited as the Wildlife and Countryside (Ringing of Certain Birds) Regulations 1982, and shall come into operation on 28th September 1982.

(2) These regulations apply for the purposes of references in section 6(5) of the Act[1].

(3) In these regulations:

"approved supplier" means any supplier specified in Schedule 1 to these regulations;

"close ring" means a continuous ring or band, without any break or join, for ringing a bird;

"ring" means any ring or band for ringing a bird;

"Secretary of State" means the Secretary of State for the Environment;

"the Act" means the Wildlife and Countryside Act 1981;

and cognate expressions shall be construed accordingly.

(4) Any reference in these regulations to a bird to which these regulations apply is a reference to a bird included in Part I of Schedule 3 which was bred in captivity.

Ringing

2. Any bird to which these regulations apply which immediately before the date on which these regulations come into operation was close ringed, or was otherwise ringed for the purpose of being shown for competition, may continue to be so ringed for the period of three years beginning on that date.

3. (1) Subject as mentioned in regulation 2 above, any bird to which these regulations apply shall be close ringed with a ring of a size no larger than the size specified in Schedule 2 to these regulations.

(2) Any such ring as is mentioned in paragraph (1) above shall be obtained from an approved supplier, and the application for the ring shall—

(a) be made by the keeper, or prospective keeper, of the bird to be ringed;

(b) provide details of its parents, or prospective parents; and

(c) in the case of a bird in being, specify its age and (where known) its sex.

---

[1] P. 151 above.

SCHEDULE 1

APPROVED SUPPLIERS

1. The British Bird Council
   35 Chatham Road
   Kingston-upon-Thames
   Surrey
   KT1 3AB.

2. The International Ornithological Association
   7 Cleve Road
   Sidcup
   Kent
   DA14 4RF

SCHEDULE 2

SIZES OF RING

Common name	Scientific name	Size of ring (internal diameter, in millimetres)
Blackbird	*Turdus merula*	4.4
Brambling	*Fringilla montifringilla*	2.7
Bullfinch	*Pyrrhula pyrrhula*	2.5
Bunting, Reed	*Emberiza schoeniculus*	2.7
Chaffinch	*Fringilla coelebs*	2.7
Dunnock	*Prunella modularis*	2.9
Goldfinch	*Carduelis carduelis*	2.5
Greenfinch	*Carduelis chloris*	2.9
Jackdaw	*Corvus monedula*	7.1
Jay	*Garrulus glandarius*	6.0
Linnet	*Carduelis cannabina*	2.5
Magpie	*Pica pica*	7.1
Owl, Barn	*Tyto alba*	9.5
Redpoll	*Carduelis flammea*	2.4
Siskin	*Carduelis spinus*	2.4
Starling	*Sturnus vulgaris*	4.4
Thrush, Song	*Turdus philomelos*	3.9
Twite	*Carduelis flavirostris*	2.4
Yellowhammer	*Emberiza citrinella*	2.9

Wildlife and Countryside (Registration and Ringing of Certain Captive Birds) Regulations 1982

S.I. 1982 No. 1221

The Secretary of State for the Environment as respects England, the Secretary of State for Scotland as respects Scotland and the Secretary of State for Wales as respects Wales, in exercise of the powers conferred by section 7(1) and (2) of the Wildlife and Countryside Act 1981[1], hereby make the following regulations:

Title, commencement, and interpretation

1. (1) These regulations may be cited as the Wildlife and Countryside (Registration and Ringing of Certain Captive Birds) Regulations 1982, and shall come into operation on 28th September 1982.

(2) In these regulations—

"keeper" means the person who keeps a bird or has a bird in his possession or under his control;

"registration" includes re-registration;

"ring" means any ring or band for ringing a bird;

"the Act" means the Wildlife and Countryside Act 1981;

"the Secretary of State" means the Secretary of State for the Environment;

and cognate expressions shall be construed accordingly.

(3) In these regulations, any reference to a bird to which these regulations apply is a reference to any bird included in Schedule 4 to the Act[2] which any person keeps or has in his possession or under his control.

Transitional arrangements

2. Nothing in these regulations shall require any bird to be registered—

    (a) before the expiration of the period of six weeks beginning on the date on which these regulations come into operation; or

    (b) in a case where an application for the registration of the bird is received by the Secretary of State within the said period, before the date on which he notifies the applicant of his decision on the application.

Registration

3. (1) The Secretary of State[3] shall, for the purposes of section 7(1) of the Act[4], maintain a register of birds to which these regulations apply.

(2) An application for registration[5] shall be made by the keeper[6], or prospective keeper, of the bird to which the application relates on a form obtained from the Secretary of State.

(3) The Secretary of State shall not register any bird which is required by regulation 5 of these regulations to be ringed, unless he is satisfied that the bird has been ringed as required.

---

[1] P. 152 above.
[2] P. 196 above.
[3] "The Secretary of State" defined by reg. 1(2) above.
[4] P. 152 above.
[5] "Registration" defined by reg. 1(2) above.
[6] "Keeper" defined by reg. 1(2) above.

(4) The Secretary of State may make such reasonable charge for registration as he thinks fit.

Termination of registration

4. (1) Subject to paragraph (1A) below, any registration[1] effected before 1st April 1991 shall cease to have effect on 1st September 1993, and any registration effected on or after 1st April 1991 shall cease to have effect at the expiration of a period of three years beginning with the day on which the registration is effected.

(1A) Any registration of a bird for which—

(*a*) the immediately preceding registration ceased to have effect in accordance with paragraph (2)(*a*)(ii) below because the registered bird has escaped into the wild or in accordance with paragraph (2)(*b*) below,

(*b*) the application for registration is made by the keeper[2] who was the keeper of the bird when the immediately preceding registration ceased to have effect, and

(*c*) the application for registration is made before the date on which the previous registration would have ceased to have effect but for the application of paragraph (2) below.

shall cease to have effect at the time at which the immediately preceding registration of that bird would have expired under paragraph (1) above had paragraph (2) below not applied.[3]

(2) Notwithstanding paragraph (1) above, any registration shall cease to have effect—

(*a*) when the registered bird—

   (i) dies;

   (ii) escapes or is released into the wild;

   (iii) is disposed of by way of sale or otherwise;

   (iv) is exported;

(*b*) when, in the case of a bird required by regulation 5 of these regulations to be ringed, the ring[4] is removed or the writing or numbering on the ring ceases to be legible;

(*c*) when the registered bird is kept or possessed by or is under the control of a person other than its registered keeper, unless it is intended at the time when the bird begins to be so kept, possessed or controlled that it will be returned to its registered keeper within the specified period and the bird is so returned, and in this sub-paragraph "the specified period" means—

   (i) where the bird will not be kept continuously at its registered address, a period of 3 weeks, and

   (ii) where the bird will be kept continuously at its registered address, a period of 6 weeks;

(*d*) when the registered bird is kept or possessed by or is under the control of its registered keeper but ceases to be kept at its registered address, unless—

   (i) it is intended at the time when the bird ceases to be so kept that it will be returned to its registered address within 3 weeks and the bird is so returned, or

   (ii) the Secretary of State[5] is notified in writing before the bird ceases to be so kept of the new address at which it will be kept and the date from which it will be so kept.

(3) In paragraph (2)(*c*) and (*d*) above, "registered keeper" in relation to a registered bird means the person who made the application in respect of which the bird is registered by the Secretary of State, and "registered address" means the address at which the bird was kept at the date of registration by the Secretary of State, or, if an address has been notified to the Secretary of State under paragraph (2)(*d*)(ii) above, the address so notified or last so notified.[6]

---

[1] "Registration" defined by reg. 1(2), p. 318 above.
[2] "Keeper" defined by reg. 1(2), p. 318 above.
[3] Regulation 4(1), (1A), substituted by the Wildlife and Countryside (Registration and Ringing of Certain Captive Birds) (Amendment) Regulations 1991, S.I. 1991/478, which came into force on 1 April 1991, reg. 2.

[4] "Ring" defined by reg. 1(2), p. 318 above.
[5] "The Secretary of State" defined by reg. 1(2), p. 318 above.
[6] Regulation 4(2)(*c*),(*d*) and 4(3) substituted by S.I. 1991/478, reg. 3.

Ringing

5. (1) Every bird to which these regulations apply shall be ringed with a ring[1] obtained from the Secretary of State.[2,3]

(2) Any person who rings a bird under this regulation shall complete a declaration of ringing on a form obtained from the Secretary of State, and return it to him.

Former schedule omitted by S.I. 1994/1152, reg. 2(b).

[1] "Ring" defined by reg. 1(2), p. 318 above.
[2] "The Secretary of State" defined by reg. 1(2), p. 318 above.
[3] Regulation 5(1) substituted by the Wildlife and Countryside (Registration and Ringing of Certain Captive Birds) (Amendment) Regulations 1994, S.I. 1994/1152, which came into force on 24 May 1994, reg. 2(a).

Wildlife and Countryside (Claims for Compensation under section 30) Regulations 1982

S.I. 1982 No. 1346

The Secretary of State for the Environment as respects England, the Secretary of State for Scotland as respects Scotland and the Secretary of State for Wales as respects Wales, in exercise of the powers conferred by section 30(2), (3) and (10) of the Wildlife and Countryside Act 1981[1], hereby make the following regulations:

Title, commencement and interpretation

1. (1) These regulations may be cited as the Wildlife and Countryside (Claims for Compensation under section 30) Regulations 1982, and shall come into operation on 21st October 1982.

    (2) In these regulations, "the Act" means the Wildlife and Countryside Act 1981.

Time within which claims are to be made

2. A claim for compensation under section 30(2) of the Act[1] shall be made within six months from the date on which the Secretary of State gives notice under paragraph 6(1) or (2) of Schedule 11 to the Act[2] of his decision in respect of the order to which the claim relates.

3. A claim for compensation under section 30(3) of the Act shall be made within six months from the expiration of the period specified in section 29(5)(c) of the Act, as modified by section 29(6) or (7) of the Act.

4. The Secretary of State may, if he thinks fit, at any time extend the period within which a claim for compensation is required to be made under regulation 2 or 3 above.

Manner in which claims are to be made

5. A claim for compensation under section 30(2) or (3) of the Act shall be made to the Nature Conservancy Council[3] in writing and shall be delivered at or sent by pre-paid post to the offices of the Council.

---

[1] P. 172 above.
[2] P. 207 above.
[3] For "Nature Conservancy Council" see s. 27A of the Act at p. 167 above; Environmental Protection Act 1990 (c. 43), s. 139, sch. 11, para. 10, p. 242 above, Natural Heritage (Scotland) Act 1991 (c. 28), s. 14, sch. 4, para. 8, p. 260 above.

The Deer (Close Seasons) (Scotland) Order 1984

S.I. 1984 No. 76 (S. 5)

In exercise of the powers conferred upon me by section 21(2) of the Deer (Scotland) Act 1959[1] and of all other powers enabling me in that behalf, and after consultation with such organisations as appear to me to represent persons likely to be affected by this Order, I hereby make the following Order:

Citation and commencement

1. (1) This Order may be cited as the Deer (Close Seasons) (Scotland) Order 1984, and shall come into operation on 1st May 1984.

Close Seasons for certain species of deer

2. Subject to the provisions of section 33 of the Deer (Scotland) Act 1959[2], no person shall take or wilfully kill or injure any deer of any of the species mentioned in the Schedule to this Order during the periods hereby fixed in each year and specified in the said Schedule in relation respectively to male and female deer of any such species.

Revocation

3. The Deer (Close Seasons) (Scotland) Order 1966[3] is hereby revoked.

SCHEDULE

Species		Periods
Fallow deer (*Dama dama*)	Male —	1st May to 31st July both dates inclusive
	Female —	16th February to 20th October both dates inclusive
Roe deer (*Capreolus capreolus*)	Male —	21st October to 31st March both dates inclusive
	Female —	1st April to 20th October both dates inclusive
Sika deer (*Cervus nippon*)	Male —	21st October to 30th June both dates inclusive
	Female —	16th February to 20th October both dates inclusive
Red/Sika deer hybrids (*Cervus elaphus/Cervus nippon*)	Male —	21st October to 30th June both dates inclusive
	Female —	16th February to 20th October both dates inclusive

[1] P. 50 above. [2] P. 59 above. [3] S.I. 1966/56.

The Deer (Firearms etc.) (Scotland) Order 1985

S.I. 1985 No. 1168 (S. 94)

In exercise of the powers conferred upon me by section 23A(1) of the Deer (Scotland) Act 1959[1] and of all other powers enabling me in that behalf, and after consultation in accordance with section 23A(2) of that Act with such organisations as appear to me to represent persons likely to be interested in or affected by this order, I hereby make the following order, a draft of which has been laid before Parliament and approved by a resolution of each House of Parliament:

1. (1) This order may be cited as the Deer (Firearms etc.) (Scotland) Order 1985 and shall come into operation on 21st October 1985.

   (2) In this order unless the context otherwise requires—

   "Act" means the Deer (Scotland) Act 1959;

   "roe deer" means deer of the species *Capreolus capreolus*;

   "shot gun" has the meaning assigned to it by section 57(4) of the Firearms Act 1968[2];

   "slaughtering instrument" has the meaning assigned to it by section 57(4) of the Firearms Act 1968.

2. No person shall use in connection with the killing or taking of deer any firearm, ammunition or sight except as is declared lawful by this order and in the circumstances provided therefor.

3. It shall be lawful to use a rifle which is capable of firing the following lawful ammunition—

   (a) for shooting deer of any species, a bullet of an expanding type designed to deform in a predictable manner of not less than 100 grains (6.48 grams) with a muzzle velocity of not less than 2,450 feet per second (746.76 metres per second) and a muzzle energy of not less than 1,750 foot pounds (2,373 joules); or

   (b) for shooting roe deer, a bullet of an expanding type designed to deform in a predictable manner of not less than 50 grains (3.24 grams) with a muzzle velocity of not less than 2,450 feet per second (746.76 metres per second) and a muzzle energy of not less than 1,000 foot pounds (1,356 joules).

4. Where an occupier of agricultural land or of enclosed woodlands has reasonable grounds for believing that serious damage will be caused to crops, pasture, trees or human or animal foodstuffs on that land if the deer are not killed, it shall be lawful for any of the persons described in paragraphs (c), (d) and (e) of section 33(3) of the Act[3] to use a shot gun whose gauge is not less than 12 bore and which is loaded with the following lawful ammunition—

   (a) for shooting deer of any species, a single rifled non-spherical projectile weighing not less than 380 grains (24.62 grams); or

---

[1] P. 52 above.   [2] 1968 c. 27.   [3] P. 59 above.

(b) for shooting deer of any species, a cartridge purporting to contain not less than 550 grains (35.64 grams) of shot, none of which is less than 0.268 inches (6.81 millimetres) in diameter, that is to say size SSG; or

(c) for shooting roe deer, a cartridge purporting to contain not less than 450 grains (29.16 grams) of shot, none of which is less than 0.203 inches (5.16 millimetres) in diameter, that is to say size AAA,

for the purpose of taking or killing any deer found on any arable land, garden grounds or land laid down in permanent grass (other than moorland and unenclosed land) and forming part of that land or on enclosed woodland, as the case may be.

....

5. It shall be lawful to use—

   (a) a slaughtering instrument using any ammunition intended for use in it;

   (b) a sight which is not a light-intensifying, heat-sensitive or other special sighting device for night shooting.

....

6. Notwithstanding the provisions of this order, it shall be lawful for any person authorised for the purpose by the Secretary of State to take or kill deer for any scientific, veterinary or related purpose by any means specified in the authorisation.

....

7. This order is without prejudice to any action to which section 33(1) of the Act applies.[4]

---

[4] P. 59 above.

The Environmental Assessment (Afforestation) Regulations 1988

S.I. 1988 No. 1207

Whereas both Houses of Parliament have approved by resolution a draft of these Regulations;

The Minister of Agriculture, Fisheries and Food, the Secretary of State for Scotland and the Secretary of State for Wales, acting jointly, being Ministers designated[1] for the purposes of section 2(2) of the European Communities Act 1972[2] in relation to measures relating to the requirement for an assessment of the impact on the environment of projects likely to have significant effects on the environment, in exercise of the powers conferred upon them by the said section 2(2) and of all other powers enabling them in that behalf, hereby make the following Regulations:

Title, application and commencement

1. (1) These Regulations, which apply throughout Great Britain, may be cited as the Environmental Assessment (Afforestation) Regulations 1988 and shall come into force on the third day after the day on which they are made[3].

(2) These Regulations apply in any case where an application for a grant or loan in respect of an afforestation project was received by the Commissioners on or after 15th July 1988.

Interpretation

2. In these Regulations—

"afforestation project" means a proposal for the initial planting of land with trees for forestry purposes;

"the Commissioners" means the Forestry Commissioners constituted under the Forestry Acts 1919 to 1945 and continued in existence by the Forestry Act 1967[4];

"environmental information" means the environmental statement prepared by the applicant for a grant or loan in respect of an afforestation project, any representations made by any authority or body required by these Regulations to be consulted, and any representations duly made by any other body or person about the likely environmental effects of the afforestation project;

"environmental statement" means such a statement as is described in the Schedule;

"grant or loan" means a grant or loan under section 1 of the Forestry Act 1979[5];

"the Minister" means, in relation to England, the Minister of Agriculture, Fisheries and Food, in relation to Scotland, the Secretary of State for Scotland, and in relation to Wales, the Secretary of State for Wales.

Prohibition of grant or loan without consideration of environmental information

3. The Commissioners[6] shall make no grant or loan for an afforestation project[7] where in their opinion the project will be likely to have significant effects on the environment, and may lead to

[1] S.I. 1988/785.
[2] 1972 c. 68.
[3] These Regulations came into force on 15 July 1988.
[4] P. 66 above.
[5] P. 142 above.
[6] "The Commissioners" defined by reg. 2 above.
[7] "Afforestation project" defined by reg. 2 above.

adverse ecological changes, by reason inter alia of its nature, size or location, unless they have first taken into consideration environmental information[1] in respect of that project.

....

Opinion of Commissioners in advance of application for grant or loan

4. (1) A person may, before applying for a grant or loan in respect of an afforestation project[2], make a written application to the Commissioners[3] for their opinion in writing on whether environmental information[4] would be required in relation to that project.

(2) An application pursuant to paragraph (1) above shall be accompanied by—

(*a*) a map or plan sufficient to identify the land on which the proposed planting would be carried out, and to show the extent of the proposed planting;

(*b*) a brief description of the nature of the proposed planting and of its possible effects on the environment; and

(*c*) such further information or representations as the applicant may wish to provide.

(3) Where the Commissioners consider that they have not been provided with sufficient information to enable them to give an opinion they shall notify the applicant of the points on which they require further information.

(4) The Commissioners shall give the applicant written notification of the opinion they have formed on the question raised within 4 weeks beginning with the date of the request, or such longer period as they may agree with him in writing, and where their opinion is that consideration of environmental information would be required, they shall state their reasons for it.

(5) Where the Commissioners have not given their written opinion by the end of the period provided for by paragraph (4) above, it shall be presumed that in their opinion environmental information would not be required.

(6) Where the Commissioners express the opinion that environmental information would be required, the applicant may apply in writing to the Minister[5] for a direction on the matter, following the procedure provided in regulation 6.

....

Procedure where an environmental statement is required

5. (1) Where it appears to the Commissioners[6] that an afforestation project[7] in respect of which an application is made for a grant or loan is a project in respect of which environmental information[8] is required, but no environmental statement[9] has been submitted with the application, they shall within 4 weeks beginning with the date of receipt of the application, or such longer period as they may agree with the applicant in writing, notify the applicant in writing of the opinion they have formed, stating their reasons for it, and that no grant or loan can be considered for the project without consideration of environmental information.

(2) The applicant may within 4 weeks beginning with the date of the notification referred to in paragraph (1) above inform the Commissioners in writing—

(*a*) that he accepts their view and proposes to provide an environmental statement; or

(*b*) that he proposes to apply in writing to the Minister[10] for his direction on the matter as provided by regulation 6.

(3) If the applicant takes no action in accordance with paragraph (2) above within the period specified the grant or loan applied for shall be deemed to be refused at the end of that period.

---

[1] "Environmental information" defined by reg. 2, p. 325 above.

[2] "Afforestation project" defined by reg. 2, p. 325 above.

[3] "The Commissioners" defined by reg. 2, p. 325 above.

[4] "Environmental information" defined by reg. 2, p. 325 above.

[5] "The Minister" defined by reg. 2, p. 325 above.

[6] "The Commissioners" defined by reg. 2, p. 325 above.

[7] "Afforestation project" defined by reg. 2, p. 325 above.

[8] "Environmental information" defined by reg. 2, p. 325 above.

[9] "Environmental statement" defined by reg. 2, p. 325 above.

[10] "The Minister" defined by reg. 2, p. 325 above.

(4) The Commissioners shall not determine any application for which environmental information is required otherwise than by refusing the grant or loan applied for unless—

(a) they receive an environmental statement and regulation 8(1) is complied with; or

(b) the Minister directs that consideration of environmental information is not required.

(5) Where the Commissioners receive an environmental statement relating to an application they shall, if regulation 8(1) has been complied with, proceed to deal with the application.

Applications for Ministers' directions

6. (1) Every application to the Minister[1] for a direction under regulation 4(6) shall be accompanied by, or by copies of—

(a) the application to the Commissioners[2] for their opinion;

(b) the documents which accompanied that application, or were called for by the Commissioners under regulation 4(3);

(c) the opinion of the Commissioners, with their reasons for it; and

(d) any representations which the applicant wishes to make.

(2) Every application to the Minister for a direction under regulation 5(2)(b) shall be accompanied by, or by copies of—

(a) the application for a grant or loan;

(b) any documents which accompanied that application;

(c) the opinion of the Commissioners, with their reasons for it; and

(d) any representations which the applicant wishes to make.

(3) Where the Minister considers that the documents put before him in pursuance of paragraph (1) or (2) above do not provide him with sufficient information to enable him to give a direction he shall notify the applicant in writing of the points on which he requires further information, and may make a written request to the Commissioners for such information as they may be able to provide on the points raised.

(4) The Minister shall, within 4 weeks beginning with the date of receipt of the application, or such longer period as he may reasonably require, direct whether or not consideration of environmental information[3] is required before a grant or loan may be made for the project.

(5) The Minister shall forthwith upon giving his direction send copies thereof to the applicant and the Commissioners, and where he directs that consideration of environmental information is required he shall state his reasons for making that direction.

Minister's power to give directions of his own motion

7. The Minister[4] may of his own motion give a direction that consideration of environmental information[5] is required in any case in which the Commissioners[6] have decided to the contrary.

Publicity for environmental statement

8. (1) Where environmental information[7] is required under these Regulations by the Commissioners[8] or by direction of the Minister[9] the applicant shall—

[1] "The Minister" defined by reg. 2, p. 325 above.
[2] "The Commissioners" defined by reg. 2, p. 325 above.
[3] "Environmental information" defined by reg. 2, p. 325 above.
[4] "The Minister" defined by reg. 2, p. 325 above.
[5] "Environmental information" defined by reg. 2, p. 325 above.
[6] "The Commissioners" defined by reg. 2, p. 325 above.
[7] "Environmental information" defined by reg. 2, p. 325 above.
[8] "The Commissioners" defined by reg. 2, p. 325 above.
[9] "The Minister" defined by reg. 2, p. 325 above.

(a) by advertisement in at least two local newspapers nominated by the Commissioners give notice of the afforestation project[1], notifying members of the public that any person wishing to make representations regarding the project should make them in writing to the Commissioners at the address specified in the advertisement within a specified period being not less than 28 days from the date of the advertisement.

(b) make available for inspection by members of the public at all reasonable times at an office of the Commissioners or at some other convenient place nominated by them (such times and place to be stated in the advertisement referred to in subparagraph (a) above), for a period of at least 21 days following the publication of the advertisement, the details of the project and of the environmental statement[2] relating to it, and shall ensure that a reasonable number of copies of the statement are made available;

(c) state in the advertisement referred to in subparagraph (a) above the address at which copies of the environmental statement may be obtained and, if a charge is to be made for a copy, the amount of the charge.

(2) Where the Commissioners receive an environmental statement relating to an application to which regulation 3 applies they shall consult—

(a) the Nature Conservancy Council[3];

(b) the Countryside Commission or Scottish Natural Heritage[4], as appropriate; and

(c) any local authority, any other public authority and any statutory body which appears to them to have an interest in the afforestation project in question.

(3) Where under this regulation the Commissioners consult any authority or body about any environmental statement they shall give not less than 4 weeks' notice to such authority or body that such statement is to be taken into consideration, shall not consider the statement until after the expiration of the period of such notice, and shall, in considering the statement, take into account any representations received from such authority or body.

(4) The Commissioners shall consider the application and the environmental statement and any representations and comments made thereon by any person, body or authority, and shall communicate their decision as to whether or not to make a grant or loan for the project in writing to such person, body or authority and by means of public advertisements in the newspapers which they nominated for the purposes of the advertisements referred to in paragraph (1) above.

(5) Where an applicant for a grant or loan submits an environmental statement to the Commissioners he shall provide them with a sufficient number of copies of the statement or parts thereof to enable them to comply with paragraph (2) above plus one extra copy.

Provision of information

9. Where a person has applied, or to the Commissioners'[5] knowledge proposes to apply, for a grant or loan in circumstances in which environmental information[6] is required under these Regulations, the Commissioners shall—

(a) inform the authorities and bodies listed in regulation 8(2) of the application, and request them to make available to the applicant any information in their possession which he or they may consider relevant to the preparation of his environmental statement[7]; and

(b) inform the applicant of what they have done under paragraph (a) above and that he shall sup-

---

[1] "Afforestation project" defined by reg. 2, p. 325 above.
[2] "Environmental statement" defined by reg. 2, p. 325 above.
[3] "Nature Conservancy Council" is construed as a reference to the Nature Conservancy Council for England or the Countryside Council for Wales, as appropriate: Environmental Protection Act 1990 (c. 43), s. 139, sch. 11, para. 10, p. 242 above.
[4] "The Countryside Commission" includes reference to the Countryside Council for Wales in respect of Wales:

Environmental Protection Act 1990 (c. 43), s. 139, sch. 11, para. 4, p. 240 above; words "Scottish Natural Heritage" substituted by the Natural Heritage (Scotland) Act 1991 (c. 28), s. 14(4), p. 254 above.
[5] "The Commissioners" defined by reg. 2, p. 325 above.
[6] "Environmental information" defined by reg. 2, p. 325 above.
[7] "Environmental statement" defined by reg. 2, p. 325 above.

ply such authorities and bodies with such further information about the afforestation project as they may reasonably request.

Further information and evidence relating to environmental statements

10. (1) The Commissioners[1], when considering an application in relation to which an environmental statement[2] has been provided, may in writing require the applicant to provide such further information as may be specified concerning any matter which is required to be, or may be, dealt with in the statement, and where in the opinion of the Commissioners—

(a) the applicant could (having regard in particular to current knowledge and methods of assessment) provide further information about any matter mentioned in paragraph 3 of the Schedule, and

(b) further information is reasonably required for the proper consideration of the likely environmental effects of the proposed project,

they shall notify the applicant in writing to that effect, and the applicant shall provide that further information.

(2) The Commissioners may in writing require an applicant to produce such evidence as they may reasonably call for to verify any information in his environmental statement.

Charges

11. (1) A reasonable charge reflecting the costs of printing, copying and distribution may be made to the public for copies of an environmental statement[3] made available to them under regulation 8 and for copies in excess of one copy for each authority or body consulted under that regulation.

(2) An authority or body providing information under regulation 9, having been requested to do so, may make a reasonable charge reflecting the costs of making available information which they had in their possession.

SCHEDULE

(Regulation 2)

1. An environmental statement comprises a document or documents providing, for the purpose of assessing the likely impact of the proposed afforestation project upon the environment, the information specified in paragraph 2 below (referred to in this Schedule as "the specified information").

2. The specified information is—

(a) a description of the afforestation project[4] proposed, comprising information about the site of the project and the design and the extent of the planting proposed;

(b) the data necessary to identify and assess the main effects which the project is likely to have on the environment;

(c) a description of the likely significant effects of the project, direct and indirect, on the environment, explained by reference to its possible impact on—

human beings;
flora;
fauna;
soil;
water;
air;
climate;

---

[1] "The Commissioners" defined by reg. 2, p. 325 above.
[2] "Environmental statement" defined by reg. 2, p. 325 above.
[3] "Environmental statement" defined by reg. 2, p. 325 above.
[4] "Afforestation project" defined by reg. 2, p. 325 above.

the landscape;
the interaction between any of the foregoing;
material assets (including the architectural and archaeological heritage);
the cultural heritage;

(d) where significant adverse effects are identified with respect to any of the foregoing, a description of the measures envisaged in order to avoid, reduce or remedy those effects; and

(e) a summary in non-technical language of the information specified above.

3. An environmental statement may include, by way of explanation or amplification of any specified information, further information on any of the following matters:

(a) the physical characteristics of the project, and the land-use requirements during the planting and subsequent stages;

(b) the main characteristics of the production processes proposed, including the nature and quality of the materials to be used;

(c) the estimated type and quantity of expected residues and emissions (including pollutants of water, air or soil, noise, vibration, light, heat and radiation) resulting from the project when planting is completed;

(d) (in outline) the main alternatives (if any) studied by the applicant and an indication of the main reasons for his choice, taking into account the environmental effects;

(e) the likely significant direct and indirect effects on the environment of the project which may result from—

(i) the use of natural resources;

(ii) the emission of pollutants, the creation of nuisances and the elimination of waste;

(f) the forecasting methods used to assess any effects on the environment about which information is given under subparagraph (e); and

(g) any difficulties, such as technical deficiencies or lack of knowledge, encountered in compiling any specified information.

In subparagraph (e) "effects" includes secondary, cumulative, short, medium and long-term, permanent and temporary, positive and negative effects.

4. Where further information is included in an environmental statement pursuant to paragraph 3 a non-technical summary of that information shall be provided.

The Conservation of Seals (Common Seals) (Shetland Islands Area) Order 1991

S.I. 1991 No. 2638 (S. 206)

Whereas having consulted with the Natural Environment Research Council under section 3(1) of the Conservation of Seals Act 1970[1] it appears to the Secretary of State necessary for the proper conservation of seals to make this Order;

Now, therefore, in exercise of the powers conferred on him by sections 3(1) and 14(2) of the said Act of 1970 and of all other powers enabling him in that behalf, the Secretary of State hereby makes the following Order:

---

1. This order may be cited as the Conservation of Seals (Common Seals) (Shetland Islands Area) Order 1991 and shall come into force on 19th December 1991.

2. Any person is hereby prohibited from killing, injuring or taking of seals of the species known as *Phoca vitulina* (common seals), in the Shetland Islands Area and within the seaward limits of the territorial waters adjacent thereto.

3. The Conservation of Seals (Common Seals) (Shetland Islands Area) Order 1990[2] is hereby revoked.

[1] P. 136 above.   [2] S.I. 1990/2337.

The Conservation of Seals (England) Order 1993

S.I. 1993 No. 2876

In exercise of the powers conferred upon me by section 3(1) of the Conservation of Seals Act 1970[1], and after consultation with the Natural Environment Research Council as required by that section, I hereby make the following Order:

1. (1) This Order may be cited as the Conservation of Seals (England) Order 1993 and shall come into force on 19th December 1993.

   (2) Without prejudice to its earlier revocation this Order shall cease to have effect on the expiration of three years beginning with the date of its coming into force.

2. There is hereby prohibited within the territorial limits set out in article 3 below, the killing, injuring or taking of seals of the species known as *Halichoerus grypus* (grey seals) and *Phoca vitulina* (common seals).

3. For the purposes of article 2 above, the territorial limits of this Order are:

   (*a*) the counties of Cleveland, Durham, East Sussex, Essex, Greater London, Humberside, Kent, Lincolnshire, Norfolk, North Yorkshire, Northumberland, Suffolk, Tyne and Wear; and

   (*b*) those territorial waters adjacent to England which are:

      (i) to the south of a line drawn at 055° true from the point on the mainland at 55° 48'.67 North latitude and 02° 02'.0 West longitude; and

      (ii) adjacent to any of the counties specified in paragraph (*a*) above and, in the case of East Sussex, not further west than a line drawn true South from Newhaven Breakwater Head Light which is at 50° 46'.5 North latitude and 00° 03'.6 East longitude.

[1] P. 136 above.

The Conservation (Natural Habitats, &c.) Regulations 1994

S.I. 1994 No. 2716

Arrangement of regulations

Part I: Introductory provisions

Part II: Conservation of natural habitats and habitats of species

European sites

Register of European sites

Management agreements

Control of potentially damaging operations

Special nature conservation orders

Part III: Protection of species

Part IV: Adaptation of planning and other controls

The Conservation (Natural Habitats &c.) Regulations 1994

The Secretary of State for the Environment, as respects England, the Secretary of State for Wales, as respects Wales, and the Secretary of State for Scotland, as respects Scotland, being designated[1] Ministers for the purposes of section 2(2) of the European Communities Act 1972[2] in relation to measures relating to the conservation of natural habitats and of wild fauna and flora, in exercise of the powers conferred upon them by the said section 2 and of all other powers enabling them in that behalf, hereby make the following Regulations, a draft of which has been laid before and approved by a resolution of each House of Parliament:

Part I: Introductory provisions

Citation and commencement

1. (1) These Regulations may be cited as the Conservation (Natural Habitats, &c.) Regulations 1994.

   (2) These Regulations shall come into force on the tenth day after that on which they are made[3].

Interpretation and application

2. (1) In these Regulations—

   "agriculture Minister" means the Minister of Agriculture, Fisheries and Food or the Secretary of State;

   "competent authority" shall be construed in accordance with regulation 6[4];

   "destroy", in relation to an egg, includes doing anything to the egg which is calculated to prevent it from hatching, and "destruction" shall be construed accordingly;

   "enactment" includes a local enactment and an enactment contained in subordinate legislation within the meaning of the Interpretation Act 1978[5];

   "European site" has the meaning given by regulation 10[6] and "European marine site" means a European site which consists of, or so far as it consists of, marine areas;

   "functions" includes powers and duties;

   "the Habitats Directive" has the meaning given by regulation 3(1);

   "land" incudes land covered by water and as respects Scotland includes salmon fishings;

   "livestock" includes any animal which is kept—

   (*a*) for the provision of food, skins or fur,

   (*b*) for the purpose of its use in the carrying on of any agricultural activity, or

   (*c*) for the provision or improvement of shooting or fishing;

   "local planning authority" means—

   (*a*) in England and Wales, except as otherwise provided, any authority having any function as a local planning authority or mineral planning authority under the Town and Country Planning Act 1990[7], and

---

[1] S.I. 1992/2870.
[2] 1972 c. 68.
[3] These Regulations came into force on 30 October 1994.
[4] P. 340 below.
[5] 1978 c. 30.
[6] P. 342 below.
[7] 1990 c. 8.

(*b*) in Scotland, a planning authority within the meaning of section 172(1) of the Local Government (Scotland) Act 1973[1];

"management agreement" means an agreement entered into, or having effect as if entered into, under regulation 16[2];

"marine area" means any land covered (continuously or intermittently) by tidal waters or any part of the sea in or adjacent to Great Britain up to the seaward limit of territorial waters;

"Natura 2000" means the European network of special areas of conservation, and special protection areas under the Wild Birds Directive, provided for by Article 3(1) of the Habitats Directive;

"nature conservation body", and "appropriate nature conservation body" in relation to England, Wales or Scotland, have the meaning given by regulation 4[3];

"occupier", for the purposes of Part III (protection of species), includes, in relation to any land other than the foreshore, any person having any right of hunting, shooting, fishing or taking game or fish;

"planning authority", in Scotland, means a planning authority within the meaning of section 172(1) of the Local Government (Scotland) Act 1973;

"the register" means the register of European sites in Great Britain provided for by regulation 11;

"relevant authorities", in relation to marine areas and European marine sites, shall be construed in accordance with regulation 5[4];

"statutory undertaker" has the same meaning as in the National Parks and Access to the Countryside Act 1949[5];

"the Wild Birds Directive" means Council Directive 79/409/EEC[6] on the conservation of wild birds.

(2) Unless the context otherwise requires, expressions used in these Regulations and in the Habitats Directive have the same meaning as in that Directive.

The following expressions, in particular, are defined in Article 1 of that Directive—

"priority natural habitat types" and "priority species";

"site" and "site of Community importance"; and

"special area of conservation".

(3) In these Regulations, unless otherwise indicated—

(*a*) any reference to a numbered regulation or Schedule is to the regulation or Schedule in these Regulations which bears that number, and

(*b*) any reference in a regulation or Schedule to a numbered paragraph is to the paragraph of that regulation or Schedule which bears that number.

(4) Subject to regulation 68[7] (which provides for Part IV to be construed as one with the Town and Country Planning Act 1990), these Regulations apply to the Isles of Scilly as if the Isles were a county and the Council of the Isles were a county council.

(5) For the purposes of these Regulations the territorial waters of the United Kingdom adjacent to Great Britain shall be treated as part of Great Britain and references to England, Wales and Scotland shall be construed as including the adjacent territorial waters.

For the purposes of this paragraph—

(*a*) territorial waters include any waters landward of the baselines from which the breadth of the territorial sea is measured; and

(*b*) any question as to whether territorial waters are to be treated as adjacent to England, Wales or Scotland shall be determined by the Secretary of State or, for any purpose in relation to

---

[1] 1973 c. 65.
[2] P. 344 below.
[3] P. 340 below.
[4] P. 340 below.
[5] P. 5 above.
[6] O.J. No. L103, 25.4.79 p. 1. The Wild Birds Directive is at Annex F of PPG 9 at p. 436 below.
[7] P. 373 below.

which the Minister of Agriculture, Fisheries and Food has responsibility, by the Secretary of State and that Minister acting jointly.

....

Implementation of Directive

3. (1) These Regulations make provision for the purpose of implementing, for Great Britain, Council Directive 92/43/EEC[1] on the conservation of natural habitats and of wild fauna and flora (referred to in these Regulations as "the Habitats Directive").

(2) The Secretary of State, the Minister of Agriculture, Fisheries and Food and the nature conservation bodies shall exercise their functions under the enactments relating to nature conservation so as to secure compliance with the requirements of the Habitats Directive.

Those enactments include—

Part III of the National Parks and Access to the Countryside Act 1949[2],

section 49A of the Countryside (Scotland) Act 1967[3] (management agreements),

section 15 of the Countryside Act 1968[4] (areas of special scientific interest),

Part I and sections 28 to 38 of the Wildlife and Countryside Act 1981[5],

sections 131 to 134 of the Environmental Protection Act 1990[6],

sections 2, 3, 5, 6, 7 and 11 of the Natural Heritage (Scotland) Act 1991[7], and these Regulations.

(3) In relation to marine areas any competent authority[8] having functions[9] relevant to marine conservation shall exercise those functions so as to secure compliance with the requirements of the Habitats Directive[10].

This applies, in particular, to functions under the following enactments—

the Sea Fisheries Acts within the meaning of section 1 of the Sea Fisheries (Wildlife Conservation) Act 1992[11],

the Dockyard Ports Regulation Act 1865[12],

section 2(2) of the Military Lands Act 1990[13] (provisions as to use of sea, tidal water or shore),

the Harbours Act 1964[14],

Part II of the Control of Pollution Act 1974[15],

sections 36 and 37 of the Wildlife and Countryside Act 1981[16] (marine nature reserves),

sections 120 to 122 of the Civic Government (Scotland) Act 1982[17] (control of the seashore, adjacent waters and inland waters),

the Water Resources Act 1991[18],

the Land Drainage Act 1991[19], and

these Regulations.

---

[1] O.J. No. L206, 22.7.92 p. 7. The Habitats Directive is at Annex G of PPG 9 at p. 000 below.

[2] P. 14 above.

[3] P. 109 above.

[4] P. 121 above.

[5] Pp. 168–180 above.

[6] P. 230 above.

[7] P. 245 above.

[8] "Competent authority" shall be construed in accordance with reg. 6, p. 340 below: reg. 2(1).

[9] "Functions" defined by reg. 2(1), p. 337 above.

[10] "The Habitats Directive" defined by reg. 3(1) above.

[11] P. 293 above.

[12] 1865 c. 125.

[13] 1900 c. 56; the power conferred by s. 2(2) was extended by s. 7 of the Lands Powers (Defence) Act 1958 (c. 30).

[14] 1964 c. 40;' relevant amendments were made by Part III of the Docks and Harbours Act 1966 (c. 28), sch. 6 to the Transport Act 1981 (c. 56) and s. 63 of, and sch. 3 to, the Transport and Works Act 1992 (c. 42).

[15] 1974 c. 40.

[16] P. 178 above.

[17] 1982 c. 45.

[18] 1991 c. 57. Part of this Act is reproduced at p. 281 above.

[19] 1991 c. 59. Part of this Act is reproduced at p. 288 above.

(4) Without prejudice to the preceding provisions, every competent authority in the exercise of any of their functions, shall have regard to the requirements of the Habitats Directive so far as they may be affected by the exercise of those functions.

Nature conservation bodies

4. In these Regulations "nature conservation body" means the Nature Conservancy Council for England[1], the Countryside Council for Wales[2] or Scottish Natural Heritage[3]; and references to "the appropriate nature conservation body", in relation to England, Wales or Scotland, shall be construed accordingly.

Relevant authorities in relation to marine areas and European marine sites

5. For the purpose of these Regulations the relevant authorities, in relation to a marine area[4] or European marine site[5], are such of the following as have functions[6] in relation to land[7] or waters within or adjacent to that area or site—

(a) a nature conservation body[8];

(b) a county council, district council, London borough council or, in Scotland, a regional, islands or district council;

(c) the National Rivers Authority, a water undertaker or sewerage undertaker, or an internal drainage board;

(d) a navigation authority within the meaning of the Water Resources Act 1991[10];

(e) a harbour authority within the meaning of the Harbours Act 1964[11];

(f) a lighthouse authority;

(g) a river purification board or a district salmon fishery board;

(h) a local fisheries committee constituted under the Sea Fisheries Regulation Act 1966[12] or any authority exercising the powers of such a committee.

Competent authorities generally

6. (1) For the purposes of these Regulations the expression "competent authority" includes any Minister, government department, public or statutory undertaker[13], public body of any description or person holding a public office.

The expression also includes any person exercising any function of a competent authority in the United Kingdom.

(2) In paragraph (1)—

(a) "public body" includes any local authority, joint board or joint committee; and

(b) "public office" means—

(a) an office under Her Majesty,

(b) an office created or continued in existence by a public general Act of Parliament, or

---

[1] The Nature Conservancy Council for England, also known as English Nature, is established by the Environmental Protection Act 1990 (c. 43), s. 128, p. 229 above.

[2] The Countryside Council for Wales is established by the Environmental Protection Act 1990 (c. 43), s. 128, p. 229 above.

[3] Scottish Natural Heritage is established by the Natural Heritage (Scotland) Act 1991 (c. 28), s. 1, p. 245 above.

[4] "Marine area" defined by reg. 2(1), p. 338 above.

[5] "European marine site" defined by reg. 2(1), p. 337 above.

[6] "Functions" defined by reg. 2(1), p. 337 above.

[7] "Land" defined by reg. 2(1), p. 337 above.

[8] "Nature conservation body" has the meaning given by reg. 4 above: reg. 2(1).

[9] See definition at p. 282 above, note 9.

[10] "Harbour authority" is defined in s. 57 of that Act.

[11] 1966 c. 38.

[12] "Statutory undertaker" defined by reg. 2(1), p. 338 above.

(c) an office the remuneration in respect of which is paid out of money provided by Parliament.

(3) In paragraph (2)(a)—

"local authority"—

(a) in relation to England, means a county council, district council or London borough council, the Common Council of the City of London, the sub-treasurer of the Inner Temple, the under treasurer of the Middle Temple or a parish council,

(b) in relation to Wales, means a county council, district council or community council, and

(c) in relation to Scotland, means a regional, islands, or district council;

"joint board" and "joint committee" in relation to England and Wales mean—

(a) a joint or special planning board constituted for a National Park by order under paragraph 1 or 3 of Schedule 17 to the Local Government Act 1972[1], or a joint planning board within the meaning of section 2 of the Town and Country Planning Act 1990, and

(b) a joint committee appointed under section 102(1)(b) of the Local Government Act 1972,

and in relation to Scotland have the same meaning as in the Local Government (Scotland) Act 1973[2].

Part II: Conservation of natural habitats and habitats of species

European sites

Selection of sites eligible for identification as of Community importance

7. (1) On the basis of the criteria set out in Annex III (Stage 1) to the Habitats Directive[3], and relevant scientific information, the Secretary of State shall propose a list of sites[4] indicating with respect to each site—

(a) which natural habitat types in Annex I to the Directive the site hosts, and

(b) which species in Annex II to the Directive that are native to Great Britain the site hosts.

(2) For animal species ranging over wide areas these sites shall correspond to the places within the natural range of such species which present the physical or biological factors essential to their life and reproduction.

For aquatic species which range over wide areas, such sites shall be proposed only where there is a clearly identifiable area representing the physical and biological factors essential to their life and reproduction.

(3) Where appropriate the Secretary of State may propose modification of the list in the light of the results of the surveillance referred to in Article 11 of the Habitats Directives[5].

(4) The list shall be transmitted to the Commission on or before 5th June 1995, together with information on each site including—

(a) a map of the site,

(b) its name, location and extent, and

(c) the data resulting from application of the criteria specified in Annex III (Stage 1),

provided in a format established by the Commission.

---

[1] 1972 c. 70.
[2] 1973 c. 65; the expressions "joint board" and "joint committee" are defined in s. 235(1) of the Act.
[3] The Directive is at Annex G of PPG 9, p. 446 below.

[4] "Site" is defined in Article 1 of the Habitats Directive at p. 448 below: reg. 2(2).
[5] P. 451 below.

Adoption of list of sites: designation of special areas of conservation

8. (1) Once a site of Community importance[1] in Great Britain has been adopted in accordance with the procedure laid down in paragraph 2 of Article 4 of the Habitats Directive[2], the Secretary of State shall designate that site as a special area of conservation[3] as soon as possible and within six years at most.

(2) The Secretary of State shall establish priorities for the designation of sites in the light of—

(a) the importance of the sites for the maintenance or restoration at a favourable conservation status of—

(i) a natural habitat type in Annex I to the Habitats Directive, or

(ii) a species in Annex II to the Directive,

and for the coherence of Natura 2000[4]; and

(b) the threats of degradation or destruction to which those sites are exposed.

Consultation as to inclusion of site omitted from the list

9. If consultation is initiated by the Commission in accordance with Article 5(1) of the Habitats Directive[5] with respect to a site[6] in Great Britain hosting a priority natural habitat type or priority species[7] and—

(a) the Secretary of State agrees that the site should be added to the list transmitted in accordance with regulation 7, or

(b) the Council, acting on a proposal from the Commission in pursuance of paragraph 2 of Article 5 of the Habitats Directive, so decides,

the site shall be treated as added to the list as from the date of that agreement or decision.

Meaning of "European site" in these Regulations

10. (1) In these Regulations a "European site" means—

(a) a special area of conservation[8],

(b) a site of Community importance[9] which has been placed on the list referred to in the third sub-paragraph of Article 4(2) of the Habitats Directive[10],

(c) a site hosting a priority natural habitat type or priority species[11] in respect of which consultation has been initiated under Article 5(1) of the Habitats Directive, during the consultation period or pending a decision of the Council under Article 5(3), or

(d) an area classified pursuant to Article 4(1) or (2) of the Wild Birds Directive[12].

(2) Sites which are European sites by virtue only of paragraph (1)(c) are not within regulations 20(1)[13] and (2), 24[14] and 48[15] (which relate to the approval of certain plans and projects); but this is without prejudice to their protection under other provisions of these Regulations.

---

[1] "Site of Community importance" is defined in Article 1 of the Habitats Directive at p. 448 below: reg. 2(2).

[2] The Habitats Directive is at Annex G of PPG 9, p. 446 below.

[3] "Special area of conservation" is defined in Article 1 of the Habitats Directive at p. 448 below: reg. 2(2).

[4] "Natura 2000" defined by reg. 2(1), p. 338 above.

[5] The Habitats Directive is at Annex G of PPG 9, p. 446 below.

[6] "Site" is defined in Article 1 of the Habitats Directive at p. 448 below: reg. 2(2).

[7] "Priority natural habitat types" and "priority species" are defined in Article 1 of the Habitats Directive at p. 447 below: reg. 2(2).

[8] "Special area of conservation" is defined in Article 1 of the Habitats Directive at p. 448 below: reg. 2(2).

[9] "Site of Community importance" is defined in Article 1 of the Habitats Directive at p. 448 below: reg. 2(2).

[10] The Habitats Directive is at Annex G of PPG 9, p. 446 below.

[11] "Priority natural habitat types" and "priority species" are defined in Article 1 of the Habitats Directive at p. 447 below: reg. 2(2).

[12] The Wild Birds Directive is at Annex F of PPG 9, p. 436 below.

[13] P. 347 below.

[14] P. 349 below.

[15] P. 361 below.

Register of European sites

Duty to compile and maintain register of European sites

11. (1) The Secretary of State shall compile and maintain, in such form as he thinks fit, a register of European sites[1] in Great Britain.

(2) He shall include in the register—

(a) special areas of conservation[2], as soon as they are designated by him;

(b) sites of Community importance[3] as soon as they are placed on the list referred to in the third sub-paragraph of Article 4(2) of the Habitats Directive, until they are designated as special areas of conservation;

(c) any site hosting a priority natural habitat type or priority species[4] in respect of which consultation is initiated under Article 5(1) of the Habitats Directive, during the consultation period or pending a Council decision under Article 5(3); and

(d) areas classified by him pursuant to Article 4(1) or (2) of the Wild Birds Directive[5], as soon as they are so classified or, if they have been classified before the commencement of these Regulations, as soon as practicable after commencement.

(3) He may, if appropriate, amend the entry in the register relating to a European site.

(4) He shall remove the relevant entry—

(a) if a special area of conservation is declassified by the Commission under Article 9 of the Habitats Directive; or

(b) if a site otherwise ceases to fall within any of the categories listed in paragraph (2) above.

(5) He shall keep a copy of the register available for public inspection at all reasonable hours and free of charge.

....

Notification to appropriate nature conservation body

12. (1) The Secretary of State shall notify the appropriate nature conservation body[6] as soon as may be after including a site[7] in the register[8], amending an entry in the register or removing an entry from the register.

(2) Notification of the inclusion of a site in the register shall be accompanied by a copy of the register entry.

(3) Notification of the amendment of an entry in the register shall be accompanied by a copy of the amended entry.

(4) Each nature conservation body[9] shall keep copies of the register entries relating to European sites[10] in their area available for public inspection at all reasonable hours and free of charge.

....

Notice to landowners, relevant authorities, &c.

13. (1) As soon as practicable after a nature conservation body[11] receive notification under regulation 12 they shall give notice to—

---

[1] "European site" has the meaning given by reg. 10, p. 342 above: reg. 2(1).

[2] "Special area of conservation" is defined in Article 1 of the Habitats Directive at p. 448 below: reg. 2(2).

[3] "Site of Community importance" is defined in Article 1 of the Habitats Directive at p. 448 below: reg. 2(2).

[4] "Priority natural habitat types" and "priority species" are defined in Article 1 of the Habitats Directive at p. 447 below: reg. 2(2).

[5] The Wild Birds Directive is at Annex F of PPG 9 at p. 436 below.

[6] "Appropriate nature conservation body" has the meaning given by reg. 4, p. 340 above: reg. 2(1).

[7] "Site" is defined in Article 1 of the Habitats Directive at p. 448 below: reg. 2(2).

[8] "The register" defined by reg. 2(1), p. 338 above.

[9] "Nature conservation body" has the meaning given by reg. 4, p. 340 above: reg. 2(1).

[10] "European site" has the meaning given by reg. 10, p. 342 above: reg. 2(1).

[11] "Nature conservation body" has the meaning given by reg. 4, p. 340 above: reg. 2(1).

(a) every owner or occupier of land[1] within the site[2],

(b) every local planning authority[3] in whose area the site, or any part of it, is situated, and

(c) such other persons or bodies as the Secretary of State may direct.

(2) Notice of the inclusion of a site in the register, or of the amendment of an entry in the register[4], shall be accompanied by a copy of so much of the relevant register entry as relates to land owned or occupied by or, as the case may be, to land within the area of, the person or authority to whom the notice is given.

(3) The Secretary of State may give directions as to the form and content of notices to be given under this regulation.

Local registration: England and Wales

14. An entry in the register[5] relating to a European site[6] in England and Wales is a local land charge.

Local registers: Scotland

15. (1) A planning authority[7] in Scotland shall keep available at their principal office for free public inspection a register of all the European sites[8] of which they have been given notice under regulation 13(1)(b)[9].

(2) A planning authority[10] in Scotland may keep available at any other of their offices for free public inspection such part of the register referred to in paragraph (1) as appears to them to relate to that part of their area in which such office is situated.

(3) A planning authority shall supply to any person, on payment of such reasonable fee as they may determine, a copy, certified by the proper office of the authority to be a true copy, of any entry in the register kept by them under paragraph (1).

Management agreements

Management agreements

16. (1) The appropriate nature conservation body[11] may enter into an agreement (a "management agreement") with every owner, lessee and occupier of land[12] forming part of a European site[13], or land adjacent to such a site, for the management, conservation, restoration or protection of the site, or any part of it.

(2) A management agreement may impose such restrictions as may be expedient for the purposes of the agreement on the exercise of rights over the land by the persons who can be bound by the agreement.

(3) A management agreement—

(a) may provide for the management of the land in such manner, the carrying out thereon of such work and the doing thereon of such other things as may be expedient for the purposes of the agreement;

(b) may provide for any of the matters mentioned in sub-paragraph (a) being carried out, or for the costs thereof being defrayed, either by the said owner or other persons or by the appropriate nature conservation body, or partly in one way and partly in another;

[1] "Land" defined by reg. 2(1), p. 337 above.
[2] "Site" is defined in Article 1 of the Habitats Directive at p. 448 below: reg. 2(2).
[3] "Local planning authority" defined by reg. 2(1), p. 337 above.
[4] "The register" defined by reg. 2(1), p. 338 above.
[5] "The register" defined by reg. 2(1), p. 338 above.
[6] "European site" has the meaning given by reg. 10, p. 342 above: reg. 2(1).
[7] "Planning authority" defined by reg. 2(1), p. 338 above.
[8] "European site" has the meaning given by reg. 10, p. 342 above.
[9] Above.
[10] "Planning authority" defined by reg. 2(1), p. 338 above.
[11] "Appropriate nature conservation body" has the meaning given by reg. 4, p. 340 above: reg. 2(1).
[12] "Land" defined by reg. 2(1), p. 337 above.
[13] "European site" has the meaning given by reg. 10, p. 342 above: reg. 2(1).

(c) may contain such other provisions as to the making of payments by the appropriate nature conservation body, and in particular for the payment by them of compensation for the effect of the restrictions mentioned in paragraph (2), as may be specified in the agreement.

(4) Where land in England and Wales is subject to a management agreement, the appropriate nature conservation body shall, as respects the enforcement of the agreement against persons other than the original contracting party, have the like rights as if—

(a) they had at all material times been the absolute owners in possession of ascertained land adjacent to the land subject to the agreement and capable of being benefited by the agreement, and

(b) the management agreement had been expressed to be for the benefit of that adjacent land;

and section 84 of the Law of Property Act 1925[1] (which enables the Lands Tribunal to discharge or modify restrictive covenants) shall not apply to the agreement.

(5) A management agreement affecting land in Scotland may be registered either—

(a) in a case where the land affected by the agreement is registered in that register, in the Land Register of Scotland, or

(b) in any other case, in the General Register of Sasines;

and, on being so recorded, it shall be enforceable at the instance of the appropriate nature conservation body against any person having an interest in the land and against any person deriving title from him:

Provided that a management agreement shall not be so enforceable against a third party who has *bona fide* onerously acquired right (whether completed by infeftment or not) to his interest in the land prior to the agreement being recorded as aforesaid, or against any person deriving title from such third party.

Continuation in force of existing agreement, &c.

17. (1) Any agreement previously entered into under—

(a) section 16 of the National Parks and Access to the Countryside Act 1949[2] (nature reserves),

(b) section 15 of the Countryside Act 1968[3] (areas of special scientific interest), or

(c) section 49A of the Countryside (Scotland) Act 1967[4] (management agreements),

in relation to land[5] which on or after the commencement of these Regulations becomes land within a European site[6], or adjacent to such a site, shall have effect as if entered into under regulation 16 above.

Regulation 32(1)(b) (power of compulsory acquisition in case of breach of agreement)[7] shall apply accordingly.

(2) Any other thing done or deemed to have been done under any provision of Part III[8] or VI of the National Parks and Access to the Countryside Act 1949, or under section 49A of the Countryside (Scotland) Act 1967, in respect of any land prior to that land becoming land within a European site, or adjacent to such a site, shall continue to have effect as if done under the corresponding provision of these Regulations.

For the purposes of this paragraph Part III of the 1949 Act shall be deemed to include section 15 of the Countryside Act 1968 and anything done or deemed to be done under that section and to which this paragraph applies shall have effect as if done or deemed to be done under section 16 of the 1949 Act.

---

[1] 1925 c. 20; by virtue of s. 28(1) of the Law of Property Act 1969 (c. 59) s. 84 has effect as set out in sch. 3 to that Act.
[2] P. 15 above.
[3] P. 121 above.
[4] P. 109 above.
[5] "Land" defined by reg. 2(1), p. 337 above.
[6] "European site" has the meaning given by reg. 10, p. 342 above: reg. 2(1).
[7] P. 353 below.
[8] P. 14 above.

(3) Any reference in an outlying enactment to a nature reserve within the meaning of section 15 of the National Parks and Access to the Countryside Act 1949 shall be construed as including a European site.

For this purpose an "outlying enactment" means an enactment not contained in, or in an instrument made under, the National Parks and Access to the Countryside Act 1949 or the Wildlife and Countryside Act 1981.

Control of potentially damaging operations

Notification of potentially damaging operations

18. (1) Any notification in force in relation to a European site under Section 28 of the Wildlife and Countryside Act 1981[1] (areas of special scientific interest) specifying—

(a) the flora, fauna, or geological or physiographical features by reason of which the land is of special interest, and

(b) any operations appearing to the appropriate nature conservation body to be likely to damage that flora or fauna or those features,

shall have effect for the purposes of these Regulations.

(2) The appropriate nature conservation body[2] may, for the purpose of securing compliance with the requirements of the Habitats Directive[3], at any time amend the notification with respect to any of the matters mentioned in paragraph (1)(a) or (b).

(3) Notice of any amendment shall be given—

(a) to every owner and occupier of land[4] within the site who in the opinion of the appropriate nature conservation body may be affected by the amendment, and

(b) to the local planning authority[5];

and the amendment shall come into force in relation to an owner or occupier upon such notice being given to him.

(4) The provisions of—

(a) section 28(11) of the Wildlife and Countryside Act 1981 (notification to be local land charge in England and Wales), and

(b) section 28(12) to (12B) of that Act (local registration of notification in Scotland),

apply, with the necessary modifications, in relation to an amendment of a notification under this regulation as in relation to the original notification.

....

Restriction on carrying out operations specified in notification

19. (1) The owner or occupier of any land[6] within a European site[7] shall not carry out, or cause or permit to be carried out, on that land any operation specified in a notification in force in relation to the site under regulation 18, unless—

(a) one of them has given the appropriate nature conservation body[8] written notice of a proposal to carry out the operation, specifying its nature and the land on which it is proposed to carry it out, and

(b) one of the conditions specified in paragraph (2) is fulfilled.

(2) Those conditions are—

---

[1] P. 168 above.
[2] "Appropriate nature conservation body" has the meaning given by reg. 4, p. 340 above: reg. 2(1).
[3] The Habitats Directive is at Annex G of PPG 9 at p. 446 below.
[4] "Land" defined by reg. 2(1), p. 337 above.
[5] "Local planning authority" defined by reg. 2(1), p. 337 above.

[6] "Land" defined by reg. 2(1), p. 337 above.
[7] "European site" has the meaning given by reg. 10, p. 342 above: reg. 2(1).
[8] "Appropriate nature conservation body" has the meaning given by reg. 4, p. 340 above: reg. 2(1).

(a) that the operation is carried out with the written consent of the appropriate nature conservation body;

(b) that the operation is carried out in accordance with the terms of a management agreement;

(c) that four months have expired from the giving of the notice under paragraph (1)(a).

(3) A person who, without reasonable excuse, contravenes paragraph (1) commits an offence and is liable on summary conviction to a fine not exceeding level 4 on the standard scale[1].

(4) For the purposes of paragraph (3) it is a reasonable excuse for a person to carry out an operation—

(a) that the operation was an emergency operation particulars of which (including details of the emergency) were notified to the appropriate nature conservation body as soon as practicable after the commencement of the operation; or

(b) that the operation was authorised by a planning permission granted on an application under Part III of the Town and Country Planning Act 1990[2] or Part III of the Town and Country Planning (Scotland) Act 1972[3].

(5) The appropriate nature conservation body has power to enforce this regulation; but nothing in this paragraph shall be construed as authorising the institution of proceedings in Scotland for an offence.

(6) Proceedings in England and Wales for an offence under this regulation shall not, without the consent of the Director of Public Prosecutions, be taken by a person other than the appropriate nature conservation body.

Supplementary provisions as to consents

20. (1) Where it appears to the appropriate nature conservation body[4] that an application for consent under regulation 19(2)(a) relates to an operation which is or forms part of a plan or project which—

(a) is not directly connected with or necessary to the management of the site, and

(b) is likely to have a significant effect on the site (either alone or in combination with other plans or projects),

they shall make an appropriate assessment of the implications for the site in view of that site's conservation objectives.

(2) In the light of the conclusions of the assessment, they may give consent for the operation only after having ascertained that the plan or project will not adversely affect the integrity of the site.

(3) The above provisions do not apply in relation to a site which is a European site[5] by reason only of regulation 10(1)(c)[6] (site protected in accordance with Article 5(4)).

(4) Where in any case, whether in pursuance of this regulation or otherwise, the appropriate nature conservation body have not given consent for an operation, but they consider that there is a risk that the operation may nevertheless be carried out, they shall notify the Secretary of State.

(5) They shall take such steps as are requisite to secure that any such notification is given at least one month before the expiry of the period mentioned in regulation 19(2)(c) (period after which operation may be carried out in absence of consent).

---

[1] The current fine at level 4 is £2,500: Criminal Justice Act 1991 (c. 53), s. 17 which came into force on 1 October 1992: S.I. 1992/333, S.I. 1992/2118.

[2] 1990 c. 8.

[3] 1972 c. 52.

[4] "Appropriate nature conservation body" has the meaning given by reg. 4, p. 340 above: reg. 2(1).

[5] "European site" has the meaning given by reg. 10, p. 342 above: reg. 2(1).

[6] P. 342 above.

Provision as to existing notices and consents

21. (1) Any notice or consent previously given under section 28(5)(*a*) or (6)(*a*) of the Wildlife and Countryside Act 1981[1] in relation to land[2] which on or after the commencement of these Regulations becomes land within a European site[3] shall have effect, subject as follows, as if given under regulation 19(1)(*a*)[4] or (2)(*a*) above.

(2) The appropriate nature conservation body[5] shall review any such consent as regards its compatibility with the conservation objectives of the site, and may modify or withdraw it.

(3) Notice of any such modification or withdrawal of consent shall be given to every owner and occupier of land within the site who in the opinion of the appropriate nature conservation body may be affected by it; and the modification or withdrawal shall come into force in relation to an owner or occupier upon such notice being given to him.

(4) The modification or withdrawal of a consent shall not affect anything done in reliance on the consent before the modification or withdrawal takes effect.

(5) Where or to the extent that an operation ceases to be covered by a consent by reason of the consent being modified or withdrawn, the period after which in accordance with regulation 19(2)(*c*) the operation may be carried out in the absence of consent shall be four months from the giving of notice of the modification or withdrawal under paragraph (3) above.

(6) Regulation 20(4) and (5) (provisions as to notification of Secretary of State) apply in such a case, with the following modifications—

(*a*) for the reference to consent not having been given substitute a reference to consent being modified or withdrawn;

(*b*) for the reference to the period specified in regulation 19(2)(*c*) substitute a reference to the period specified in paragraph (5) above.

Special nature conservation orders

Power to make special nature conservation order

22. (1) The Secretary of State may, after consultation with the appropriate nature conservation body[6], make in respect of any land[7] within a European site[8] an order (a "special nature conservation order") specifying operations which appear to him to be likely to destroy or damage the flora, fauna, or geological or physiographical features by reason of which the land is a European site.

(2) A special nature conservation order may be amended or revoked by a further order.

(3) Schedule 1[9] has effect with respect to the making, confirmation and coming into operation of special nature conservation orders and amending or revoking orders.

(4) A special nature conservation order in relation to land in England and Wales is a local land charge.

(5) A special nature conservation order in relation to land in Scotland shall be registered either—

(*a*) in a case where the land affected by the order is registered in that Register, in the Land Register of Scotland; or

(*b*) in any other case, in the appropriate Division of the General Register of Sasines.

---

[1] P. 169 above.
[2] "Land" defined by reg. 2(1), p. 337 above.
[3] "European site" has the meaning given by reg. 10, p. 342 above: reg. 2(1).
[4] P. 346 above.
[5] "Appropriate nature conservation body" has the meaning given by reg. 4, p. 340 above: reg. 2(1).
[6] "Appropriate nature conservation body" has the meaning given by reg. 4, p. 340 above: reg. 2(1).
[7] "Land" defined by reg. 2(1), p. 337 above.
[8] "European site" has the meaning given by reg. 10, p. 342 above: reg. 2(1).
[9] P. 391 below.

(6) A report submitted by a nature conservation body[1] to the Secretary of State under paragraph 20 of Schedule 6 to the Environmental Protection Act 1990[2] or section 10(2) of the Natural Heritage (Scotland) Act 1991[3] shall set out particulars of any land in their area as respects which a special nature conservation order has come into operation during the year to which the report relates.

Restriction on carrying out operations specified in order

23. (1) No person shall carry out on any land[4] within a European site[5] in respect of which a special nature conservation order[6] is in force any operation specified in the order, unless the operation is carried out, or caused or permitted to be carried out, by the owner or occupier of the land and—

(a) one of them has, after the making of the order, given the appropriate nature conservation body[7] written notice of a proposal to carry out the operation, specifying its nature and the land on which it is proposed to carry it out, and

(b) one of the conditions specified in paragraph (2) is fulfilled.

(2) Those conditions are—

(a) that the operation is carried out with the written consent of the appropriate nature conservation body;

(b) that the operation is carried out in accordance with the terms of a management agreement[8].

(3) A person who, without reasonable excuse, contravenes paragraph (1) commits an offence and is liable—

(a) on summary conviction, to a fine not exceeding the statutory maximum;

(b) on conviction on indictment, to a fine.

(4) For the purposes of paragraph (3) it is a reasonable excuse for a person to carry out an operation—

(a) that the operation was an emergency operation particulars of which (including details of the emergency) were notified to the appropriate nature conservation body as soon as practicable after the commencement of the operation; or

(b) that the operation was authorised by a planning permission granted on an application under Part III of the Town and Country Planning Act 1990 or Part III of the Town and Country Planning (Scotland) Act 1972.

Supplementary provisions as to consents

24. (1) Where it appears to the appropriate nature conservation body[9] that an application for consent under regulation 23(2)(a) relates to an operation which is or forms part of a plan or project which—

(a) is not directly connected with or necessary to the management of the site, and

(b) is likely to have a significant effect on the site (either alone or in combination with other plans or projects),

they shall make an appropriate assessment of the implications for the site in view of that site's conservation objectives.

---

[1] "Nature conservation body" has the meaning given by reg. 4, p. 340 above: reg. 2(1).

[2] P. 237 above.

[3] P. 251 above.

[4] "Land" defined by reg. 2(1), p. 337 above.

[5] "European site" has the meaning given by reg. 10, p. 342 above: reg. 2(1).

[6] "Special nature conservation order" defined by reg. 22, p. 348 above.

[7] "Appropriate nature conservation body" has the meaning given by reg. 4, p. 340 above: reg. 2(1).

[8] "Management agreement" defined by reg. 2(1), p. 338 above.

[9] "Appropriate nature conservation body" has the meaning given by reg. 4, p. 340 above: reg. 2(1).

(2) In the light of the conclusions of the assessment, they may give consent for the operation only after having ascertained that the plan or project will not adversely affect the integrity of the site.

(3) Where the appropriate nature conservation body refuse consent in accordance with paragraph (2) they shall give reasons for their decision.

(4) The owner or occupier of the land in question may—

(*a*) within two months of receiving notice of the refusal of consent, or

(*b*) if no notice of a decision is received by him within three months of an application for consent being made,

by notice in writing to the appropriate nature conservation body require them to refer the matter forthwith to the Secretary of State.

(5) If on the matter being referred to the Secretary of State he is satisfied that, there being no alternative solutions, the plan or project must be carried out for imperative reasons of overriding public interest (which, subject to paragraph (6), may be of a social or economic nature), he may direct the appropriate nature conservation body to give consent to the operation.

(6) Where the site concerned hosts a priority natural habitat type or a priority species[1], the reasons referred to in paragraph (5) must be either—

(*a*) reasons relating to human health, public safety or beneficial consequences of primary importance to the environment, or

(*b*) other reasons which in the opinion of the European Commission are imperative reasons of overriding public interest.

(7) Where the Secretary of State directs the appropriate nature conservation body to give consent under this regulation, he shall secure that such compensatory measures are taken as are necessary to ensure that the overall coherence of Natura 2000[2] is protected.

(8) This regulation does not apply in relation to a site which is a European site[3] by reason only of regulation 10(1)(*c*)[4] (site protected in accordance with Article 5(4)).

Compensation for effect of order

25. (1) Where a special nature conservation order[5] is made, the appropriate nature conservation body[6] shall pay compensation to any person having at the time of the making of the order an interest in land[7] comprised in an agricultural unit comprising land to which the order relates who, on a claim made to the appropriate nature conservation body within the time and in the manner prescribed by regulations, shows that the value of his interest is less than it would have been if the order had not been made.

(2) For this purpose an "agricultural unit" means land which is occupied as a unit for agricultural purposes, including any dwelling-house or other building occupied by the same person for the purpose of farming the land.

(3) No claim for compensation shall be made under this regulation in respect of an order unless the Secretary of State has given notice under paragraph 6(1) or (2) of Schedule 1[8] of his decision in respect of the order.

---

[1] "Priority natural habitat types" and "priority species" are defined in Article 1 of the Habitats Directive at p. 447 below: reg. 2(2).

[2] "Natura 2000" defined by reg. 2(1), p. 338 above.

[3] "European site" has the meaning given by reg. 10, p. 342 above: reg. 2(1).

[4] P. 342 above.

[5] "Special nature conservation order" defined by reg. 22, p. 348 above.

[6] "Appropriate nature conservation body" has the meaning given by reg. 4, p. 340 above: reg. 2(1).

[7] "Land" defined by reg. 2(1), p. 337 above.

[8] P. 392 below.

Restoration where order contravened

26. (1) Where a person is convicted of an offence under regulation 23[1], the court by which he is convicted may, in addition to dealing with him in any other way, make an order requiring him to carry out, within such period as may be specified in the order, such operations for the purpose of restoring the land to its former condition as may be so specified.

(2) An order under this regulation made on conviction on indictment shall be treated for the purposes of section 30 of the Criminal Appeal Act 1968[2] (effect of appeals on orders for the restitution of property) as an order for the restitution of property.

(3) In the case of an order under this regulation made by a magistrates' court the period specified in the order shall not begin to run—

(*a*) in any case until the expiration of the period for the time being prescribed by law for the giving of notice of appeal against a decision of a magistrates' court;

(*b*) where notice of appeal is given within the period so prescribed, until determination of the appeal.

(4) At any time before an order under this regulation has been complied with or fully complied with, the court by which it was made may, on the application of the person against whom it was made, discharge or vary the order if it appears to the court that a change in circumstances has made compliance or full compliance with the order impracticable or unnecessary.

(5) If a person fails without reasonable excuse to comply with an order under this regulation, he commits an offence and is liable on summary conviction to a fine not exceeding level 5 on the standard scale[3]; and if the failure continues after conviction, he may be proceeded against for a further offence from time to time until the order is complied with.

(6) If, within the period specified in an order under this regulation, any operations specified in the order have not been carried out, the appropriate nature conservation body[4] may enter the land and carry out those operations and recover from the person against whom the order was made any expenses reasonably incurred by them in doing so.

(7) In the application of this regulation to Scotland—

(*a*) paragraphs (2) and (3) shall not apply, and

(*b*) for the purposes of any appeal or review, an order under this regulation is a sentence.

Continuation in force of existing orders, &c.

27. (1) Where an order is in force under section 29 of the Wildlife and Countryside Act 1981[5] (special protection for certain areas of special scientific interest) in relation to land[6] which on or after the commencement of these Regulations becomes land within a European site[7], the order shall have effect as if made under regulation 22 above[8].

(2) Any notice previously given under section 29(4)(*a*) (notice by owner or occupier of proposal to carry out operation) shall have effect as if given under regulation 23(1)(*a*)[9] and, if the appropriate nature conservation body[10] have neither given nor refused consent, shall be dealt with under these Regulations.

(3) Any consent previously given under section 29(5)(*a*) shall be reviewed by the appropriate nature conservation body as regards its compatibility with the conservation objectives of the site, and may be modified or withdrawn.

---

[1] P. 349 above.

[2] 1968 c. 19; s. 30 was substituted by para. 28 of sch. 15 to the Criminal Justice Act 1988 (c. 33).

[3] The current fine at level 5 is £5,000: Criminal Justice Act 1991 (c. 53), s. 17 which came into force on 1 October 1992: S.I. 1992/333, S.I. 1992/2118.

[4] "Appropriate nature conservation body" has the meaning given by reg. 4, p. 340 above: reg. 2(1).

[5] P. 171 above.

[6] "Land" defined by reg. 2(1), p. 337 above.

[7] "European site" has the meaning given by reg. 10, p. 342 above: reg. 2(1).

[8] P. 348 above.

[9] P. 349 above.

[10] "Appropriate nature conservation body" has the meaning given by reg. 4, p. 340 above: reg. 2(1).

(4) Notice of any such modification or withdrawal of consent shall be given to every owner and occupier of land within the site who in the opinion of the appropriate nature conservation body may be affected by it; and the modification or withdrawal shall come into force in relation to an owner or occupier upon such notice being given to him.

(5) The modification or withdrawal of a consent shall not affect anything done in reliance on the consent before the modification or withdrawal takes effect.

(6) Section 29(5)(c), (6) and (7) shall cease to apply and the carrying out, or continuation, of any operation on land within a European site which is not otherwise authorised in accordance with these Regulations shall be subject to the prohibition in regulation 23(1).

Byelaws

Power to make byelaws

28. (1) The appropriate nature conservation body[1] may make byelaws for the protection of a European site[2] under section 20 of the National Parks and Access to the Countryside Act 1949[3] (byelaws for protection of nature reserves).

(2) Without prejudice to the generality of paragraph (1), byelaws under that section as it applies by virtue of this regulation may make provision of any of the following kinds.

(3) They may—

(a) provide for prohibiting or restricting the entry into, or movement within, the site of persons, vehicles, boats and animals;

(b) prohibit or restrict the killing, taking, molesting or disturbance of living creatures of any description in the site, the taking, destruction[4] or disturbance of eggs of any such creature, the taking of, or interference with, vegetation of any description in the site, or the doing of anything in the site which will interfere with the soil or damage any object in the site;

(c) contain provisions prohibiting the depositing of rubbish and the leaving of litter in the site;

(d) prohibit or restrict, or provide for prohibiting or restricting, the lighting of fires in the site or the doing of anything likely to cause a fire in the site.

(4) They may prohibit or restrict any activity referred to in paragraph (3) within such area surrounding or adjoining the site as appears to the appropriate nature conservation body requisite for the protection of the site.

(5) They may provide for the issue, on such terms and subject to such conditions as may be specified in the byelaws, of permits authorising—

(a) entry into the site or any such surrounding or adjoining area as is mentioned in paragraph (4), or

(b) the doing of anything within the site, or any such surrounding or adjoining area,

where such entry, or doing that thing, would otherwise be unlawful under the byelaws.

(6) They may be made so as to relate either to the whole or to any part of the site, or of any such surrounding or adjoining area as is mentioned in paragraph (4), and may make different provision for different parts thereof.

(7) This regulation does not apply in relation to a European marine site (but see regulation 36[5]).

Byelaws: limitation on effect

29. Byelaws under section 20 of the National Parks and Access to the Countryside Act 1949[6] as it applies by virtue of regulation 28 shall not interfere with—

---

[1] "Appropriate nature conservation body" has the meaning given by reg. 4, p. 340 above: reg. 2(1).
[2] "European site" has the meaning given by reg. 10, p. 342 above: reg. 2(1).
[3] P. 17 above.

[4] "Destroy" defined by reg. 2(1), p. 337 above.
[5] P. 355 below; "European marine site" defined by reg. 2(1), p. 337 above.
[6] P. 17 above.

(a) the exercise by any person of a right vested in him as owner, lessee or occupier of land[1] in the European site[2], or in any such surrounding or adjoining area as is mentioned in paragraph (4) of that regulation;

(b) the exercise of any public right of way;

(c) the exercise of any functions of statutory undertakers[3];

(d) the exercise of any functions of an internal drainage board, a district salmon fishery board or the Commissioners appointed under the Tweed Fisheries Act 1969[4]; or

(e) the running of a telecommunications code system or the exercise of any right conferred by or in accordance with the telecommunications code on the operator of any such system.

Compensation for effect of byelaws

30. Where the exercise of any right vested in a person, whether by reason of his being entitled to any interest in land or by virtue of a licence or agreement, is prevented or hindered by the coming into operation of byelaws under section 20 of the National Parks and Access to the Countryside Act 1949[5] as it applies by virtue of regulation 28, he shall be entitled to receive from the appropriate nature conservation body[6] compensation in respect thereof.

Continuation in force of existing byelaws

31. Any byelaws in force under section 20 of the National Parks and Access to the Countryside Act 1949[7] in relation to land[8] which on or after the commencement of these Regulations becomes land within a European site[9], or adjacent to such a site, shall have effect as if made under the said section 20 as it applies by virtue of regulation 28 and shall be construed as if originally so made.

Powers of compulsory acquisition

Powers of compulsory acquisition

32. (1) Where the appropriate nature conservation body[10] are satisfied—

(a) that they are unable, as respects any interest in land[11] within a European site[12], to conclude a management agreement[13] on terms appearing to them to be reasonable, or

(b) where they have entered into a management agreement as respects such an interest, that a breach of the agreement has occurred which prevents or impairs the satisfactory management of the European site.

they may acquire that interest compulsorily.

(2) Such a breach as is mentioned in paragraph (1)(b) shall not be treated as having occurred by virtue of any act or omission capable of remedy unless there has been default in remedying it within a reasonable time after notice given by the appropriate nature conservation body requiring the remedying thereof.

(3) Any dispute arising whether there has been such a breach of a management agreement shall be determined—

---

[1] "Land" defined by reg. 2(1), p. 337 above.

[2] "European site" has the meaning given by reg. 10, p. 342 above: reg. 2(1).

[3] "Statutory undertaker" defined by reg. 2(1), p. 338 above.

[4] 1969 c. xxiv.

[5] P. 17 above.

[6] "Appropriate nature conservation body" has the meaning given by reg. 4, p. 340 above: reg. 2(1).

[7] P. 17 above.

[8] "Land" defined by reg. 2(1), p. 337 above.

[9] "European site" has the meaning given by reg. 10, p. 342 above: reg. 2(1).

[10] "Appropriate nature conservation body" has the meaning given by reg. 4, p. 340 above: reg. 2(1).

[11] "Land" defined by reg. 2(1), p. 337 above.

[12] "European site" has the meaning given by reg. 10, p. 342 above: reg. 2(1).

[13] "Management agreement" defined by reg. 2(1), p. 338 above.

(a) in the case of land in England and Wales, by an arbitrator appointed by the Lord Chancellor;

(b) in the case of land in Scotland, by an arbiter appointed by the Lord President of the Court of Session.

Special provisions as to European marine sites

Marking of site and advice by nature conservation bodies

33. (1) The appropriate nature conservation body[1] may install markers indicating the existence and extent of a European marine site[2].

This power is exercisable subject to the obtaining of any necessary consent under section 34 of the Coast Protection Act 1949[3] (restriction of works detrimental to navigation).

(2) As soon as possible after a site becomes a European marine site, the appropriate nature conservation body shall advise other relevant authorities as to—

(a) the conservation objectives for that site, and

(b) any operations which may cause deterioration of natural habitats or the habitats of species, or disturbance of species, for which the site has been designated.

Management scheme for European marine site

34. (1) The relevant authorities[4], or any of them, may establish for a European marine site[5] a management scheme under which their functions[6] (including any power to make byelaws) shall be exercised so as to secure in relation to that site compliance with the requirements of the Habitats Directive[7].

(2) Only one management scheme may be made for each European marine site.

(3) A management scheme may be amended from time to time.

(4) As soon as a management scheme has been established, or is amended, a copy of it shall be sent by the relevant authority or authorities concerned to the appropriate nature conservation body[8].

Direction to establish or amend management scheme

35. (1) The relevant Minister[9] may give directions to the relevant authorities[10], or any of them, as to the establishment of a management scheme for a European marine site[11].

(2) Directions may, in particular—

(a) require conservation measures specified in the direction to be included in the scheme;

(b) appoint one of the relevant authorities to co-ordinate the establishment of the scheme;

(c) set time limits within which any steps are to be taken;

(d) provide that the approval of the Minister is required before the scheme is established; and

(e) require any relevant authority to supply to the Minister such information concerning the establishment of the scheme as may be specified in the direction.

---

[1] "Appropriate nature conservation body" has the meaning given by reg. 4, p. 340 above: reg. 2(1).

[2] "European marine site" defined by reg. 2(1), p. 337 above.

[3] 1949 c. 74; s. 34 was amended by s. 36(1) to (4) of the Merchant Shipping Act 1988 (c. 12).

[4] "Relevant authorities" defined by reg. 2(1), p. 338 above.

[5] "European marine site" defined by reg. 2(1), p. 337 above.

[6] "Functions" defined by reg. 2(1), p. 337 above.

[7] The Habitats Directive is at Annex G of PPG 9 at p. 446 below.

[8] "Appropriate nature conservation body" has the meaning given by reg. 4, p. 340 above: reg. 2(1).

[9] "The relevant Minister" defined by para. (5) below.

[10] "Relevant authorities" defined by reg. 2(1), p. 338 above.

[11] "European marine site" defined by reg. 2(1), p. 337 above.

(3) The relevant Minister may give directions to the relevant authorities, or any of them, as to the amendment of a management scheme for a European marine site, either generally or in any particular respect.

(4) Any direction under this regulation shall be in writing and may be varied or revoked by a further direction.

(5) In this regulation "the relevant Minister" means, in relation to a site in England, the Secretary of State and the Minister of Agriculture, Fisheries and Food acting jointly and in any other case the Secretary of State.

Byelaws for protection of European marine site

36. (1) The appropriate nature conservation body[1] may make byelaws for the protection of a European marine site[2] under section 37 of the Wildlife and Countryside Act 1981[3] (byelaws for protection of marine nature reserves).

(2) The provisions of subsections (2) to (11) of that section apply in relation to byelaws made by virtue of this regulation with the substitution for the references to marine nature reserves of references to European marine sites.

(3) Nothing in byelaws made by virtue of this regulation shall interfere with the exercise of any functions of a relevant authority[4], any functions[5] conferred by or under an enactment[6] (whenever passed) or any right of any person (whenever vested).

Miscellaneous

Nature conservation policy in planning contexts

37. (1) For the purposes of the planning enactments mentioned below, policies in respect of the conservation of the natural beauty and amenity of the land[7] shall be taken to include policies encouraging the management of features of the landscape which are of major importance for wild flora and fauna.

Such features are those which, by virtue of their linear and continuous structure (such as rivers with their banks or the traditional systems of marking field boundaries) or their function as stepping stones (such as ponds or small woods), are essential for the migration, dispersal and genetic exchange of wild species.

(2) The enactments referred to in paragraph (1) are—

(*a*) in the Town and Country Planning Act 1990[8], section 12(3A) (unitary development plans), section 31(3) (structure plans) and section 36(3)[9] (local plans);

(*b*) in the Town and Country Planning (Scotland) Act 1972[10], section 5(3)(*a*) (structure plans) and section 9(3)(*a*) (local plans)[11].

---

[1] "Appropriate nature conservation body" has the meaning given by reg. 4, p. 340 above: reg. 2(1).
[2] "European marine site" defined by reg. 2(1), p. 337 above.
[3] P. 179 above.
[4] "Relevant authorities" defined by reg. 2(1), p. 338 above.
[5] "Functions" defined by reg. 2(1), p. 337 above.
[6] "Enactment" defined by reg. 2(1), p. 337 above.

[7] "Land" defined by reg. 2(1), p. 337 above.
[8] 1990 c. 8.
[9] S. 12(3A) was inserted, and ss. 31(3) and 36(3) were substituted, by paras. 2(1), 16 and 17 respectively of sch. 4 to the Planning and Compensation Act 1991 (c. 34).
[10] 1972 c. 52.
[11] The relevant passages in ss. 5(3)(*a*) and 9(3)(*a*) were inserted by paras. 3 and 4 of sch. 13 to the Planning and Compensation Act 1991 (c. 34).

Part III: Protection of species

Protection of animals

European protected species of animals

38. The species of animals listed in Annex IV(*a*) to the Habitats Directive whose natural range includes any area in Great Britain are listed in Schedule 2 to these Regulations[1].

References in these Regulations to a "European protected species" of animal are to any of those species.

Protection of wild animals of European protected species

39. (1) It is an offence—

(*a*) deliberately to capture or kill a wild animal of a European protected species[2];

(*b*) deliberately to disturb any such animal;

(*c*) deliberately to take or destroy[3] the eggs of such an animal; or

(*d*) to damage or destroy a breeding site or resting place of such an animal.

(2) It is an offence to keep, transport, sell or exchange, or offer for sale or exchange, any live or dead wild animal of a European protected species, or any part of, or anything derived from, such an animal.

(3) Paragraphs (1) and (2) apply to all stages of the life of the animals to which they apply.

(4) A person shall not be guilty of an offence under paragraph (2) if he shows—

(*a*) that the animal had not been taken or killed, or had been lawfully taken or killed, or

(*b*) that the animal or other thing in question had been lawfully sold (whether to him or any other person).

For this purpose "lawfully" means without any contravention of these Regulations or Part I of the Wildlife and Countryside Act 1981[4].

(5) In any proceedings for an offence under this regulation, the animal in question shall be presumed to have been a wild animal unless the contrary is shown.

(6) A person guilty of an offence under this regulation is liable on summary conviction to a fine not exceeding level 5 on the standard scale[5].

Exceptions from regulation 39

40. (1) Nothing in regulation 39 shall make unlawful—

(*a*) anything done in pursuance of a requirement by the agriculture Minister[6] under section 98 of the Agriculture Act 1947[7] or section 39 of the Agriculture (Scotland) Act 1948[8] (prevention of damage by pests); or

(*b*) anything done under, or in pursuance of an order made under, the Animal Health Act 1981[9].

(2) Nothing in regulation 39(1)(*b*) or (*d*) shall make unlawful anything done within a dwelling-house.

---

[1] P. 393 below.

[2] "European protected species" of animal defined by reg. 38 above.

[3] "Destroy" defined by reg. 2(1), p. 337 above.

[4] P. 146 above.

[5] The current fine at level 5 is £5,000: Criminal Justice Act 1991 (c. 53), s. 17 which came into force on 1 October 1992: S.I. 1992/333, S.I. 1992/2118.

[6] "Agriculture Minister" defined by reg. 2(1), p. 337 above.

[7] 1947 c. 48; s. 98 was amended by the Prevention of Damage by Pests Act 1949 (c. 55) and the Pests Act 1954 (c. 68).

[8] 1948 c. 45; s. 39 was amended by the Prevention of Damage by Pests Act 1949 (c. 55), the Pests Act 1954 (c. 68) and the Deer (Amendment) (Scotland) Act 1982 (c. 19).

[9] 1981 c. 22; the Act was amended by the Animal Health and Welfare Act 1984 (c. 40) and the Environmental Protection Act 1990 (c. 43).

(3) Notwithstanding anything in regulation 39, a person shall not be guilty of an offence by reason of—

(a) the taking of a wild animal of a European protected species[1] if he shows that the animal had been disabled otherwise than by his unlawful act and was taken solely for the purpose of tending it and releasing it when no longer disabled;

(b) the killing of such an animal if he shows that the animal has been so seriously disabled otherwise than by his unlawful act that there was no reasonable chance of its recovering; or

(c) any act made unlawful by that regulation if he shows that the act was the incidental result of a lawful operation and could not reasonably have been avoided.

(4) A person shall not be entitled to rely on the defence provided by paragraph (2) or (3)(c) as respects anything done in relation to a bat otherwise than in the living area of a dwelling-house unless he had notified the appropriate nature conservation body[2] of the proposed action or operation and allowed them a reasonable time to advise him as to whether it should be carried out and, if so, the method to be used.

(5) Notwithstanding anything in regulation 39 a person—

(a) being the owner or occupier[3], or any person authorised by the owner or occupier, of the land[4] on which the action authorised is taken, or

(b) authorised by the local authority[5] for the area within which the action authorised is taken.

shall not be guilty of an offence by reason of the killing or disturbing of an animal of a European protected species if he shows that his action was necessary for the purpose of preventing serious damage to livestock[6], foodstuffs, crops, vegetables, fruit, growing timber or any other form of property or fisheries.

(6) A person may not rely on the defence provided by paragraph (5) as respects action taken at any time if it had become apparent before that time that the action would prove necessary for the purpose mentioned in that paragraph and either—

(a) a licence under regulation 44[7] authorising that action had not been applied for as soon as reasonably practicable after that fact had become apparent, or

(b) an application for such a licence had been determined.

(7) In paragraph (5) "local authority" means—

(a) in relation to England and Wales, a county, district or London borough council and includes the Common Council of the City of London, and

(b) in Scotland, a regional, islands or district council.

Prohibition of certain methods of taking or killing wild animals

41. (1) This regulation applies in relation to the taking or killing of a wild animal—

(a) of any of the species listed in Schedule 3 to these Regulations[8] (which shows the species listed in Annex V(a) to the Habitats Directive, and to which Article 15 applies, whose natural range includes any area of Great Britain), or

(b) of a European protected species[9], where the taking or killing of such animals is permitted in accordance with these Regulations.

(2) It is an offence to use for the purpose of taking or killing any such wild animal—

(a) any of the means listed in paragraph (3) or (4) below, or

---

[1] "European protected species" of animal defined by reg. 38, p. 356 above.
[2] "Appropriate nature conservation body" has the meaning given by reg. 4, p. 340 above: reg. 2(1).
[3] "Occupier" defined by reg. 2(1), p. 338 above.
[4] "Land" defined by reg. 2(1), p. 337 above.

[5] "Local authority" defined by para. (7) below.
[6] "Livestock" defined by reg. 2(1), p. 337 above.
[7] P. 359 below.
[8] P. 394 below.
[9] "European protected species" of animal defined by reg. 38, p. 356 above.

(b) any form of taking or killing from the modes of transport listed in paragraph (5) below.

(3) The prohibited means of taking or killing of mammals are—

(a) blind or mutilated animals used as live decoys;

(b) tape recorders;

(c) electrical and electronic devices capable of killing or stunning;

(d) artificial light sources;

(e) mirrors and other dazzling devices;

(f) devices for illuminating targets;

(g) sighting devices for night shooting comprising an electronic image magnifier or image converter;

(h) explosives;

(i) nets which are non-selective according to their principle or their conditions of use;

(j) traps which are non-selective according to their principle or their conditions of use;

(k) crossbows;

(l) poisons and poisoned or anaesthetic bait;

(m) gassing or smoking out;

(n) semi-automatic or automatic weapons with a magazine capable of holding more than two rounds of ammunition.

(4) The prohibited means of taking or killing fish are—

(a) poison;

(b) explosives.

(5) The prohibited modes of transport are—

(a) aircraft;

(b) moving motor vehicles.

(6) A person guilty of an offence under this regulation is liable on summary conviction to a fine not exceeding level 5 on the standard scale[1].

Protection of plants

European protected species of plants

42. The species of plants listed in Annex IV(b) to the Habitats Directive whose natural range includes any area in Great Britain are listed in Schedule 4 to these Regulations[2].

References in these Regulations to a "European protected species" of plant are to any of those species.

....

Protection of wild plants of European protected species

43. (1) It is an offence deliberately to pick, collect, cut, uproot or destroy a wild plant of a European protected species[3].

(2) It is an offence to keep, transport, sell or exchange, or offer for sale or exchange, any live or dead wild plant of a European protected species, or any part of, or anything derived from, such a plant.

(3) Paragraphs (1) and (2) apply to all stages of the biological cycle of the plants to which they apply.

---

[1] The current fine at level 5 is £5,000: Criminal Justice Act 1991 (c. 53), s. 17 which came into force on 1 October 1992: S.I. 1992/333, S.I. 1992/2118.

[2] P. 395 below.

[3] "European protected species" of plant defined by reg. 42 above.

(4) A person shall not be guilty of an offence under paragraph (1), by reason of any act made unlawful by that paragraph if he shows that the act was an incidental result of a lawful operation and could not reasonably have been avoided.

(5) A person shall not be guilty of an offence under paragraph (2) if he shows that the plant or other thing in question had been lawfully sold (whether to him or any other person).

For this purpose "lawfully" means without any contravention of these Regulations or Part I of the Wildlife and Countryside Act 1981[1].

(6) In any proceedings for an offence under this regulation, the plant in question shall be presumed to have been a wild plant unless the contrary is shown.

(7) A person guilty of an offence under this section is liable on summary conviction to a fine not exceeding level 4 on the standard scale[2].

Power to grant licences

Grant of licences for certain purposes

44. (1) Regulations 39[3], 41[4] and 43 do not apply to anything done for any of the following purposes under and in accordance with the terms of a licence granted by the appropriate authority[5].

(2) The purposes referred to in paragraph (1) are—

(a) scientific or educational purposes;

(b) ringing or marking, or examining any ring or mark on, wild animals;

(c) conserving wild animals or wild plants or introducing them to particular areas;

(d) protecting any zoological or botanical collection;

(e) preserving public health or public safety or other imperative reasons of overriding public interest including those of a social or economic nature and beneficial consequences of primary importance for the environment;

(f) preventing the spread of disease; or

(g) preventing serious damage to livestock[6], foodstuffs for livestock, crops, vegetables, fruit, growing timber or any other form of property or to fisheries.

(3) The appropriate authority shall not grant a licence under this regulation unless they are satisfied—

(a) that there is no satisfactory alternative, and

(b) that the action authorised will not be detrimental to the maintenance of the population of the species concerned at a favourable conservation status in their natural range.

(4) For the purposes of this regulation "the appropriate authority" means—

(a) in the case of a licence under any of sub-paragraphs (a) to (d) of paragraph (2), the appropriate nature conservation body[7]; and

(b) in the case of a licence under any of sub-paragraphs (e) to (g) of that paragraph, the agriculture Minister[8].

(5) The agriculture Minister shall from time to time consult with the nature conservation bodies[9] as to the exercise of his functions[10] under this regulation; and he shall not grant a licence of any description unless he has been advised by the appropriate nature conservation body as to the circumstances in which, in their opinion, licences of that description should be granted.

---

[1] P. 146 above.

[2] The current fine at level 4 is £2,500: Criminal Justice Act 1991 (c. 53), s. 17 which came into force on 1 October 1992: S.I. 1992/333, S.I. 1992/2118.

[3] P. 356.

[4] P. 357.

[5] "The appropriate authority" defined by para. (4) below.

[6] "Livestock" defined by reg. 2(1), p. 337 above.

[7] "Appropriate nature conservation body" has the meaning given by reg. 4, p. 340 above: reg. 2(1).

[8] "Agriculture Minister" defined by reg. 2(1), p. 337 above.

[9] "Nature conservation body" has the meaning given by reg. 4, p. 340 above: reg. 2(1).

[10] "Functions" defined by reg. 2(1), p. 337 above.

Licences: supplementary provisions

45. (1) A licence under regulation 44—

(*a*) may be, to any degree, general or specific;

(*b*) may be granted either to persons of a class or to a particular person; and

(*c*) may be subject to compliance with any specified conditions.

(2) For the purposes of a licence under regulation 44 the definition of a class of persons may be framed by reference to any circumstances whatever including, in particular, their being authorised by any other person.

(3) A licence under regulation 44 may be modified or revoked at any time by the appropriate authority; but otherwise shall be valid for the period stated in the licence.

(4) A licence under regulation 44 which authorises any person to kill wild animals shall specify the area within which and the methods by which the wild animals may be killed and shall not be granted for a period of more than two years.

(5) It shall be a defence in proceedings for an offence under section 8(*b*) of the Protection of Animals Act 1911[1] or section 7(*b*) of the Protection of Animals (Scotland) Act 1912[2] (which restrict the placing on land of poison and poisonous substances) to show that—

(*a*) the act alleged to constitute the offence was done under and in accordance with the terms of a licence under regulation 44, and

(*b*) any conditions specified in the licence were complied with.

(6) The appropriate authority may charge for a licence under regulation 44 such reasonable sum (if any) as they may determine.

False statements made for obtaining licence

46. (1) A person commits an offence who, for the purposes of obtaining, whether for himself or another, the grant of a licence under regulation 44[3]—

(a) makes a statement or representation, or furnishes a document or information, which he knows to be false in a material particular, or

(b) recklessly makes a statement or representation, or furnishes a document or information, which is false in a material particular.

(2) A person guilty of an offence under this regulation is liable on summary conviction to a fine not exceeding level 4 on the standard scale[4].

Part IV: Adaptation of planning and other controls

Introductory

Application of provisions of this Part

47. (1) The requirements of—

(*a*) regulations 48 and 49 (requirement to consider effect on European sites), and

(*b*) regulations 50 and 51 (requirement to review certain existing decisions and consents, &c.),

apply, subject to and in accordance with the provisions of regulations 54 to 85[5], in relation to the matters specified in those provisions.

---

[1] 1911 c. 27; s. 8 was amended by s. 1 of the Protection of Animals (Amendment) Act 1927 (c. 27).

[2] 1912 c. 14.

[3] P. 359 above.

[4] The current fine at level 4 is £2,500: Criminal Justice Act 1991 (c. 53), s. 17 which came into force on 1 October 1992: S.I. 1992/333, S.I. 1992/2118.

[5] Pp. 364–381 below.

(2) Supplementary provision is made by—

(a) regulation 52[1] (co-ordination where more than one competent authority involved), and

(b) regulation 53[2] (compensatory measures where plan or project is agreed to notwithstanding a negative assessment of the implications for a European site).

General provisions for protection of European sites

Assessment of implications for European site

48. (1) A competent authority[3], before deciding to undertake, or give any consent, permission or other authorisation for, a plan or project which—

(a) is likely to have a significant effect on a European site[4] in Great Britain (either alone or in combination with other plans or projects), and

(b) is not directly connected with or necessary to the management of the site,

shall make an appropriate assessment of the implications for the site in view of that site's conservation objectives.

(2) A person applying for any such consent, permission or other authorisation shall provide such information as the competent authority may reasonably require for the purposes of the assessment.

(3) The competent authority shall for the purposes of the assessment consult the appropriate nature conservation body[5] and have regard to any representations made by that body within such reasonable time as the authority may specify.

(4) They shall also, if they consider it appropriate, take the opinion of the general public; and if they do so, they shall take such steps for that purpose as they consider appropriate.

(5) In the light of the conclusions of the assessment, and subject to regulation 49, the authority shall agree to the plan or project only after having ascertained that it will not adversely affect the integrity of the European site.

(6) In considering whether a plan or project will adversely affect the integrity of the site, the authority shall have regard to the manner in which it is proposed to be carried out or to any conditions or restrictions subject to which they propose that the consent, permission or other authorisation should be given.

(7) This regulation does not apply in relation to a site which is a European site by reason only of regulation 10(1)(c)[6] (site protected in accordance with Article 5(4)).

....

Considerations of overriding public interest

49. (1) If they are satisfied that, there being no alternative solutions, the plan or project must be carried out for imperative reasons of overriding public interest (which, subject to paragraph (2), may be of a social or economic nature), the competent authority[7] may agree to the plan or project notwithstanding a negative assessment of the implications for the site.

(2) Where the site concerned hosts a priority natural habitat type or a priority species[8], the reasons referred to in paragraph (1) must be either—

(a) reasons relating to human health, public safety or beneficial consequences of primary importance to the environment, or

[1] P. 363 below.
[2] P. 363 below.
[3] "Competent authority" shall be construed in accordance with reg. 6, p. 340 above: reg. 2(1).
[4] "European site" has the meaning given by reg. 10, p. 342 above: reg. 2(1).
[5] "Appropriate nature conservation body" has the meaning given by reg. 4, p. 340 above: reg. 2(1).
[6] P. 342 above.
[7] "Competent authority" shall be construed in accordance with reg. 6, p. 340 above: reg. 2(1).
[8] "Priority natural habitat types" and "priority species" are defined in Article 1 of the Habitats Directive at p. 447 below: reg. 2(2).

(*b*) other reasons which in the opinion of the European Commission are imperative reasons of overriding public interest.

(3) Where a competent authority other than the Secretary of State desire to obtain the opinion of the European Commission as to whether reasons are to be considered imperative reasons of overriding public interest, they shall submit a written request to the Secretary of State—

(*a*) identifying the matter on which an opinion is sought, and

(*b*) accompanied by any documents or information which may be required.

(4) The Secretary of State may thereupon, if he thinks fit, seek the opinion of the Commission; and if he does so, he shall upon receiving the Commission's opinion transmit it to the authority.

(5) Where an authority other than the Secretary of State propose to agree to a plan or project under this regulation notwithstanding a negative assessment of the implications for a European site[1], they shall notify the Secretary of State.

Having notified the Secretary of State, they shall not agree to the plan or project before the end of the period of 21 days beginning with the day notified to them by the Secretary of State as that on which their notification was received by him, unless the Secretary of State notifies them that they may do so.

(6) In any such case the Secretary of State may give directions to the authority prohibiting them from agreeing to the plan or project, either indefinitely or during such period as may be specified in the direction.

This power is without prejudice to any other power of the Secretary of State in relation to the decision in question.

....

Review of existing decisions and consents, &c.

50. (1) Where before the date on which a site[2] becomes a European site[3] or, if later, the commencement of these Regulations, a competent authority[4] have decided to undertake, or have given any consent, permission or other authorisation for, a plan or project to which regulation 48(1)[5] would apply if it were to be reconsidered as of that date, the authority shall as soon as reasonably practicable, review their decision or, as the case may be, the consent, permission or other authorisation, and shall affirm, modify or revoke it.

(2) They shall for that purpose make an appropriate assessment of the implications for the site in view of that site's conservation objectives; and the provisions of regulation 48(2) to (4) shall apply, with the appropriate modifications, in relation to such a review.

(3) Subject to the following provisions of this Part, any review required by this regulation shall be carried out under existing statutory procedures where such procedures exist, and if none exist the Secretary of State may give directions as to the procedure to be followed.

(4) Nothing in this regulation shall affect anything done in pursuance of the decision, or the consent, permission or other authorisation, before the date mentioned in paragraph (1).

....

Consideration on review

51. (1) The following provisions apply where a decision, or a consent, permission or other authorisation, falls to be reviewed under regulation 50.

(2) Subject as follows, the provisions of regulation 48(5) and (6) and regulation 49 shall apply, with the appropriate modifications, in relation to the decision on the review.

---

[1] "European site" has the meaning given by reg. 10, p. 342 above: reg. 2(1).

[2] "Site" is defined in Article 1 of the Habitats Directive at p. 448 below: reg. 2(2).

[3] "European site" has the meaning given by reg. 10, p. 342 above: reg. 2(1).

[4] "Competent authority" shall be construed in accordance with reg. 6, p. 340 above: reg. 2(1).

[5] P. 361 above.

(3) The decision, or the consent, permission or other authorisation, may be affirmed if it appears to the authority reviewing it that other action taken or to be taken by them, or by another authority, will secure that the plan or project does not adversely affect the integrity of the site.

Where that object may be attained in a number of ways, the authority or authorities concerned shall seek to secure that the action taken is the least onerous to those affected.

(4) The Secretary of State may issue guidance to authorities for the purposes of paragraph (3) as to the manner of determining which of different ways should be adopted for securing that the plan or project does not have any such effect, and in particular—

(a) the order of application of different controls, and

(b) the extent to which account should be taken of the possible exercise of other powers;

and the authorities concerned shall have regard to any guidance so issued in discharging their functions under that paragraph.

(5) Any modification or revocation effected in pursuance of this regulation shall be carried out under existing statutory procedures where such procedures exist.

If none exist, the Secretary of State may give directions as to the procedure to be followed.

Co-ordination where more than one competent authority involved

52. (1) The following provisions apply where a plan or project—

(a) is undertaken by more than one competent authority[1],

(b) requires the consent, permission or other authorisation of more than one competent authority, or

(c) is undertaken by one or more competent authorities and requires the consent, permission or other authorisation of one or more other competent authorities.

(2) Nothing in regulation 48(1)[2] or 50(2)[3] requires a competent authority to assess any implications of a plan or project which would be more appropriately assessed under that provision by another competent authority.

(3) The Secretary of State may issue guidance to authorities for the purposes of regulations 48 to 51 as to the circumstances in which an authority may or should adopt the reasoning or conclusions of another competent authority as to whether a plan or project—

(a) is likely to have a significant effect on a European site[4], or

(b) will adversely affect the integrity of a European site;

and the authorities involved shall have regard to any guidance so issued in discharging their functions under those regulations.

(4) In determining whether a plan or project should be agreed to under regulation 49(1)[5] (considerations of overriding public interest) a competent authority other than the Secretary of State shall seek and have regard to the views of the other competent authority or authorities involved.

Compensatory measures

53. Where in accordance with regulation 49[6] (considerations of overriding public interest)—

(a) a plan or project is agreed to, notwithstanding a negative assessment of the implications for a European site[7], or

---

[1] "Competent authority" shall be construed in accordance with reg. 6, p. 340 above: reg. 2(1).

[2] P. 361 above.

[3] P. 362 above.

[4] "European site" has the meaning given by reg. 10, p. 342 above: reg. 2(1).

[5] P. 361 above.

[6] P. 361 above.

[7] "European site" has the meaning given by reg. 10, p. 342 above: reg. 2(1).

(b) a decision, or a consent, permission or other authorisation, is affirmed on review, notwith-standing such an assessment,

the Secretary of State shall secure that any necessary compensatory measures are taken to ensure that the overall coherence of Natura 2000[1] is protected.

Planning

Grant of planning permission

54. (1) Regulations 48[2] and 49[3] (requirement to consider effect on European site[4]) apply, in England and Wales, in relation to—

(a) granting planning permission on an application under Part III of the Town and Country Planning Act 1990[5];

(b) granting planning permission, or upholding a decision of the local planning authority[6] to grant planning permission (whether or not subject to the same conditions and limitations as those imposed by the local planning authority), on determining an appeal under section 78[7] of that Act in respect of such an application;

(c) granting planning permission under—

 (i) section 141(2)(a) of that Act (action by Secretary of State in relation to purchase notice),

 (ii) section 177(1)(a)[8] of that Act (powers of Secretary of State on appeal against enforce-ment notice), or

 (iii) section 196(5)[9] of that Act as originally enacted (powers of Secretary of State on refer-ence or appeal as to established use certificate);

(d) directing under section 90(1), (2) or (2A)[10] of that Act (development with government autho-risation), or under section 5(1) of the Pipe-lines Act 1962[11], that planning permission shall be deemed to be granted;

(e) making—

 (i) an order under section 102[12] of that Act (order requiring discontinuance of use or removal of buildings or works), including an order made under that section by virtue of section 104 (powers of Secretary of State), which grants planning permission, or

 (ii) an order under paragraph 1 of Schedule 9[13] to that Act (order requiring discontinuance of mineral working), including an order made under that paragraph by virtue of para-graph 11 of that Schedule (default powers of Secretary of State), which grants planning permission,

 or confirming any such order under section 103 of that Act;

(f) directing under—

 (i) section 141(3) of that Act (action by Secretary of State in relation to purchase notice), or

 (ii) section 35(5) of the Planning (Listed Buildings and Conservation Areas) Act 1990[14] (action by Secretary of State in relation to listed building purchase notice),

that if an application is made for planning permission it shall be granted.

---

[1] "Natura 2000" defined by reg. 2(1), p. 338 above.

[2] P. 361 above.

[3] P. 361 above.

[4] "European site" has the meaning given by reg. 10, p. 342 above: reg. 2(1).

[5] 1990 c. 8.

[6] "Local planning authority" defined by reg. 2(1), p. 337 above.

[7] S. 78 was amended by s. 17(2) of the Planning and Compensation Act 1991 (c. 34).

[8] S. 177(1)(a) was substituted by para. 24(1)(a) of sch. 7 to the Planning and Compensation Act 1991 (c. 34).

[9] S. 196(5) was repealed by para. 33(e) of sch. 7 to the Planning and Compensation Act 1991 (c. 34) but that repeal does not apply to appeals arising out of applications made under s. 192(1) (as originally enacted) before 27 July 1992.

[10] S. 90(2A) was inserted by s. 16(1) of the Transport and Works Act 1992 (c. 42).

[11] 1962 c. 58.

[12] S. 102 was amended by para. 6 of sch. 1, and para. 12 of sch. 7, to the Planning and Compensation Act 1992 (c. 34).

[13] Para. 1 of sch. 9 was amended by para. 15 of sch. 1 to the Planning and Compensation Act 1991 (c. 34).

[14] 1990 c. 9.

(2) Regulations 48 and 49 (requirement to consider effect on European site) apply, in Scotland, in relation to—

(a) granting planning permission on an application under Part III of the Town and Country Planning (Scotland) Act 1972[1];

(b) granting planning permission, or upholding a decision of the planning authority[2] to grant planning permission (whether or not subject to the same conditions and limitations as those imposed by the local planning authority), on determining an appeal under section 33 (appeals) of that Act in respect of such an application;

(c) granting planning permission under—

   (i) section 172(2) of that Act (action by Secretary of State in relation to purchase notice).

   (ii) section 85(5)[3] of that Act (powers of Secretary of State on appeal against enforcement notice), or

   (iii) section 91(3)[4] of that Act as originally enacted (powers of Secretary of State on reference or appeal as to established use certificate);

(d) directing under section 37(1)[5] (development with government authorisation) of that Act, or under section 5(1) of the Pipe-lines Act 1962 or paragraph 7 of Schedule 8 to the Electricity Act 1989[6], that planning permission shall be deemed to be granted;

(e) making an order under section 49[7] of that Act (order requiring discontinuance of use or removal of buildings or works), including an order made under that section by virtue of section 260 (default powers of Secretary of State), which grants planning permission, or confirming any such order;

(f) directing under—

   (i) section 172(3) of that Act (powers of Secretary of State in relation to purchase notice), or

   (ii) paragraph 2(6) of Schedule 17 to that Act (powers of Secretary of State in relation to listed building purchase notice),

that if an application is made for planning permission it shall be granted.

(3) Where regulations 48 and 49 apply, the competent authority[8] may, if they consider that any adverse effects of the plan or project on the integrity of a European site[9] would be avoided if the planning permission were subject to conditions or limitations, grant planning permission or, as the case may be, take action which results in planning permission being granted or deemed to be granted subject to those conditions or limitations.

(4) Where regulations 48 and 49 apply, outline planning permission shall not be granted unless the competent authority are satisfied (whether by reason of the conditions and limitations to which the outline planning permission is to be made subject, or otherwise) that no development likely adversely to affect the integrity of a European site could be carried out under the permission, whether before or after obtaining approval of any reserved matters.

In this paragraph "outline planning permission" and "reserved matters" have the same meaning as in section 92 of the Town and Country Planning Act 1990 or section 39 of the Town and Country Planning (Scotland) Act 1972.

---

[1] 1972 c. 52.

[2] "Planning authority" defined by reg. 2(1), p. 338 above.

[3] S. 85(5) was amended by para. 20 of sch. 13 to, and pt. IV of sch. 19 to the Planning and Compensation Act 1991 (c. 34).

[4] S. 91(3) was repealed by para. 26(b) of sch. 13 to the Planning and Compensation Act 1991 (c. 34) but that repeal does not apply to appeals arising out of applications made under s. 90(2) (as originally enacted) before 27th September 1992.

[5] S. 37(1) was amended by pt. 1 of sch. 4 to the Local Government and Planning (Scotland) Act 1982 (c. 43).

[6] 1989 c. 29; para. 7 is repealed insofar as it extends to England and Wales by pt. II of sch. 1 to the Planning (Consequential Provisions) Act 1990 (c. 11).

[7] S. 49 was amended by s. 172(2) of the Local Government (Scotland) Act 1973 (c. 65), ss. 26 and 35 of the Town and Country Planning (Minerals) Act 1981 (c. 36) and para. 5 of sch. 8, and para. 16 of sch. 13, to the Planning and Compensation Act 1991 (c. 34).

[8] "Competent authority" shall be construed in accordance with reg. 6, p. 340 above: reg. 2(1).

[9] "European site" has the meaning given by reg. 10, p. 342 above: reg. 2(1).

Planning permission: duty to review

55. (1) Subject to the following provisions of this regulation, regulations 50[1] and 51[2] (requirement to review certain decisions and consents, &c.) apply to any planning permission or deemed planning permission, unless—

(a) the development to which it related has been completed, or

(b) it was granted subject to a condition as to the time within which the development to which it related was to be begun and that time has expired without the development having been begun, or

(c) it was granted for a limited period and that period has expired.

(2) Regulations 50 and 51 do not apply to planning permission granted or deemed to have been granted—

(a) a development order (but see regulations 60 to 64 below[3]);

(b) by virtue of the adoption of a simplified planning zone scheme or of alterations to such a scheme (but see regulation 65 below[4]);

(c) by virtue of the taking effect of an order designating an enterprise zone under Schedule 32 to the Local Government, Planning and Land Act 1980[5], or by virtue of the approval of a modified enterprise zone scheme (but see regulation 66 below[6]).

(3) Planning permission deemed to be granted by virtue of—

(a) a direction under section 90(1) of the Town and Country Planning Act 1990 or section 37(1) of the Town and Country Planning (Scotland) Act 1972 in respect of development for which an authorisation has been granted under section 1 or 3 of the Pipe-lines Act 1962[7],

(b) a direction under section 5(1) of the Pipe-lines Act 1962,

(c) a direction under section 90(1) of the Town and Country Planning Act 1990 or section 37(1) of the Town and Country Planning (Scotland) Act 1972 in respect of development for which a consent has been given under section 36 or 37 of the Electricity Act 1989.

(d) a direction under section 90(2) of the Town and Country Planning Act 1990 or paragraph 7 of Schedule 8 to the Electricity Act 1989, or

(e) a direction under section 90(2A) of the Town and Country Planning Act 1990 (which relates to development in pursuance of an order under section 1 or 3 of the Transport and Works Act 1992[8]),

shall be reviewed in accordance with the following provisions of this Part in conjunction with the review of the underlying authorisation, consent or order.

(4) In the case of planning permission deemed to have been granted in any other case by a direction under section 90(1) of the Town and Country Planning Act 1990 or section 37(1) of the Town and Country Planning (Scotland) Act 1972, the local planning authority[9] shall—

(a) identify any such permission which they consider falls to be reviewed under regulations 50 and 51, and

(b) refer the matter to the government department which made the direction;

and the department shall, if it agrees that the planning permission does fall to be so reviewed, thereupon review the direction in accordance with those regulations.

(5) Save as otherwise expressly provided, regulations 50 and 51 do not apply to planning permission granted or deemed to be granted by a public general Act of Parliament.

---

[1] P. 362 above.
[2] P. 362 above.
[3] Pp. 370–372 below.
[4] P. 372 below.
[5] 1980 c. 65.
[6] P. 372 below.
[7] 1962 c. 58.
[8] 1992 c. 42.
[9] "Local planning authority" defined by reg. 2(1), p. 337 above.

(6) Subject to paragraphs (3) and (4), where planning permission granted by the Secretary of State falls to be reviewed under regulations 50 and 51—

(a) it shall be reviewed by the local planning authority, and

(b) the power conferred by section 97 of the Town and Country Planning Act 1990 or section 42 of the Town and Country Planning (Scotland) Act 1972 (revocation or modification of planning permission) shall be exercisable by that authority as in relation to planning permission granted on an application under Part III of that Act.

In a non-metropolitan county in England and Wales the function of reviewing any such planning permission shall be exercised by the district planning authority unless it relates to a county matter (within the meaning of Schedule 1 to the Town and Country Planning Act 1990) in which case it shall be exercised by the county planning authority.

Planning permission: consideration on review

56. (1) In reviewing any planning permission or deemed planning permission in pursuance of regulations 50[1] and 51[2], the competent authority[3] shall, in England and Wales—

(a) consider whether any adverse effects could be overcome by planning obligations under section 106[4] of the Town and Country Planning Act 1990 being entered into, and

(b) if they consider that those effects could be so overcome, invite those concerned to enter into such obligations;

and so far as the adverse effects are not thus overcome the authority shall make such order under section 97 of that Act (power to revoke or modify planning permission), or under section 102 of or paragraph 1 of Schedule 9 to that Act (order requiring discontinuance of use, &c.), as may be required.

(2) In reviewing any planning permission or deemed planning permission in pursuance of regulations 50 and 51, the competent authority shall, in Scotland—

(a) consider whether any adverse effects could be overcome by an agreement under section 50 (agreements regulating development or use of land) of the Town and Country Planning (Scotland) Act 1972 being entered into, and

(b) if they consider that those effects could be so overcome, invite those concerned to enter into such an agreement;

and so far as the adverse effects are not thus overcome, the authority shall make such order under section 42 of that Act[5] (power to revoke or modify planning permission), or under section 49 of that Act[6] (orders requiring discontinuance of use, &c.) as may be required.

(3) Where the authority ascertain that the carrying out or, as the case may be, the continuation of the development would adversely affect the integrity of a European site[7], they nevertheless need not proceed under regulations 50 and 51 if and so long as they consider that there is no likelihood of the development being carried out or continued.

Effect of orders made on review: England and Wales

57. (1) An order under section 97 of the Town and Country Planning Act 1990[8] (power to revoke or modify planning permission) made pursuant to regulation 55[9] shall take effect upon service of

[1] P. 362 above.
[2] P. 362 above.
[3] "Competent authority" shall be construed in accordance with reg. 6, p. 340 above: reg. 2(1).
[4] S. 106 was substituted by s. 12(1) of the Planning and Compensation Act 1991 (c. 34).
[5] S. 42 was amended by s. 172(2) of the Local Government (Scotland) Act 1973 (c. 65) and ss. 26 and 35 of the Town and Country Planning (Minerals) Act 1981 (c. 36).

[6] S. 49 was amended by s. 172(2) of the Local Government (Scotland) Act 1973 (c. 65), ss. 26 and 35 of the Town and Country Planning (Minerals) Act 1981 (c. 36) and para. 5 of sch. 8, and para. 16 of sch. 13 to the Planning and Compensation Act 1991 (c. 34).
[7] "European site" has the meaning given by reg. 10, p. 342 above: reg. 2(1).
[8] 1990 c. 8.
[9] P. 366 above.

the notices required by section 98(2) of that Act or, where there is more than one such notice and those notices are served at different times, upon the service of the last such notice to be served.

(2) Where the Secretary of State determines not to confirm such an order, the order shall cease to have effect from the time of that determination, and the permission revoked or modified by the order shall thereafter have effect as if the order had never been made, and—

(a) any period specified in the permission for the taking of any action, being a period which had not expired prior to the date upon which the order took effect under paragraph (1) above, shall be extended by a period equal to that during which the order had effect; and

(b) there shall be substituted for any date specified in the permission as being a date by which any action should be taken, not being a date falling prior to the date upon which the order took effect under paragraph (1) above, such date as post-dates the specified date by a period equal to that during which the order had effect.

(3) An order under section 102 of, or under paragraph 1 of Schedule 9 to, the Town and Country Planning Act 1990 (order requiring discontinuance of use, &c.) made pursuant to regulation 55 shall insofar as it requires the discontinuance of a use of land[1] or imposes conditions upon the continuance of a use of land, take effect upon service of the notices required by section 103(3) or, where there is more than one such notice and those notices are served at different times, upon service of the last such notice to be served.

(4) Where the Secretary of State determines not to confirm any such order, the order shall cease to have effect from the time of that determination and the use which by the order was discontinued or upon whose continuance conditions were imposed—

(a) may thereafter be continued as if the order had never been made, and

(b) be treated for the purposes of the Town and Country Planning Act 1990 as if it had continued without interruption or modification throughout the period during which the order had effect.

(5) An order under section 97 of that Act (power to revoke or modify planning permission) made in pursuance of regulation 55 shall not affect so much of the development authorised by the permission as was carried out prior to the order taking effect.

(6) An order under section 102 of, or under paragraph 1 of Schedule 9 to, that Act (order requiring discontinuance of use, &c.) made in pursuance of regulation 55 shall not affect anything done prior to the site becoming a European site[2] or, if later, the commencement of these Regulations.

....

Effect of orders made on review: Scotland

58. (1) An order under section 42 of the Town and Country Planning (Scotland) Act 1972 (power to revoke or modify planning permission) made pursuant to regulation 55[3] shall take effect upon service of the notices required by subsection (3) of that section or, where there is more than one such notice and those notices are served at different times, upon the service of the last such notice to be served.

(2) Where the Secretary of State determines not to confirm such an order, the order shall cease to have effect from the time of that determination, and the permission revoked or modified by the order shall thereafter have effect as if the order had never been made, and—

(a) any period specified in the permission for the taking of any action, being a period which had not expired prior to the date upon which the order took effect under paragraph (1) above, shall be extended by a period equal to that during which the order had effect; and

(b) there shall be substituted for any date specified in the permission as being a date by which any action should be taken, not being a date falling prior to that date upon which the order

---

[1] "Land" defined by reg. 2(1), p. 337 above.
[2] "European site" has the meaning given by reg. 10, p.
342 above: reg. 2(1).
[3] P. 366 above.

took effect under paragraph (1) above, such date as post-dates the specified date by a period equal to that during which the order had effect.

(3) An order under section 49 of the Town and Country Planning (Scotland) Act 1972 (order requiring discontinuance of use, &c.) made pursuant to regulation 55 shall, insofar as it requires the discontinuance of a use of land[1] or imposes conditions upon the continuance of a use of land, take effect upon service of the notices required by subsection (5) of that section or, where there is more than one such notice and those notices are served at different times, upon service of the last such notice to be served.

(4) Where the Secretary of State determines not to confirm any such order, the order shall cease to have effect from the time of that determination and the use which by the order was discontinued or upon whose continuance conditions were imposed—

(a) may thereafter be continued as if the order had never been made, and

(b) shall be treated for the purposes of the Town and Country Planning (Scotland) Act 1972 as if it had continued without interruption throughout the period during which the order had effect.

(5) An order under section 42 of that Act (power to modify or revoke planning permission) made in pursuance of regulation 55 shall not affect so much of the development authorised by the permission as was carried out prior to the site becoming a European site[2] or, if later, the commencement of these Regulations.

(6) An order under section 49 of that Act (order requiring discontinuance of use, &c.) made in pursuance of regulation 55 above shall not affect any use made of the land prior to the site becoming a European site or, if later, the commencement of these Regulations.

....

Planning permission: supplementary provisions as to compensation

59. (1) Where the Secretary of State determines not to confirm—

(a) an order under section 97 of the Town and Country Planning Act 1990 (revocation or modification of planning permission) which has taken effect under regulation 57(1), or

(b) an order under section 42 of the Town and Country Planning (Scotland) Act 1972 (revocation or modification of planning permission) which has taken effect under regulation 58(1),

any claim for compensation under section 107 of the Act of 1990 or section 153 of the Act of 1972 shall be limited to any loss or damage directly attributable to the permission being suspended or temporarily modified for the duration of the period between the order so taking effect and the Secretary of State determining not to confirm the order.

(2) Where the Secretary of State determines not to confirm—

(a) an order under section 102 of the Town and Country Planning Act 1990 (order requiring discontinuance of use, &c.) which has taken effect under regulation 57(3) above, or

(b) an order under section 49 of the Town and Country Planning (Scotland) Act 1972 (order requiring discontinuance of use, &c.) which has taken effect under regulation 58(3) above,

any claim for compensation under section 115 of the Act of 1990 or section 159 of the Act of 1972 shall be limited to any loss or damage directly attributable to any right to continue a use of the land being, by virtue of the order, suspended or subject to conditions for the duration of the period between the order so taking effect and the Secretary of State determining not to confirm the order.

(3) Where compensation is payable in respect of—

(a) an order under section 97 of the Town and Country Planning Act 1990, or

(b) any order mentioned in section 115(1) of that Act (compensation in respect of orders under s. 102, &c.), or to which that section applies by virtue of section 115(5),

---

[1] "Land" defined by reg. 2(1), p. 337 above.   [2] "European site" has the meaning given by reg. 10, p. 342 above: reg. 2(1).

and the order has been made pursuant to regulation 50, the question as to the amount of the compensation shall be referred, by the authority liable to pay the compensation, to and be determined by the Lands Tribunal unless and to the extent that in any particular case the Secretary of State has indicated in writing that such a reference and determination may be dispensed with.

(4) Where compensation is payable in respect of—

(a) an order under section 42 of the Town and Country Planning (Scotland) Act 1972 (revocation or modification of planning permission), or

(b) any order mentioned in section 153(1) of that Act (compensation in respect of orders under s. 49),

and the order has been made pursuant to regulation 50[1], the question as to the amount of the compensation shall be referred, by the authority liable to pay the compensation, to and be determined by the Lands Tribunal for Scotland unless and to the extent that in any particular case the Secretary of State has indicated in writing that such a reference and determination may be dispensed with.

General development orders

60. (1) It shall be a condition of any planning permission granted by a general development order, whether made before or after the commencement of these Regulations, that development which—

(a) is likely to have a significant effect on a European site[2] in Great Britain (either alone or in combination with other plans or projects), and

(b) is not directly connected with or necessary to the management of the site,

shall not be begun until the developer has received written notification of the approval of the local planning authority[3] under regulation 62[4].

(2) It shall be a condition of any planning permission granted by a general development order made before the commencement of these Regulations that development which—

(a) is likely to have a significant effect on a European site in Great Britain (either alone or in combination with other plans or projects), and

(b) is not directly connected with or necessary to the management of the site,

and which was begun but not completed before the commencement of these Regulations, shall not be continued until the developer has received written notification of the approval of the local planning authority under regulation 62.

(3) Nothing in this regulation shall affect anything done before the commencement of these Regulations.

General development orders: opinion of appropriate nature conservation body

61. (1) Where it is intended to carry out development in reliance on the permission granted by a general development order, application may be made in writing to the appropriate nature conservation body[5] for their opinion whether the development is likely to have such an effect as is mentioned in regulation 60(1)(a) or (2)(a).

The application shall give details of the development which is intended to be carried out.

(2) On receiving such an application, the appropriate nature conservation body shall consider whether the development is likely to have such an effect.

---

[1] P. 362 above.
[2] "European site" has the meaning given by reg. 10, p. 342 above: reg. 2(1).
[3] "Local planning authority" defined by reg. 2(1), p. 337
above.
[4] P. 371 below.
[5] "Appropriate nature conservation body" has the meaning given by reg. 4, p. 340 above: reg. 2(1).

(3) Where they consider that they have sufficient information to conclude that the development will, or will not, have such an effect, they shall in writing notify the applicant and the local planning authority[1] of their opinion.

(4) If they consider that they have insufficient information to reach either of those conclusions, they shall notify the applicant in writing indicating in what respects they consider the information insufficient; and the applicant may supply further information with a view to enabling them to reach a decision on the application.

(5) The opinion of the appropriate nature conservation body, notified in accordance with paragraph (3), that the development is not likely to have such an effect as is mentioned in regulation 60(1)(a) or (2)(a)[2] shall be conclusive of that question for the purpose of reliance on the planning permission granted by a general development order.

General development orders: approval of local planning authority

62. (1) Where it is intended to carry out development in reliance upon the permission granted by a general development order, application may be made in writing to the local planning authority[3] for their approval.

(2) The application shall—

(a) give details of the development which is intended to be carried out; and

(b) be accompanied by—

    (i) a copy of any relevant notification by the appropriate nature conservation body[4] under regulation 61, and

    (ii) any fee required to be paid.

(3) For the purposes of their consideration of the application the local planning authority shall assume that the development is likely to have such an effect as is mentioned in regulation 60(1)(a) or (2)(a)[5].

(4) The authority shall send a copy of the application to the appropriate nature conservation body and shall take account of any representations made by them.

(5) If in their representations the appropriate nature conservation body state their opinion that the development is not likely to have such an effect as is mentioned in regulation 60(1)(a) or (2)(a), the local planning authority shall send a copy of the representations to the applicant; and the sending of that copy shall have the same effect as a notification by the appropriate nature conservation body of its opinion under regulation 61(3).

(6) In any other case the local planning authority shall, taking account of any representations made by the appropriate nature conservation body, make an appropriate assessment of the implications of the development for the European site[6] in view of that site's conservation objectives.

In the light of the conclusions of the assessment the authority shall approve the development only after having ascertained that it will not adversely affect the integrity of the site.

General development orders: supplementary

63. (1) The local planning authority[7] for the purposes of regulations 60 to 62 shall be the authority to whom an application for approval under regulation 62 would fall to be made if it were an application for planning permission.

---

[1] "Local planning authority" defined by reg. 2(1), p. 337 above.

[2] P. 370 above.

[3] "Local planning authority" defined by reg. 2(1), p. 337 above.

[4] "Appropriate nature conservation body" has the meaning given by reg. 4, p. 340 above: reg. 2(1).

[5] P. 370 above.

[6] "European site" has the meaning given by reg. 10, p. 342 above: reg. 2(1).

[7] "Local planning authority" defined by reg. 2(1), p. 337 above.

(2) The fee payable in connection with an application for such approval is—

(a) £25 in the case of applications made before 3rd January 1995, and

(b) £30 in the case of applications made on or after that date.

(3) Approval required by regulation 60 shall be treated—

(a) for the purposes of the provisions of the Town and Country Planning Act 1990[1], or the Town and Country Planning (Scotland) Act 1972[2], relating to appeals, as approval required by a condition imposed on a grant of planning permission; and

(b) for the purposes of the provisions of any general development order relating to the time within which notice of a decision should be made, as approval required by a condition attached to a grant of planning permission.

Special development orders

64. (1) A special development order made after the commencement of these Regulations may not grant planning permission for development which—

(a) is likely to have a significant effect on a European site[3] in Great Britain (either alone or in combination with other plans or projects), and

(b) is not directly connected with or necessary to the management of the site;

and any such order made before the commencement of these Regulations shall, on and after that date, cease to have effect to grant such permission, whether or not the development authorised by the permission has been begun.

(2) Nothing in this regulation shall affect anything done before the commencement of these Regulations.

Simplified planning zones

65. The adoption or approval of a simplified planning zone scheme after the commencement of these Regulations shall not have effect to grant planning permission for development which—

(a) is likely to have a significant effect on a European site[4] in Great Britain (either alone or in combination with other plans or projects), and

(b) is not directly connected with or necessary to the management of the site;

and every simplified planning zone scheme already in force shall cease to have effect to grant such permission, whether or not the development authorised by the permission has been begun.

Enterprise zones

66. An order designating an enterprise zone, or the approval of a modified scheme, if made or given after the commencement of these Regulations, shall not have effect to grant planning permission for development which—

(a) is likely to have a significant effect on a European site[5] in Great Britain (either alone or in combination with other plans or projects), and

(b) is not directly connected with or necessary to the management of the site;

and where the order or approval was made or given before that date, the permission granted by virtue of the taking effect of the order or the modifications shall, from that date, cease to have effect to grant planning permission for such development, whether or not the development authorised by the permission has been begun.

[1] 1990 c. 8.
[2] 1972 c. 52.
[3] "European site" has the meaning given by reg. 10, p. 342 above: reg. 2(1).

[4] "European site" has the meaning given by reg. 10, p. 342 above: reg. 2(1).
[5] "European site" has the meaning given by reg. 10, p. 342 above: reg. 2(1).

Simplified planning zones and enterprise zones: supplementary provisions as to compensation

67. (1) Where in England and Wales—

(a) planning permission is withdrawn by regulation 65 or 66, and

(b) development authorised by the permission had been begun but not completed before the commencement of these Regulations, and

(c) on an application made under Part III of the Town and Country Planning Act 1990 before the end of the period of 12 months beginning with the date of commencement of these Regulations, planning permission for the development is refused or is granted subject to conditions other than those imposed by the scheme,

section 107(1)(a) of that Act (compensation in respect of abortive expenditure) shall apply as if the permission granted by the scheme had been granted by the local planning authority[1] under Part III of that Act and had been revoked or modified by an order under section 97 of that Act.

(2) Where in Scotland—

(a) planning permission is withdrawn by regulation 65 or 66, and

(b) development authorised by the permission had been begun but not completed before the commencement of these Regulations, and

(c) on an application made under Part III of the Town and Country Planning (Scotland) Act 1972 before the end of the period of 12 months beginning with the date of commencement of these Regulations, planning permission for the development is refused or is granted subject to conditions other than those imposed by the scheme,

section 153(1)(a) of that Act (compensation in respect of abortive expenditure) shall apply as if the permission granted by the scheme had been granted by the local planning authority under Part III of that Act and had been revoked or modified by an order under section 42 of that Act.

(3) Paragraphs (1) and (2) above do not apply in relation to planning permission for the development of operational land by statutory undertakers[2].

Construction as one with planning legislation

68. Regulations 54 to 67 shall be construed as one—

(a) in England and Wales, with the Town and Country Planning Act 1990; and

(b) in Scotland, with the Town and Country Planning (Scotland) Act 1972.

Highways and roads

Construction or improvement of highways or roads

69. (1) Regulations 48 and 49[3] (requirement to consider effect on European site) apply in relation to any plan or project—

(a) by the Secretary of State—

(i) to construct a new highway or to improve, within the meaning of the Highways Act 1980[4], an existing highway, or

(ii) to construct a new road or to improve, within the meaning of the Roads (Scotland) Act 1984[5], an existing road; or

(b) by a local highway authority or local roads authority, to carry out within the boundaries of a road any works required for the improvement of the road.

---

[1] "Local planning authority" defined by reg. 2(1), p. 337 above.

[2] "Statutory undertaker" defined by reg. 2(1), p. 338 above.

[3] P. 361 above.

[4] 1980 c. 66; the expression "improvement" is defined in s. 329(1) of the Act.

[5] 1984 c. 54; the expression "improvement" is defined in s. 151(1) of the Act.

(2) Regulations 50 and 51[1] (requirement to review certain decisions and consents, &c.) apply to any such plan or project as is mentioned in paragraph (1) unless the works have been completed before the site[2] became a European site[3] or, if later, the commencement of these Regulations.

Cycle tracks and other ancillary works

70. As from the commencement of these Regulations, section 3(1) of the Cycle Tracks Act 1984[4] and section 152(4) of the Roads (Scotland) Act 1984 shall cease to have effect to deem planning permission to be granted for development which—

(a) is likely to have a significant effect on a European site[5] in Great Britain (either alone or in combination with other plans or projects), and

(b) is not directly connected with or necessary to the management of the site,

whether or not the development authorised by the permission has been begun.

Electricity

Consents under Electricity Act 1989: application of general requirements

71. (1) Regulations 48 and 49[6] (requirement to consider effect on European site) apply in relation to the granting of—

(a) consent under section 36 of the Electricity Act 1989[7] to construct, extend or operate a generating station, or

(b) consent under section 37 of that Act to install an electric line above ground.

(2) Where in such a case the Secretary of State considers that any adverse effects of the plan or project on the integrity of a European site[8] would be avoided if the consent were subject to conditions, he may grant consent subject to those conditions.

(3) Regulations 50 and 51 (requirement to review existing decisions and consents, &c.) apply to such a consent as is mentioned in paragraph (1) unless—

(a) the works to which the consent relates have been completed before the site became a European site or, if later, the commencement of these Regulations, or

(b) the consent was granted subject to a condition as to the time within which the works to which it relates were to be begun and that time has expired without them having been begun, or

(c) it was granted for a limited period and that period has expired.

Where the consent is for, or includes, the operation of a generating station, the works shall be treated as completed when, in reliance on the consent, the generating station is first operated.

(4) Where on the review of such a consent the Secretary of State considers that any adverse effects on the integrity of a European site of the carrying out or, as the case may be, the continuation of the plan or project would be avoided by a variation of the consent, he may vary the consent accordingly.

(5) In conjunction with the review of any such consent the Secretary of State shall review any direction deeming planning permission to be granted for the plan or project and may vary or revoke it.

---

[1] P. 362 above.
[2] "Site" is defined in Article 1 of the Habitats Directive at p. 448 below: reg. 2(2).
[3] "European site" has the meaning given by reg. 10, p. 342 above: reg. 2(1).
[4] 1984 c. 38.
[5] "European site" has the meaning given by reg. 10, p. 342 above: reg. 2(1).
[6] P. 361 above.
[7] 1989 c. 29.
[8] "European site" has the meaning given by reg. 10, p. 342 above: reg. 2(1).

Consents under the Electricity Act 1989: procedure on review

72. (1) Where the Secretary of State decides in pursuance of regulation 71 to revoke or vary a consent under the Electricity Act 1989, or a direction deeming planning permission to be granted, he shall serve notice on—

(*a*) the person to whom the consent was granted or, as the case may be, in whose favour the direction was made,

(*b*) in the case of a consent under section 36 of the Electricity Act 1989, any other person proposing to operate the generating station in question, and

(*c*) any other person who in his opinion will be affected by the revocation or variation,

informing them of the decision and specifying a period of not less than 28 days within which any person on whom the notice is served may make representations to him.

(2) The Secretary of State shall also serve notice on—

(*a*) the relevant planning authority within the meaning of paragraph 2(6) of Schedule 8 to the Electricity Act 1989, and

(*b*) the appropriate nature conservation body[1],

informing them of the decision and inviting their representations within the specified period.

(3) The Secretary of State shall consider whether to proceed with the revocation or variation, and shall have regard to any representations made to him in accordance with paragraph (1) or (2).

(4) If within the specified period a person on whom notice was served under paragraph (1), or the relevant planning authority, so requires, the Secretary of State shall before deciding whether to proceed with the revocation or variation give—

(*a*) to them, and

(*b*) to any other person on whom notice under paragraph (1) or (2) was required to be served,

an opportunity of appearing before, and being heard by, a person appointed by the Secretary of State for the purpose.

Consents under Electricity Act 1989: effect of review

73. (1) The revocation or variation pursuant to regulation 71[2] of a consent under section 36 or 37 of the Electricity Act 1989, or a direction deeming planning permission to be granted, shall take effect upon service of the notices required by regulation 72(1) or, where there is more than one such notice and those notices are served at different times, from the date on which the last of them was served.

(2) Where the Secretary of State decides not to proceed with the revocation or variation, the consent or direction shall have effect again from the time of that decision, and shall thereafter have effect as if—

(*a*) any period specified in the consent or direction for the taking of any action, being a period which had not expired prior to the date mentioned in paragraph (1), were extended by a period equal to that during which the revocation or variation had effect; and

(*b*) there were substituted for any date specified in the consent or direction as being a date by which any action should be taken, not being a date falling prior to that date mentioned in paragraph (1), such date as post-dates the specified date by a period equal to that during which the revocation or variation had effect;

---

[1] "Appropriate nature conservation body" has the meaning given by reg. 4, p. 340 above: reg. 2(1).

[2] P. 374 above.

(3) The revocation or variation pursuant to regulation 71 of consent under section 36 or 37 of the Electricity Act 1989, or a direction deeming planning permission to be granted, shall not affect anything done under the consent or direction prior to the revocation or variation taking effect.

....

Consents under Electricity Act 1989: compensation for revocation or variation

74. (1) Where a direction deeming planning permission to be granted is revoked or varied pursuant to regulation 71[1], that permission shall be treated—

(*a*) for the purposes of Part IV of the Town and Country Planning Act 1990 (compensation) as having been revoked or modified by order under section 97 of that Act, or

(*b*) for the purposes of Part VIII of the Town and Country Planning (Scotland) Act 1972 (compensation) as having been revoked or modified by order under section 42 of that Act.

(2) Where a consent under section 36 or 37 of the Electricity Act 1989 is revoked or varied pursuant to regulation 71, Part IV of the Town and Country Planning Act 1990 or Part VIII of the Town and Country Planning (Scotland) Act 1972 (compensation) shall apply as if—

(*a*) the consent had been planning permission granted on an application under that Act and had been revoked or modified by order under section 97 of the 1990 Act or section 42 of the 1972 Act; and

(*b*) each of those Parts provided that the Secretary of State was the person liable to pay any compensation provided for by that Part.

This paragraph shall not have effect to confer any right to compensation for any expenditure, loss or damage for which compensation is payable by virtue of paragraph (1) above.

(3) Where the Secretary of State decides not to proceed with the revocation or variation of a consent under section 36 or 37 of the Electricity Act 1989, or a direction deeming planning permission to be granted, any claim for compensation by virtue of this regulation shall be limited to any loss or damage directly attributable to the consent or direction ceasing to have effect or being varied for the duration of the period between the revocation or variation taking effect under regulation 73(1) and the Secretary of State deciding not to proceed with it.

(4) Where compensation is payable by virtue of this regulation, the question as to the amount of the compensation shall be referred to and determined by the Lands Tribunal, or the Lands Tribunal for Scotland, unless and to the extent that in any particular case the Secretary of State has indicated in writing that such a reference and determination may be dispensed with.

Pipe-lines

Authorisations under the Pipe-lines Act 1962: application of general requirements

75. (1) Regulations 48 and 49[2] (requirement to consider effect on European site) apply in relation to the granting of a pipe-line construction or diversion authorisation under the Pipe-lines Act 1962[3].

(2) Where in such a case the Secretary of State considers that any adverse effects of the plan or project on the integrity of a European site[4] would be avoided by granting an authorisation for the execution of works for the placing of the proposed pipe-line or, as the case may be, the portion of the pipe-line to be diverted, along a modified route, he may, subject to the provisions of Schedule 1 to the Pipe-lines Act 1962, grant such an authorisation.

(3) Regulations 50 and 51[5] (requirement to review existing decisions and consents, &c.) apply to a pipe-line construction or diversion authorisation under the Pipe-lines Act 1962 unless—

(*a*) the works to which the authorisation relates have been completed before the site became a European site or, if later, the commencement of these Regulations, or

[1] P. 374 above.
[2] P. 361 above.
[3] 1962 c. 58.

[4] "European site" has the meaning given by reg. 10, p. 342 above: reg. 2(1).
[5] P. 362 above.

(b) the authorisation was granted subject to a condition as to the time within which the works to which it relates were to be begun and that time has expired without them having been begun, or

(c) it was granted for a limited period and that period has expired.

(4) Where on the review of such an authorisation the Secretary of State considers that any adverse effects on the integrity of a European site of the carrying out or, as the case may be, the continuation of the plan or project would be avoided by a variation of the authorisation, he may vary it accordingly.

(5) In conjunction with the review of any such authorisation the Secretary of State shall review any direction deeming planning permission to be granted for the plan or project and may vary or revoke it.

Authorisations under the Pipe-lines Act 1962: procedure on review

76. (1) Where the Secretary of State decides in pursuance of regulation 75 to revoke or vary an authorisation under the Pipe-lines Act 1962, or a direction deeming planning permission to be granted, he shall serve notice on—

(a) the person to whom the authorisation was granted or, as the case may be, in whose favour the direction was made, and

(b) any other person who in his opinion will be affected by the revocation or variation,

informing them of the decision and specifying a period of not less than 28 days within which any person on whom the notice is served may make representations to him.

(2) The Secretary of State shall also serve notice on—

(a) the local planning authority[1], and

(b) the appropriate nature conservation body[2],

informing them of the decision and inviting their representations within the specified period.

(3) The Secretary of State shall consider whether to proceed with the revocation or variation , and shall have regard to any representations made to him in accordance with paragraph (1) or (2).

(4) If within the specified period a person on whom notice was served under paragraph (1), or the local planning authority, so requires, the Secretary of State shall before deciding whether to proceed with the revocation or variation give—

(a) to them, and

(b) to any other person on whom notice under paragraph (1) or (2) was required to be served,

an opportunity of appearing before, and being heard by, a person appointed by the Secretary of State for the purpose.

Authorisations under the Pipe-lines Act 1962: effect of review

77. (1) The revocation or variation pursuant to regulation 75[3] of an authorisation under the Pipe-lines Act 1962, or of a direction deeming planning permission to be granted, shall take effect upon service of the notices required by regulation 76(1) or, where there is more than one such notice and those notices are served at different times, upon the service of the last such notice to be served.

(2) Where the Secretary of State decides not to proceed with the revocation or variation, the authorisation or direction shall have effect again from the time of that decision, and shall thereafter have effect as if—

---

[1] "Local planning authority" defined by reg. 2(1), p. 337 above.

[2] "Appropriate nature conservation body" has the meaning given by reg. 4, p. 340 above: reg. 2(1).

[3] P. 376 above.

(a) any period specified in the authorisation or direction for the taking of any action, being a period which had not expired prior to the date mentioned in paragraph (1), were extended by a period equal to that during which the revocation or variation had effect; and

(b) there were substituted for any date specified in the authorisation or direction as being a date by which any action should be taken, not being a date falling prior to that date mentioned in paragraph (1), such date as post-dates the specified date by a period equal to that during which the revocation or variation had effect.

(3) The revocation or variation pursuant to regulation 75 of an authorisation under the Pipe-lines Act 1962, or a direction deeming planning permission to be granted, shall not affect anything done under the authorisation or direction prior to the revocation or variation taking effect.

Authorisations under the Pipe-lines Act 1962: compensation for revocation or variation

78. (1) Where a direction deeming planning permission to be granted is revoked or varied pursuant to regulation 75[1], that permission shall be treated—

(a) for the purposes of Part IV of the Town and Country Planning Act 1990[2] (compensation) as having been revoked or modified by order under section 97 of that Act, or

(b) for the purposes of Part VIII of the Town and Country Planning (Scotland) Act 1972[3] (compensation) as having been revoked or modified by order under section 42 of that Act.

(2) Where an authorisation under the Pipe-lines Act 1962 is revoked or varied pursuant to regulation 75, Part IV of the Town and Country Planning Act 1990 or Part VIII of the Town and Country Planning (Scotland) Act 1972 (compensation) shall apply as if—

(a) the authorisation had been planning permission granted on an application under that Act and had been revoked or modified by order under section 97 of the 1990 Act or section 42 of the 1972 Act; and

(b) each of those Parts provided that the Secretary of State was the person liable to pay any compensation provided for by that Part.

This paragraph shall not have effect to confer any right to compensation for any expenditure, loss or damage for which compensation is payable by virtue of paragraph (1) above.

(3) Where the Secretary of State decides not to proceed with the revocation or variation of an authorisation under the Pipe-lines Act 1962, or a direction deeming planning permission to be granted, any claim for compensation by virtue of this regulation shall be limited to any loss or damage directly attributable to the authorisation or direction ceasing to have effect or being varied for the duration of the period between the revocation or variation taking effect under regulation 77(1)[4] and the Secretary of State deciding not to proceed with it.

(4) Where compensation is payable by virtue of this regulation, the question as to the amount of the compensation shall be referred to and determined by the Lands Tribunal, or the Lands Tribunal for Scotland, unless and to the extent that in any particular case the Secretary of State has indicated in writing that such a reference and determination may be dispensed with.

Transport and works

Orders under the Transport and Works Act 1992: application of general requirements

79. (1) Regulations 48 and 49[5] (requirement to consider effect on European site) apply in relation to the making of an order under section 1 or 3 of the Transport and Works Act 1992[6].

(2) Where in such a case the Secretary of State considers that any adverse effects of the plan or project on the integrity of a European site[7] would be avoided by making modifications to the proposals, he may make an order subject to those modifications.

---

[1] P. 376 above.
[2] 1990 c. 8.
[3] 1972 c. 52.
[4] P. 377 above.

[5] P. 361 above.
[6] 1992 c. 42.
[7] "European site" has the meaning given by reg. 10, p. 342 above: reg. 2(1).

(3) Regulations 50 and 51[1] (requirement to review existing decisions and consents, &c.) apply to an order under section 1 or 3 of the Transport and Works Act 1992 unless the works to which the order relates have been completed before the site became a European site.

(4) Where on the review of such an order the Secretary of State considers that any adverse effects on the integrity of a European site of the carrying out or, as the case may be, the continuation of the plan or project would be avoided by a variation of the order, he may vary it accordingly.

(5) In conjunction with the review of any such order the Secretary of State shall review any direction deeming planning permission to be granted for the plan or project and may vary or revoke it.

Orders under the Transport and Works Act 1992: procedure on review

80. (1) Where the Secretary of State decides in pursuance of regulation 79 to revoke or vary an order under the Transport and Works Act 1992, or a direction deeming planning permission to be granted, he shall serve notice on—

(a) the person (if any) on whose application the order was made or, as the case may be, in whose favour the direction was made, and

(b) any other person who in his opinion will be affected by the revocation or variation,

informing them of the decision and specifying a period of not less than 28 days within which any person on whom the notice is served may make representations to him.

(2) The Secretary of State shall also serve notice on—

(a) the local planning authority[2], and

(b) the appropriate nature conservation body[3],

informing them of the decision and inviting their representations within the specified period.

(3) The Secretary of State shall consider whether to proceed with the revocation or variation, and shall have regard to any representations made to him in accordance with paragraph (1) or (2).

(4) If within the specified period a person on whom notice was served under paragraph (1), or the local planning authority, so requires, the Secretary of State shall before deciding whether to proceed with the revocation or variation of the order or direction give—

(a) to them,

(b) to any other person on whom notice under paragraph (1) or (2) was required to be served,

an opportunity of appearing before, and being heard by, a person appointed by the Secretary of State for the purpose.

Orders under the Transport and Works Act 1992: effect of review

81. (1) The revocation or variation pursuant to regulation 79[4] of an order under the Transport and Works Act 1992, or of a direction deeming planning permission to be granted, shall take effect upon service of the notices required by regulation 80(1) or, where there is more than one such notice and those notices are served at different times, upon the service of the last such notice to be served.

(2) Where the Secretary of State decides not to proceed with the revocation or variation, the order or direction shall have effect again from the time of that decision, and shall thereafter have effect as if—

---

[1] P. 362 above.
[2] "Local planning authority" defined by reg. 2(1), p. 337 above.

[3] "Appropriate nature conservation body" has the meaning given by reg. 4, p. 340 above: reg. 2(1).
[4] P. 378 above.

(*a*) any period specified in the order or direction for the taking of any action, being a period which had not expired prior to the date mentioned in paragraph (1), were extended by a period equal to that during which the revocation or variation had effect; and

(*b*) there were substituted for any date specified in the order or direction as being a date by which any action should be taken, not being a date falling prior to that date mentioned in paragraph (1), such date as post-dates the specified date by a period equal to that during which the revocation or variation had effect.

(3) The revocation or variation pursuant to regulation 79 of an order under section 1 or 3 of the Transport and Works Act 1992, or of a direction deeming planning permission to be granted, shall not affect anything done under the order or direction prior to the revocation or variation taking effect.

....

Orders under the Transport and Works Act 1992: compensation for revocation or variation

82. (1) Where a direction deeming planning permission to be granted is revoked or varied pursuant to regulation 79[1], that permission shall be treated for the purposes of Part IV of the Town and Country Planning Act 1990 (compensation) as having been revoked or modified by order under section 97 of that Act.

(2) Where an order under section 1 or 3 of the Transport and Works Act 1992 is revoked or varied pursuant to regulation 79, Part IV of the Town and Country Planning Act 1990 shall apply as if—

(*a*) the order had been planning permission granted on an application under that Act and had been revoked or modified by order under section 97 of that Act; and

(*b*) that Part provided that the Secretary of State was the person liable to pay any compensation provided for by that Part.

This paragraph shall not have effect to confer any right to compensation for any expenditure, loss or damage for which compensation is payable by virtue of paragraph (1) above.

(3) Where the Secretary of State decides not to proceed with the revocation or variation of an order under section 1 or 3 of the Transport and Works Act 1992, or a direction deeming planning permission to be granted, any claim for compensation by virtue of this regulation shall be limited to any loss or damage directly attributable to the order or direction ceasing to have effect or being varied for the duration of the period between the revocation or variation taking effect under regulation 81(1) and the Secretary of State deciding not to proceed with it.

(4) Where compensation is payable by virtue of this regulation, the question as to the amount of the compensation shall be referred to and determined by the Lands Tribunal unless and to the extent that in any particular case the Secretary of State has indicated in writing that such a reference and determination may be dispensed with.

Environmental controls

Authorisations under Part I of the Environmental Protection Act 1990

83. (1) Regulations 48 and 49[2] (requirement to consider effect on European site) apply in relation to the granting of an authorisation under Part I of the Environmental Protection Act 1990[3] (integrated pollution control and local authority air pollution control).

(2) Where in such a case the competent authority[4] consider that any adverse effects of the plan or project on the integrity of a European site[5] would be avoided if the authorisation were subject to conditions, they may grant an authorisation, or cause an authorisation to be granted, subject to those conditions.

---

[1] P. 378 above.
[2] P. 361 above.
[3] 1990 c. 43.

[4] "Competent authority" shall be construed in accordance with reg. 6, p. 340 above: reg. 2(1).
[5] "European site" has the meaning given by reg. 10, p. 342 above: reg. 2(1).

(3) Regulations 50 and 51[1] (requirement to review existing decisions and consents, &c.) apply to any such authorisation as is mentioned in paragraph (1).

(4) Where on the review of such an authorisation the competent authority consider that any adverse effects on the integrity of a European site of the carrying out or, as the case may be, the continuation of activities authorised by it would be avoided by a variation of the authorisation, they may vary it, or cause it to be varied, accordingly.

(5) Where any question arises as to agreeing to a plan or project, or affirming an authorisation on review, under regulation 49 (considerations of overriding public interest), the competent authority shall refer the matter to the Secretary of State who shall determine the matter in accordance with that regulation and give directions to the authority accordingly.

Licences under Part II of the Environmental Protection Act 1990

84. (1) Regulations 48 and 49[2] (requirement to consider effect on European site) apply in relation to—

(a) the granting of a waste management licence under Part II of the Environmental Protection Act 1990.

(b) the passing of a resolution under section 54 of that Act (provisions as to land occupied by disposal authorities themselves), and

(c) the granting of a disposal licence under Part I of the Control of Pollution Act 1974[3] and the passing of a resolution under section 11 of that Act[4].

(2) Where in such a case the competent authority[5] consider that any adverse effects of the plan or project on the integrity of a European site[6] would be avoided by making any licence subject to conditions, they may grant a licence, or cause a licence to be granted, or, as the case may be, pass a resolution, subject to those conditions.

(3) Regulations 50 and 51[7] (requirement to review existing decisions and consents, &c.) apply to any such licence or resolution as is mentioned in paragraph (1).

(4) Where on the review of such a licence or resolution the competent authority consider that any adverse effects on the integrity of a European site of the carrying out or, as the case may be, the continuation of the activities authorised by it would be avoided by a variation of the licence or resolution, they may vary it, or cause it to be varied, accordingly.

Discharge consents under water pollution legislation

85. (1) Regulations 48 and 49[8] (requirement to consider effect on European site) apply in relation to the giving of consent under—

(a) Chapter II of Part III to the Water Resources Act 1991[9] (control of pollution of water resources), or

(b) Part II of the Control of Pollution Act 1974[10] (which makes corresponding provision for Scotland).

(2) Where in such a case the competent authority[11] consider that any adverse effects of the plan or project on the integrity of a European site[12] would be avoided by making any consent subject to conditions, they may give consent, or cause it to be given, subject to those conditions.

---

[1] P. 362 above.
[2] P. 361 above.
[3] 1974 c. 40.
[4] The relevant provisions of pt. 1, and s. 11, were repealed by the Environmental Protection Act 1990 (c. 43) subject to savings (see s. 77 of that Act).
[5] "Competent authority" shall be construed in accordance with reg. 6, p. 340 above: reg. 2(1).
[6] "European site" has the meaning given by reg. 10, p. 342 above: reg. 2(1).
[7] P. 362 above.
[8] P. 361 above.
[9] 1991 c. 57.
[10] 1974 c. 40.
[11] "Competent authority" shall be construed in accordance with reg. 6, p. 340 above: reg. 2(1).
[12] "European site" has the meaning given by reg. 10, p. 342 above: reg. 2(1).

(3) Regulations 50 and 51[1] (requirement to review existing decisions and consents, &c.) apply to any such consent as is mentioned in paragraph (1).

(4) Where on the review of such a consent the competent authority consider that any adverse effects on the integrity of a European site of the carrying out or, as the case may be, the continuation of the activities authorised by it would be avoided by a variation of the consent, they may vary it, or cause it to be varied, accordingly.

Part V: Supplementary provisions

Supplementary provisions as to management agreements

Powers of limited owners, &c. to enter into management agreements

86. (1) In the case of settled land in England and Wales—

   (*a*) the tenant for life may enter into a management agreement[2] relating to the land[3], or any part of it, either for consideration or gratuitously;

   (*b*) the Settled Land Act 1925[4] shall apply as if the power conferred by subparagraph (*a*) had been conferred by that Act; and

   (*c*) for the purposes of section 72 of that Act (which relates to the mode of giving effect to a disposition by a tenant for life and to the operation thereof), and of any other relevant statutory provision, entering into a management agreement shall be treated as a disposition.

   The above provisions of this paragraph shall be construed as one with the Settled Land Act 1925.

(2) Section 28 of the Law of Property Act 1925[5] (which confers the powers of a tenant for life on trustees for sale) shall apply as if the power of a tenant for life under paragraph (1)(*a*) above had been conferred by the Settled Land Act 1925.

(3) A university or college to which the Universities and College Estates Act 1925[6] applies may enter into a management agreement relating to any land belonging to it in England and Wales either for consideration or gratuitously.

   That Act shall apply as if the power conferred by this paragraph had been conferred by that Act.

(4) In the case of glebe land or other land belonging to an ecclesiastical benefice—

   (*a*) the incumbent of the benefice, and

   (*b*) in the case of land which is part of the endowment of any other ecclesiastical corporation, the corporation,

may with the consent of the Church Commissioners enter into a management agreement either for consideration or gratuitously.

   The Ecclesiastical Leasing Acts shall apply as if the power conferred by this paragraph had been conferred by those Acts, except that the consent of the patron of an ecclesiastical benefice shall not be requisite.

(5) In the case of any land in Scotland, any person being—

   (*a*) the liferenter, or

   (*b*) the heir of entail,

in possession of the land shall have power to enter into a management agreement relating to the land or any part of it.

---

[1] P. 362 above.
[2] "Management agreement" defined by reg. 2(1), p. 338 above.
[3] "Land" defined by reg. 2(1), p. 337 above.
[4] 1925 c. 18.
[5] 1925 c. 20.
[6] 1925 c. 24.

(6) The Trusts (Scotland) Act 1921[1] shall have effect as if among the powers conferred on trustees by section 4 of that Act (which relates to the general powers of trustees) there were included a power to enter into management agreements relating to the trust estate or any part of it.

Supplementary provisions as to potentially damaging operations

Carrying out of operation after expiry of period

87. (1) If before the expiry of the period of four months referred to in regulation 19(2)(c)[2] the relevant person[3] agrees in writing with the appropriate nature conservation body[4] that, subject as follows, the condition specified in that provision shall not apply in relation to the operation in question, then, subject as follows, regulation 19(2) shall as from the date of the agreement have effect in relation to the operation (as regards both the owner or the occupier of the land in question) as if sub-paragraph (c) were omitted.

(2) If after such an agreement has been made the relevant person (whether a party to the agreement or not) gives written notice to the appropriate nature conservation body that he wishes to terminate the agreement, then as from the giving of the notice regulation 19(2) shall have effect in relation to the operation in question (as regards both the owner and the occupier of the land in question) as if paragraph (c) specified the condition that one month, or any longer period specified in the notice, has expired from the giving of the notice under this paragraph.

(3) In paragraphs (1) and (2) above "the relevant person"—

(a) in case where the notice under regulation 19(1)(a) was given by the owner of the land in question, means the owner of that land;

(b) in a case where that notice was given by the occupier of that land, means the occupier of that land.

Duties of agriculture Ministers with respect to European sites

88. (1) Where an application for a farm capital grant[5] is made as respects expenditure incurred or to be incurred for the purpose of activities on land[6] within a European site[7], the Minister responsible for determining the application—

(a) shall, so far as may be consistent with the purposes of the grant provisions[8], so exercise his functions thereunder as to further the conservation of the flora, fauna, or geological or physiographical features by reason of which the land is a European site; and

(b) where the appropriate nature conservation body[9] have objected to the making of the grant on the ground that the activities in question have destroyed or damaged or will destroy or damage that flora or fauna or those features, shall not make the grant except after considering the objection and, in the case of land in England, after consulting with the Secretary of State.

(2) Where in consequence of an objection by the appropriate nature conservation body, an application for a grant as respects expenditure to be incurred is refused on the ground that the activities in question will have such an effect as is mentioned in paragraph (1)(b), the appropriate nature conservation body shall, within three months of their receiving notice of the Minister's decision, offer to enter into, in the terms of a draft submitted to the applicant, a management agreement—

(a) imposing restrictions as respects those activities, and

(b) providing for the making by them of payments to the applicant.

---

[1] 1921 c. 58.
[2] P. 347 above.
[3] "The relevant person" defined by para. 3 below.
[4] "Appropriate nature conservation body" has the meaning given by reg. 4, p. 340 above: reg. 2(1).
[5] "Farm capital grant" defined by para. 3 below.

[6] "Land" defined by reg. 2(1), p. 337 above.
[7] "European site" has the meaning given by reg. 10, p. 342 above: reg. 2(1).
[8] "Grant provisions" defined by para. 3 below.
[9] "Appropriate nature conservation body" has the meaning given by reg. 4, p. 340 above: reg. 2(1).

(3) In this regulation—

"farm capital grant" means—

(*a*) a grant under a scheme made under section 29 of the Agriculture Act 1970[1], or

(*b*) a grant under regulations made under section 2(2) of the European Communities Act 1972[2] to a person carrying on an agricultural business within the meaning of those regulations in respect of expenditure incurred or to be incurred for the purposes of or in connection with that business, being expenditure of a capital nature or incurred in connection with expenditure of a capital nature; and

"grant provisions" means—

(i) in the case of such a grant as is mentioned in paragraph (*a*) above, the scheme under which the grant is made and section 29 of the Agriculture Act 1970, and

(ii) in the case of such a grant as is mentioned in paragraph (*b*) above, the regulations under which the grant is made and the Community instrument in pursuance of which the regulations were made.

Payments under certain agreements offered by authorities

89. (1) This regulation applies where the appropriate nature conservation body[3] offers to enter into a management agreement[4] providing for the making of payments by them to—

(*a*) a person who has given notice under regulation 19(1)(*a*)[5] or 23(1)(*a*)[6], or

(*b*) a person whose application for a farm capital grant within the meaning of regulation 88 has been refused in consequence of an objection by that body.

(2) Subject to paragraph (3), the said payments shall be of such amounts as may be determined by the offeror in accordance with guidance given—

(*a*) in England, by the Minister of Agriculture, Fisheries and Food and the Secretary of State, or

(*b*) in Wales or Scotland, by the Secretary of State.

(3) If the offeree so requires within one month of receiving the offer, the determination of those amounts shall be referred to an arbitrator to be appointed, in default of agreement, by the Secretary of State.

(4) Where the amounts determined by the arbitrator exceed those determined by the offeror, the offeror shall—

(*a*) amend the offer so as to give effect to the arbitrator's determination, or

(*b*) except in the case of an offer made to a person whose application for a farm capital grant has been refused in consequence of an objection by the offeror, withdraw the offer.

(5) In the application of this regulation in Scotland references to an arbitrator shall be construed as references to an arbiter.

Powers of entry

90. (1) A person authorised in writing by the appropriate nature conservation body[7] may, at any reasonable time and (if required to do so) upon producing evidence that he is so authorised, enter any land[8]—

---

[1] 1970 c. 40; s. 29 was amended by s. 15(1) of the Agriculture (Miscellaneous Provisions) Act 1976 (c. 55).

[2] 1972 c. 68.

[3] "Appropriate nature conservation body" has the meaning given by reg. 4, p. 340 above: reg. 2(1).

[4] "Management agreement" defined by reg. 2(1), p. 338 above.

[5] P. 346 above.

[6] P. 349 above.

[7] "Appropriate nature conservation body" has the meaning given by reg. 4, p. 340 above: reg. 2(1).

[8] "Land" defined by reg. 2(1), p. 337 above.

(a) to ascertain whether a special nature conservation order[1] should be made in relation to that land, or if an offence under regulation 23[2] is being, or has been, committed on that land; or

(b) to ascertain the amount of any compensation payable under regulation 25[3] in respect of an interest in that land.

But nothing in this paragraph shall authorise any person to enter a dwelling.

(2) A person shall not demand admission as of right to any land which is occupied unless either—

(a) 24 hours' notice of the intended entry has been given to the occupier, or

(b) the purpose of the entry is to ascertain if an offence under regulation 23 is being, or has been, committed on that land.

(3) A person who intentionally obstructs a person in the exercise of his powers under this regulation commits an offence and is liable on summary conviction to a fine not exceeding level 3 on the standard scale[4].

Compensation: amount and assessment

91. (1) The following provisions have effect as to compensation under regulation 25(1)[5] (effect of special nature conservation order: decrease in value of agricultural unit).

(2) The amount of the compensation shall be the difference between the value of the interest in question and what it would have been had the order not been made.

(3) For this purpose—

(a) an interest in land shall be valued as at the time when the order is made; and

(b) where a person, by reason of his having more than one interest in land, makes more than one claim in respect of the same order, his various interests shall be valued together.

(4) Section 10 of the Land Compensation Act 1973[6] (mortgages, trusts for sale and settlements) or section 10 of the Land Compensation (Scotland) Act 1973[7] apply in relation to compensation under regulation 25(1) as in relation to compensation under Part I of that Act.

(5) For the purposes of assessing compensation under regulation 25(1), the rules set out in section 5 of the Land Compensation Act 1961[8] or section 12 of the Land Compensation (Scotland) Act 1963[9] have effect, so far as applicable and subject to any necessary modifications, as they have effect for the purpose of assessing compensation for the compulsory acquisition of an interest in land.

Compensation: other supplementary provisions

92. (1) The following provisions have effect in relation to compensation under regulation 25[10] (compensation for effect of special nature conservation order).

(2) The compensation shall carry interest, at the rate for the time being prescribed under section 32 of the Land Compensation Act 1961 or section 40 of the Land Compensation (Scotland) Act 1963[11], from the date of the claim until payment.

(3) Except in so far as may be provided by regulations, any question of disputed compensation shall be referred to and determined by the Lands Tribunal or the Lands Tribunal for Scotland.

(4) In relation to the determination of any such question, the provisions of sections 2 and 4 of the Land Compensation Act 1961 or sections 9 and 11 of the Land Compensation (Scotland) Act

[1] "Special nature conservation order" defined by reg. 22, p. 348 above.
[2] P. 349 above.
[3] P. 350 above.
[4] The current fine at level 3 is £1,000: Criminal Justice Act 1991 (c. 53), s. 17 which came into force on 1 October 1992: S.I. 1992/333, S.I. 1992/2118.
[5] P. 350 above.
[6] 1973 c. 26.
[7] 1973 c. 56.
[8] 1961 c. 33.
[9] 1963 c. 51.
[10] P. 350 above.
[11] 1961 c. 33; 1963 c. 51.

1963 (procedure and costs) shall apply, subject to any necessary modifications and to the provisions of any regulations.

Compensation: procedural provisions

93. (1) The power to make regulations under section 30 of the Wildlife and Countryside Act 1981[1] (provisions as to compensation where order made under section 29 of that Act) shall be exercisable so as to make provision for the purposes of these Regulations corresponding to those for which provision may be made under that section.

(2) The references in regulation 25[2] to matters being prescribed by regulations, and in regulation 92(3) and (4) to matters being provided by regulations, are to their being so prescribed or provided.

(3) Any regulations in force under section 30 on the commencement of these Regulations shall have effect for the purposes of these Regulations as if made under that section as applied by this regulation.

Supplementary provisions as to byelaws

Procedure for making byelaws, penalties, &c.

94. (1) Sections 236 to 238 of the Local Government Act 1972[3] or sections 201 to 204 of the Local Government (Scotland) Act 1973[4] (procedure, &c. for byelaws; offences against byelaws; evidence of byelaws) apply to all byelaws made under section 20 of the National Parks and Access to the Countryside Act 1949[5] as it applies by virtue of regulation 28 as if the appropriate nature conservation body[6] were a local authority within the meaning of that Act.

(2) In relation to byelaws so made the confirming authority for the purposes of the said section 236 or section 201 shall be the Secretary of State.

(3) The appropriate nature conservation body shall have power to enforce byelaws made by them:

Provided that nothing in this paragraph shall be construed as authorising the institution of proceedings in Scotland for an offence.

Powers of entry

95. (1) For the purpose of surveying land[7] , or of estimating its value, in connection with any claim for compensation payable under regulation 30[8] in respect of that or any other land, an officer of the Valuation Office or person duly authorised in writing by the authority from whom the compensation is claimed may enter upon the land.

(2) A person authorised under this regulation to enter upon any land shall, if so required, produce evidence of his authority before entering.

(3) A person shall not under this regulation demand admission as of right to any land which is occupied unless at least 14 days' notice in writing of the intended entry has been given to the occupier.

(4) A person who intentionally obstructs a person in the exercise of his powers under this regulation commits an offence and is liable on summary conviction to a fine not exceeding level 3 on the standard scale[9].

[1] P. 172 above.
[2] P. 350 above.
[3] 1972 c. 70.
[4] 1973 c. 65.
[5] P. 17 above.
[6] "Appropriate nature conservation body" has the meaning given by reg. 4, p. 340 above: reg. 2(1).
[7] "Land" defined by reg. 2(1), p. 337 above.
[8] P. 353 above.
[9] The current fine at level 3 is £1,000: Criminal Justice Act 1991 (c. 53), s. 17 which came into force on 1 October 1992: S.I. 1992/333, S.I. 1992/2118.

Compensation: England and Wales

96. (1) The following provisions have effect as to compensation under regulation 30[1] (compensation for effect of byelaws) in respect of land[2] in England and Wales.

(2) Any dispute arising on a claim for any such compensation shall be determined by the Lands Tribunal.

(3) For the purposes of any such reference to the Lands Tribunal, section 4 of the Land Compensation Act 1961[3] (which relates to costs) has effect with the substitution for references to the acquiring authority of references to the authority from whom the compensation in question is claimed.

(4) Rules (2) to (4) of the Rules set out in section 5 of that Act (which provides rules for valuation on a compulsory acquisition) apply to the calculation of any such compensation, in so far as it is calculated by reference to the depreciation of the value of an interest in land.

(5) In the case of an interest in land subject to a mortgage—

(*a*) any such compensation in respect of the depreciation of that interest shall be calculated as if the interest were not subject to the mortgage;

(*b*) a claim or application for the payment of any such compensation may be made by any person who when the byelaws giving rise to the compensation were made was the mortgagee of the interest, or by any person claiming under such a person, but without prejudice to the making of a claim or application by any other person;

(*c*) a mortgagee shall not be entitled to any such compensation in respect of his interest as such; and

(*d*) any compensation payable in respect of the interest subject to the mortgage shall be paid to the mortgagee or, where there is more than one mortgagee, to the first mortgagee, and shall in either case be applied by him as if it were proceeds of sale.

Compensation: Scotland

97. (1) The following provisions have effect as to compensation under regulation 30[4] (compensation for effect of byelaws) in respect of land[5] in Scotland.

(2) Any dispute arising on a claim for any such compensation shall be determined by the Lands Tribunal for Scotland.

(3) For the purposes of any such reference to the Lands Tribunal for Scotland section 8 of the Land Compensation (Scotland) Act 1963[6] (which relates to expenses) has effect with the substitution for references to the acquiring authority, of references to the authority from whom the compensation in question is claimed.

(4) Rules (2) to (4) of the Rules set out in section 12 of that Act (which provides rules for valuation on a compulsory acquisition) apply to the calculation of any such compensation, in so far as it is calculated by reference to the depreciation of the value of an interest in land.

(5) In the case of an interest in land subject to a heritable security—

(*a*) any such compensation in respect of the depreciation of that interest shall be calculated as if the interest were not subject to the heritable security;

(*b*) a claim or application for the payment of any such compensation may be made by any person who when the byelaws giving rise to the compensation were made was the creditor in a heritable security of the interest, or by any person claiming under such a person, but without prejudice to the making of a claim or application by any other person;

[1] P. 353 above.
[2] "Land" defined by reg. 2(1), p. 337above.
[3] 1961 c. 33.
[4] P. 353.
[5] "Land" defined by reg. 2(1), p. 337 above.
[6] 1963 c. 51.

(c) a creditor in a heritable security shall not be entitled to any such compensation in respect of his interest as such; and

(d) any compensation payable in respect of the interest subject to the heritable security shall be paid to the creditor or, where there is more than one creditor in a heritable security, to the creditor whose heritable security has priority over any other heritable securities secured on the land, and shall in either case be applied by him as if it were proceeds of sale.

Supplementary provisions as to compulsory acquisition

Supplementary provisions as to acquisition of land

98. (1) The powers of compulsory acquisition conferred on the appropriate nature conservation body[1] by regulation 32[2] are exercisable in any particular case on their being authorised so to do by the Secretary of State.

(2) In that regulation and in this regulation "land" includes any interest in land.

For this purpose "interest", in relation to land, includes any estate in land and any right over land, whether the right is exercisable by virtue of the ownership of an interest in land or by virtue of a licence or agreement, and in particular includes sporting rights.

(3) The Acquisition of Land Act 1981[3] applies in relation to any acquisition under these Regulations of land in England and Wales, and the Compulsory Purchase Act 1965[4] applies with any necessary modifications in relation to the acquisition of any interest in land in England and Wales.

(4) In relation to the compulsory acquisition of land in Scotland, the Acquisition of Land (Authorisation Procedure) (Scotland) Act 1947[5] shall apply as if these Regulations had been in force immediately before the commencement of that Act and as if in paragraph (a) of subsection (1) of section 1 thereof, in Part I of the First Schedule thereto and in the Second Schedule thereto references to a local authority included Scottish Natural Heritage:

Provided that section 2 of the said Act (which confers temporary powers for the speedy acquisition of land in urgent cases) shall not apply to any such compulsory acquisition as is mentioned in this paragraph.

The provisions of the Lands Clauses Acts incorporated with these Regulations by virtue of paragraph 1 of the Second Schedule to the Acquisition of Land (Authorisation Procedure) (Scotland) Act 1947, as applied by this paragraph, shall apply with the necessary modifications in relation to the compulsory acquisition of any interest in land, being an interest not falling within the definition of "lands" contained in the Lands Clauses Acts.

Powers of entry

99. (1) For the purpose of surveying land[6] in connection with the acquisition thereof or of any interest therein, whether by agreement or compulsorily, in the exercise of any power conferred by these Regulations, a person duly authorised in writing by the authority having power so to acquire the land or interest may enter upon the land.

(2) A person authorised under this regulation to enter upon any land shall, if so required, produce evidence of his authority before entering.

(3) A person shall not under this regulation demand admission as of right to any land which is occupied unless at least 14 days' notice in writing of the intended entry has been given to the occupier.

---

[1] "Appropriate nature conservation body" has the meaning given by reg. 4, p. 340 above: reg. 2(1).
[2] P. 353 above.
[3] 1981 c. 67.
[4] 1965 c. 56.
[5] 1947 c. 42.
[6] "Land" defined by reg. 2(1), p. 337 above.

(4) A person who intentionally obstructs a person in the exercise of his powers under this regulation commits an offence and is liable on summary conviction to a fine not exceeding level 3 on the standard scale[1].

Supplementary provisions as to protection of species

Attempts and possession of means of committing offence

100. (1) A person who attempts to commit an offence under Part III of these Regulations[2] is guilty of an offence and punishable in like manner as for that offence.

(2) A person who, for the purposes of committing an offence under Part III of these Regulations, has in his possession anything capable of being used for committing the offence is guilty of an offence and punishable in like manner as for that offence.

(3) References below to an offence under Part III include an offence under this regulation.

Enforcement

101. (1) If a constable suspects with reasonable cause that any person is committing or has committed an offence under Part III of these Regulations[3], the constable may without warrant—

(a) stop and search that person if the constable suspects with reasonable cause that evidence of the commission of the offence is to be found on that person;

(b) search or examine any thing which that person may then be using or have in his possession if the constable suspects with reasonable cause that evidence of the commission of the offence is to be found on that thing;

(c) seize and detain for the purposes of proceedings under that Part any thing which may be evidence of the commission of the offence or may be liable to be forfeited under regulation 103.

(2) If a constable suspects with reasonable cause that any person is committing an offence under Part III of these Regulations, he may, for the purposes of exercising the powers conferred by paragraph (1) or arresting a person in accordance with section 25 of the Police and Criminal Evidence Act 1984[4] for such an offence, enter any land[5] other than a dwelling-house.

(3) If a justice of the peace is satisfied by information on oath that there are reasonable grounds for suspecting that an offence under regulation 39[6], 41[7] or 43[8] has been committed and that evidence of the offence may be found on any premises, he may grant a warrant to any constable (with or without other persons) to enter upon and search those premises for the purpose of obtaining that evidence.

In the application of this paragraph to Scotland, the reference to a justice of the peace includes a sheriff.

Proceedings for offences: venue, time limits

102. (1) An offence under Part III of these Regulations[9] shall, for the purposes of conferring jurisdiction, be deemed to have been committed in any place where the offender is found or to which he is first brought after the commission of the offence.

(2) Summary proceedings for—

(a) any offence under regulation 39(1)[10] involving the taking or killing of a wild animal, and

(b) any offence under regulation 43(1)[11],

---

[1] The current fine at level 3 is £1,000: Criminal Justice Act 1991 (c. 53), s. 17 which came into force on 1 October 1992: S.I. 1992/333, S.I. 1992/2118.
[2] P. 356 above.
[3] P. 356 above.
[4] 1984 c. 60.
[5] "Land" defined by reg. 2(1), p. 337 above.
[6] P. 356 above.
[7] P. 357 above.
[8] P. 358 above.
[9] P. 356 above.
[10] P. 356 above.
[11] P. 358 above.

may be brought within a period of six months from the date on which evidence sufficient in the opinion of the prosecutor to warrant the proceedings came to his knowledge.

But no such proceedings shall be brought by virtue of this paragraph more than two years after the commission of the offence.

(3) For the purposes of paragraph (2) a certificate signed by or on behalf of the prosecutor and stating the date on which such evidence as aforesaid came to his knowledge shall be conclusive evidence of that fact; and a certificate stating that matter and purporting to be so signed shall be deemed to be so signed unless the contrary is proved.

Power of court to order forfeiture

103. (1) The court by which a person is convicted of an offence under Part III of these Regulations[1]—

(a) shall order the forfeiture of any animal, plant or other thing in respect of which the offence was committed; and

(b) may order the forfeiture of any vehicle, animal, weapon or other thing which was used to commit the offence.

(2) In paragraph (1)(b) "vehicle" includes aircraft, hovercraft and boat.

Saving for other protective provisions

104. Nothing in these Regulations shall be construed as excluding the application of the provisions of Part I of the Wildlife and Countryside Act 1981[2] (protection of wildlife) in relation to animals or plants also protected under Part III of these Regulations[3].

Powers of drainage authorities

105. (1) Where the appropriate nature conservation body[4] or any other person enter into an agreement with a drainage authority for the doing by that authority of any work on land in a European site[5], no limitation imposed by law on the capacity of the drainage authority by virtue of its constitution shall operate so as to prevent the authority carrying out the agreement.

(2) In paragraph (1) "drainage authority" means the National Rivers Authority or an internal drainage board.

Offences by bodies corporate, &c.

106. (1) Where an offence under these Regulations committed by a body corporate is proved to have been committed with the consent or connivance of, or to be attributable to any neglect on the part of, a director, manager, secretary or other similar officer of the body corporate, or a person purporting to act in any such capacity, he as well as the body corporate is guilty of the offence and liable to be proceeded against and punished accordingly.

For this purpose "director", in relation to a body corporate whose affairs are managed by its members, means any member of the body.

(2) Where an offence under these Regulations committed by a Scottish partnership is proved to have been committed with the consent or connivance of, or to be attributable to neglect on the part of, a partner, he (as well as the partnership) is guilty of the offence and liable to be proceeded against and punished accordingly.

---

[1] P. 356 above.
[2] P. 146 above.
[3] P. 356 above.

[4] "Appropriate nature conservation body" has the meaning given by reg. 4, p. 340 above: reg. 2(1).
[5] "European site" has the meaning given by reg. 10, p. 342 above: reg. 2(1).

Local inquiries

107. (1) The Secretary of State may cause a local inquiry to be held for the purposes of the exercise of any of his functions under these Regulations.

(2) The provisions of section 250(2) to (5) of the Local Government Act 1972[1] or section 210(4) to (8) of the Local Government (Scotland) Act 1973[2] (local inquiries: evidence and costs) apply in relation to an inquiry held under this regulation.

Service of notices

108. (1) Section 329 of the Town and Country Planning Act 1990[3] or section 269 of the Town and Country Planning (Scotland) Act 1972[4] (service of notices) apply to notices and other documents required or authorised to be served under these Regulations.

(2) Paragraph (1) does not apply to the service of any notice required or authorised to be served under the Acquisition of Land Act 1981[5] or the Acquisition of Land (Authorisation Procedure) (Scotland) Act 1947[6], as applied by these Regulations.

SCHEDULE 1

(Regulation 22(3))

PROCEDURE IN CONNECTION WITH ORDERS UNDER REGULATION 22.

Coming into operation

1. (1) An original order[7] or a restrictive amending order[8] takes effect on its being made.

(2) The Secretary of State shall consider every such order[9], and the order shall cease to have effect nine months after it is made unless he has previously given notice under paragraph 6 that he has considered it and does not propose to amend or revoke it, or has revoked it.

(3) Subject to paragraphs 3(1) and 4(4), a revoking order[10], or an amending order[11] which is not restrictive, does not take effect until confirmed by the Secretary of State.

(4) An amending or revoking order requiring confirmation shall stand revoked if the Secretary of State gives notice under paragraph 6 below that it is not to be confirmed.

Publicity for orders

2. (1) The Secretary of State shall, where an order has been made, give notice setting out the order (or describing its general effect) and stating that it has taken effect or, as the case may be, that it has been made and requires confirmation.

(2) The notice shall—

(a) name a place in the area in which the land to which the order relates is situated where a copy of the order may be inspected free of charge at all reasonable hours; and

(b) specify the time (not being less than 28 days from the date of the first publication of the notice) within which, and the manner in which, representations or objections with respect to the order may be made.

(3) The notice shall be given—

(a) by publication in the Gazette[12] and also at least one local newspaper circulating in the area in which the land to which the order relates is situated;

---

[1] 1972 c. 70.
[2] 1973 c. 65.
[3] 1990 c. 8.
[4] 1972 c. 52.
[5] 1981 c. 67.
[6] 1947 c. 42.
[7] "Original order" defined by para. 8 below.

[8] "Restrictive amending order" defined by para. 8 below.
[9] "Order" means an order under reg. 22, p. 348 above: para. 8 below.
[10] "Revoking order" defined by para. 8 below.
[11] "Amending order" defined by para. 8 below.
[12] "The Gazette" defined by para. 8 below.

(*b*) by serving a like notice—

   (i) on every owner and occupier of that land (subject to sub-paragraph (4) below); and

   (ii) on the local planning authority[1] within whose area the land is situated.

(4) The Secretary of State may, in any particular case, direct that it shall not be necessary to comply with sub-paragraph (3)(*b*)(i); but if he so directs in the case of any land, then in addition to publication the notice shall be addressed to "The owners and any occupiers" of the land (describing it) and a copy or copies of the notice shall be affixed to some conspicuous object or objects on the land.

Unopposed orders

3. (1) Where an order has taken effect immediately and no representations or objections are duly made in respect of it or any so made are withdrawn, the Secretary of State shall, as soon as practicable after considering the order, decide either to take no action on it or to make an order amending or revoking it.

   An amending or revoking order under this sub-paragraph takes effect immediately and does not require confirmation nor shall any representation or objection with respect to it be entertained.

(2) Where an order requiring confirmation is made and no representations or objections are duly made in respect of it, or any so made are withdrawn, the Secretary of State may confirm the order (with or without modification).

Opposed orders

4. (1) If any representation or objection duly made with respect to an order is not withdrawn, then, as soon as practicable in the case of an order having immediate effect and before confirming an order requiring confirmation, the Secretary of State shall either—

(*a*) cause a local inquiry to be held; or

(*b*) afford any person by whom a representation or objection has been duly made and not withdrawn an opportunity of being heard by a person appointed by the Secretary of State for the purpose.

(2) On considering any representations or objections duly made and the report of any person appointed to hold the inquiry or to hear representations or objections, the Secretary of State—

(*a*) if the order has already taken effect, shall decide either to take no action on the order, or to make an order amending or revoking it as he thinks appropriate in the light of the report, representations or objections; and

(*b*) if the order requires confirmation, may confirm it (with or without modifications).

(3) The provisions of section 250(2) to (5) of the Local Government Act 1972[2] or section 210(4) to (8) of the Local Government (Scotland) Act 1973[3] (local inquiries: evidence and costs) apply in relation to an inquiry held under this paragraph.

(4) An amending or revoking order made by virtue of sub-paragraph (2) above takes effect immediately and does not require confirmation nor shall any representation or objection with respect to it be entertained.

Restriction on power to amend orders or confirm them with modifications

5. The Secretary of State shall not by virtue of paragraphs 3(1) or 4(2) amend an order which has taken effect, or confirm any other order with modifications, so as to extend the area to which the order applies.

Notice of final decision on order

6. (1) The Secretary of State shall as soon as practicable after making an order by virtue of paragraphs 3(1) or 4(2) give notice—

(*a*) setting out the order (or describing its effect) and stating that it has taken effect; and

(*b*) naming a place in the area in which the land to which the order relates is situated where a copy of the order may be inspected free of charge at all reasonable hours.

(2) The Secretary of State shall give notice of any of the following decisions of his as soon as practicable after making the decision—

(*a*) a decision under paragraph 3(1) or 4(2) to take no action on an order which has already taken effect;

---

[1] "Local planning authority" defined by reg. 2(1), p. 337 above.

[2] 1972 c. 70.

[3] 1973 c. 65.

(b) a decision to confirm or not to confirm an order requiring confirmation under this Schedule.

(3) A notice under this paragraph of a decision to confirm an order shall—

(a) set out the order as confirmed (or describe its general effect) and state the day on which the order took effect; and

(b) name a place in the area in which the land to which the order relates is situated where a copy of the order as confirmed may be inspected free of charge at all reasonable hours.

(4) Notice under this paragraph shall be given by publishing it in accordance with paragraph 2(3) and serving a copy of it on any person on whom a notice was required to be served under paragraph 2(3) or (4).

Proceedings for questioning validity of orders

7. (1) This paragraph applies to any order which has taken effect and as to which the Secretary of State has given notice under paragraph 6 of a decision of his to take no action or to amend the order in accordance with paragraph 4; and in this paragraph "the relevant notice" means that notice.

(2) If any person is aggrieved by an order to which this paragraph applies and desires to question its validity on the ground that it is not within the powers of regulation 22, or that any of the requirements of this Schedule have not been complied with in relation to it, he may within six weeks from the date of the relevant notice make an application to the court under this paragraph.

(3) On any such application the court may, if satisfied that the order is not within those powers or that the interests of the applicant have been substantially prejudiced by a failure to comply with any of those requirements—

(a) in England and Wales, quash the order, or any provision of the order, either generally or in so far as it affects the interests of the applicant; or

(b) in Scotland, make such declarator as seems to the court to be appropriate.

(4) Except as provided by this paragraph, the validity of an order shall not be questioned in any legal proceedings whatsoever.

(5) In this paragraph "the court" means the High Court in relation to England and Wales and the Court of Session in relation to Scotland.

Interpretation

8. In this Schedule—

"amending order" and "revoking order" mean an order which amends or, as the case may be, revokes a previous order;

"the Gazette" means—

(a) if the order relates in whole or in part to land in England and Wales, the London Gazette; and

(b) if the order relates in whole or in part to land in Scotland, the Edinburgh Gazette;

"order" means an order under regulation 22;

"original order" means an order other than an amending or revoking order; and

"restrictive amending order" means an amending order which extends the area to which a previous order applies.

SCHEDULE 2

(Regulation 38)

EUROPEAN PROTECTED SPECIES OF ANIMALS

Common name	Scientific name
Bats, Horseshoe (all species)	*Rhinolophidae*
Bats, Typical (all species)	*Vespertilionidae*
Butterfly, Large Blue	*Maculinea arion*
Cat, Wild	*Felis silvestris*

Common name	Scientific name
Dolphins, porpoises and whales (all species)	*Cetacea*
Dormouse	*Muscardinus avellanarius*
Lizard, Sand	*Lacerta agilis*
Newt, Great Crested (or Warty)	*Triturus cristatus*
Otter, Common	*Lutra lutra*
Snake, Smooth	*Coronella austriaca*
Sturgeon	*Acipenser sturio*
Toad, Natterjack	*Bufo calamita*
Turtles, Marine	*Caretta caretta* *Chelonia mydas* *Lepidochelys kempii* *Eretmochelys imbricata* *Dermochelys coriacea*

NOTE. The common name or names given in the first column of this Schedule are included by way of guidance only; in the event of any dispute or proceedings, the common name or names shall not be taken into account.

SCHEDULE 3

(Regulation 41(1)(*a*))

ANIMALS WHICH MAY NOT BE TAKEN OR KILLED IN CERTAIN WAYS

Common name	Scientific name
Barbel	*Barbus barbus*
Grayling	*Thymallus thymallus*
Hare, Mountain	*Lepus timidus*
Lamprey, River	*Lampetra fluviatilis*
Marten, Pine	*Martes martes*
Polecat	*Mustela putorius* (*otherwise known as Putorius putorius*)
Salmon, Atlantic	*Salmo salar* (*only in fresh water*)
Seal, Bearded	*Erignathus barbatus*
Seal, Common	*Phoca vitulina*
Seal, Grey	*Halichoerus grypus*
Seal, Harp	*Phoca groenlandica* (*otherwise known as Pagophilus groenlandicus*)
Seal, Hooded	*Cystophora cristata*
Seal, Ringed	*Phoca hispida* (*otherwise known as Pusa hispida*)
Shad, Allis	*Alosa alosa*
Shad, Twaite	*Alosa fallax*
Vendace	*Coregonus albula*
Whitefish	*Coregonus lavaretus*

NOTE. The common name or names given in the first column of this Schedule are included by way of guidance only; in the event of any dispute or proceedings, the common name or names shall not be taken into account.

SCHEDULE 4

(Regulation 42)

EUROPEAN PROTECTED SPECIES OF PLANTS

Common name	Scientific name
Dock, Shore	*Rumex rupestris*
Fern, Killarney	*Trichomanes speciosum*
Gentian, Early	*Gentianella anglica*
Lady's-slipper	*Cypripedium calceolus*
Marshwort, Creeping	*Apium repens*
Naiad, slender	*Najas flexilis*
Orchid, Fen	*Liparis loeselii*
Plantain, Floating-leaved water	*Luronium natans*
Saxifrage, Yellow Marsh	*Saxifraga hirculus*

NOTE. The common name or names given in the first column of this Schedule are included by way of guidance only; in the event of any dispute or proceedings, the common name or names shall not be taken into account.

List of Wild Birds (Sundays) Orders

The orders set out below were made under the Protection of Birds Act 1954, s. 2(1). This Act was repealed by the Wildlife and Countryside Act 1981. The power to make similar orders is re-enacted in s. 2(3) of the 1981 Act. The orders below are set out on the ground that they have effect under the 1981 Act pursuant to s. 17(2) of the Interpretation Act 1978.

The prescribed areas are described in the Orders by reference to local government areas in existence before the reorganisation of local government in 1974 under the Local Government Act 1972. For the statutory provisions relating to prescribed areas see s. 2 of the Wildlife and Countryside Act 1981, p. 147 above.

The Wild Birds (Sundays) Order 1955, S.I. 1955/1286

This Order came into operation on 1 September 1955.

The Order prescribes the following areas:

The administrative counties of Caernarvon, Carmarthen, Devon, Isle of Ely, Montgomery, Norfolk, Pembroke, and York, North Riding and York, West Riding;
The county boroughs of Doncaster, Great Yarmouth and Leeds.

The Wild Birds (Sundays) Order 1956, S.I. 1956/1310

This Order came into operation on 1 September 1956.

The Order prescribes the following areas:

The administrative counties of Brecknock, Cardigan, Denbigh and Merioneth.

The Wild Birds (Sundays) Order 1957, S.I. 1957/429

This Order came into operation on 1 April 1957.

The Order prescribes the following areas:

The administrative counties of Cornwall, Glamorgan and Somerset.

The Wild Birds (Sunday in Anglesey) Order 1963, S.I. 1963/1700

This Order came into operation on 1 November 1963.

The Order prescribes the following areas:

The administrative county of Anglesey.

List of Orders establishing Areas of Special Protection for Birds

The Protection of Birds Act 1954 made provision for areas to be established as bird sanctuaries by order. The 1954 Act also provided that certain orders made under the Wild Birds Protection Acts, 1880 to 1939, be deemed as made under it. This Act was repealed b the Wildlife and Countryside Act 1981. The power to make similar orders was re-enacted in s. 3(1) of the 1981 Act and, under that Act, the areas are known as Areas of Special Protection for Birds (AOSPs). The orders made prior to the 1981 Act are set out below on the ground that they have effect under the 1981 Act pursuant to s. 17(2) of the Interpretation Act 1978.

For the statutory provisions relating to Areas of Special Protection for Birds see s. 3, Wildlife and Countryside Act 1981, p. 148 above. Reference should be made to the order relating to an area for its provisions including the prohibitions imposed and the area of land which is the subject of the order. The list of orders made before the 1981 Act is not definitive and there may be other existing orders which have not been located. The list below has been compiled from information provided to the editor by the European Wildlife Division of the Department of the Environment.

Orders made under the Wildlife and Countryside Act 1981, s. 3(1)

Area	Order (S.I. No.)
Berry Head and Berry Head (Southern Redoubt), Devon	1984/1471; 1988/1479
The Easington Lagoons, Humberside	1987/1163
The Easington Lagoons (No. 2)	1993/2059
Gull Island and Warren Shore and Needs Ore Point, Hampshire	1984/578
The Horsey Estate, Norfolk	1988/324

Orders made prior to the Wildlife and Countryside Act 1981

Area	Order (S.I. No.)
Abberton Reservoir, Essex	1967/365
Brean Down, Somerset	1968/562
Burry Estuary, Glamorgan	1963/1244; 1969/1795
Charlton's Pond, Billingham, Durham	1968/564
Cleddau, Haverfordwest, Pembrokeshire	1970/72
Cley Marshes, Norfolk	1966/536
Coquet Island, Northumberland	1964/1096; 1978/1074
Durleigh Reservoir, Somerset	1964/1989
Fairburn Ings and Newton Ings, Fairburn, West Yorkshire	1980/401
Farne Islands, Northumberland	1980/402
Fetlar Island, Shetlands	1968/755 (S. 80)
Foulney Island, Cumbria	1980/1839
Gibraltar Point, Lincolnshire	1971/557
Havergate Island, Suffolk	1961/1077

Area	*Order (S.I. No.)*
Hanningfield Reservoir, Essex	1978/1075
Horse Island, Ardrossan, Ayr	1963/120 (S. 4)
Hornsea Mere, Humberside	1980/403
Humber Estuary, Yorks./Lincs.	1955/1532; 1963/1808
Inchmickery, Midlothian	1963/119 (S. 3)
Lady Isle, Firth of Clyde	1955/1854 (S. 145)
Loch Eye, Fearn and Tain, Ross and Cromarty	1974/1596 (S. 141)
Loch Garten, Inverness	1960/760 (S. 36)
Low Parks, Hamilton, Lanark	1958/281 (S. 15)
Poole Harbour, Dorset	1978/1258
Porth Reservoir, Melancoose, Cornwall	1964/1097
Possil Marsh, Glasgow	1956/333 (S. 10)
Southport, Lancashire	1956/692
Tamar Lake, Devon and Cornwall	1960/2144
Trethias Island, Cornwall	1959/2009
Walmsley, Cornwall	1961/865
Washington New Town, Tyne and Wear	1980/404; 1980/944
Wheldrake Ings, North Yorkshire	1978/1259
Wicken Sedge Fen, Cambs.	1957/1015
Wyre-Lune, Lancashire	1963/1796; 1963/2000

List of Orders Designating Environmentally Sensitive Areas

This list sets out the orders designating environmentally sensitive areas (ESAs) under s. 18 of the Agriculture Act 1986, p. 216 above. The dates in brackets following the statutory instrument number are the dates upon which the orders came into force. The areas are defined by reference to maps which can be inspected at the offices set out in the orders. The list includes the Counties and Regions where the areas are located.

England

Avon Valley

Order: S.I. 1993/84 (13.2.93) amended by S.I. 1994/927 (30.4.94) and S.I. 1995/197 (28.2.95).

Counties: Dorset, Hampshire and Wiltshire.

Blackdown Hills

Order: S.I. 1994/707 (6.4.94).

Counties: Devon and Somerset

Breckland

Order: S.I. 1993/455 (27.3.93) amended by S.I. 1994/923 (30.4.94) and S.I. 1995/198 (28.2.95).

Counties: Cambridgeshire, Norfolk and Suffolk.

This order replaces a previous designation under S.I. 1987/2029 (1.1.88) now revoked.

The Broads

Order: S.I. 1992/54 (5.2.92) amended by S.I. 1994/929 (30.4.94).

Counties: Norfolk and Suffolk.

This order replaces a previous designation under S.I. 1986/2254 (1.3.87) now revoked.

Clun

Order: S.I. 1993/456 (27.3.93) amended by S.I. 1994/921 (30.4.94) and S.I. 1995/190 (28.2.95).

County: Shropshire.

This order replaces a previous designation under S.I. 1987/2031 (1.1.88) (Shropshire Borders) now revoked.

Cotswold Hills

Order: S.I. 1994/708 (6.4.94) amended by S.I. 1995/200 (28.2.95).

Counties: Avon, Gloucestershire, Hereford and Worcester and Warwickshire.

Dartmoor

Order: S.I. 1994/710 (6.4.94).

County: Devon.

Essex Coast

Order: S.I. 1994/711 (6.4.94).

County: Essex.

Exmoor

Order: S.I. 1993/83 (13.2.93) amended by S.I. 1994/928 (30.4.94) S.I. 1995/195 (28.2.95) and S.I. 1995/960 (21.4.95).

Counties: Devon and Somerset.

Lake District

Order: S.I. 1993/85 (13.2.93) amended by S.I. 1994/925 (30.4.94) and S.I. 1995/193 (28.2.95).

County: Cumbria.

North Peak

Order: S.I. 1993/457 (27.3.93) amended by S.I. 1994/922 (30.4.94) and S.I. 1995/189 (28.2.95).

Counties: Greater Manchester, Derbyshire, South Yorkshire and West Yorkshire.

This order replaces a previous designation under S.I. 1987/2030 (1.1.88) now revoked.

North Kent Marshes

Order: S.I. 1993/82 (13.2.93) amended by S.I. 1994/918 (30.4.94) and S.I. 1995/199 (28.2.95).

County: Kent.

Pennine Dales

Order: S.I. 1992/55 (5.2.92) amended by S.I. 1992/301 (25.2.92), S.I. 1993/460 (27.3.93) and S.I. 1994/930 (30.4.94).

Counties: Cumbria, Durham, North Yorkshire and Northumberland.

This order replaces a previous designation under S.I. 1986/2253 (1.3.87) now revoked.

Somerset Levels and Moors

Order: S.I. 1992/53 (5.2.92) amended by S.I. 1994/932 (30.4.94).

County: Somerset.

This order replaces a previous designation under S.I. 1986/2252 (1.3.87) now revoked.

Shropshire Hills

Order: S.I. 1994/709 (6.4.94).

County: Shropshire.

South Downs

Order: S.I. 1992/52 (5.2.92) amended by S.I. 1994/931 (30.4.94).

Counties: Hampshire, East and West Sussex.

This order replaces a previous designation under S.I. 1986/2249 (1.3.87) now revoked.

Suffolk River Valleys

Order: S.I. 1993/458 (27.3.93) amended by S.I. 1994/920 (30.4.94) and S.I. 1995/194 (28.2.95).

County: Essex and Suffolk.

This order replaces a previous designation under S.I. 1987/2033 (1.1.88) now revoked.

South Wessex Downs

Order: S.I. 1993/86 (13.2.93) amended by S.I. 1994/924 (30.4.94).

Counties: Dorset, Hampshire and Wiltshire.

South West Peak

Order: S.I. 1993/87 (13.2.93) amended by S.I. 1994/926 (30.4.94) and S.I. 1995/192 (28.2.95).

Counties: Cheshire, Derbyshire and Staffordshire.

Test Valley

Order: S.I. 1993/459 (27.3.93) amended by S.I. 1994/919 (30.4.94) and S.I. 1995/191 (28.2.95).

County: Hampshire.

This order replaces a previous designation under S.I. 1987/2034 (1.1.88) now revoked.

Upper Thames Tributaries

Order: S.I. 1994/712 (6.4.94).

Counties: Buckinghamshire, Gloucestershire, Northamptonshire and Oxfordshire.

West Penwith

Order: S.I. 1986/2251 (1.3.87) amended by S.I. 1992/51 (5.2.92) and S.I. 1994/933 (30.4.94).

County: Cornwall.

Scotland

Argyll Islands

Order: S.I. 1993/3136 (S. 297) (13.1.94) amended by S.I. 1994/3067 (S. 161) (30.12.94).

Area within the Argyll and Bute District of Strathclyde Region.

Breadalbane

Order: S.I. 1992/1920 (S. 196) (3.9.92) as amended by S.I. 1992/2063 (S. 210) (2.9.92) and S.I. 1994/3067 (S. 161) (30.12.94).

Area partly within the Perth and Kinross District of Tayside Region and partly within the Stirling District of Central Region.

This order replaces a previous designation under S.I. 1987/653 (S. 53) (7.5.87) now revoked.

Cairngorms Straths

Order: S.I. 1993/2345 (S. 245) (19.10.93) amended by S.I. 1994/3067 (S. 161) (30.12.94).

Area partly within the Gordon, the Kincardine and Deeside and the Moray Districts of Grampian Region and partly within the Badenoch and Strathspey District of Highland Region.

Central Borders

Order: S.I. 1993/2767 (S. 255) (8.12.93) amended by S.I. 1994/3067 (S. 161) (30.12.94).

Area within the Ettrick and Lauderdale and Roxburgh Districts of Borders Region.

This order replaces a previous designation under S.I. 1988/494 (S. 143) (14.4.88) (Whitlaw and Eildon) now revoked.

Central Southern Uplands

Order: S.I. 1993/996 (S. 142) (6.5.93) amended by S.I. 1994/3067 (S. 161) (30.12.94).

Area partly within the Cumnock and Doon Valley, the Clydesdale and East Kilbride Districts of Strathclyde Region; partly within the Nithsdale and Annandale and Eskdale Districts of Dumfries and Galloway Region and partly within the Ettrick and Lauderdale, Tweeddale and Roxburgh Districts of the Borders Region.

Loch Lomond

Order: S.I. 1992/1919 (S. 195) (3.9.92) as amended by S.I. 1992/2062 (S. 209) (2.9.92) and S.I. 1994/3067 (S. 161) (30.12.94).

Area partly within the Killin and Stirling District of Central Region and partly within the Dumbarton District of Strathclyde Region and located at the southern extremity of the Highlands stretching from Balloch in the South to Glenfalloch in the North.

This order replaces a previous designation under S.I. 1987/654 (S. 54) (7.5.87) now revoked.

Machair of the Uists and Benbecula, Barra and Vatersay

Order: S.I. 1993/3149 (S. 298) (13.1.94) amended by S.I. 1994/3067 (S. 161) (30.12.94).

Area in the Western Isles.

This order replaces a previous designation under S.I. 198/495 (S. 57) (14.4.88) now revoked.

Shetland Islands

Order: S.I. 1993/3150 (S. 299) (13.1.94) amended by S.I. 1994/3067 (S. 161) (30.12.94).

Stewartry

Order: S.I. 1993/2768 (S. 256) (8.12.93) amended by S.I. 1994/3067 (S. 161) (30.12.94).

Area within the Stewartry, Nithsdale and Wigtown Districts of Dumfries and Galloway Region.

This order replaces a previous designation under S.I. 1988/493 (S. 55) (14.4.88) now revoked.

Western Southern Uplands

Order: S.I. 1993/997 (S. 143) (6.5.93) amended by S.I. 1994/3067 (S. 161) (30.12.94).

Area partly within the Cumnock and Doon Valley and the Kyle and Carrick District of Strathclyde Region and partly within the Nithsdale, Wigtown and Stewartry Districts of Dumfries and Galloway Region.

Wales

Cambrian Mountains

Order: S.I. 1986/2257 (1.3.87) amended by S.I. 1988/173 (1.3.88), S.I. 1992/1359 (30.6.92), S.I. 1992/2342 (22.10.92) and S.I. 1995/243 (1.3.95).

Extension: S.I. 1987/2026 (1.1.88) amended by S.I. 1988/173 (1.3.88), S.I. 1994/240 (1.3.94) and S.I. 1995/242 (1.3.95).

Counties: Dyfed and Powys.

Clwydian Range

Order: S.I. 1994/238 (1.3.94) amended by S.I. 1995/242 (1.3.95).

County: Clwyd.

Lleyn Peninsula

Order: S.I. 1987/2027 (1.1.88) amended by S.I. 1988/173 (1.3.88), S.I. 1994/241 (1.3.94) and S.I. 1995/242 (1.3.95).

County: Gwynedd.

Preseli

Order: S.I. 1994/239 (1.3.94) amended by S.I. 1995/242 (1.3.95).

Area within the Districts of Preseli Pembrokeshire and South Pembrokeshire in the County of Dyfed.

Radnor

Order: S.I. 1993/1211 (31.5.93) amended by S.I. 1994/1989 (Welsh Language Provisions) (1.9.94) and S.I. 1995/242 (1.3.95).

Area within the District of Radnorshire in the County of Powys.

Ynys Môn

Order: S.I. 1993/1210 (31.5.93) amended by S.I. 1993/2422 (1.11.93), S.I. 1994/1990 (Welsh Language Provisions) (1.9.94) and S.I. 1995/242 (1.3.95).

Area within the District of Ynys Môn—Isle of Anglesey in the County of Gwynedd.

Part III

Policy Guidance

This section contains Planning Policy Guidance 9 on Nature Conservation, relating to England, and Scottish Office Circular No. 6/1995 concerning the implementation of the EC Habitats and Birds Directives in Scotland.

At the time of writing this manual there is no published guidance to local planning authorities in Wales concerning the Habitats Directive. In relation to nature conservation, the Welsh Office Circulars 52/87, *Nature Conservation*, and 1/92, *Planning Controls over Sites of Special Scientific Interest*, are extant in Wales[1].

This part does not refer to all the guidance notes and advice to planning authorities that are relevant to nature conservation. Guidance notes that relate to other areas of planning also concern nature conservation. These are published in the form of Planning Policy Guidance notes (PPGs), Minerals Planning Guidance Notes (MPGs) and Circulars by the Department of the Environment and the Welsh Office, and National Planning Policy Guidelines (NPPGs), Circulars and Planning Advice Notes (PANs) by the Scottish Office.

PPG 9 lists the addresses of English Nature and the Joint Nature Conservation Committee. A list of the addresses of the Countryside Council for Wales, Scottish Natural Heritage and other organisations is at p. 502.

---

[1] These circulars were issued as joint circulars with the Department of the Environment; in respect of England, however, they are cancelled by PPG 9, paragraph 50.

Planning Policy Guidance: Nature Conservation

Department of the Environment PPG 9: October 1994

Planning Policy Guidance notes set out the Government's policies on different aspects of planning. Local planning authorities must take their contents into account in preparing their development plans. The guidance may also be material to decisions on individual planning applications and appeals.

This PPG gives guidance on how the Government's policies for the conservation of our natural heritage are to be reflected in land use planning. It embodies the Government's commitment to sustainable development and to conserving the diversity of our wildlife.

This guidance:

— sets out the Government's objectives for nature conservation, and the framework for safeguarding our natural heritage under domestic and international law;

— describes the key role of local planning authorities and English Nature;

— emphasises the importance of both designated sites and undesignated areas for nature conservation;

— advises on the treatment of nature conservation issues in development plans;

— states development control criteria, particularly for Sites of Special Scientific Interest and sites with additional national and international designations;

— contributes to the implementation of the EC Directive on the Conservation of Natural Habitats and of Wild Fauna and Flora (the Habitats Directive);

— elaborates on minerals development and nature conservation, and on the development control implications of species protection.

Contents

Key to abbreviations

AOSP — Area of Special Protection for birds

DOE — Department of the Environment

EA   — Environmental Assessment

GCR — Geological Conservation Review

GDO — General Development Order

JNCC — Joint Nature Conservation Committee

LNR — Local Nature Reserve

MNR — Marine Nature Reserve

MPG — Minerals Planning Guidance note

NCC — Nature Conservancy Council

NCR — Nature Conservation Review

NNR — National Nature Reserve

NRA — National Rivers Authority

PPG — Planning Policy Guidance note

SAC — Special Area of Conservation

SPA　— Special Protection Area

SSSI　— Site of Special Scientific Interest

Planning Policy Guidance: Nature Conservation

Introduction

1. The wildlife of Britain is an integral part of its countryside, towns and coasts. The 1990 White Paper *This Common Inheritance* made plain the Government's commitment to sustainable development, and in particular to conserving the natural heritage for the benefit of this and future generations.[1] In January 1994 the Government published a national strategy looking at the principles of sustainable development and the processes for implementing and monitoring them.[2] The United Kingdom signed the Biodiversity Convention at the UN Conference on Environment and Development held in Brazil in June 1992. Biodiversity (biological diversity) can be simply defined as "the sum total of life's variety on earth". The Convention includes provisions on habitat conservation and impact assessment. It requires that the components of diversity should be used sustainably; that is, in a way and at a rate which does not lead to their long-term decline, and which maintains their potential to meet the needs of present and future generations. These concepts are not new to the United Kingdom. In response to the Convention the Government published in January 1994 an Action Plan setting out the UK's conservation strategy for the next 10 and 20 years.[3]

2. The Government's objectives for nature conservation are to ensure that its policies contribute to the conservation of the abundance and diversity of British wildlife and its habitats, or minimise the adverse effects on wildlife where conflict of interest is unavoidable, and to meet its international responsibilities and obligations for nature conservation. Sound stewardship of wildlife and natural features is not a task for Government alone. It depends also on the decisions made by local planning authorities, landowners and others who influence the development and use of land.

3. One of the essential tasks for Government, local authorities, and all public agencies concerned with the use of land and natural resources is to make adequate provision for development and economic growth whilst ensuring effective conservation of wildlife and natural features as an important element of a clean and healthy natural environment. The conservation of nature is important. Attractive environments, where attention is given to nature conservation, are essential to social and economic well-being. With careful planning and control, conservation and development can be compatible.

4. The key to the conservation of wildlife is the protection of the habitat on which it depends. The Wildlife and Countryside Act 1981 introduced the most comprehensive system of wildlife conservation ever seen in this country, based on a network of Sites of Special Scientific Interest (SSSIs). But protection of wildlife is not an objective which applies only in SSSIs; it depends on the wise use and management of the nation's land resources as a whole. The Government looks to local authorities to keep themselves informed of the state of the natural environment locally, and to take account of nature conservation interests wherever relevant to local decisions.

5. This Planning Policy Guidance note (PPG) sets out the principles and policies that apply to the integration of nature conservation priorities and land use planning. But others may also be relevant to nature conservation issues—for example PPG7, which provides guidance on the need to balance economic, conservation, agricultural and other factors in considering development in the countryside; PPG12, which makes clear that the planning (and especially the development plans) system can contribute to sustainable development and that plan policies and proposals should be subject to appropriate environmental appraisal; PPG13, which advises on mitigating the impact of transport proposals on the natural environment; PPG17 on the interaction of nature conservation with sport and recreation; PPG20 on coastal planning; and PPG21 on tourism.

6. This PPG first describes the main statutory nature conservation obligations, under both domestic and international law. (Annex A describes the different types of designation under that legislation,

---

[1] Cm 1200.
[2] *Sustainable Development: The UK Strategy*, Cm 2426.
[3] *Biodiversity: The UK Action Plan*, Cm 2427.

and the protection that results). The PPG then explains how nature conservation objectives should be reflected in regional planning guidance and development plans. It goes on to describe the planning controls that help to protect SSSIs, including those of international importance. In particular, it takes account of the implementation of the Habitats Directive, adopted by the Council of the European Communities in May 1992. Annex B shows classified and identified potential sites of international importance, and Annex C advises on development control in such areas in accordance with the Conservation (Natural Habitats &c.) Regulations 1994 (the Habitats Regulations).

Statutory Framework

7. Successive Governments since 1949 have built up and applied a framework of statutory measures to safeguard the natural heritage. This consists of both conservation and planning legislation and has been strengthened significantly in recent years.

Legislative landmarks in nature conservation

The National Parks and Access to the Countryside Act 1949[1]

Introduced the concept of National Nature Reserves (NNRs) and SSSIs, important for their flora and fauna, geological or physiographical (landform) features; and conferred powers on local authorities to create nature reserves.

The Countryside Act 1968[2]

Strengthened many of the powers given under the 1949 Act and imposed on every Minister, government department and public body a duty to have regard to the desirability of conserving the natural beauty and amenity of the countryside in the exercise of their functions relating to land. Annex D advises on the implications of this duty for local authorities.

The Wildlife and Countryside Act 1981[3]

Strengthened the protection for SSSIs, provided additional safeguards for particular types of area, and restricted the killing, taking from the wild and disturbance of various species.

The Wildlife and Countryside (Amendment) Act 1985[4]

Further strengthened the protection for SSSIs by making it operative immediately on notification by the Nature Conservancy Council.

The Environmental Protection Act 1990[5]

Established three country conservation councils and the Joint Nature Conservation Committee to succeed the Nature Conservancy Council; and provided further protection for SSSIs.

The Planning and Compensation Act 1991

Improved local planning authorities' abilities to safeguard conservation and amenity areas by strengthening their planning enforcement and development control powers. It also required structure, local and unitary development plans to include policies in respect of the conservation of the natural beauty and amenity of the land.

---

[1] P. 5 above.
[2] P. 112 above.
[3] P. 143 above.
[4] The amendments made by the Wildlife and Countryside (Amendment) Act 1985 are noted at the appro-

priate points within the Acts in this manual. In particular the amendments made in respect of SSSIs are at s. 28 of the Wildlife and Countryside Act 1981, p. 168 above.
[5] P. 228 above.

The Conservation (Natural Habitats &c.) Regulations 1994 (the Habitats Regulations)[1]

Formally transpose the requirements of the EC Habitats Directive into national law. They build on the existing nature conservation legislation for the protection of habitats and species listed in the Directive and apply its considerations in respect of development control and pollution control legislation. They also introduce a new system for the conservation of certain marine areas.

International Obligations and Interests

8. Species other than man do not recognise national boundaries and effective nature conservation cannot depend solely on national action. The Government attaches great importance to the various international obligations it has assumed, is determined to honour them and to encourage other countries similarly to honour theirs. These international obligations underlie much of our legislative framework for conservation. This PPG outlines the specific consequences for local planning authorities.

Key international obligations

The Bern Convention on the Conservation of European Wildlife and Natural Habitats

Carries obligations to conserve wild plants, birds and other animals, with particular emphasis on endangered and vulnerable species and their habitats. The provisions of the Convention underlie the EC Habitats Directive (see below) as well as the UK's wildlife legislation.

The Ramsar Convention on Wetlands of International Importance especially as Waterfowl Habitat

Requires the conservation of wetlands, especially sites listed under the Convention. The Convention is reproduced at Annex E.

EC Council Directive on the Conservation of Wild Birds: The Birds Directive

Applies to birds, their eggs, nests and habitats. It provides for the protection, management and control of all species of naturally occurring wild birds in the European territory of Member States (Article 1); requires Member States to take measures to preserve a sufficient diversity of habitats for all species of wild birds naturally occurring within their territories (Articles 2 and 3) in order to maintain populations at ecologically and scientifically sound levels, and requires Member States to take special measures to conserve the habitat of certain particularly rare species and of migratory species (Article 4). The Directive is reproduced at Annex F.

EC Council Directive on the Conservation of Natural Habitats and of Wild Fauna and Flora: The Habitats Directive

Contributes to the conservation of biodiversity by requiring Member States to take measures to maintain or restore natural habitats and wild species at a favourable conservation status in the Community, giving effect to both site and species protection objectives. The Directive was adopted by the Council in May 1992. Following a period of consultation, sites to be designated as Special Areas of Conservation (SACs) must be agreed with the EC Commission by June 1998. The Habitats Directive is reproduced at Annex G. Article 7 modifies the Birds Directive.

The Bonn Convention on the Conservation of Migratory Species of Wild Animals

Requires the protection of endangered migratory species listed, and encourages separate international agreements covering particular species. An agreement covering the Conservation of Bats in Europe came into force in January 1994. It deals with the need to protect bats and their feeding and roosting areas.

---

[1] P. 333 above.

EC Council Directive on the Assessment of the Effects of certain Public and Private Projects on the Environment

Requires environmental assessment to be carried out, before a decision is taken on whether development consent should be granted for certain types of project which are likely to have significant environmental effects.

The Role of English Nature

9. The Nature Conservancy Council for England (English Nature) is the agency responsible in England for advising central and local government on nature conservation, and for monitoring, research and promotion of wildlife and natural features. They:

   — establish, maintain and manage nature reserves;

   — notify and protect SSSIs;

   — advise Ministers on policies affecting nature conservation and their implementation;

   — provide advice and disseminate knowledge about nature conservation;

   — commission and support research;

   — advise on, or issue licences under, the Wildlife and Countryside Act 1981 and the Protection of Badgers Act 1992.

10. English Nature can advise local authorities and others on a wide range of conservation issues. They have a statutory role in development plan preparation and development control. They should be approached through their local offices, which are listed at Annex H.

11. English Nature, the Countryside Council for Wales and Scottish Natural Heritage are required to exercise certain functions jointly through the Joint Nature Conservation Committee (JNCC). This promotes Great Britain-wide and international nature conservation, carries out joint monitoring and research, sets common standards and advises central government.

Designated sites

12. Many important sites for nature conservation have been designated under the statutes and international conventions outlined above. Annex A describes in more detail the obligations, designations and protection afforded them under conservation legislation. The Secretary of State wishes to ensure that these obligations are fully met, and that, as far as possible and consistent with the objectives of the designation, these sites are protected from damage and destruction, with their important scientific features conserved by appropriate management.

13. All National Nature Reserves (NNRs), terrestrial Ramsar Sites, Special Protection Areas (SPAs) and (in future) Special Areas of Conservation (SACs) are also SSSIs under national legislation. In addition, some SSSIs have been identified as potentially qualifying for SPA classification but are currently subject to further survey or consultation work before decisions can be taken about their classification. Similarly, candidate SACs will be identified on a list which the Government must send to the Commission by June 1995. For the purpose of considering development proposals affecting them, potential SPAs and candidate SACs included in the list sent to the European Commission should be treated in the same way as classified SPAs and designated SACs. Sites which the Government and the Commission have agreed as Sites of Community Importance which are to be designated as SACs attract the same legal protection as if they had already been designated. Advice about such areas is available from English Nature.[1] A location

---

[1] Information on important bird sites is available in *Important Bird Areas in the United Kingdom*, published by the Royal Society for the Protection of Birds in co-operation with English Nature, the Countryside Council for Wales, Scottish Natural Heritage and the JNCC, 1990 (ISBN 0–903138–46–8); and *Protecting Internationally Important Bird Sites—A Review of the EEC Special Protection Area Network in Great Britain*, Nature Conservancy Council,

Site designations

Importance	Site Designation and explanation	UK statutory designation
Sites of *international* importance	**Ramsar Sites** listed under the Convention on Wetlands of International Importance	SSSI
	Special protection Areas (SPAs) classified under the EC Directive on the Conservation of Wild Birds	SSSI; SPA
	Special Areas of Conservation (SACs) to be designated under the EC Directive on the Conservation of Natural Habitats and of Wild Fauna and Flora (the Habitats Directive)	SSSI; SAC
Sites of *national* importance*	**National Nature Reserves (NNRs)** declared under section 19 of the National Parks and Access to the Countryside Act 1949 or section 35 of the Wildlife and Countryside Act 1981	SSSI
	Sites of Special Scientific Interest (SSSIs) notified under section 28 of the Wildlife and Countryside Act 1981	SSSI
Sites of *regional/local* importance	**Local Nature Reserves (LNRs)** designated by local authorities under section 21 of the National Parks and Access to the Countryside Act 1949	LNR
	Non-statutory Nature Reserves established and managed by a variety of public and private bodies eg county wildlife trusts, Royal Society for the Protection of Birds	—
	Sites of Importance for Nature Conservation Sites of importance for Nature Conservation or equivalent. These are usually adopted by local authorities for planning purposes. The name and status of this type of site varies considerably	—

Note: *Biological SSSIs collectively form a national series of sites; those SSSIs identified under the Nature Conservation Review and Geological Conservation Review criteria are key sites of national importance.

map and list of classified and potential SPAs and listed Ramsar Sites as at September 1994 is at Annex B.

Nature Conservation outside Designated Sites

14. Our natural wildlife heritage is not confined to the various statutorily designated sites but is found throughout the countryside and in many urban and coastal areas. Lowland England, for example, retains many remnants of ancient woodland, which have nature conservation and amenity value as well as economic use for timber production. Many urban sites for nature conservation have an enhanced local importance as a consequence of the relative lack of wildlife sites in built-up areas. Endangered species protected under the 1981 Act may be found in many places not notified as SSSIs.

15. Many sites of local nature conservation importance are given designations by local authorities and by local conservation organisations. These sites are important to local communities, often affording people the only opportunity of direct contact with nature, especially in urban areas.

1990 (ISBN 0–86139–633–2). In addition the Government intends to publish regular information through English Nature to local planning authorities about those sites which have been designated or agreed as Sites of Community Importance to be designated as SACs and those which have been declared as potential or candidate sites.

Statutory and non-statutory sites, together with countryside features which provide wildlife corridors, links or stepping stones from one habitat to another, all help to form a network necessary to ensure the maintenance of the current range and diversity of our flora, fauna, geological and landform features and the survival of important species. In some areas the maintenance of traditional agricultural practices is important for nature conservation objectives. Sensitive landscaping and planting, the creation, maintenance and management of landscape features important to wildlife, and the skilled adaptation of derelict areas can provide extended habitats.

16. The Habitats Directive requires Member States to endeavour to encourage the management of features of the landscape which are of major importance for wild flora and fauna (see paragraph 23 below). These features are those which, because of their linear and continuous structure or their function as stepping stones, are essential for migration, dispersal and genetic exchange. Examples given in the Directive are rivers with their banks, traditional field boundary systems [such as hedgerows], ponds and small woods.

17. Regionally important geological/geomorphological sites are being identified by local conservation groups with the involvement in many cases of local authorities. These sites provide valuable educational facilities, and supplement sites notified as SSSIs as a result of the Geological Conservation Review.

18. Local planning authorities should have regard to the relative significance of international, national, local and informal designations in considering the weight to be attached to nature conservation interests. They should only apply local designations to sites of substantive nature conservation value, and take care to avoid unnecessary constraints on development.

Nature Conservation and Land Use Planning

19. The Government's general policy on nature conservation is outlined in the introduction. Nature conservation objectives should be taken into account in all planning activities which affect rural and coastal land use, and in urban areas where there is wildlife of local importance. They should be reflected in regional planning guidance, structure plans, unitary development plans and local plans. General policy advice on plan preparation is set out in PPG12. This includes guidance that plan policies and proposals should be subject to appropriate environmental appraisal in the plan preparation process.

20. Specific advice on nature conservation issues in structure and local plan preparation is available from English Nature. The voluntary sector has developed a wide range of expertise and makes a vital contribution to nature conservation. National bodies such as the Royal Society for the Protection of Birds and the Royal Society for Nature Conservation, and local bodies such as the county wildlife trusts and urban conservation groups, can provide valuable advice.

Regional and strategic planning guidance

21. Nature conservation issues are not confined by administrative boundaries, and should be addressed on a strategic basis. Regional planning guidance notes issued by the Department of the Environment include nature conservation issues but the form of that guidance means that the issue is addressed very generally. Local authorities should aim to ensure that regional nature conservation issues are brought before the regional planning conferences.

Structure plans

22. Structure plans and part I of unitary development plans set out general policies and proposals on key strategic issues, taking account of the appropriate published national and regional policy guidance. They should identify key sites of nature conservation importance, such as SSSIs, NNRs, SPAs, SACs and Ramsar sites, to establish a strategic framework and exemplify the particular characteristics of nature conservation interest in the plan area in their national and international context. Policies to be applied to these sites should reflect their relative significance (see

paragraph 18 above), and place particular emphasis on the protection of internationally important sites (see paragraph 37 below and Annex C). The detailed policies in local plans and part II of unitary development plans should conform to this framework.

23. Structure plans, local plans and unitary development plans must include policies in respect of the conservation of the natural beauty and amenity of the land. Arising from article 10 of the Habitats Directive, regulation 37 of the Conservation (Natural Habitats &c.) Regulations 1994 (the Habitats Regulations)[1] states that such policies shall include policies encouraging the management of features of the landscape which are of major importance for wild flora and fauna (see paragraph 16 above). Suitable planning conditions and obligations may serve to promote such management.

Local plans

24. Local plans and part II of unitary development plans should identify relevant international, national and local nature conservation interests. They should ensure that the protection and enhancement of those interests is properly provided for in development and land-use policies, and place particular emphasis on the strength of protection afforded to international designations. Plans should offer reasonable certainty to developers, landowners and residents alike about the weight that will be given to nature conservation interests in reaching planning decisions. Nature conservation issues should be included in the surveys of local authority areas required by sections 11 and 30 of the Town and Country Planning Act 1990 to ensure that the plans are based on fully adequate information about local species, habitats, geology and landform. Plans should be concerned not only with designated areas but also with other land of conservation value (see paragraph 23 above) and the possible provision of new habitats. They should take account of locally-prepared nature conservation strategies, which should in turn be consistent with development plan policies.

25. Local plans should include planning policies to be applied to nature conservation sites, indicating the criteria against which a development affecting a site will be judged. They should have regard to the advice in this PPG on the relevant significance of different designations (paragraph 18), and on policies for SSSIs (paragraph 29); NNRs and NCR and GCR sites (paragraph 36); SPAs and SACs (paragraph 37 and Annex C); and potential SPAs, candidate SACs and Ramsar sites (paragraphs 13 and C7 of Annex C). The plan proposals map should identify the areas to which these policies apply, including any sites identified as of local nature conservation importance. Minerals and waste local plans should also take account of nature conservation interests, especially in respect of designated sites.

26. Authorities should take account of nature conservation considerations in assessing sites for any development proposals in the plan. In some cases the reduced importance of keeping agricultural land in production may enable development to be directed towards land which is not of the best and most versatile agricultural quality, rather than to alternative sites which may be of greater nature conservation interest; special protection applies to the best and most versatile agricultural land (see PPG7).

Nature Conservation and Development Control

27. Nature conservation can be a significant material consideration in determining many planning applications, especially in or near SSSIs, where there are statutory requirements to consult English Nature. But local planning authorities should not refuse permission if development can be subject to conditions that will prevent damaging impacts on wildlife habitats or important physical features, or if other material factors are sufficient to override nature conservation considerations.

---

[1] P. 355 above.

28. Where there is a risk of damage to a designated site, the planning authority should consider the use of conditions or planning obligations in the interests of nature conservation. Conditions can be used, for example, to require areas to be fenced or bounded off to protect them, or to restrict operations or uses to specific times of year. Planning obligations can accompany permissions in order to secure long-term management, to provide funds for management, or to provide nature conservation features to compensate for any such features lost when development takes place. Full guidance on planning conditions is provided by DoE Circular 1/85 and on planning obligations in DoE Circular 16/91.

Sites of Special Scientific Interest

29. The key importance of SSSIs means that development proposals in or likely to affect them must be subject to special scrutiny. The paragraphs below give details. Paragraphs 27 and 28 are also relevant.

Consultation with English Nature

30. Under the General Development Order (GDO), planning authorities must consult English Nature before granting permission for the development of land *in* an SSSI. Such consultation should take place as soon as possible and authorities may not determine any application to develop such a site within 14 days of initiating consultation. For their part, English Nature will respond as quickly as possible. The authority should tell the agency if it intends to grant permission against their advice, so that the agency can consider before the applicant is informed of the authority's decision whether to ask the Secretary of State to call-in the application. SSSIs can be seriously damaged or even destroyed by development outside their boundaries. The GDO also requires a local planning authority to consult about planning applications in any consultation area *around* an SSSI defined by English Nature. An authority is also required to consult where an application is for development which is *likely to affect* an SSSI, even if the application site falls outside the SSSI and any consultation area.

31. The Government has requested English Nature to give priority to defining consultation areas around sites of international importance. It has also asked them to define the consultation areas as narrowly as is consistent with protecting the scientific interest of these particularly important sites. A consultation area may extend up to a maximum of 2 kilometres from the boundary of an SSSI. Normally it will not extend beyond about 500 metres, although for areas such as wetlands it may extend as far as the 2 kilometre maximum. The boundaries of such consultation areas will be notified to local planning authorities by English Nature. When notifying a consultation area English Nature may advise that they wish to be consulted only about certain types of development. They may also advise a local authority that they would like to be consulted about other types of development (for example a major industrial facility) beyond the 2 kilometre maximum.

32. Where a consultation area has not been defined, the planning authority should give particular attention to any planning application in the vicinity of an SSSI so as to decide whether or not such consultation is needed. The planning authority should bear in mind the possibility that certain developments may affect a site some distance away. (For example a wetland site might have its water table lowered as a result of water abstraction some considerable distance away; and a river SSSI might be affected by an upstream development.) Consultation is not required on proposals, such as minor house extensions, that would clearly have no effect on a nearby SSSI. But, where there is any doubt whether or not there is likely to be an effect, the local planning authority should contact the appropriate office of English Nature for advice. Annex H provides contact points.

33. A local planning authority should inform English Nature of decisions on all applications for the development of land about which they were consulted.

Recreational activities

34. The permission granted by the GDO for the temporary use of land for war games, motorsports and clay pigeon shooting does not apply in SSSIs. This means that a planning application is

required for all such uses of land within an SSSI; nature conservation and other relevant considerations can therefore be taken properly into account before the land is so used. It does not mean that no such activities can take place in SSSIs under any circumstances. A local planning authority should make a proper assessment and not reject an application out of hand. Some SSSIs are seasonal in their sensitivity; others can accommodate recreational activities without risk to their features of special interest. In some cases an authority may be able to mitigate potential damage to its satisfaction by imposing conditions to regulate the proposed use.

35. Where appropriate, an authority may also wish to consider making a direction under Article 4 of the GDO to withdraw permitted development rights for other activities, in particular in SSSIs. In such cases a planning application will be required.

Special procedures to protect sites of particular importance

36. Whilst all SSSIs form part of a national series and are subject to the basic procedures outlined in paragraphs 29–35 above, some have additional designations conferred on them for specific reasons (see paragraph 13 above and Annex A). When weighing the case for proposed development in NNRs and in NCR and GCR sites against nature conservation interests, a planning authority is expected to pay particular regard to their national importance. On the advice of English Nature, the Secretary of State will normally call-in for his own decision planning applications with a significant effect on these sites. He may also call-in other applications affecting SSSIs if they raise planning issues of more than local importance.

Implementation of the Habitats Directive

37. The UK is bound by the terms of the EC Birds and Habitats Directives (reproduced in Annexes F and G). Special considerations therefore apply to SPAs and in future to SACs. The Conservation (Natural Habitats &c.) Regulations 1994 (the Habitats Regulations) provide for the designation of SACs, pursuant to the Habitats Directive. They apply specific provisions of the Habitats Directive to future SACs and to existing and future SPAs classified pursuant to the Birds Directive. The provisions of the Habitats Directive are summarised in Annex A, paragraph A15. The procedures described in Annex C for SPAs and SACs, in conjunction with the statutory duties imposed by the Habitats Regulations, fulfil the assessment and decision-making requirements of the Habitats Directive in respect of the land use planning system.

Environmental assessment

38. Environmental assessment (EA) is mandatory for projects of the kinds listed in Schedule 1 to the Town and Country Planning (Assessment of Environmental Effects) Regulations 1988. For projects of a kind listed in Schedule 2 to the Regulations (Schedule 2 projects), EA is required if the particular development proposed would be likely to have significant environmental effects by virtue of factors such as its nature, size or location.

39. DOE Circular 15/88 advises that consideration should be given to the need for EA where a Schedule 2 project is likely to have significant effects on the special character of an SSSI, and that any views expressed by the Nature Conservancy Council, now succeeded by English Nature, should be taken into account. It also advises that the environmental effects of any proposed development either in or close to an SPA or Ramsar site should be subjected to the most rigorous examination; the same applies to potential SPAs or to SACs from the point they are placed on the candidate list. In practice the effect of Schedule 2 development on an SSSI will often be such as to require EA. Whilst each case should be judged on its merits, EA would normally be required where a Ramsar site or a potential or classified SPA, or a candidate, agreed or designated SAC could be affected. Where a local planning authority is uncertain about the significance of a project's likely effects on the environment, it should consult English Nature.

Minerals matters including peat extraction

40. Minerals are a valuable natural resource and can only be worked where they are found. However some mineral deposits occur within or underlying sites of importance for nature conservation.

Guidance on drawing up policies for minerals in development plans and on the handling of new applications for mineral working which would affect SSSIs is contained in the series of Minerals Planning Guidance Notes (MPGs) issued by DOE, and in particular MPGs 1,2,6,7 and 10. Applications in or likely to affect SSSIs should be the subject of the most rigorous examination, and English Nature must be consulted on such applications. The need for the mineral must be balanced against environmental and other relevant considerations. Where planning permission is given, conditions will normally be required relating to the winning and working of the minerals and the restoration and aftercare of the site. Particular attention should be paid to the proposed end-use of the site in framing those conditions. Special considerations apply to applications which are likely significantly to affect SPAs, SACs and Ramsar sites (see box following paragraph C10 of Annex C).

41. Guidance on the provisions for registration of permissions for the winning and working of minerals or the depositing of mineral wastes, originally granted under Interim Development Orders, is in MPG8. Advice on preparation of schemes of conditions for these sites is in MPG9, including reference to the need to protect, as far as possible, sensitive areas of environmental or ecological importance.

42. Extraction of minerals can create new types of habitat in areas where they were formerly rare or absent, while quarry faces may provide a valuable supplement to natural rock outcrops since features of geological importance may be revealed during quarrying operations. Mineral planning authorities and mineral companies should bear in mind opportunities for habitat creation and enhancement even where conservation is not the primary end-use of a site. Planning conditions, particularly on longer-life sites, may need to allow for some flexibility to accommodate changes to schemes should these become necessary. Consideration should also be given to arrangements for continuing management of restored nature conservation sites, beyond the end of the aftercare period.

43. Proposals for the working of peat should be subject to special consideration. Peat is formed from accumulated remains of plants, mainly sedges and sphagnum mosses, which grow in waterlogged conditions. Resources of peat which may be of commercial quality for mineral extraction are generally found in lowland areas which, in their natural state, formed raised mires (domes of peat) or fen (sedge) peats. They provide particularly distinctive and rare habitats. Peatlands are listed as habitat types for protection at a favourable conservation status under the Habitats Directive, some types having priority status. Large areas of the original peatlands have been drained for agriculture, developed, or cut for peat for commercial or domestic purposes. The Department of the Environment's Working Group, set up to advise about nature conservation, peat extraction and other land use matters affecting peatlands (Commons Hansard, 7 July 1992, col. 158) published its report in 1994. The Working Group took the requirements of the Habitats Directive into account. A draft MPG on peat provision in England which takes account of the Working Group's report has been issued for consultation. Mineral planning authorities should consult English Nature about any proposals for peat working which could affect sites of nature conservation importance. The Secretary of State will consider calling in any such applications on the advice of these agencies. Aspects of proposals for peat extraction which would need particular attention include the hydrological and ecological implications, methods of working, and intentions and methods for site reclamation.

Protection of Species

44. Part 1 of the Wildlife and Countryside Act 1981[1] sets out the protection which is afforded to wild animals and plants. Every five years, the Schedules to the Act relating to protected animals (Schedule 5) and plants (Schedule 8) are reviewed. Local authorities are notified of any amendments and additions to those Schedules as a result of the review and are bound by the Act to take steps to bring to the attention of the public and of school children in particular the provisions of

---

[1] P. 146 above.

Part 1 of the Act. The protection offered by the Act is additional to that offered by the planning system.

45. Certain plant and animal species, including all wild birds, are protected under the 1981 Act. Some other animals are protected under their own legislation (for example the Protection of Badgers Act 1992). It is an offence to ill-treat any animal; to kill, injure, sell or take protected species (with certain exceptions); or intentionally to damage, destroy or obstruct their places of shelter. Bats enjoy additional protection. It is an offence to kill, injure or disturb bats found in the non-living areas of a dwelling house (that is, in the loft) or in any other place without first notifying English Nature.

46. The Conservation (Natural Habitats, &c.) Regulations 1994 (the Habitats Regulations) implement the requirements of the Habitats Directive for species listed in Annex IV of the Directive (see Annex G to this PPG). It is an offence deliberately to kill, injure, take or disturb listed animal species; to destroy their resting places or breeding sites; or to pick, collect, cut, uproot or otherwise destroy listed plant species.

47. The presence of a protected species is a material consideration when a local planning authority is considering a development proposal which, if carried out, would be likely to result in harm to the species or its habitat. Local authorities should consult English Nature before granting planning permission. They should consider attaching appropriate planning conditions or entering into planning obligations under which the developer would take steps to secure the protection of the species, particularly if a species listed in Annex IV to the Habitats Directive would be affected. They should also advise developers that they must conform with any statutory species protection provisions affecting the site concerned.

48. English Nature are responsible for issuing licences under section 10(1)(d) of the Protection of Badgers Act 1992[1] to permit interference with a badger sett, in the course of development (which includes building and construction work). Although consideration of the case for granting a licence is separate from the process of applying for planning permission, a local authority should advise anyone submitting an application for development in an area where there are known to be badger setts that they must comply with the provisions of the Act. Local authorities and all other public bodies also need a licence in respect of any development which they themselves carry out in any areas where there are known to be badger setts. For further information see Home Office Circular 100/91.

Lawful Development Certificates

49. If a local planning authority is considering an application for a lawful development certificate[2], and the development or use appear *prima facie* to involve a contravention of the 1981 Act, they should draw its requirements to the applicant's attention. They cannot however have regard to possible contravention of the 1981 Act in determining the application. A lawful development certificate relates only to the lawfulness of the use of land or buildings under planning legislation. It remains the applicant's responsibility to comply with all other legislation. A local authority should however notify English Nature of any lawful development certificate application relating to an SSSI.

Cancellation of Advice

50. DOE Circulars 32/81, 24/82, 27/87 and 1/92 are hereby cancelled.

---

[1] P. 298 above.

[2] Under s. 191 or 192 of the Town and Country Planning Act 1990 (as amended).

ANNEX A

DESIGNATED SITES

A1. This Annex describes the various designations under British law and other agreements, and the protection offered under conservation legislation.

A2. **Sites of Special Scientific Interest (SSSIs)** are identified by English Nature. Guidelines for the selection of biological SSSIs were published by their predecessor, the Nature Conservancy Council (NCC), in 1989. These will be updated and guidelines for geological sites will be published in due course by the Joint Nature Conservation Committee. English Nature must notify the sites to their owners and occupiers, the local planning authority, the National Rivers Authority and the Secretary of State. Interested parties may make representations to English Nature following the initial notification of an SSSI. The council must consider all such representations and decide within 9 months of the original notification whether or not it should stand.

A3. The Wildlife and Countryside Act 1981 also required English Nature to renotify SSSIs designated under previous legislation. This renotification is virtually complete.

A4. All sites of national and international importance on land (including National Nature Reserve (NNRs), Nature Conservation Review (NCR) and Geological Conservation Review (GCR) sites, Special Protection Areas (SPAs), Special Areas of Conservation (SACs) and Ramsar Sites) are notified as SSSIs.

A5. In line with the concepts explained in the 1947 Government White Paper (Cmnd. 7122 and Cmnd. 7235), which led to the National Parks and Access to the Countryside Act 1949, within the SSSI series certain "key areas" have been identified where nature conservation should be the primary purpose of control and management of the site. These "key areas" embody the basic principle that adequate examples of all major semi-natural and natural ecosystems in Britain should be set aside and managed so as to maintain their environment (including physical structure), with their characteristic communities of plants and animals, in a satisfactory state.

A6. A comprehensive survey and assessment of biological sites of national and international importance was published by the Cambridge University Press on behalf of the former NCC and the Natural Environment Research Council in 1977. The Review describes the main habitat types in Britain and sets out the criteria in selecting the "key" sites listed in Volume 2 of the review. These sites are known as **NCR sites.** Since its publication the former NCC and now the JNCC have identified additional important sites and have added them to the list of NCR sites. Notification of these NCR sites is included in the notification of SSSIs.

A7. Between 1977 and 1989 the former NCC conducted a similar comprehensive survey and assessment of geological sites. The Review is intended to identify, assess and describe all those British geological and geomorphological areas where conservation is essential for education and research in the earth sciences. These sites are known as **GCR sites.** Notification of GCR sites is included in the notification of SSSIs.

A8. To protect SSSIs from operations outside the scope of planning controls, English Nature specify to their owners and occupiers the operations which they consider to be harmful to their conservation interest. Owners and occupiers are required either to notify English Nature of potentially damaging operations and may not undertake them for 4 months (longer by agreement) unless they are in accordance with the terms of a management agreement or to have the consent of English Nature.

A9. Local authorities are required to register all notifications of SSSIs as a local land charge. They are also asked to help protect them by alerting English Nature if they become aware of any threat to the special interest of the site, such as a change in farming techniques, an application for development of land or coast protection works. In all cases, English Nature should be advised about development affecting SSSIs (see paragraph 30 of the PPG).

A10. As further protection, the Secretary of State may make a **Nature Conservation Order** to protect any sites of national or international importance. Such an order extends the period for the negotiation of a management agreement to up to 12 months (or longer by agreement). If agreement still cannot be reached, English Nature may apply to the Secretary of State for confirmation of a Compulsory Purchase Order.

A11. **Limestone pavements**, fissured by natural erosion, are of physiographical, and sometimes biological, interest. They are identified as a priority habitat type in the Habitats Directive. Those in this country, mainly in the north of England, are among the best examples in the world. In the past, pavements have been vulnerable to exploitation for use in garden rockeries and decorative walling. English Nature and the Countryside Commission are required to notify local planning authorities of limestone pavements which they consider to be of special interest. Under section 34[1] of and Schedule 11[2] to the Wildlife and Countryside Act 1981, the

---

[1] P. 176 above.   [2] P. 206 above.

Secretary of State or the relevant local planning authority may then make a **Limestone Pavement Order** designating the land concerned and prohibiting the removal or disturbance of limestone on or in it.

A12. An order takes effect on being made. County Planning Authorities may revoke their own Orders but the Secretary of State is required to consider each Order made by other authorities or by him. He must give notice within 9 months that he intends either to revoke, amend, or allow the Order to remain in force; if he takes no action, the Order ceases to have effect. No compensation is payable. There are procedures for objections to be made against Orders and for challenging Orders in the Courts.

A13. The removal of limestone from Order land requires a planning permission granted on a specific application under Part III of the Town and Country Planning Act 1990. The General Development Order does not grant permission for such development.

A14. **National Nature Reserves (NNRs)** are areas of national, and sometimes international, importance which are owned or leased by English Nature or bodies approved by them, or are managed in accordance with Nature Reserve Agreements with landowners and occupiers. The essential characteristic of NNRs is that they are primarily used for nature conservation.

A15. **Special Protection Areas (SPAs) and Special Areas of Conservation (SACs)** are intended to protect the habitats of threatened species of wildlife.

— Article 4 of the Birds Directive requires that special measures be taken to conserve the habitat of the species listed in Annex I of the Directive in order to ensure their survival and reproduction in their area of distribution. In particular, Member States are required to classify the most suitable areas for these species as SPAs. Similar measures are to be taken in respect of regularly occurring migratory species not listed in Annex I.

— Article 2 of the Habitats Directive states that the Directive's aim is to contribute towards bio-diversity through conserving natural habitats and wild fauna and flora of Community importance. Measures taken pursuant to the Directive are to take account of economic, social and cultural requirements and regional and local characteristics.

— Article 3 of the Habitats Directive requires Member States to contribute, according to the selection and designation procedure set out in Article 4 and Annex III, to a coherent Community-wide network of SACs called Natura 2000. The SACs will be selected for their importance as natural habitat types and as habitats of the species listed in Annexes I and II of the Directive. All Birds Directive SPAs will also be part of the Natura 2000 network under Article 3(1) of the Habitats Directive.

— Article 6(2) of the Habitats Directive requires Member States to take appropriate steps to avoid, in SACs and SPAs, significant deterioration of natural habitats and the habitats of species as well as disturbance of the species for which the sites have been designated.

— Article 6(3) and (4) of the Habitats Directive requires that proposed developments,[1] not directly connected with or necessary to site management, which are likely to have a significant effect on an SAC or an SPA, either individually or in combination with other plans or projects, should be assessed according to their implications for the site's conservation objectives. The development may go ahead if, as a result of that assessment, it is found that it will not adversely affect the integrity of the site. If the assessment shows there will be a negative effect, the scheme may only be allowed if there is no alternative solution and if there are imperative reasons of overriding public interest, including those of a social or economic nature. In such instances, Member States must take compensatory measures to preserve the overall coherence of the Natura 2000 network. There are special considerations for sites which host priority natural habitat types or priority species, which are particularly at risk and are marked with * in Annexes I and II to the Habitats Directive (see Annex G of this PPG). In such cases, schemes can only be considered in terms of overriding reasons of human health and public safety, or beneficial consequences of primary importance for the environment or, further to an opinion from the European Commission following consultation by the Government, other imperative reasons of overriding public interest.

— Article 7 of the Habitats Directive applies Articles 6(2), (3) and (4) of that Directive to the Birds Directive. These provisions supersede the first sentence of Article 4(4) of the Birds Directive.

— Article 10 of the Habitats Directive requires Member States to encourage in their land-use planning and development policies the management of landscape features which are of major importance for wild fauna and flora (see paragraph 16 of this PPG).

---

[1] Development in this context does not include development plans, since the plan itself cannot authorise development that would affect the site.

A16. The Conservation (Natural Habitats, &c.) Regulations 1994 (the Habitats Regulations) make provision for the purposes of implementing the Habitats Directive. Among other things, they apply the relevant requirements of Article 6 to specified provisions of the Town and Country Planning Act 1990, the Pipe-lines Act 1962, the Highways Act 1980, the Cycle Tracks Act 1984, the Electricity Act 1989 and the Transport and Works Act 1992. They also provide for the designation of SACs under the Habitats Directive. In the Regulations, SACs and SPAs classified pursuant to the Birds Directive, are known as European sites.

A17. The **Ramsar Convention** requires signatory states to protect wetlands that are of international importance, particularly as waterfowl habitats. **Ramsar sites** are listed by the Secretary of State. The provisions of the Ramsar Convention include requirements for contracting parties to promote wetlands generally and to:

a. "formulate and implement their planning so as to promote the conservation of the wetlands included in the list, and as far as possible the wise use of wetlands in their territory";

b. "designate alternative sites of the original habitat type should the development of any of the presently designated sites become necessary in the urgent national interest".

A18. **Biogenetic Reserve.** A number of National Nature Reserves and some important SSSIs have been identified as Biogenetic Reserves under a Council of Europe programme for the conservation of heathlands and dry grasslands. Sites of international importance are designated by the Secretary of State in the light of recommendations made by English Nature. These recommendations are made only after consultation with local authorities and the owners and occupiers of the land concerned. The Secretary of State takes any comments into account before reaching a decision. Relevant local authorities are informed of any designations by English Nature.

A19. **Marine Nature Reserves (MNRs)** are designated under the Wildlife and Countryside Act 1981 to conserve marine flora or fauna or geological or physiographical features or to allow study of such features. Following an application by English Nature, the Secretary of State may apply such a designation to any areas of land covered (continuously or intermittently) by tidal waters or to parts of the sea up to the seaward limits of territorial waters. An MNR has already been established at Lundy. a voluntary marine park has been established at the Isles of Scilly.

A20. English Nature may make byelaws for the protection of MNRs, except where these would interfere with the byelaw-making functions already vested in another authority. Local authorities can contribute to the successful operation of reserves by making complementary byelaws to control activities on the foreshore or other parts of MNRs within their boundaries.

A21. **Areas of Special Protection for Birds (AOSPs)** are established under the Wildlife and Countryside Act 1981 by orders made by the Secretary of State after appropriate consultation with owners and occupiers. The purpose of such orders is normally to provide sanctuary to particularly vulnerable groups of birds. The protection given by such Orders can vary to meet particular circumstances. AOSPs replace the establishment of **Bird Sanctuaries** under the Protection of Birds Act 1954 but sanctuaries established under that Act still enjoy protection.

A22. **Local Nature Reserves (LNRs)** may be established by local authorities under section 21 of the National Parks and Access to the Countryside Act 1949[1]. These habitats of local significance can make a useful contribution both to nature conservation and to the opportunities for the public to see, learn about, and enjoy wildlife. Authorities are required to consult English Nature about the establishment of such a reserve. English Nature can give practical help and, in some circumstances, grants, as well as advice on byelaws to protect the reserve. Such byelaws should follow the model available from the Department of the Environment and require confirmation by the Secretary of State.

ANNEX B*
CLASSIFIED SPECIAL PROTECTION AREAS, POTENTIAL SPECIAL PROTECTION AREAS AND LISTED RAMSAR SITES

* Annex B contains a map which is not reproduced in this Manual. The map indicates the location of the areas set out below.

KEY   SR: Special Protection Area/Ramsar; R: Ramsar; S: Special Protection Area

CLASSIFIED SPECIAL PROTECTION AREAS AND LISTED RAMSAR SITES

[1] P. 19 above.

1(SR)	Lindisfarne
2(SR)	Holburn Moss
3(S)	Farne Islands
4(S)	Coquet Island
5(R)	Irthinghead Mires
6(SR)	Upper Solway Flats & Marshes
7(S)	Moor House
8(R)	Esthwaite Water
9(SR)	Leighton Moss
10(SR)	Lower Derwent Valley
11(S)	Ribbel Estuary
12(SR)	Martin Mere
13(SR)	Alt Estuary
14(R)	Rostherne Mere
15(SR)	The Dee Estuary
16(SR)	Rutland Water
17(SR)	The Wash
18(SR)	North Norfolk Coast
19(SR)	Ouse Washes
20(R)	Chippenham Fen
21(R)	Redgrave & Lopham Fen
22(SR)	Broadland (including Bure Marshes, and Hickling Broad and Horsey Mere)
23(SR)	Colne Estuary
24(SR)	Minsmere—Walberswick
25(S)	Orfordness Havergate
26(SR)	Abberton Reservoir
27(SR)	Old Hall Marshes
28(SR)	The Swale
29(SR)	Walmore Common
30(SR)	Upper Severn Estuary
31(R)	Bridgwater Bay
32(S)	Chew Valley Lake
33(SR)	Exe Estuary
34(SR)	Chesil Beach & The Fleet
35(SR)	Chichester & Langstone Harbours
36(SR)	Pagham Harbour
37(S)	Flamborough Head & Bempton Cliffs
38(S)	Hornsea Mere
39(SR)	Gibraltar Point
40(SR)	Nene Washes
41(S)	Great Yarmouth North Denes
42(S)	Porton Down
43(S)	Bowland Fells
44(SR)	Hamford Water
45(SR)	Benfleet and Southend Marshes
46(SR)	Medway Estuary and Marshes
47(SR)	Stodmarsh
48(S)	Wealden Heaths Phase 1
49(R)	Thursley and Ockley Bogs
50(SR)	New Forest
51(S)	Salisbury Plain
52(R)	Malham Tarn
53(SR)	Derwent Ings
54(SR)	Dengie
55(SR)	Rockliffe Marshes
56(R)	Roydon Common
57(SR)	Stour and Orwell Estuary
58(SR)	Thanet Coast & Sandwich Bay
59(SR)	Humber Flats Marshes & Coast
60(R)	Midland Meres and Mosses

POTENTIAL SPECIAL PROTECTION AREAS[1]

101 Northumberland Coast
102 Teesmouth & Cleveland Coast
103 North Yorkshire Moors
104 Thorne and Hatfield Moors
105 Brecklands
106 Breydon Water
107 Benacre Broad to Easton Bavents
108 Alde-Ore Estuary
109 Deben Estuary
110 Blackwater Estuary
111 River Crouch Marshes
112 Foulness
113 Lee Valley
114 Thames Estuary & Marshes
115 Dungeness to Pett Levels
116 Ashdown Forest
117 London Reservoirs and Gravel Pits
118 Thames Basin Heaths
119 Wealdon Heaths Phase 2 (formerly Woolmer Forest)
120 Arun Valley (formerly Amberley)
121 Portsmouth Harbour
122 Southampton Water & Solent Marshes
123 Avon Valley
124 Dorset Heathlands
125 Poole Harbour
126 East Devon Heaths
127 Tamar Estuaries Complex
128 Somerset Levels & Moors
129 Severn Estuary
130 Mersey Estuary
131 South Pennine Moors (formerly Yorkshire Dale Moorlands)
132 Ribble & Alt Estuaries
133 Morecambe Bay
134 Duddon Estuary
135 North Pennine Moors

ANNEX C

DEVELOPMENT CONTROL FOR SPECIAL PROTECTION AREAS AND SPECIAL AREAS OF CONSERVATION

Classification of SPAs and SACs

C1. When consultations take place preparatory to the classification of an SPA or designation of an SAC, local planning authorities will be asked to consider all extant planning permissions which may affect the proposed area (i.e. those permissions which have not been implemented at all, and those which have not been completely implemented). They should consider for each whether the implementation of that permission would have a significant effect on the ecological value of the site. If so, they should say so in their response to the consultation.

C2. Regulations 50[1], 51, 55[2] and 56 of the Conservation (Natural Habitats, &c.) Regulations 1994 (the Habitats Regulations) require the local planning authority to review extant planning permissions[3] which are likely to

---

[1] This map and list include those areas identified on the basis of scientific advice as potentially qualifying for classification as SPAs in England. For the purposes of considering development proposals affecting them, these sites should be treated in the same way as classified SPAs (see paragraphs 13 and C7 of this PPG). The Government has asked the JNCC to review this list. When the outcome of this review is announced the Government will provide local planning authorities with a revised list of potential SPAs.

[2] P. 362 above.
[3] P. 366 above.
[4] Excluding planning permission deemed to be granted under s. 90(1), (2) or (2A) of the Town and Country Planning Act 1990 in connection with the Pipe-lines Act 1962, the Electricity Act 1989 or the Transport and Works Act 1992. Such reviews will be carried out by the Secretary of State, as will those of other deemed permissions under s. 90(1) (see reg. 55(3) and (4)). The local planning authority must

have a significant effect on a site, either individually or in combination with other development, and to take any appropriate action. This requirement applies to:

existing SPAs (listed in Annex B) when the Regulations come into force;

future SPAs when they are classified; and

SACs when the Government and the European Commission agree the site as a Site of Community Importance to be designated as an SAC. (Local authorities will be notified when sites are agreed).

C3. Local authorities must review permissions as soon as is reasonably practicable. They should have identified any relevant permissions during the consultations referred to in paragraph C1 above. The Department will have considered whether they should be a factor in deciding the boundaries of the site under the requirements of the Birds and Habitats Directives. The review will need to ascertain whether implementation of any permission which is likely to have a significant effect on the site, and is not directly connected with or necessary to its management, would adversely affect its integrity (see box following paragraph C10). English Nature will advise on individual cases. If the integrity of the site would be adversely affected, and if the permission does not fulfil the conditions under which a new development proposal affecting the site would be approved (see box following paragraph C10), then the authority must take appropriate action to remove the potential for harm, unless there is no likelihood of the development being carried out or continued.

C4. If local authorities consider that planning obligations restricting or regulating the use of the land would safeguard the integrity of the site they must invite those concerned to enter into them. Otherwise they must modify or revoke the permission, or make a discontinuance order. They should also take such action if a developer proceeds with damaging development while they are endeavouring to secure a planning obligation. Regulation 57[1] provides that modification, revocation or discontinuance orders take effect when served. They must however be confirmed by the Secretary of State. Where compensation is payable, the authority must refer the amount to the Lands Tribunal unless the Secretary of State indicates otherwise (see regulation 59[2]).

C5. PPG23, *Planning and Pollution*, advises that local planning authorities should not seek to duplicate controls which are the statutory responsibility of other bodies (including local planning authorities in their non-planning functions). Regulations 83[3], 84 and 85 require the review of authorisations under the Environmental Protection Act 1990 granted by Her Majesty's Inspectorate of Pollution for integrated pollution control and by local authorities for air pollution control; of waste management licences under the 1990 Act granted by waste regulation authorities; and of water discharge consents under the Water Resources Act 1991 granted by the National Rivers Authority. If in reviewing a planning permission local planning authorities consider that action falls to be taken under regulations 83, 84 or 85 they should inform the relevant authority. They should only exercise planning powers under regulation 56 if powers under the other regimes are not available or if their exercise could not achieve what is required. In carrying out reviews and in exercising their own powers local planning authorities must have regard to the provision in regulation 51 that the action to be taken should be the least onerous to those affected.

C6. Advice on amendments to the General Development Order is at paragraphs C12–C16 below. Regulations 64[4], 65, and 66 provide that existing Special Development Orders, Simplified Planning Zone schemes and Enterprise Zone schemes cease to have effect to grant planning permission for development which is likely to have a significant effect on a classified SPA or an SAC agreed by the Commission and the Government as a Site of Community Importance to be designated as an SAC. Existing Special Development Orders relate to Urban Development Corporations, former New Town Development Corporations, Atomic Energy Establishments and Telecommunications Networks on Railway Operational Land. The Regulations also prevent new Special Development Orders and SPZ and EZ schemes from granting planning permission for development which is likely significantly to affect a classified SPA or agreed SAC.

Development affecting SPAs and SACs

C7. Regulations 48[5], 49, and 54[6] restrict the granting of planning permission for development which is likely significantly to affect an SPA or SAC, and which is not directly connected with or necessary to the management of the site. They apply to planning decisions taken on or after the date the Regulations come into force, regardless of when the application was submitted. They apply to classified SPAs, and to SACs from the point where

consider whether any of these other permissions under s. 90(1) should in their opinion be reviewed. If so they must refer the matter to the Government Department which made the direction deeming permission to be granted. They should take similar action in the case of deemed permissions connected with the Pipe-lines, Electricity and Transport and Works Acts. See para. C6 below regarding permissions granted by Development Orders and

Simplified Planning Zone and Enterprise Zone schemes, which are also excluded from review (reg. 55(2) refers).

[1] P. 367 above.
[2] P. 369 above.
[3] P. 380 above.
[4] P. 372 above.
[5] P. 361 above.
[6] P. 364 above.

the Commission and the Government agree the site as a Site of Community Importance to be designated as an SAC. They do not apply to potential SPAs or to candidate SACs before they have been agreed with the Commission, but as a matter of policy the Government wishes development proposals affecting them to be considered in the same way as if they had already been classified or designated (see paragraph 13 of this PPG). The Government has chosen to apply the same considerations to listed Ramsar sites.

C8. On land, SPAs and in future SACs will already have been notified to authorities as SSSIs. An authority is required under the GDO to consult English Nature before granting planning permission for development affecting an SSSI; regulation 48 incorporates a similar requirement for development affecting an SPA or SAC. In responding, these bodies will advise if the SSSI forms part of a designated or potential SPA or SAC or is otherwise of particular significance in terms of the Birds or Habitats Directives. They will also advise whether in their opinion the proposed development would significantly affect the ecological value for which the site was identified, and if appropriate will suggest what measures might be taken to avoid such effects.

C9. The Secretary of State will normally call in for his own decision planning applications which are likely significantly to affect sites of international importance; he will have regard to the advice of English Nature on which applications are likely to have such effects. Where a planning application likely to affect such a site is not called in, the Government expects the papers inviting local authority members to take a particular decision to indicate clearly that the relevant factors have been fully addressed, whether or not the authority is minded to allow the development. Planning authorities should be prepared to explain their reasons, particularly if they do not decide the case in accordance with the recommendations of English Nature. Regulation 49 requires an authority proposing to allow development which would adversely affect an SPA or SAC to notify the Secretary of State in advance.

C10. The approach to be taken in considering a development proposal that would affect an SPA or SAC is set out in the box below, whether the decision-taker is the Secretary of State or the local planning authority.

CONSIDERATION OF DEVELOPMENT PROPOSALS AFFECTING SPAs AND SACs[1]

The decision-taker must first establish whether the proposed development is directly connected with or necessary to site management for nature conservation and whether it is **likely to have a significant effect** on an SPA or SAC. Taking account of advice from English Nature, they should consider whether the effect of the proposal on the site, either individually or in combination with other proposals, is likely to be significant in terms of the ecological objectives for which the site was classified or designated. If the initial assessment is inconclusive, a fuller assessment will be needed to establish the effects of the proposed development on the site.

If the decision-taker concludes that a proposed development unconnected with site management is likely significantly to affect an SPA or SAC, they must then assess its implications in view of the **site's conservation objectives** (i.e. the reasons for which the site was classified or designated), so as to ascertain whether or not it will adversely affect the integrity of the site. The advice of English Nature and the citation issued by them saying why the site was classified or designated will need to be carefully considered. The **integrity of a site** is the coherence of its ecological structure and function, across its whole area, that enables it to sustain the habitat, complex of habitats and/or the levels of populations of the species for which it was classified. The scope and content of an **appropriate assessment** will depend on the location, size and significance of the proposed project. English Nature will advise on a case-by-case basis.

According to the nature conservation value of the site, they will identify whether particular aspects such as hydrology, disturbance or land-take should be specifically addressed. In the simplest cases, a general statement from them of the impact of the development may suffice. The assessment required under the Habitats Regulations does not correspond to an environmental assessment, although for some projects EA will be necessary (see paragraphs 38–39 of this PPG). In such cases it will be appropriate to use the information assembled for the purposes of the EA also for the assessment required by the Habitats Regulations.

If the decision-taker ascertains that the proposed development will adversely affect the integrity of the site, and this effect will not be removed by conditions, they must not grant planning permission except in the following closely defined circumstances. They must first be satisfied that there are no **alternative solutions**. They should consider whether there are or are likely to be suitable and available sites which are reasonable alternatives for the proposed development, or different, practicable approaches which would have a lesser impact. They should bear in mind the advice of English Nature. In their own interests applicants should demonstrate that they have fully considered alternative solutions.

---

[1] See also para. C7 regarding potential SPAs, candidate SACs, and Ramsar sites.

CONSIDERATION OF DEVELOPMENT PROPOSALS AFFECTING SPAs AND SACS

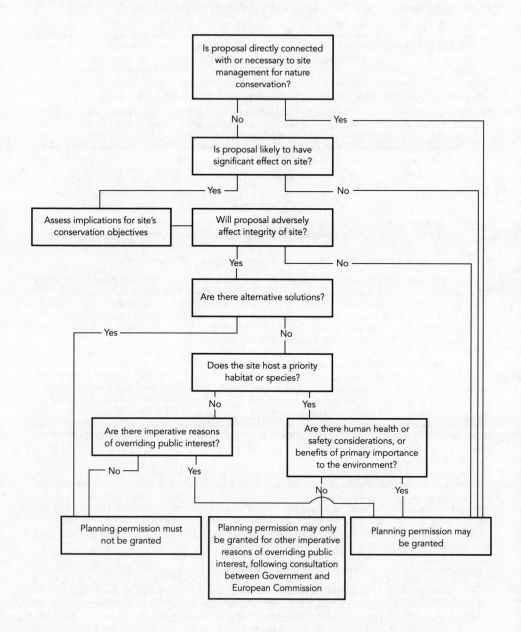

If there is no alternative solution, and the site does not host a priority natural habitat type or species defined in the Habitats Directive,[1] planning permission must not be granted unless the proposed development has to be carried out **for imperative reasons of overriding public interest,** including those of a social or economic nature. Such reasons would need to be sufficient to override the ecological importance of the designation.[2]

If the site hosts a priority habitat or species, and there is no alternative solution, the only considerations which can justify the grant of planning permission are those which relate to human health, public safety, or beneficial consequences of primary importance to the environment (unless the European Commission is of the opinion that there are other imperative reasons of overriding public interest—any such consultation with the Commission must be carried out by the Government).

This process is represented in the flow chart opposite.

If planning permission is granted for a development which would adversely affect the integrity of an SPA or SAC, regulation 53[3] requires the Secretary of State to secure that any necessary compensatory measures are taken to ensure that the overall coherence of the Community-wide network of SPAs and SACs known as Natura 2000 is protected.

Local authority and Crown development affecting SPAs and SACs

C11. Applications made by local planning authorities, or for the development of their land, are now subject to normal planning procedures (with some modifications). The Government has announced its intention to end Crown exemption from planning laws, with certain exceptions including trunk road and motorway development, which is subject to separate procedures designed to produce the same effect as planning legislation. Regulation 69[4] achieves the same result for trunk road or motorway construction or improvement projects carried out by the Secretary of State under the Highways Act 1980 as the Regulations do for development requiring planning permission. Pending legislation altering Crown exemption, local planning authorities will continue to be consulted about proposals for Crown development under the procedures in DOE Circular 18/84. Where such proposals are likely to affect a site of international importance, authorities should apply the same tests in framing their advice as under the Habitats Regulations. The Secretaries of State will do likewise in deciding whether planning clearance should be given for proposals which are the subject of unresolved objections from a local planning authority.

Permitted Development Rights, SPAs and SACs

C12. Article 3 of the Town and Country Planning General Development Order (GDO) grants a general planning permission (subject to specified conditions and limitations) for the types of development set out in Schedule 2 to the GDO. These permitted development rights largely apply to developments which are uncontentious, and which, if they required individual consideration, would place an unnecessary burden on householders or other developers and on local planning authorities. Other permitted development rights relate to developments which are controlled through other approval procedures, and to developments by statutory undertakers and local authorities in the performance of their statutory duties.

C13. Regulations 60–63[5] ensure that any permission granted under the GDO is not in breach of the terms of the Habitats Directive. They prevent any development which is likely significantly to affect a classified SPA, or a site which the Government and the European Commission have agreed as a site to be designated as an SAC (see paragraph 13 of this PPG), or a designated SAC from benefiting from permitted development rights unless the local planning authority have decided, after consulting English Nature, that it would not adversely affect the integrity of the site.

C14. The flow chart at page 430 explains the process developers should follow to find out whether the particular development they propose would benefit from a permitted development right. It identifies the role of the local planning authority and English Nature.[6] Additional information is given in the box following paragraph c. 16.

---

[1] Priority habitats and species are indicated by an asterisk in Annexes I and II of the Habitats Directive. The citation saying why the site was designated will show whether it hosts a priority habitat or species.

[2] Reg. 52(4) requires a "competent authority", other than the Secretary of State, in determining whether to agree on grounds of overriding public interest, to seek and have regard to the views of any other competent authorities involved.

[3] P. 363 above.

[4] P. 373 above.

[5] P. 370 above.

[6] This process does not remove the responsibilities of owners and occupiers or developers to undertake other consultations with English Nature under other legislation, for example s. 28 of the Wildlife and Countryside Act 1981 (as amended). However, consultees may send single notification, covering one or more consultation procedures, so long as these separate procedures are made clear in the notice.

PERMITTED DEVELOPMENT RIGHTS, SPAs AND SACs

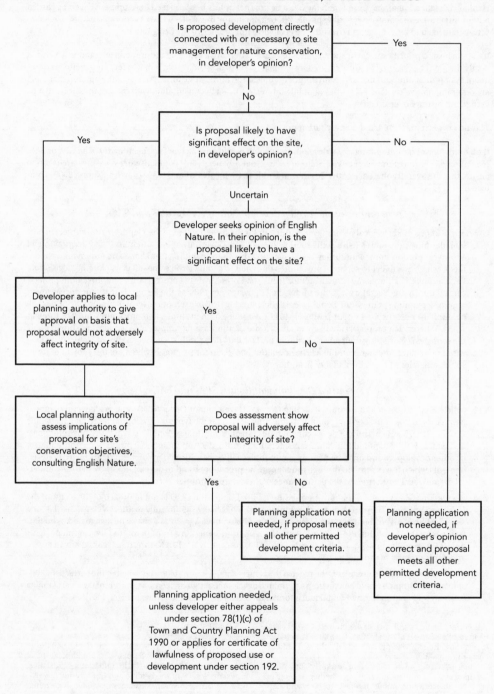

C15. The local planning authority would enter the process at the point where either the developer or English Nature decided that the proposal would be likely to have a significant effect on the site. If the developer wished to pursue the proposal further, the local planning authority would undertake an assessment of the implications of the proposal for the site's conservation objectives. After consulting English Nature, the local planning authority would decide whether or not the proposal would adversely affect the integrity of the site. If the authority concluded that it would have such an effect and the developer wished to proceed a planning application would be required. Regulation 63(2) provides for a fee to be paid to the local planning authority for undertaking this assessment. Advice on significant effect, appropriate assessment and site integrity is contained in the box after paragraph C10.

C16. English Nature will respond within 21 days from the receipt of all information necessary to enable them to form an opinion, both to requests from:

a developer for their opinion as to whether a development is likely to have a significant effect on a site; and

a local planning authority for advice about whether a development will adversely affect the integrity of a site.

If the information provided is inadequate or incomplete, English Nature will advise what additional information they need.

PERMITTED DEVELOPMENT RIGHTS AND THE DEVELOPER

Developers should bear in mind that if they proceed with a development in or near an SPA or SAC on the assumption that it benefits from a permitted development right, without first checking whether it is likely to have a significant effect on the site, they run the risk of undertaking the project without the benefit of planning permission and being liable to enforcement proceedings.

If developers are uncertain whether their proposal is likely to have a significant effect on the site, they should seek an opinion from English Nature, through the appropriate local office (see Annex H). There is no charge for this. Developers should provide the following information:

(a) A short description of the proposed development or works showing:

  (i) their broad purpose;
 (ii) their physical extent, including the area of land or water likely to be covered;
(iii) any residues likely to be produced and proposals for disposal, and any emissions to air, water, soil, and by noise, vibration, heat, light or radiation;
 (iv) the timetable for the proposed development.

(b) A map (or maps) showing the location of the proposed development in relation to the SPA/SAC boundary and the position of all proposed buildings, service access routes and works (whether permanent or temporary).

(c) A description of possible direct or indirect effects (including disturbance) on the wildlife, water quality, hydrology, geological or landform features of the site.

(d) Information about any measures the developer proposes to incorporate into the project to prevent, reduce, ameliorate or offset any landtake, residues or emissions.

To inform their initial consideration about whether to consult English Nature, developers may obtain a copy of the citation giving the reasons for designation or classification from the appropriate local office of English Nature (see Annex H). A copy of the citation is provided to relevant local authorities and to owners and occupiers of a site during the consultation process which precedes designation or classification.

Unauthorised developments affecting SPAs and SACs

C17. Local planning authorities will need to implement specific administrative procedures to prevent, or quickly remedy, any alleged breach of planning control which has, or is likely to have, a significant effect on an SPA or SAC. If a continuing breach of planning control is likely to result in serious long-term harm to a site, the authority should consider the simultaneous service of a stop notice with the related enforcement notice, to prohibit environmentally harmful activity which would otherwise continue for the duration of an enforcement appeal. Where the significant effect on an SPA or SAC appears to result from an alleged breach of a planning condition, it may be more effective to issue an enforcement notice, reinforced by a stop notice, rather than serve a breach of condition notice. This is because a minimum period of 28 days must be allowed for compliance with a breach of condition notice, during which period irremediable harm to the natural habitat may occur. Alternatively, or additionally, the authority may consider submitting an immediate application to the High Court, or County Court, for the grant of an interim planning enforcement injunction while they prepare to take other action to enforce against a breach of control which is having a significant effect on an SPA or SAC. Advice on enforcement is given in PPG18 and DOE Circular 21/91.

ANNEX D

LOCAL AUTHORITY ACTION UNDER THE COUNTRYSIDE ACT 1968

D1. In exercising their functions relating to land under any enactment, local authorities are required by section 11 of the Countryside Act 1968[1] "to have regard to the desirability of conserving the natural beauty and amenity of the countryside". This includes safeguarding wildlife and geologically and physiographically important features. It extends to urban as well as rural areas.

D2. This is a responsibility which local authorities should take seriously and which should be shared with the whole community. Voluntary bodies and the business community may have a particularly important part to play as catalysts to mobilise wider support. Measures which local authorities should consider include:

— the use of local authority byelaws to support local nature conservation objectives;

— the making of tree preservation orders under section 198 of the Town and Country Planning Act 1990;

— the creation of new wildlife habitats through restoration of mineral workings and reclamation of derelict land;

— pond restoration and creation;

— entering into management agreements with owners or occupiers of land (under section 39 of the Wildlife and Countryside Act 1981), and the giving of loans/grants;

— managing local authority land so that account is taken of its wildlife interest, for example in the sympathetic treatment of roadside verges, open spaces and parks and in environmental improvement schemes, both domestic and industrial;

— educational activities, such as the establishment of nature conservation areas in school grounds and the provision of information about conservation.

ANNEX E

CONVENTION ON WETLANDS OF INTERNATIONAL IMPORTANCE ESPECIALLY AS WATERFOWL HABITAT

RAMSAR, 2.2.1971
AS AMENDED BY THE PROTOCOL OF 3.12.1982

The Contracting Parties,

Recognizing the interdependence of Man and his environment;

Considering the fundamental ecological functions of wetlands as regulators of water regimes and as habitats supporting a characteristic flora and fauna, especially waterfowl;

Being convinced that wetlands constitute a resource of great economic, cultural, scientific, and recreational value, the loss of which would be irreparable;

Desiring to stem the progressive encroachment on and loss of wetlands now and in the future;

Recognizing that waterfowl in their seasonal migrations may transcend frontiers and so should be regarded as an international resource;

Being confident that the conservation of wetlands and their flora and fauna can be ensured by combining farsighted national policies with co-ordinated international action;

Have agreed as follows:

Article 1

1. For the purpose of this Convention wetlands are areas of marsh, fen, peatland or water, whether natural or artificial, permanent or temporary, with water that is static or flowing, fresh, brackish or salt, including areas of marine water the depth of which at low tide does not exceed six metres.

---

[1] P. 118 above.

2. For the purpose of this Convention waterfowl are birds ecologically dependent on wetlands.

Article 2

1. Each Contracting Party shall designate suitable wetlands within its territory for inclusion in a List of Wetlands of International Importance, hereinafter referred to as "the list" which is maintained by the bureau established under Article 8. The boundaries of each wetland shall be precisely described and also delimited on a map and they may incorporate riparian and coastal zones adjacent to the wetlands, and islands or bodies of marine water deeper than six metres at low tide lying within the wetlands, especially where these have importance as waterfowl habitat.

2. Wetlands should be selected for the List on account of their international significance in terms of ecology, botany, zoology, limnology or hydrology. In the first instance wetlands of international importance to waterfowl at any season should be included.

3. The inclusion of a wetland in the list does not prejudice the exclusive sovereign rights of the Contracting Party in whose territory the wetland is situated.

4. Each Contracting Party shall designate at lease one wetland to be included in the List when signing this Convention or when depositing its instrument of ratification or accession as provided in Article 9.

5. Any Contracting Party shall have the right to add to the List further wetlands situated within its territory, to extend the boundaries of those wetlands already included by it in the List, or, because of its urgent national interests, to delete or restrict the boundaries of wetlands already included by it in the List and shall, at the earliest possible time, inform the organization or government responsible for the continuing bureau duties specified in Article 8 of any such changes.

6. Each Contracting Party shall consider its international responsibilities for the conservation, management and wise use of migratory stocks of waterfowl, both when designating entries for the List and when exercising its right to change entries in the List relating to wetlands within its territory.

Article 3

1. The Contracting Parties shall formulate and implement their planning so as to promote the conservation of the wetlands included in the List, and as far as possible the wise use of wetlands in their territory.

2. Each Contracting Party shall arrange to be informed at the earliest possible time if the ecological character of any wetland in its territory and included in the List has changed, is changing or is likely to change as the result of technological developments, pollution or other human interference. Information on such changes shall be passed without delay to the organization or government responsible for the continuing bureau duties specified in Article 8.

Article 4

1. Each Contracting Party shall promote the conservation of wetlands and waterfowl by establishing nature reserves on wetlands, whether they are included in the List or not, and provide adequately for their wardening.

2. Where a Contracting Party in its urgent national interest, deletes or restricts the boundaries of a wetland included in the List, it should as far as possible compensate for any loss of wetland resources, and in particular it should create additional nature reserves for waterfowl and for the protection, either in the same area or elsewhere, of an adequate portion of the original habitat.

3. The Contracting Parties shall encourage research and the exchange of data and publications regarding wetlands and their flora and fauna.

4. The Contracting Parties shall endeavour through management to increase waterfowl populations on appropriate wetlands.

5. The Contracting Parties shall promote the training of personnel competent in the fields of wetland research, management and wardening.

Article 5

1. The Contracting Parties shall consult with each other about implementing obligations arising from the Convention especially in the case of a wetland extending over the territories of more than one Contracting Party or where a water system is shared by Contracting Parties. They shall at the same time endeavour to co-ordinate and support present and future policies and regulations concerning the conservation of wetlands and their flora and fauna.

Article 6[1]

1. The Contracting Parties shall, as the necessity arises, convene Conferences on the Conservation of Wetlands and Waterfowl.

2. The Conferences shall have an advisory character and shall be competent, inter alia:

   (*a*) to discuss the implementation of this Convention;

   (*b*) to discuss additions to and changes in the List;

   (*c*) to consider information regarding changes in the ecological character of wetlands included in the List provided in accordance with paragraph 2 of Article 3;

   (*d*) to make general or specific recommendations to the Contracting Parties regarding the conservation, management and wise use of wetlands and their flora and fauna;

   (*e*) to request relevant international bodies to prepare reports and statistics on matters which are essentially international in character affecting wetlands.

3. The Contracting Parties shall ensure that those responsible at all levels for wetlands management shall be informed of, and take into consideration, recommendations of such Conferences concerning the conservation, management and wise use of wetlands and their flora and fauna.

Article 7[1]

1. The representatives of the Contracting Parties at such Conferences should include persons who are experts on wetlands or waterfowl by reason of knowledge and experience gained in scientific, administrative or other appropriate capacities.

2. Each of the Contracting Parties represented at a Conference shall have one vote, recommendations being adopted by a simple majority of the votes cast, provided that not less than half the Contracting Parties cast votes.

Article 8

1. The International Union for Conservation of Nature and Natural Resources shall perform the continuing bureau duties under this Convention until such time as another organization or government is appointed by a majority of two-thirds of all Contracting Parties.

2. The continuing bureau duties shall be, inter alia:

   (*a*) to assist in the convening and organizing of Conferences specified in Article 6;

   (*b*) to maintain the List of Wetlands of International Importance and to be informed by the Contracting Parties of any additions, extensions, deletions or restrictions concerning wetlands included in the List provided in accordance with paragraph 5 of Article 2;

   (*c*) to be informed by the Contracting Parties of any changes in the ecological character of wetlands included in the List provided in accordance with paragraph 2 of Article[3] ;

   (*d*) to forward notification of any alterations to the List, or changes in character of wetlands included therein, to all Contracting Parties and to arrange for these matters to be discussed at the next Conference;

   (*e*) to make known to the Contracting Party concerned, the recommendations of the Conferences in respect of such alterations to the List or of changes in the character of wetlands included therein.

Article 9

1. This Convention shall remain open for signature indefinitely.

2. Any member of the United Nations or of one of the Specialized Agencies or of the International Atomic Energy Agency or Party to the Statute of the International Court of Justice may become a Party to this Convention by:

   (*a*) signature without reservation as to ratification;

   (*b*) signature subject to ratification followed by ratification;

   (*c*) accession.

3. Ratification or accession shall be effected by the deposit of an instrument of ratification or accession with the Director-General of the United Nations Educational, Scientific and Cultural Organization (hereinafter referred to as "the Depositary").

---

[1] These articles have been amended by the Conference of the Parties on 28.5.1987.

Article 10

1. This Convention shall enter into force four months after seven States have become Parties to this Convention in accordance with paragraph 2 of Article 9.

2. Thereafter this Convention shall enter into force for each Contracting Party four months after the day of its signature without reservation as to ratification, or its deposit of an instrument of ratification or accession.

Article 10 bis

1. The Convention may be amended at a meeting of the Contracting Parties convened for that purpose in accordance with this article.

2. Proposals for amendment may be made by any Contracting Party.

3. The text of any proposed amendment and the reasons for it shall be communicated to the organization or government performing the continuing bureau duties under the Convention (hereinafter referred to as "the Bureau") and shall promptly be communicated by the Bureau to all Contracting Parties. Any comments on the text by the Contracting Parties shall be communicated to the Bureau within three months of the date on which the amendments were communicated to the Contracting Parties by the Bureau. The Bureau shall, immediately after the last day for submission of comments, communicate to the Contracting Parties all comments submitted by that day.

4. A meeting of Contracting Parties to consider an amendment communicated in accordance with paragraph 3 shall be convened by the Bureau upon the written request of one third of the Contracting Parties. The Bureau shall consult the Parties concerning the time and venue of the meeting.

5. Amendments shall be adopted by a two-thirds majority of the Contracting Parties present and voting.

6. An amendment adopted shall enter into force for the Contracting Parties which have accepted it on the first day of the fourth month following the date on which two thirds of the Contracting Parties have deposited an instrument of acceptance with the Depositary. For each Contracting Party, which deposits an instrument of acceptance after the date on which two thirds of the Contracting Parties have deposited an instrument of acceptance, the amendment shall enter into force on the first day of the fourth month following the date of the deposit of its instrument of acceptance.

Article 11

1. This Convention shall continue in force for an indefinite period.

2. Any Contracting Party may denounce this Convention after a period of five years from the date on which it entered into force for that Party by giving written notice thereof to the Depository. Denunciation shall take effect four months after the day on which notice thereof is received by the Depository.

Article 12

1. The Depositary shall inform all States that have signed and acceded to this Convention as soon as possible of:

   (*a*) signatures to the Convention;

   (*b*) deposits of instruments of ratification of this Convention;

   (*c*) deposits of instruments of accession to this Convention;

   (*d*) the date of entry into force of this Convention;

   (*e*) notifications of denunciation of this Convention.

2. When this Convention has entered into force, the Depository shall have it registered with the Secretariat of the United Nations in accordance with Article 102 of the Charter.

IN WITNESS WHEREOF, the undersigned, being duly authorized to that effect, have signed this Convention.

DONE at Ramsar this 2nd day of February 1971, in a single original in the English, French, German and Russian languages, all texts being equally authentic which shall be deposited with the Depositary which shall send true copies thereof to all Contracting Parties.

ARTICLES 6 AND 7 OF THE CONVENTION ON WETLANDS OF INTERNATIONAL IMPORTANCE ESPECIALLY AS WATERFOWL HABITAT AS AMENDED BY THE CONFERENCE OF THE PARTIES ON 28.5.1987

(AMENDMENTS ARE REPRODUCED BELOW IN ITALICS)

Article 6

1. *There shall be established a Conference of the Contracting Parties to review and promote the implementation of this Convention. The Bureau referred to in Article 8, paragraph I, shall convene ordinary meetings of the Conference of the Contracting Parties at intervals of not more than three years, unless the Conference decides otherwise, and extraordinary meetings at the written requests of at least one third of the Contracting Parties. Each ordinary meeting of the Conference of the Contracting Parties shall determine the time and venue of the next ordinary meeting.*

2. *The Conference of the Contracting Parties shall be competent:*

   (*a*) to discuss the implementation of this Convention;

   (*b*) to discuss additions to and changes in the List;

   (*c*) to consider information regarding changes in the ecological character of wetlands included in the List provided in accordance with paragraph 2 of Article 3;

   (*d*) to make general or specific recommendations to the Contracting Parties regarding the conservation, management and wise use of wetlands and their flora and fauna;

   (*e*) to request relevant international bodies to prepare reports and statistics on matters which are essentially international in character affecting wetlands;

   (*f*) *to adopt other recommendations, or resolutions, to promote the functioning of this Convention.*

3. The Contracting Parties shall ensure that those responsible at all levels for wetlands management shall be informed of, and take into consideration, recommendations of such Conferences concerning the conservation, management and wise use of wetlands and their flora and fauna.

4. *The Conference of the Contracting Parties shall adopt rules of procedure for each of its meetings.*

5. *The Conference of the Contracting Parties shall establish and keep under review the financial regulations of this Convention. At each of its ordinary meetings, it shall adopt the budget for the next financial period by a two-third majority of Contracting Parties present and voting.*

6. *Each Contracting party shall contribute to the budget according to a scale of contributions adopted by unanimity of the Contracting Parties present and voting at a meeting of the ordinary Conference of the Contracting Parties.*

Article 7

1. The representatives of the Contracting Parties at such Conferences should include persons who are experts on wetlands or waterfowl by reason of knowledge and experience gained in scientific, administrative or other appropriate capacities.

2. *Each of the Contracting Parties represented at a Conference shall have one vote, recommendations, resolutions and decisions being adopted by a simple majority of the Contracting Parties present and voting, unless otherwise provided for in this Convention.*

ANNEX F[1]

COUNCIL DIRECTIVE
OF 2 APRIL 1979 ON THE CONSERVATION OF WILD BIRDS
(79/409/EEC)

THE COUNCIL OF THE EUROPEAN COMMUNITIES

Having regard to the Treaty establishing the European Economic Community, and in particular Article 235 thereof,

Having regard to the proposal from the Commission,[2]

Having regard to the opinion of the European Parliament,[3]

Having regard to the opinion of the Economic and Social Committee,[4]

---

[1] **Case: Birds Directive** *R v Secretary of State for the Environment ex parte Royal Society for the Protection of Birds: House of Lords, 9 February 1995..*

[2] OJ No C 24, 1.2.1977, p. 3; OJ No C 201, 23.8.1977, p. 2.
[3] OJ No C 163, 11.7.1977, p. 28.
[4] OJ No C 152, 29.6.1977, p. 3.

Whereas the Council declaration of 22 November 1973 on the programme of action of the European Communities on the environment[1] calls for specific action to protect birds, supplemented by the resolution of the Council of the European Communities and of the representatives of the Governments of the Member States meeting within the the Council of 17 May 1977 on the continuation and implementation of a European Community policy and action programme on the environment;[2]

Whereas a large number of species of wild birds naturally occurring in the European territory of the Member States are declining in number, very rapidly in some cases; whereas this decline represents a serious threat to the conservation of the natural environment, particularly because of the biological balances threatened thereby;

Whereas the species of wild birds naturally occurring in the European Territory of the Member States are mainly migratory species; whereas such species constitute a common heritage and whereas effective bird protection is typically a trans-frontier environment problem entailing common responsibilities;

Whereas the conditions of life for birds in Greenland are fundamentally different from those in the other regions of the European territory of the Member States on account of the general circumstances and in particular the climate, the low density of population and the exceptional size and geographical situation of the island;

Whereas therefore this Directive should not apply to Greenland;

Whereas the conservation of the species of wild birds naturally occurring in the European territory of the Member States is necessary to attain, within the operation of the common market, of the Community's objectives regarding the improvement of living conditions, a harmonious development of economic activities throughout the Community and a continuous and balanced expansion, but the necessary specific powers to act have not been provided for in the Treaty;

Whereas the measures to be taken must apply to the various factors which may affect the numbers of birds, namely the repercussions of man's activities and in particular the destruction and pollution of their habitats, capture and killing by man and the trade resulting from such practices; whereas the stringency of such measures should be adapted to the particular situation of the various species within the framework of a conservation policy;

Whereas conservation is aimed at the long-term protection and management of natural resources as an integral part of the heritage of the peoples of Europe; whereas it makes it possible to control natural resources and governs their use on the basis of the measures necessary for the maintenance and adjustment of the natural balances between species as far as is reasonably possible;

Whereas the preservation, maintenance or restoration of a sufficient diversity and area of habitats is essential to the conservation of all species of birds; whereas certain species of birds should be the subject of special conservation measures concerning their habitats in order to ensure their survival and reproduction in their area of distribution; whereas such measures must also take account of migratory species and be coordinated with a view to setting up a coherent whole;

Whereas, in order to prevent commercial interests from exerting a possible harmful pressure on exploitation levels it is necessary to impose a general ban on marketing and to restrict all derogation to those species whose biological status so permits, account being taken of the specific conditions obtaining in the different regions;

Whereas, because of their high population level, geographical distribution and reproductive rate in the Community as a whole, certain species may be hunted, which constitutes acceptable exploitation; where certain limits are established and respected, such hunting must be compatible with maintenance of the population of these species at a satisfactory level;

Whereas the various means, devices or methods of large-scale or non-selective capture or killing and hunting with certain forms of transport must be banned because of the excessive pressure which they exert or may exert on the numbers of the species concerned;

Whereas, because of the importance which may be attached to certain specific situations, provision should be made for the possibility of derogations on certain conditions and subject to monitoring by the Commission;

Whereas the conservation of birds and, in particular, migratory birds still presents problems which call for scientific research; whereas such research will also make it possible to assess the effectiveness of the measures taken;

Whereas care should be taken in consultation with the Commission to see that the introduction of any species of wild bird not naturally occurring in the European territory of the Member States does not cause harm to local flora and fauna;

Whereas the Commission will every three years prepare and transmit to the Member States a composite report based on information submitted by the Member States on the application of natural provisions introduced pursuant to this Directive;

---

[1] OJ No C 112, 20.12.1973, p. 40.　　　[2] OJ No C 139, 13.6.1977, p. 1.

Whereas it is necessary to adapt certain Annexes rapidly in the light of technical and scientific progress; whereas, to facilitate the implementation of the measures needed for this purpose, provision should be made for a procedure establishing close cooperation between the Member States and the Commission in a Committee for Adaptation to Technical and Scientific Progress,

HAS ADOPTED THIS DIRECTIVE:

Article 1

1. This Directive relates to the conservation of all species of naturally occurring birds in the wild state in the European territory of the Member States to which the Treaty applies. It covers the protection, management and control of these species and lays down rules for their exploitation.

2. It shall apply to birds, their eggs, nests and habitats.

3. This Directive shall not apply to Greenland.

Article 2

Member States shall take the requisite measures to maintain the population of the species referred to in Article 1 at a level which corresponds in particular to ecological, scientific and cultural requirements, while taking account of economic and recreational requirements, or to adapt the population of these species to that level.

Article 3

1. In the light of the requirements referred to in Article 2, Member States shall take the requisite measures to preserve, maintain or re-establish a sufficient diversity and area of habitats for all the species of birds referred to in Article 1.

2. The preservation, maintenance and re-establishment of biotopes and habitats shall include primarily the following measures:

   (a) creation of protected areas;

   (b) upkeep and management in accordance with the ecological needs of habitats inside and outside the protected zones;

   (c) re-establishment of destroyed biotopes;

   (d) creation of biotopes.

Article 4

1. The species mentioned in Annex I shall be the subject of special conservation measures concerning their habitat in order to ensure their survival and reproduction in their area of distribution.

   In this connection, account shall be taken of:

   (a) species in danger of extinction;

   (b) species vulnerable to specific changes in their habitat;

   (c) species considered rare because of small populations or restricted local distribution;

   (d) other species requiring particular attention for reasons of the specific nature of their habitat.

   Trends and variations in population levels shall be taken into account as a background for evaluations.

   Member States shall classify in particular the most suitable territories in number and size as special protection areas for the conservation of these species, taking into account their protection requirements in the geographical sea and land area where this Directive applies.

2. Member States shall take similar measures for regularly occurring migratory species not listed in Annex I, bearing in mind their need for protection in the geographical sea and land area where this Directive applies, as regards their breeding, moulting and wintering areas and staging posts along their migration routes. To this end, Member States shall pay particular attention to the protection of wetlands and particularly to wetlands of international importance.

3. Member States shall send the Commission all relevant information so that it may take appropriate initiatives with a view to the coordination necessary to ensure that the areas provided for in paragraphs 1 and 2 above form a coherent whole which meets the protection requirements of these species in the geographical sea and land area where this Directive applies.

4. In respect of the protection areas referred to in paragraphs 1 and 2 above, Member States shall take appropriate steps to avoid pollution or deterioration of habitats or any disturbances affecting the birds, in so far as these would be significant having regard to the objectives of this Article. Outside these protection areas, Member States shall also strive to avoid pollution or deterioration of habitats.

Article 5

Without prejudice to Articles 7 and 9, Member States shall take the requisite measures to establish a general system of protection for all species of birds referred to in Article 1, prohibiting in particular:

(a) deliberate killing or capture by any method;

(b) deliberate destruction of, or damage to, their nests and eggs or removal of their nests;

(c) taking their eggs in the wild and keeping these eggs even if empty;

(d) deliberate disturbance of these birds particularly during the period of breeding and rearing, in so far as disturbance would be significant having regard to the objectives of this Directive;

(e) keeping birds of species the hunting and capture of which is prohibited.

Article 6

1. Without prejudice to the provisions of paragraphs 2 and 3, Member States shall prohibit, for all the bird species referred to in Article 1, the sale, transport for sale, keeping for sale and the offering for sale of live or dead birds and of any readily recognisable parts or derivatives of such birds.

2. The activities referred to in paragraph 1 shall not be prohibited in respect of the species referred to in Annex III/1, provided that the birds have been legally killed or captured or otherwise legally acquired.

3. Member States may, for the species listed in Annex III/2, allow within their territory the activities referred to in paragraph 1, making provision for certain restrictions, provided the birds have been legally killed or captured or otherwise legally acquired.

Member States wishing to grant such authorisation shall first of all consult the Commission with a view to examining jointly with the latter whether the marketing of specimens of such species would result or could reasonably be expected to result in the population levels, geographical distribution or reproductive rate of the species being endangered throughout the Community. Should this examination prove that the intended authorisation will, in the view of the Commission, result in any one of the aforementioned species being thus endangered or in the possibility of their being thus endangered, the Commission shall forward a reasoned recommendation to the Member State concerned stating its opposition to the marketing of the species in question. Should the Commission consider that no such risk exists, it will inform the Member State concerned accordingly.

The Commission's recommendation shall be published in the *Official Journal of the European Communities*.

Member States granting authorisation pursuant to this paragraph shall verify at regular intervals that the conditions governing the granting of such authorisation continue to be fulfilled.

4. The Commission shall carry out studies on the biological status of the species listed in Annex III/3 and on the effects of marketing on such status.

It shall submit, at the latest four months before the time limit referred to in Article 18(1) of this Directive, a report and its proposals to the Committee referred to in Article 16, with a view to a decision on the entry of such species in Annex III/2.

Pending this decision, the Member States may apply existing national rules to such species without prejudice to paragraph 3 hereof.

Article 7

1. Owing to their population level, geographical distribution and reproductive rate throughout the Community, the species listed in Annex II may be hunted under national legislation. Member States shall ensure that the hunting of these species does not jeopardise conservation efforts in their distribution area.

2. The species referred to in Annex II/1 may be hunted in the geographical sea and land area where this Directive applies.

3. The species referred to in Annex II/2 may be hunted only in the Member States in respect of which they are indicated.

4. Member States shall ensure that the practice of hunting, including falconry if practised, as carried on in accordance with the national measures in force, complies with the principles of wise use and ecologically balanced

control of the species of birds concerned and that this practice is compatible as regards the population of these species, in particular migratory species, with the measures resulting from Article 2. They shall see in particular that the species to which hunting laws apply are not hunted during the rearing season nor during the various stages of reproduction. In the case of migratory species, they shall see in particular that the species to which hunting regulations apply are not hunted during their period of reproduction or during their return to their rearing grounds. Member States shall send the Commission all relevant information on the practical application of their hunting regulations.

Article 8

1. In respect of the hunting, capture or killing of birds under this Directive, Member States shall prohibit the use of all means, arrangements or methods used for the large-scale or non-selective capture or killing of birds or capable of causing the local disappearing of a species, in particular the use of those listed in Annex IV(*a*).

2. Moreover, Member States shall prohibit any hunting from the modes of transport and under the conditions mentioned in Annex IV(*b*).

Article 9

1. Member States may derogate from the provisions of Articles 5, 6, 7 and 8, where there is no other satisfactory solution, for the following reasons:

   (*a*) — in the interests of public health and safety,

   — in the interests of air safety,

   — to prevent serious damage to crops, livestock, forests, fisheries and water,

   — for the protection of flora and fauna;

   (*b*) for the purposes of research and teaching, of re-population, of re-introduction and for the breeding necessary for these purposes;

   (*c*) to permit, under strictly supervised conditions and on a selective basis, the capture, keeping or other judicious use of certain birds in small numbers.

2. The derogations must specify:

   — the species which are subject to the derogations,

   — the means, arrangements or methods authorised for capture or killing,

   — the conditions of risk and the circumstances of time and place under which such derogations may be granted,

   — the authority empowered to declare that the required conditions obtain and to decide what means, arrangements or methods may be used, within what limits and by whom,

   — the controls which will be carried out.

3. Each year the Member States shall send a report to the Commission on the implementation of this Article.

4. On the basis of the information available to it, and in particular the information communicated to it pursuant to paragraph 3, the Commission shall at all times ensure that the consequences of these derogations are not incompatible with this Directive. It shall take appropriate steps to this end.

Article 10

1. Member States shall encourage research and any work required as a basis for the protection, management and use of the population of all species of bird referred to in Article 1.

2. Particular attention shall be paid to research and work on the subjects listed in Annex V. Member States shall send the Commission any information required to enable it to take appropriate measures for the coordination of the research and work referred to in this Article.

Article 11

Member States shall see that any introduction of species of bird which do not occur naturally in the wild state in the European territory of the Member States does not prejudice the local flora and fauna. In this connection they shall consult the Commission.

Article 12

1. Member States shall forward to the Commission every three years, starting from the date of expiry of the time limit referred to in Article 18(1), a report on the implementation of national provisions taken thereunder.

2. The Commission shall prepare every three years a composite report based on the information referred to in paragraph 1. That part of the draft report covering the information supplied by a Member State shall be forwarded to the authorities of the Member State in question for verification. The final version of the report shall be forwarded to the Member States.

Article 13

Application of the measures taken pursuant to this Directive may not lead to deterioration in the present situation as regards the conservation of species of birds referred to in Article 1.

Article 14

Member States may introduce stricter protective measures than those provided for under this Directive.

Article 15

Such amendments as are necessary for adapting Annexes I and V to this Directive to technical and scientific progress and the amendments referred to in the second paragraph of Article 6(4) shall be adopted in accordance with the procedure laid down in Article 17.

Article 16

1. For the purposes of the amendments referred to in Article 15 of this Directive, a Committee for the Adaptation to Technical and Scientific Progress (hereinafter called "the Committee"), consisting of representatives of the Member States and chaired by a representative of the Commission, is hereby set up.

2. The Committee shall draw up its rules of procedure.

Article 17

1. Where the procedure laid down in this Article is to be followed, matters shall be referred to the Committee by its chairman, either on his own initiative or at the request of the representative of a Member State.

2. The Commission representative shall submit to the Committee a draft of the measures to be taken. The Committee shall deliver its opinion on the draft within a time limit set by the chairman having regard to the urgency of the matter. It shall act by a majority of 41 votes, the votes of the Member States being weighted as provided in Article 148(2) of the Treaty. The Chairman shall not vote.

3. (a) The Commission shall adopt the measures envisaged where they are in accordance with the opinion of the Committee.

   (b) Where the measures envisaged are not in accordance with the opinion of the Committee, or if no opinion is delivered, the Commission shall without delay submit a proposal to the Council concerning the measures to be adopted. The Council shall act by a qualified majority.

   (c) If, within three months of the proposal being submitted to it, the Council has not acted, the proposed measures shall be adopted by the Commission.

Article 18

1. Member States shall bring into force the laws, regulations and administrative provisions necessary to comply with this Directive within two years of its notification. They shall forthwith inform the Commission thereof.

2. Member States shall communicate to the Commission the texts of the main provisions of national law which they adopt in the field governed by this Directive.

Article 19

This Directive is addressed to the Member States.

Done at Luxembourg, 2 April 1979.

ANNEX I [TO THE BIRDS DIRECTIVE]

1. *Gavia stellata*	Red-throated Diver	42. *Pernis apivorus*	Honey Buzzard
2. *Gavia arctica*	Black-throated Diver	43. *Elanus caeruleus*	Black-shouldered Kite
3. *Gavia immer*	Great Northern Diver	44. *Milvus migrans*	Black Kite
4. *Podiceps auritus*	Slavonian Grebe	45. *Milvus milvus*	Red Kite
5. *Pterodroma madeira*	Freira	46. *Haliaeetus albicilla*	White-tailed Eagle
6. *Petrodroma feae*	Gon-gon	47. *Gypaetus barbatus*	Bearded Vulture
7. *Bulweria bulwerii*	Bulwer's Petrel	48. *Neophron percnopterus*	Egyptian Vulture
8. *Calonectris diomedea*	Cory's Shearwater	49. *Gyps fulvus*	Griffon Vulture
9. *Puffinus puffinus mauretanicus*	Manx Shearwater (Balaeric subspecies)	50. *Aegypius monachus*	Black Vulture
10. *Puffinus assimilis*	Little Shearwater	51. *Circaetus gallicus*	Short-toed Eagle
11. *Pelagodroma marina*	Frigate Petrel	52. *Circus aeruginosus*	Marsh Harrier
12. *Hydrobates pelagicus*	Storm Petrel	53. *Circus cyaneus*	Hen Harrier
13. *Oceanodroma leucorhoa*	Leach's Storm-petrel	54. *Circus macrourus*	Pallid Harrier
14. *Oceanodroma castro*	Madeiran Storm-petrel	55. *Circus pygargus*	Montagu's Harrier
15. *Phalacrocorax carbo sinensis*	Commorant (continental subspecies)	56. *Accipiter gentilis arrigonii*	Goshawk (Corsican–Sardinian subspecies)
16. *Phalacrocorax aristotelis desmarestii*	Shag (Mediterranean subspecies)	57. *Accipiter nisus granti*	Sparrowhawk (Canarian–Madeirian subspecies)
17. *Phalacrocorax pygmeus*	Pygmy Cormorant	58. *Accipiter brevipes*	Levant Sparrowhawk
18. *Pelecanus onocrotalus*	White Pelican	59. *Buteo rufinus*	Long-legged Buzzard
19. *Pelecanus crispus*	Dalmatian Pelican	60. *Aquila pomarina*	Lesser Spotted Eagle
20. *Botaurus stellaris*	Bittern	61. *Aquila clanga*	Spotted Eagle
21. *Ixobrychus minutus*	Little Bittern	62. *Aquila heliaca*	Imperial Eagle
22. *Nycticorax nycticorax*	Night Heron	63. *Aquila adalberti*	Spanish Imperial Eagle
23. *Ardeola ralloides*	Squacco Heron	64. *Aquila chrysaetos*	Golden Eagle
24. *Egrett garzetta*	Little Egret	65. *Hieraaetus pennatus*	Booted Eagle
25. *Egretta alba*	Great White Egret	66. *Hieraaetus fasciatus*	Bonelli's Eagle
26. *Ardea purpurea*	Purple Heron	67. *Pandion haliaetus*	Osprey
27. *Ciconia nigra*	Black Stork	68. *Falco naumanni*	Lesser Kestrel
28. *Ciconia ciconia*	White Stork	69. *Falco columbarius*	Merlin
29. *Plegadis falcinellus*	Glossy Ibis	70. *Falco eleonorae*	Eleonora's Falcon
30. *Platalea leucorodia*	Spoonbill	71. *Falco biarmicus*	Lanner Falcon
31. *Phoenicopterus ruber*	Greater Flamingo	72. *Falco peregrinus*	Peregrine
32. *Cygnus bewickii* (*Cygnus columbianus bewickii*)	Bewick's Swan	73. *Bonasa bonasia*	Hazel Grouse
33. *Cygnus cygnus*	Whooper Swan	74. *Lagopus mutus pyrenaicus*	Ptarmigan (Pyrenean subspecies)
34. *Anser albifrons flavirostris*	White-fronted Goose (Greenland subspecies)	75. *Lagopus mutus helveticus*	Ptarmigan (Alpine subspecies)
35. *Anser erythropus*	Lesser White-fronted Goose	76. *Tetrao tetrix tetrix*	Black Grouse (continental subspecies)
36. *Branta leucopsis*	Barnacle Goose	77. *Tetrao urogallus*	Capercaillie
37. *Branta ruficollis*	Red-breasted Goose	78. *Alectoris graeca saxatilis*	Rock Partridge (Alpine subspecies)
38. *Tadoma ferruginea*	Ruddy Shelduck	79. *Alectoris graeca whitaken*	Rock Partridge (Sicilian subspecies)
39. *Marmaronetta angustirostris*	Marbled Teal	80. *Alectoris barbara*	Barbary Partridge
40. *Aythya nyroca*	White-eyed Pochard		
41. *Oxyura leucocephala*	White-headed Duck		

81.	*Perdix perdix italica*	Partridge (Italian subspecies)	121.	*Pterocles alchata*	Pin-tailed Sandgrouse
82.	*Perdix perdix hispaniensis*	Partridge (Iberian subspecies)	122.	*Columba palumbus azorica*	Woodpigeon (Azores subspecies)
83.	*Porzana porzana*	Spotted Crake	123.	*Columba trocaz*	Long-toed Pigeon
84.	*Porzana parva*	Little Crake	124.	*Columba bollii*	Bolle's Laurel Pigeon
85.	*Porzana pusilla*	Baillon's Crake	125.	*Columba junoniae*	Laurel Pigeon
86.	*Crex crex*	Corncrake	126.	*Bubo bubo*	Eagle Owl
87.	*Porphyrio porphyrio*	Purple Gallinule	127.	*Nyctea scandiaca*	Snowy Owl
88.	*Fulica cristata*	Crested Coot	128.	*Glaucidium passerinum*	Pygmy Owl
89.	*Turnix sytvatica*	Andalusian Hemipode	129.	*Asio flammeus*	Short-eared owl
			130.	*Aegolius funereus*	Tengmalm's Owl
90.	*Grus grus*	Crane	131.	*Caprimulgus europaeus*	Nightjar
91.	*Tetrax tetrax*	Little Bustard	132.	*Apus caffer*	White-rumped Swift
92.	*Chlamydotis undulata*	Houbara	133.	*Alcedo atthis*	Kingfisher
93.	*Otis tarda*	Great Bustard	134.	*Coracias garrulus*	Roller
94.	*Himantopus himantopus*	Black-winged Stilt	135.	*Picus canus*	Grey-headed Woodpecker
95.	*Recurvirostra avosetta*	Avocet	136.	*Dryocopus martius*	Black Woodpecker
96.	*Burhinus oedicnemus*	Stone Curlew	137.	*Dendrocopos major canariensis*	Great Spotted Woodpecker (Teneriffe subspecies)
97.	*Cursorius cursor*	Cream-coloured Courser	138.	*Dendrocopos major thanneri*	Great Spotted Woodpecker (Gran Canaria subspecies)
98.	*Glareola pratincola*	Collared Pratincole	139.	*Dendrocopos syriacus*	Syrian Woodpecker
99.	*Charadrius morinellus* (*Eudromias morinellus*)	Dotterel	140.	*Dendrocopos medius*	Middle Spotted Woodpecker
100.	*Pluvialis apricaria*	Golden Plover	141.	*Dendrocopos leucotos*	White-backed Woodpecker
101.	*Hoplopterus spinosus*	Spur-winged Plover			
102.	*Philomachus pugnax*	Ruff	142.	*Picoides tridactylus*	Three-toed Woodpecker
103.	*Gallinago media*	Great Snipe	143.	*Cherosophilius duponti*	Dupont's Lark
104.	*Numenius tenuirostris*	Slender-billed Curlew	144.	*Melanocorypha calandra*	Calandra Lark
105.	*Tringa glareola*	Wood Sandpiper	145.	*Calandrella brachy-dactyla*	Short-toed Lark
106.	*Phalaropus lobatus*	Red-necked Phalarope	146.	*Galerida theklae*	Thekla Lark
			147.	*Lullula arborea*	Woodlark
107.	*Larus melanocephalus*	Mediterranean Gull	148.	*Anthus campestris*	Tawny Pipit
108.	*Larus genei*	Slender-billed Gull	149.	*Troglodytes troglodytes fridanensis*	Wren (Fair Isle subspecies)
109.	*Larus audouinii*	Audouin's Gull			
110.	*Gelochelidon nilotica*	Gull-billed Tern	150.	*Luscinia svecica*	Bluethroat
111.	*Sterna caspia*	Caspian Tern	151.	*Saxicola dacotiae*	Canary Islands Stonechat
112.	*Sterna sandvicensis*	Sandwich Tern	152.	*Oenanthe leucura*	Black Wheatear
113.	*Sterna dougallii*	Roseate Tern	153.	*Acrocephalus melano-pogon*	Moustached Warbler
114.	*Sterna hirundo*	Common Tern			
115.	*Sterna paradisaea*	Arctic Tern	154.	*Acrocephalus paludicola*	Aquatic Warbler
116.	*Sterna albifrons*	Little Tern	155.	*Hippolais olivetorum*	Olive-tree Warbler
117.	*Chlidonias hybridus*	Whiskered Tern	156.	*Sylvia sarda*	Marmora's Warbler
118.	*Chlidonias niger*	Black Tern	157.	*Sylvia undata*	Dartford Warbler
119.	*Uria aalge ibiricus*	Guillemot (Iberian subspecies)	158.	*Sylvia rueppelli*	Rüppell's Warbler
120.	*Pterocles orientalis*	Black-bellied Sandgrouse	159.	*Sylvia nisoria*	Barred Warbler

160.	*Ficedula parva*	Red-breasted Flycatcher
161.	*Ficedula semitorquata*	Semi-collared Flycatcher
162.	*Ficedula albicollis*	Collared Flycatcher
163.	*Sitta krueperi*	Krüper's Nuthatch
164.	*Sitta whiteheadi*	Corsican Nuthatch
165.	*Lanius collurio*	Red-backed Shrike
166.	*Lanius minor*	Lesser Grey Shrike
167.	*Pyrrhocorax pyrrhoco-rax*	Chough
168.	*Fringilla coelebs ombriosa*	Chaffinch (Hierro subspecies)
169.	*Fringilla teydea*	Canary Island Chaffinch
170.	*Loxia scotica*	Scottish Crossbill
171.	*Bucanetes githagineus*	Trumpeter Finch
172.	*Pyrrhula murin*	Azores Bullfinch
173.	*Emberiza cineracea*	Cinereous Bunting
174.	*Emberiza hortulana*	Ortolan Bunting
175.	*Emberiza caesia*	Cretzschmar's Bunting

ANNEX II/1 [TO THE BIRDS DIRECTIVE]

ANSERIFORMES

1.	*Anser fabalis*	Bean goose
2.	*Anser anser*	Greylag goose
3.	*Branta canadensis*	Canada goose
4.	*Anas penelope*	Wigeon
5.	*Anas strepera*	Gadwall
6.	*Anas crecca*	Teal
7.	*Anas platyrhynchus*	Mallard
8.	*Anas acuta*	Pintail
9.	*Anas querquedula*	Garganey
10.	*Anas clypeata*	Shoveler
11.	*Aythya ferina*	Pochard
12.	*Aythya fuligula*	Tufted duck

GALLIFORMES

13.	*Lagopus lagopus scoticus et hibernicus*	Red grouse
14.	*Lagopus mutus*	Ptarmigan
15.	*Alectoris graeca*	Rock partridge
16.	*Alectoris rufa*	Red-legged partridge
17.	*Perdix perdix*	Partridge
18.	*Phasianus colchicus*	Pheasant

GRUIFORMES

| 19. | *Fulica atra* | Coot |

CHARADRIIFORMES

20.	*Lymnocryptes minimus*	Jack snipe
21.	*Gallinago gallinago*	Snipe
22.	*Scolopax rusticola*	Woodcock

COLUMBIFORMES

| 23. | *Columba livia* | Rock dove |
| 24. | *Columba palumbus* | Wood pigeon |

ANNEX II/2 [TO THE BIRDS DIRECTIVE]

25.	*Cygnus olor*	Mute swan
26.	*Anser brachyrhynchus**	Pink-footed goose
27.	*Anser albifrons**	White-fronted goose
28.	*Branta bernicla*	Brent goose
29.	*Netta rufina*	Red-crested pochard
30.	*Aythya marila**	Scaup
31.	*Somateria mollissima*	Eider
32.	*Clangula hyemalis**	Long-tailed duck
33.	*Melanitta nigra**	Common scoter
34.	*Melanitta fusca**	Velvet scoter
35.	*Bucephala clangula**	Golden-eye
36.	*Mergus serrator*	Red-breasted merganser
37.	*Mergus merganser*	Goosander
38.	*Bonasia bonasia (Tetrastes bonasia)*	Hazel hen
39.	*Tetrao tetrix (Lyrurus tetrix)**	Black grouse
40.	*Tetrao urogallus**	Capercaillie
41.	*Alectoris barbara*	Barbary patridge
42.	*Coturnix coturnix*	Quail
43.	*Meleagris gallopavo*	Wild turkey
44.	*Rallus aquaticus*	Water rail
45.	*Gallinula chloropus**	Moorhen
46.	*Haematopus ostralegus*	Oystercatcher
47.	*Pluvialis apricaria**	Golden plover
48.	*Pluvialis squatarola**	Grey plover
49.	*Vanellus vanellus*	Lapwing
50.	*Calidris canutus*	Knot
51.	*Philomachus pugnax*	Ruff Reeve
52.	*Limosa limosa*	Black-tailed godwit
53.	*Limosa lapponica**	Bar-tailed godwit
54.	*Numenius phaeopus**	Whimbrel
55.	*Numenius arquata**	Curlew
56.	*Tringa erythropus*	Spotted redshank

* denotes hunting of the species may be authorised under Article 7(3).

57.	*Tringa totanus**	Redshank	65. *Streptopelia decaoctoa*	Collared turtle dove
58.	*Tringa nebularia*	Greenshank	66. *Streptopeli turtur*	Turtle dove
59.	*Larus ridibundus*	Black-headed gull	67. *Alauda arvensis*	Skylark
60.	*Larus canus*	Common gull	68. *Turdus merula*	Blackbird
61.	*Larus fuscus*	Lesser black-backed gull	69. *Turdus pilaris*	Fieldfare
62.	*Larus argentatus*	Herring gull	70. *Turdus philomelos*	Song-thrush
63.	*Larus marinus*	Greater black-backed gull	71. *Turdus iliacus*	Redwing
64.	*Columba oenas*	Stock dove	72. *Turdus viscivorus*	Mistle-thrush

ANNEX III/1 [TO THE BIRDS DIRECTIVE]

1.	*Anas platyrhynchos*	Mallard	4. *Alectoris barbara*	Barbary Partridge
2.	*Lagopus lagopus scoticus et hibernicus*	Red Grouse	5. *Perdix perdix*	Partridge
			6. *Phasianus colchicus*	Pheasant
3.	*Alectoris rufa*	Red-legged Partridge	7. *Columba palumbus*	Wood Pigeon

ANNEX III/2 [TO THE BIRDS DIRECTIVE]

8.	*Anser albifrons albifrons*	White-fronted Goose (Continental race)	18. *Melanitta nigra*	Common Scoter
			19. *Lagopus mutus*	Ptarmigan
9.	*Anser anser*	Greylag Goose	20. *Tetrao tetrix britannicus*	Black grouse (British population)
10.	*Anas penelope*	Wigeon		
11.	*Anas crecca*	Teal	21. *Tetrao urogallus*	Capercaillie
12.	*Anas acuta*	Pintail	22. *Fulica atra*	Coot
13.	*Anas clypeata*	Shoveler	23. *Pluvialis apricaria*	Golden Plover
14.	*Aythya ferina*	Pochard	24. *Lymnocryptes minimus*	Jack Snipe
15.	*Aythya fuligula*	Tufted Duck	25. *Gallinago gallinago*	Snipe
16.	*Aythya marila*	Scaup	26. *Scolopax rusticola*	Woodcock
17.	*Somateri mollissima*	Eider		

ANNEX IV [TO THE BIRDS DIRECTIVE]

(*a*) — Snares, limes, hooks, live birds which are blind or mutilated used as decoys, tape recorders, electrocuting devices.

— Artificial light sources, mirror, devices for illuminating targets, sighting devices for night shooting comprising an electronic image magnifier or image converter.

— Explosives.

— Nets, traps, poisoned or anaesthetic bait.

— Semi-automatic or automatic weapons with a magazine capable of holding more than two rounds of ammunition.

(*b*) — Aircraft, motor vehicles.

— Boats driven at a speed exceeding five kilometres per hour. On the open sea, Member States may, for safety reasons, authorize the use of motor-boats with a maximum speed of 18 kilometres per hour. Member States shall inform the Commission of any authorizations granted.

ANNEX V [TO THE BIRDS DIRECTIVE]

(*a*) National lists of species in danger of extinction or particularly endangered species, taking into account their geographical distribution.

(*b*) Listing and ecological description of areas particularly important to migratory species on their migratory routes and as wintering and nesting grounds.

(*c*) Listing of data on the population levels of migratory species as shown by ringing.

(*d*) Assessing the influence of methods of taking wild birds on population levels.

(*e*) Developing or refining ecological methods for preventing the type of damage caused by birds.

(*f*) Determining the role of certain species as indicators of pollution.

(*g*) Studying the adverse effect of chemical pollution on population levels of bird species.

ANNEX G

COUNCIL DIRECTIVE 92/43/EEC
OF 21 MAY 1992
ON THE CONSERVATION OF NATURAL HABITATS AND OF WILD FAUNA AND FLORA

THE COUNCIL OF THE EUROPEAN COMMUNITIES

Having regard to the Treaty establishing the European Economic Community, and in particular Article 130s thereof,

Having regard to the proposal from the Commission,[1]

Having regard to the opinion of the European Parliament,[2]

Having regard to the opinion of the Economic and Social Committee,[3]

Whereas the preservation, protection and improvement of the quality of the environment, including the conservation of natural habitats and of wild fauna and flora, are an essential objective of general interest pursued by the Community, as stated in Article 130r of the Treaty;

Whereas the European Community policy and action programme on the environment (1987 to 1992)[4] makes provision for measures regarding the conservation of nature and natural resources;

Whereas, the main aim of this Directive being to promote the maintenance of biodiversity, taking account of economic, social, cultural and regional requirements, this Directive makes a contribution to the general objective of sustainable development; whereas the maintenance of such biodiversity may in certain cases require the maintenance, or indeed the encouragement, of human activities;

Whereas, in the European territory of the Member States, natural habitats are continuing to deteriorate and an increasing number of wild species are seriously threatened; whereas given that the threatened habitats and species form part of the Community's natural heritage and the threats to them are often of a transboundary nature, it is necessary to take measures at Community level in order to conserve them;

Whereas, in view of the threats to certain types of natural habitat and certain species, it is necessary to define them as having priority in order to favour the early implementation of measures to conserve them;

Whereas in order to ensure the restoration or maintenance of natural habitats and species of Community interest at a favourable conservation status, it is necessary to designate special areas of conservation in order to create a coherent European ecological network according to a specified timetable;

Whereas all the areas designated, including those classified now or in the future as special protection areas pursuant to Council Directive 79/409/EEC of 2 April 1979 on the conservation of wild birds,[5] will have to be incorporated into the coherent European ecological network;

Whereas it is appropriate, in each area designated, to implement the necessary measures having regard to the conservation objectives pursued;

Whereas sites eligible for designation as special areas of conservation are proposed by the Member States but whereas a procedure must nevertheless be laid down to allow the designation in exceptional cases of a site which has not been proposed by a Member State but which the Community considers essential for either the maintenance or the survival of a priority natural habitat type or a priority species;

Whereas an appropriate assessment must be made of any plan or programme likely to have a significant effect on the conservation objectives of a site which has been designated or is designated in future;

---

[1] OJ No C 247, 21.9.1988, p. 3; and OJ No C 195, 3.8.1990, p. 1.
[2] OJ No C 75, 20.3.1991, p. 12.
[3] OJ No C 31, 6.2.1991, p. 25.

[4] OJ No C 328, 7.12.1987, p. 1.
[5] OJ No L 103, 25.4.1979, p. 1. Directive at last amended by Directive 91/244/EEC (OJ No L 115, 8.5.1991, p. 41).

Whereas it is recognised that the adoption of measures intended to promote the conservation of priority natural habitats and priority species of Community interest is a common responsibility of all Member States; whereas this may, however, impose an excessive financial burden on certain Member States given, on the one hand, the uneven distribution of such habitats and species throughout the Community and, on the other hand, the fact that the "polluter pays" principle can have only limited application in the special case of nature conservation;

Whereas it is therefore agreed that, in this exceptional case, a contribution by means of Community co-financing should be provided for within the limits of the resources made available under the Community's decisions;

Whereas land-use planning and development policies should encourage the management of features of the landscape which are of major importance for wild fauna and flora;

Whereas a system should be set up for surveillance of the conservation status of the natural habitats and species covered by this Directive;

Whereas a general system of protection is required for certain species of flora and fauna to complement Directive 79/409/EEC; whereas provision should be made for management measures for certain species, if their conservation status so warrants including the prohibition of certain means of capture or killing, whilst providing for the possibility of derogations on certain conditions;

Whereas, with the aim of ensuring that the implementation of this Directive is monitored, the Commission will periodically prepare a composite report based, *inter alia*, on the information sent to it by the Member States regarding the application of national provisions adopted under this Directive;

Whereas the improvement of scientific and technical knowledge is essential for the implementation of this Directive; whereas it is consequently appropriate to encourage the necessary research and scientific work;

Whereas technical and scientific progress mean that it must be possible to adapt the Annexes; whereas a procedure should be established whereby the Council can amend the Annexes;

Whereas a regulatory committee should be set up to assist the Commission in the implementation of this Directive and in particular when decisions on Community co-financing are taken;

Whereas provision should be made for supplementary measures governing the re-introduction of certain native species of fauna and flora and the possible introduction of non-native species;

Whereas education and general information relating to the objectives of this Directive are essential for ensuring its effective implementation,

HAS ADOPTED THIS DIRECTIVE:

DEFINITIONS

Article 1

For the purpose of this Directive:

(a) *conservation* means a series of measures required to maintain or restore the natural habitats and the populations of species of wild fauna and flora at a favourable status as defined in (e) and (i);

(b) *natural habitats* means terrestrial or aquatic areas distinguished by geographic, abiotic and biotic features, whether entirely natural or semi-natural;

(c) *natural habitat types of Community interest* means those which, within the territory referred to in Article 2:

    (i) are in danger of disappearance in their natural range;

    or

    (ii) have a small natural range following their regression or by reason of their intrinsically restricted area;

    or

    (iii) present outstanding examples of typical characteristics of one or more of the five following biogeographical regions: Alpine, Atlantic, Continental, Macaronesian and Mediterranean.

    Such habitat types are listed or may be listed in Annex I;

(d) *priority natural habitat types* means natural habitat types in danger of disappearance, which are present on the territory referred to in Article 2 and for the conservation of which the Community has particular responsibility in view of the proportion of their natural range which falls within the territory referred to in Article 2; these priority natural habitat types are indicated by an asterisk (*) in Annex I;

(e) *conservation status of a natural habitat* means the sum of the influences acting on a natural habitat and its typical species that may affect its long-term natural distribution, structure and functions as well as the long-term survival of its typical species within the territory referred to in Article 2.

The conservation status of a natural habitat will be taken as "favourable" when:

— its natural range and areas it covers within that range are stable or increasing, and

— the species structure and functions which are necessary for its long-term maintenance exist and are likely to continue to exist for the foreseeable future, and

— the conservation status of its typical species is favourable as defined in (*i*);

(*f*)   *habitat of a species* means an environment defined by specific abiotic and biotic factors, in which the species lives at any stage of its biological cycle;

(*g*)   *species of Community interest* means species which, within the territory referred to in Article 2, are:

    (i)   endangered, except those species whose natural range is marginal in that territory and which are not endangered or vulnerable in the western palearctic region; or

    (ii)   vulnerable, i.e. believed likely to move into the endangered category in the near future if the causal factors continue operating; or

    (iii)   rare, i.e. with small populations that are not at present endangered or vulnerable, but are at risk. The species are located within restricted geographical areas or are thinly scattered over a more extensive range; or

    (iv)   endemic and requiring particular attention by reason of the specific nature of their habitat and/or the potential impact of their exploitation on their habitat and/or the potential impact of their exploitation on their conservation status.

Such species are listed or may be listed in Annex II and/or Annex IV or V;

(*h*)   *priority species* means species referred to in (*g*)(i) for the conservation of which the Community has particular responsibility in view of the proportion of their natural range which falls within the territory referred to in Article 2; these priority species are indicated by an asterisk (*) in Annex II;

(*i*)   *conservation status of a species* means the sum of the influences acting on the species concerned that may affect the long-term distribution and abundance of its populations within the territory referred to in Article 2;

The *conservation status* will be taken as "favourable" when:

— population dynamics data on the species concerned indicate that it is maintaining itself on a long-term basis as a viable component of its natural habitats, and

— the natural range of the species is neither being reduced nor is likely to be reduced for the foreseeable future, and

— there is, and will probably continue to be, a sufficiently large habitat to maintain its populations on a long-term basis;

(*j*)   *site* means a geographically defined area whose extent is clearly delineated;

(*k*)   *site of Community importance* means a site which, in the biogeographical region or regions to which it belongs, contributes significantly to the maintenance or restoration at a favourable conservation status of a natural habitat type in Annex I or of a species in Annex II and may also contribute significantly to the coherence of Natura 2000 referred to in Article 3, and/or contributes significantly to the maintenance of biological diversity within the biogeographical region or regions concerned.

For animal species ranging over wide areas, sites of Community importance shall correspond to the places within the natural range of such species which present the physical or biological factors essential to their life and reproduction;

(*l*)   *special area of conservation* means a site of Community importance designated by the Member States through a statutory, administrative and/or contractual act where the necessary conservation measures are applied for the maintenance or restoration, at a favourable conservation status, of the natural habitats and/or the populations of the species for which the site is designated;

(*m*)   *specimen* means any animal or plant, whether alive or dead, of the species listed in Annex IV and Annex V, any part or derivative thereof, as well as any other goods which appear, from an accompanying document, the packaging or a mark or label, or from any other circumstances, to be parts or derivatives of animals or plants of those species;

(*n*)   *the committee* means the committee set up pursuant to Article 20.

Article 2

1.   The aim of this Directive shall be to contribute towards ensuring bio-diversity through the conservation of natural habitats and of wild fauna and flora in the European territory of the Member States to which the Treaty applies.

2. Measures taken pursuant to this Directive shall be designed to maintain or restore, at favourable conservation status, natural habitats and species of wild fauna and flora of Community interest.

3. Measures taken pursuant to this Directive shall take account of economic, social and cultural requirements and regional and local characteristics.

CONSERVATION OF NATURAL HABITATS AND HABITATS OF SPECIES

Article 3

1. A coherent European ecological network of special areas of conservation shall be set up under the title Natura 2000. This network, composed of sites hosting the natural habitat types listed in Annex I and habitats of the species listed in Annex II, shall enable the natural habitat types and the species' habitats concerned to be maintained or, where appropriate, restored at a favourable conservation status in their natural range.

   The Natura 2000 network shall include the special protection areas classified by the Member States pursuant to Directive 79/409/EEC.

2. Each Member State shall contribute to the creation of Natura 2000 in proportion to the representation within its territory of the natural habitat types and the habitats of species referred to in paragraph 1. To that effect each Member State shall designate, in accordance with Article 4, sites as special areas of conservation taking account of the objectives set out in paragraph 1.

3. Where they consider it necessary, Member States shall endeavour to improve the ecological coherence of Natura 2000 by maintaining, and where appropriate developing, features of the landscape which are of major importance for wild fauna and flora, as referred to in Article 10.

Article 4

1. On the basis of the criteria set out in Annex III (Stage 1) and relevant scientific information, each Member State shall propose a list of sites indicating which natural habitat types in Annex I and which species in Annex II that are native to its territory the sites host. For animal species ranging over wide areas these sites shall correspond to the places within the natural range of such species which present the physical or biological factors essential to their life and reproduction. For aquatic species which range over wide areas, such sites will be proposed only where there is a clearly identifiable area representing the physical and biological factors essential to their life and reproduction. Where appropriate, Member States shall propose adaptation of the list in the light of the results of the surveillance referred to in Article 11.

   The list shall be transmitted to the Commission, within three years of the notification of this Directive, together with information on each site. That information shall include a map of the site, its name, location, extent and the data resulting from application of the criteria specified in Annex III (Stage 1) provided in a format established by the Commission in accordance with the procedure laid down in Article 21.

2. On the basis of the criteria set out in Annex III (Stage 2) and in the framework both of each of the five biogeographical regions referred to in Article 1(c)(iii) and of the whole of the territory referred to in Article 2(1), the Commission shall establish, in agreement with each Member State, a draft list of sites of Community importance drawn from the Member States' lists identifying those which host one or more priority natural habitat types or priority species.

   Member States whose sites hosting one or more priority natural habitat types and priority species represent more than 5% of their national territory may, in agreement with the Commission, request that the criteria listed in Annex III (Stage 2) be applied more flexibly in selecting all the sites of Community importance in their territory.

   The list of sites selected as sites of Community importance, identifying those which host one or more priority natural habitat types or priority species, shall be adopted by the Commission in accordance with the procedure laid down in Article 21.

3. The list referred to in paragraph 2 shall be established within six years of the notification of this Directive.

4. Once a site of Community importance has been adopted in accordance with the procedure laid down in paragraph 2, the Member State concerned shall designate that site as a special area of conservation as soon as possible and within six years at most, establishing priorities in the light of the importance of the sites for the maintenance or restoration, at a favourable conservation status, of a natural habitat type in Annex I or a species in Annex II and for the coherence of Natura 2000, and in the light of the threats of degradation or destruction to which those sites are exposed.

5. As soon as a site is placed on the list referred to in the third subparagraph of paragraph 2 it shall be subject to Article 6(2), (3) and (4).

Article 5

1. In exceptional cases where the Commission finds that a national list as referred to in Article 4(1) fails to mention a site hosting a priority natural habitat type or priority species which, on the basis of relevant and reliable scientific information, it considers to be essential for the maintenance of that priority natural habitat type or for the survival of that priority species, a bilateral consultation procedure shall be initiated between that Member State and the Commission for the purpose of comparing the scientific data used by each.

2. If, on expiry of a consultation period not exceeding six months, the dispute remains unresolved, the Commission shall forward to the Council a proposal relating to the selection of the site as a site of Community importance.

3. The Council, acting unanimously, shall take a decision within three months of the date of referral.

4. During the consultation period and pending a Council decision, the site concerned shall be subject to Article 6(2).

Article 6

1. For special areas of conservation, Member States shall establish the necessary conservation measures involving, if need be, appropriate management plans specifically designed for the sites or integrated into other development plans, and appropriate statutory, administrative or contractual measures which correspond to the ecological requirements of the natural habitat types in Annex I and the species in Annex II present on the sites.

2. Member States shall take appropriate steps to avoid, in the special areas of conservation, the deterioration of natural habitats and the habitats of species as well as disturbance of the species for which the areas have been designated, in so far as such disturbance could be significant in relation to the objectives of this Directive.

3. Any plan or project not directly connected with or necessary to the management of the site but likely to have a significant effect thereon, either individually or in combination with other plans or projects, shall be subject to appropriate assessment of its implications for the site in view of the site's conservation objectives. In the light of the conclusions of the assessment of the implications for the site and subject to the provisions of paragraph 4, the competent national authorities shall agree to the plan or project only after having ascertained that it will not adversely affect the integrity of the site concerned and, if appropriate, after having obtained the opinion of the general public.

4. If, in spite of a negative assessment of the implications for the site and in the absence of alternative solutions, a plan or project must nevertheless be carried out for imperative reasons of overriding public interest, including those of a social or economic nature, the Member State shall take all compensatory measures necessary to ensure that the overall coherence of Natura 2000 is protected. It shall inform the Commission of the compensatory measures adopted.

   Whereas the site concerned hosts a priority natural habitat type and/or a priority species, the only considerations which may be raised are those relating to human health or public safety, to beneficial consequences of primary importance for the environment or, further to an opinion from the Commission, to other imperative reasons of overriding public interest.

Article 7

Obligations arising under Article 6(2), (3) and (4) of this Directive shall replace any obligations arising under the first sentence of Article 4(4) of Directive 79/409/EEC in respect of areas classified pursuant to Article 4(1) or similarly recognised under Article 4(2) thereof, as from the date of implementation of this Directive or the date of classification or recognition by a Member State under Directive 79/409/EEC, where the latter date is later.

Article 8

1. In parallel with their proposals for sites eligible for designation as special areas of conservation, hosting priority natural habitat types and/or priority species, the Member States shall send, as appropriate, to the Commission their estimates relating to the Community co-financing which they consider necessary to allow them to meet their obligations pursuant to Article 6(1).

2. In agreement with each of the Member States concerned, the Commission shall identify, for sites of Community importance for which co-financing is sought, those measures essential for the maintenance or re-establishment at a favourable conservation status of the priority natural habitat types and priority species on the sites concerned, as well as the total costs arising from those measures.

3. The Commission, in agreement with the Member States concerned, shall assess the financing, including co-financing, required for the operation of the measures referred to in paragraph 2, taking into account, amongst

other things, the concentration on the Member State's territory of priority natural habitat types and/or priority species and the relative burdens which the required measures entail.

4. According to the assessment referred to in paragraphs 2 and 3, the Commission shall adopt, having regard to the available sources of funding under the relevant Community instruments and according to the procedure set out in Article 21, a prioritised action framework of measures involving co-financing to be taken when the site has been designated under Article 4(4).

5. The measures which have not been retained in the action framework for lack of sufficient resources, as well as those included in the above mentioned action framework which have not received the necessary co-financing or have only been partially co-financed, shall be reconsidered in accordance with the procedure set out in Article 21, in the context of the two-yearly review of the action framework and may, in the meantime, be postponed by the Member States pending such review. This review shall take into account, as appropriate, the new situation of the site concerned.

6. In areas where the measures dependent on co-financing are postponed, Member States shall refrain from any new measures likely to result in deterioration of those areas.

Article 9

The Commission, acting in accordance with the procedure laid down in Article 21, shall periodically review the contribution of Natura 2000 towards achievement of the objectives set out in Article 2 and 3. In this context, a special area of conservation may be considered for declassification where this is warranted by natural developments noted as a result of the surveillance provided for in Article 11.

Article 10

Member States shall endeavour, where they consider it necessary, in their land-use planning and development policies and, in particular, with a view to improving the ecological coherence of the Natura 2000 network, to encourage the management of features of the landscape which are of major importance for wild fauna and flora.

Such features are those which, by virtue of their linear and continuous structure (such as rivers with their banks or the traditional systems for marking field boundaries) or their function as stepping stones (such as ponds or small woods), are essential for the migration, dispersal and genetic exchange of wild species.

Article 11

Member States shall undertake surveillance of the conservation status of the natural habitats and species referred to in Article 2 with particular regard to priority natural habitat types and priority species.

PROTECTION OF SPECIES

Article 12

1. Member States shall take the requisite measures to establish a system of strict protection for the animal species listed in Annex IV(*a*) in their natural range, prohibiting:

   (*a*) all forms of deliberate capture or killing of specimens of these species in the wild;

   (*b*) deliberate disturbance of these species, particularly during the period of breeding, rearing, hibernation and migration;

   (*c*) deliberate destruction or taking of eggs from the wild;

   (*d*) deterioration or destruction of breeding sites or resting places.

2. For the species, Member States shall prohibit the keeping, transport and sale or exchange, and offering for sale or exchange, of specimens taken from the wild, except for those taken legally before this Directive is implemented.

3. The prohibition referred to in paragraph 1(*a*) and (*b*) and paragraph 2 shall apply to all stages of life of the animals to which this Article applies.

4. Member States shall establish a system to monitor the incidental capture and killing of the animal species listed in Annex IV(*a*). In the light of the information gathered, Member States shall take further research or conservation measures as required to ensure that incidental capture and killing does not have a significant negative impact on the species concerned.

Article 13

1. Member States shall take the requisite measures to establish a system of strict protection for the plant species listed in Annex IV(*b*), prohibiting:

   (*a*) the deliberate picking, collecting, cutting, uprooting or destruction of such plants in their natural range in the wild;

   (*b*) the keeping, transport and sale or exchange and offering for sale or exchange of specimens of such species taken in the wild, except for those taken legally before this Directive is implemented.

2. The prohibitions referred to in paragraph 1(*a*) and (*b*) shall apply to all stages of the biological cycle of the plants to which this Article applies.

Article 14

1. If, in the light of the surveillance provided for in Article 11, Member States deem it necessary, they shall take measures to ensure that the taking in the wild of specimens of species of wild fauna and flora listed in Annex V as well as their exploitation is compatible with their being maintained at a favourable conservation status.

2. Where such measures are deemed necessary, they shall include continuation of the surveillance provided for in Article 11. Such measures may also include in particular:

   — regulations regarding access to certain property,

   — temporary or local prohibition of the taking of specimens in the wild and exploitation of certain populations,

   — regulation of the periods and/or methods of taking specimens,

   — application, when specimens are taken, of hunting and fishing rules which take account of the conservation of such populations,

   — establishment of a system of licences for taking specimens or of quotas,

   — regulation of the purchase, sale, offering for sale, keeping for sale or transport for sale of specimens.

   — breeding in captivity of animal species as well as artificial propagation of plant species, under strictly controlled conditions, with a view to reducing the taking of specimens from the wild,

   — assessment of the effect of the measures adopted.

Article 15

In respect of the capture or killing of species of wild fauna listed in Annex V(*a*) and in cases where, in accordance with Article 16, derogations are applied to the taking, capture or killing of species listed in Annex IV(*a*), Member States shall prohibit the use of all indiscriminate means capable of causing local disappearance of, or serious disturbance to, populations of such species, and in particular:

   (*a*) use of the means of capture and killing listed in Annex VI(*a*);

   (*b*) any form of capture and killing from the modes of transport referred to in Annex VI(*b*).

Article 16

1. Provided that there is no satisfactory alternative and the derogation is not detrimental to the maintenance of the populations of the species concerned at a favourable conservation status in their natural range, Member States may derogate from the provisions of Articles 12, 13, 14 and 15(*a*) and (*b*):

   (*a*) in the interest of protecting wild fauna and flora and conserving natural habitats;

   (*b*) to prevent serious damage, in particular to crops, livestock, forests, fisheries and water and other types of property;

   (*c*) in the interests of public health and public safety, or for other imperative reasons of overriding public interest, including those of a social or economic nature and beneficial consequences of primary importance for the environment;

   (*d*) for the purpose of research and education, of repopulating and re-introducing these species and for the breeding operations necessary for these purposes, including the artificial propagation of plants;

   (*e*) to allow, under strictly supervised conditions, on a selective basis and to a limited extent, the taking or keeping of certain specimens of the species listed in Annex IV in limited numbers specified by the competent national authorities.

2. Member States shall forward to the Commission every two years a report in accordance with the format established by the Committee on the derogations applied under paragraph 1. The Commission shall give its opinion on these derogations within a maximum time limit of 12 months following receipt of the report and shall give an account to the Committee.

3. The report shall specify:

   (a) the species which are subject to the derogations and the reason for the derogation, including the nature of the risk, with, if appropriate, a reference to alternatives rejected and scientific data used;

   (b) the means, devices or methods authorised for the capture or killing of animal species and the reasons for their use;

   (c) the circumstances of when and where such derogations are granted;

   (d) the authority empowered to declare and check that the required conditions obtain and to decide what means, devices or methods may be used, within what limits and by what agencies, and which persons are to carry out the task;

   (e) the supervisory measures used and the results obtained.

INFORMATION

Article 17

1. Every six years from the date of expiry of the period laid down in Article 23, Member States shall draw up a report on the implementation of the measures taken under this Directive. This report shall include in particular information concerning the conservation measures referred to in Article 6(1) as well as evaluation of the impact of those measures on the conservation status of the natural habitat types of Annex I and the species in Annex II and the main results of the surveillance referred to in Article 11. The report, in accordance with the format established by the committee, shall be forwarded to the Commission and made accessible to the public.

2. The Commission shall prepare a composite report based on the reports referred to in paragraph 1. This report shall include an appropriate evaluation of the progress achieved and, in particular, of the contribution of Natura 2000 to the achievement of the objectives set out in Article 3. A draft of the part of the report covering the information supplied by a Member State shall be forwarded to the Member State in question for verification. After submission to the committee, the final version of the report shall be published by the Commission, not later than two years after receipt of the reports referred to in paragraph 1, and shall be forwarded to the Member States, the European Parliament, the Council and the Economic and Social Committee.

3. Member States may mark areas designated under this Directive by means of Community notices designed for that purpose by the committee.

RESEARCH

Article 18

1. Member States and the Commission shall encourage the necessary research and scientific work having regard to the objectives set out in Article 2 and the obligation referred to in Article 11. They shall exchange information for the purposes of proper coordination of research carried out at Member State and at Community level.

2. Particular attention shall be paid to scientific work necessary for the implementation of Articles 4 and 10, and transboundary cooperative research between Member States shall be encouraged.

PROCEDURE FOR AMENDING THE ANNEXES

Article 19

Such amendments as are necessary for adapting Annexes I, II, III, V and VI to technical and scientific progress shall be adopted by the Council acting by qualified majority on a proposal from the Commission.

Such amendments as are necessary for adapting Annex IV to technical and scientific progress shall be adopted by the Council acting unanimously on a proposal from the Commission.

COMMITTEE

Article 20

The Commission shall be assisted by a committee consisting of representatives of the Member States and chaired by a representative of the Commission.

Article 21

1. The representative of the Commission shall submit to the committee a draft of the measures to be taken. The committee shall deliver its opinion on the draft within a time limit which the Chairman may lay down according to the urgency of the matter. The opinion shall be delivered by the majority laid down in Article 148(2) of the Treaty in the case of decisions which the Council is required to adopt on a proposal from the Commission. The votes of the representatives of the Member States within the committee shall be weighted in the manner set out in that Article. The Chairman shall not vote.

2. The Commission shall adopt the measures envisaged if they are in accordance with the opinion of the committee.

   If the measures envisaged are not in accordance with the opinion of the committee, or if no opinion is delivered, the Commission shall, without delay, submit to the Council a proposal relating to the measures to be taken. The Council shall act by a qualified majority.

   If, on the expiry of three months from the date of referral to the Council, the Council has not acted, the proposed measures shall be adopted by the Commission.

SUPPLEMENTARY PROVISIONS

Article 22

In implementing the provisions of this Directive, Member States shall:

(a) study the desirability of re-introducing species in Annex IV, that are native to their territory where this might contribute to their conservation, provided that an investigation, also taking into account experience in other Member States or elsewhere, has established that such re-introduction contributes effectively to re-establishing these species at a favourable conservation status and that it takes place only after proper consultation of the public concerned:

(b) ensure that the deliberate introduction into the wild of any species which is not native to their territory is regulated so as not to prejudice natural habitats within their natural range or the wild native fauna and flora and, if they consider it necessary, prohibit such introduction. The results of the assessment undertaken shall be forwarded to the committee for information;

(c) promote education and general information on the need to protect species of wild fauna and flora and to conserve their habitats and natural habitats.

FINAL PROVISIONS

Article 23

1. Member States shall bring into force the laws, regulations and administrative provisions necessary to comply with this Directive within two years of its notification. They shall forthwith inform the Commission thereof.

2. When Member States adopt such measures, they shall contain a reference to this Directive or be accompanied by such reference on the occasion of their official publication. The methods of making such a reference shall be laid down by the Member States.

3. Member States shall communicate to the Commission the main provisions of national law which they adopt in the field covered by this Directive.

Article 24

This Directive is addressed to the Member States.

Done at Brussels, 21 May 1992.

ANNEX I [TO THE HABITATS DIRECTIVE]

NATURAL HABITAT TYPES OF COMMUNITY INTEREST WHOSE CONSERVATION REQUIRES THE DESIGNATION OF SPECIAL AREAS OF CONSERVATION

Interpretation

Code: The hierarchical classification of habitats produced through the Corine programme[1] (Corine biotopes project) is the reference work for this Annex. Most types of natural habitat quoted are accompanied by the corresponding Corine code listed in the Technical Handbook, Volume 1, pp. 73–109, Corine/Biotope/89/2.2, 19 May 1988, partially updated 14 February 1989.

The sign "×" combining codes indicates associated habitat types, e.g. 35.2 × 64.1—Open grassland with *Corynephorus* and *Agrostis* (35.2), in combination with continental dunes (64.1).

The sign "*" indicates priority habitat types.

COASTAL AND HALOPHYTIC HABITATS

Open sea and tidal areas

11.25	Sandbanks which are slightly covered by sea water all the time
11.34	* Posidonia beds
13.2	Estuaries
14	Mudflats and sandflats not covered by sea-water at low tide
21	* Lagoons
—	Large shallow inlets and bays
—	Reefs
—	Marine "columns" in shallow water made by leaking gases

Sea cliffs and shingle or stony beaches

17.2	Annual vegetation of drift lines
17.3	Perennial vegetation of stony banks
18.21	Vegetated sea cliffs of the Atlantic and Baltic coasts
18.22	Vegetated sea cliffs of the Mediterranean coasts (with endemic *Limonium spp.*)
18.23	Vegetated sea cliffs of the Macaronesian coasts (flora endemic to these coasts)

Atlantic and continental salt marshes and salt meadows

15.11	*Salicornia* and other annuals colonising mud and sand
15.12	Spartina swards (*Spartinion*)
15.13	Atlantic salt meadows (*Glauco-Puccinellietalia*)
15.14	* Continental salt meadows (*Puccinellietalia distantis*)

Mediterranean and thermo-Atlantic salt marshes and salt meadows

15.15	Mediterranean salt meadows (*Juncetalia maritimi*)
15.16	Mediterranean and thermo-Atlantic halophilous scrubs (*Arthrocnemetalia fructicosae*)
15.17	Iberia halo-nitrophilous scrubs (*Pegano-Salsoletea*)

Salt and gypsum continental steppes

15.18	* Salt steppes (*Limonietalia*)
15.19	* Gypsum steppes (*Gypsophiletalia*)

COASTAL SAND DUNES AND CONTINENTAL DUNES

Sea dunes of the Atlantic, North Sea and Baltic coasts

16.211 Embyronic shifting dunes

---

[1] Corine Council Decision 85/338/EEC of 27 June 1985 (OJ No L 176, 6.7.1985, p. 14).

16.212   Shifting dunes along the shoreline with *Ammophila arenaria* (white dunes)
16.221 to 16.227 * Fixed dunes with herbaceous vegetation (grey dunes):
                  16.221 *Galio-Koelerion albescentis*
                  16.222 *Euphorbio-Helichrysion*
                  16.223 *Crucianellion maritimae*
                  16.224 *Euphorbia terracina*
                  16.225 *Mesobromion*
                  16.226 *Trifolio-Gerantietea sanguinei, Galio maritimi-Geranion sanguinei*
                  16.227 *Thero-Airion, Botrychio-Polygaletum, Tuberarion guttatae*
16.23   * Decalcified fixed dunes with *Empetrum nigrum*
16.24   * Eu-atlantic decalcified fixed dunes (*Calluno-Ulicetea*)
16.25   Dunes with *Hyppophae rhamnoides*
16.26   Dunes with *Salix arenaria*
16.29   Wooded dunes of the Atlantic coast
16.31 to 16.35   Humid dune slacks
1.A   Machairs (* Ireland)

Sea dunes of the Mediterranean coast

16.223   *Crucianellion maritimae* fixed beach dunes
16.224   Dunes with *Euphorbia terracina*
16.228   *Malcolmietalia* dune grasslands
16.229   *Brachypodietalia* dune grasslands with annuals
16.27   * Dune juniper thickets (*Juniperus spp.*)
16.28   Dune scleorophyllous scrubs (*Cisto-Lavenduletalia*)
16.29 × 42.8   * Wooded dunes with *Pinus pinea* and/or *Pinus pinaster*

Continental dunes, old and decalcified

64.1 × 31.223 Dry sandy heaths with *Calluna* and *Genista*
64.1 × 31.227 Dry sandy heaths with *Calluna* and *Empetrum nigrum*
64.1 × 35.2   Open grassland with *Corynephorus* and *Agrostis* of continental dunes

FRESHWATER HABITATS

Standing water

22.11 × 22.31   Oligotrophic waters containing very few minerals of Atlantic sandy plains with amphibious vegetation: *Lobelia, Littorelia* and *Isoetes*
22.11 × 22.34   Oligotrophic waters containing very few minerals of West Mediterranean sandy plains with *Isoetes*
22.11 × (22.31 and 22.32) Oligotrophic waters in medio-European and perialpine area with amphibious vegetation: Littorella or Isoetes or annual vegetation on exposed banks (*Nanocyperetalia*)
22.12 × 22.44   Hard oligo-mesotrophic waters with benthic vegetation of chara formations
22.13   Natural eutrophic lakes with *Magnopotamion* or *Hydrocharition*-type vegetation
22.14   Dystrophic lakes
22.34   * Mediterranean temporary ponds
—   * Turloughs (Ireland)

Running water

Sections of water courses with natural or semi-natural dynamics (minor, average and major beds) where the water quality shows no significant deterioration
24.221 and 24.222 Alpine rivers and the herbaceous vegetation along their banks
24.223   Alpine rivers and their ligneous vegetation with *Myricaria germanica*
24.224   Alpine rivers and their ligneous vegetation with *Salix elaegnos*
24.225   Constantly flowing Mediterranean rivers with *Glaucium flavum*
24.4   Floating vegetation of Ranunculus of plain and submountainous rivers
24.52   *Chenopodietum rubri* of submountainous rivers
24.53   Constantly flowing Mediterranean rivers: *Paspalo-Agrostidion* and hanging curtains of Salix and *Populus alba*
—   Intermittently flowing Mediterranean rivers

Temperate heath and scrub

31.11   Northern Atlantic wet heaths with *Erica tetralix*
31.12   * Southern Atlantic wet heaths with *Erica ciliaris* and *Erica tetralix*
31.2   Dry heaths (all subtypes)
31.234   * Dry coastal heaths with *Erica vagans* and *Ulex maritimus*
31.3   * Endemic Macaronesian dry heaths
31.4   Alpine and subalpine heaths
31.5   * Scrub with *Pinus mugo* and *Rhododendron hirsutum* (*Mugo-Rhododenretum hirsuti*)
31.622   Sub-Arctic willow scrub
31.7   Endemic oro-Mediterranean heaths with gorse

Sclerophyllous scrub (Matorral)

Sub-Mediterranean and temperate

31.82   Stable *Buxus sempervirens* formations on calcareous rock slopes (*Berberidion p.*)
31.842   Mountain *Genista purgans* formations
31.88   *Juniperus communis* formations on calcareous heaths or grasslands
31.89   * *Cistus palhinhae* formations on maritime wet heaths (*Junipero-Cistetum palhinhae*)

Mediterranean arborescent matorral

32.131 to 32.135   Juniper formations
32.17   * Matorral with *Zyziphus*
32.18   * Matorral with *Laurus nobilis*

Thermo-Mediterranean and pre-steppe brush

32.216   Laurel thickets
32.217   Low formations of euphorbia close to cliffs
32.22 to 32.26 All types

Phrygana

33.1 *Astragalo-Plantaginetum subulatae phrygana*
33.3 *Sarcopoterium spinosum phrygana*
33.4 Cretan formations (*Euphorbieto-Verbascion*)

Natural and semi-natural grassland formations

Natural grasslands

34.11   * Karstic calcareous grasslands (*Alysso-Sedion albi*)
34.12   * Xeric sand calcareous grasslands (*Koelerion glaucae*)
34.2   Calaminarian grasslands
36.314   Siliceous Pyrenean grasslands with *Festuca eskia*
36.32   Siliceous alpine and boreal grasslands
36.36   Siliceous Festuca *indigesta* Iberian grasslands
36.41 to 36.45 Alpine calcareous grasslands
36.5   Macaronesian mountain grasslands

Semi-natural dry grasslands and scrubland facies

34.31 to 34.34   On calcareous substrates (*Festuco Brometalia*) (*important orchid sites)
34.5   * Pseudo-steppe with grasses and annuals (*Thero-Brachypodietea*)
35.1   * Species-rich *Nardus* grasslands, on siliceous substrates in mountain areas (and sub-mountain areas, in continental Europe)

Sclerophyllous grazed forests (dehesas)

32.11 With *Quercus suber* and/or *Quercus ilex*

Semi-natural tall-herb humid meadows

37.31	Molinia meadows on chalk and clay (*Eu-Molinion*)
37.4	Mediterranean tall-herb and rush meadows (*Molinio-Holoschoenion*)
37.7 and 37.8	Eutrophic tall herbs
—	*Cnidion venosae* meadows liable to flooding

Mesophile grasslands

38.2	Lowland hay meadows (*Alopecurus pratensis, Sanguisorba officinalis*)
38.3	Mountain hay meadows (British types with *Geranium sylvaticum*)

RAISED BOGS AND MIRES AND FENS

Sphagnum acid bogs

51.1	* Active raised bogs
51.2	Degraded raised bogs (still capable of natural regeneration)
52.1 and 52.2	Blanket bog (*active only)
54.5	Transition mires and quaking bogs
54.6	Depressions on peat substrates (*Rhynchosporion*)

Calcareous fens

53.3	* Calcareous fens with *Cladium mariscus* and *Carex davalliana*
54.12	* Petrifying springs with tufa formation (*Cratoneurion*)
54.2	Alkaline fens
54.3	* Alpine pioneer formations of *Caricion bicolorisatrofuscae*

ROCKY HABITATS AND CAVES

Scree

61.1	Siliceous
61.2	Eutric
61.3	Western Mediterranean and alpine thermophilous
61.4	Balkan
61.5	Medio-European siliceous
61.6	* Medio-European calcareous

Chasmophytic vegetation on rocky slopes

62.1 and 62.1A	Calcareous sub-types
62.2	Silicicolous sub-types
62.3	Pioneer vegetation of rock surfaces
62.4	* Limestone pavements

Other rocky habitats

65 Caves not open to the public
— Fields of lava and natural excavations
— Submerged or partly submerged sea caves
— Permanent glaciers

FORESTS

(Sub)natural woodland vegetation comprising native species forming forests of tall trees, with typical undergrowth, and meeting the following criteria: rare or residual, and/or hosting species of Community interest

Forests of temperate Europe

41.11	*Luzulo-Fagetum* beech forests
41.12	Beech forests with Ilex and *Taxus*, rich in epiphytes (*Ilici-Fagion*)
41.13	*Asperulo-Fagetum* beech forests

41.15	Subalpine beech woods with *Acer* and *Rumex arifolius*
41.16	Calcareous beech forest (*Cephalanthero-Fagion*)
41.24	*Stellario-Carpinetum* oak-hornbeam forests
41.26	*Galio-Carpinetum* oak-hornbeam forests
41.4	* *Tilio-Acerion* ravine forests
41.51	Old acidophilous oak woods with *Quercus robur* on sandy plains
41.53	Old oak woods with *Ilex* and *Blechnum* in the British Isles
41.86	*Fraxinus angustifolia* woods
42.51	* Caledonian forest
44.A1 to 44.A4	* Bog woodland
44.3	* Residual alluvial forests (*Alnion glutinosoincanae*)
44.4	Mixed oak–elm–ash forests of great rivers

Mediterranean deciduous forests

41.181	* Apennine beech forests with *Taxus* and *Ilex*
41.184	* Apennine beech forests with *Abies alba* and beech forests with *Abies nebrodensis*
41.6	Galicio-Portuguese oak woods with *Quercus robur* and *Quercus pyrenaica*
41.77	*Quercus faginea* woods (Iberian Peninsula)
41.85	*Quercus trojana* woods (Italy and Greece)
41.9	Chestnut woods
41.1A × 42.17	Hellenic beech forests with *Abies borisii-regis*
41.1B	*Quercus frainetto* woods
42.A1	Cypress forests (*Acero-Cupression*)
44.17	*Salix alba* and *Populus alba* galleries
44.52	Riparian formations on intermittent Mediterranean water courses with *Rhododendron ponticum*, *Salix* and others
44.7	Oriental plane woods (*Platanion orientalis*)
44.8	Thermo-Mediterranean riparian galleries (*Nerio-Tamariceteae*) and south-west Iberian Peninsula riparian galleries (*Securinegion tinctoriae*)

Mediterranean sclerophyllous forests

41.7C	Cretan *Quercus brachyphylla* forests
45.1	*Olea* and *Ceratonia* forests
45.2	*Quercus suber* forests
45.3	*Quercus ilex* forests
45.5	*Quercus macrolepis* forests
45.61 to 45.63	* Macaronesian laurel forests (*Laurus, Ocotea*)
45.7	* Palm groves of *Phoenix*
45.8	Forests of *Ilex aquifolium*

Alpine and subalpine coniferous forests

42.21 to 42.23	Acidophilous forests (*Vaccinio-Piceetea*)
42.31 and 42.32	Alpine forests with larch and *Pinus cembra*
42.4	*Pinus uncinata* forests (*on gypsum or limestone)

Mediterranean mountainous coniferous forest

42.14	* Apennine *Abies alba* and *Picea excelsa* forests
42.19	*Abies pinsapo* forests
42.61 to 42.66	* Mediterranean pine forests with endemic black pines
42.8	Mediterranean pine forests with endemic Mesogean pines, including *Pinus mugo* and *Pinus leucodermis*
42.9	Macaronesian pine forests (endemic)
42.A2 to 42.A5 and 42.A8	* Endemic Mediterranean forests with *Juniperus* spp.
42.A6	* *Tetraclinis articulata* forests (Andalusia)
42.A71 to 42.A73	* *Taxus baccata* woods

ANNEX II [TO THE HABITATS DIRECTIVE]

ANIMAL AND PLANT SPECIES OF COMMUNITY INTEREST WHOSE CONSERVATION REQUIRES THE DESIGNATION OF SPECIAL AREAS OF CONSERVATION

Interpretation

(a) Annex II follows on from Annex I for the establishment of a consistent network of special areas of conservation.

(b) The species listed in this Annex are indicated:

— by the name of the species or subspecies, or

— by the body of species belonging to higher taxon or to a designated part of that taxon.

The abbreviation "spp." after the name of a family or genus designates all the species belonging to that family or genus.

(c) *Symbols*

An asterisk (*) before the name of a species indicates that the species is a priority species.

Most species listed in this Annex are also listed in Annex IV.

Where a species appears in this Annex but does not appear in either Annex IV or Annex V, the species name is followed by the symbol (o); where a species which appears in this Annex also appears in Annex V but does not appear in Annex IV, its name is followed by the symbol (V).

(a) ANIMALS

VERTEBRATES

MAMMALS

INSECTIVORA

Talpidae

* Galemys pyrenaicus

CHIROPTERA

Rhinolophidae

Rhinolophus blasii
Rhinolophus euryale
Rhinolophus ferrumequinum
Rhinolophus hipposideros
Rhinolophus mehelyi

Vespertilionidae

Barbastella barbastellus
Miniopterus schreibersi
Myotis bechsteini
Myotis blythi
Myotis capaccinnii
Myotis dasycneme
Myotis emarginatus
Myotis myotis

RODENTIA

Sciuridae

Spermophilus citellus

Castoridae

Castor fiber

Microtidae

Microtus cabrerae
* Microtus oeconomus arenicola

CARNIVORA

Canidae

* Canis lupus (Spanish populations: only those south of the Duero; Greek populations: only those south of the 39th parallel)

Ursidae

* Ursus arctos

Mustelidae

Lutra lutra
Mustela lutreola

Felidae

Lynx lynx
* Lynx pardina

Phocidae

Halichoerus grypus (V)
* Monachus monachus
Phoca vitulina (V)

ARTIODACTYLA

Cervidae

* Cervus elaphus corsicanus

Bovidae

Capra aegagrus (natural populations)
* Capra pyrenaica pyrenaica
Ovis ammon musimon (natural populations—Corsica and Sardinia)
Rupicapra rupicapra balcanica
* Rupicapra ornata

CETACEA

Tursiops truncatus
Phocoena phocoena

REPTILES

TESTUDINATA

Testudinidae

Testudo hermanni
Testudo graeca
Testudo marginata

Cheloniidae

* Caretta caretta

Emydidae

Emys orbicularis
Mauremys caspica
Mauremys leprosa

SAURIA

Lacertidae

Lacerta monticola
Lacerta schreiberi
Gallotia galloti insulanagae
* Gallotia simonyi
Podarcis lilfordi
Podarcis pityusensis

Scinidae

Chalcides occidentalis

Gekkonidae

Phyllodactylus europaeus

OPHIDIA

Colubridae

Elaphe quatuorlineata
Elaphe situla

Viperidae

* Vipera schweizeri
Vipera ursinii

AMPHIBIANS

CAUDATA

Salamandiidae

Chioglossa lusitanica
Mertensiella luschani
* Salamandra salamandra aurorae
Salamandrina teridigitata
Triturus cristatus

Proteidae

Proteus anguinus

Plethodontidae

Speleomantes ambrosii
Speleomantes flavus
Speleomantes genei

Speleomantes imperialis
Speleomantes supramontes

ANURA

Discoglossidae

Bombina bombina
Bombina variegata
Discoglossus jeaneae
Discoglossus montalentii
Discoglossus sardus
* Alytes muletensis

Ranidae

Rana latastei

Pelobatidae

* Pelobates fuscus insubricus

FISH

PETROMYZONIFORMES

Petromyzonidae

Eudontomyzon spp. (o)
Lampetra fluviatilis (V)
Lampetra planeri (o)
Lethenteron zanandrai (V)
Petromyzon marinus (o)

ACIPENSERIFORMES

Acipenseridae

* Acipenser naccarii
* Acipenser sturio

ATHERINIFORMES

Cyprinodontidae

Aphanius iberus (o)
Aphanius fasciatus (o)
* Valencia hispanica

SALMONIFORMES

Salmonidae

Hucho hucho (natural populations) (V)
Salmo salar (only in fresh water) (V)
Salmo marmoradus (o)
Salmo macrostigma (o)

Coregonidae

* Coregonus oxyrhynchus (anadromous populations in certain sectors of the North Sea)

CYPRINIFORMES

Cyprinidae

Alburnus vulturius (o)
Albrnus albidus (o)
Anaecypris hispanica
Aspius aspius (o)
Barbus plebejus (V)
Barbus meridionalis (V)
Barbus capito (V)
Barbus comiza (V)

Chalcalburnus chalcoides (o)
Chondrostoma soetta (o)
Chrondrostoma polylepis (o)
Chondrostoma genei (o)
Chrondrostoma lusitanicum (o)
Chondrostoma toxostroma (o)

Gobio albipinnatus (o)
Gobio uranoscopus (o)
Iberocypris palaciosi (o)
* Ladigesocypris ghigii (o)
Leuciscus lucomonis (o)
Leuciscus souffia (o)
Phoxinellus spp. (o)
Rutilus pigus (o)
Rutilus rubilio (o)
Rutilus arcasii (o)
Rutilus macrolepidotus (o)
Rutilus lemmingii (o)
Rutilus friesii meidingeri (o)
Rutilus alburnoides (o)
Rhodeus sericeus amarus (o)
Scardinius graecus (o)

Cobitidae

Cobitis conspersa (o)
Cobitis larvata (o)
Cobitis trichonica (o)
Cobitis taenia (o)
Misgurnis fossilis (o)
Sabanejewia aurata (o)

PERCIFORMES

Percidae

Gymnocephalus schraetzer (V)
Zingel spp. [(o) except Zingel asper and Zingel zingel (V)]

Gobiidae

Pomatoschistus canestrini (o)
Padogobius panizzai (o)
Padogobius nigricans (o)

CLUPEIFORMES

Clupeidae

Alosa spp. (V)

SCORPAENIFORMES

Cottidae

Cottus ferruginosus (o)
Cottus petiti (o)
Cottus gobio (o)

SILURIFORMES

Siluridae

Silurus aristotelis (V)

INVERTEBRATES

ARTHROPODS

CRUSTACAE

Decapoda

Austropotamobius pallipes (V)

INSECTA

Coleoptera

Buprestis splendens
* Carabus olympiae
Cerambyx cerdo
Cucujus cinnaberinus
Dytiscus latissimus
Graphoderus bilineatus
Limoniscus violaceus (o)
Lucanus cervus (o)
Morimus funereus (o)
* Osmoderma eremita
* Rosalia alpina

Lepidoptera

* Callimorpha quadripunctata (o)
Coenonympha oedippus
Erebia calcaria
Erebia christi
Eriogaster catax
Euphydryas aurinia (o)
Graellsia isbellae (V)
Hypodryas maturna
Lycaena dispar
Maculinea nausithous
Maculinea teleius
Melanagria arge
Papilio hospiton
Plebicula golgus

Mantodea

Apteromantis aptera

Odonata

Coenagrion hylas (o)
Coenagrion mercuriale (o)
Cordulegaster trinacriae
Gomphus graslinii
Leucorrhina pectoralis
Lindenia tetraphylla
Macromia splendens
Ophiogomphus cecilia
Oxygastra curtisii

Orthoptera

Baetica ustulata

MOLLUSCS

GASTROPODA

Caseolus calculus
Caseolus commixta
Caseolus sphaerula
Discula leacockiana

Discula tabellata
Discus defloratus
Discus guerinianus
Elona quimperiana
Geomalacus maculosus
Geomitra moniziana
Helix subplicata
Leiostyla abbreviata
Leiostyla cassida
Leiostyla corneocostata
Leiostyla gibba
Leiostyla lamellosa
Vertigo angustior (o)
Vertigo genesii (o)
Vertigo geyeri (o)
Vertigo moulinsiana (o)

BIVALVIA

Unionoida

Margaritifera margaritifera (V)
Unio crassus

(b) PLANTS

PTERIDOPHYTA

ASPLENIACEAE

Asplenium jahandiezii (Litard.) Rouy

BLECHNACEAE

Woodwardia radicans (L.) Sm.

DICKSONIACEAE

Culcita macrocarpa C. Presl

DRYOPTERIDACEAE

* Dryopteris corleyi Fraser-Jenk.

HYMENOPHYLLACEAE

Trichomanes speciosum Willd.

ISOETACEAE

Isoetes boryana Durieu
Isoetes malinverniana Ces. & De Not.

MARSILEACEAE

Marsilea batardae Launert
Marsilea quadrifolia L.
Marsilea strigosa Willd.

OPHIOGLOSSACEAE

Botrychium simplex Hitchc.
Ophioglossum polyphyllum A. Braun

GYMNOSPERMAE

PINACEAE

* Abies nebrodensis (Lojac.) Mattei

ANGIOSPERMAE

ALISMATACEA

Caldesia parnassifolia (L.) parl.

Luronium natans (L.) Raf.

AMARYLLIDACEAE

Leucojum nicaeese Ard.
Narcissus asturiensis (Jordan) Pugsley
Narcissus calcicola Mendonça
Narcissus cyclamineus DC.
Narcissus fernandesii G. Pedro
Narcissus humilis (Cav.) Traub
* Narcissus nevadensis Pugsley
Narcissus pseudonarcissus L. subsp. nobilis
   (Haw.) A. Fernandes
Narcissus scaberulus Henriq.
Narcissus triandrus (Salisb.) D. A. Webb subsp.
   capax (Salisb.) D. A. Webb
Narcissus viridiflorus Schousboe

BORAGINACEA

* Anchusa crispa Viv.
* Lithodora nitida (H. Ern) R. Fernandes
Myosotis lusitanica Schuster
Myosotis rehsteineri Wartm.
Myosotis retusifolia R. Afonso
Omphalodes kuzinskyana Willk.
* Omphalodes littoralis Lehm.
Solenanthus albanicus (Degen & al.) Degen &
   Baldacci
* Symphytum cycladense Pawl.

CAMPANULACEAE

Asyneuma giganteum (Boiss.) Bornm.
* Campanula sabatia De Not.
Jasione crispa (Pourret) Samp. subsp.
   serpentinica Pinto da Silva
Jasione lusitanica A. DC.

CARYOPHYLLACEA

* Arenaria nevadensis Boiss. & Reuter
Arenaria provincialis Chater & Halliday
Dianthus cintranus Boiss. & Reuter subsp.
   cintranus Boiss. & Reuter
Dianthus marizii (Samp.) Samp.
Dianthus rupicola Biv.
* Gypsophila papillosa P. Porta
Herniaria algarvica Chaudri
Herniaria berlengiana (Chaudhri) Franco
* Herniaria latfolia Lapeyr. subsp. litardierei gamis
Herniaria maritima Link
Moehringia tommasinii Marches.
Petrocoptis grandiflora Rothm.
Petrocoptis montsicciana O. Bolos & Rivas Mart.
Petrocoptis pseudoviscosa Fernandez Casas
Silene cintrana Rothm.
* Silena hicesiae Brullo & Signorello
Silene hifacensis Rouy ex Willk.
* Silene holzmanii Heldr. ex Boiss.
Silene longicilia (Brot.) Otth.
Silene mariana Pau
* Silene orphanidis Boiss.
* Silene rothmaleri Pinto da Silva
* Silene velutina Pouret ex Loisel.

CHENOPODIAECEAE

* Bassia saxicola (Guss.) A. J. Scott
* Kochia saxicola Guss.
* Salicornia veneta Pignatti & Lausi

CISTACEAE

Cistus palhinhae Ingram
Halimium verticillatum (Brot.) Sennen
Helianthemum alypoides Losa & Rivas Goday
Helianthemum caput-felis Boiss
* Tuberaria major (Willk.) Pinto da Silva & Roseira

COMPOSITAE

* Anthemis glaberrima (Rech. f.) Greuter
* Artemisia granatensis Boiss.
* Aster pyrenaeus Desf. ex DC.
* Aster sorrentinii (Tod) Lojac.
Carduus myriacanthus Salzm. ex DC.
* Centaurea alba L. subsp. heldreichii (Halacsy) Dostal
* Centaurea alba L. subsp. princeps (Boiss. & Heldr.) Gugler
* Centaurea attica Nyman subsp. megarensis (Halacsy & Hayek) Dostal
* Centaurea balearica J. D. Rodriguez
* Centaurea borjae Valdes-Berm. & Rivas Goday
* Centaurea citricolour Font Quer
Centaurea corymbosa Pourett
Centaurea gadorensis G. Bianca
* Centaurea horrida Badaro
* Centaurea kalambakensis Freyn & Sint.
Centaurea kartschiana Scop.
* Centaurea lactiflora Halacsy
Centaurea micrantha Hoffmanns. & Link subsp. herminii (Rouy) Dostal
* Centaurea niederi Heldr.
* Centaurea peucedanifolia Boiss. & Orph.
* Centaurea pinnata Pau
Centaurea pulvinata (G. Bianca) G. Bianca
Centaurea rothmalerana (Arènes) Dostal
Centaurea vicentina Mariz
* Crepis crocifolia Boiss. & Heldr.
Crepis granatensis (Wilk.) B. Bianca & M. Cueto
Erigeron frigidus Boiss. ex DC.
Hymenostemma pseudanthemis (Kunze) Willd.
* Jurinea cyanoides (L.) Reichenb.
* Jurinea fontqueri Cuatrec.
* Lamyropsis microcephala (Moris) Dittrich & Greuter
Leontodon microcephalus (Boiss. ex DC.) Boiss.
Leontodon boryi Boiss.
* Leontodon siculus (Guss.) Finch & Sell
Leuzea longifolia Hoffmanns. & Link
Ligularia sibirica (L.) Cass.
Santolina impressa Hoffmanns. & Link
Santolina semidentata Hoffmanns. & Link
* Senecio elodes Boiss. ex DC.
Senecio nevadensis Boiss. & Reuter

CONVOLVULACEAE

* Convolvulus argyrothamnus Greuter
* Convolvulus Fernandes Pinto da Silva & Teles

CRUCIFERAE

Alyssum pyrenaicum Lapeyr.
Arabis sadina (Samp.) P. Cout.
* Biscutella neustrica Bonnet
Biscutella vincentina (Samp.) Rothm.
Boleum asperum (Pers.) Desvaux
Brassica glabrescens Polidini
Brassica insularis Moris
* Brassica macrocarpa Guss.
Coincya cintrana (P. Cout.) Pinto da Silva
* Coincya rupestris Rouy
* Coronopus navasii Pau
Diplotaxis ibicensis (Pau) Gomez-Campo
* Diplotaxis siettiana Maire
Diplotaxis vicentina (P. Cout.) Rothm.
Erucastrum palustre (Pirona) Vis.
* Iberis arbuscula Runemark
Iberis procumbens Lange subsp. microcarpa Franco & Pinto da Silva
* Ionopsidium acaule (Desf.) Reichenb.
Ionopsidium savianum (Caruel) Ball ex Arcang.
Sisymbrium cavanillesianum Valdes & Castroviejo
Sisymbrium supinum L.

CYPERACEAE

* Carex panormitana Guss.
Eleocharis carniolica Koch

DIOSCOREACEAE

* Borderea chouardii (Gaussen) Heslot

DROSERACEAE

Aldrovanda vesiculosa L.

EUPHORBIACEAE

* Euphorbia margalidiana Kuhbier & Lewejohann
Euphorbia transtagana Boiss.

GENTIANACEAE

* Centaurium rigualii Esteve Cheuca
* Centaurium somedanum Lainz
Gentiana ligustica R. de Vilm. & Chopinet
Gentianella angelica (Pugsley) E. F. Warburg

GERANIACEA

* Erodium astragaloides Boiss. & Reuter
Erodium paularense Fernandez-Gonzalez & Izco
* Erodium rupicola Boiss.

GRAMINEAE

Avenula hackelii (Henriq.) Holub
Bromus grossus Desf. ex DC.
Coleanthus subtilis (Tratt.) Seidl
Festuca brigantina (Markgr.-Dannenb.) Markgr.-Dannenb.
Festuca duriotagana Franco & R. Afonso
Festuca elegans Boiss.
Festuca henriquesii Hack.
Festuca sumilusitanica Franco & R. Afonso
Guadinia hispanica Stace & Tutin

Holcus setiglumis Boiss. & Reuter subsp.
  duriensis Pinto da Silva
Micropyropsis tuberosa Romero—Zarco &
  Cabezudo
Pseudarrhenatherum pallens (Link) J. Holub
Puccinellia pungens (Pau) Paunero
* Stipa austroitalica Martinovsky
* Stipa bavarica Martinovsky & H. Scholz
* Stipa veneta Moraldo

GROSSULARIACEAE
* Ribes sardum Martelli

HYPERICACEAE
* Hypericum aciferum (Greuter) N. K. B. Robson

JUNCACEAE
Juncus valvatus Link

LABIATAE
Dracocephalum austriacum L.
* Micromeria taygetea P. H. Davis
Nepata dirphya (Boiss.) Heldr. ex Halacsy
* Nepeta sphaciotica P. H. Davis
Origanum dictamnus L.
Sideritis incana subsp. glauca (Cav.) Malagarriga
Sideritis javalambrensis Pau
Sideritis serrata Cav. ex Lag.
Teucrium lepicephalum Pau
Teucrium turredanum Losa & Rivas Goday
* Thymus camphoratus Hoffmanns. & Link
Thymus carnosus Boiss.
* Thymus cephalotos L.

LEGUMINOSAE
Anthyllis hystrix Cardona, Contandr. & E. Sierra
* Astragalus algarbiensis Coss. ex Bunge
* Astragalus aquilanus Anzalone
Astragalus centralpinus Braun-Blanquet
* Astragalus maritimus Moris
Astragalus tremolsianus Pau
* Astragalus verrucosus Moris
* Cytisus aeolicus Guss. ex Lindl.
Genista dorycnifolia Font Quer
Genista holopetala (Fleischm. ex Koch) Baldacci
Melilotus segetalis(Brot.) Ser. subsp. fallax Franco
* Ononis hackelii Lange
Trifolium saxatile All.
* Vicia bifoliolata J. D. Rodriguez

LENTIBULARIACEAE
Pinguicula nevadensis (Lindb.) Casper

LILIACEAE
Allium grosii Font Quer
* Androcymbrium rechingeri Greuter
* Asphodelus bento-rainhae P.Silva
Hyancinthoides vincentina (Hoffmanns. & Link)
  Rothm.
* Muscari gussonei (Parl.) Tod.

LINACEAE
* Linum muelleri Moris

LYTHRACEAE
* Lythrum flexuosum Lag.

MALVACEAE
Kosteletzkya pentacarpos (L.) Ledeb.

NAJADACEAE
Najas flexilus (Willd.) Rostk. & W. L. Schmidt

ORCHIDACEAE
* Cephalanthera cucullata Boiss. & Heldr.
Cypripedium calceolus L.
Liparis loeselii (L.) Rich.
* Ophrys lunulata Parl.

PAEONIACEAE
Paeonia cambessedesii (Willk.) Willk.
Paeonia parnassica Tzanoudakis
Paeonia clusii F. C. Stern subsp. rhodia (Stearn)
  Tzanoudakis

PALMAE
Phoenix theophrasti Greuter

PLANTAGINACEAE
Plantago algarbiensis Samp.
Plantago almogravensis Franco

PLUMBAGINACEAE
Armeria berlengensis Daveau
* Armeria helodes Martini & Pold
Armeria negleta Girard
Armeria pseudarmeria (Murray) Mansfeld
* Armeria rouyana Daveau
Armeria soleirolii (Duby) Godron
Armeria velutina Welv. ex Boiss. & Reuter
Limonium dodartii (Girard) O. Kuntze subsp.
  lusitanicum (Daveau) Franco
* Limonium insulare (Beg. & Landi) Arrig. & Diana
Limonium lanceolatum (Hoffmanns. & Link)
  Franco
Limonium multiflorum Erben
* Limonium pseudolaetum Arrig. & Diana
* Limonium strictissimum (Salzmann) Arrig.

POLYGONACEAE
Polygonum praelongum Coode & Cullen
Rumex rupestris Le Gall

PRIMULACEAE
Androsace mathildae Levier
Androsace pyrenaica Lam.
* Primula apennina Widmer
Primula palinuri Petagna
Soldanella villosa Darracq.

RANUNCULACEAE
* Acontium corsicum Gayer
Adonis distorta Ten.
Aquilegia bertolonii Schott
Aquilegia kitaibelii Schott
* Aquilegia pyrenaica D. C. subsp. cazorlensis
  (Heywood) Galiano

* Consolida samia P. H. Davis
Pulsatilla patens (L.) Miller
* Ranunculus weyleri Mares

RESEDACEAE

* Reseda decursiva Fossk.

ROSACEAE

Potentilla delphinensis Gren. & Godron

RUBIACEAE

* Galium lotorale Guss.
* Galium viridiflorum Boiss. & Reuter

SALICACEAE

Salix salvifolia Brot. subsp. australis Franco

SANTALACEAE

Thesium ebracteatum Hayne

SAXIFRAGACEAE

Saxifraga berica (Beguinot) D. A. Webb
Saxifraga florulenta Moretti
Saxifraga hirculus L.
Saxifraga tombeanensis Boiss. ex Engl.

SCROPHULARIAECEAE

Antirrhinum charidemi Lange
Chaenorrhinum serpyllifolium (Lange) Lange
  subsp. lusitanicum R. Fernandes
* Euphrasia genargentea (Feoli) Diana
Euphrasia marchesettii Wettst. ex Marches.
Linaria algarviana Chav.
Linaria coutinhoi Valdés
* Linaria ficalhoana Rouy
Linaria flava (Poiret) Desf.
* Linaria hellenica Turrill
* Linaria ricardoi Cout.
* Linaria tursica B. Valdes & Cabezudo
Linaria tonzigii Lona
Odontites granatensis Boiss.
Verbascum litigosum Samp.
Veronica micrantha Hoffmanns. & Link
* Veronica oetaea L.-A. Gustavson

SELAGINACEAE

* Globularia stygia Orph. ex Boiss.

SOLANACEAE

Atropa baetica Willk.

THYMELAEACEAE

Daphne petraea Leybold
* Daphne rodiguezii Texidor

ULMACEAE

Zeklova albelicea (Lam.) Boiss.

UMBELLIFERAE

* Angelica heterocarpa Lloyd
Angelica palustris (Besser) Hoffm.
* Apium bermejoi Llorens
Apium repens (Jacq.) Lag.

Athamanta cortiana Ferrarini
* Bupleurum capillare Boiss. & Heldr.
* Bupleurum kakiskalae Greuter
Eryngium alpinum L.
* Eryngium vivipartum Gay
* Laserpitium longiradium Boiss.
* Naufraga balearica Constans & Cannon
* Oenanthe conioides Lange
Petagnia saniculifolia Guss.
Rouya polygama (Desf.) Coincy
* Seseli intricatum Boiss.
Thorella verticillatinundata (Thore) Brig.

VALERIANACEAE

Centranthus trinervis (Viv.) Beguinot

VIOLACEAE

* Viola hispida Lam.
Viola jaubertiana Mares & Vigineix

Lower plants

BRYOPHYTA

Bruchia vogesiaca Schwaegr. (o)
* Bryoerythrophyllum machadoanum (Sergio)
  M. Hill (o)
Buxbaumia viridis (Moug. ex Lam. & DC.) Brid.
  ex Moug. & Nestl. (o)
Dichelyma capillaceum (With.) Myr. (o)
Dicranum viride (Sull. & Lesq.) Lindb. (o)
Distichophyllum carinatum Dix. & Nich. (o)
Drepanocladus vernicocus (Mitt.) Warnst. (o)
Jungermannia handelii (Schiffn.) Amak. (o)
Mannia triandra (Scop.) Grolle (o)
* Marsupella profunda Lindb. (o)
Meesia longiseta Hedw. (o)
Nothothylas orbicularis (Schwein.) Sull. (o)
Orthotrichum rogeri Brid. (o)
Petalophyllm ralfsii Nees & Goot. ex Lehm. (o)
Riccia breidleri Jur. ex Steph. (o)
Riella helicophylla (Mont.) Hook. (o)
Scapania massolongi (K. Muell.) K. Muell. (o)
Sphagnum pylaisii Brid. (o)
Tayloria rudolphiana (Gasrov) B. & G. (o)

SPECIES FOR MACARONESIA

PTERIDOPHYTA

HYMENOPHYLLACEAE

Hymenophyllum maderensis Gibby & Lovis

DRYOPTERIDACEAE

* Polystichum drepanum (Sw.) C. Presl.

ISOETACEAE

Isoetes azorica Durieu & Paiva

MARSILIACEAE

* Marsilea azorica Launert & Paiva

ANGIOSPERMAE

ASCLEPIADACEAE

 Caralluma burchardii N. E. Brown
 * Ceropegia chyrsantha Svent.

BORAGINACEAE

 Echium candicans L. fil.
 * Echium gentianoides Webb & Coincy
 Myosotis azorica H. C. Watson
 Myosotis maritima Hochst. in Seub.

CAMPANULACEAE

 * Azorina vidalii (H. C. Watson) Feer
 Musschia aurea (L. f.) DC.
 * Musschia wollastonii Lowe

CAPRIFOLIACEAE

 * Sambucus palmensis Link

CARYOPHYLLACEAE

 Spergularia azorica (Kindb.) Lebel

CELASTRACEAE

 Maytenus umbellata (R. Br.) Mabb.

CHENOPODIACEAE

 Beta patula Ait.

CISTACEA

 Cistus chinamadensis Banares & Romero
 * Helianthemum bystropogophyllum Svent.

COMPOSITAE

 Andryala crithmifolia Ait.
 * Argyranthemum lidii Humphries
 Argyranthemum thalassophylum (Svent.)
  Hump.
 Argyranthemum winterii (Svent.) Humphries
 * Atractylis arbuscula Svent. & Michaelis
 Atractylis preauxiana Schultz.
 Calendula maderensis DC.
 Cheirolophus duranii (Burchard) Holub
 Cheirolophus ghomerytus (Svent.) Holub
 Cheirolophus junonianus (Svent.) Holub
 Cheirolophus massonianus (Lowe) Hansen
 Cirsium latifolium Lowe
 Helichrysum gossypinum Webb
 Helichrysum oligocephala (Svent. & Bzamw.)
 * Lactuca watsoniana Trel.
 * Onopordum nogalessi Svent.
 * Onopordum carduelinum Bolle
 * Pericallis hadrosoma Svent.
 Phagnalon benetti Lowe
 Stemmacantha cynaroides (Chr. Son. in Buch)
  Ditt
 Sventenia bupleuroides Font Quer
 * Tanacetum ptarmiciflorum Webb & Berth

CONVOLVULACEAE

 * Convolvulus caput-medusae Lowe
 * Convolvulus lopez-socasii Svent.
 * Convolvulus massonii A. Dietr.

CRASSULACEAE

 Aeonium gomeraense Praeger
 Aoenium saundersii Bolle
 Aichryson dumosum (Lowe) Praeg.
 Monanthes wildpretti Banares & Scholz
 Sedum brissemoretti Raymond-Hamet

CRUCIFERAE

 * Crambe arborea Webb ex Christ
 Crambe laevigata DC. ex Christ
 * Crambe sventenii R. Petters ex Bramwell & Sund.
 * Parolinia schizogynoides Svent.
 Sinapidendron rupestre (Ait.) Lowe

CYPERACEAE

 Carex malato-belizii Raymond

DIPSACACEAE

 Scabiosa nitens Roemer & J. A. Schultes

ERICACEAE

 Erica scoparia L. subsp. azorica (Hochst.)
  D. A. Webb

EUPHORBIACEAE

 * Euphorbi handiensis Burchard
 Euphorbia lambii Svent.
 Euphorbia stygiana H. C. Watson

GERANIAECEAE

 * Geranium maderense P. F. Yeo

GRAMINEAE

 Deschampsia maderensis (Haeck. & Born.)
 Phalaris maderensis (Menezes) Menezes

LABIATAE

 * Sideritis cystosiphon Svent.
 * Sideritis discolor (Webb ex de Noe) Bolle
 Sideritis infernalis Bolle
 Sideritis marmorea Bolle
 Teucrium abutiloides L'Hér
 Teucrium betonicum L'Hér

LEGUMINOSAE

 * Anagyris latifolia Brouss. ex Willd.
 Anthyllis lemanniana Lowe
 * Dorycnium spectabile Webb & Berthel
 * Lotus azoricus P. W. Ball
 Lotus callis-viridis D. Bramwell & D. H. Davis
 Lotus kunkelii (E. Chueca) D. Bramwell & al.
 * Teline rosmarinifolia Webb & Berthel.
 * Teline salsoloides Arco & Acebes.
 Vicia dennesiana H. C. Watson

LILIACEAE

 * Androcymbium psammophilum Svent.
 Scilla maderensis Menezes
 Semele maderensis Costa

LORANTHACEAE

 Arceuthobium azoricum Wiens & Hawksw

MYRICACEAE

 * Myrica rivas-martinezii Santos.

OLEACEAE

 Jasminum azoricum L.
 Picconia azorica (Tutin) Knobl.

ORCHIDACEAE

 Goodyera macrophyll Lowe

PITTOSPORACEAE

 * Pittosporum coriaceum Dryand. ex Ait.

PLANTAGINACEAE

 Plantago malato-belizii Lawalree

PLUMBAGINACEAE

 * Limonium arborescens (Brouss.) Kuntze
 Limonium dendroides Svent.
 * Limonium spectabile (Svent.) Kunkel &
Sunding]
 * Limonium sventenii Santos & Fernandez Galvan

POLYGONACEAE

 Rumex azoricus Rech. fil.

RHAMNACEAE

 Frangula azorica Tutin

ROSACEAE

 * Bencomia brachystachya Svent.
 Bencomia sphaerocarpa Svent.
 * Chamaemeles coriacea Lindl.
 Dendriopterium pulidoi Svent.
 Marcetella maderensis (Born.) Svent.
 Prunus lusitanica L. subsp. azorica (Mouillef.)
  Franco
 Sorbus maderensis (Lowe) Docle

SANTALACEAE

 Kunkeliella subsucculenta Kammer

SCROPHULARIACEAE

 * Europrasia azorica Wats
 Euphrasia grandiflora Hochst. ex Seub.
 * Isoplexis chalcantha Svent. & O'Shanahan
 Isoplexis isabelliana (Webb & Berthel.) Masferrer
 Odontites holliana (Lowe) Benth.
 Sibthorpia peregrina L.

SELAGINACEAE

 * Globularia ascanii D. Bramwell & Kunkel
 * Globularia sarcophylla Svent.

SOLANACEAE

 * Solanum lidii Sunding

UMBELLIFERAE

 Ammi trifoliatum (H. C. Watson) Trelease
 Bupleurum handiense (Bolle) Kunkel
 Chaerophyllum azoricum Trelease
 Ferula latipinna Santos
 Melanoselinum decipiens (Schrader & Wendl.)
  Hoffm.
 Monizia edulis Lowe
 Oenanthe divaricata (R. Br.) Mabb.
 Sanicula azorica Guthnick ex Seub.

VIOLACEAE

 Viola paradoxa Lowe

Lower plants

BRYOPHYTA

 * Echinodium spinosum (Mitt.) Jur. (o)
 * Thamnobryum fernandesii Sergio (o)

ANNEX III [TO THE DIRECTIVE]

CRITERIA FOR SELECTING SITES ELIGIBLE FOR IDENTIFICATION AS SITES OF COMMUNITY IMPORTANCE AND DESIGNATION
AS SPECIAL AREAS OF CONSERVATION

*Stage 1: Assessment at national level of the relative importance of sites for each natural habitat type
in Annex I and each species in Annex II (including priority natural habitat types and priority species)*

A. *Site assessment criteria for a given natural habitat type in Annex I*

 (a) Degree of representativity of the natural habitat type on the site.

 (b) Area of the site covered by the natural habitat type in relation to the total area covered by that natural habitat type within national territory.

 (c) Degree of conservation of the structure and functions of the natural habitat type concerned and restoration possibilities.

 (d) Global assessment of the value of the site for conservation of the natural habitat type concerned.

B. *Site assessment criteria for a given species in Annex II*

 (a) Size and density of the population of the species present on the site in relation to the populations present within national territory.

 (b) Degree of conservation of the features of the habitat which are important for the species concerned and restoration possibilities.

(c) Degree of isolation of the population present on the site in relation to the natural range of the species.

(d) Global assessment of the value of the site for conservation of the species concerned.

C. On the basis of these criteria, Member States will classify the sites which they propose on the national list as sites eligible for identification as sites of Community importance according to their relative value for the conservation of each natural habitat type in Annex I or each species in Annex II.

D. That list will show the sites containing the priority natural habitat types and priority species selected by the Member States on the basis of the criteria in A and B above.

Stage 2: Assessment of the Community importance of the sites included on the national lists

1. All the sites identified by the Member States in Stage 1 which contain priority natural habitat types and/or species will be considered as sites of Community importance.

2. The assessment of the Community importance of other sites on Member States' lists, i.e. their contribution to maintaining or re-establishing, at a favourable conservation status, a natural habitat in Annex I or a species in Annex II and/or to the coherence of Natura 2000 will take account of the following criteria:

(a) relative value of the site at national level;

(b) geographical situation of the site in relation to migration of species in Annex II and whether it belongs to a continuous ecosystem situated on both sides of one or more internal Community frontiers;

(c) total area of the site;

(d) number of natural habitat types in Annex I and species in Annex II present on the site;

(e) global ecological value of the site for the biogeographical regions concerned and/or for the whole of the territory referred to in Article 2, as regards both the characteristic or unique aspect of its features and the way they are combined.

ANNEX IV [TO THE HABITATS DIRECTIVE]

ANIMAL AND PLANT SPECIES OF COMMUNITY INTEREST IN NEED OF STRICT PROTECTION

The species listed in this Annex are indicated:

— by the name of species or subspecies, or

— by the body of species belonging to a higher taxon or to a designated part of that taxon.

The abbreviation "spp." after the name of a family or genus designates all the species belonging to that family or genus.

(a) ANIMALS

VERTEBRATES

MAMMALS

INSECTIVORA

Erinaceidae

Erinaceus algirus

Soricidae

Crocidura canariensis

Talpidae

Galemys pyrenaicus

MICROCHIROPTERA

All species

RODENTIA

Gliridae

All species except Gilis glis and Eliomys quercinus

Sciuridae

Citellus citellus

Sciurus anomalus

Castoridae

Castor fiber

Cricetidae

Cricetus cricetus

Microtidae

Microtus cabrerae

Microtus oeconomus arenicola

Zapodidae

Sicista betulina

Hystricidae

Hystrix cristata

CARNIVORA

Canidae

Canis lupus (except Spanish populations north of the Duero and Greek populations north of the 39th parallel)

Ursidae

Ursus arctos

Mustelidae

Lutra lutra
Mustela lutreola

Felidae

Felis silvestris
Lynx lynx
Lynx pardina

Phocidae

Monachus monachus

ARTIODACTYLA

Cervidae

Cervus elaphus corsicanus

Bovidae

Capra aegagrus (natural populations)
Capra pyrenaica pyrenaica
Ovis ammon musimon (natural populations—Corsica and Sardinia)
Rupicapra rupicapra balcanica
Rupicapra ornata

CETACEA

All species

REPTILES

TESTUDINATA

Testudinidae

Testudo hermanni
Testudo graeca
Testudo marginata

Cheloniidae

Caretta caretta
Chelonia mydas
Lepidochelys kempii
Eretmochelys imbricata

Dermochelyidae

Dermochelys coriacea

Emydidae

Emys orbicularis
Mauremys caspica
Mauremys leprosa

SAURIA

Lacertidae

Algyroides fitzingeri
Algyroides marchi
Algyroides moreoticus
Algyroides nigropunctatus

Lacerta agilis
Lacerta bedriagae
Lacerta danfordi
Lacerta dugesi
Lacerta graeca
Lacerta horvathi
Lacerta monticola
Lacerta schreiberi
Lacerta trilineata
Lacerta viridis
Gallotia atlantica
Gallotia galloti
Gallotia galloti insulanagae
Gallotia simonyi
Gallotia stehlini
Ophisops elegans
Podarcis erhardii
Podarcis filfolensis
Podarcis hispanica atrata
Podarcis lilfordi
Podarcis melisellensis
Podarcis milensis
Podarcis muralis
Podarcis peloponnesiaca
Podarcis pityusensis
Podarcis sicula
Podarcis taurica
Podarcis tiliguerta
Podarcis wagleriana

Scincidae

Ablepharus kitaibelli
Chalcides bedriagai
Chalcides occidentalis
Chalcides ocellatus
Chalcides sexlineatus
Chalcides viridianus
Ophiomorus punctatissimus

Gekkonidae

Cyrtopodion kotschyi
Phyllodactylus europaeus
Tarentola angustimentalis
Tarentola boettgeri
Tarentola delalandii
Tarentola gomerensis

Agamidae

Stellio stellio

Chamaeleontidae

Chamaeleo chamaeleon

Anguidae

Ophisaurus apodus

OPHIDIA

Colubridae

Coluber caspius
Coluber hippocrepis
Coluber jugularis
Coluber laurenti

Coluber najadum
Coluber nummifer
Coluber viridiflavus
Coronella austriaca
Eirenis modesta
Elaphe longissima
Elaphe quatuorlineata
Elaphe situla
Natrix natrix cetti
Natrix natrix corsa
Natrix tessellata
Telescopus falax

Viperidae

Vipera ammodytes
Vipera schweizeri
Vipera seoanni (except Spanish populations)
Vipera ursinii
Vipera xanthina

Boidae

Eryx jaculus

AMPHIBIANS

CAUDATA

Salamandridae

Chioglossa lusitanica
Euproctus asper
Euproctus montanus
Eupoctus platycephalus
Salamandra atra
Salamandra aurorae
Salamandra lanzai
Salamandra luschani
Salamandrina terdigitata
Triturus carnifex
Triturus cristatus
Triturus italicus
Triturus karelinii
Triturus marmoratus

Proteidae

Proteus anguinus

Plethodontidae

Speleomantes ambrosii
Speleomantes flavus
Speleomantes genei
Speleomantes imperialis
Speleomantes italicus
Speleomantes supramontes

ANURA

Discoglossidae

Bombina bombina
Bombina variegata
Discoglossus galganoi
Discoglossus jeanneae
Discoglossus montalentii
Discoglossus pictus
Discoglossus sardus

Alytes cisternasii
Alytes muletensis
Alytes obstetricans

Ranidae

Rana arvalis
Rana dalmatina
Rana graeca
Rana iberica
Rana italica
Rana latastei
Rana lessonae

Pelobatidae

Pelobates cultripes
Pelobates fuscus
Pelobates syriacus

Bufonidae

Bufo calamita
Bufo viridis

Hylidae

Hyla arborea
Hyla meridionalis
Hyla sarda

FISH

ACIPENSERIFORMES

Acipenseridae

Acipenser naccarii
Acipenser sturio

ATHERINIFORMES

Cyprinodontidae

Valencia hispanica

CYPRINIFORMES

Cyprinidae

Anaecypris hispanica

PERCIFORMES

Percidae

Zingel asper

SALMONIFORMES

Coregonidae

Coregonus oxyrhynchus (anadromous
populations in certain sectors of the North
Sea)

INVERTEBRATES

ARTHROPODS

INSECTA

Coleoptera

Buprestis splendens
Carabus olympiae
Cerambyx cerdo
Cucujus cinnaberinus

Dytiscus latissimus
Graphoderus bilineatus
Osmoderma eremita
Rosalia alpina

Lepidoptera

Apatura metis
Coenonympha hero
Coenonympha oedippus
Erebia calcaria
Erebia christi
Erebia sudetica
Eriogaster catax
Fabriciana elisa
Hypodryas maturna
Hyles hippophaes
Lopinga achine
Lycaena dispar
Maculinea arion
Maculinea nausithous
Maculinea teleius
Melanagria arge
Papilio alexanor
Papilio hospiton
Parnassius apollo
Parnassius mnemosyne
Plebicula golgus
Proserpinus proserpina
Zerynthia polyxena

Mantodea

Apteromantis aptera

Odonata

Aeshna viridis
Cordulegaster trinacriae
Gomphus graslinii
Leucorrhina albifrons
Leucorrhina caudalis
Leucorrhina pectoralis
Lindenia tetraphylla
Macromia splendens
Ophiogomphus cecilia
Oxygastra curtisii
Stylurus flavipes
Sympecma braueri

Orthoptera

Baetica ustulata
Saga pedo

ARACHNIDA

Araneae

Macrothele calpeiana

MOLLUSCS

GASTROPODA

Prosobranchia

Patella feruginea

Stylommatophora

Caseolus calculus
Caseolus commixta
Caseolus sphaerula
Discula leacockiana
Discula tabellata
Discula testudinalis
Discula turricula
Discus defloratus
Discus guerinianus
Elona quimperiana
Geomalacus maculosus
Geomitra moniziana
Helix subplicata
Leiostyla abbreviata
Leiostyla cassida
Leiostyla corneocostata
Leiostyla gibba
Leiostyla lamellosa

BIVALVIA

Anisomyaria

Lithophaga lithophaga
Pinna nobilis

Unionoida

Margaritifera auricularia
Unio crassus

ECHINODERMATA

Echinoidea

Centrostephanus longispinus

(*b*) PLANTS

Annex IV(*b*) contains all the plant species listed in Annex II (*b*)[1] plus those mentioned below.

PTERIDOPHYTA

ASPLENIACEAE

Asplenium hemionitis L.

ANGIOSPERMAE

AGAVACEAE

Dracaena draco (L.) L.

AMARYLLIDACEAE

Narcissus longispathus Pugsley
Narcissus triandrus L.

BERBERIDACEAE

Berberis maderensis Lowe

CAMPANULACEAE

Campanula morettiana Reichenb.
Physoplexis comosa (L.) Schur.

---

[1] Except bryophytes in Annex II(*b*).

CARYOPHYLLACEAE

Moehringia fontqueri Pau

COMPOSITAE

Argyranthemum pinnatifidum (L.f.) Lowe subsp.
   succulentum (Lowe) C. J. Humphries
Helichrysum sibthorpii Rouy
Picris willkommii (Schultz Bip.) Nyman
Santolina elegans Boiss. ex DC.
Senecio caespitosus Brot.
Senecio lagascanus DC. subsp. lusitanicus
   (P. Cout.) Pinto da Silva
Wagenitzia lancifolia (Sieber ex Sprengel) Dostal

CRUCIFERAE

Murbeckiella sousae Rothm.

EUPHORBIACEAE

Euphorbia nevadensis Boiss. & Reuter

GESNERIACEAE

Jankaea heldreichii (Boiss.) Boiss.
Ramonda serbica Pancic

IRIDACEAE

Crocus etruscus Parl.
Iris boissieri Henriq.
Iris marisca Ricci & Colasante

LABIATAE

Rosmarinus tomentosus Huber-Morath & Maire
Teucrium charidemi Sandwith
Thymus capitellatus Hoffmanns. & Link
Thymus villosus L. subsp. villosus L.

LILIACEAE

Androcymbium europeum (Lange) K. Richter
Bellevalia heckelli Freyn
Colchicum corsicum Baker
Colchicum cousturieri Greuter
Fritillaria conica Rix
Fritillaria drenovskii Dogen & Stoy.
Fritillaria gussichiae (Degen & Doerfler) Rix
Fritillaria obliqua Ker-Gawl.
Fritillaria rhodocanakis Orph. ex Baker

Ornithogalum reverchonii Degen & Herv.-Bass.
Scilla beirana Samp.
Scilla odorata Link

ORCHIDACEAE

Ophrys argolica Fleischm.
Orchis scopulorum Simsmerh.
Spiranthes aestivalis (Poiret) L. C. M. Richard

PRIMULACEAE

Androsace cylindrica DC.
Primula glaucescens Moretti
Primula spectabilis Tratt.

RANUNCULACEAE

Aquilegia alpina L.

SAPOTACEAE

Sideroxylon marmulano Banks ex Lowe

SAXIFRAGACEAE

Saxifraga cintrana Kuzinsky ex Willk.
Saxifraga portosanctana Boiss.
Saxifraga presolanensis Engl.
Saxifraga valdensis DC.
Saxifraga vayredana Luizet

SCROPHULARIACEAE

Antirrhinum lopesianum Rothm.
Lindernia procumbens (Krocker) Philcox

SOLANACEAE

Mandragora officinarum L.

THYMELAEACEAE

Thymelaea broterana P. Cout.

UMBELLIFERAE

Bunium brevifolium Lowe

VIOLACEAE

Viola athois W. Becker
Viola cazorlensis Gandoger
Viola delphinantha Boiss.

ANNEX V

ANIMAL AND PLANT SPECIES OF COMMUNITY INTEREST WHOSE TAKING IN THE WILD AND EXPLOITATION MAY BE SUBJECT
TO MANAGEMENT MEASURES

The species listed in this Annex are indicated:

— by the name of the species or subspecies, or

— by the body of species belonging to a higher taxon or to a designated part of that taxon.

The abbreviation "spp." after the name of a family or genus designates all the species belonging to that family or
genus.

(*a*) ANIMALS

VERTEBRATES

MAMMALS

CARNIVORA

Canidae

Canis aureus
Canis lupus (Spanish populations north of the Duera and Greek populations north of the 39th parallel)

Mustelidae

Martes martes
Mustela putorius

Phocidae

All species not mentioned in Annex IV

Viverridae

Genetta genetta
Herpestes ichneumon

DUPLICIDENTATA

Leporidae

Lepus timidus

ARTIODACTYLA

Bovidae

Capra ibex
Capra pyrenaica (except Capra pyrenaica pyrenaica)
Rupicapra rupicapra (except Rupicapra rupicapra balcanica and rupicapra ornata)

AMPHIBIANS

ANURA

Ranidae

Rana esculenta
Rana perezi
Rana ridibunda
Rana temporaria

FISH

PETROMYZONIFORMES

Petromyzonidae

Lampetra fluviatilis
Lethenteron zanandrai

ACIPENSERIFORMES

Acipenseridae

All species not mentioned in Annex IV

SALMONIFORMES

Salmonidae

Thymallus thymallus
Coregonus spp. (except Coregonus oxyrhynchus—

anadromous populations in certain sectors of the North Sea)
Hucho hucho
Salmo salar (only in fresh water)

Cyprinidae

Barbus spp.

PERCIFORMES

Percidae

Gymnocephalus schraetzer
Zingel zingel

CLUPEIFORMES

Clupeidae

Alosa spp.

SILURIFORMES

Siluridae

Silurus aristotelis

INVERTEBRATES

COELENTERATA

CNIDARIA

Corallium rubrum

MOLLUSCA

GASTROPODA—STYLOMMATOPHORA

Helicidae

Helix pomatia

BIVALVIA—UNIONOIDA

Margaritiferidae

Margaritifera margaritifera

Unionidae

Microcondylaea compressa
Unio elongatulus

ANNELIDA

HIRUDINOIDEA—ARHYNCHOBDELLAE

Hirudinidae

Hirundo medicinalis

ARTHROPODA

CRUSTACEA—DECAPODA

Astacidae

Astacus astacus
Austropotamobius pallipes
Austropotamobius torrentium

Scyllaridae

Scyllarides latus

INSECTA–LEPIDOPTERA

Saturniidae

Graellsia isabellae

(b) PLANTS

ALGAE

RHODOPHYTA

CORALLINACEAE

    Lithothamnium coralloides Crouan frat.
Phymatholithon calcareum (Poll.) Adey &
  McKibbin

LICHENES

CLADONIACEAE

    Cladonia L. subgenus Cladina (Nyl.) Vain

BRYOPHYTA

MUSCI

LEUCOBRYACEAE

    Leucobryum glaucum (Hedw.) Angstr.

SPHAGNACEAE

    Sphagnum L. spp. (except Sphagnum pylassi
Brid.)

PTERIDOPHYTA

    Lycopodium spp.

ANGIOSPERMAE

AMARYLLIDACEAE

    Galanthus nivalis L.
Narcissus bulbocodium L.
Narcissus juncifolius Lagasca

COMPOSITAE

    Arnica montana L.
Artemisia eriantha Ten
Artemisia genipi Weber
Doronicum plantagineum L. subsp. tournefortii
  (Rouy) P. Cout.

CRUCIFERAE

    Alyssum pintadasilvae Dudley.
Malcolmia lacera (L.) DC. subsp. graccilima
  (Samp.) Franco
Murbeckiella pinnatifida (Lam.) Rothm. subsp.
  herminii (Rivas-Martinez) Greuter & Burdet

GENTIANACEAE

    Gentiana lutea L.

IRIDACEAE

    Iris lusitanica Ker-Gawler

LABIATAE

    Teucrium salviastrum Schreber subsp.
  salviastrum Schreber

LEGUMINOSAE

    Anthyllis lusitanica Cullen & Pinto da Silva
Dorycnium pentaphyllum Scop. subsp.
  transmontana Franco
Ulex densus Welw. ex Webb.

LILIACEAE

    Lilium rubrum Lmk
Ruscus aculeatus L.

PLUMBAGINACEAE

    Armeria sampaio (Bernis) Nieto Feliner

ROSACEAE

    Rubus genevieri Boreau subsp. herminii (Samp.)
  P. Cout.

SCROPHULARIACEAE

    Anarrhinum longipedicelatum R. Fernandes
Euphrasia mendonçae Samp.
Scrophularia grandiflora DC. subsp. grandiflora
  DC.
Scrophularia berminii Hoffmanns & Link
Scrophularia sublyrata Brot.

COMPOSITAE

    Leuzea rhaponticoides Graells

ANNEX VI [TO THE HABITATS DIRECTIVE]

PROHIBITED METHODS AND MEANS OF CAPTURE AND KILLING AND MODES OF TRANSPORT

(a) Non-selective means

MAMMALS

— Blind or mutilated animals used as live decoys

— Tape recorders

— Electrical and electronic devices capable of killing or
  stunning

— Artificial light sources

— Mirrors and other dazzling devices

— Devices for illuminating targets

— Sighting devices for night shooting comprising an
  electronic image magnifier or image converter

— Explosives

— Nets which are non-selective according to their
  principle or their conditions of use

— Traps which are non-selective according to their
  principle or their conditions of use

— Crossbows

— Poisons and poisoned or anaesthetic bait

— Gassing or smoking out

— Semi-automatic or automatic weapons with a magazine capable of holding more than two rounds of ammunition

FISH

— Poison

— Explosives

(b) *Modes of transport*

— Aircraft

— Moving motor vehicles

ANNEX H

ADDRESSES OF THE JOINT NATURE CONSERVATION COMMITTEE AND ENGLISH NATURE

JOINT NATURE CONSERVATION COMMITTEE

Monkstone House
City Road
Peterborough
Cambridgeshire
PE1 1JY
Tel: 01733 62626

ENGLISH NATURE

SCHA Headquarters
Northminster House
Peterborough
Cambridgeshire PE1 1UA
Tel: 01733 340345

Local Offices

(Northumberland, Tyne and Wear, Cleveland, Durham)
Archbold House
Archbold Terrace
Newcastle upon Tyne NE2 1EG
Tel: 0191 2816316

(Cumbria)
Blackwell
Bowness-on-Windermere
Cumbria LA23 3JR
Tel: 015394 45286

(Berks, Bucks, Oxon)
Foxhold House
Thornfold Road
Crookham Common
Newbury
Berks RG15 8EL
Tel: 01635 268881

(Kent)
The Countryside Management Centre
Coldharbour Farm
Wye
Ashford
Kent TN25 5DB
Tel: 01233 812525

(Avon, Somerset)
Roughmoor
Bishop's Hull
Taunton
Somerset
TA1 5AA
Tel: 01823 283211

(Cheshire, Shropshire, Staffs, West Midlands)
Attingham Park
Shrewsbury
Shropshire SY4 4TW
Tel: 01743 709611

(West Sussex, East Sussex, Surrey)
The Old Candlemakers
West Street
Lewes
East Sussex BN7 2NZ
Tel: 01273 476595

(London)
Room 801
Chancery House
Chancery Lane
London WC2A 1SP
Tel: 0171 831 6922

(Hants, Isle of Wight)
1 Southampton Road
Lyndhurst
Hants SO43 7BU
Tel: 01703 283944

(Wilts)
Prince Maurice Court
Hambleton Avenue
Devizes
Wilts SN10 2RT
Tel: 01380 726344

(Dorset)
Slepe Farm
Arne
Wareham
Dorset BH20 5BN
Tel: 01823 556688

(Devon)
The Old Mill House
37 North Street
Okehampton
Devon EX20 1ER
Tel: 01837 55045

(Cornwall)
Trelissick
Feock
Truro
Cornwall TR3 6QQ
Tel: 01872 865261

(Norfolk)
60 Bracondale
Norwich NR1 2BE
Tel: 01603 620558

(Suffolk)
Norman Tower House
1–2 Crown Street
Bury St Edmunds
Suffolk IP33 1QX
Tel: 01284 762218

(Essex, Herts)
Harbour House
Hythe Quay
Colchester
Essex CO2 8JF
Tel: 01206 796666

(Notts, Leics, Lincs)
The Maltings
Wharf Road
Grantham
Lincs
NG31 6BH
Tel: 01476 68431

(Beds, Cambs, Northants)
Ham Lane House
Ham Lane
Orton Waterville
Peterborough PE2 5UR
Tel: 01733 391100

(Gloucs, Hereford and Worcester)
Masefield House
Wells Road
Malvern Wells
Worcs WR14 4PA
Tel: 01684 560616

(Derbyshire)
Manor Barn
Over Haddon
Bakewell
Derbyshire DE45 1JE
Tel: 01629 815095

(Warwickshire)
10/11 Butchers Row
Banbury
Oxon OX16 8JH
Tel: 01295 257601

(North Yorks, North Humberside)
The Institute for Applied Biology
The University of York
York YO1 5DD
Tel: 01904 432700

(North Yorks–Craven and Richmond only)
Thornborough Hall
Leyburn
North Yorks
DL8 5AB
Tel: 01969 23447

(South Yorks, West Yorks, South Humberside)
44 Bond Street
Wakefield
South Yorks WF1 2QP
Tel: 01924 387010

(Manchester, Merseyside, Lancashire and the Cheshire
districts of Ellesmere Port and Neston, Halton and
Warrington)
Pier House
Wallgate
Wigan
WN3 4AL
Tel: 01942 820342

Scottish Office Circular No. 6/1995

NATURE CONSERVATION: IMPLEMENTATION IN SCOTLAND OF EC DIRECTIVES ON THE CONSERVATION OF NATURAL HABITATS AND OF WILD FLORA AND FAUNA AND THE CONSERVATION OF WILD BIRDS.
THE HABITATS AND BIRDS DIRECTIVES

The Chief Executive, Regional, Islands and District Councils
Chief Constables
Director, River Purification Boards
Director, Central Scotland Water Development Board
Chief Executive, Scottish Natural Heritage
Chief Executive/Managing Director, New Town
Development Corporations
Clerk, District Salmon Fishery Boards
Secretary, Harbour and Port Authorities
Secretary, Lighthouse Authorities
Secretary, Scottish Power plc
Secretary, Scottish Hydro-Electric plc

6 March 1995

CONTENTS

NATURE CONSERVATION: IMPLEMENTATION IN SCOTLAND OF EC DIRECTIVES ON THE CONSERVATION OF NATURAL HABITATS AND OF WILD FLORA AND FAUNA AND THE CONSERVATION OF WILD BIRDS ("THE HABITATS AND BIRDS DIRECTIVES")

Introduction

1. This Circular provides advice on the implementation in Scotland of Directive 92/43/EEC on the Conservation of Natural Habitats and of Wild Flora and Fauna (the Habitats Directive) and further guidance on Directive 79/409/EEC on the Conservation of Wild Birds (the Birds Directive), with particular reference to the Conservation (Natural Habitats &c) Regulations 1994 (the Habitats

Regulations). Circular SDD 1/1988 is hereby cancelled. Circular Env 13/1991 is supplemented and reinforced by this Circular and paragraph 10 is now superseded. Circular Env 1/1993 gives guidance on the aims, functions and organisation of Scottish Natural Heritage (SNH) which has a key advisory and executive role in the implementation of the UK's EC and other international nature conservation obligations.

2. The Circular is addressed to a wide range of public authorities the exercise of whose functions will be immediately or potentially affected by the Regulations. Copies of the Circular are also being sent to a wide range of public bodies and statutory undertakers upon whose activities the Regulations will have an immediate impact or are likely to have an impact in future as implementation of the Directives progresses. Chief Constables will wish to note in particular the changes to species' protection legislation and the range of new statutory offences introduced by the Habitats Regulations.

3. The Habitats Regulations came into effect on 30 October 1994[1]. The Regulations are made under the European Communities Act 1972 and they cover Scotland, England and Wales. Copies of the Regulations (SI 1994/2716) are available from HMSO price £8.70.

The purpose of the regulations

4. These Regulations transpose the Habitats Directive into GB law. They apply to sites that will be designated as Special Areas of Conservation (SACs) under the Habitats Directive and to sites classified as Special Protection Areas (SPAs) under the Birds Directive. These are referred to collectively in the Regulations as European sites. The network of sites across the European Community will be known as Natura 2000. The Regulations also introduce some technical measures which supplement the species provisions of the Wildlife and Countryside Act 1981.

The Habitats Directive

5. The Habitats Directive aims to contribute to the conservation of biodiversity by requiring Member States to take measures designed to maintain or restore certain natural habitats and wild species at a favourable conservation status in the Community, giving effect to both site and species protection objectives. The Directive transposes the Bern Convention on European Wildlife and Natural Habitats into Community law. Article 7 modifies the Birds Directive in relation to the protection of SPAs. The Directive is reproduced as *Annex A*.[2]

The Birds Directive

6. The Birds Directive applies to birds, their eggs, nests and habitats. It provides for the protection, management and control of all species of naturally occurring wild birds in the European territory of Member States (Article 1); requires Member States to take sufficient measures to preserve a sufficient diversity of habitats for all species of wild birds naturally occurring within their territories (Articles 2 and 3) in order to maintain populations at ecologically and scientifically sound levels, and requires Member States to take special measures to conserve the habitat of certain particularly rare species and of migratory species (Article 4). The Directive is reproduced as *Annex B*.[3]

Key general duties and obligations

7. The Habitats Regulations set out some key general duties and obligations:

- duties are placed on the Secretary of State and Scottish Natural Heritage (SNH) to exercise their nature conservation functions to secure compliance with the requirements of the Habitats Directive (Regulation 3(2));

- Ministers and all relevant public authorities are required to exercise their functions relevant to *marine conservation* so as to secure compliance with the requirements of the Habitats Directive (Regulation 3(3));

---

[1] The Regulations are set out at p. 333 above.
[2] As the Directive is also annexed to PPG9, it is not set out at Annex A. The Directive is at Annex G to PPG9, p. 446 above.

[3] As the Directive is also annexed to PPG9, it is not set out at Annex A. The Directive is at Annex F to PPG9, p. 436 above.

- Ministers and all relevant public authorities are required in the exercise of any of their functions to have regard to the requirements of the Habitats Directive (Regulation 3(4));

- public authorities are obliged not to permit developments or operations damaging to an interest to be protected within a European site, unless there are imperative reasons of overriding public interest;

- public authorities such as local authorities and river purification boards are obliged to review existing planning permissions which have not yet been implemented and analogous consents, and to modify or revoke them if their effect would be damaging to the conservation interests of European sites.

Site selection and designation

8. There are currently some 140 classified and potential SPAs in Scotland, covering approximately 6% of Scotland's land area. So far 42 of these have been classified, totalling around 70,000 hectares. A list of classified SPAs and potential SPAs is attached as *Annex C*. Where a site lies within more than one authority it is shown against each. The statutory nature conservation agencies (in Scotland SNH) are currently reviewing the list of potential SPAs and any changes to the existing list will be notified to local authorities and other bodies with an interest. SPAs are classified by the Secretary of State following consultations with owners and occupiers and other local interests which are carried out on his behalf by SNH. The Government is committed to completing the programme of SPA classifications required by the Birds Directive as quickly as practicable.

9. SACs are to be selected in accordance with the scientific criteria laid down in the Habitats Directive. Article 2(3) states that measures taken pursuant to the Directive shall take account of economic, social and cultural requirements and regional and local characteristics. The Government will initiate consultations shortly with owners and occupiers and other interests on a list of sites which might qualify for SAC designation prior to submitting a draft list of sites to the European Commission. A definitive list of sites is to be agreed with the Commission by 1998 and all these sites are to be designated by 2004.

Protection of SAC and SPA interests

10. The Habitats Directive applies a common protection regime to SACs and SPAs. Article 6(2) of the Directive requires Member States to:

"take appropriate steps to avoid [in European sites] the deterioration of natural habitats and the habitats of species as well as disturbance of the species for which the sites have been designated, in so far as such disturbance could be significant in relation to the objectives of the Directive."

Any plan or project likely to have a significant effect on a European site and which is not directly connected with or necessary to the management of that site must undergo an appropriate assessment as required by Article 6(3) of the Directive. The Directive further requires that plans or projects that would adversely affect the integrity of the site may go ahead only under certain circumstances, set out in the next paragraph. The scope and content of what constitutes an appropriate assessment will depend on the location, size and significance of the plan or project. For further guidance on this and on significant effect and site integrity see *Annex D Appendix A*.

11. The circumstances referred to in paragraph 10 are:

11.1 that there are no alternative solutions; and

11.2 that there are imperative reasons of overriding public interest, including, for sites not hosting a priority habitat type and/or a priority species, those of a social or economic nature.

If the site concerned hosts a priority natural habitat type and/or a priority species (as defined in Article 1 of the Habitats Directive), the only considerations which may be taken into account are those relating to human health or public safety, to beneficial consequences of primary importance for the environment or, further to an opinion from the Commission, to other imperative reasons of overriding public interest.

12. The Directive's requirement is to protect the interest for which a European site has been designated. Thus the need for appropriate assessment extends to plans or projects *outwith* the boundary of the site in order to determine their implications for the interest to be protected *within* the site. Public authorities should bear this requirement in mind and consult SNH if they are in any doubt about whether a development or operation outside a European site would have a significant effect on it.

13. It is important to recognise that the Directive does not impose a general prohibition on development or other activities affecting European sites. On the contrary, much of our wildlife and important habitats readily co-exist with man's activities, indeed in many cases rely on it. Thus, for the most part, the sustainable management and use of areas which are or become European sites, which has continued over many years and has maintained the high conservation value for which the site is recognised, will meet the aims of the Directive and may continue unchanged. Moreover, proposals for new development or other uses need to be assessed for their impact on the interest to be protected in a European site. If appropriate assessment indicates that there would be no adverse effect on the integrity of the site, the Directive will not prevent the development or other uses going ahead simply because it happens to be within the boundaries of such a site.

Potential SPAs and SACs

14. Some sites have been identified as potentially qualifying for SPA classification but are currently subject to further survey or consultation work before decisions can be taken about their classification. Similarly sites which might qualify for SAC designation will be on a list which the Government will publish for consultation soon and thereafter a draft list will be sent to the European Commission. For the purpose of considering development proposals or other uses of land affecting them, potential SPAs and SACs should be treated in the same way as classified SPAs. Sites which the Commission and the Government have agreed as Sites of Community Importance (within the meaning of Article 4(2) of the Habitats Directive) which are to be designated as SACs attract the same legal protection as if they had already been designated.

15. When consultations take place about the possible classification of a SPA or SAC, planning authorities will be asked to consider all extant planning permissions and analogous consents which may affect the proposed area (ie those permissions which have not been implemented at all, and those which have not been completely implemented). They should consider for each whether that consent or the implementation of that permission would have a significant effect on the ecological value of the site. If so, they should say so in their response to the consultation.

The effects of the Habitats Regulations

16. Detailed advice and guidance on the provisions of the Habitats Regulations is attached as *Annex D*.

The effects of nature conservation provisions

17. The Government will not propose to the European Commission any land-based sites for SAC designation which have not been notified and confirmed as Sites of Special Scientific Interest (SSSIs). Similarly, no land-based site will be classified by the Secretary of State as a SPA under the Birds Directive until it has been notified and confirmed as a SSSI. As SSSIs all land-based European sites will already be subject to the provisions of the existing nature conservation legislation in the Wildlife and Countryside Act 1981 and related provisions in the Countryside Act 1968. Specific nature conservation provisions in the Habitats Regulations build on these existing provisions and on those for nature reserves contained in the National Parks and Access to the Countryside Act 1949. In particular:

- SNH is given the power to amend the lists of potentially damaging operations which form part of an SSSI notification when this is necessary to bring them into line with the ecological objectives of a European site;

- this may lead to SNH on occasion having to modify or revoke Potentially Damaging Operation (PDO) consents granted on an SSSI before it had become a European site;

- the existing time limit under the Wildlife and Countryside Act after which a potentially damaging operation notified to SNH may be carried out without SNH's consent does not apply to a special nature conservation order protecting a European site. In many such cases SNH will in practice already have offered a management agreement, and affected owners/occupiers may seek arbitration if they disagree with the financial terms of the management agreement offered;

- if no management agreement can be concluded, or if an agreement has been breached so that the satisfactory management of the site has been prevented or impaired, SNH will in extreme circumstances be obliged to initiate compulsory purchase procedures. If this should become necessary, the area or interest to be purchased would be as limited as possible. The Government expects SNH to make every effort to address the neglect or inappropriate management of land by offering voluntary management agreements;

- SNH may make byelaws to protect European sites from damage by parties other than the owner/occupier, and these byelaws may also apply to adjacent land.

Species protection

18. The Habitats Directive gives effect to the aspects of the Bern Convention which do not relate to birds. The species protection provisions of the Wildlife and Countryside Act 1981—which are described in detail in Annex 2 to Circular Env 13/1991—were in most respects consistent with the requirements of the Directive though some changes were necessary. The Regulations implement the requirements of the Directive for those species which are covered by the Directive through provisions which broadly parallel certain sections of the 1981 Act. In particular, Regulations 38–46 and Schedules 2–4 make provision to the following effect:

- addition of "disturbance" to the list of offences affecting protected animal species (for species not covered by the Directive still found in section 9 of the 1981 Act[1]) and the replacement of "intentionally" by "deliberately";

- the deletion of "intentionally" from the offence of damage or destruction of places of shelter or protection (breeding sites or resting places);

- the addition of "cutting" and "collecting" to the list of offences concerning protected plant species (otherwise found in section 13 of the 1981 Act[2]);

- the addition of all stages of the biological cycle to plant protection provision;

- the addition of a new proviso for the issue of licences under the present section 16(3)[3] to ensure that they cannot be issued unless there is no satisfactory alternative and the action authorised will not be detrimental to the maintenance of the species population at a favourable conservation status;

- to provide that, subject to the above proviso, licences can be issued for imperative reasons of overriding public interest;

- the addition of certain species to the Regulations' equivalent of Schedule 6 of the 1981 Act to ensure that all British native Annex IV and V mammals and fish are subject to Article 15 of the Directive (which prohibits particular means of taking or killing wild animals, and any form of taking or killing a wild animal from an aircraft or moving motor vehicle).

19. The requirements of the Birds Directive to protect, manage and control all species of naturally occurring wild birds are met by the relevant sections of the Wildlife and Countryside Act 1981.

The Effects of Provisions Relating to Planning Permissions, Permitted Development Rights and Analogous Consents

20. The Regulations set out measures to ensure that the Habitats Directive is implemented in the domain of planning law and that the relevant competent authorities are obliged not to consent to operations or developments damaging to European sites. In outline:

[1] P. 153 above.
[2] P. 156 above.

[3] P. 158 above.

- authorities are obliged not to permit developments or operations damaging to the integrity of European sites unless there are imperative reasons of overriding public interest for the development to be undertaken;

- authorities are obliged to review existing permissions which have not yet been implemented, and to modify or revoke them if their implementation would be damaging to the conservation interests of European sites;

- provision already exists under the Town and Country Planning (Scotland) Act 1972 for developers to be compensated when a planning permission is modified or revoked. The Secretary of State will consider sympathetically any requests from local authorities for the reimbursement of the costs of compensation necessarily incurred by them in modifying or revoking planning permissions under the Habitats Regulations;

- the Secretary of State must be notified if an authority proposes to permit a damaging development or operation to go ahead for the reasons of overriding public interest set out in the Directive;

- the General Permitted Development Order (GPDO) no longer has effect to grant permission for developments damaging to the integrity of European sites. If a development permitted under that Order is likely to have a significant effect on the site and is not directly connected with or necessary to its management, specific approval for the development must be sought from the planning authority. Similar provision is made with regard to development in Simplified Planning Zones and Enterprise Zones. If a developer is in doubt about whether a proposed development permitted under the GPDO may affect a European site, he may consult SNH.

The effects of other control provisions

21. As well as implementing the Directive in the field of planning, the Regulations make provision to achieve similar results in relation to:

    21.1 road construction or improvement projects proposed by the Secretary of State;

    21.2 construction and diversion of pipe-lines under the Pipe-lines Act 1962; and

    21.3 construction of generating stations and installation of electric lines above ground under the Electricity Act 1989.

    The Regulations also make provision to ensure that the existing integrated pollution control, waste management and water discharge consents procedures are compatible with the requirements of the Directive.

Effects in the marine environment

22. The Regulations contain an innovative set of measures to secure the protection of European sites in the marine environment. In summary the Regulations provide that:

    - all relevant authorities (such as harbour authorities, local authorities, and River Purification Authorities) having functions relevant to marine conservation are obliged to exercise those functions to protect the integrity of European marine sites. This means, for instance, that authorities will be obliged not to authorise discharges where this would damage the conservation interests of such sites (unless there are imperative reasons of overriding public interest);

    - Ministers are also obliged to use their powers to protect the conservation interest of European marine sites (with the particular implication in Scotland that Ministers will use their powers under the Inshore Fishing (Scotland) Act 1984 to regulate fishing activities where this is necessary to protect European marine sites);

    - SNH will inform relevant authorities of the conservation objectives of marine sites. It will be for the relevant authorities to decide how to use their powers to protect the integrity of European marine sites;

    - where there is a complex interaction of different management issues, the relevant authorities may co-operate in developing a management scheme for the site, which will be sent to SNH (although SNH has no authority over these other authorities). Co-operation with the users of the marine environment, such as fishermen, will be essential;

- Ministers have reserve powers to direct that a management scheme should be established under a lead agency, to require prior Ministerial approval of the scheme, or to direct what should be in the scheme;

- byelaws may be made by SNH to protect marine sites but, as with the existing provisions for marine nature reserves, the byelaws must not interfere with private rights. However, SNH may enter into voluntary management agreements with the holders of private salmon fishing rights in the marine environment if it is desirable to restrict the exercise of those rights to protect the integrity of a European marine site.

None of the provisions affects international rights of innocent passage.

European sites: development plans

23. Over time development plans must clearly refer to European sites. Structure plans will indicate their broad locations and local plans will identify the sites in detail. The accompanying tests should emphasise the very strict protection which must be afforded to the interests for which European sites are designated and the implications this has for development proposals which would adversely affect those interests. This will be particularly useful in local plans which are a key reference source for the public and developers in making an early assessment of development proposals.

Conservation outside European sites

24. Article 10 of the Habitats Directive require Member States to endeavour, where they consider it necessary, in their land use planning and development policies to encourage the management of features of the landscape which are of major importance for wild flora and fauna. These features are those which, because of their linear and continuous structure or their function as "stepping stones", are essential for migration, dispersal and genetic exchange. Examples given in the Directive are rivers with their banks, traditional field boundary systems, ponds and small woods. The requirements of Article 10 are transposed by Regulation 37 of the Habitats Regulations.

25. Structure plans, local plans and Indicative Forestry Strategies proposed in response to SDD Circular 13/1990 should include policies that respect the need to conserve and enhance our natural heritage, in accordance with current national policy and the UK's international obligations. In particular, these policies should seek to improve the ecological coherence of the Natura 2000 network in accordance with the requirements of Article 10. Regulation 37 requires that such policies shall include policies encouraging the management of features of the landscape which are of major importance for wild flora and fauna. Suitable planning conditions and obligations may serve to promote such management.

26. Circular Env 13/1991 provided advice and guidance to local authorities and other agencies on their role in nature conservation, including nature conservation outside statutorily designated sites (ie in the wider countryside and urban areas). The Government, bearing in mind the obligation now imposed on all relevant public authorities to have regard to the requirements of the Habitats Directive in the exercise of their functions, strongly commends that advice and guidance. The Government's policies and plans in respect of broader measures to conserve and enhance the rural and marine environments are set out in the Biodiversity Action Plan published in January 1994 (Cm 2428, HMSO £18.50). Government policy towards the protection of SSSIs which do not qualify for designation as a European site remains unchanged. The protection of these SSSIs will have an important contribution to make in meeting the requirements of Article 10 of the Directive and Regulation 37 of the Habitats Regulations.

Further legislation

27. Further minor Regulations will be introduced in early course bringing the exercise by relevant authorities of powers under specific statutes into line with the requirements of the Habitats Directive.

Ramsar sites

28. The UK is a contracting party to the Ramsar Convention on Wetlands of International Importance, especially as waterfowl habitat. The full text of the Convention is set out in Cmnd 6465 (May 1976)[1]. The Convention requires contracting parties to designate suitable wetlands ("Ramsar sites") for inclusion in a list of wetlands of international importance and to formulate and implement their planning so as to promote the conservation of the wetlands included in the list, and as far as possible the wise use of wetlands in their territory. The Convention also requires that where a contracting party in its urgent national interest deletes or restricts the boundaries of a wetland included in the list it shall as far as possible compensate for this by designating and protecting alternative wetland areas of similar habitat.

29. Ramsar sites, like SPAs and SACs,. are designated by the Secretary of State and areas proposed for designation are similarly notified as SSSIs. The procedure for designating Ramsar sites is the same as that for the classification of SPAs, and where, as in the great majority of cases, such sites are also to be considered for classification as SPAs, the procedure for consultation and consideration will be a combined one.

30. For those sites which qualify for designation only under the Ramsar Convention (and not as SAC or SPA) the Government has chosen as a matter of policy to apply the same considerations to their protection as if they were classified as SPAs. SNH will be able to advise planning authorities on the conservation of Ramsar sites.

Natural heritage policy guidance

31. The Government is preparing for issue later this year a natural heritage policy guidance document aimed primarily at local authorities and other public bodies. The Government believe that the legislative measures set out in the Habitats Regulations, taken together with the continuing protection of SSSIs and the broader measures to conserve and enhance the rural and marine environments set out in the UK Biodiversity Action Plan present a firm foundation for achieving effective conservation gains in partnership with those who earn their living from the countryside and the sea.

Enquiries

32. Any enquiries about this circular should be addressed to James McTernan (0131-244 4095) or Eamon Murphy (0131-244 4415).

T G BIRLEY
Rural Affairs and Natural Heritage Division

[1] The Ramsar Convention is set out at Annex E to PPG9, p. 432 above.

ANNEX A

COUNCIL DIRECTIVE 92/43/EEC
OF 21 MAY 1992
ON THE CONSERVATION OF NATURAL HABITATS AND OF WILD FAUNA
AND FLORA

This directive is also set out at Annex G to PPG9, p. 446 above, and is accordingly not reproduced here.

ANNEX B

COUNCIL DIRECTIVE
OF 2 APRIL 1979 ON THE CONSERVATION OF WILD BIRDS
(79/409/EEC)

This directive is also set out at Annex F to PPG9, p. 436 above, and is accordingly not reproduced here.

ANNEX C

SPECIAL PROTECTION AREAS

1. CLASSIFIED SITES AS AT 3 FEBRUARY 1995

Local Authority	*Site*
Borders	Hoselaw Loch
Dumfries and Galloway	Loch Ken and Dee Marshes
	Upper Solway Flats and Marshes
Fife	Cameron Reservoir
	Forth Islands
Grampian	Loch of Skene
	Fowlsheugh
	Glen Tanar
	Loch Spynie
Highland	Handa
	Priest Island
	Rum
	Loch Maree
	Loch Eye
	Abernethy Forest
	Loch Vaa
Lothian	Forth Islands
	Gladhouse Reservoir
	Fala Flow
Orkney	Copinsay
	Marwick Head
	Sule Skerry and Stack
Shetland	Hermaness & Saxa Vord, Unst
	Fair isle
	Fetlar

Local Authority	*Site*
Strathclyde	Treshnish Isles
	Gruinart Flats, Islay
	Bridgend Flats, Islay
	Laggan Peninsula, Islay
	Eilean na Muice Duibhe, Islay
	Glac na Criche, Islay
	Feur Lochain, Islay
	Ailsa Craig
Tayside	Loch of Kinnordy
	Loch of Lintrathen
	Montrose Basin
	South Tayside Goose Roosts
Western Isles	Mingulay and Berneray
	Monach Isles
	Loch Druidibeg/a'Machair
	Flannan Isles
	St Kilda
	Shiant Isles

2. POTENTIAL SITES AS AT 18 NOVEMBER 1994

Local Authority	*Site*
Borders	Westwater
	St Abb's Head to Fast Castle
	Greenlaw Moor and Hule Moss
Central	Flanders Moss and Lake of Menteith
	Firth of Forth
	Loch Lomond
Dumfries and Galloway	Castle Loch Dumfries
	Lochinch and Torrs Warren
	Wigtown Bay
Fife	Eden Estuary, Tentsmuir Point and Abertay Sands
	Firth of Forth
	Firth of Tay
Grampian	Moray Basin Firths and Bays
	Loch of Strathbeg
	Ythan Estuary, Sands of Forvie and Meikle Lochs
	Cairngorms
	Troup, Pennan & Lion Heads
	St Cyrus
	Buchan Ness to Collieston Coast
	Rosehearty to Fraserburgh Coast
	Loch Oire
	Muir of Dinnet
	An Socach—Carn a Gheoidh
	Caenlochan
Highland	Pentland Firth Islands
	The Peatlands
	Caithness Lochs
	Caithness Cliffs
	Cape Wrath
	Inverpolly, Loch Urigill & Nearby Lochs
	Loch Ruthven and Nearby Lochs
	Central Highland Hills and Glens
	Assynt Lochs

Local Authority	*Site*
	Loch Stack, Loch Nam Brac and Nearby Locks
	Loch Shin and Nearby Lochs
	Moray Basin Firths and Bays
	Beinn Dearg
	Ben Wyvis
	Glengarry Lochs
	Loch Tarff and Nearby Lochs
	North Inverness Lochs
	River Spey—Insh Marshes
	Cairngorms
	Drumochter Hills
	Monadhliath
	Alvie
	Ben Alder
	Kinveachy
	Creag Meagaidh
Lothian	Firth of Forth
Orkney	Pentland Firth Islands
	West Westray
	Papa Westray (North Hill and Holm)
	Lochs of Harray and Stenness
	Hoy
	West Mainland Moors
	North Mainland Coast
	South Westray Coast
	East Sanday
	Rousay
	North Ronaldsay Coast
	Southeastern Stronsay
	Eday
	Mill Dam, Shapinsay
	Orphir and Stenness Hills
	Keelylang
	Loch of Isbister
Shetland	Ramna Stacks and Gruney
	North Roe and Tingon, Mainland Shetland
	Papa Stour
	Foula
	Noss
	Croussa Field and The Heogs
	Mousa
	Sumburgh Head
	Lochs of Spiggie and Brow
	Blackpark and Gutcher, Yell
	Moorland Areas, Central Shetland
	West Burrafirth
	Hill of Colvadale and Sobul
Strathclyde	Loch Lomond
	Tiree and Coll
	Rhinns of Islay
	Islay: the Oa
	Inner Clyde Estuary
	Rhunahaorine Point
	Machrihanish and Tangy Loch
	North Colonsay and Western Cliffs
	Sanda
Tayside	Drumochter Hills
	Caenlochan

Local Authority	Site
	Tay-isla Valley
	Loch Leven
	Firth of Tay
	Eden Estuary, Tentsmuir Point and Abertay Sands
Western Isles	North Rona and Sula Sgeir
	West Sound of Harris
	South Uist Machair and Lochs
	West Sound of Barra
	Balranald
	Baleshare and Kirkibost
	Loch Scadavay
	Lewis Peatlands
	North Harris Mountains

ANNEX D

DETAILS OF THE HABITATS REGULATIONS

Contents

THE CONSERVATION (NATURAL HABITATS &C) REGULATIONS 1994[1]

NOTE: This Annex provides advice and guidance on the content of the Conservation (Natural Habitats &c) Regulations and on related matters with particular reference to the implications for local authorities, river purification authorities and other public bodies.

PART I (GENERAL)

1. Part I (*Regulations 1–6*) contains introductory provisions. *Regulation 3(2)* places a duty on the Secretary of State and Scottish Natural Heritage (SNH) to exercise their functions under the enactments relating to nature conservation so as to secure compliance with the requirements of the Habitats Directive. These enactments include relevant provisions of the Wildlife and Countryside Act 1981, the Natural Heritage (Scotland) Act 1991 and the Habitats Regulations themselves.

2. *Regulation 3(3)* places a duty on any competent authority having functions relevant to marine conservation to exercise these functions, in relation to marine areas, so as to secure compliance with the requirements of the Habitats Directive. This key duty is the basis for securing the protection of European marine sites. The duty applies in particular to functions under certain enactments specified in *Regulation 3(3)*.

3. Without prejudice to the duties specified above, *Regulation 3(4)* places a duty on *every* competent authority in the exercise of *any* of their functions to have regard to the requirements of the Habitats Directive so far as they may be affected by the exercise of these functions. "Competent authority" is defined in *Regulation 6* as including any Minister, government department, public or statutory undertaker, public body of any description or person holding a public office.

4. *Regulation 5* specifies which are relevant authorities in relation to a marine area or a European marine site. These are, if they have functions in relation to land or waters within or adjacent to that area or site:

   SNH; local authorities; harbour authorities; lighthouse authorities; river purification authorities; district salmon fishery boards.

PART II (CONSERVATION OF NATURAL HABITATS AND HABITATS OF SPECIES)

European sites

5. *Regulations 7–15* make provision for the selection, registration and notification of sites to be protected under the Directive ("European sites").

6. *Regulations 7–9* reflect the requirements of Article 4 and 5 of the Directive in relation to site selection. The Government is required to send to the European Commission by 5 June 1995 a list of sites containing habitat types listed in Annex I to the Directive and/or species listed in Annex II. The Commission and the Government are required to reach agreement by June 1998 on the list of sites to be adopted, following which the Government should complete formal SAC designation as soon as possible and by June 2004 at the latest.

7. *Regulation 10* defines the meaning of "European site" as used in the Regulations. It is *not* confined only to SPAs which have been classified and SACs which have been designated. It includes also:

   7.1 Sites of Community Importance which have been adopted by the Commission pending designation as SAC (Article 4 refers); and

   7.2 Sites hosting a priority habitat or species during the period of consultation between the Commission and the UK Government initiated if the Commission, in exceptional cases, considers that the UK's list ought to have included these sites (Article 5 refers).

8. *Regulations 11–15* (which are in part modelled on the arrangements under the Wildlife and Countryside Act 1981 for maintaining a register of SSSIs) provide for the compilation and maintenance of a register of European sites in Great Britain. In practice the Secretary of State for Scotland (*per* The Scottish Office Environment Department at the address shown in the Circular) will maintain a register of European sites in Scotland. A copy of the register will be available for public inspection at all reasonable hours and free of charge. The Secretary of State shall also notify SNH of sites included in the register and of any amendments; and SNH will keep a copy of the register of European sites in Scotland available for public inspection at all reasonable hours and free of charge.

9. SNH is required under *Regulation 13(1)* to give notice to all owners and occupiers of land within a European site, to the planning authorities concerned and to such other persons or bodies as the Secretary of State may direct, as soon as practicable after it receives notice of inclusion of a site in the register or of an amendment.

---

[1] The Regulations are set out at p. 333 above.

10. Planning authorities are required to keep available at their principal office for free public inspection a register of all the European sites of which they have been given notice by SNH (*Regulation 15(1)*). They may also keep available for free public inspection at any other of their offices such part of the register as appears to them to relate to that part of their area in which such office is situated. Planning authorities are also required to supply on request, on payment of such reasonable fee as they may determine, certified true copies of any entry in the register kept by them.

11. These provisions have immediate effect in relation to the 42 SPAs in Scotland already classified administratively by the Secretary of State and which now become the first sites to be included in the register. Additions/amendments to the register will be made as more SPAs are classified, when a list of Sites of Community Importance is adopted and when SACs are designated.

Management agreements

12. *Regulation 16* is based on SNH's existing power under section 16 of the National Parks and Access to the Countryside Act 1949[1] in relation to nature reserves. It empowers SNH to enter into management agreements with any owner, lessee or occupier of land forming part of a European site, or land adjacent to such a site, for the management, conservation, restoration or protection of the site or any part of it.

13. *Regulation 17* provides that any management agreements in force on or after the commencement of the Regulations which relate to land within or adjacent to a European site shall have effect as if entered into under *Regulation 16*. If SNH considers that an existing agreement requires amendment or replacement to secure compliance with the Directive in relation to a European site, it will seek to enter negotiations with the owner or occupier on a new or revised agreement. The agreements referred to in this Regulation are not only those entered into under Section 16 of the 1949 Act but also includes those under Section 15 of the Countryside Act 1968[2] and Section 49A of the Countryside (Scotland) Act 1967[3].

Control of potentially damaging operations

14. *Regulations 18–21* build on the existing provisions of section 28 of the Wildlife and Countryside Act 1981[4] to ensure the protection of European sites in accordance with the requirements of the Habitats Directive. Notifications of SSSIs by SNH or its predecessors, including the list of potentially damaging operations (PDOs) which may not be carried out without consultation with SNH, remain in force (*Regulation 21*). Owners and occupiers are required to notify SNH of their intention to undertake a PDO and are then precluded for a period of 4 months (or longer by agreement) from carrying out the operation unless the proposal is in accordance with the terms of a management agreement between the owner/occupier and SNH or has the consent of SNH (*Regulation 19*). SNH is obliged not to consent to PDOs which are likely to have an adverse effect on the integrity of the site (*Regulation 20(2)*).

15. In some cases the current lists of PDOs and consents given hitherto by SNH or its predecessors may not meet the Directive's requirements for the protection of a European site. *Regulation 18* therefore enables SNH to amend SSSI notifications, including the PDO list: notice of any amendment must be given to every owner/occupier concerned and to the local planning authority. The Secretary of State also expects SNH to notify him of any such amendments.

16. If SNH considers that there is a risk of the PDO going ahead without consent 4 months after notice of intent has been given to SNH, SNH must inform the Secretary of State at least one month before expiry of the consultation period (*Regulation 20(4) and (5)*). This is to enable the Secretary of State to consider whether other action (eg. a special nature conservation order) should be taken to protect the site.

17. *Regulation 21* requires SNH to review and, where necessary, modify or withdraw consents, including those given at the time of the original SSSI notification, unless they were given under a management agreement. Any changes must be notified to the owners/occupiers concerned. Owners/occupiers would, unless other action is taken, be able to carry out the PDO without consent 4 months after notice of withdrawal of consent. However in practice SNH is likely in such cases to offer a management agreement. If SNH considers that there is a risk of the PDO going ahead after 4 months, it is obliged to inform the Secretary of State at least one month before the expiry of the 4 month period.

Special Nature Conservation Orders

18. *Regulations 22–27* build on the existing provisions of sections 29–31 of the Wildlife and Countryside Act 1981[5] which enable the Secretary of State to intervene to protect threatened sites of national importance.

---

[1] P. 15 above.
[2] P. 121 above.
[3] P. 109 above.

[4] P. 168 above.
[5] P. 171 above.

19. *Regulation 22(1)* provides that the Secretary of State may, after consultation with SNH, make a Special Nature Conservation Order (SNCO) specifying PDO(s) which may damage the features by reason of which the land is a European site. (In practice a SNCO is likely to be made only if there is a risk of a PDO going ahead without consent.) Carrying out of the PDO(s) is then prohibited under *Regulation 23(1) and (2) unless* the owner/occupier has given written notice of intent *and* the operation is carried out either with SNH's written consent *or* in accordance with a management agreement. There is provision for objections or representations to be made to the making of a SNCO and in such circumstances the Secretary of State is required to hold a local inquiry or a hearing and to consider the objections or representations and the report of the inquiry before reaching a final decision on the Order. In any event he must reach a decision on what action (if any) to take in relation to the Order within 9 months of its being made. The detailed procedure is set out in Schedule 1 to the Regulations.

20. Unlike land subject to Orders made under section 29 of the 1981 Act, there is no time limit during which SNH may respond to a notice of intent to carry out a PDO on land subject to a SNCO. In practice therefore a SNCO, if confirmed, imposes an absolute obligation not to carry out without consent the operations specified in the Order. Regulation 24 provides that SNH can give consent to a PDO specified in a SNCO only if it has ascertained that the plan or project to which it relates would not adversely affect the integrity of the site. If consent is refused, SNH is obliged to give reasons for its decision; the owner or occupier of the land in question may then, within 2 months of refusal, require SNH to refer the matter to the Secretary of State. If the Secretary of State is satisfied that, there being no alternative solutions, the plan or project concerned must be carried out for imperative reasons of overriding public interest, he may direct SNH to give consent to the operation. This Regulation does not apply to a site which is a European site by reason only of *Regulation 10 (1((c)))*.

21. *Regulation 25* provides that where a SNCO is made SNH shall pay compensation to any person having an interest in an agricultural unit comprising land to which the Order relates only if the Secretary of State has given notice setting out both the Order *and* his decision either to take no action or to confirm or not to confirm the Order. This Regulation is based on the little used section 30 of the 1981 Act. In practice SNH is likely to have offered a management agreement in response to a PDO to which it cannot give consent; and the offer of a management agreement (with recourse to arbitration if necessary) will remain on the table after a SNCO is made. The provisions relating to management agreements are not restricted to agricultural units so the Government expects that *Regulation 25* will seldom if ever be used.

22. *Regulation 26* provides that an owner or occupier may be required to carry out restoration measures if convicted of carrying out a PDO without consent. *Regulation 27* provides that where there is in place an order under section 29 of the 1981 Act, this will in effect become a SNCO when the land becomes a European site. SNH is required by *Regulation 27(3)* to review any consent previously given under Section 29(5)(a) of the 1981 Act as regards its compatibility with the conservation objectives of the site, and it may modify or withdraw the consent. Under *Regulation 27(4)*, SNH must give notice of any such modification or withdrawal of consent to every owner and occupier of land within the site who in SNH's opinion may be affected by it. SNH would be likely at that stage to indicate its willingness to enter into a management agreement with the owners and occupiers affected. *Regulation 27(5)* provides that the withdrawal or modification of a consent does not affect anything done in reliance on the consent before the modification or withdrawal takes effect.

Byelaws

23. *Regulation 28* empowers SNH to make byelaws for the protection of a European site; and these may apply to surrounding or adjoining land. Byelaws are subject to confirmation by the Secretary of State. *Regulation 29* provides that byelaws cannot interfere with the rights of owners and occupiers of land to which the byelaws apply; the exercise of any public right of way or the exercise of any functions of statutory undertakers or district salmon fishery board; or the running of a telecommunications code system or the rights of its operator.

24. *Regulation 31* provides that byelaws already in force on a nature reserve will have effect as if made under *Regulation 28* if that reserve becomes a European site.

Powers of compulsory acquisition

25. *Regulation 32* provides that SNH may initiate compulsory purchase procedures where:

25.1 no management agreement can be concluded between SNH and an owner or occupier on terms SNH considers reasonable; or

25.2 an agreement has been breached, so that satisfactory management of a European site has been prevented or impaired.

If this should become necessary, the area to be purchased will be as limited as possible. There is provision for arbitration to determine whether such a breach of a management agreement has occurred. An act or omission which can be and is remedied within reasonable time is not a breach. Where a site is threatened by a PDO the

Government expects that resort where necessary to a Special Nature Conservation Order will be sufficient to protect the site. The Government also expects SNH to make every effort to address the neglect or inappropriate management of land by offering voluntary positive management agreements. Compulsory purchase is therefore a last resort measure which should only be necessary in extreme and exceptional circumstances.

European marine sites

26. *Regulations 33–36* make special provision as to the protection of European marine sites. They need to be read with the key duties set out in Regulation 3, in particular *Regulation 3(3)*. The general framework for the protection of European marine sites is set out in paragraph 22 of the main Circular. This approach is consistent with the Government's policy towards coastal zone management generally and with the objectives and targets relating to marine conservation set out in the Biodiversity Action Plan published in January 1994. The Government favours an approach which requires all relevant authorities to cooperate with each other and with other interests in developing management schemes for European marine sites. However it has no wish to see onerous or complex arrangements put in place if these are not necessary to achieve the appropriate management of a site. Moreover the Government hopes that management schemes will be developed from existing working arrangements where these cover European marine sites and that "re-inventing the wheel" will be avoided. The Government considers that, as will be the case on land, existing uses of marine sites will usually be compatible with the requirements of the Directive. In particular the Directive encourages *sustainable* fishing in relation to the particular interests for which a SAC is designated and *not* the exclusion of all fishing activity.

27. European marine sites may include inter-tidal areas (the foreshore) or sub-tidal areas (permanently covered by the sea). The SSSI system extends to inter-tidal areas but not to the sub-tidal, and there is no equivalent marine designation; hence the need for a new set of measures. However where a European marine site includes an inter-tidal area, the relevant nature conservation provisions, mainly in relation to SSSIs and the rights and activities of owners and occupiers, should be taken into account in any scheme of management for the site.

28. *Regulation 33* empowers SNH to install markers indicating the existence and extent of European marine sites. It also requires SNH, as soon as possible after a site becomes a European marine site, to advise other relevant authorities as to:

28.1 the conservation objectives of the site; and

28.2 any operations which may cause deterioration of natural habitats or the habitats for species, or disturbance of species, for which the site has been designated.

29. *Regulation 34* provides that the relevant authorities, or any of them, may establish for a European marine site a management scheme under which their functions shall be exercised so as to secure compliance with the requirements of the Directive in relation to that site. As soon as a scheme has been established, or is amended, the relevant authority or authorities must send a copy to SNH.

30. *Regulation 35* gives Ministers reserve powers to direct that a management scheme should be established under a lead agency, to require prior Ministerial approval of the scheme, or to direct what should be in the scheme.

31. *Regulation 36* extends to European marine sites SNH's existing power under the Wildlife and Countryside Act 1981 to make byelaws for the protection of marine nature reserves. Such byelaws, which are subject to confirmation by the Secretary of State, cannot interfere with any functions of a relevant authority, functions conferred under an enactment or any private rights.

Nature conservation policy in planning contexts

32. Paragraphs 23–36 of the main Circular provide advice on the Directives' implications for development plans both in relation to European sites and to the wider countryside and marine environment outside these designated areas. These paragraphs include advice on *Regulation 37* which transposes Article 10 of the Habitats Directive.

33. The forthcoming natural heritage policy guidance document, referred to in paragraph 31 of the main Circular, will offer detailed advice on planning issues relating to the natural heritage in a consolidated form. In the meantime, some advice on the impact of nature conservation policy and legislation on planning can be found in NPPGs 1, 4 and 6; and in SDD Circular 13/1990 "Indicative Forestry Strategies" which underlines the Government's wish to encourage the expansion of forestry in an environmentally sensitive way.

Part III (Protection of Species)

34. *Regulations 38–46* make provision for protection of species and habitats—see paragraph 18 of main Circular.

PART IV (ADAPTATION OF PLANNING AND OTHER CONTROLS)

Introduction/general provisions for protection of European sites

35. *Regulations 47–51* are core provisions which are of fundamental importance in understanding the other provisions of this Part of the Regulations. In particular, Regulation 47 provides that the requirements of:

   (a) *Regulations 48 and 49*, which specify the requirement on competent authorities to undertake appropriate assessments to consider the effect of plans or projects on European sites; and

   (b) *Regulations 50 and 51*, which specify the requirement on competent authorities to review certain *existing* decisions and consents in relation to their effect on European sites

   apply to the matters specified in *Regulations 54–85*. Thus the detailed provisions in those Regulations should be read with the general requirements of *Regulations 48–51*.

   NB. By virtue of *Regulation 48(7)*, this Part of the Regulations, does not apply to sites which are European sites only by reason of *Regulation 10(1)(c)*. For general ease of understanding, however, the guidance below refers generally to European sites or to SPAs and SACs.

36. *Regulations 52 and 53* make provision which is supplementary to the general purpose and effect of this Part. *Regulation 52* applies in situations where more than one competent authority is involved in a plan or project. *Regulation 53* transposes Article 6(4) of the Habitats Directive. Where a plan or project is agreed to, notwithstanding an assessment which indicates that it would be likely to have an adverse effect on the integrity of a European site, the Secretary of State must secure that any necessary compensatory measures are taken to protect the overall coherence of the Natura 2000 network. Such measures could include the designation of another area as a European site.

Duty to review extant permissions

37. *Regulations 50, 51, 55 and 56* of the Regulations require the planning authority to review extant planning permissions[1] which are likely to have a significant effect on a site, either individually or in combination with other development, and to take any appropriate action. This requirement applies to:

   existing SPAs when the Regulations came into force and those classified since then (listed in Annex C to the main Circular);

   future SPAs when they are classified; and

   SACs when the Government and the European Commission agree the site as a Site of Community Importance to be classified as a SAC. (Planning authorities will be notified when sites are agreed.)

38. Planning authorities are required by *Regulation 50(1)* to review permissions as soon as is reasonably practicable. They should have identified any relevant permissions during the consultations referred to in paragraph 15 of the main Circular. The review will need to ascertain whether implementation of any permission which is likely to have a significant effect on the site, and is not directly connected with or necessary to its management, would adversely affect its integrity (see *Appendix A*). The planning authority must consult SNH and have regard to any representations made by it within such reasonable time as the authority may specify (*Regulations 48(3) and 50(2)*). If the integrity of the site would be adversely affected, and if the permission does not fulfil the conditions under which a new development proposal affecting the site would be approved, then the authority must take appropriate action to remove the potential for harm, unless there is no likelihood of the development being carried out or continued (see *Regulation 56(3)*).

39. If planning authorities consider that agreements made under section 50 would safeguard the integrity of the site *Regulation 56(2)* requires them to invite those concerned to enter into them. Otherwise they must modify or revoke the permission, or make a discontinuance order. They should also take such action if a developer proceeds with damaging development while they are endeavouring to secure a section 50 agreement. *Regulation 58* provides that modification, revocation or discontinuance orders take effect when served. They must however be confirmed by the Secretary of State, in order to have continuing effect. Where compensation is payable

---

[1] Excluding planning permission deemed to be granted by virtue of section 37 of the Town and Country Planning (Scotland) Act 1972 in respect of developments authorised under the Pipe-lines Act 1962 or for which consent has been given under the Electricity Act 1989. Such reviews will be carried out by the Secretary of State (see *Regulation 55(3)*). The planning authority must identify any other permissions deemed to have been granted under section 37 which they consider fall to be reviewed and refer the matter to the relevant Government Department. If the Department agrees with the planning authority on this, it must review the permission accordingly (see *Regulation 55(4)*). See also paragraph 41 below regarding permissions granted by Development Orders and Simplified Planning Zone and Enterprise Zone schemes, which are also excluded from review (*Regulation 55(2)* refers).

in the event of the order not being confirmed, the authority must refer the amount to the Lands Tribunal for Scotland unless the Secretary of State indicates otherwise (see *Regulation 59*).

40. The Government advise that planning authorities should not seek to duplicate controls which are the statutory responsibility of other bodies (including planning authorities in their non-planning functions). *Regulations 83, 84 and 85* require the review of authorisations under the Environmental Protection Act 1990 granted by Her Majesty's Industrial Pollution Inspectorate or the River Purification Authority for integrated pollution control and by local authorities for air pollution control; of waste management licences under the 1990 Act granted by local authorities (district or islands councils until April 1995); and of effluent discharge consents under the Control of Pollution Act 1974 granted by the river purification authority. As a matter of policy, if in reviewing a planning permission planning authorities consider that action calls to be taken under *Regulations 83, 84 or 85* they should inform the relevant authority. Further, they should exercise planning powers under *Regulation 56* only if powers under the other regimes are not available or if their exercise could not achieve what is required. In carrying out reviews and in exercising their own powers planning authorities must have regard to the provision in *Regulation 51* that the action to be taken to secure that the integrity of the site is not adversely affected should be the least onerous to those affected.

41. Advice on amendments to the General Permitted Development Order (GPDO) and General Development Procedure Order (GDPO) is at paragraphs 47–55 below. *Regulations 64, 65 and 66* provide that existing Special Development Orders, Simplified Planning Zone schemes and Enterprise Zone schemes cease to have effect to grant planning permission for development which is likely to have a significant effect on a classified SPA or a site agreed by the Commission and the Government as a Site of Community Importance to be designated as an SAC. (Existing Special Development Orders relate to New Town Development Corporations.) The Regulations also prevent new Special Development Orders and SPZ and EZ schemes from granting planning permission for development which is likely significantly to affect a site classified as SPA or agreed as SAC.

Development affecting SPAs and SACs

42. *Regulations 48, 49 and 54* restrict the granting of planning permission for development which is likely significantly to affect an SPA or SAC, and which is not directly connected with or necessary to the management of the site. They apply to planning decisions taken on or after the date the Regulations came into force, regardless of when the application was submitted. They apply to sites of one of the types listed in paragraph 37 above. They do not apply to candidate SACs before they have been agreed with the European Commission or to potential SPAs, but as a matter of policy the Government wishes development proposals affecting them to be considered in the same way as if they had already been classified. The Government has chosen to apply the same considerations to listed Ramsar sites. (See also paragraphs 14 and 30 of main Circular.)

43. SPAs and in future terrestrial SACs will already have been notified to authorities as SSSIs. An authority is required under the GDPO to consult SNH before granting planning permission for development affecting an SSSI; Regulation 48 incorporates a similar requirement for development affecting a SPA or SAC. In responding, SNH will advise if the SSSI is a SPA or a SAC or is otherwise of particular significance in terms of the Birds or Habitats Directives. It will also advise whether in its opinion the proposed development would significantly affect the ecological value for which the site was identified, and if appropriate will suggest what measures might be taken in advance of permission being granted to avoid such effects.

44. Before issuing a decision on the planning application *Regulation 49(5)* requires an authority proposing to allow a development which would adversely affect a SPA or SAC, to notify the Secretary of State and to delay agreeing to the development for a period of 21 days following receipt of the notification by the Secretary of State unless permitted in writing by the Secretary of State. Planning authorities should explain the reasons for their decision particularly if they do not decide the case in accordance with the recommendations of SNH. The Secretary of State will normally call-in for his own decision planning applications which are likely to have a significant effect on sites of international importance; he will have regard to the advice of SNH on applications which are likely to have such effects. If a planning application for development likely to affect such a site is not called-in, the Government expects the planning authority to demonstrate in the decision-making process that the relevant factors have been fully addressed; this requirement applies whether or not the authority is minded to approve the application.

45. The approach to be taken in considering a development proposal that would affect a SPA or SAC is set out in *Appendix A*, whether the decision-taker is the Secretary of State or the planning authority.

Planning authority and crown development affecting SPAs and SACs

46. Applications made by planning authorities for the development of their land are subject to the planning procedures set out in the Town and Country Planning (Development by Planning Authorities) (Scotland) Regulations 1981. The Government has announced its intention to end Crown exemption from planning laws,

with certain exceptions including trunk road and motorway development which is subject to separate procedures designed to produce the same effect as planning legislation. *Regulation 69* achieves the same result as regards road construction or improvement projects carried out by the Secretary of State under the Roads (Scotland) Act 1984 as the Regulations do for development requiring planning permission. Pending legislation altering Crown exemption, planning authorities will continue to be consulted about proposals for Crown development under the procedures in SDD Circular No. 21/1984. Where such proposals are likely to affect a site of a type listed in paragraph 37 above, authorities should apply the same tests in framing their advice as under the Habitats Regulations. The Secretary of State will do likewise in deciding whether planning clearance should be given for proposals which are the subject of unresolved objections from a planning authority.

Permitted development rights: SPAs and SACs

47. Article 3 of the Town and Country Planning (General Permitted Development) (Scotland) Order 1992 (GPDO) grants a general planning permission (subject to specified conditions and limitations) for the types of development set out in Schedule 2 to the GPDO. These permitted development rights largely apply to developments which are uncontentious, and which, if they required individual consideration, would place an unnecessary burden on householders or other developers and on planning authorities. Other permitted development rights relate to developments which are controlled through other approval procedures, and to developments by statutory undertakers and local authorities in the performance of their statutory duties.

48. *Regulations 60–63* ensure that any permission granted under the GPDO is not in breach of the terms of the Habitats Directive. They prevent any development which is likely significantly to affect a European site from benefiting from permitted development rights unless the planning authority have decided, after consulting SNH, that it would not adversely affect the integrity of the site.

49. *Appendix C* explains the process developers should follow to find out whether the particular development they propose would benefit from a permitted development right. It identifies the role of the planning authority and SNH.

Permitted development rights and the developer

50. Developers should bear in mind that if they proceed with a development in or near a European site on the assumption that it benefits from a permitted development right, without first checking whether it is likely to have a significant effect on the site, they run the risk of undertaking the project without the benefit of planning permission and being liable to enforcement proceedings.

51. If developers are uncertain whether their proposal is likely to have a significant effect on the site, they may seek an opinion from SNH (*Regulation 61(1)*). There is no charge for this. An application for SNH's opinion must give details of the proposed development and, in the Department's view, this should include the following information:

    51.1 A short description of the proposed development or works showing:

    - their broad purpose;

    - their physical extent, including the area of land or water likely to be covered;

    - any residues likely to be produced and proposals for disposal, and any emissions to air, water, soil, and by noise, vibration, heat, light or radiation;

    - the timetable for the proposed development.

    51.2 A map (or maps) showing the location of the proposed development in relation to SPA/SAC boundary and the position of all proposed buildings, service access routes and works (whether permanent or temporary).

    51.3 A description of possible direct or indirect effects (including disturbance) on the wildlife, water quality, hydrology, geological or landform features of the site.

    51.4 Information about any measures the developer proposes to incorporate into the project to prevent, reduce, ameliorate or offset any landtake, residues or emissions.

52. To inform their initial consideration about whether to consult SNH, developers may obtain a copy of the citation giving the reasons for classification of the site from the appropriate local office of SNH. A copy of the citation is provided to relevant planning authorities and to owners and occupiers of a site during the pre-classification process.

53. The planning authority would enter the process at the point where either the developer or SNH decided that the proposal would be likely to have a significant effect on the site. If the developer wishes to pursue the proposal further, the planning authority would undertake an assessment of the implications of the proposal for the

site's conservation objectives. After consulting SNH, the planning authority would decide whether or not the proposal would adversely affect the integrity of the site. If the authority concluded that it would have such an effect and the developer wished to proceed an application for the authority's approval would be required. *Regulation 63(2)* provides for a fee to be paid to the planning authority in connection with the application for approval. Advice on significant effect, appropriate assessment and site integrity is contained in *Appendix A*.

54. If the authority decides, after consulting SNH, that there would be no adverse effect on the integrity of the site, the developer can go ahead. If the authority decides that there would be, the developer will have to make a full planning application. As with any other change in the law which has the effect of withdrawing PDRs, compensation may be payable. The possible right to compensation arises only where a planning application is:

54.1 submitted within 12 months of the date when the removal of PDRs come into effect (in this case 30 October 1994);

54.2 refused or granted subject to conditions other than those attached to the PDRs; and

54.3 for a development which would have benefited from those PDRs if they had not been revoked.

55. SNH will endeavour to respond within 21 days from the receipt of all information necessary to enable it to form an opinion, both to:

55.1 requests from a developer for its opinion as to whether a development is likely to have a significant effect on a site (*Regulation 61(1)*); and

55.2 applications from a planning authority under *Regulation 62(4)*, on the issue of whether a development will adversely affect the integrity of a site.

If the information provided under *Regulation 61(1)* is inadequate or incomplete, SNH will advise what additional information they need (*Regulation 61(4)*). Planning authorities must, by virtue of *Regulation 62(4)*, take account of any representations made by SNH.

Unauthorised developments affecting SPAs and SACs

56. Planning authorities will need to implement specific administrative procedures to prevent, or remedy quickly, any alleged breach of planning control which has, or is likely to have, a significant effect on a SPA or SAC. If a continuing breach of planning control is likely to result in serious long-term harm to a site, the authority should consider the simultaneous service of a stop notice with the related enforcement notice, to prohibit environmentally harmful activity which would otherwise continue for the duration of an enforcement appeal. Where the significant effect on a SPA or SAC appears to result from an alleged breach of a planning condition, it may be more effective to issue an enforcement notice, reinforced by a stop notice, rather than serve a breach of condition notice. This is because a minimum period of 28 days must be allowed for compliance with a breach of condition notice, during which period irremediable harm to the natural habitat may occur. Alternatively, or additionally, the authority may consider submitting an immediate application to the Court of Session or the Sheriff court for interdict while they prepare to take other action to enforce against a breach of control which is having a significant effect on an SPA or SAC. Advice on enforcement is given in National Planning Policy Guideline 1 (NPPG1) (The Planning System, paragraphs 62 and 63) and in Circulars Env 8/1992 and 36/1992.

Roads, cycle tracks and ancillary works (Regulations 69–70)
Consents under Electricity Act 1989 (Regulations 71–74)
Authorisations under Pipe-lines Act 1962 (Regulations 75–78)

57. These Regulations achieve broadly the same result as the other Regulations in this Part do for development requiring planning permission in respect of:

57.1 road construction and improvement projects proposed by the Secretary of State and proposed cycle track establishment projects;

57.2 construction and operation of generating stations and installation of electric lines above ground; and

57.3 construction and diversion of pipe-lines.

PART V (SUPPLEMENTARY PROVISIONS)

58. *Regulations 86–108* contain supplementary provisions which are not described in detail here. *Regulation 87* is modelled on sections 28(6A), (6B) and (6C) of the Wildlife and Countryside Act 1981[1] (as inserted by the Wildlife and Countryside (Amendment) Act 1985). *Regulation 88* is modelled on section 32 of the 1981 Act[2]. This

---

[1] P. 169 above.   [2] P. 175 above.

Regulation requires the Secretary of State, where an application for a farm capital grant relates to activities on land within a European site, to exercise his functions so far as is consistent with the purposes of the grant provisions to further the conservation of the features by reason of which the land is a European site. SNH may object to the making of a grant where this may damage or destroy these features; and the Secretary of State must consider any such objections. If grant is refused, SNH must offer to enter into a management agreement with the applicant within 3 months, imposing restrictions on these activities and providing for payments to the applicant. *Regulation 89* is modelled on section 50 of the 1981 Act[1].

59. Powers of entry to land exist for:

    59.1 persons authorised by SNH to ascertain whether a special nature conservation order should be made in relation to that land, an offence has been committed on the land or the award of compensation payable under Regulation 25 (by virtue of *Regulation 90(1)*);

    59.2 persons authorised by the Valuation Office to survey land or estimate its value in consideration of a claim for compensation under Regulation 30 (*Regulation 95(1)*); or

    59.3 persons authorised to survey land in the exercise of any power under the Regulations prior to the acquisition of an interest in the land by the prospective acquirer (*Regulation 99(1)*).

    In the first case, 24 hours notice to the occupier is required prior to entry unless it is believed an offence is being or has been committed (*Regulation 90(2)*). Otherwise, 14 days notice is required (*Regulations 95(3) and 99(3)*, respectively).

60. *Regulations 100–104* contain provisions supplementary to Part III of the Regulations relating to the protection of species.

The Scottish Office Environment Department
March 1995

ANNEX D, APPENDIX A

CONSIDERATION OF DEVELOPMENT PROPOSALS AFFECTING SPAs AND SACs[2]

1. The planning authority must first establish: (1) whether the proposed development is directly connected with or necessary to site management for nature conservation; and (2) whether it is likely to have a significant effect on a European site either individually or in combination with other plans or projects. The authority should take account of advice from SNH. If initial consideration of these issues is inconclusive, an analysis in more depth will be needed to establish the effects of the proposed development on the site.

2. If the planning authority concludes that a proposed development unconnected with site management is likely significantly to affect a European site, it must then carry out an appropriate assessment of its implications in view of the site's conservation objectives (i.e. the reasons for which the site was classified), so as to ascertain whether or not it will adversely affect the integrity of the site. The advice of SNH (as required by Regulation 48(3)) and the citation issued by it saying why the site was classified will need to be carefully considered. The integrity of a site is the coherence of its ecological structure and function, across its whole area, that enables it to sustain the habitat, complex of habitats and/or the levels of populations of the species for which it was classified. The scope and content of what constitutes an appropriate assessment will depend on the location, size and significance of the proposed project. SNH will advise on a case-by-case basis.

3. According to the nature conservation value of the site, SNH will identify whether particular aspects such as hydrology, disturbance or land-take should be specifically addressed. In the simplest cases, a general statement from SNH of the impact of the development may suffice. The assessment required under the Habitats Regulations is that which is necessary to determine the likely impact of a development proposal on the conservation interests(s) for which a European site has been classified. An assessment made under the Habitats Regulations does not exempt prospective developers from their obligations under the Environmental Assessment (Scotland) Regulations 1988 and related legislation to undertake an Environmental Assessment (EA) for certain types of project. However, in cases where EA is required in order to comply with those Regulations, it

---

[1] P. 187 above.

[2] See also paragraphs 14 and 30 regarding potential SPAs and SACs, and Ramsar sites.

will be appropriate to use the information assembled for the purposes of the EA also for the assessment required by the Habitats Regulations.

4. If the planning authority ascertains that the proposed development will adversely affect the integrity of the site, and this effect will not be removed by conditions attached to the planning permission, it must not grant planning permission except in the following closely defined circumstances. It must first be satisfied that there are no *alternative solutions*. It should consider whether there are or are likely to be suitable and available sites which are reasonable alternatives for the proposed development, or different, practicable approaches which would have a lesser impact. It should bear in mind the advice of SNH. In their own interests applicants should demonstrate that they have fully considered alternative solutions.

5. If there is no alternative solution, and the site does not host a priority natural habitat type or species defined in the Habitats Directive[1], planning permission must not be granted unless the proposed development has to be carried out for imperative reasons of overriding public interest, including those of a social or economic nature.

6. Such reasons would need to be sufficient to override the ecological importance of the classification[2].

7. If the site hosts a priority habitat or species, and there is no alternative solution, the only considerations which can justify the grant of planning permission are those which relate to human health, public safety, or beneficial consequences of primary importance to the environment (unless the European Commission is of the opinion that there are other imperative reasons of overriding public interest—any such consultation with the Commission must be carried out by the Government).

8. This process is represented in *Appendix B*.

9. If planning permission is granted for a development which would adversely affect the integrity of a SPA or SAC, *Regulation 53* requires the Secretary of State to secure that any necessary compensatory measures are taken to ensure that the overall coherence of the Community-wide network of SPAs and SACs known as Natura 2000 is protected.

---

[1] Priority habitats and species are indicated by an asterisk in Annexes I and II of the Habitats Directive. The citation saying why the site was classified will show whether it hosts a priority habitat or species.

[2] *Regulation 52(4)* requires a "competent authority", other than the Secretary of State, in determining whether to agree to a development on grounds of overriding public interest, to seek and have regard to the views of any other competent authorities involved.

ANNEX D, APPENDIX B

CONSIDERATION OF DEVELOPMENT PROPOSALS AFFECTING SPAs AND SACs

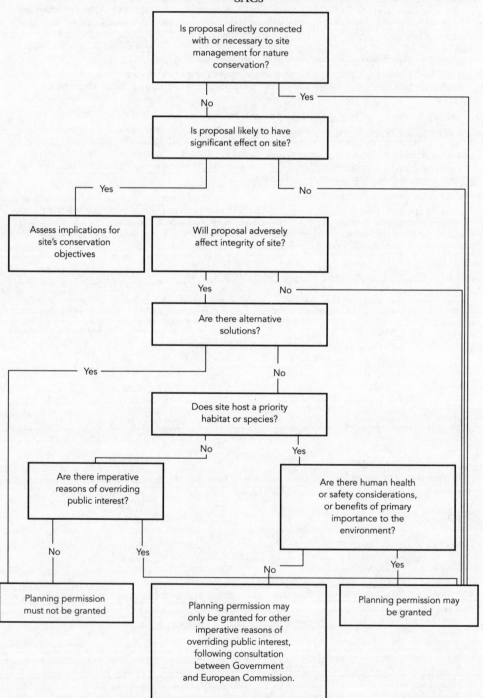

ANNEX D, APPENDIX C

PERMITTED DEVELOPMENT RIGHTS: SPAs AND SACs

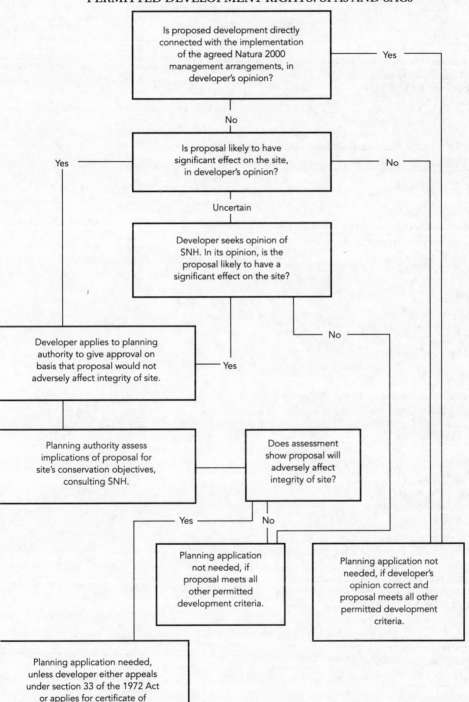

List of Addresses

Countryside Commission

Headquarters

John Dower House, Crescent Place
Cheltenham, Gloucestershire GL50 3RA
Telephone: 01242 521381
Fax: 01242 584270

Northern

4th Floor, Warwick House, Grantham Road,
Newcastle-Upon-Tyne NE2 1QX
Telephone: 0191 232 8252
Fax: 0191 222 0185

Yorkshire & Humberside

2nd Floor, Victoria Wharf, Embankment IV
Sovereign Street, Leeds LS1 4BA
Telephone: 0113 2469222
Fax: 0113 2460353

North West

7th Floor,Bridgewater House
Whitworth Street, Manchester, M1 6LT
Telephone: 0161 237 1061
Fax: 0161 237 1062

Midlands

1st Floor, Vincent House, Tindal Bridge
92–93 Edward Street, Birmingham B1 2RA
Telephone: 0121 233 9399
Fax: 0121 233 9286

Eastern

Ortona House, 110 Hills Road
Cambridge CB2 1LQ
Telephone: 01223 354462
Fax: 01223 313850

South East

4th Floor, 71 Kingsway
London WC2B 6ST
Telephone 0171 831 3510
Fax: 0171 831 1439

South West

Bridge House, Sion Place
Clifton Down, Bristol BS8 4AS
Telephone: 0117 9739966
Fax: 0117 9238086

Cyngor Cefn Gwlad Cymru
Countryside Council for Wales

Plas Penrhos
Ffordd Penrhos
Bangor
Gwynedd
LL57 2LQ
Telephone: 01248 370444
Fax: 01248 355782

Swyddfa Rhanbarthol Gogledd Cymru

Hafod Elfyn
Ffordd Penrhos
Bangor
Gwynedd
LL57 2LQ
Telephone: 01248 372333
Fax: 01248 370734

North Wales Regional Office

Hafod Elfyn
Ffordd Penrhos
Bangor
Gwynedd
LL57 2LQ

Swyddfa Rhanbarthol Dyfed Powys a´r Canolbarth

Plas Gogerddan
Aberystwyth
Dyfed
SY23 3EE
Telephone: 01970 828551
Fax: 01970 828314

Dyfed and Mid Wales Regional Office

Plas Gogerddan
Aberystwyth
Dyfed
SY23 3EE

Swyddfa Rhanbarthol De Cymru

43–45 The Parade
Y Rhath
Caerdydd
CF2 3UH
Telephone: 01222 485111
Fax: 01222 473527

South Wales Regional Office

43–45 The Parade
Roath
Cardiff
CF2 3UH

English Nature

See PPG9, Annex H, p. 476 above.

Forestry Commission

231 Corstorphine Road
Edinburgh EH12 7AT
Telephone: 0131 334 0303
Fax: 0131 334 3047

Joint Nature Conservation Committee

See PPG9, Annex H, p. 476 above.

Scottish Natural Heritage

12 Hope Terrace
Edinburgh EH9 2AS
Telephone: 0131 447 4784
Fax: 0131 446 2279

Regional Offices

South West Region

Caspian House
2 Mariner Court
8 South Avenue
Clydebank Business Park
Clydebank G81 2NR
Telephone: 0141 951 4488
Fax: 0141 951 4510

South East Region

Battleby
Redgorton
Perth PH1 3EW
Telephone: 01738 444177
Fax: 01738 444180

North West Region

Fraser Darling House
9 Culduthel Road
Inverness IV2 4AG
Telephone: 01463 239431
Fax: 01463 710713

North East Region

Wynne-Edwards House
17 Rubislaw Terrace
Aberdeen AB1 1XE
Telephone: 01224 642863
Fax: 01224 643347

Appendix I: Environment Bill

This appendix outlines the main provisions of the Environment Bill which relate to nature conservation. The Bill was introduced into the House of Lords on 1 December 1994. This appendix is based on the Bill as introduced into the House of Commons on 21 March 1995 (Bill 85) which is the most recent reprint of the Bill at the time or writing.

The new agencies

Part I of the Bill relates to the establishment of the Environment Agency and the Scottish Environment Protection Agency (SEPA). The constitution, functions, powers and duties of the new agencies are set out in this part.

In England and Wales the functions of the National Rivers Authority (NRA), waste regulation authorities, Her Majesty's Inspectorate of Pollution (HMIP) and certain functions of the Secretary of State are to be transferred to the Environment Agency. The NRA is to be abolished. A date will be appointed by the Secretary of State for the transfer of these functions. The provisions of the Water Resources Act 1991 set out in this manual will be repealed and replaced by the new provisions in Part I with the exception of section 15, which will be amended in consequence of the changes. The duty of the Agency with respect to conservation differs from the form of the duty at present imposed in relation to the NRA's functions where the Agency is formulating or considering proposals relating to its "pollution control functions". These functions comprise principally the functions at present undertaken by HMIP, by the NRA in respect of the control of pollution of water resources, functions relating to waste on land and contaminated land and certain functions at present undertaken by the Secretary of State.

There has been considerable debate concerning the conservation duties of the Environment Agency. In response to concern expressed following the publication by the Department of the Environment of a draft version of the Bill on 13 October 1994, the Bill introduced into Parliament has been modified. The Bill now provides that, in respect of proposals relating to functions other than pollution control functions, the duties to be imposed upon the Ministers and the Agency are to be similar to those at present imposed on the Ministers and the NRA under section 16 of the Water Resources Act 1991. Thus, as far as may be consistent with specified provisions, the Ministers and the Agency are to exercise any power so as

"to further the conservation and enhancement of natural beauty and the conservation of flora, fauna and geological or physiographical features of special interest".

However, in respect of proposals relating to pollution control functions, the Ministers and the Agency are

"to have regard to the desirability of conserving and enhancing natural beauty and of conserving flora, fauna and geological or physiographical features of special interest".

In Scotland, the functions of river purification authorities, of local authorities in respect of waste regulation and air pollution control, and of Her Majesty's Industrial Pollution Inspectorate, and certain functions of the Secretary of State are to be transferred to SEPA. River purification authorities are to be dissolved. A date will be appointed by the Secretary of State for the transfer of these functions. A duty is imposed on the Secretary of State and SEPA in relation to any of SEPA's functions

"to have regard to the desirability of conserving and enhancing the natural heritage of Scotland".

It is also a duty of SEPA

"to such extent as it considers desirable, generally to promote—

(a) the conservation and enhancement of the natural beauty and amenity of inland and coastal waters and of land associated with such waters; and

(b) the conservation of flora and fauna which are dependent on an aquatic environment".

In addition the Agency is required to have regard to the desirability of preserving freedom of access to places of natural beauty.

Following notification of a Natural Heritage Area or a site of special interest by Scottish Natural Heritage (SNH), SEPA is required to consult SNH before undertaking activities, or giving an authorisation, which is likely to adversely affect such an area. The Secretary of State may approve by order a code of practice issued with respect to the Agency's environmental and recreational duties.

Both agencies are required to have regard to guidance, to be given by Ministers, which must include the contribution of the agencies "towards attaining the objective of achieving sustainable development". In relation to the Environment Agency only, an amendment was made to the Bill on report to the House of Lords which provides that it shall be a principal aim of the Agency to make this contribution to sustainable development. A duty is imposed on each agency to take into account costs and benefits in exercising their powers. The Bill was amended in the House of Lords to provide a definition of "costs" as including costs to any person and costs to the environment.

It is proposed that the Agencies will take over their functions on 1 April 1996. In Scotland, the reorganisation of local government, under the Local Government etc. (Scotland) Act 1994, will also come into effect on this date.

National Parks

Part III of the Bill relates to National Parks. The purposes of National Parks, as set out in s. 5 of the National Parks and Access to the Countryside Act 1949, are to be redefined. The Bill provides that section 5(1) of the 1949 Act be replaced by the following provision:

"(1) The provisions of this Part of this Act shall have effect for the purpose—

(a) of conserving and enhancing the natural beauty, wildlife and cultural heritage of the areas specified in the next following subsection; and

(b) of promoting opportunities for the quiet enjoyment and understanding of the special qualities of those areas by the public."

The reference to quiet enjoyment was inserted by the House of Lords at the committee stage. The original wording referred to ". . . promoting opportunities for the understanding and enjoyment of the special qualities . . .". This amendment will be reviewed when the Bill is considered by the House of Commons.

A new section, 11A, is to be inserted into the 1949 Act. This provides that a National Parks authority shall seek to foster the economic and social well-being of local communities and that, in the event of a conflict between the purposes set out in the proposed section 5(1), relevant authorities are to attach greater weight to the conservation purpose set out in paragraph (a) of that subsection.

This part of the Bill also makes provision for the Secretary of State to establish independent National Park authorities which will be the sole local planning authority and mineral planning authority for the area of the Park. These authorities will be required to prepare and publish a National Park Management Plan. Amendments consequent upon the provisions of Part III are to be made to legislation, including the National Parks and Access to the Countryside Act 1949, the Countryside Act 1968, the Wildlife and Countryside Act 1981, the Norfolk and Suffolk Broads Act 1988 and the water consolidation legislation of 1991.

Hedgerows

Part IV of the Bill contains a new measure relating to hedgerows in England and Wales. Ministers are given power to make regulations providing for the protection of important hedgerows. The question of "importance" is to be determined in accordance with prescribed criteria. This provision was amended in the House of Lords to provide that the Minister shall consult certain bodies before making such regulations.

Appendix II: References to International Conventions and Agreements

Convention on Wetlands of International Importance especially as Waterfowl Habitat 1971 (the Ramsar Convention), HMSO, Cmnd. 6465: this convention together with amendments is at Annex E to PPG9, p. 432 above.

Convention on the Conservation of Migratory Species of Wild Animals 1979 (the Bonn Convention), HMSO, Treaty Series No. 87 (1990), Cm. 1332.

Convention on the Conservation of European Wildlife and Natural Habitats 1979 (the Berne Convention), HMSO, Treaty Series No. 56 (1982), Cmnd. 8783.

Amendments to Appendix 1 to the Convention on the Conservation of European Wildlife and Natural Habitats 1979, HMSO, Treaty Series No. 52 (1992), Cm. 2002.

Agreement on the Conservation of Small Cetaceans of the Baltic and North Sea 1992, HMSO, Miscellaneous Series No. 2 (1993), Cm. 2119. This agreement was ratified by the United Kingdom on 13 July 1993 and will be published in the Treaty Series.

Convention on Biological Diversity 1992, HMSO, Miscellaneous Series No. 3 (1993) Cm. 2127. This convention was ratified by the United Kingdom on 3 June 1994 and will be published in the Treaty Series.

Agreement on the Conservation of Bats in Europe 1991, HMSO, Treaty Series No. 9 (1994), Cm. 2472.

Index